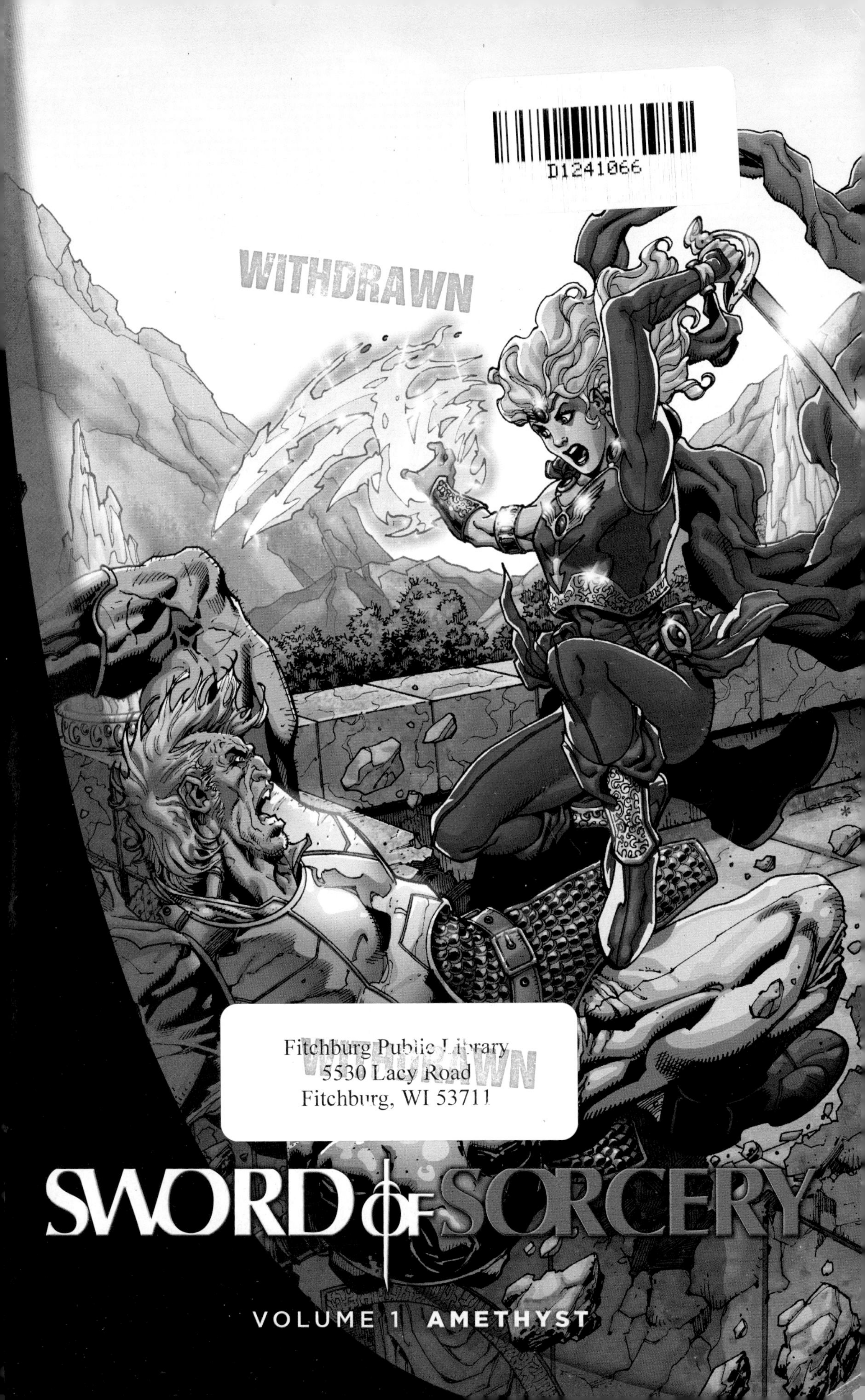

SWORD OF SORCERY

VOLUME 1 AMETHYST

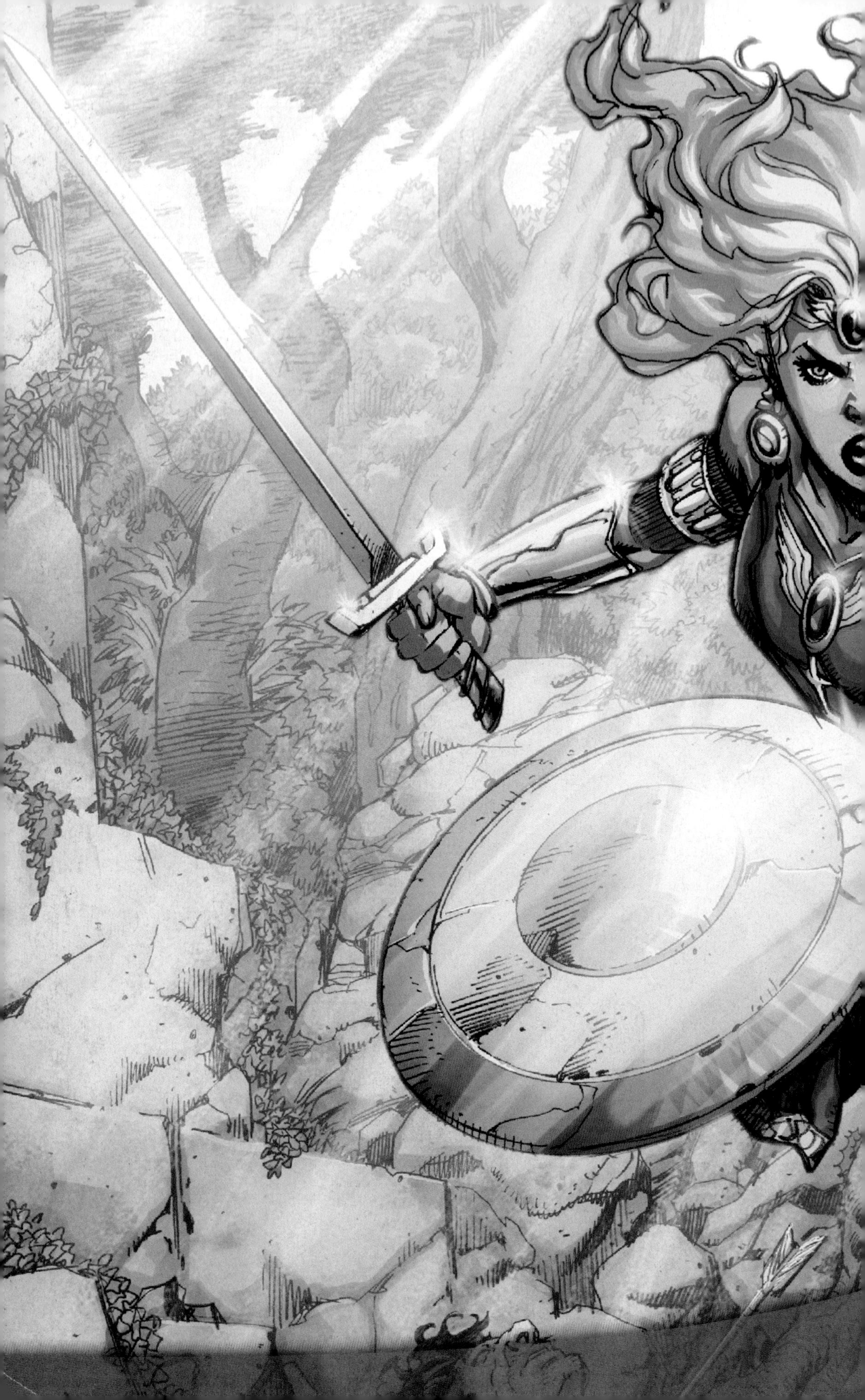

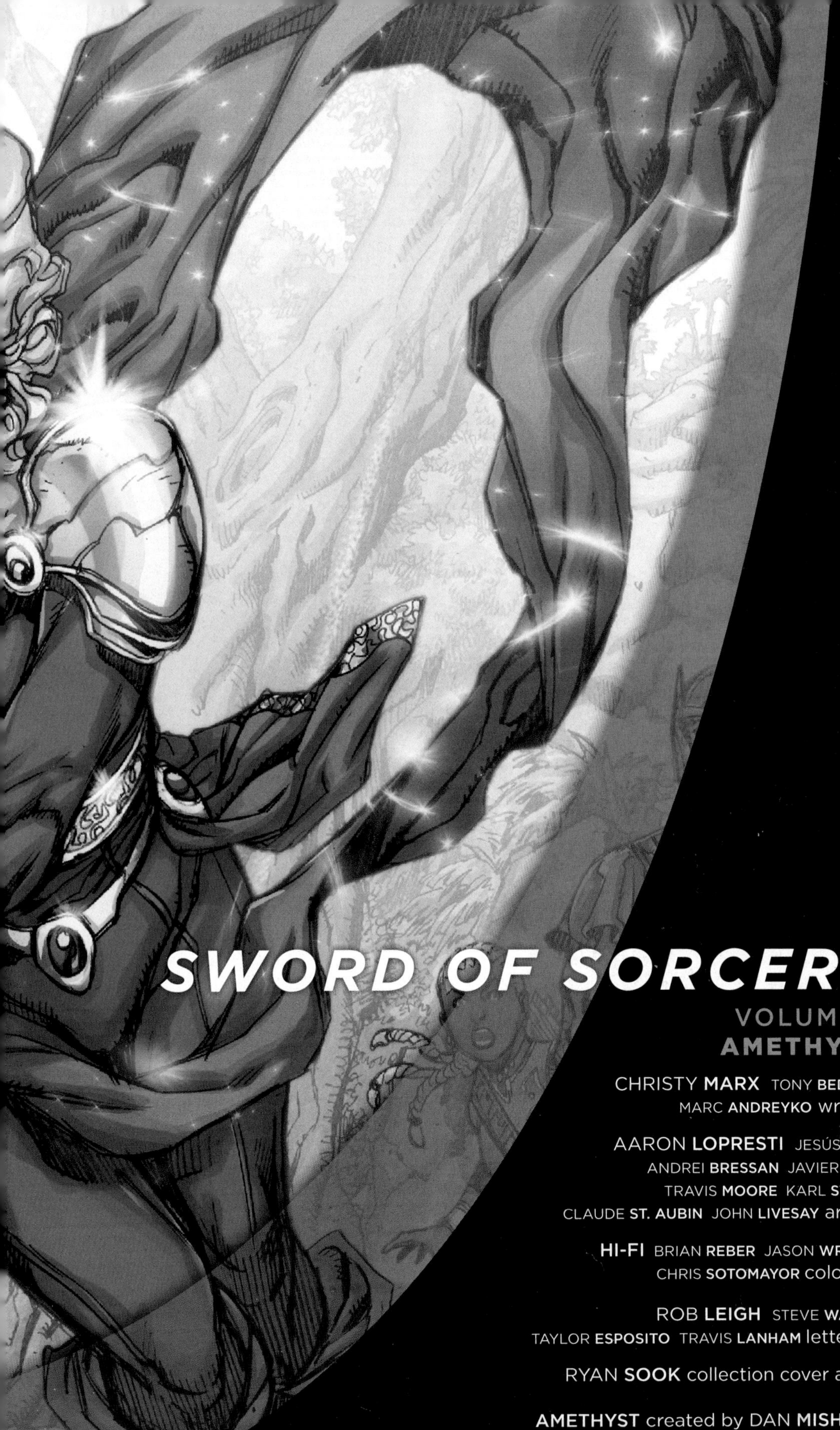

SWORD OF SORCERY

VOLUME 1
AMETHYST

CHRISTY **MARX** TONY **BEDARD**
MARC **ANDREYKO** writers

AARON **LOPRESTI** JESÚS **SAÍZ**
ANDREI **BRESSAN** JAVIER **PINA**
TRAVIS **MOORE** KARL **STORY**
CLAUDE **ST. AUBIN** JOHN **LIVESAY** artists

HI-FI BRIAN **REBER** JASON **WRIGHT**
CHRIS **SOTOMAYOR** colorists

ROB **LEIGH** STEVE **WANDS**
TAYLOR **ESPOSITO** TRAVIS **LANHAM** letterers

RYAN **SOOK** collection cover artist

AMETHYST created by DAN **MISHKIN**,
GARY **COHN** and ERNIE **COLÓN**

RACHEL GLUCKSTERN MIKE COTTON Editors – Original Series
RICKEY PURDIN DARREN SHAN ANTHONY MARQUES Assistant Editors – Original Series ROBIN WILDMAN Editor
ROBBIN BROSTERMAN Design Director – Books ROBBIE BIEDERMAN Publication Design

BOB HARRAS Senior VP – Editor-in-Chief, DC Comics

DIANE NELSON President DAN DIDIO and JIM LEE Co-Publishers GEOFF JOHNS Chief Creative Officer
JOHN ROOD Executive VP – Sales, Marketing and Business Development AMY GENKINS Senior VP – Business and Legal Affairs
NAIRI GARDINER Senior VP – Finance JEFF BOISON VP – Publishing Planning
MARK CHIARELLO VP – Art Direction and Design JOHN CUNNINGHAM VP – Marketing
TERRI CUNNINGHAM VP – Editorial Administration ALISON GILL Senior VP – Manufacturing and Operations
HANK KANALZ Senior VP – Vertigo & Integrated Publishing JAY KOGAN VP – Business and Legal Affairs, Publishing
JACK MAHAN VP – Business Affairs, Talent NICK NAPOLITANO VP – Manufacturing Administration
SUE POHJA VP – Book Sales COURTNEY SIMMONS Senior VP – Publicity BOB WAYNE Senior VP – Sales

SWORD OF SORCERY VOLUME 1: AMETHYST

Published by DC Comics. Compilation Copyright © 2013 DC Comics. All Rights Reserved.

Originally published in single magazine form in SWORD OF SORCERY 0-8, DC UNIVERSE PRESENTS 19
Copyright © 2012, 2013 DC Comics. All Rights Reserved. All characters, their distinctive likenesses and related elements
featured in this publication are trademarks of DC Comics. The stories, characters and incidents featured in this
publication are entirely fictional. DC Comics does not read or accept unsolicited ideas, stories or artwork.

DC Comics, 1700 Broadway, New York, NY 10019
A Warner Bros. Entertainment Company.
Printed by RR Donnelley, Salem, VA, USA. 7/26/13. First Printing.
ISBN: 978-1-4012-4100-1

Library of Congress Cataloging-in-Publication Data

Marx, Christy, author.
Sword of sorcery. Volume 1, Amethyst / Christy Marx, Aaron Lopresti.
pages cm
"Originally published in single magazine form in Sword of Sorcery 0-8, DC Universe Presents 19."
ISBN 978-1-4012-4100-1
1. Graphic novels. I. Lopresti, Aaron, illustrator. II. Title. III. Title: Amethyst.
PN6728.S96M37 2013
741.5'973—dc23
                                    2013003527

SUSTAINABLE
FORESTRY
INITIATIVE
Certified Chain of Custody
At Least 20% Certified Forest Content
www.sfiprogram.org
SFI-01042
APPLIES TO TEXT STOCK ONLY

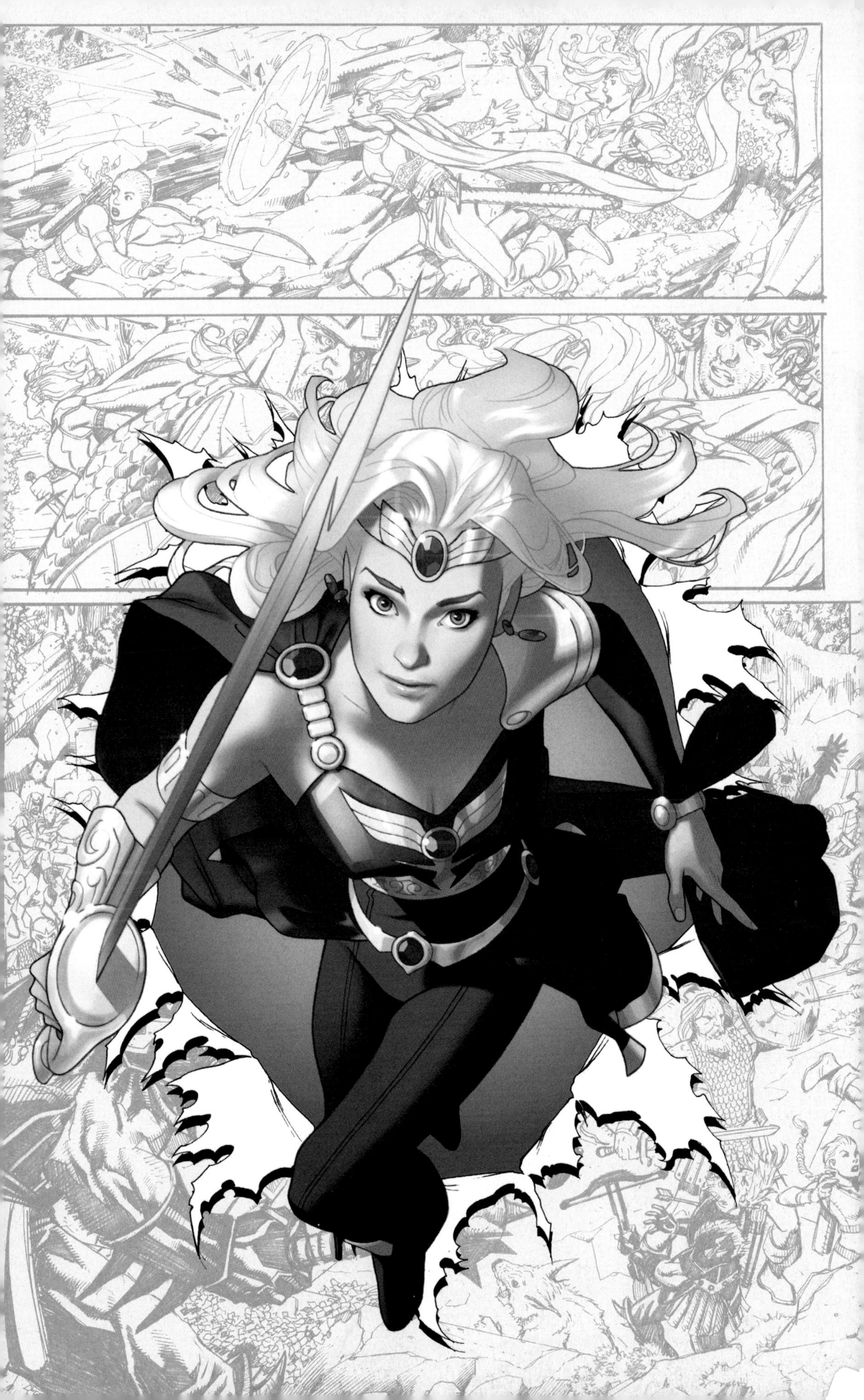

AMETHYST part one HOMECOMING

CHRISTY MARX writer AARON LOPRESTI artist cover by JOSH MIDDLETON

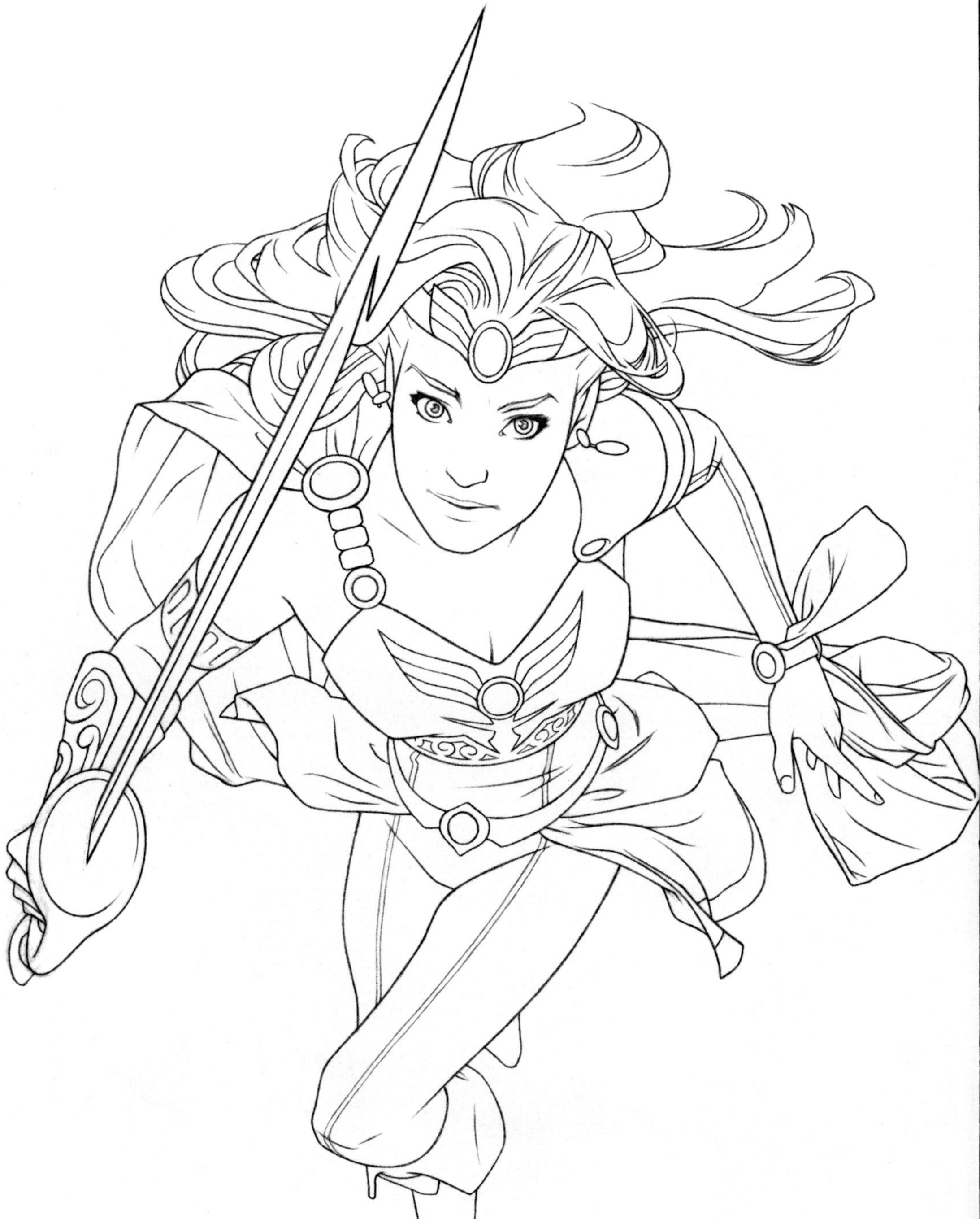

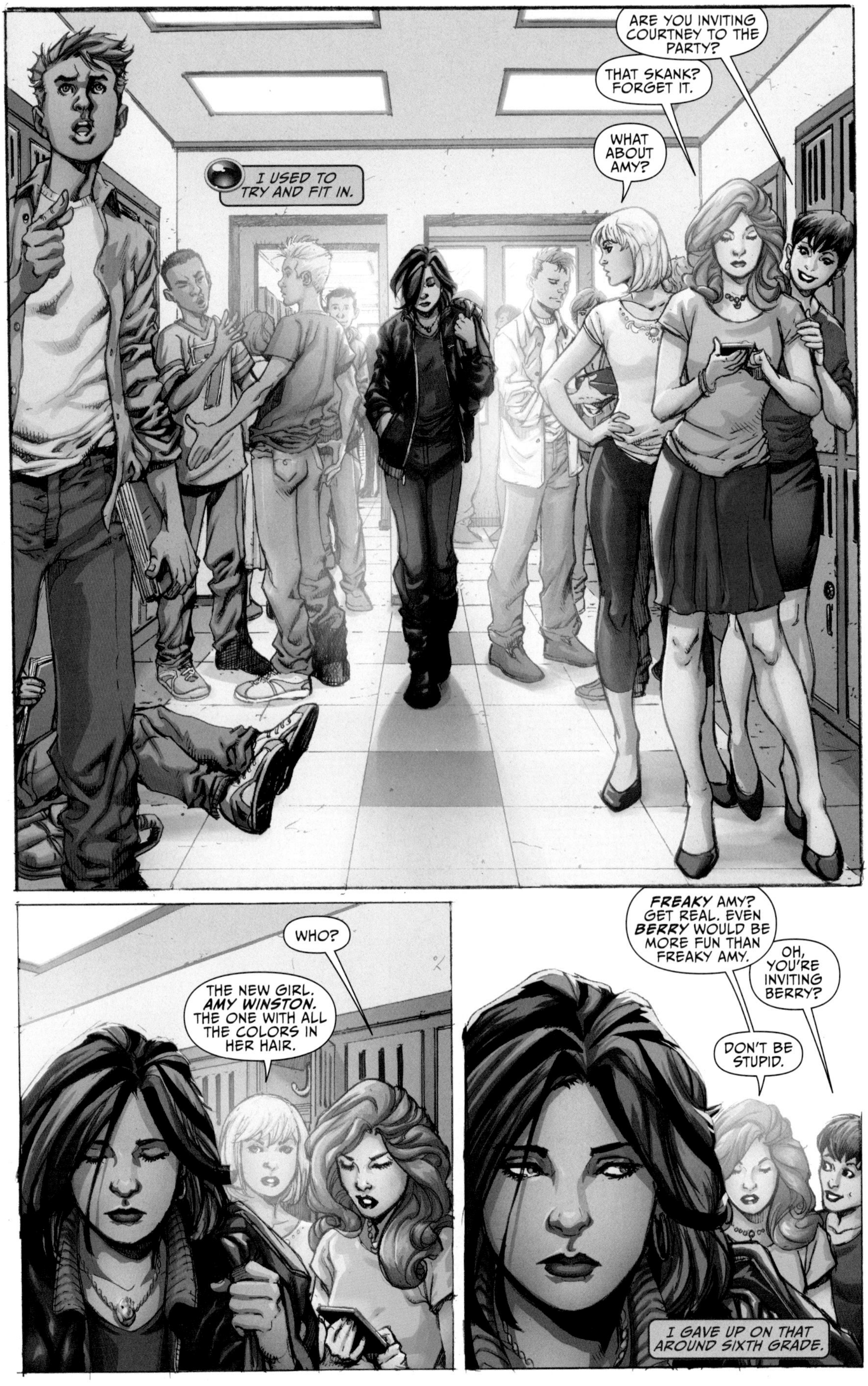
I USED TO TRY AND FIT IN.
ARE YOU INVITING COURTNEY TO THE PARTY?
THAT SKANK? FORGET IT.
WHAT ABOUT AMY?
WHO?
THE NEW GIRL. AMY WINSTON. THE ONE WITH ALL THE COLORS IN HER HAIR.
FREAKY AMY? GET REAL. EVEN BERRY WOULD BE MORE FUN THAN FREAKY AMY.
OH, YOU'RE INVITING BERRY?
DON'T BE STUPID.
I GAVE UP ON THAT AROUND SIXTH GRADE.

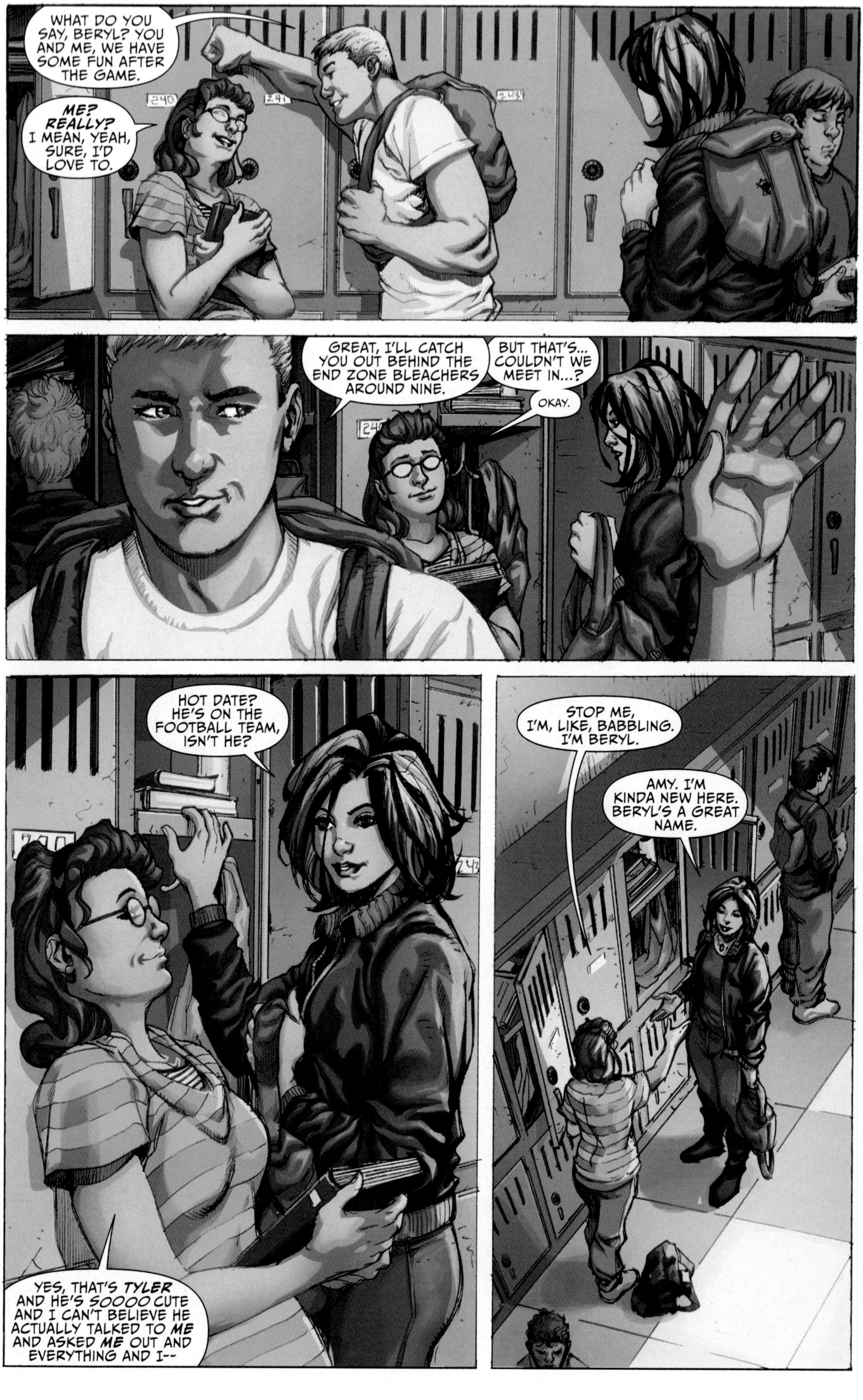
WHAT DO YOU SAY, BERYL? YOU AND ME, WE HAVE SOME FUN AFTER THE GAME.
ME? REALLY? I MEAN, YEAH, SURE, I'D LOVE TO.
GREAT, I'LL CATCH YOU OUT BEHIND THE END ZONE BLEACHERS AROUND NINE.
BUT THAT'S... COULDN'T WE MEET IN...?
OKAY.
HOT DATE? HE'S ON THE FOOTBALL TEAM, ISN'T HE?
YES, THAT'S TYLER AND HE'S SOOOO CUTE AND I CAN'T BELIEVE HE ACTUALLY TALKED TO ME AND ASKED ME OUT AND EVERYTHING AND I--
STOP ME, I'M, LIKE, BABBLING. I'M BERYL.
AMY. I'M KINDA NEW HERE. BERYL'S A GREAT NAME.

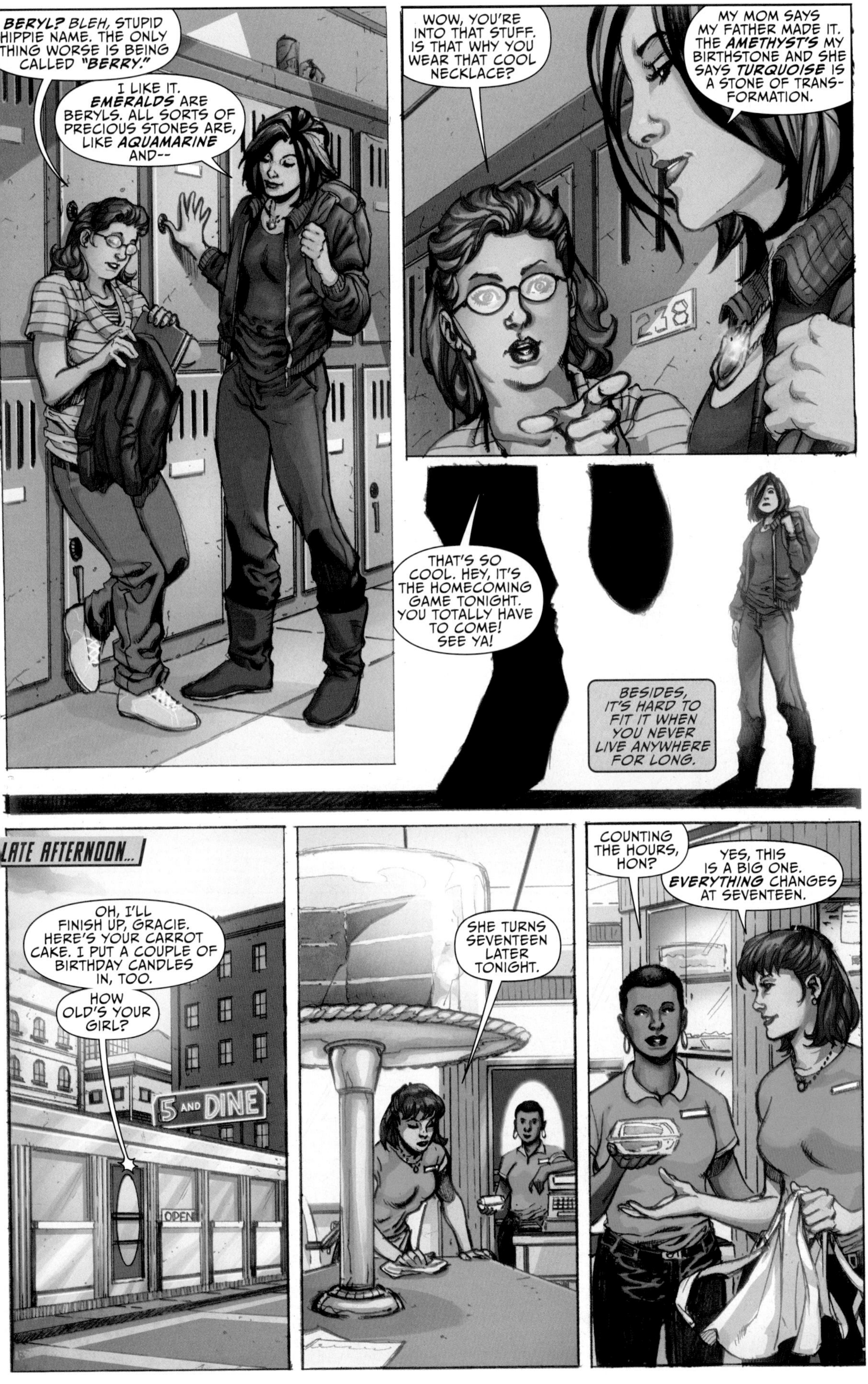
BERYL? BLEH, STUPID HIPPIE NAME. THE ONLY THING WORSE IS BEING CALLED "BERRY."
I LIKE IT. EMERALDS ARE BERYLS. ALL SORTS OF PRECIOUS STONES ARE, LIKE AQUAMARINE AND--
WOW, YOU'RE INTO THAT STUFF. IS THAT WHY YOU WEAR THAT COOL NECKLACE?
MY MOM SAYS MY FATHER MADE IT. THE AMETHYST'S MY BIRTHSTONE AND SHE SAYS TURQUOISE IS A STONE OF TRANS-FORMATION.
238
THAT'S SO COOL. HEY, IT'S THE HOMECOMING GAME TONIGHT. YOU TOTALLY HAVE TO COME! SEE YA!
BESIDES, IT'S HARD TO FIT IT WHEN YOU NEVER LIVE ANYWHERE FOR LONG.
LATE AFTERNOON...
OH, I'LL FINISH UP, GRACIE. HERE'S YOUR CARROT CAKE. I PUT A COUPLE OF BIRTHDAY CANDLES IN, TOO.
HOW OLD'S YOUR GIRL?
5 AND DINE
OPEN
SHE TURNS SEVENTEEN LATER TONIGHT.
COUNTING THE HOURS, HON?
YES, THIS IS A BIG ONE. EVERYTHING CHANGES AT SEVENTEEN.

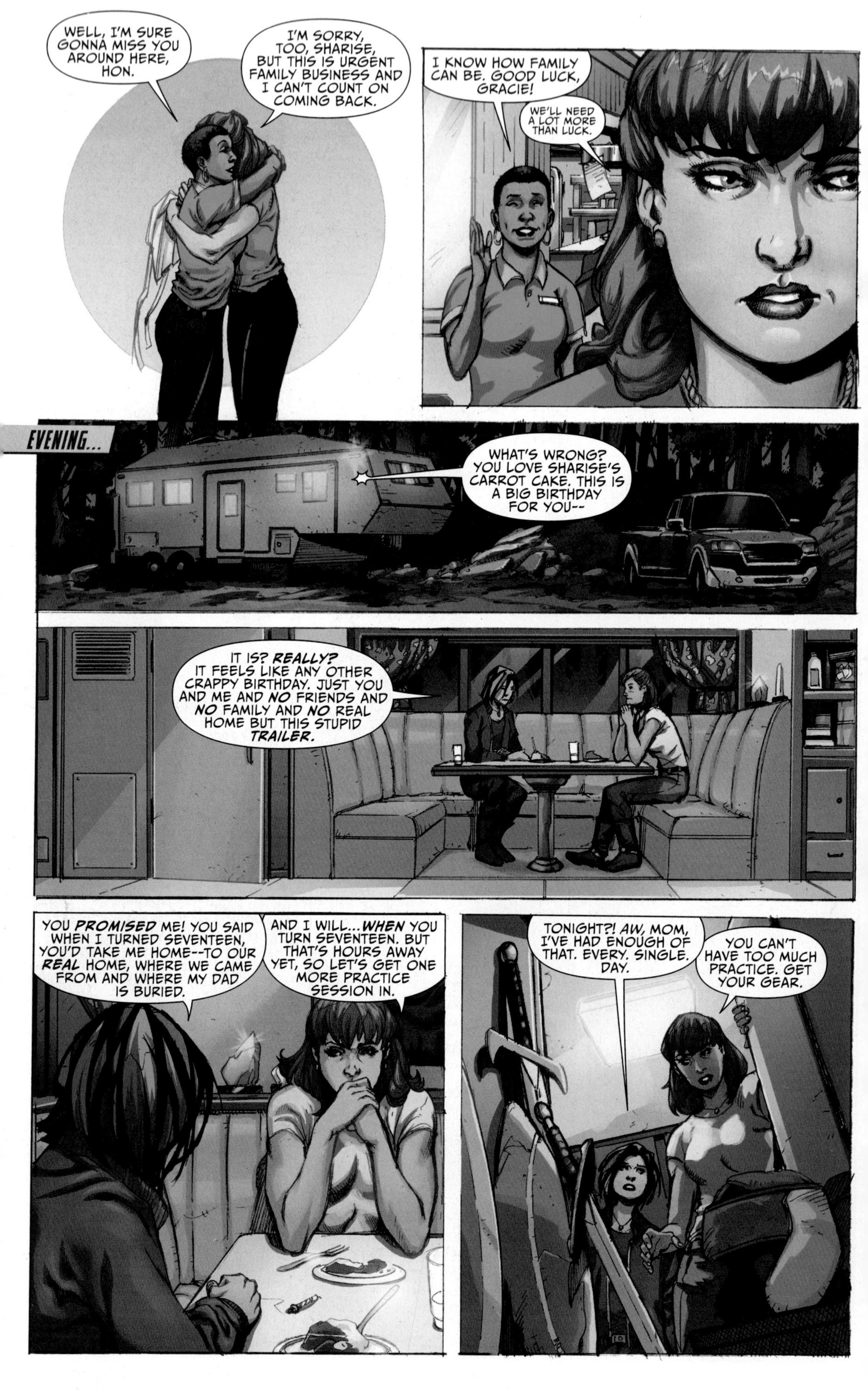

WELL, I'M SURE GONNA MISS YOU AROUND HERE, HON.
I'M SORRY, TOO, SHARISE, BUT THIS IS URGENT FAMILY BUSINESS AND I CAN'T COUNT ON COMING BACK.
I KNOW HOW FAMILY CAN BE. GOOD LUCK, GRACIE!
WE'LL NEED A LOT MORE THAN LUCK.
EVENING...
WHAT'S WRONG? YOU LOVE SHARISE'S CARROT CAKE. THIS IS A BIG BIRTHDAY FOR YOU--
IT IS? REALLY? IT FEELS LIKE ANY OTHER CRAPPY BIRTHDAY. JUST YOU AND ME AND NO FRIENDS AND NO FAMILY AND NO REAL HOME BUT THIS STUPID TRAILER.
YOU PROMISED ME! YOU SAID WHEN I TURNED SEVENTEEN, YOU'D TAKE ME HOME--TO OUR REAL HOME, WHERE WE CAME FROM AND WHERE MY DAD IS BURIED.
AND I WILL...WHEN YOU TURN SEVENTEEN. BUT THAT'S HOURS AWAY YET, SO LET'S GET ONE MORE PRACTICE SESSION IN.
TONIGHT?! AW, MOM, I'VE HAD ENOUGH OF THAT. EVERY. SINGLE. DAY.
YOU CAN'T HAVE TOO MUCH PRACTICE. GET YOUR GEAR.

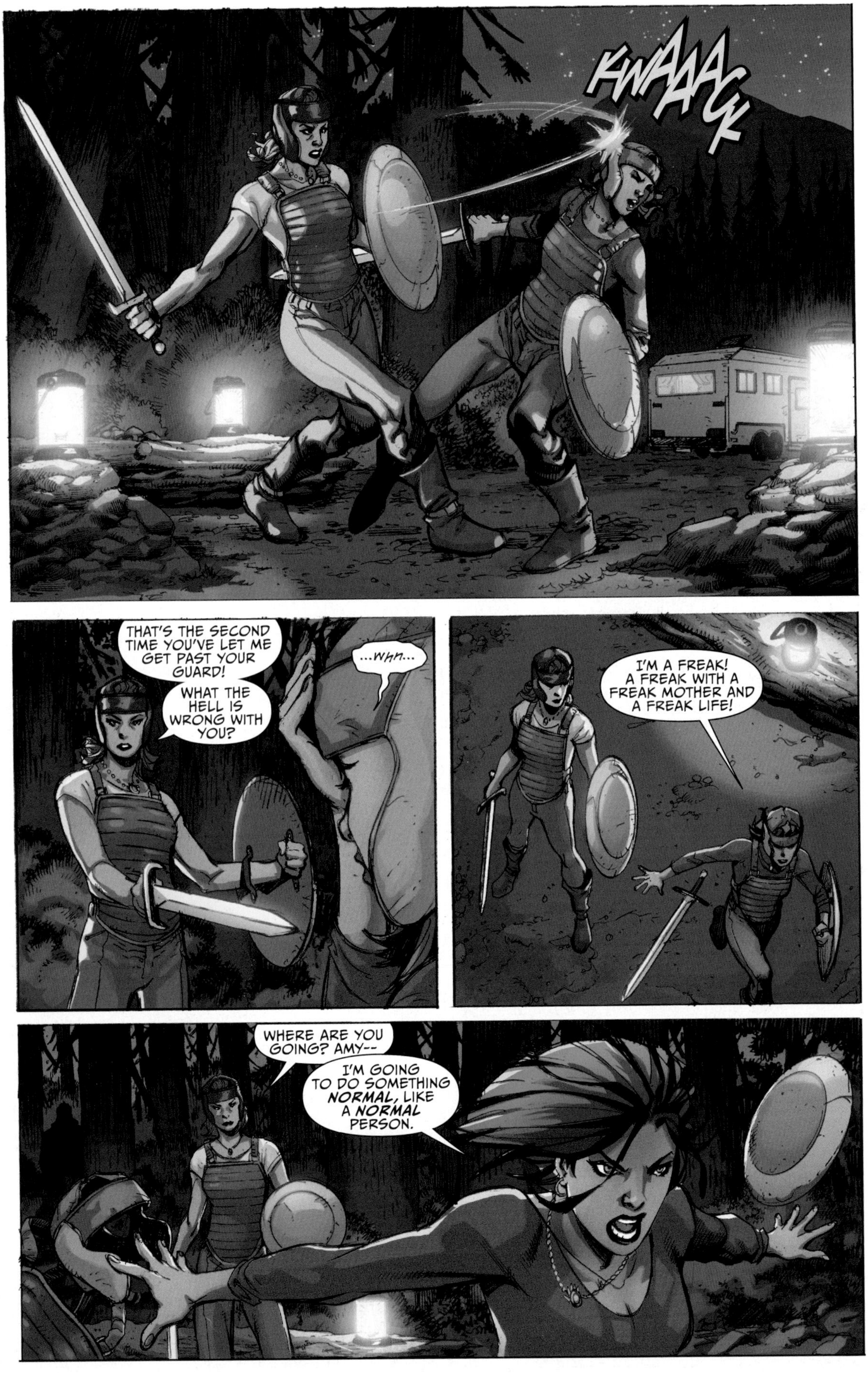
KWAAAACK
THAT'S THE SECOND TIME YOU'VE LET ME GET PAST YOUR GUARD!
WHAT THE HELL IS WRONG WITH YOU?
...whn...
I'M A FREAK! A FREAK WITH A FREAK MOTHER AND A FREAK LIFE!
WHERE ARE YOU GOING? AMY--
I'M GOING TO DO SOMETHING NORMAL, LIKE A NORMAL PERSON.

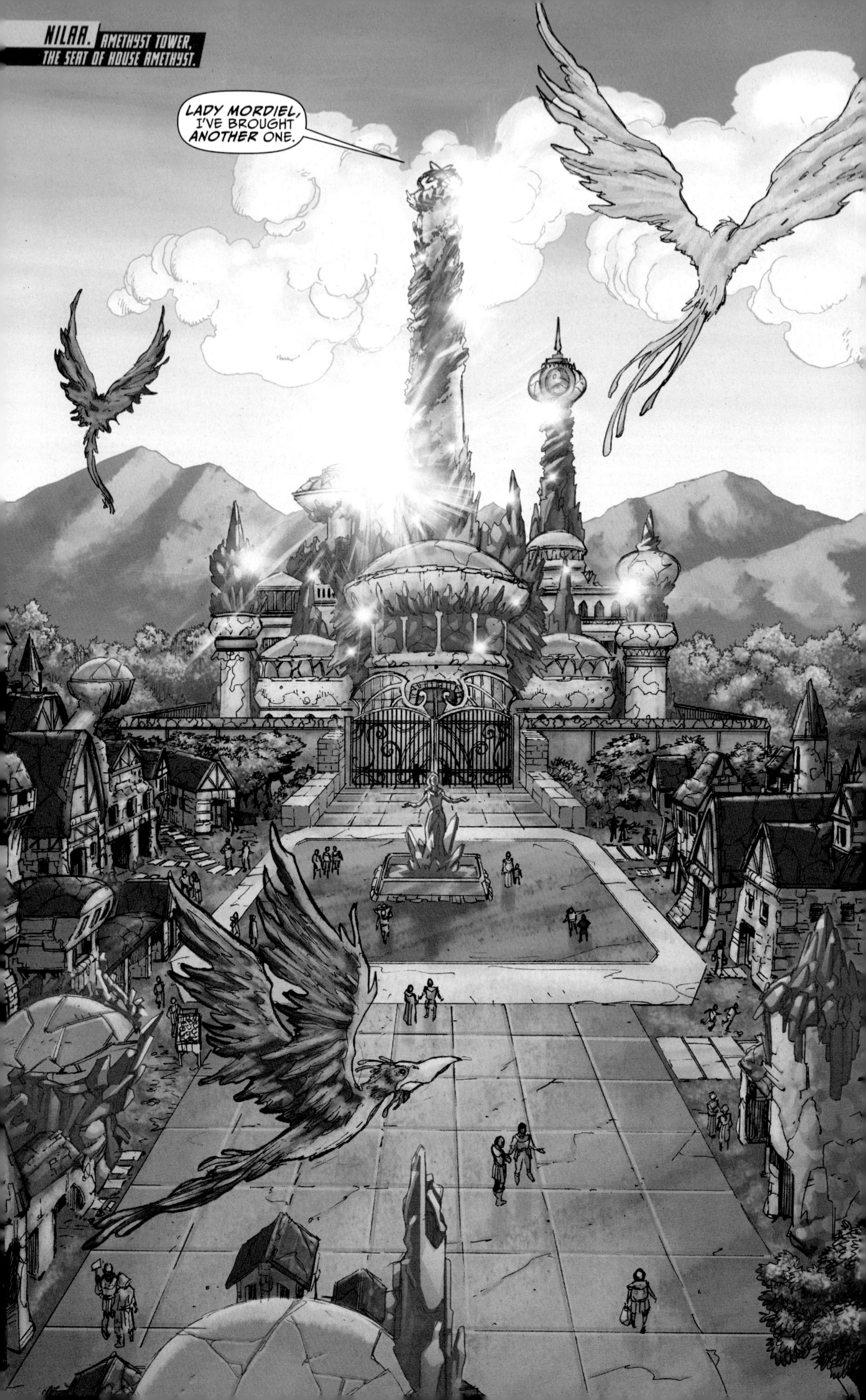
NILAAR. AMETHYST TOWER, THE SEAT OF HOUSE AMETHYST.
LADY MORDIEL, I'VE BROUGHT ANOTHER ONE.

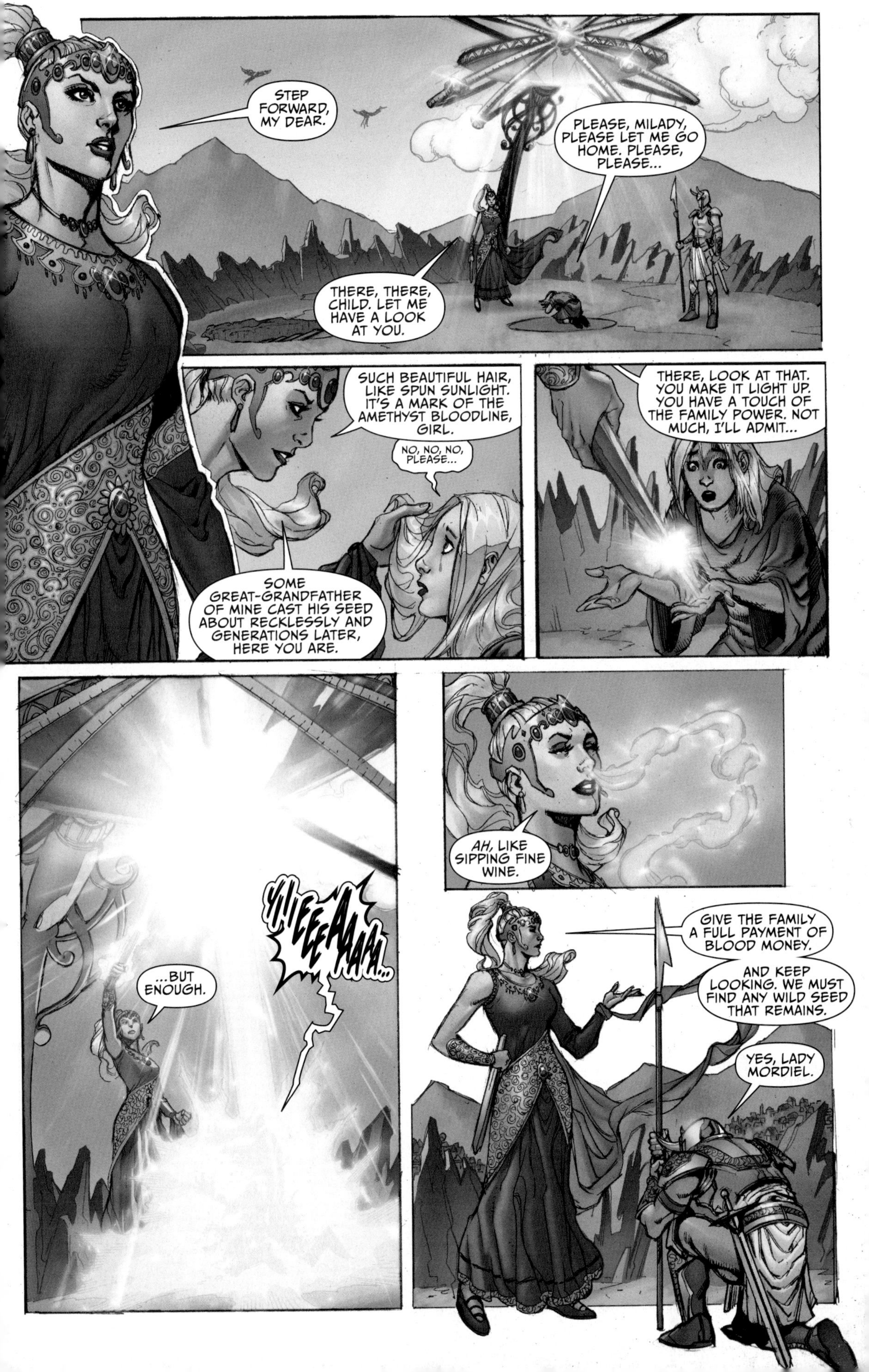
STEP FORWARD, MY DEAR.
PLEASE, MILADY, PLEASE LET ME GO HOME. PLEASE, PLEASE...
THERE, THERE, CHILD. LET ME HAVE A LOOK AT YOU.
SUCH BEAUTIFUL HAIR, LIKE SPUN SUNLIGHT. IT'S A MARK OF THE AMETHYST BLOODLINE, GIRL.
NO, NO, NO, PLEASE...
SOME GREAT-GRANDFATHER OF MINE CAST HIS SEED ABOUT RECKLESSLY AND GENERATIONS LATER, HERE YOU ARE.
THERE, LOOK AT THAT. YOU MAKE IT LIGHT UP. YOU HAVE A TOUCH OF THE FAMILY POWER. NOT MUCH, I'LL ADMIT...
...BUT ENOUGH.
YIIIEEEAAAAA...
AH, LIKE SIPPING FINE WINE.
GIVE THE FAMILY A FULL PAYMENT OF BLOOD MONEY.
AND KEEP LOOKING. WE MUST FIND ANY WILD SEED THAT REMAINS.
YES, LADY MORDIEL.

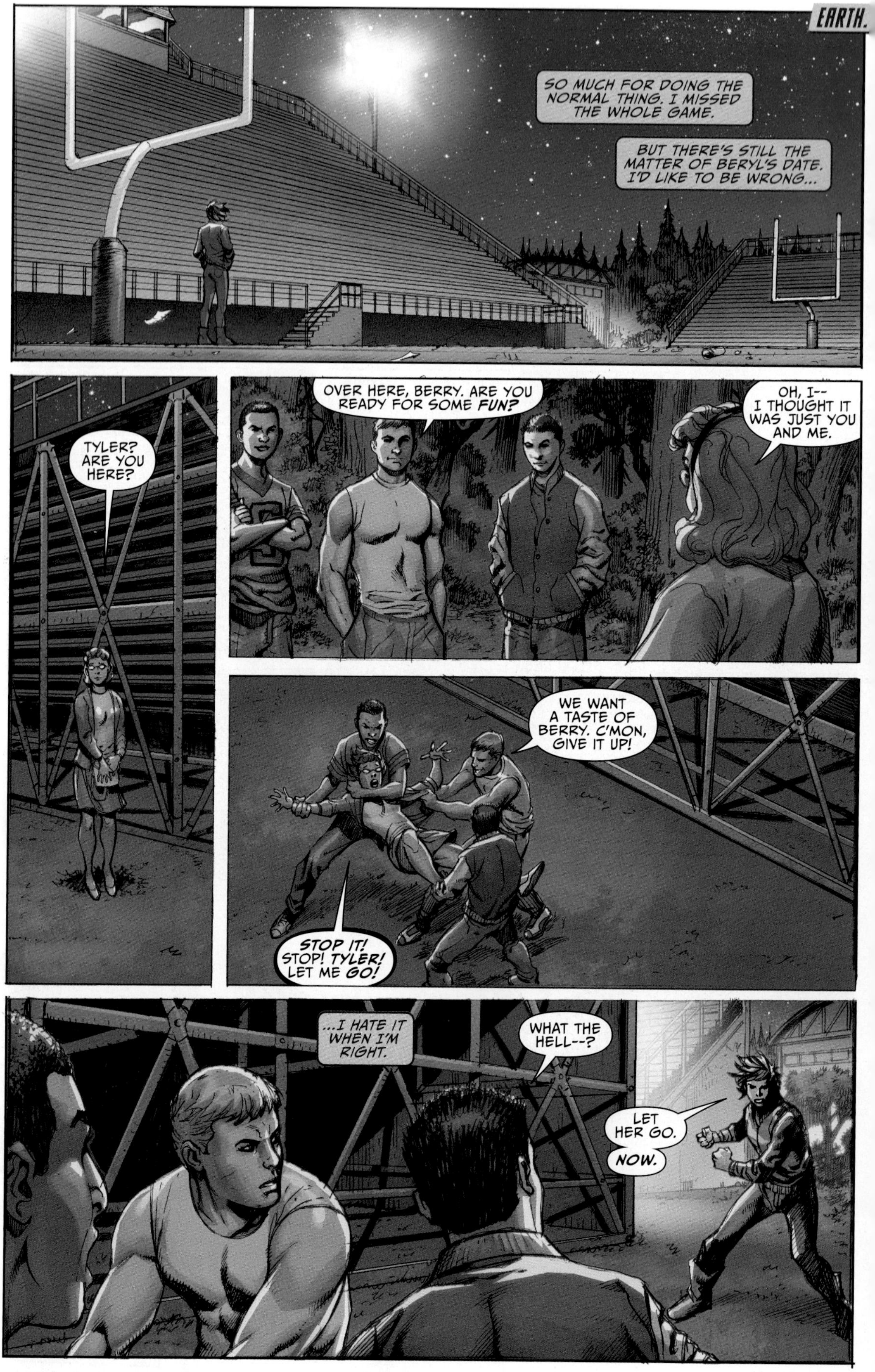
EARTH.
SO MUCH FOR DOING THE NORMAL THING. I MISSED THE WHOLE GAME.
BUT THERE'S STILL THE MATTER OF BERYL'S DATE. I'D LIKE TO BE WRONG...
TYLER? ARE YOU HERE?
OVER HERE, BERRY. ARE YOU READY FOR SOME FUN?
OH, I-- I THOUGHT IT WAS JUST YOU AND ME.
WE WANT A TASTE OF BERRY. C'MON, GIVE IT UP!
STOP IT! STOP! TYLER! LET ME GO!
...I HATE IT WHEN I'M RIGHT.
WHAT THE HELL--?
LET HER GO.
NOW.

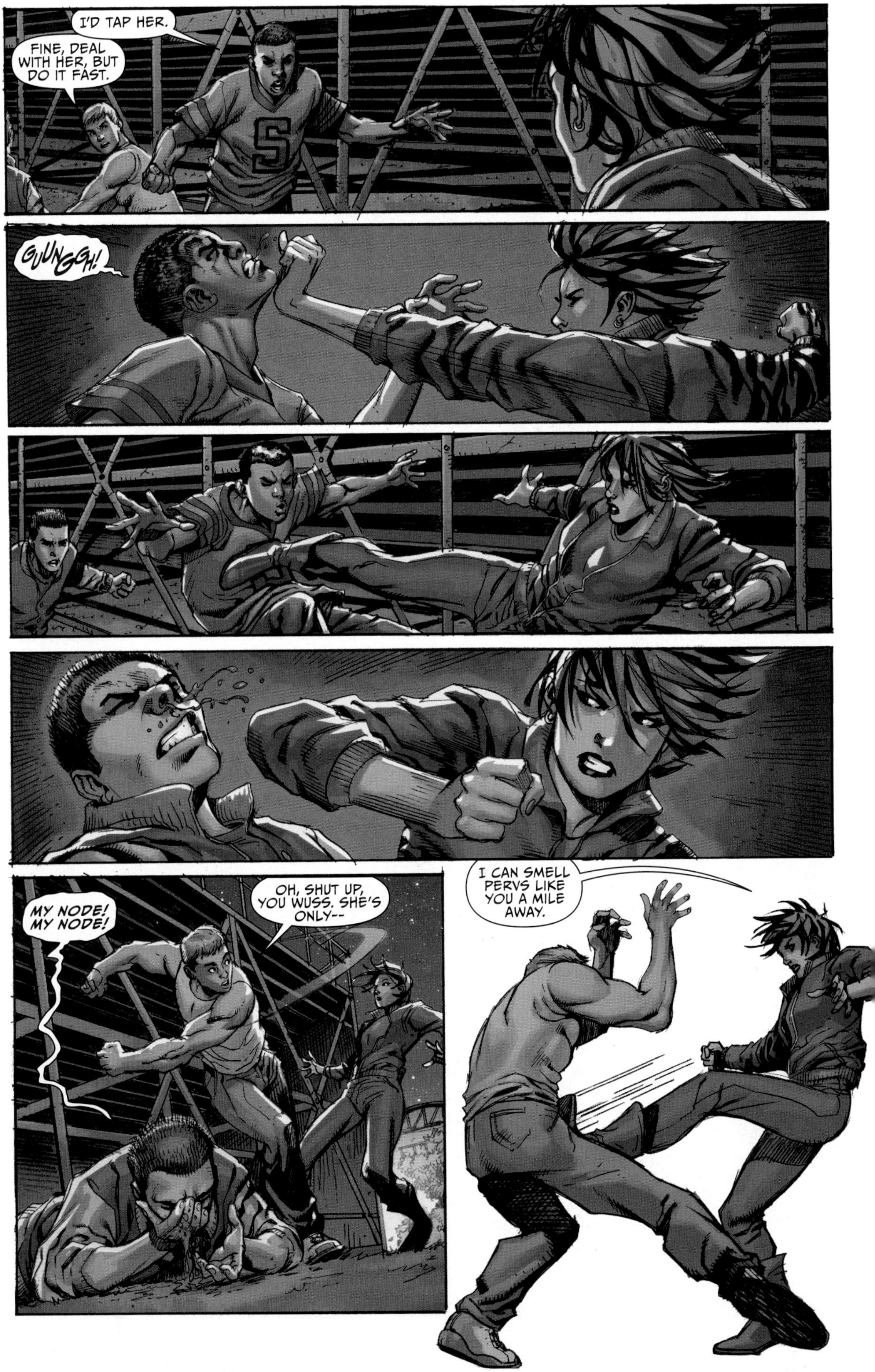
I'D TAP HER.
FINE, DEAL WITH HER, BUT DO IT FAST.
GUUNGGH!
MY NODE! MY NODE!
OH, SHUT UP, YOU WUSS. SHE'S ONLY--
I CAN SMELL PERVS LIKE YOU A MILE AWAY.

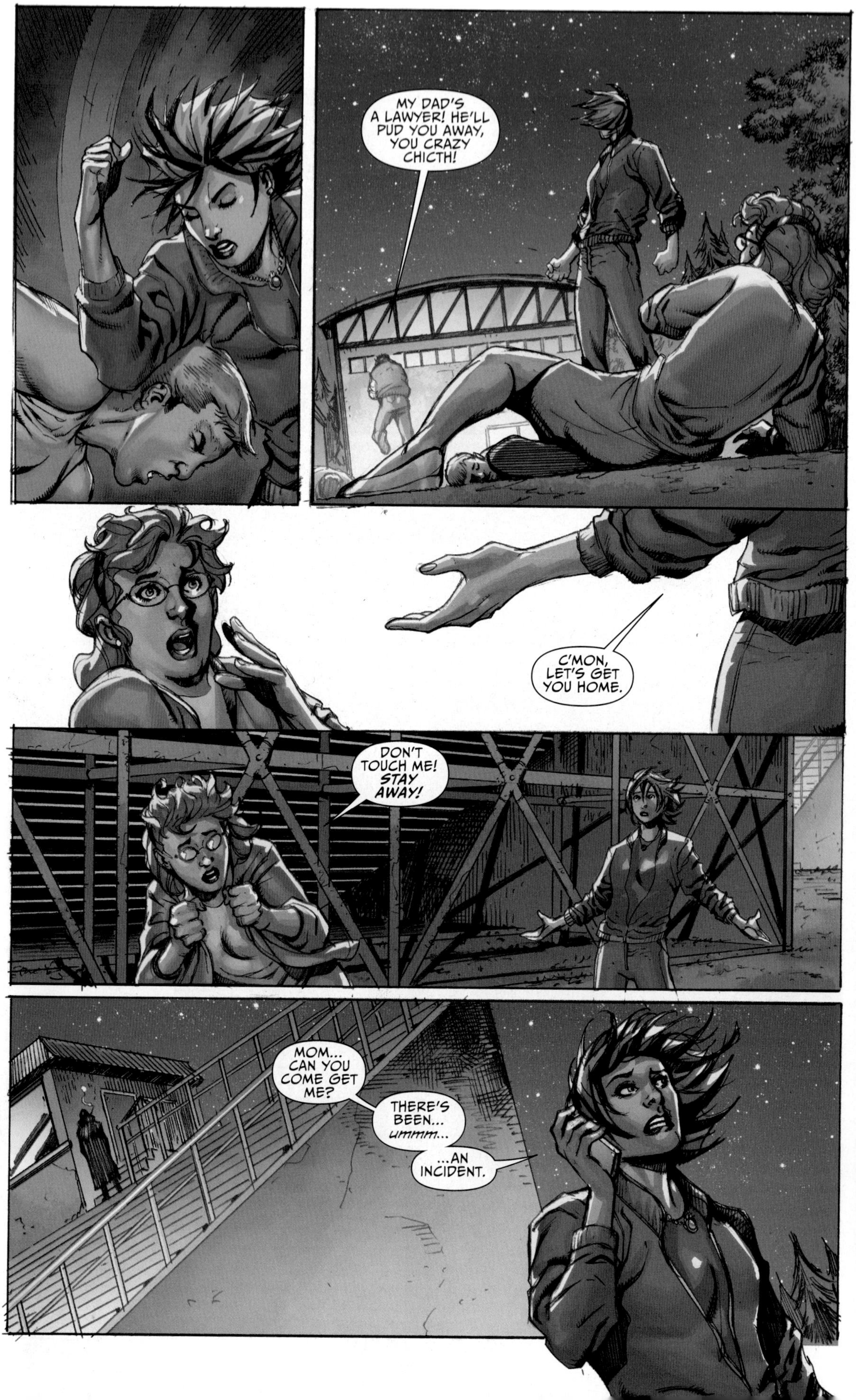
MY DAD'S A LAWYER! HE'LL PUD YOU AWAY, YOU CRAZY CHICTH!
C'MON, LET'S GET YOU HOME.
DON'T TOUCH ME! *STAY AWAY!*
MOM... CAN YOU COME GET ME?
THERE'S BEEN... *ummm...*
...AN INCIDENT.

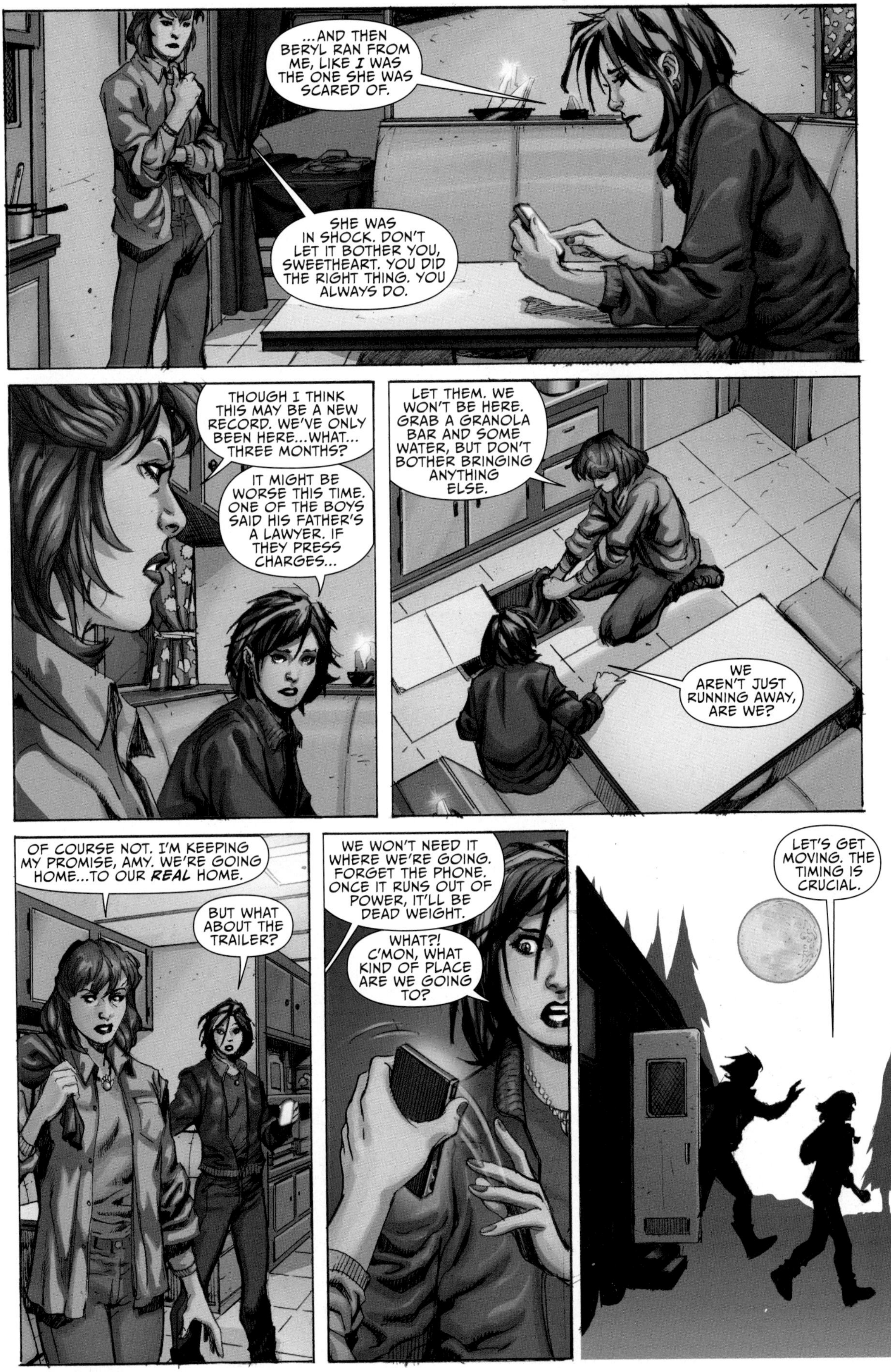
...AND THEN BERYL RAN FROM ME, LIKE I WAS THE ONE SHE WAS SCARED OF.
SHE WAS IN SHOCK. DON'T LET IT BOTHER YOU, SWEETHEART. YOU DID THE RIGHT THING. YOU ALWAYS DO.
THOUGH I THINK THIS MAY BE A NEW RECORD. WE'VE ONLY BEEN HERE...WHAT... THREE MONTHS?
IT MIGHT BE WORSE THIS TIME. ONE OF THE BOYS SAID HIS FATHER'S A LAWYER. IF THEY PRESS CHARGES...
LET THEM. WE WON'T BE HERE. GRAB A GRANOLA BAR AND SOME WATER, BUT DON'T BOTHER BRINGING ANYTHING ELSE.
WE AREN'T JUST RUNNING AWAY, ARE WE?
OF COURSE NOT. I'M KEEPING MY PROMISE, AMY. WE'RE GOING HOME...TO OUR REAL HOME.
BUT WHAT ABOUT THE TRAILER?
WE WON'T NEED IT WHERE WE'RE GOING. FORGET THE PHONE. ONCE IT RUNS OUT OF POWER, IT'LL BE DEAD WEIGHT.
WHAT?! C'MON, WHAT KIND OF PLACE ARE WE GOING TO?
LET'S GET MOVING. THE TIMING IS CRUCIAL.

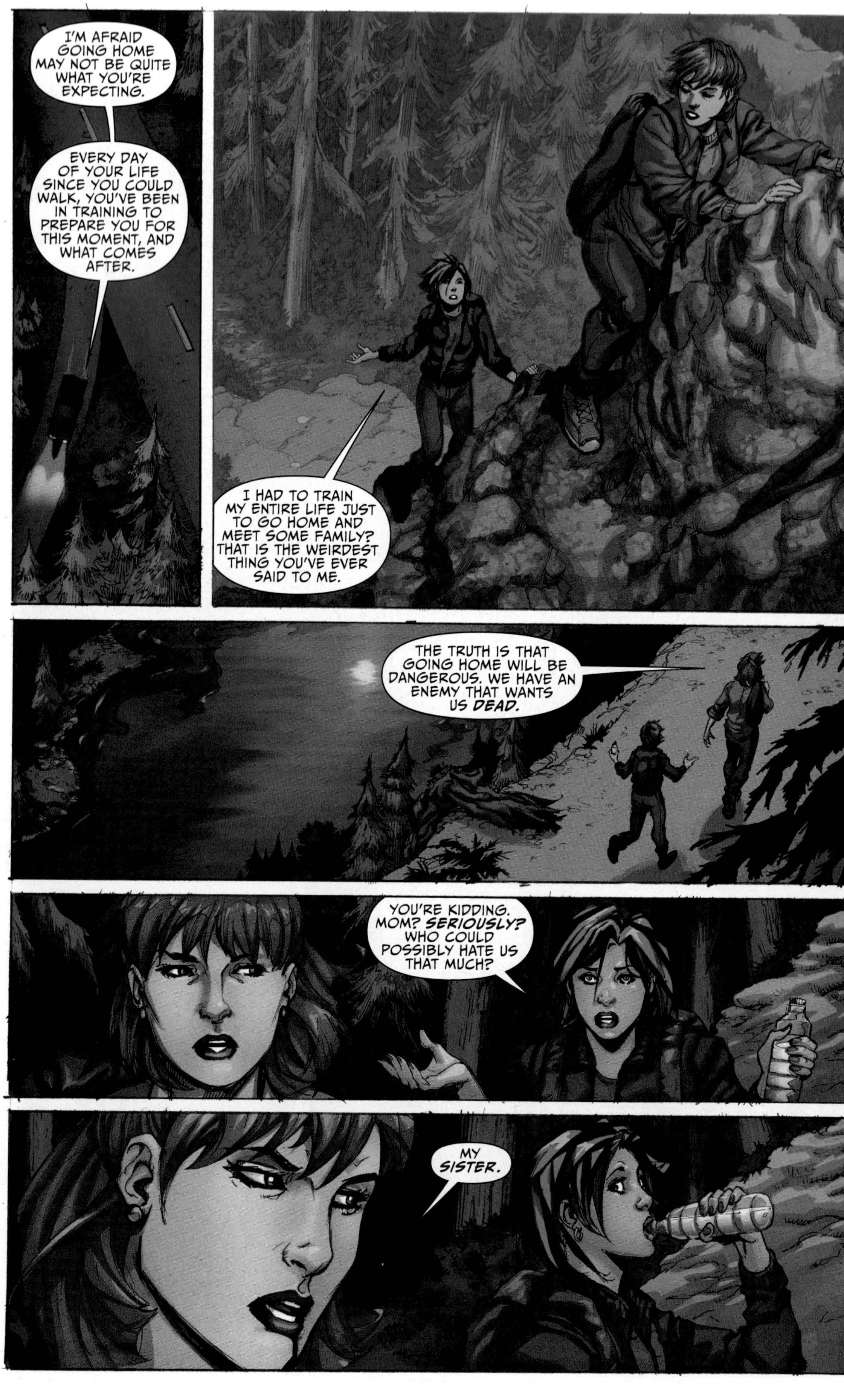
I'M AFRAID GOING HOME MAY NOT BE QUITE WHAT YOU'RE EXPECTING.
EVERY DAY OF YOUR LIFE SINCE YOU COULD WALK, YOU'VE BEEN IN TRAINING TO PREPARE YOU FOR THIS MOMENT, AND WHAT COMES AFTER.
I HAD TO TRAIN MY ENTIRE LIFE JUST TO GO HOME AND MEET SOME FAMILY? THAT IS THE WEIRDEST THING YOU'VE EVER SAID TO ME.
THE TRUTH IS THAT GOING HOME WILL BE DANGEROUS. WE HAVE AN ENEMY THAT WANTS US *DEAD.*
YOU'RE KIDDING. MOM? *SERIOUSLY?* WHO COULD POSSIBLY HATE US THAT MUCH?
MY *SISTER.*

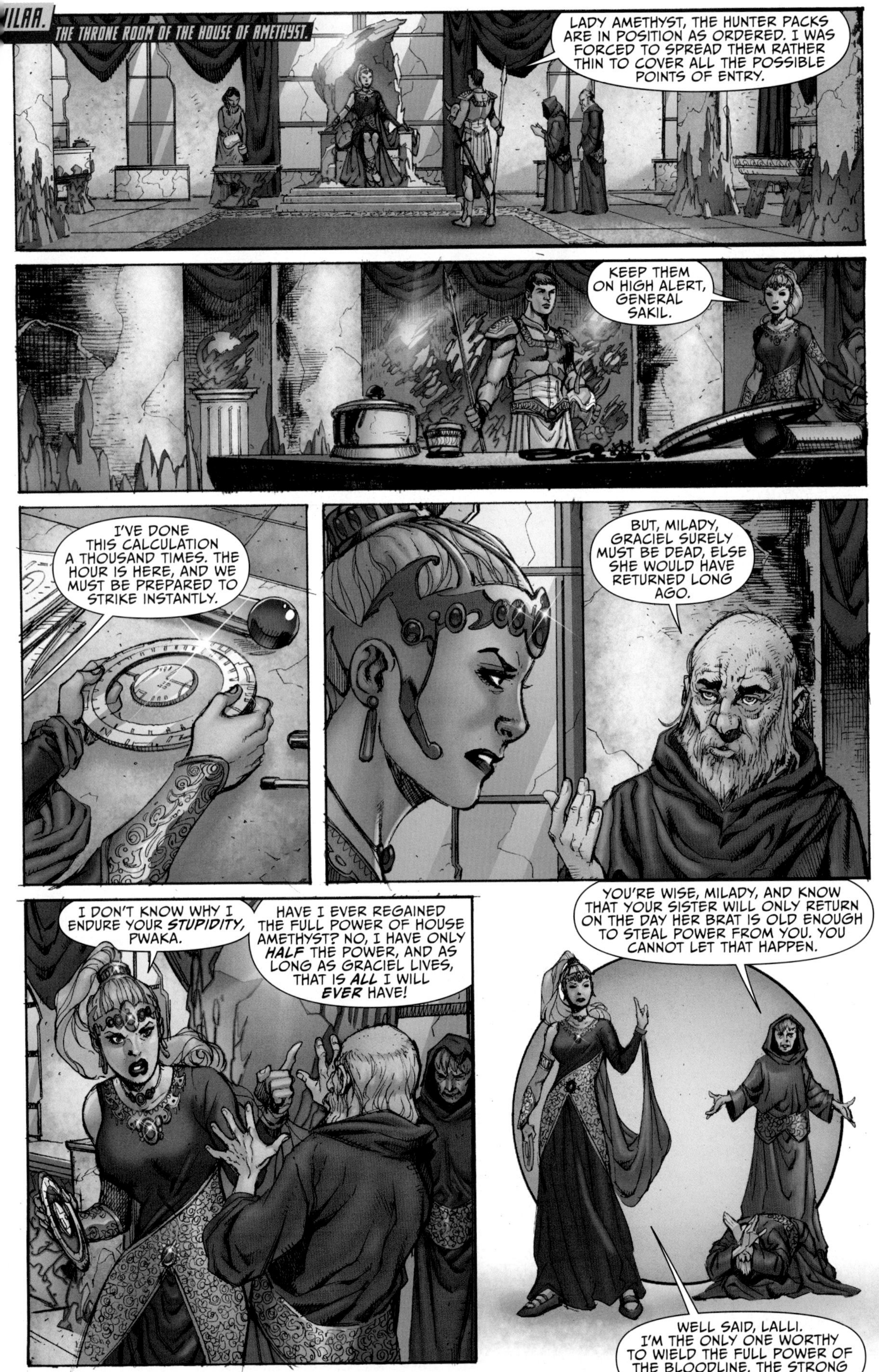
ILAA.
THE THRONE ROOM OF THE HOUSE OF AMETHYST.
LADY AMETHYST, THE HUNTER PACKS ARE IN POSITION AS ORDERED. I WAS FORCED TO SPREAD THEM RATHER THIN TO COVER ALL THE POSSIBLE POINTS OF ENTRY.
KEEP THEM ON HIGH ALERT, GENERAL SAKIL.
I'VE DONE THIS CALCULATION A THOUSAND TIMES. THE HOUR IS HERE, AND WE MUST BE PREPARED TO STRIKE INSTANTLY.
BUT, MILADY, GRACIEL SURELY MUST BE DEAD, ELSE SHE WOULD HAVE RETURNED LONG AGO.
I DON'T KNOW WHY I ENDURE YOUR STUPIDITY, PWAKA.
HAVE I EVER REGAINED THE FULL POWER OF HOUSE AMETHYST? NO, I HAVE ONLY HALF THE POWER, AND AS LONG AS GRACIEL LIVES, THAT IS ALL I WILL EVER HAVE!
YOU'RE WISE, MILADY, AND KNOW THAT YOUR SISTER WILL ONLY RETURN ON THE DAY HER BRAT IS OLD ENOUGH TO STEAL POWER FROM YOU. YOU CANNOT LET THAT HAPPEN.
WELL SAID, LALLI. I'M THE ONLY ONE WORTHY TO WIELD THE FULL POWER OF THE BLOODLINE. THE STRONG WILL DRIVE OUT THE WEAK.

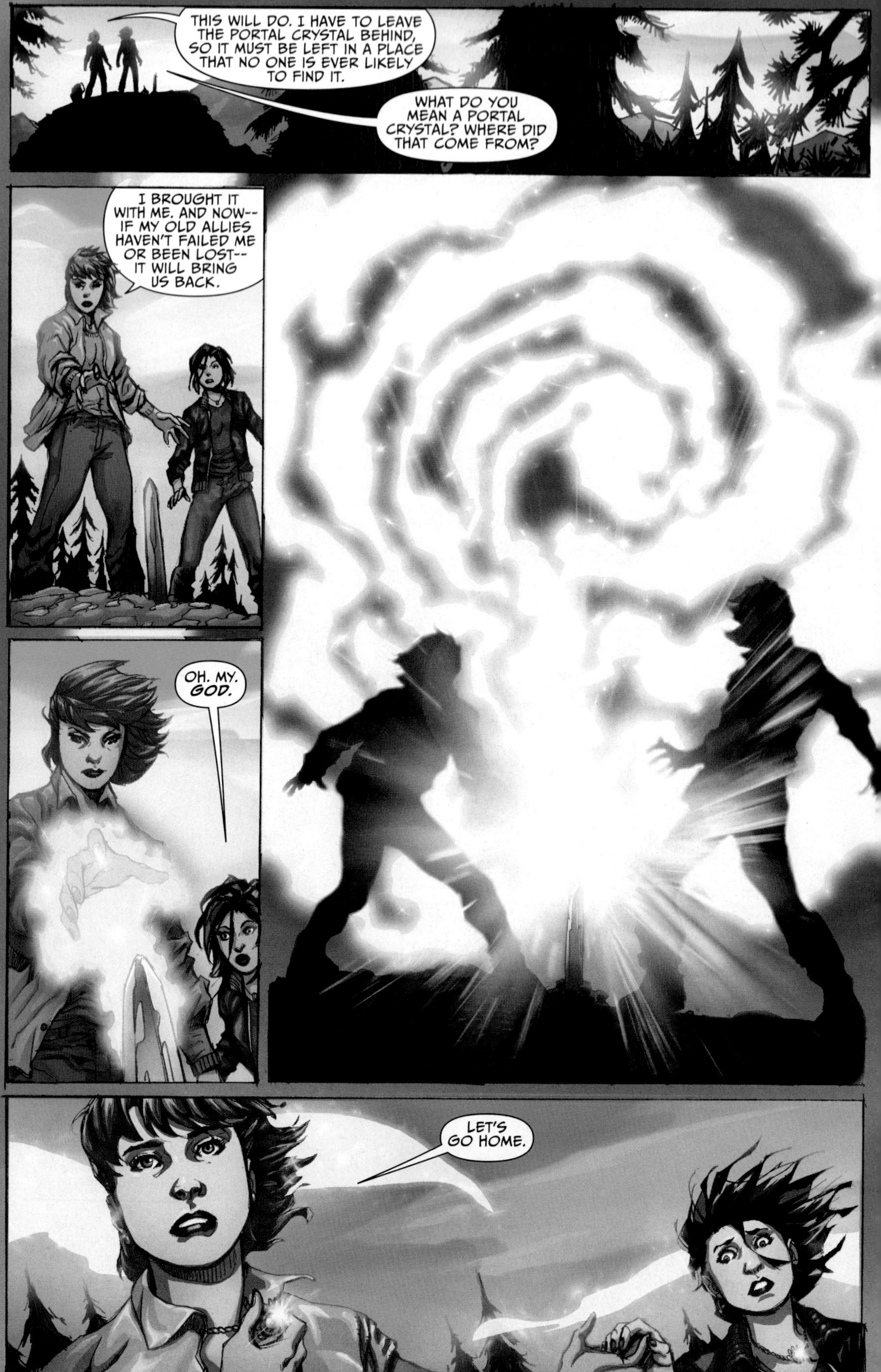
THIS WILL DO. I HAVE TO LEAVE THE PORTAL CRYSTAL BEHIND, SO IT MUST BE LEFT IN A PLACE THAT NO ONE IS EVER LIKELY TO FIND IT.
WHAT DO YOU MEAN A PORTAL CRYSTAL? WHERE DID THAT COME FROM?
I BROUGHT IT WITH ME. AND NOW-- IF MY OLD ALLIES HAVEN'T FAILED ME OR BEEN LOST-- IT WILL BRING US BACK.
OH. MY. *GOD.*
LET'S GO HOME.

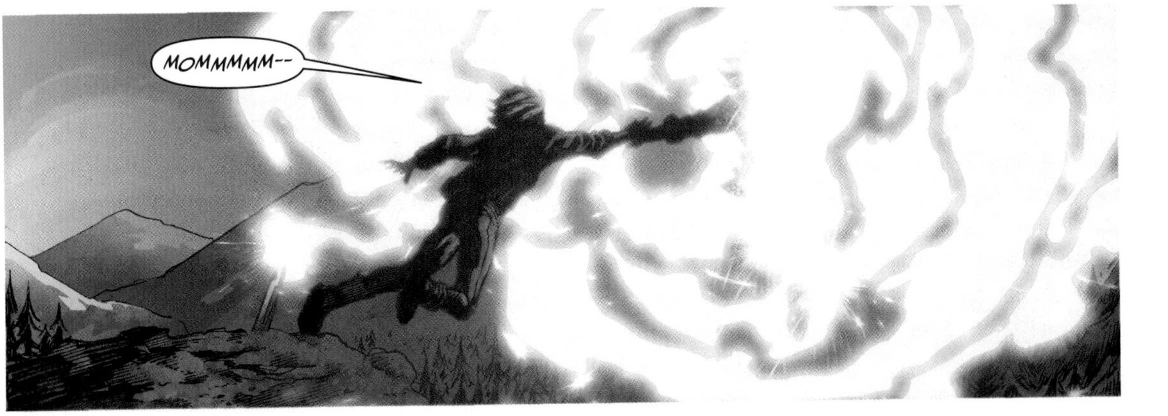
MOMMMMM--

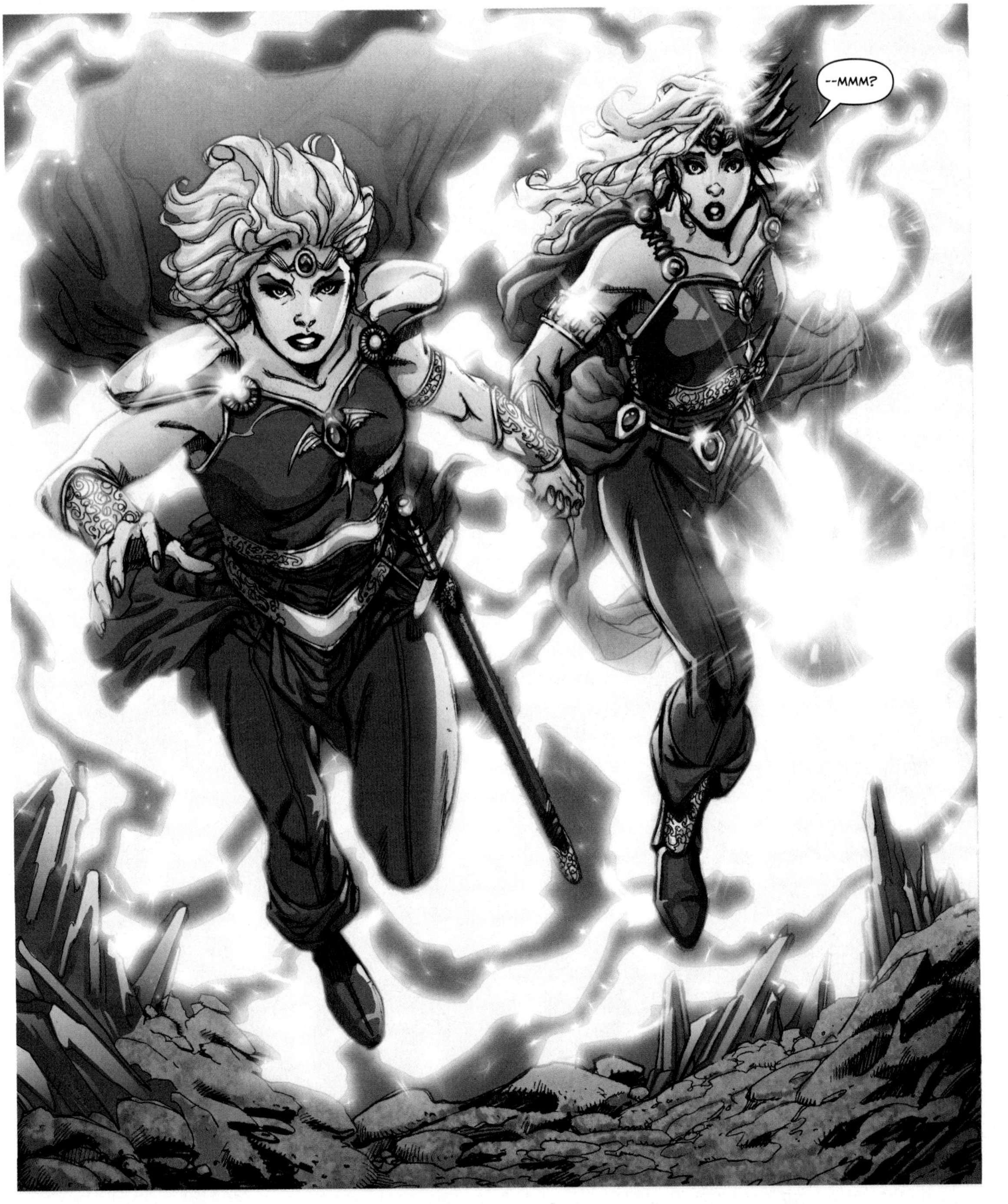
--MMM?

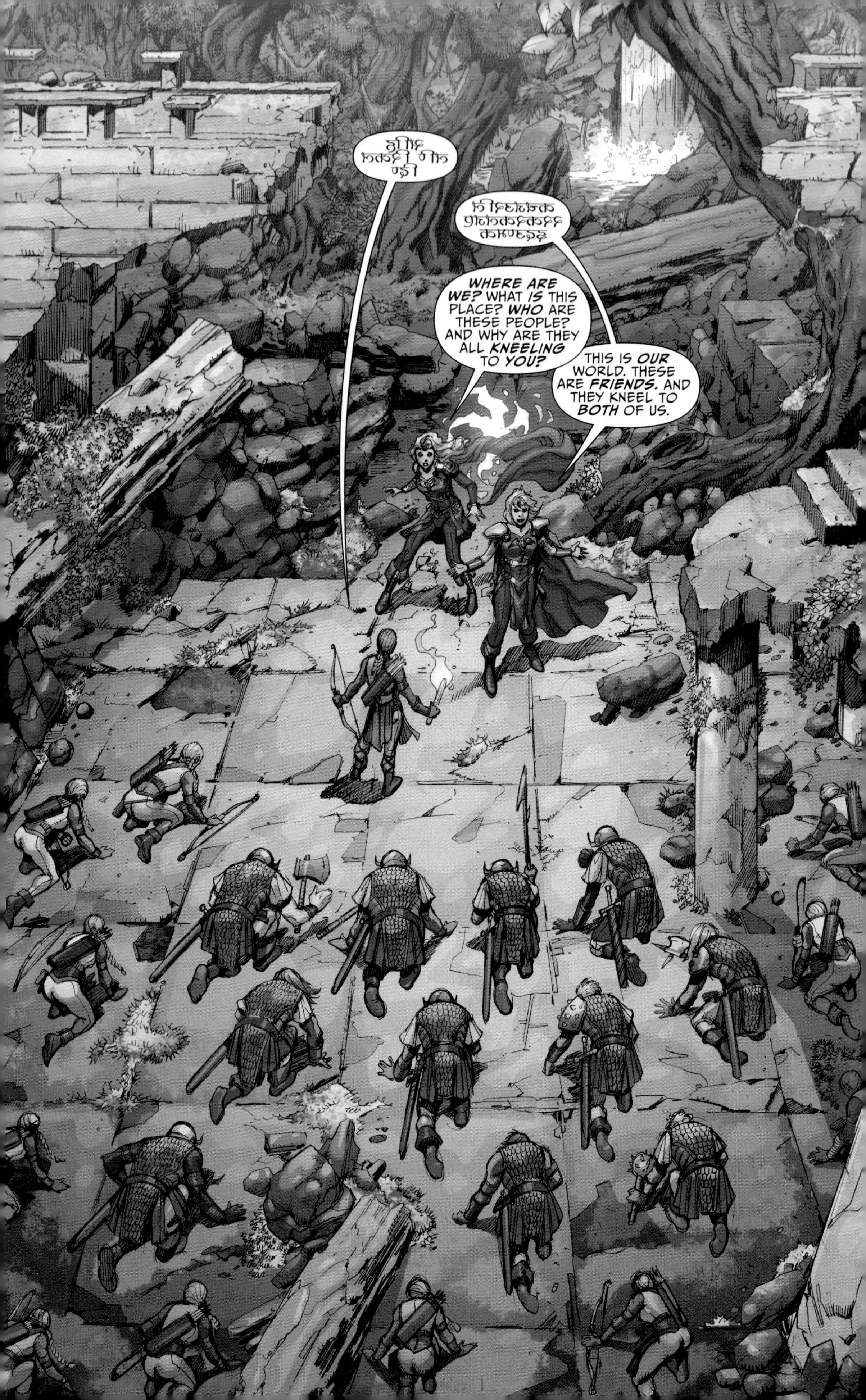
WHERE ARE WE? WHAT IS THIS PLACE? WHO ARE THESE PEOPLE? AND WHY ARE THEY ALL KNEELING TO YOU?
THIS IS OUR WORLD. THESE ARE FRIENDS. AND THEY KNEEL TO BOTH OF US.

WHAT ON EARTH AM I *WEARING?!*

WE AREN'T ON EARTH. AS I TOLD YOU, THE TURQUOISE IS A TRANSFORMATIVE STONE.

MOM, YOUR HAIR! THE COLORING IS GONE. YOU'RE...YOU'RE BLONDE.

SO ARE YOU.

THE POWER IN OUR BLOOD IS TOO STRONG TO HIDE THE TRUE COLOR.

I HAVE THE POWER TO BE BLONDE. WOW. I AM *SOOOOO* THRILLED WITH THAT.

ᚺᛖᛁᚷ ᛋᚻᚾ ᛈᛁᚻ ᚻᛏᛁᛖᛋ

ᛒᚻ ᚻᛁᚷ ᛚᚪᛋᛁᚻ ᛁᚲᚾᛁᛒᛒᛖ

WHAT LANGUAGE IS THAT? I'VE NEVER HEARD ANYTHING LIKE IT. AND WHERE *ARE* WE?

THIS WORLD IS *NILAA.* AND WE'RE GOING TO DEAL WITH THE LANGUAGE PROBLEM IN JUST A--

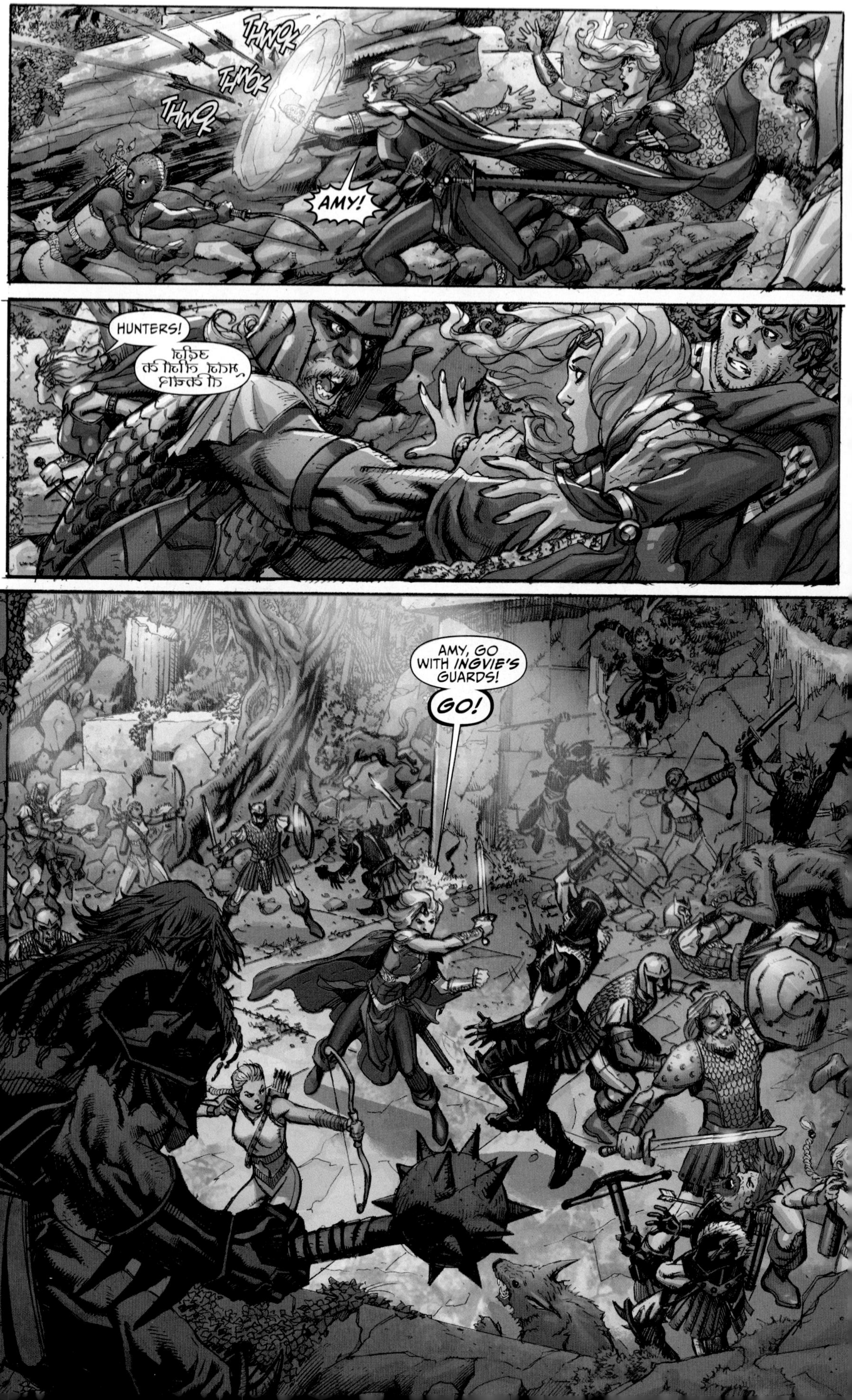
THWOK
THWOK
THWOK
AMY!
HUNTERS!
AMY, GO WITH *INGVIE'S* GUARDS!
GO!

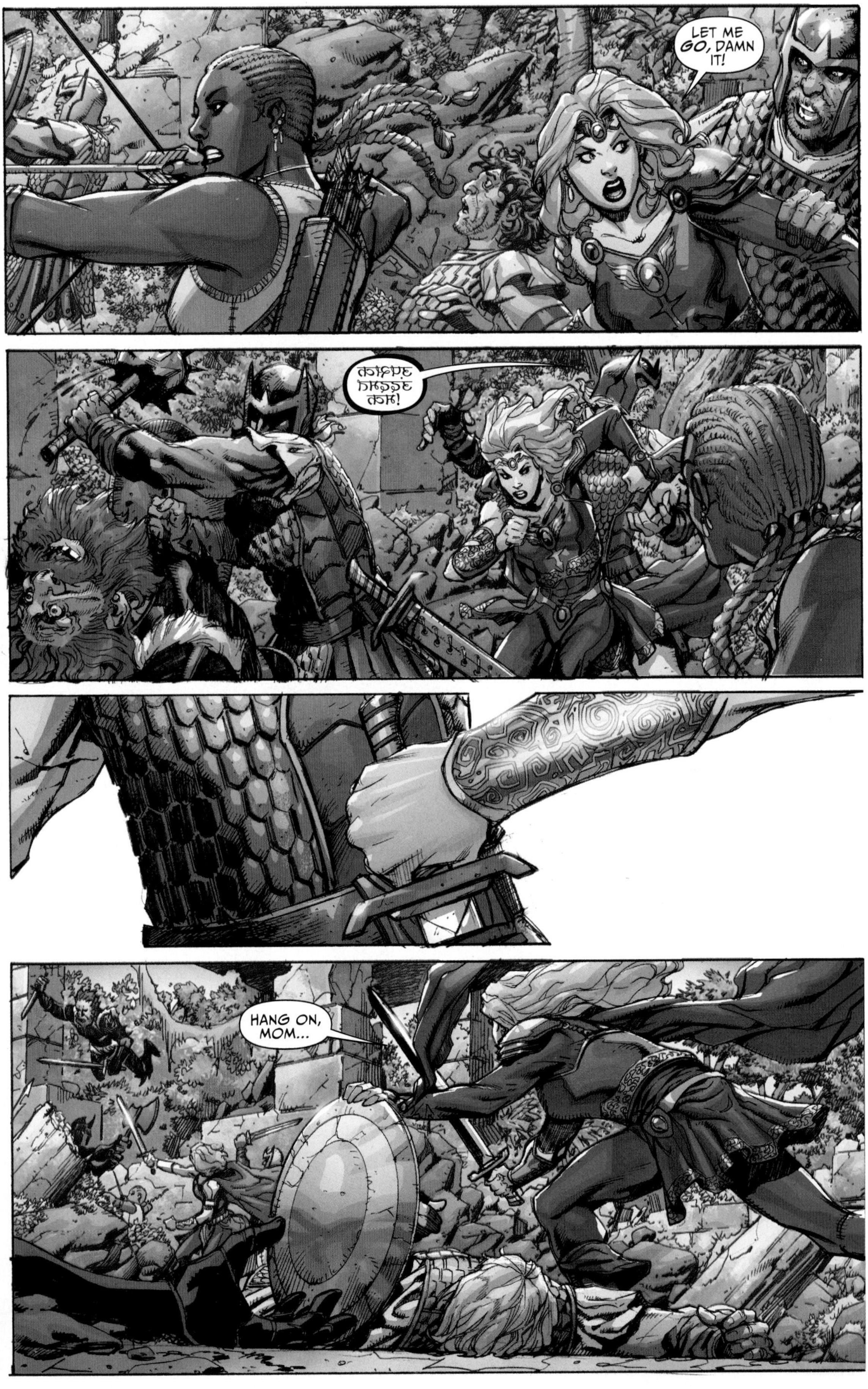
LET ME GO, DAMN IT!
HANG ON, MOM...

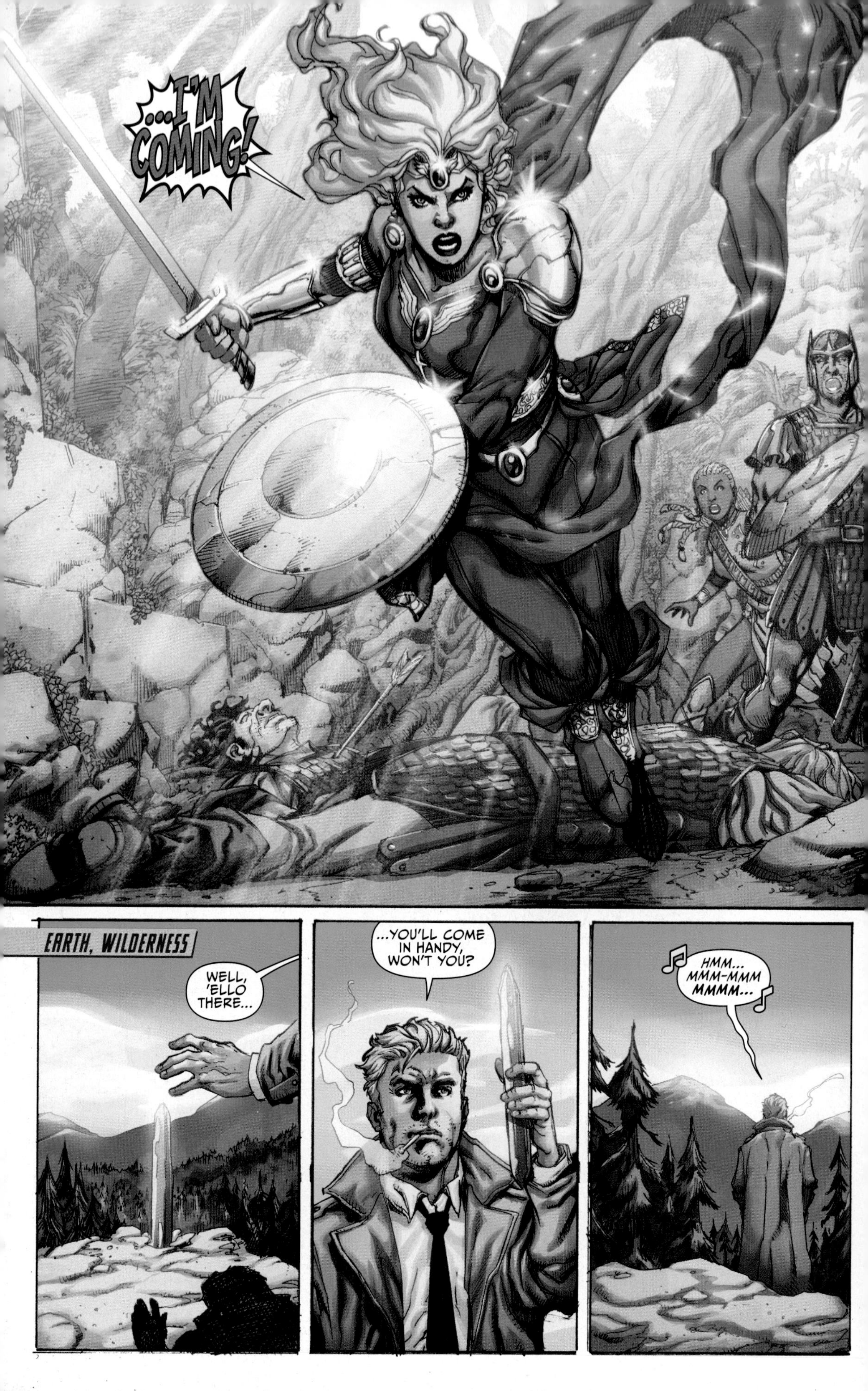
...I'M COMING!
EARTH, WILDERNESS
WELL, 'ELLO THERE...
...YOU'LL COME IN HANDY, WON'T YOU?
HMM... MMM-MMM MMMM...

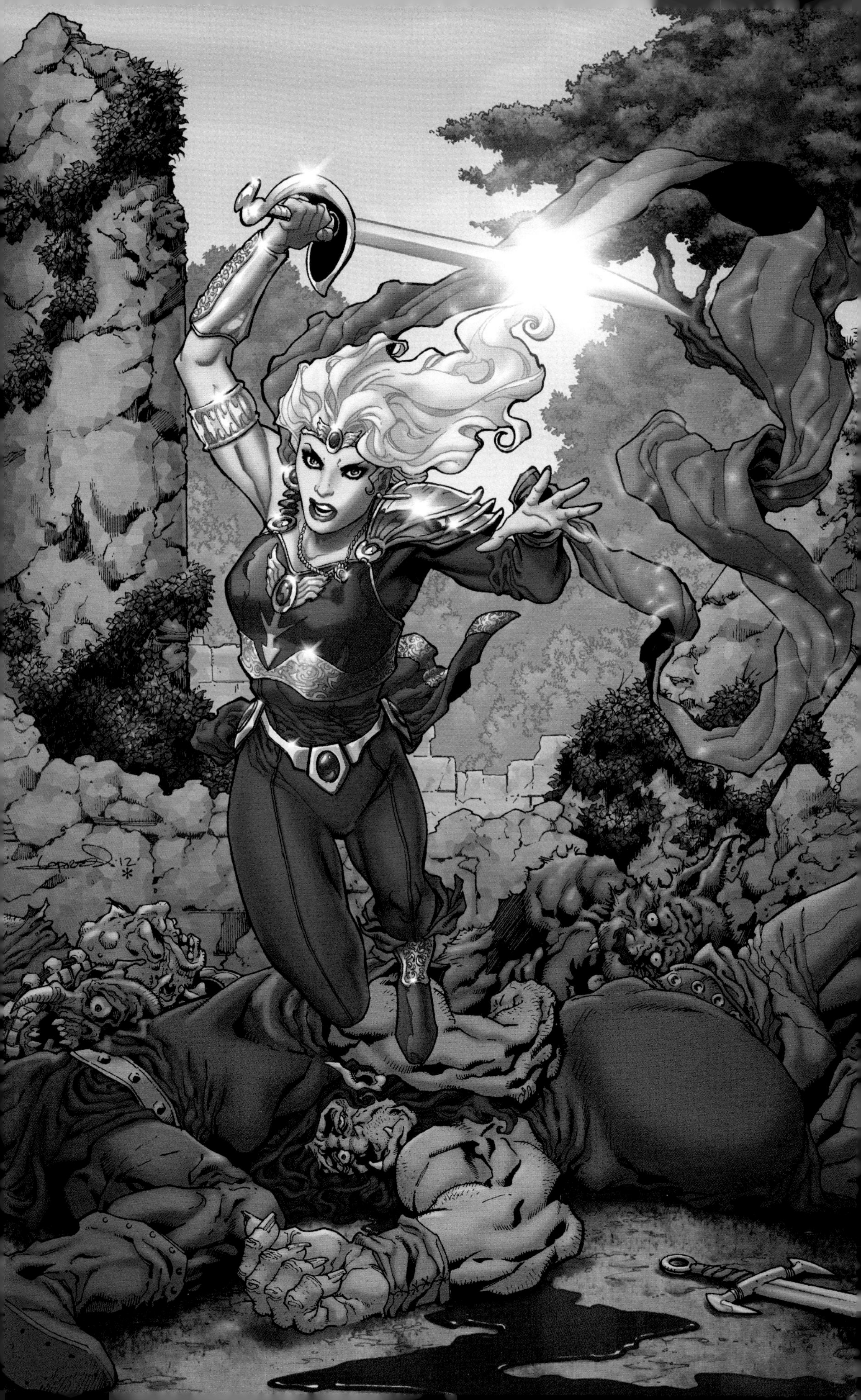

CHRISTY MARX writer AARON LOPRESTI artist cover by AARON LOPRESTI & HI-FI

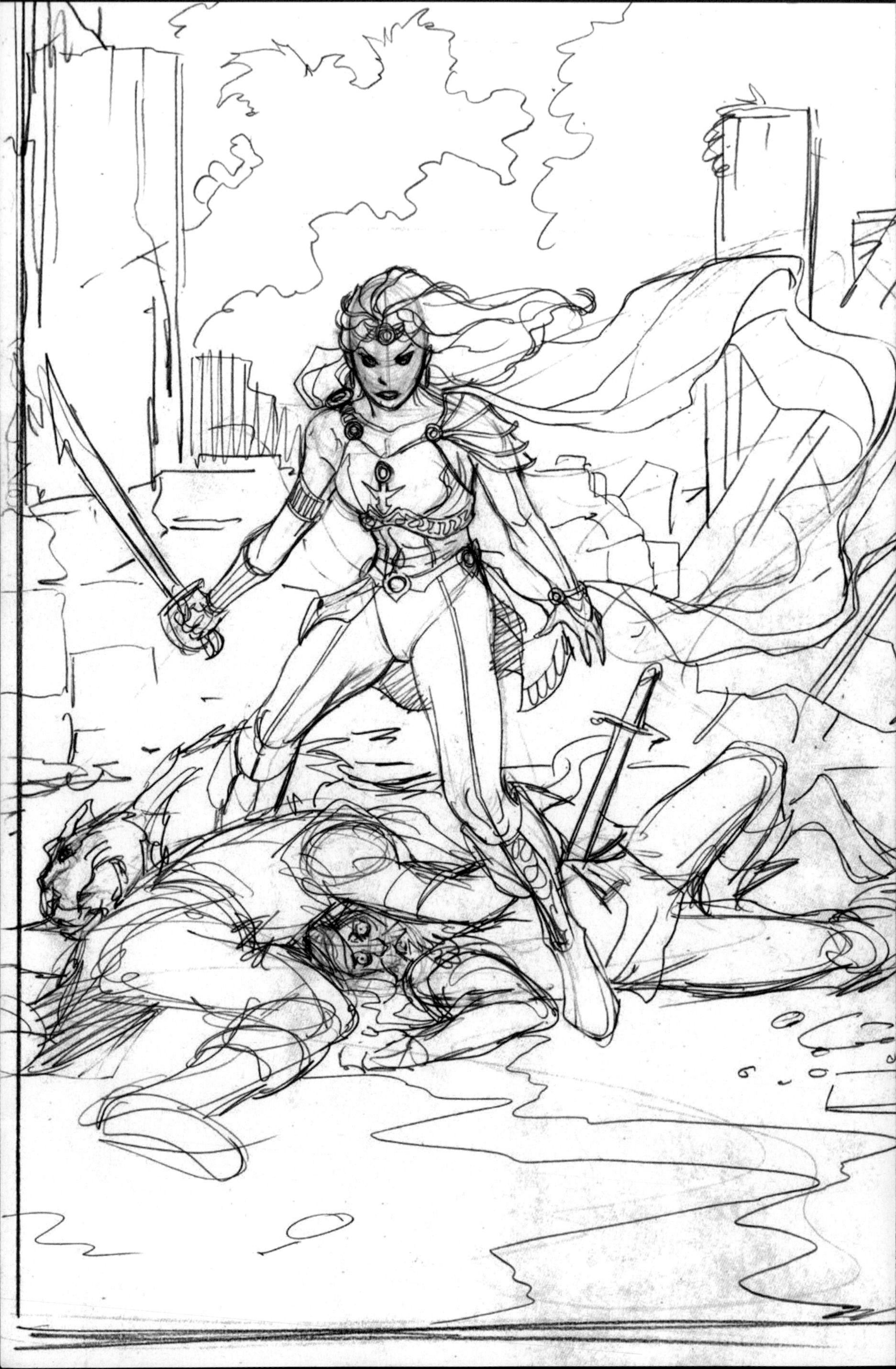

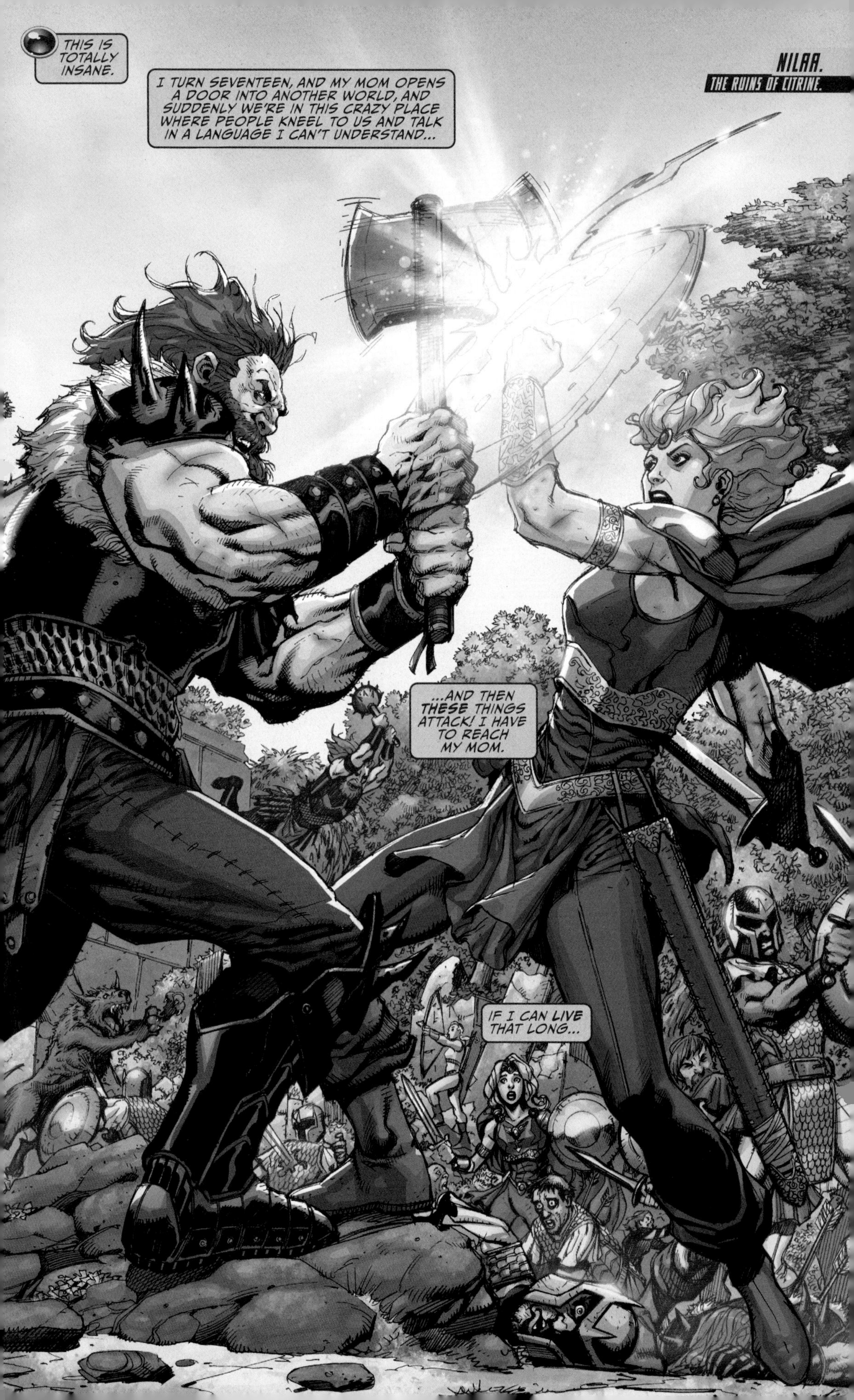
THIS IS TOTALLY INSANE.
NILAA.
THE RUINS OF CITRINE.
I TURN SEVENTEEN, AND MY MOM OPENS A DOOR INTO ANOTHER WORLD, AND SUDDENLY WE'RE IN THIS CRAZY PLACE WHERE PEOPLE KNEEL TO US AND TALK IN A LANGUAGE I CAN'T UNDERSTAND...
...AND THEN THESE THINGS ATTACK! I HAVE TO REACH MY MOM.
IF I CAN LIVE THAT LONG...

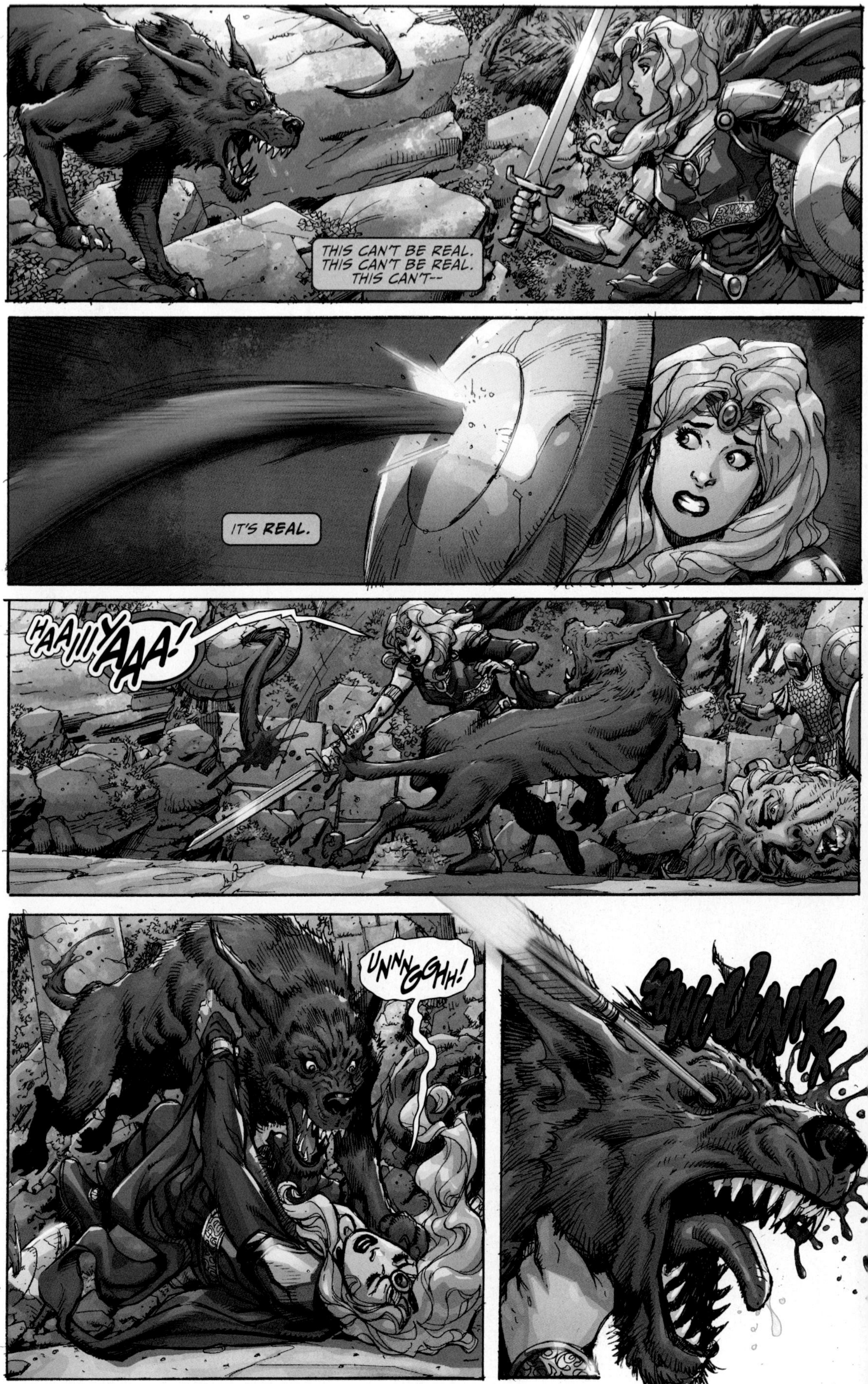
THIS CAN'T BE REAL. THIS CAN'T BE REAL. THIS CAN'T--
IT'S REAL.
HAAIIIYAAA!
UNNNGGHH!

TH-THANKS. NICE SHOOTING.

ԵՐՈՎ ԱՀՂԻԵ ՄՈ'Է ԱԹԷ

WATCH OUT!

GRRRGGGHHH... UHKKK!

GUURRrr GGGGll....

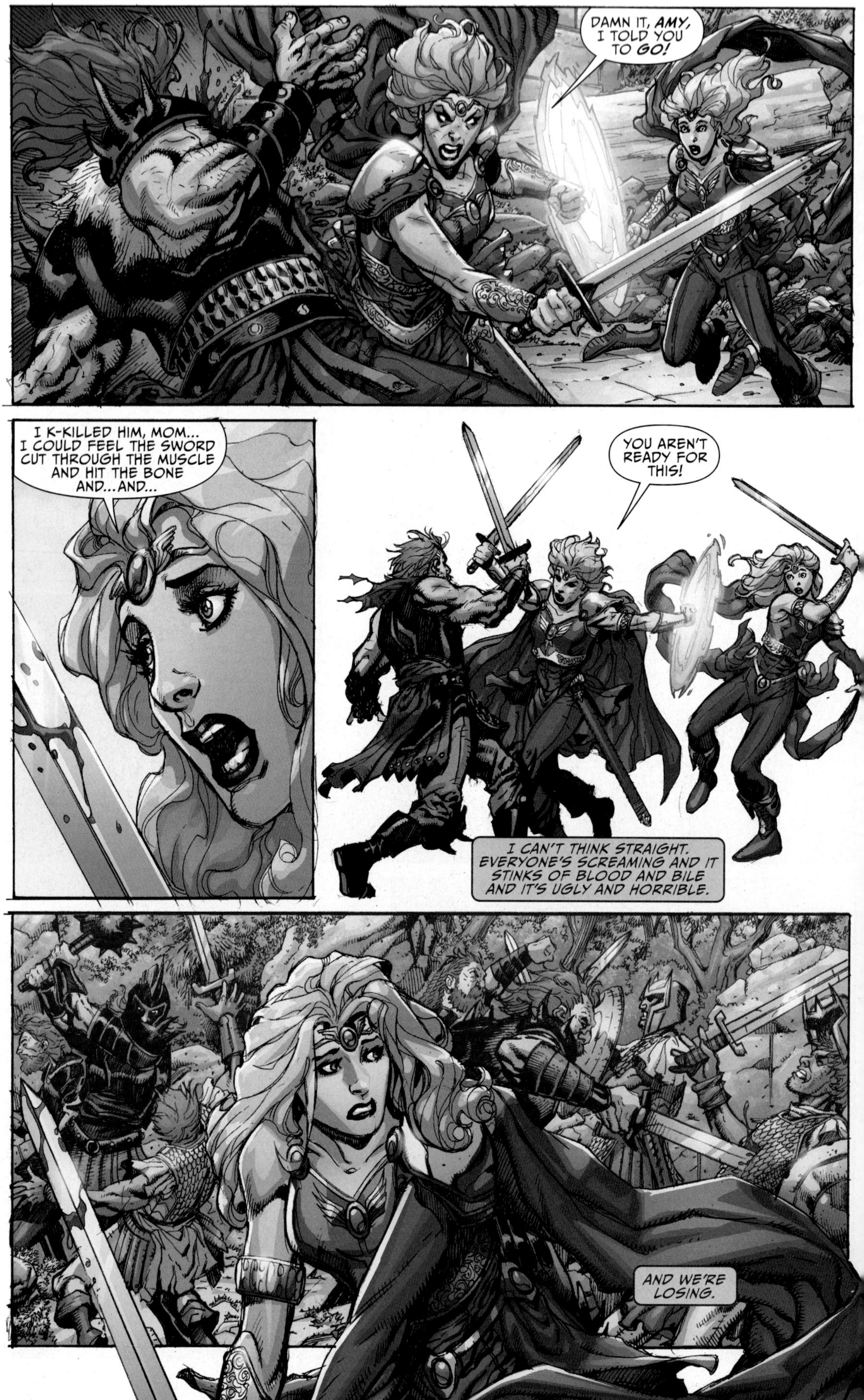
DAMN IT, AMY, I TOLD YOU TO GO!
I K-KILLED HIM, MOM... I COULD FEEL THE SWORD CUT THROUGH THE MUSCLE AND HIT THE BONE AND...AND...
YOU AREN'T READY FOR THIS!
I CAN'T THINK STRAIGHT. EVERYONE'S SCREAMING AND IT STINKS OF BLOOD AND BILE AND IT'S UGLY AND HORRIBLE.
AND WE'RE LOSING.

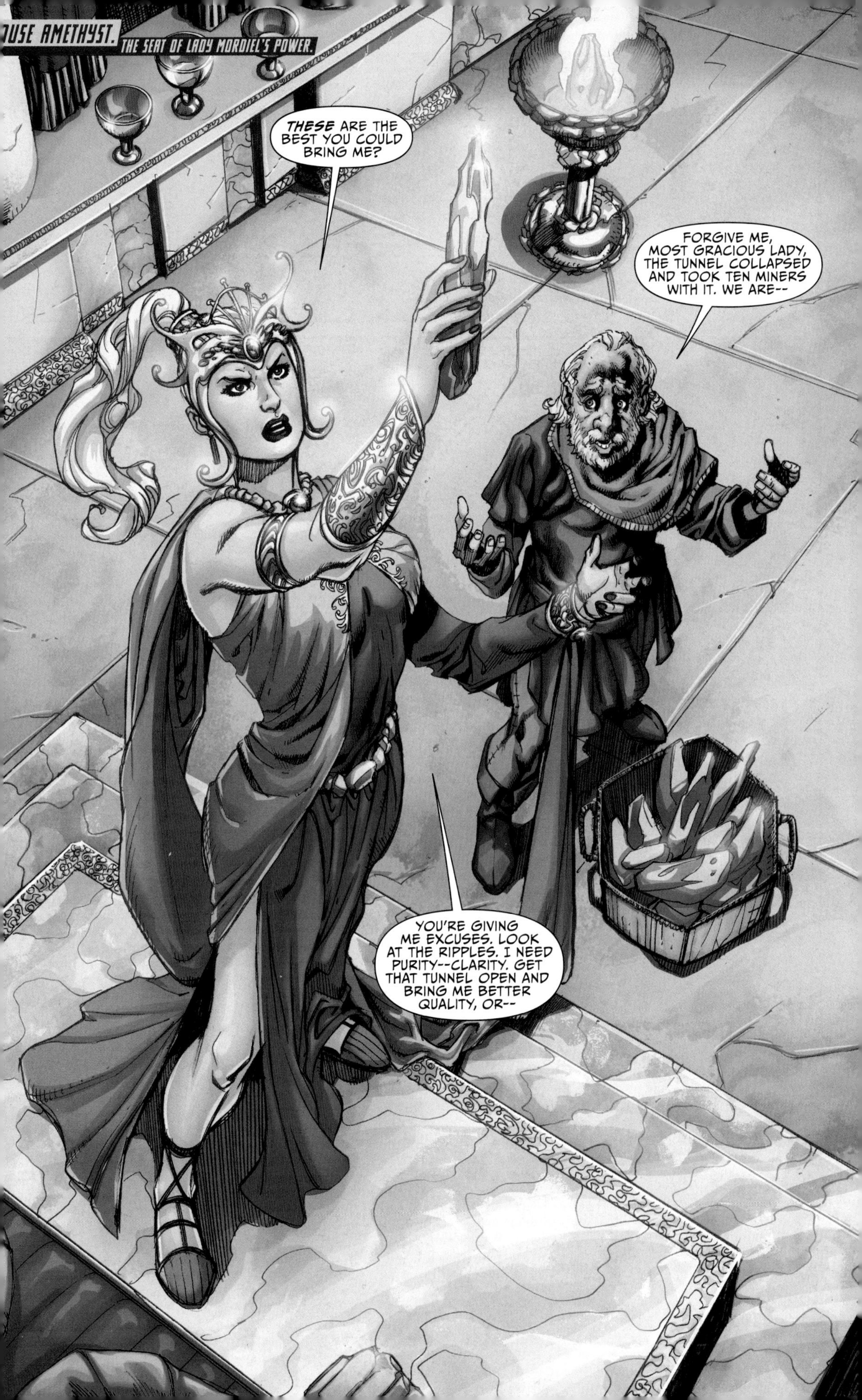

OUSE AMETHYST. THE SEAT OF LADY MORDIEL'S POWER.
THESE ARE THE BEST YOU COULD BRING ME?
FORGIVE ME, MOST GRACIOUS LADY, THE TUNNEL COLLAPSED AND TOOK TEN MINERS WITH IT. WE ARE--
YOU'RE GIVING ME EXCUSES. LOOK AT THE RIPPLES. I NEED PURITY--CLARITY. GET THAT TUNNEL OPEN AND BRING ME BETTER QUALITY, OR--

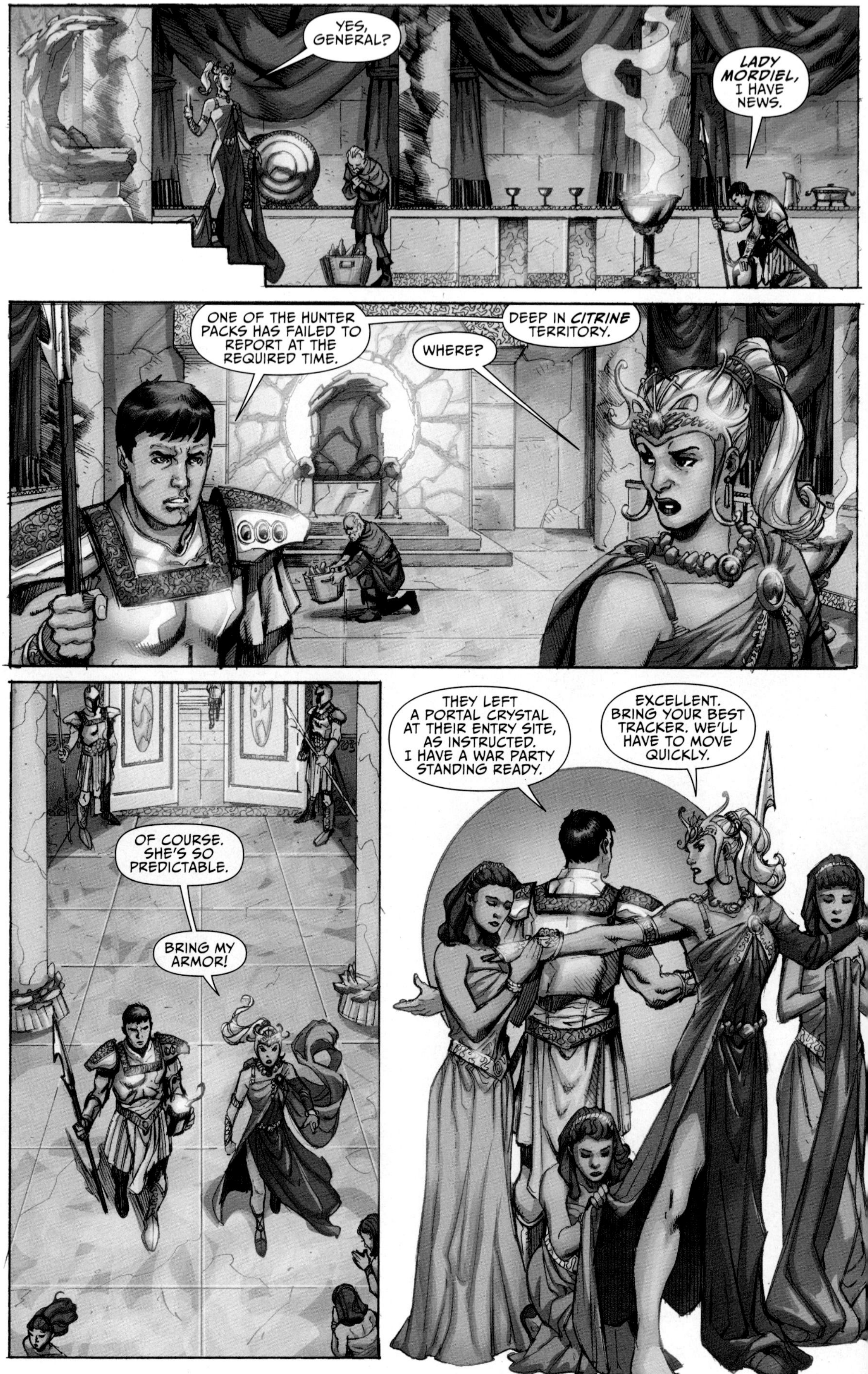
YES, GENERAL?
LADY MORDIEL, I HAVE NEWS.
ONE OF THE HUNTER PACKS HAS FAILED TO REPORT AT THE REQUIRED TIME.
WHERE?
DEEP IN CITRINE TERRITORY.
OF COURSE. SHE'S SO PREDICTABLE.
BRING MY ARMOR!
THEY LEFT A PORTAL CRYSTAL AT THEIR ENTRY SITE, AS INSTRUCTED. I HAVE A WAR PARTY STANDING READY.
EXCELLENT. BRING YOUR BEST TRACKER. WE'LL HAVE TO MOVE QUICKLY.

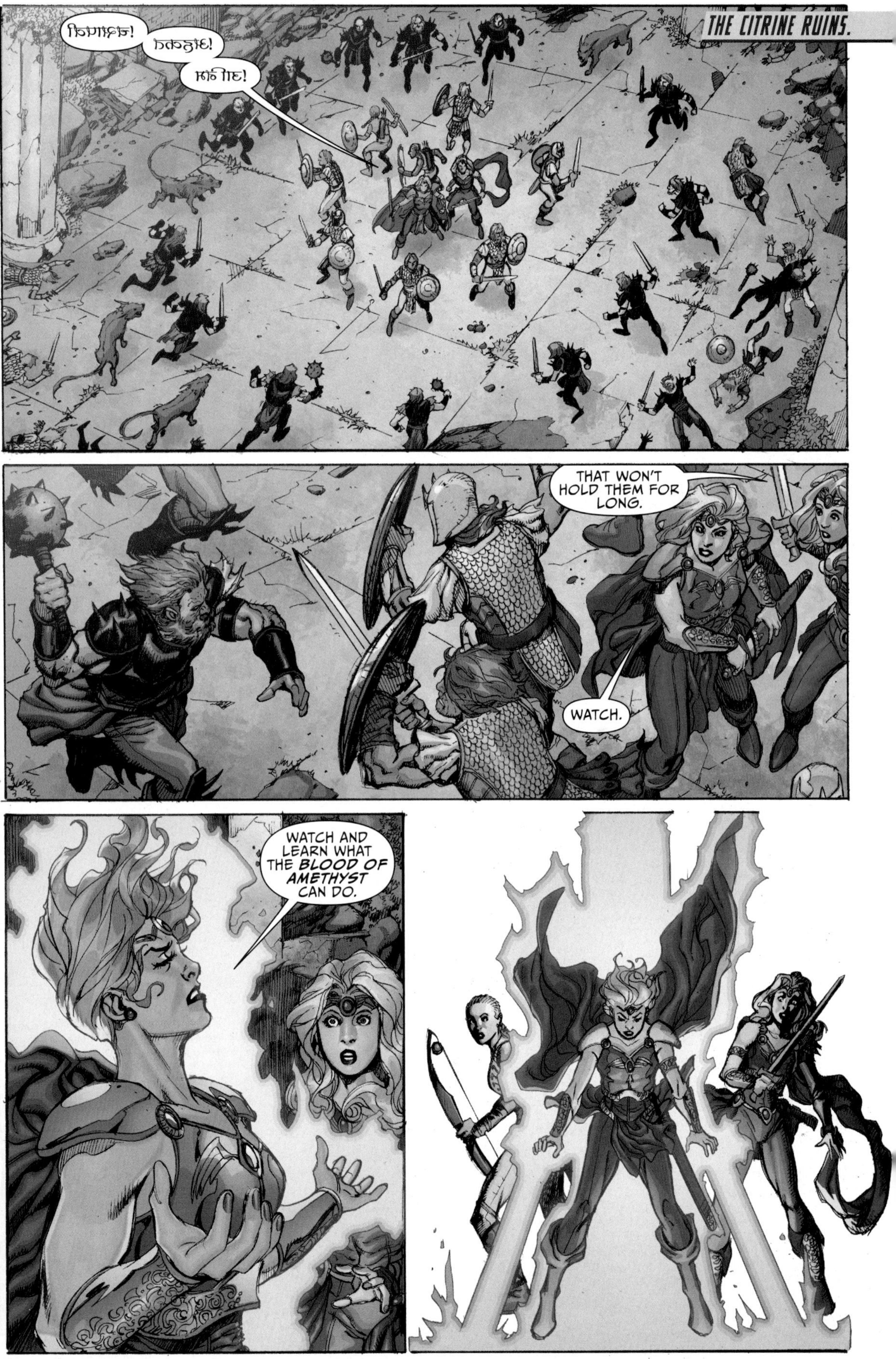
THE CITRINE RUINS.
THAT WON'T HOLD THEM FOR LONG.
WATCH.
WATCH AND LEARN WHAT THE *BLOOD OF AMETHYST* CAN DO.

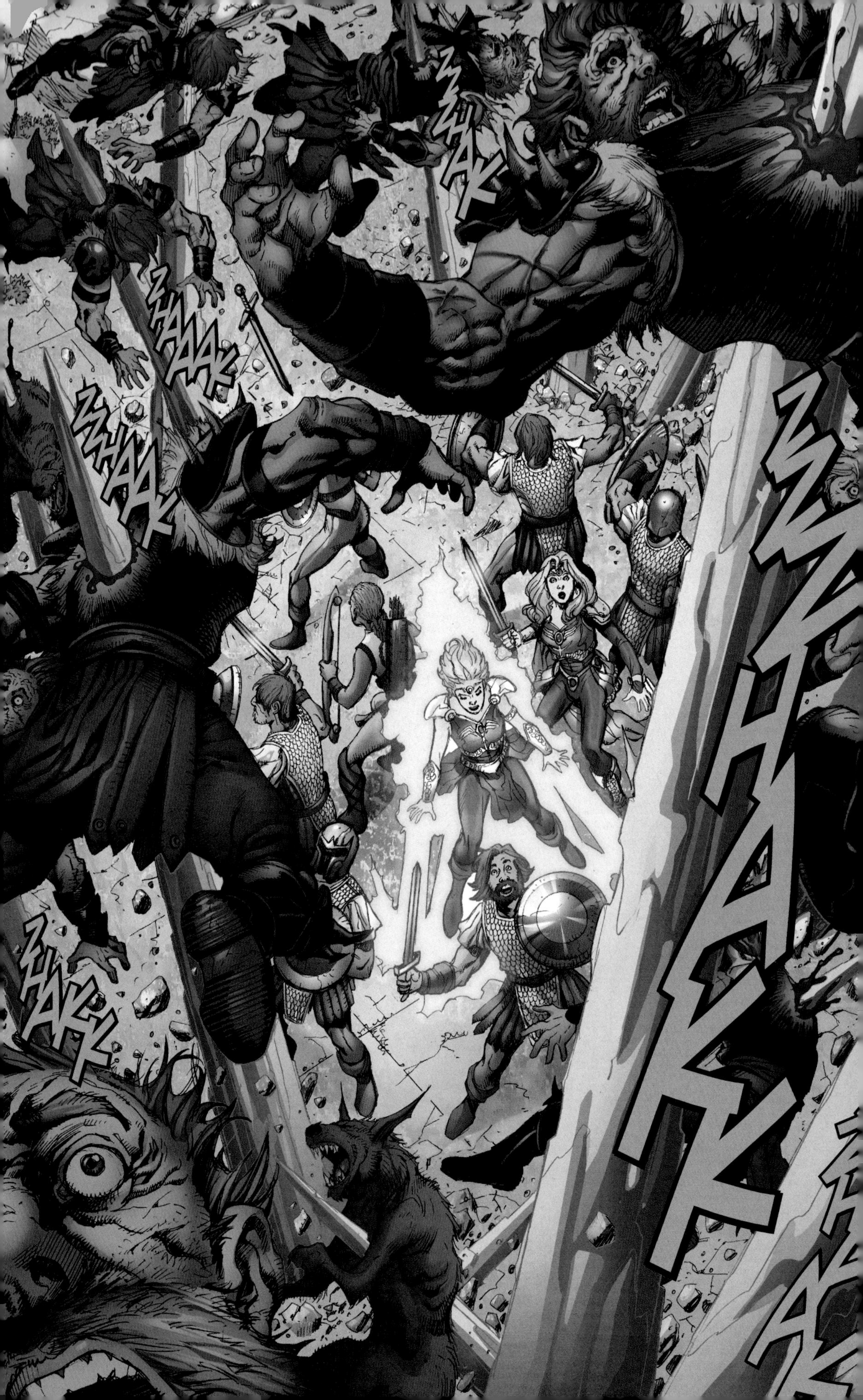
ZWHAK
ZHAAAK
ZWHAAAK

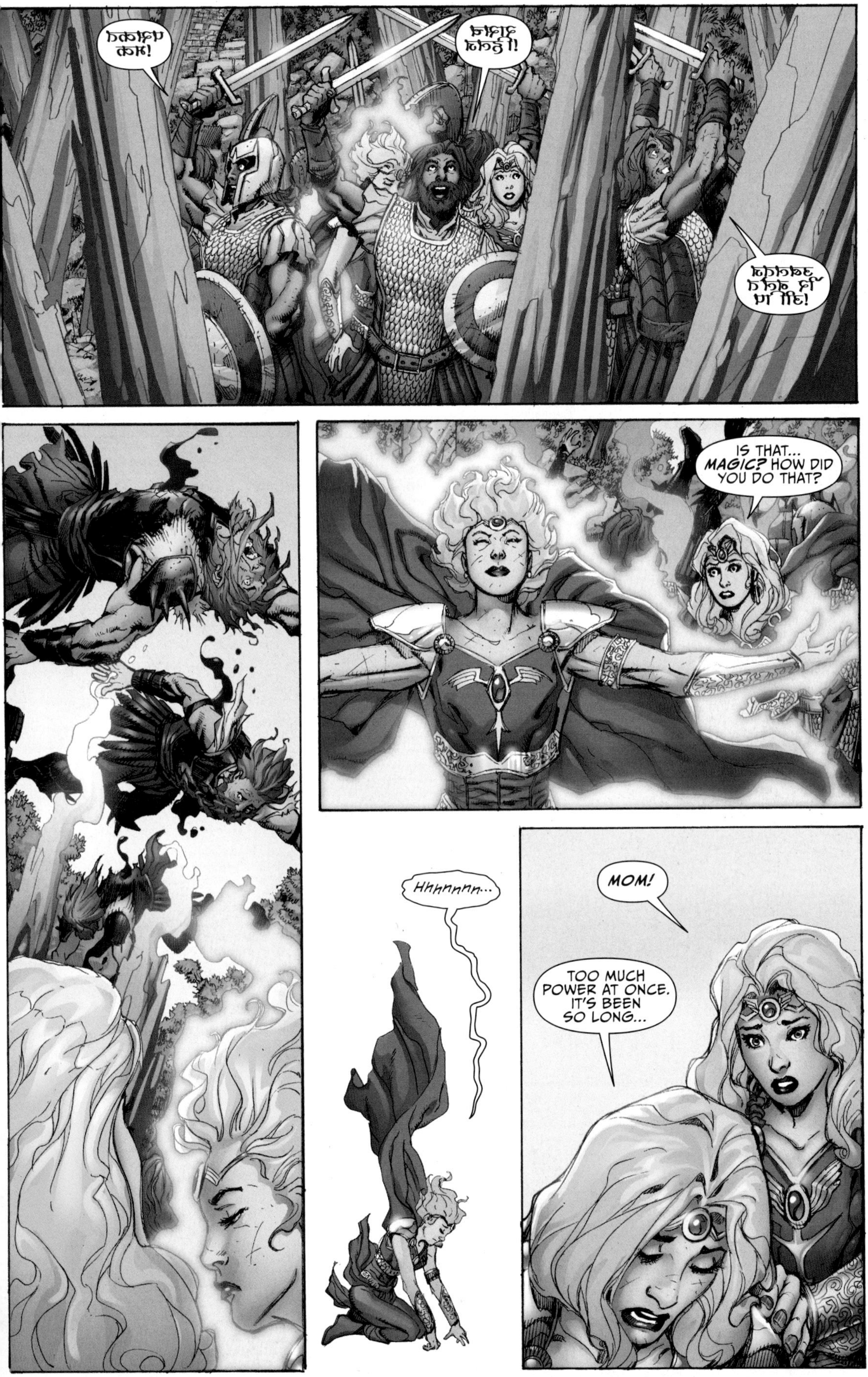
IS THAT... MAGIC? HOW DID YOU DO THAT?
Hhnnnnn...
MOM!
TOO MUCH POWER AT ONCE. IT'S BEEN SO LONG...

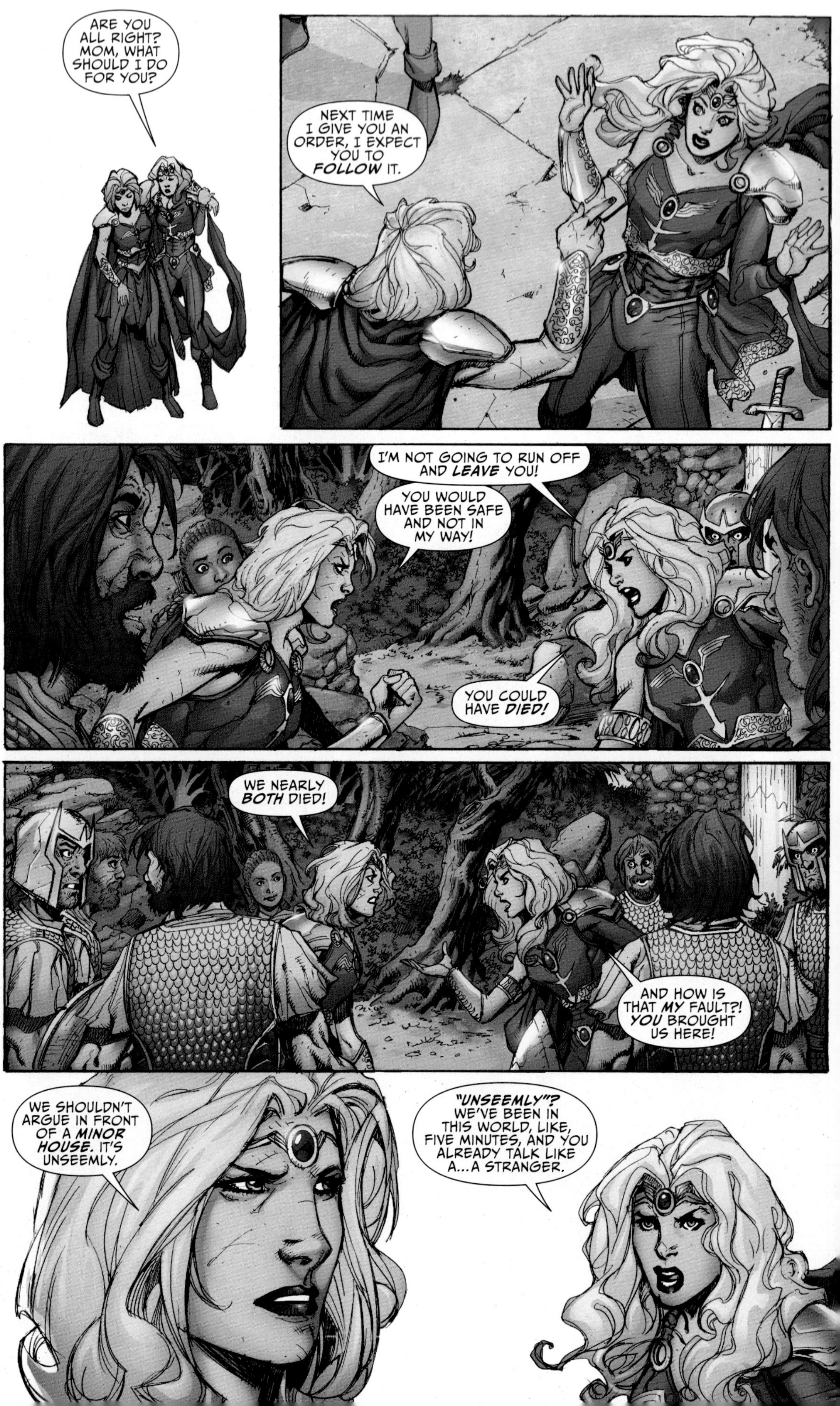
ARE YOU ALL RIGHT? MOM, WHAT SHOULD I DO FOR YOU?
NEXT TIME I GIVE YOU AN ORDER, I EXPECT YOU TO FOLLOW IT.
I'M NOT GOING TO RUN OFF AND LEAVE YOU!
YOU WOULD HAVE BEEN SAFE AND NOT IN MY WAY!
YOU COULD HAVE DIED!
WE NEARLY BOTH DIED!
AND HOW IS THAT MY FAULT?! YOU BROUGHT US HERE!
WE SHOULDN'T ARGUE IN FRONT OF A MINOR HOUSE. IT'S UNSEEMLY.
"UNSEEMLY"? WE'VE BEEN IN THIS WORLD, LIKE, FIVE MINUTES, AND YOU ALREADY TALK LIKE A...A STRANGER.

ᛁᚾᚷᛁᛖ ᛏᚺᛖ ᛏᚱᚨᚹᛖᛚ
ᛏᚺᚨᛏ ᛒᛖᚾᛖ ᛒᛟᚾᚾᚨᛁᛖ
ᛁᛋᚠᛁᛚᛖ ᛒᚨ ᛏᚺᛁᛋ
ᛋᛖ ᚺᚨᛚᛖ

INGVIE WILL DEAL WITH THE LANGUAGE PROBLEM. I NEED TO ASSESS THE INJURED. WE MUST LEAVE HERE IMMEDIATELY.

Umm, THANKS. NICE GEM, BUT--

OW!

ᛒᛁᚷ ᛁᛋ ᚺᛋ PAIN SHOULD NOT LAST LONG, PRINCESS.

DID YOU JUST SPEAK ENGLISH?

NO, PRINCESS. THE CITRINE-OF-TONGUES HAS GIVEN YOU THE COMMAND OF *ALL* LANGUAGES.

YOU'RE SPEAKING *NILAIAN.*

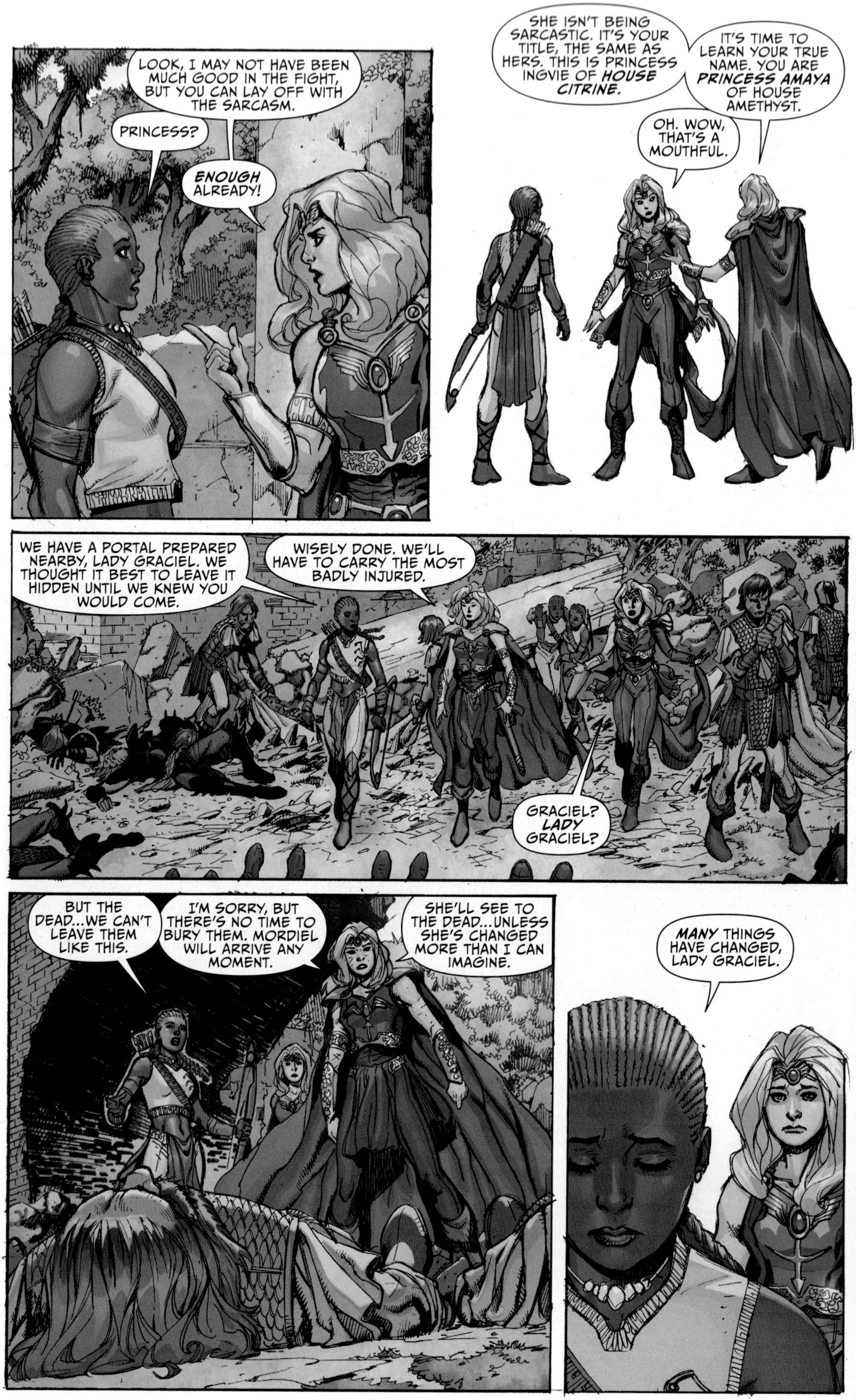
LOOK, I MAY NOT HAVE BEEN MUCH GOOD IN THE FIGHT, BUT YOU CAN LAY OFF WITH THE SARCASM.
PRINCESS?
ENOUGH ALREADY!
SHE ISN'T BEING SARCASTIC. IT'S YOUR TITLE, THE SAME AS HERS. THIS IS PRINCESS INGVIE OF HOUSE CITRINE.
IT'S TIME TO LEARN YOUR TRUE NAME. YOU ARE PRINCESS AMAYA OF HOUSE AMETHYST.
OH. WOW, THAT'S A MOUTHFUL.
WE HAVE A PORTAL PREPARED NEARBY, LADY GRACIEL. WE THOUGHT IT BEST TO LEAVE IT HIDDEN UNTIL WE KNEW YOU WOULD COME.
WISELY DONE. WE'LL HAVE TO CARRY THE MOST BADLY INJURED.
GRACIEL? LADY GRACIEL?
BUT THE DEAD...WE CAN'T LEAVE THEM LIKE THIS.
I'M SORRY, BUT THERE'S NO TIME TO BURY THEM. MORDIEL WILL ARRIVE ANY MOMENT.
SHE'LL SEE TO THE DEAD...UNLESS SHE'S CHANGED MORE THAN I CAN IMAGINE.
MANY THINGS HAVE CHANGED, LADY GRACIEL.

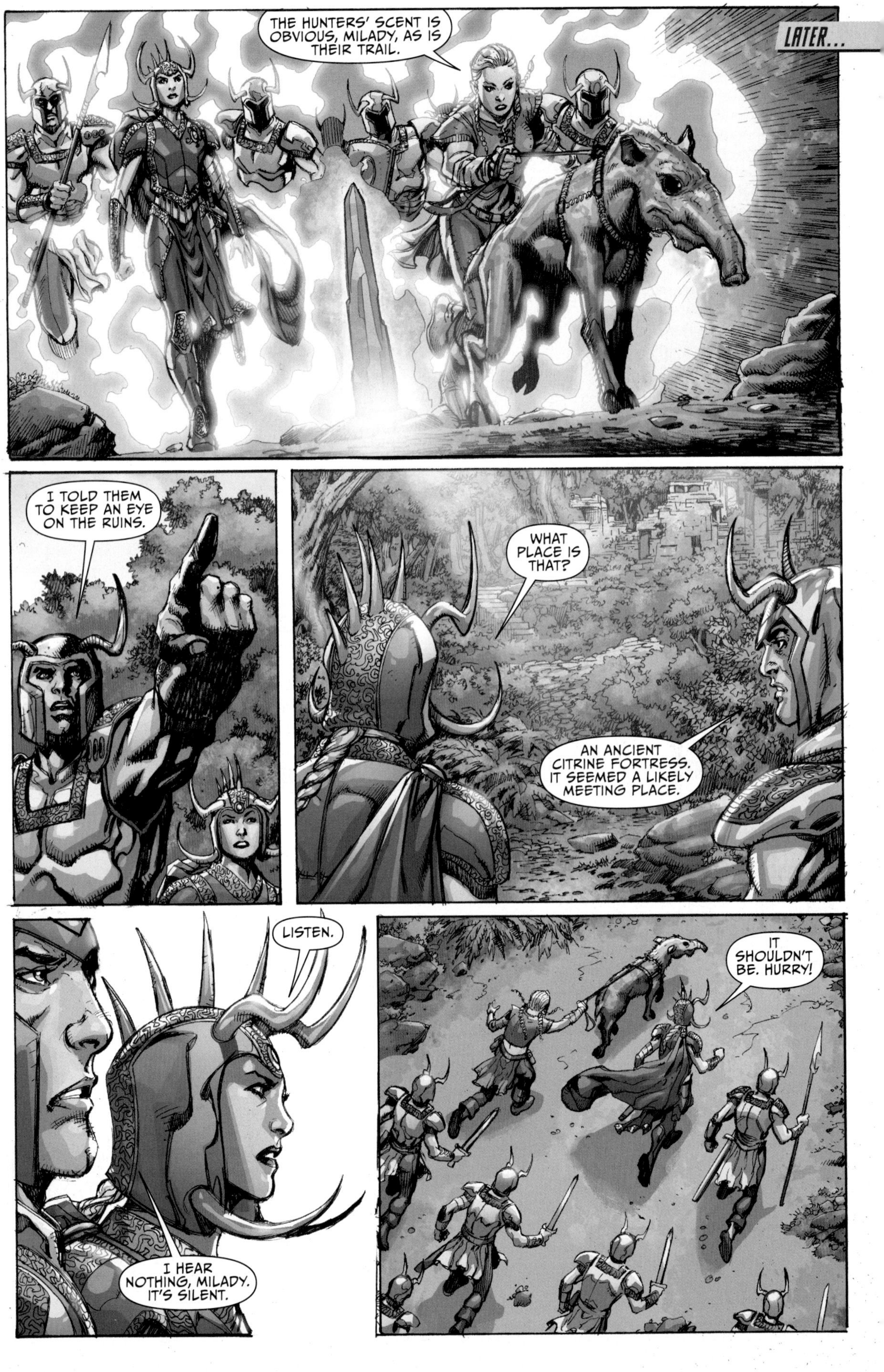
LATER...
THE HUNTERS' SCENT IS OBVIOUS, MILADY, AS IS THEIR TRAIL.
I TOLD THEM TO KEEP AN EYE ON THE RUINS.
WHAT PLACE IS THAT?
AN ANCIENT CITRINE FORTRESS. IT SEEMED A LIKELY MEETING PLACE.
LISTEN.
I HEAR NOTHING, MILADY. IT'S SILENT.
IT SHOULDN'T BE. HURRY!

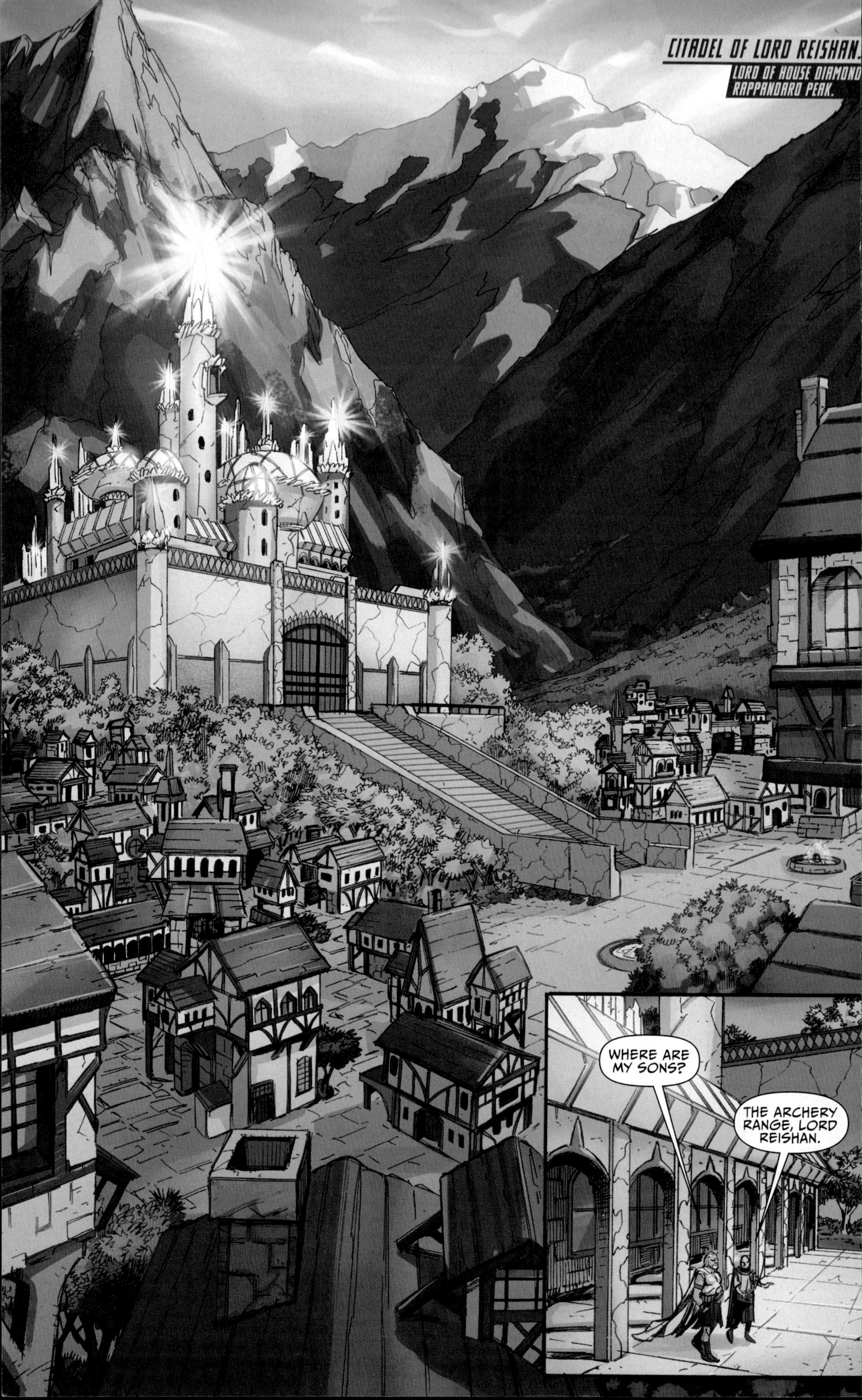
CITADEL OF LORD REISHAN.
LORD OF HOUSE DIAMOND RAPPANDARO PEAK.
WHERE ARE MY SONS?
THE ARCHERY RANGE, LORD REISHAN.

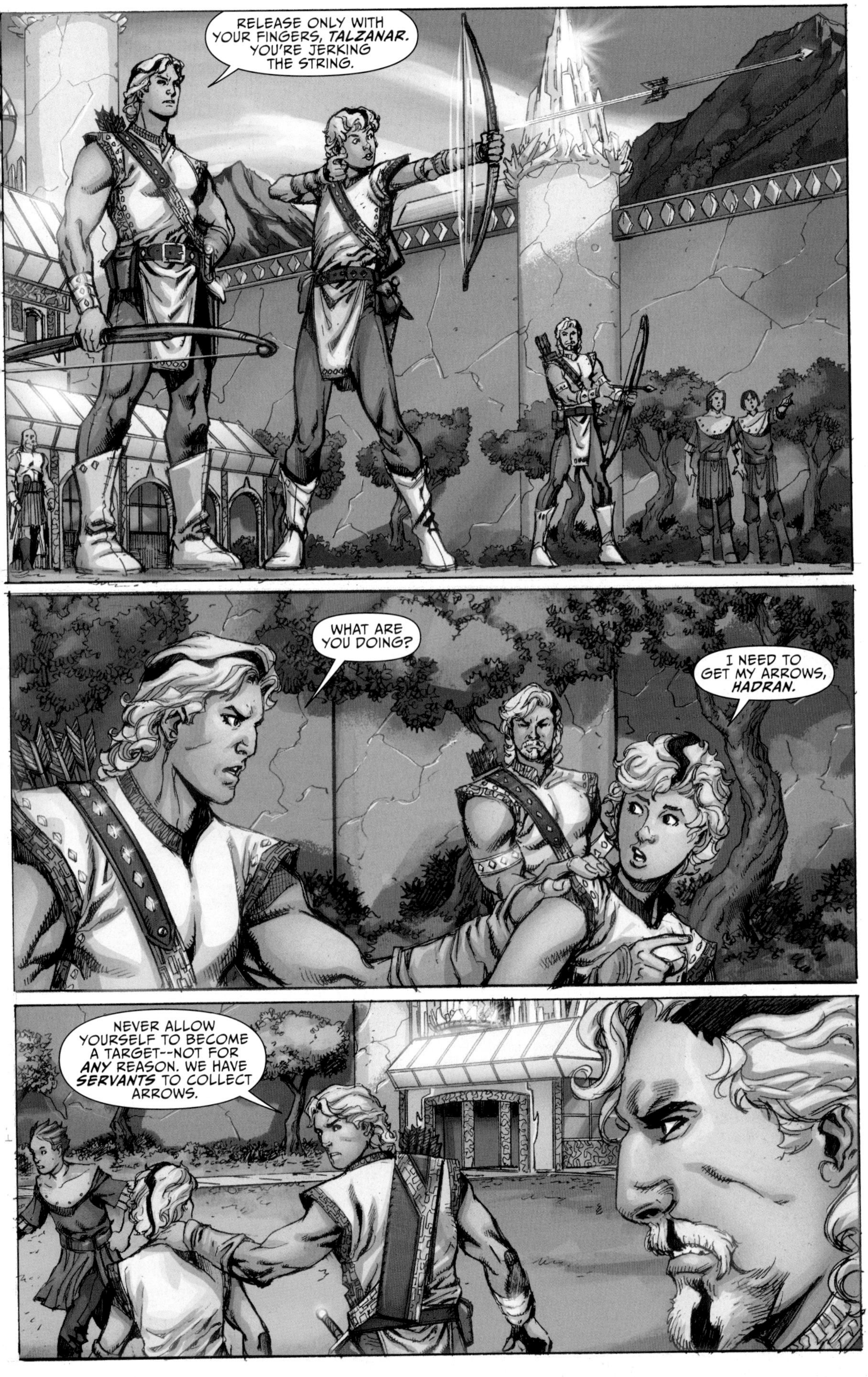
RELEASE ONLY WITH YOUR FINGERS, TALZANAR. YOU'RE JERKING THE STRING.
WHAT ARE YOU DOING?
I NEED TO GET MY ARROWS, HADRAN.
NEVER ALLOW YOURSELF TO BECOME A TARGET--NOT FOR ANY REASON. WE HAVE SERVANTS TO COLLECT ARROWS.

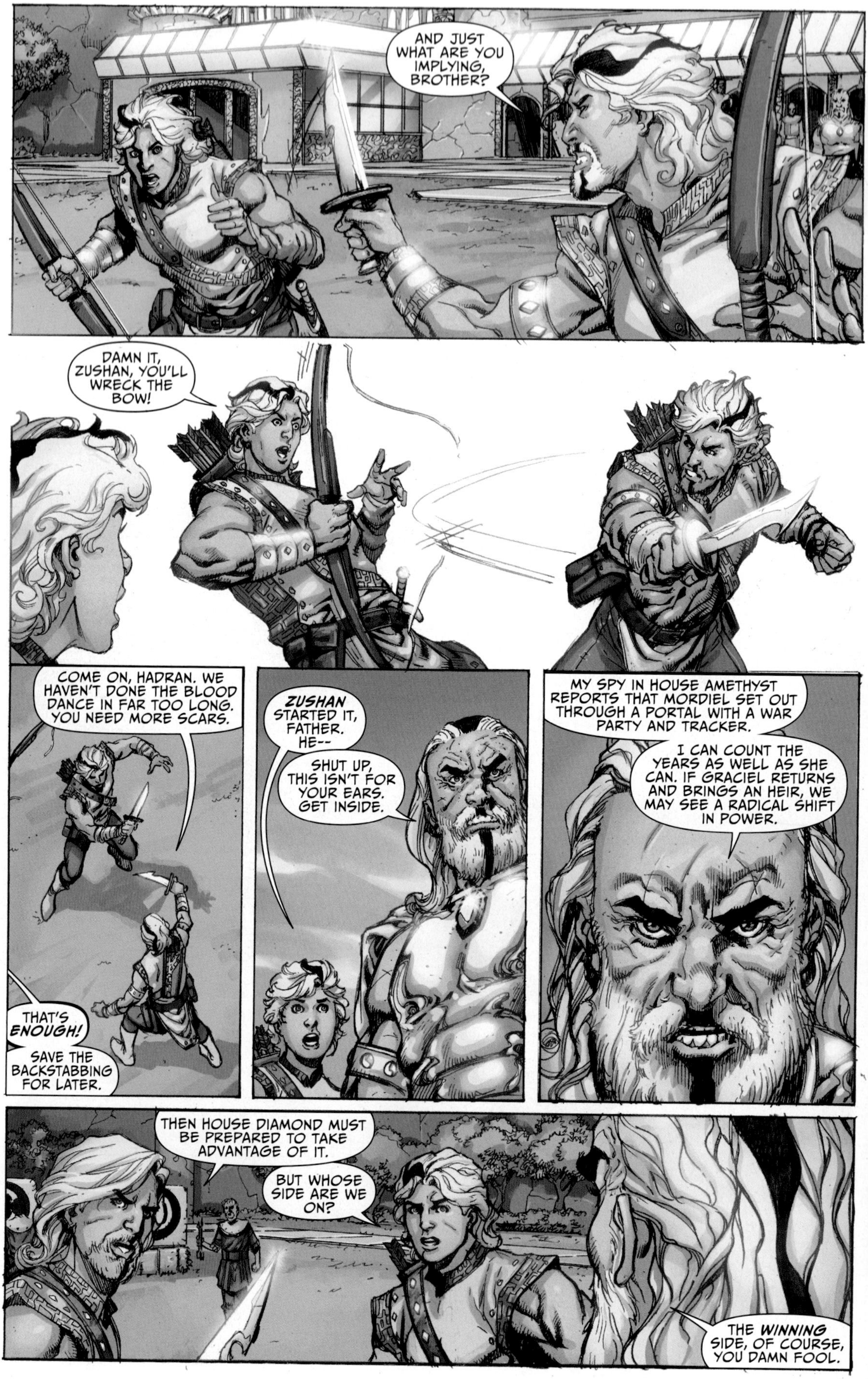
AND JUST WHAT ARE YOU IMPLYING, BROTHER?
DAMN IT, ZUSHAN, YOU'LL WRECK THE BOW!
COME ON, HADRAN. WE HAVEN'T DONE THE BLOOD DANCE IN FAR TOO LONG. YOU NEED MORE SCARS.
THAT'S *ENOUGH!*
SAVE THE BACKSTABBING FOR LATER.
ZUSHAN STARTED IT, FATHER. HE--
SHUT UP, THIS ISN'T FOR YOUR EARS. GET INSIDE.
MY SPY IN HOUSE AMETHYST REPORTS THAT MORDIEL SET OUT THROUGH A PORTAL WITH A WAR PARTY AND TRACKER.
I CAN COUNT THE YEARS AS WELL AS SHE CAN. IF GRACIEL RETURNS AND BRINGS AN HEIR, WE MAY SEE A RADICAL SHIFT IN POWER.
THEN HOUSE DIAMOND MUST BE PREPARED TO TAKE ADVANTAGE OF IT.
BUT WHOSE SIDE ARE WE ON?
THE *WINNING* SIDE, OF COURSE, YOU DAMN FOOL.

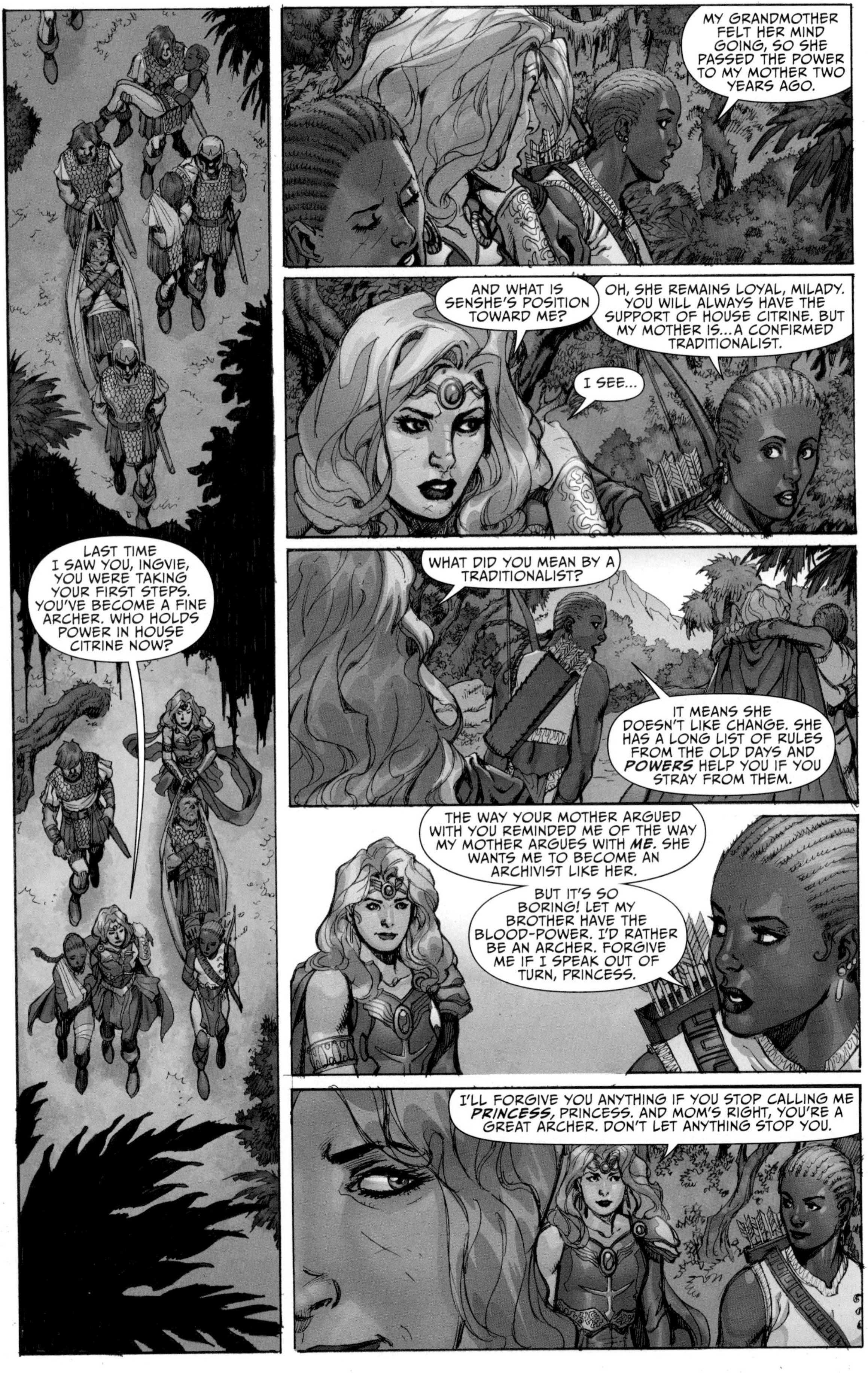
MY GRANDMOTHER FELT HER MIND GOING, SO SHE PASSED THE POWER TO MY MOTHER TWO YEARS AGO.
AND WHAT IS SENSHE'S POSITION TOWARD ME?
OH, SHE REMAINS LOYAL, MILADY. YOU WILL ALWAYS HAVE THE SUPPORT OF HOUSE CITRINE. BUT MY MOTHER IS...A CONFIRMED TRADITIONALIST.
I SEE...
LAST TIME I SAW YOU, INGVIE, YOU WERE TAKING YOUR FIRST STEPS. YOU'VE BECOME A FINE ARCHER. WHO HOLDS POWER IN HOUSE CITRINE NOW?
WHAT DID YOU MEAN BY A TRADITIONALIST?
IT MEANS SHE DOESN'T LIKE CHANGE. SHE HAS A LONG LIST OF RULES FROM THE OLD DAYS AND ***POWERS*** HELP YOU IF YOU STRAY FROM THEM.
THE WAY YOUR MOTHER ARGUED WITH YOU REMINDED ME OF THE WAY MY MOTHER ARGUES WITH ***ME.*** SHE WANTS ME TO BECOME AN ARCHIVIST LIKE HER.
BUT IT'S SO BORING! LET MY BROTHER HAVE THE BLOOD-POWER. I'D RATHER BE AN ARCHER. FORGIVE ME IF I SPEAK OUT OF TURN, PRINCESS.
I'LL FORGIVE YOU ANYTHING IF YOU STOP CALLING ME ***PRINCESS,*** PRINCESS. AND MOM'S RIGHT, YOU'RE A GREAT ARCHER. DON'T LET ANYTHING STOP YOU.

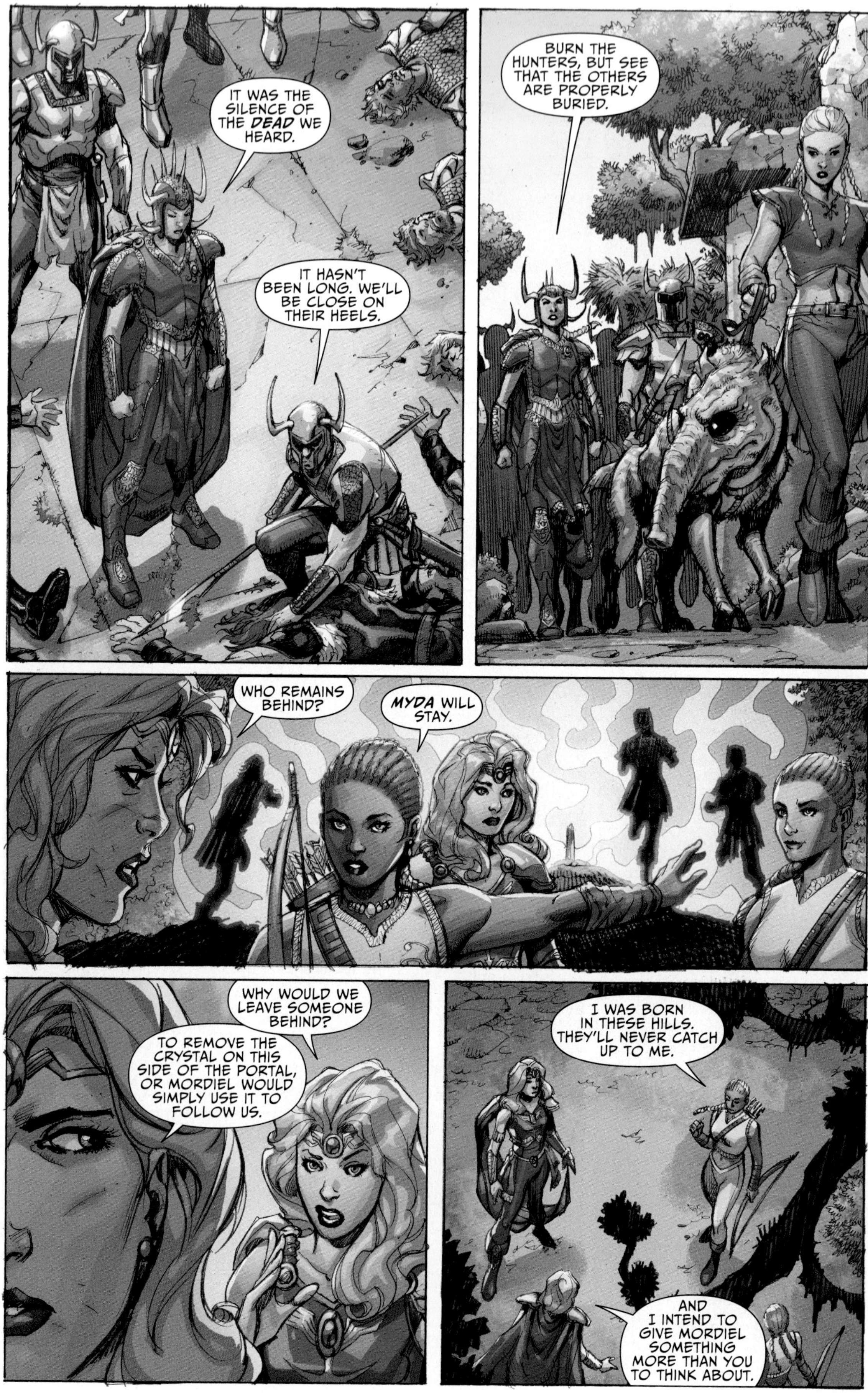
IT WAS THE SILENCE OF THE DEAD WE HEARD.
IT HASN'T BEEN LONG. WE'LL BE CLOSE ON THEIR HEELS.
BURN THE HUNTERS, BUT SEE THAT THE OTHERS ARE PROPERLY BURIED.
WHO REMAINS BEHIND?
MYDA WILL STAY.
WHY WOULD WE LEAVE SOMEONE BEHIND?
TO REMOVE THE CRYSTAL ON THIS SIDE OF THE PORTAL, OR MORDIEL WOULD SIMPLY USE IT TO FOLLOW US.
I WAS BORN IN THESE HILLS. THEY'LL NEVER CATCH UP TO ME.
AND I INTEND TO GIVE MORDIEL SOMETHING MORE THAN YOU TO THINK ABOUT.

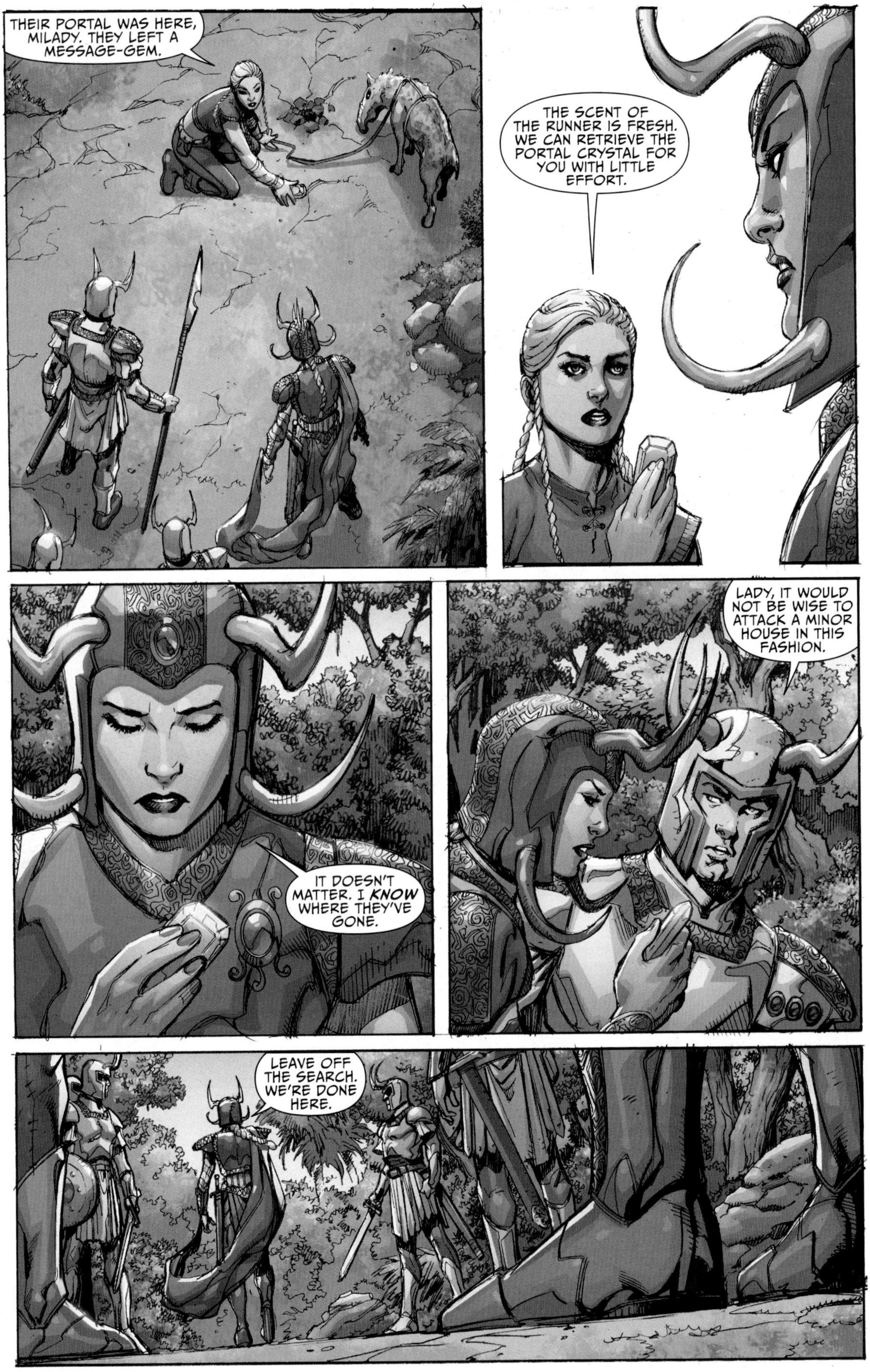
THEIR PORTAL WAS HERE, MILADY. THEY LEFT A MESSAGE-GEM.
THE SCENT OF THE RUNNER IS FRESH. WE CAN RETRIEVE THE PORTAL CRYSTAL FOR YOU WITH LITTLE EFFORT.
IT DOESN'T MATTER. I **KNOW** WHERE THEY'VE GONE.
LADY, IT WOULD NOT BE WISE TO ATTACK A MINOR HOUSE IN THIS FASHION.
LEAVE OFF THE SEARCH. WE'RE DONE HERE.

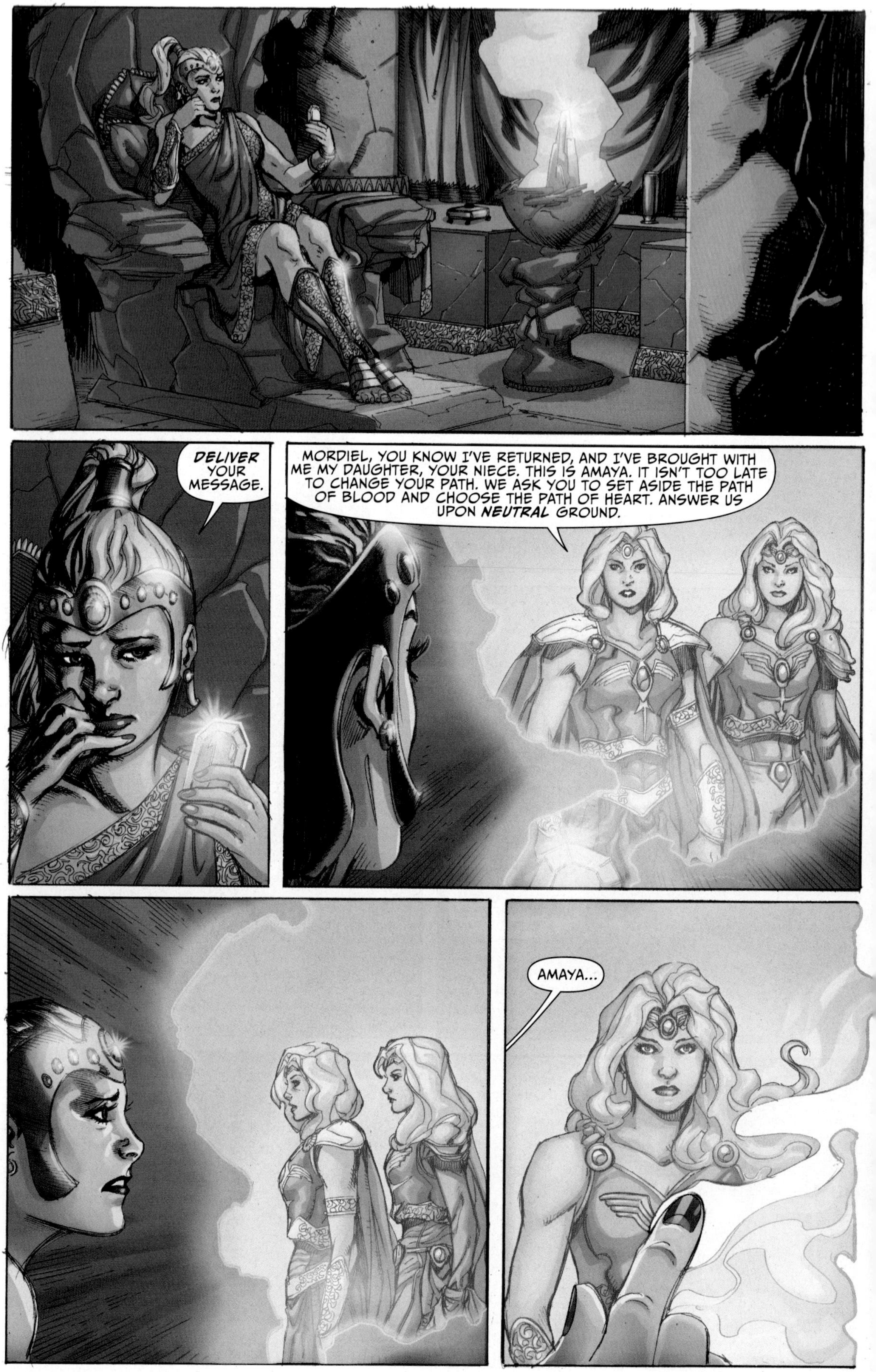

DELIVER YOUR MESSAGE.
MORDIEL, YOU KNOW I'VE RETURNED, AND I'VE BROUGHT WITH ME MY DAUGHTER, YOUR NIECE. THIS IS AMAYA. IT ISN'T TOO LATE TO CHANGE YOUR PATH. WE ASK YOU TO SET ASIDE THE PATH OF BLOOD AND CHOOSE THE PATH OF HEART. ANSWER US UPON NEUTRAL GROUND.
AMAYA...

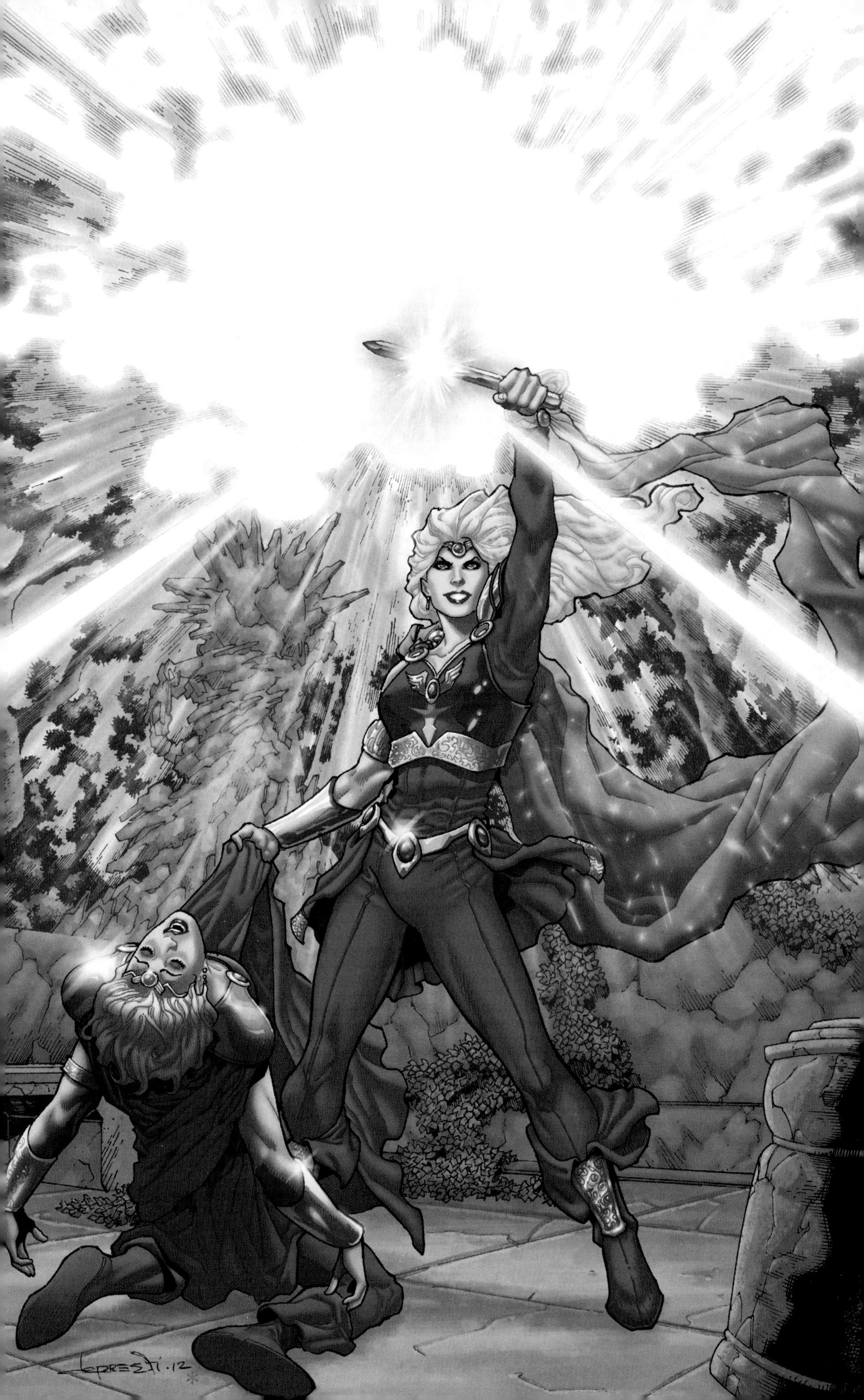

AMETHYST part three THE PATH OF HEART

CHRISTY MARX writer AARON LOPRESTI artist cover by AARON LOPRESTI & HI-FI

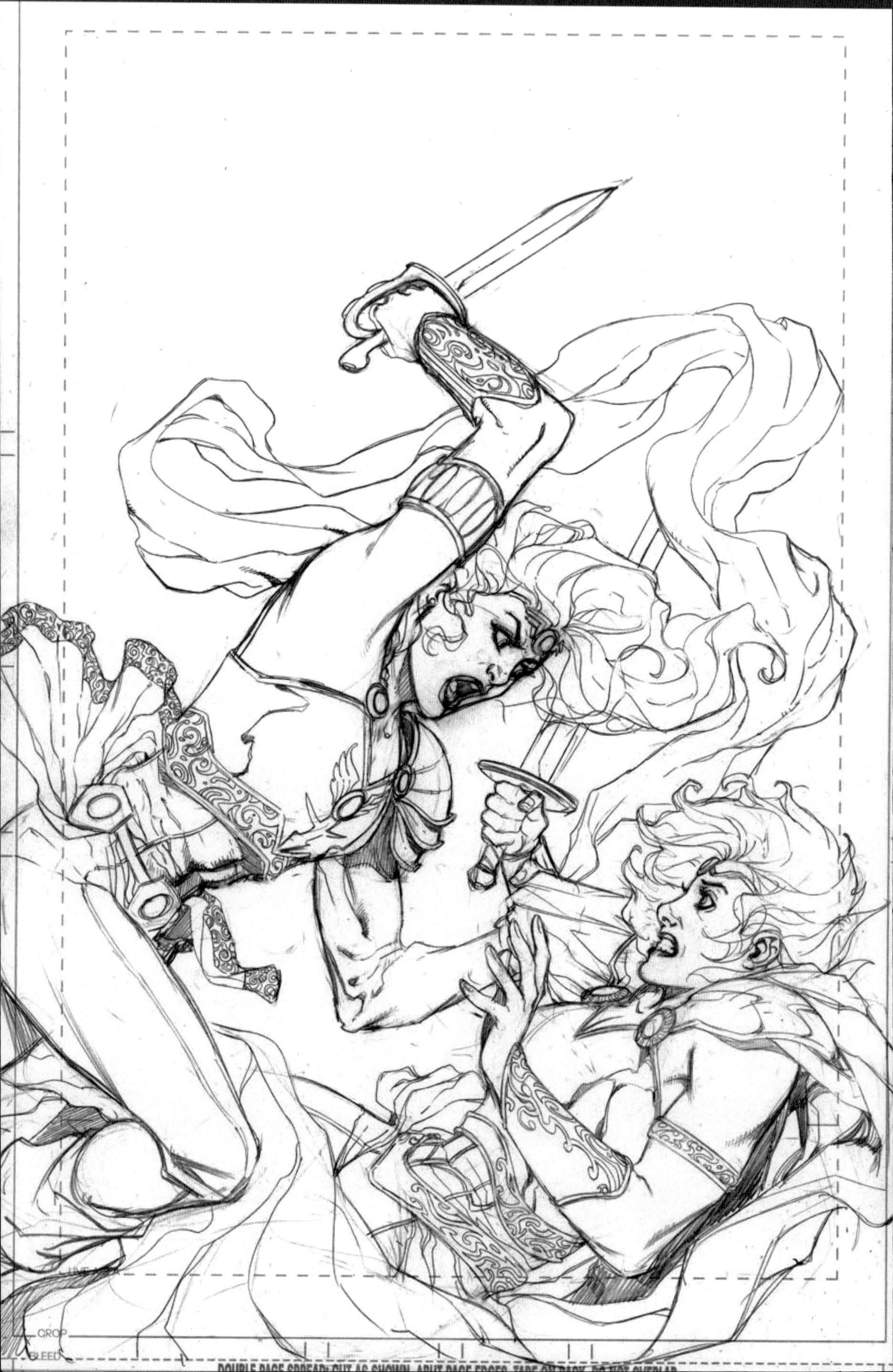
CROP
BLEED

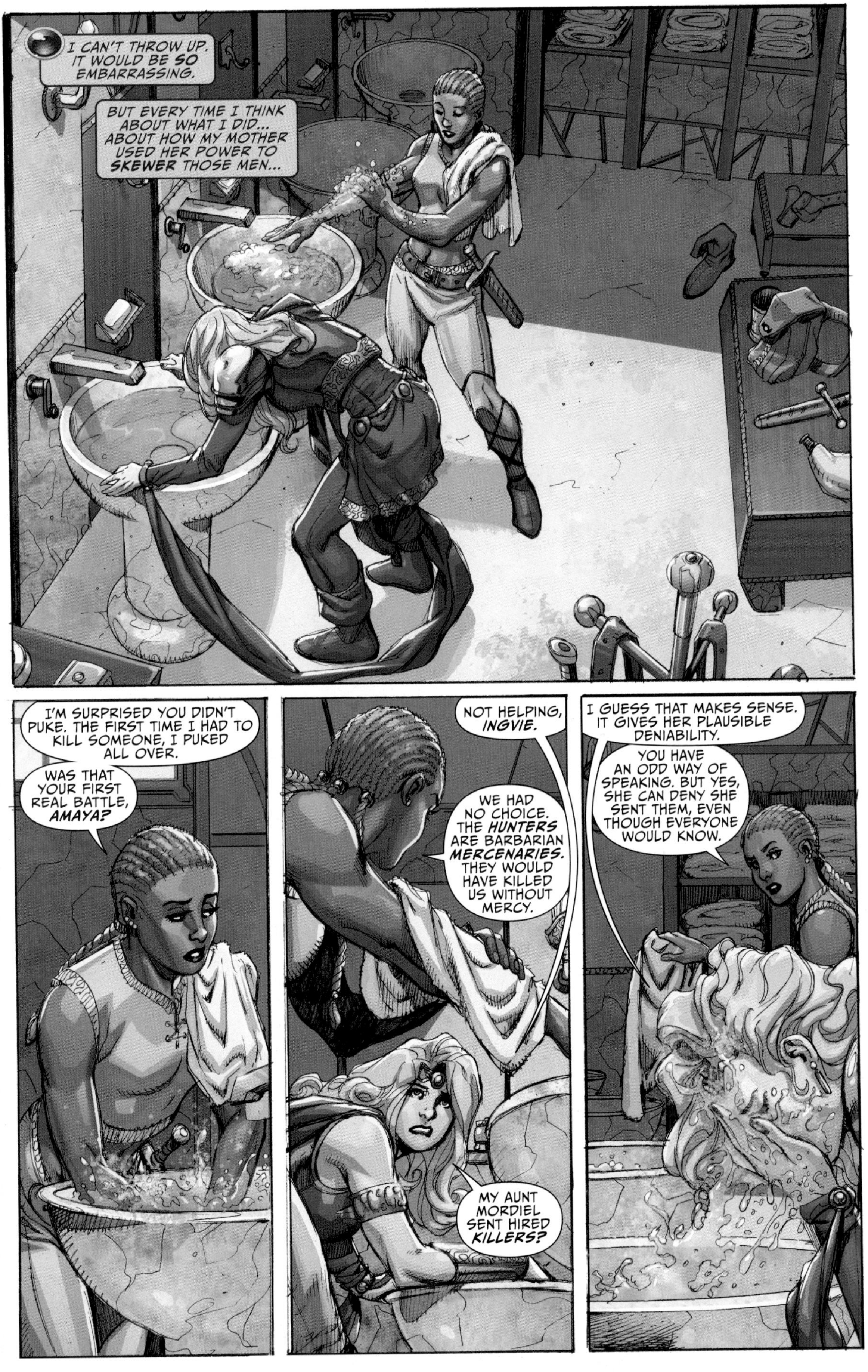

I CAN'T THROW UP. IT WOULD BE SO EMBARRASSING.
BUT EVERY TIME I THINK ABOUT WHAT I DID... ABOUT HOW MY MOTHER USED HER POWER TO SKEWER THOSE MEN...
I'M SURPRISED YOU DIDN'T PUKE. THE FIRST TIME I HAD TO KILL SOMEONE, I PUKED ALL OVER.
WAS THAT YOUR FIRST REAL BATTLE, AMAYA?
NOT HELPING, INGVIE.
WE HAD NO CHOICE. THE HUNTERS ARE BARBARIAN MERCENARIES. THEY WOULD HAVE KILLED US WITHOUT MERCY.
MY AUNT MORDIEL SENT HIRED KILLERS?
I GUESS THAT MAKES SENSE. IT GIVES HER PLAUSIBLE DENIABILITY.
YOU HAVE AN ODD WAY OF SPEAKING. BUT YES, SHE CAN DENY SHE SENT THEM, EVEN THOUGH EVERYONE WOULD KNOW.

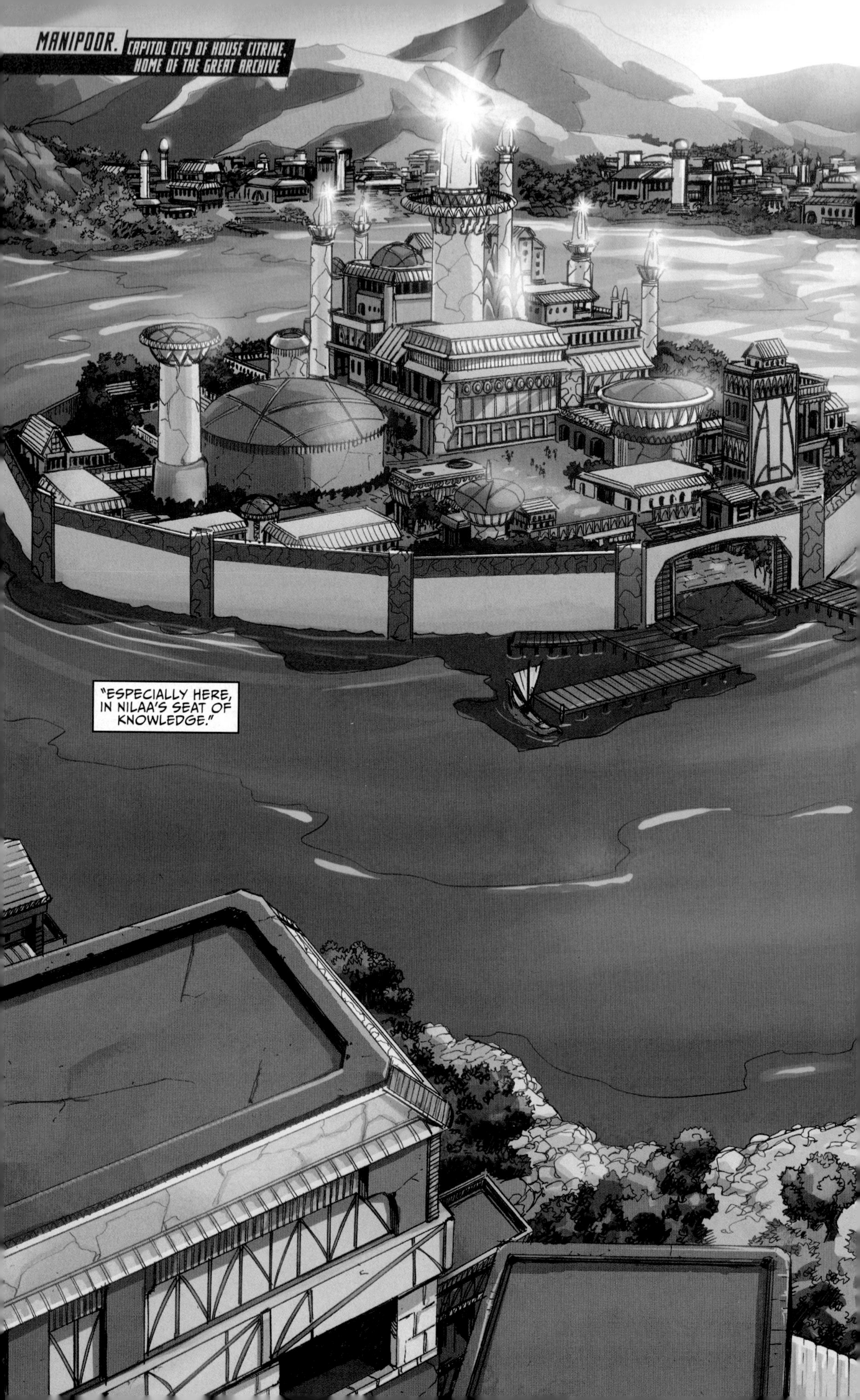
MANIPOOR.
CAPITOL CITY OF HOUSE CITRINE, HOME OF THE GREAT ARCHIVE
"ESPECIALLY HERE, IN NILAA'S SEAT OF KNOWLEDGE."

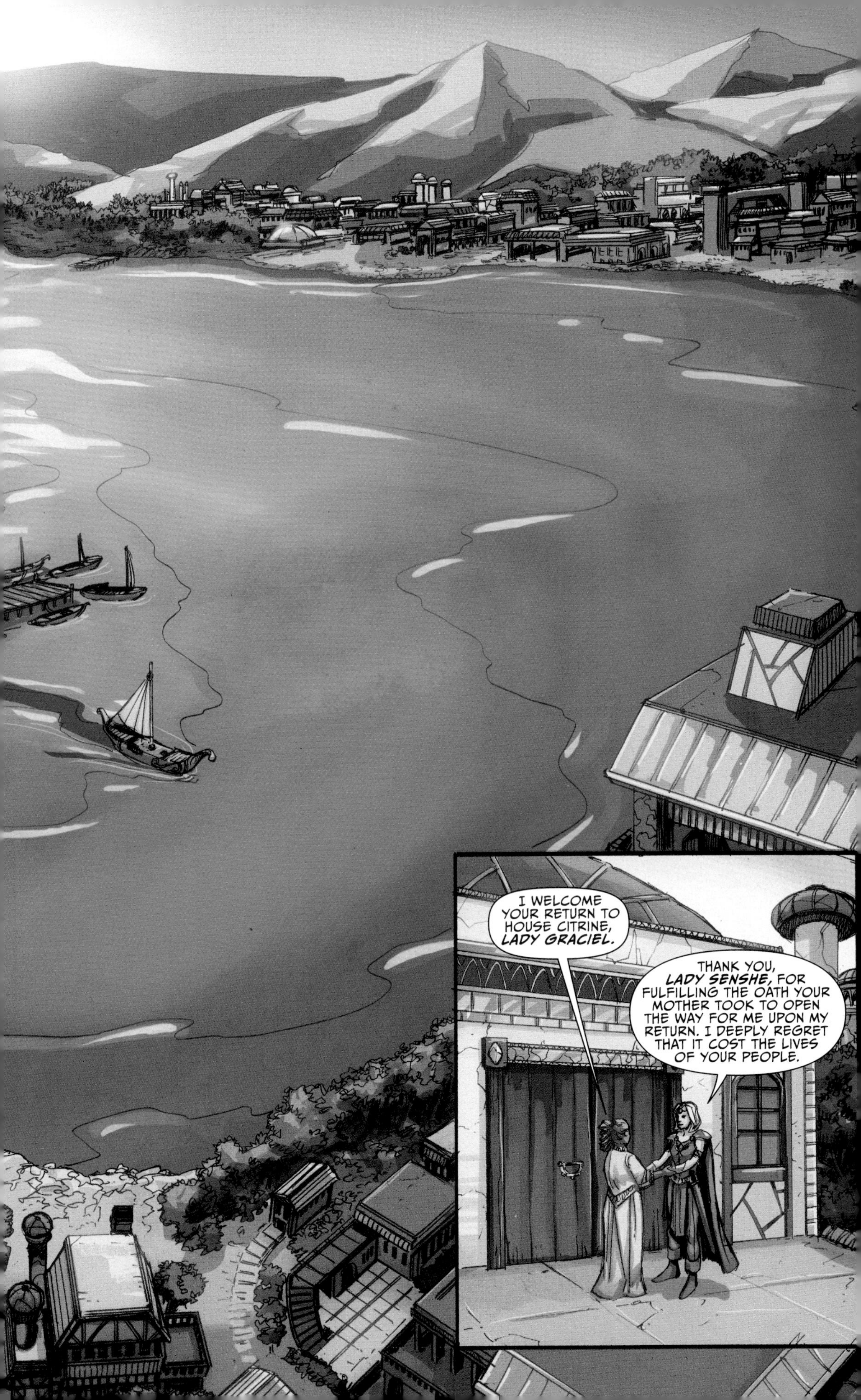
I WELCOME YOUR RETURN TO HOUSE CITRINE, LADY GRACIEL.
THANK YOU, LADY SENSHE, FOR FULFILLING THE OATH YOUR MOTHER TOOK TO OPEN THE WAY FOR ME UPON MY RETURN. I DEEPLY REGRET THAT IT COST THE LIVES OF YOUR PEOPLE.

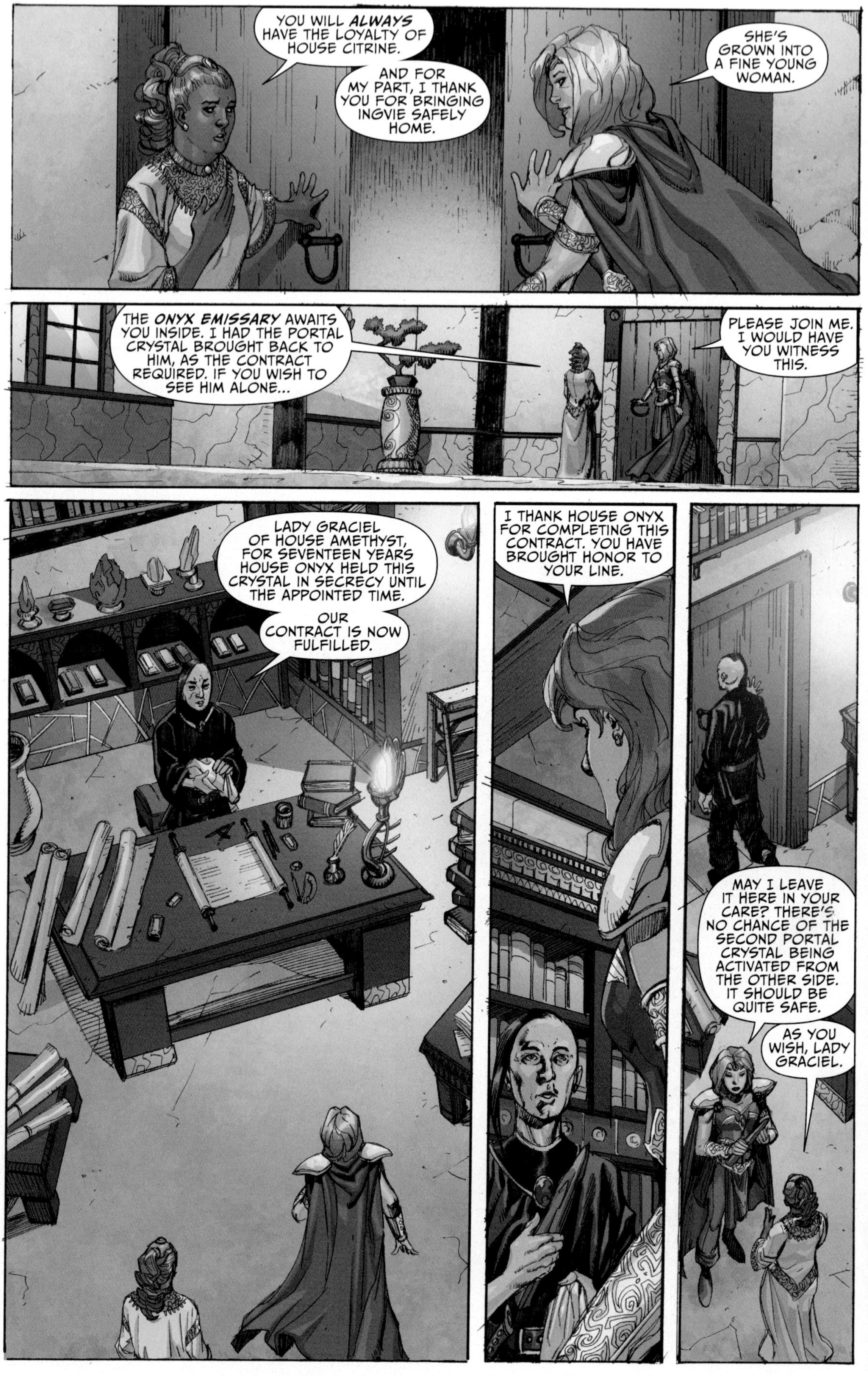

YOU WILL ALWAYS HAVE THE LOYALTY OF HOUSE CITRINE.
AND FOR MY PART, I THANK YOU FOR BRINGING INGVIE SAFELY HOME.
SHE'S GROWN INTO A FINE YOUNG WOMAN.
THE ONYX EMISSARY AWAITS YOU INSIDE. I HAD THE PORTAL CRYSTAL BROUGHT BACK TO HIM, AS THE CONTRACT REQUIRED. IF YOU WISH TO SEE HIM ALONE...
PLEASE JOIN ME. I WOULD HAVE YOU WITNESS THIS.
LADY GRACIEL OF HOUSE AMETHYST, FOR SEVENTEEN YEARS HOUSE ONYX HELD THIS CRYSTAL IN SECRECY UNTIL THE APPOINTED TIME.
OUR CONTRACT IS NOW FULFILLED.
I THANK HOUSE ONYX FOR COMPLETING THIS CONTRACT. YOU HAVE BROUGHT HONOR TO YOUR LINE.
MAY I LEAVE IT HERE IN YOUR CARE? THERE'S NO CHANCE OF THE SECOND PORTAL CRYSTAL BEING ACTIVATED FROM THE OTHER SIDE. IT SHOULD BE QUITE SAFE.
AS YOU WISH, LADY GRACIEL.

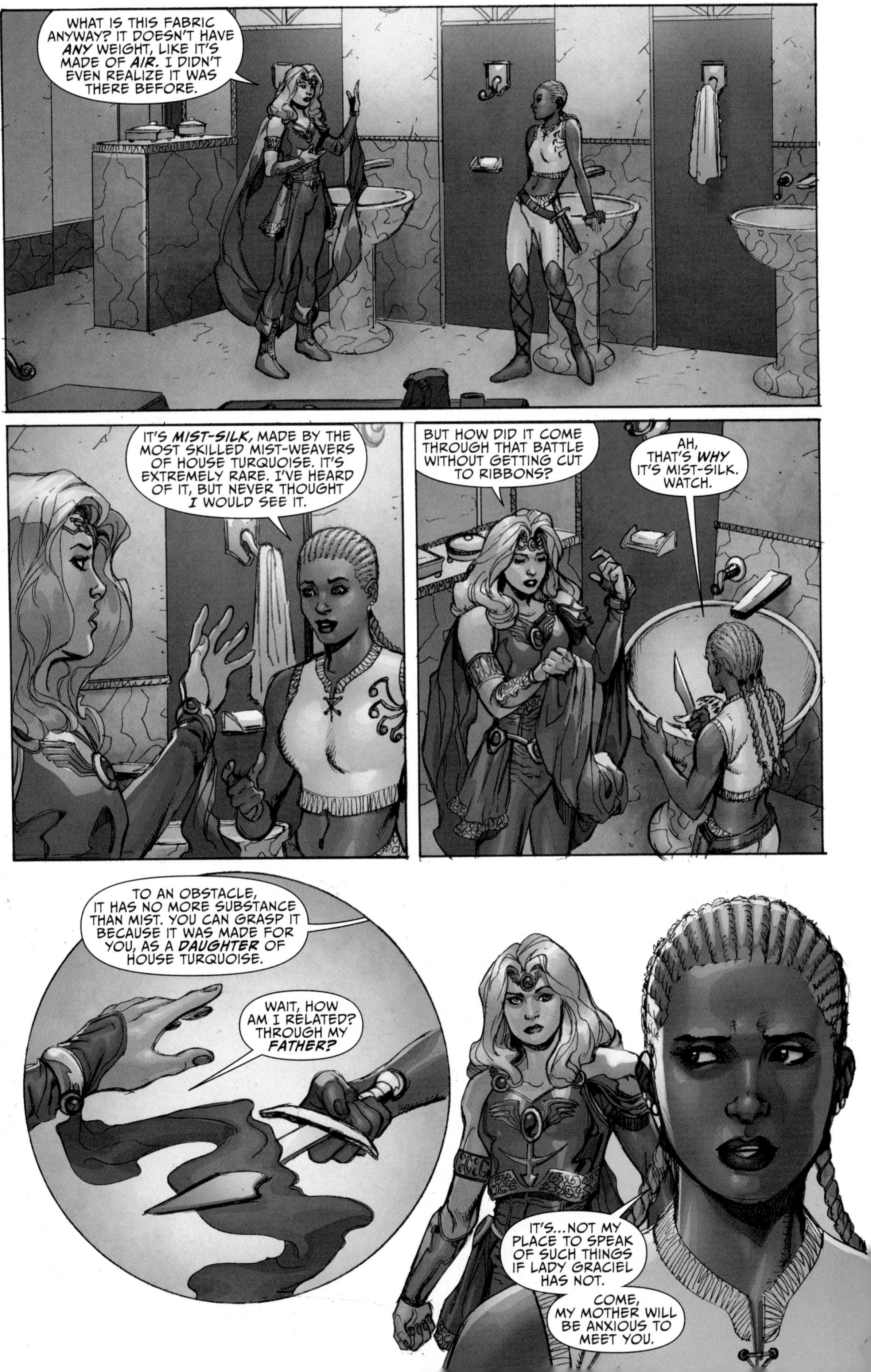
WHAT IS THIS FABRIC ANYWAY? IT DOESN'T HAVE ANY WEIGHT, LIKE IT'S MADE OF AIR. I DIDN'T EVEN REALIZE IT WAS THERE BEFORE.
IT'S MIST-SILK, MADE BY THE MOST SKILLED MIST-WEAVERS OF HOUSE TURQUOISE. IT'S EXTREMELY RARE. I'VE HEARD OF IT, BUT NEVER THOUGHT I WOULD SEE IT.
BUT HOW DID IT COME THROUGH THAT BATTLE WITHOUT GETTING CUT TO RIBBONS?
AH, THAT'S WHY IT'S MIST-SILK. WATCH.
TO AN OBSTACLE, IT HAS NO MORE SUBSTANCE THAN MIST. YOU CAN GRASP IT BECAUSE IT WAS MADE FOR YOU, AS A DAUGHTER OF HOUSE TURQUOISE.
WAIT, HOW AM I RELATED? THROUGH MY FATHER?
IT'S...NOT MY PLACE TO SPEAK OF SUCH THINGS IF LADY GRACIEL HAS NOT.
COME, MY MOTHER WILL BE ANXIOUS TO MEET YOU.

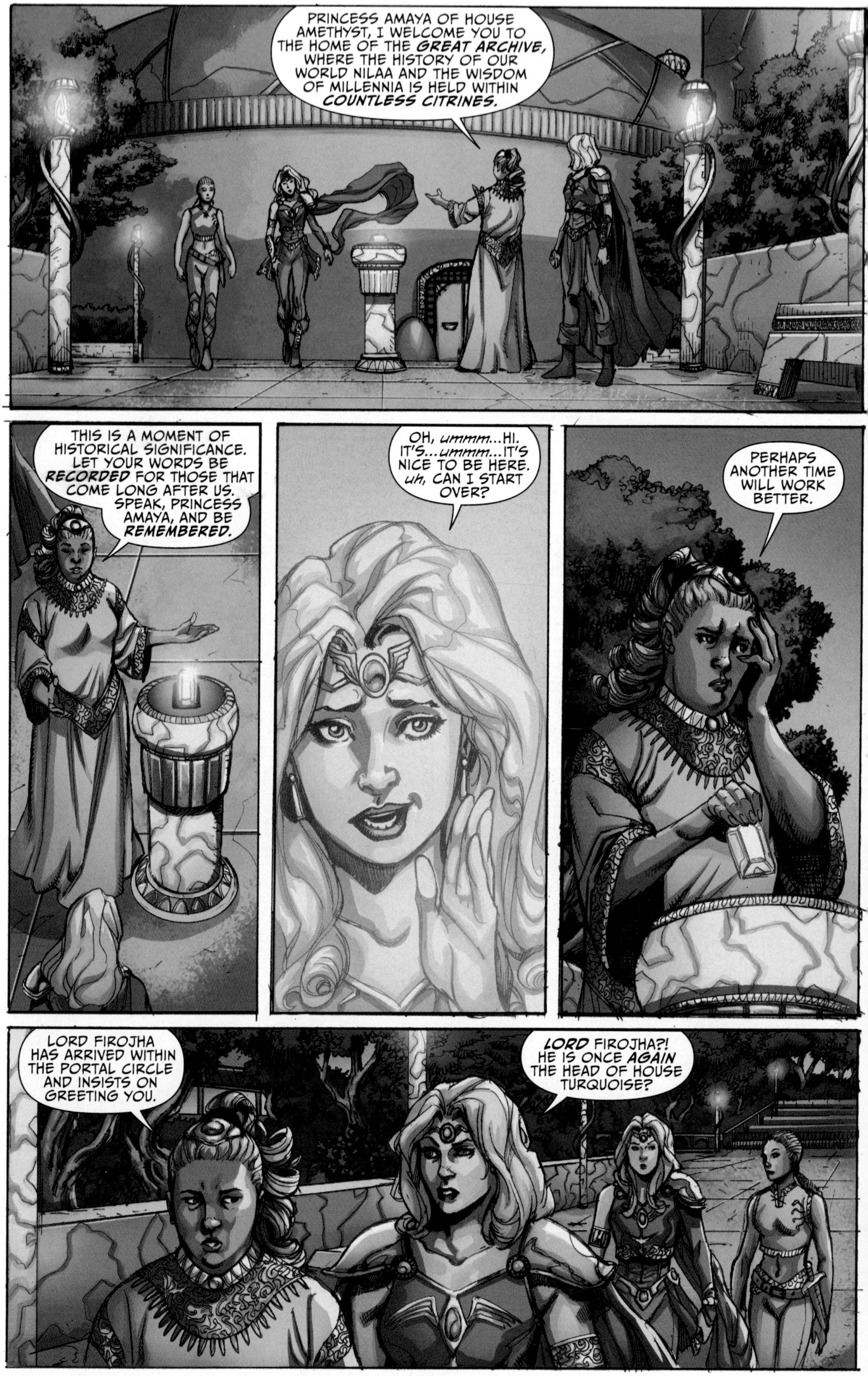
PRINCESS AMAYA OF HOUSE AMETHYST, I WELCOME YOU TO THE HOME OF THE GREAT ARCHIVE, WHERE THE HISTORY OF OUR WORLD NILAA AND THE WISDOM OF MILLENNIA IS HELD WITHIN COUNTLESS CITRINES.
THIS IS A MOMENT OF HISTORICAL SIGNIFICANCE. LET YOUR WORDS BE RECORDED FOR THOSE THAT COME LONG AFTER US. SPEAK, PRINCESS AMAYA, AND BE REMEMBERED.
OH, ummm...HI. IT'S...ummm...IT'S NICE TO BE HERE. uh, CAN I START OVER?
PERHAPS ANOTHER TIME WILL WORK BETTER.
LORD FIROJHA HAS ARRIVED WITHIN THE PORTAL CIRCLE AND INSISTS ON GREETING YOU.
LORD FIROJHA?! HE IS ONCE AGAIN THE HEAD OF HOUSE TURQUOISE?

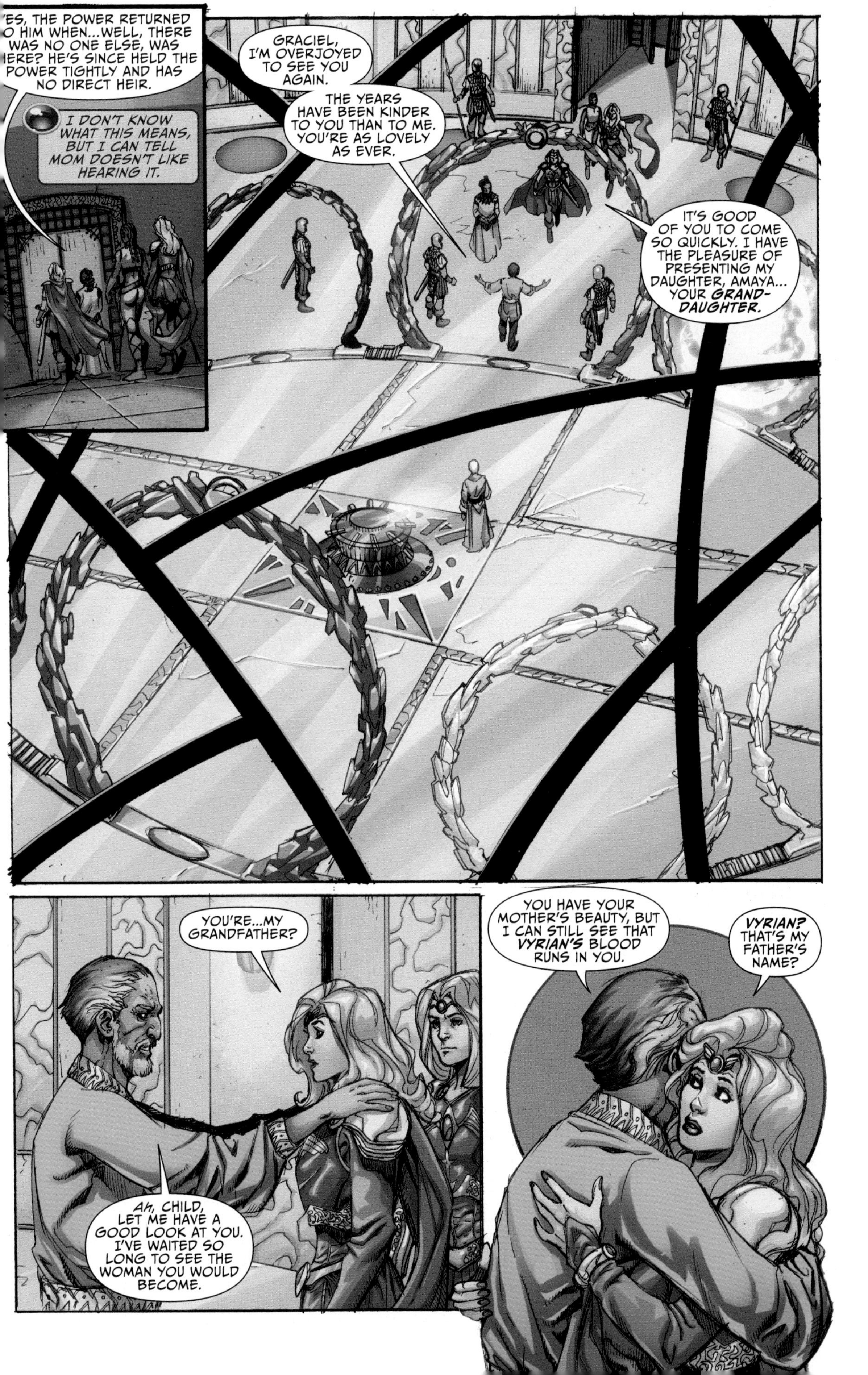
'ES, THE POWER RETURNED O HIM WHEN...WELL, THERE WAS NO ONE ELSE, WAS HERE? HE'S SINCE HELD THE POWER TIGHTLY AND HAS NO DIRECT HEIR.
I DON'T KNOW WHAT THIS MEANS, BUT I CAN TELL MOM DOESN'T LIKE HEARING IT.
GRACIEL, I'M OVERJOYED TO SEE YOU AGAIN.
THE YEARS HAVE BEEN KINDER TO YOU THAN TO ME. YOU'RE AS LOVELY AS EVER.
IT'S GOOD OF YOU TO COME SO QUICKLY. I HAVE THE PLEASURE OF PRESENTING MY DAUGHTER, AMAYA... YOUR GRAND-DAUGHTER.
YOU'RE...MY GRANDFATHER?
Ah, CHILD, LET ME HAVE A GOOD LOOK AT YOU. I'VE WAITED SO LONG TO SEE THE WOMAN YOU WOULD BECOME.
YOU HAVE YOUR MOTHER'S BEAUTY, BUT I CAN STILL SEE THAT VYRIAN'S BLOOD RUNS IN YOU.
VYRIAN? THAT'S MY FATHER'S NAME?

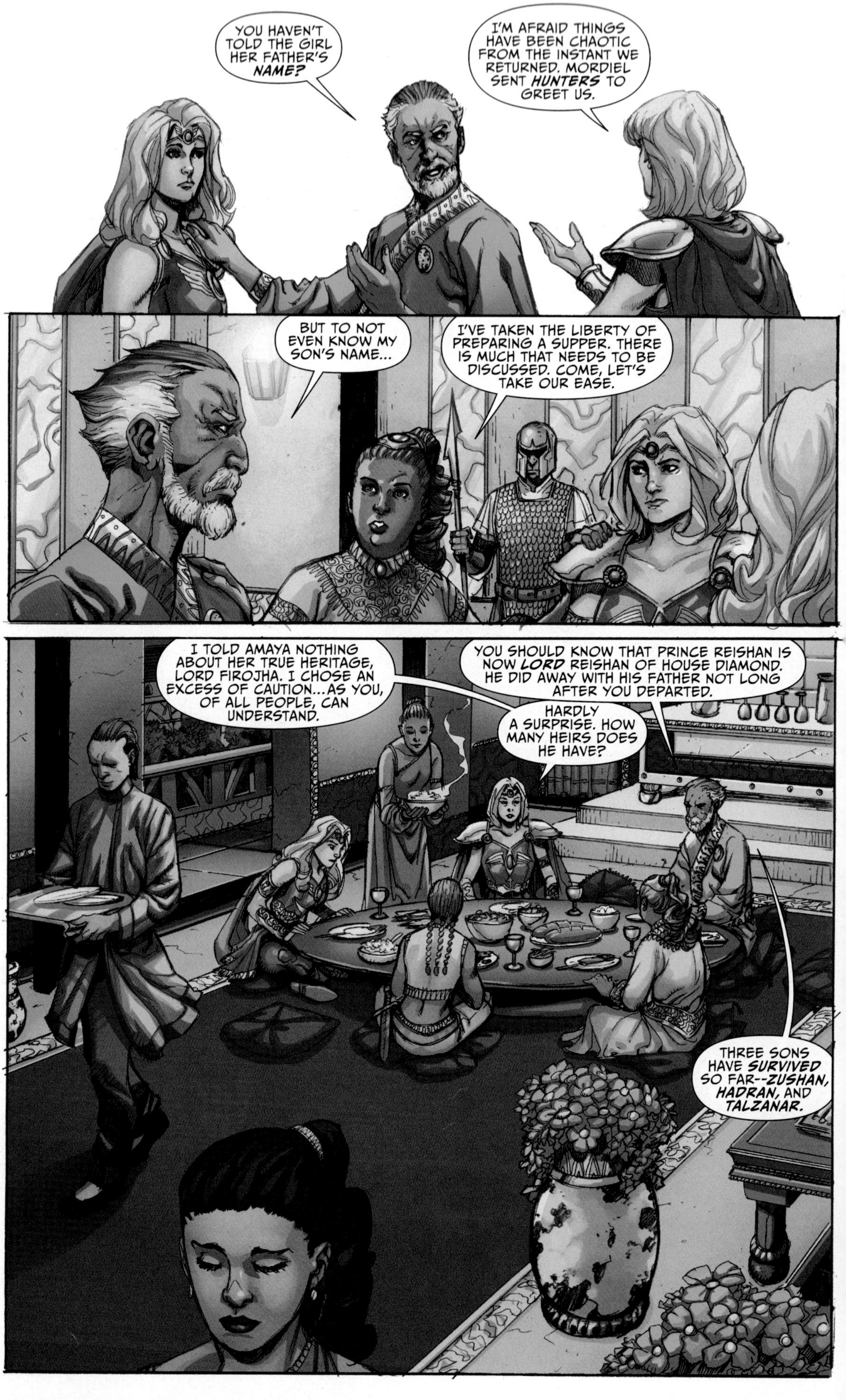
YOU HAVEN'T TOLD THE GIRL HER FATHER'S *NAME?*
I'M AFRAID THINGS HAVE BEEN CHAOTIC FROM THE INSTANT WE RETURNED. MORDIEL SENT *HUNTERS* TO GREET US.
BUT TO NOT EVEN KNOW MY SON'S NAME...
I'VE TAKEN THE LIBERTY OF PREPARING A SUPPER. THERE IS MUCH THAT NEEDS TO BE DISCUSSED. COME, LET'S TAKE OUR EASE.
I TOLD AMAYA NOTHING ABOUT HER TRUE HERITAGE, LORD FIROJHA. I CHOSE AN EXCESS OF CAUTION...AS YOU, OF ALL PEOPLE, CAN UNDERSTAND.
YOU SHOULD KNOW THAT PRINCE REISHAN IS NOW *LORD* REISHAN OF HOUSE DIAMOND. HE DID AWAY WITH HIS FATHER NOT LONG AFTER YOU DEPARTED.
HARDLY A SURPRISE. HOW MANY HEIRS DOES HE HAVE?
THREE SONS HAVE *SURVIVED* SO FAR--*ZUSHAN, HADRAN,* AND *TALZANAR.*

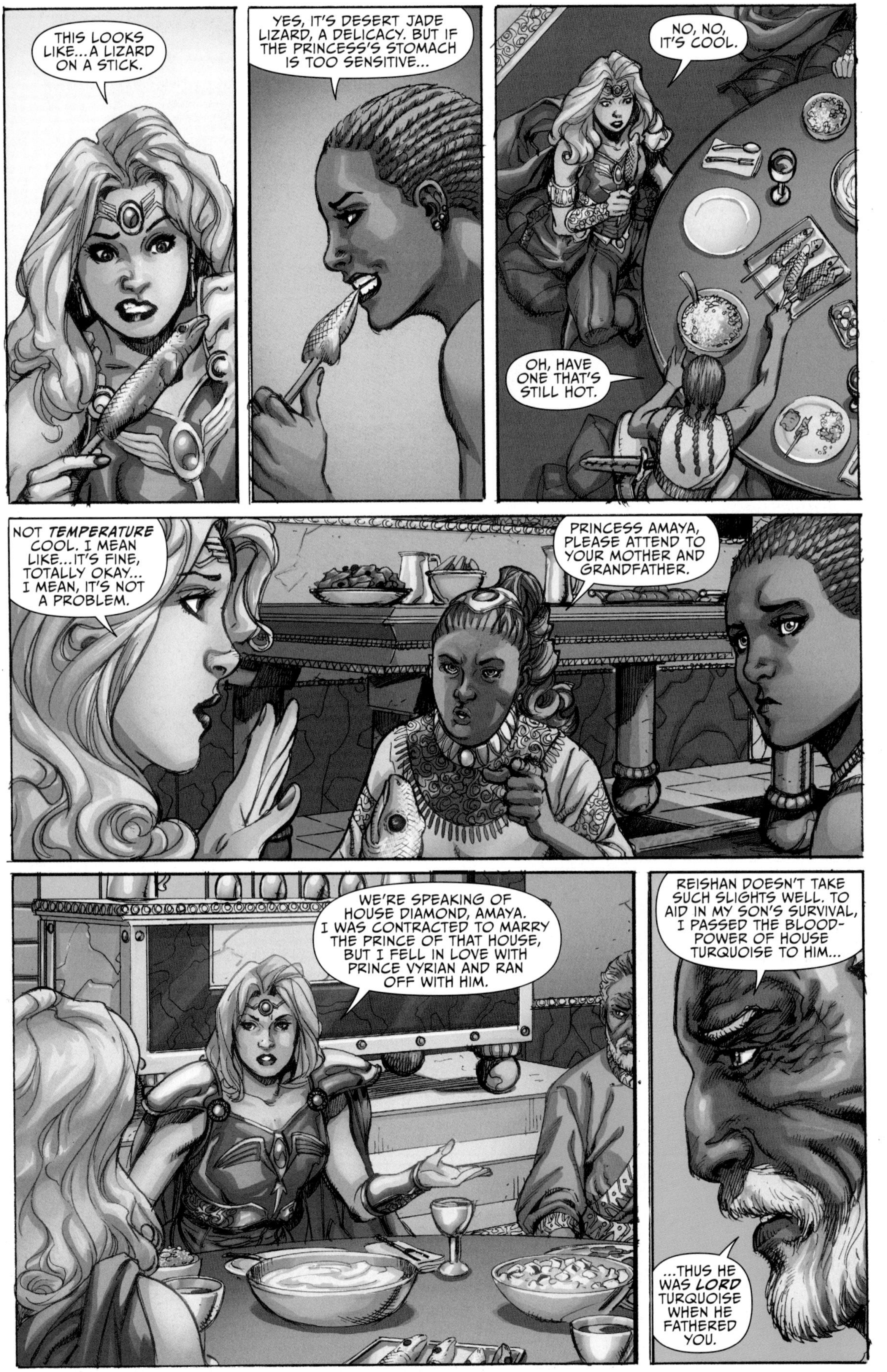
THIS LOOKS LIKE...A LIZARD ON A STICK.
YES, IT'S DESERT JADE LIZARD, A DELICACY. BUT IF THE PRINCESS'S STOMACH IS TOO SENSITIVE...
NO, NO, IT'S COOL.
OH, HAVE ONE THAT'S STILL HOT.
NOT *TEMPERATURE* COOL. I MEAN LIKE...IT'S FINE, TOTALLY OKAY... I MEAN, IT'S NOT A PROBLEM.
PRINCESS AMAYA, PLEASE ATTEND TO YOUR MOTHER AND GRANDFATHER.
WE'RE SPEAKING OF HOUSE DIAMOND, AMAYA. I WAS CONTRACTED TO MARRY THE PRINCE OF THAT HOUSE, BUT I FELL IN LOVE WITH PRINCE VYRIAN AND RAN OFF WITH HIM.
REISHAN DOESN'T TAKE SUCH SLIGHTS WELL. TO AID IN MY SON'S SURVIVAL, I PASSED THE BLOOD-POWER OF HOUSE TURQUOISE TO HIM...
...THUS HE WAS *LORD* TURQUOISE WHEN HE FATHERED YOU.

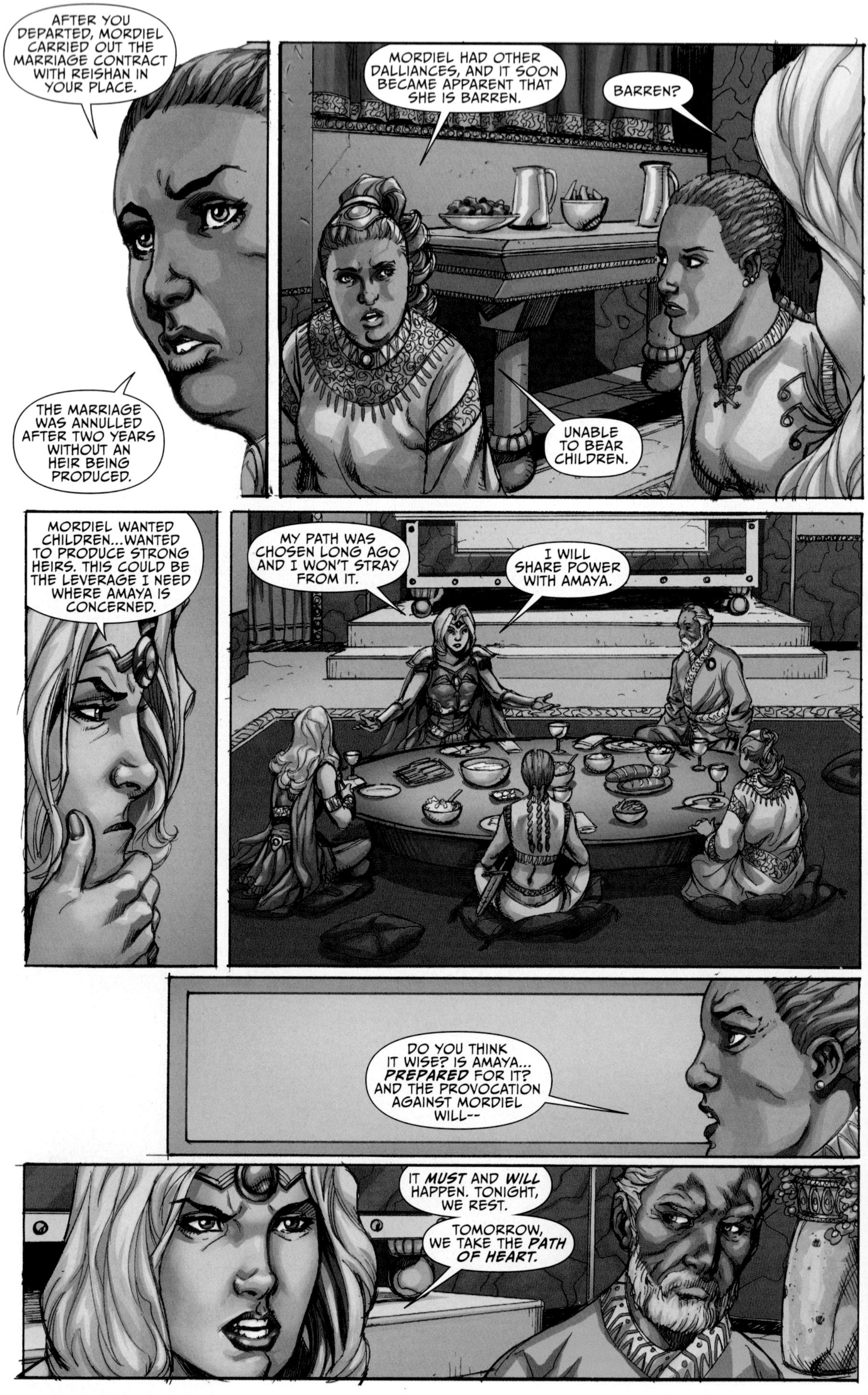
AFTER YOU DEPARTED, MORDIEL CARRIED OUT THE MARRIAGE CONTRACT WITH REISHAN IN YOUR PLACE.
THE MARRIAGE WAS ANNULLED AFTER TWO YEARS WITHOUT AN HEIR BEING PRODUCED.
MORDIEL HAD OTHER DALLIANCES, AND IT SOON BECAME APPARENT THAT SHE IS BARREN.
BARREN?
UNABLE TO BEAR CHILDREN.
MORDIEL WANTED CHILDREN...WANTED TO PRODUCE STRONG HEIRS. THIS COULD BE THE LEVERAGE I NEED WHERE AMAYA IS CONCERNED.
MY PATH WAS CHOSEN LONG AGO AND I WON'T STRAY FROM IT.
I WILL SHARE POWER WITH AMAYA.
DO YOU THINK IT WISE? IS AMAYA... ***PREPARED*** FOR IT? AND THE PROVOCATION AGAINST MORDIEL WILL--
IT ***MUST*** AND ***WILL*** HAPPEN. TONIGHT, WE REST.
TOMORROW, WE TAKE THE ***PATH OF HEART.***

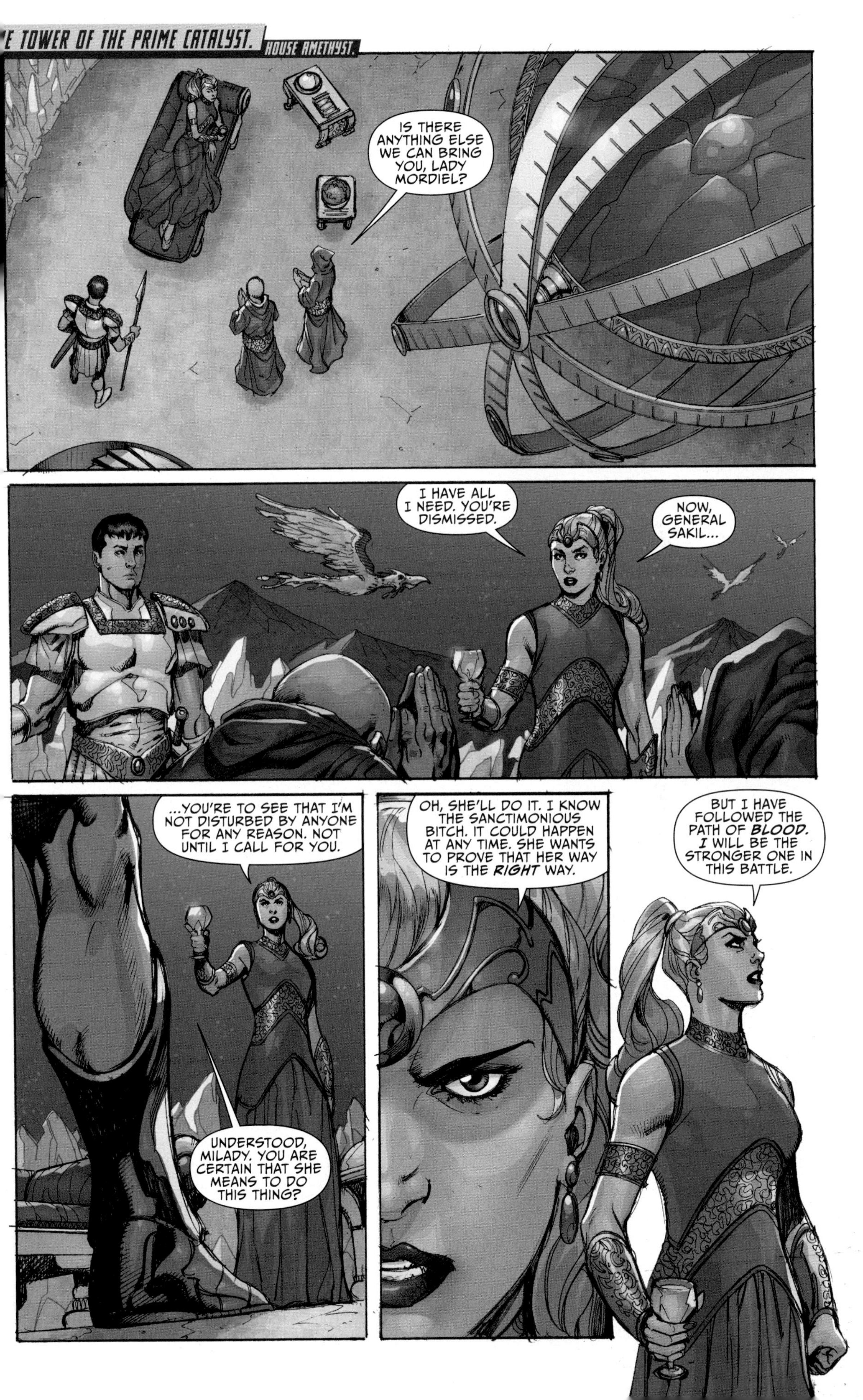
E TOWER OF THE PRIME CATALYST.
HOUSE AMETHYST.
IS THERE ANYTHING ELSE WE CAN BRING YOU, LADY MORDIEL?
I HAVE ALL I NEED. YOU'RE DISMISSED.
NOW, GENERAL SAKIL...
...YOU'RE TO SEE THAT I'M NOT DISTURBED BY ANYONE FOR ANY REASON. NOT UNTIL I CALL FOR YOU.
UNDERSTOOD, MILADY. YOU ARE CERTAIN THAT SHE MEANS TO DO THIS THING?
OH, SHE'LL DO IT. I KNOW THE SANCTIMONIOUS BITCH. IT COULD HAPPEN AT ANY TIME. SHE WANTS TO PROVE THAT HER WAY IS THE *RIGHT* WAY.
BUT I HAVE FOLLOWED THE PATH OF *BLOOD.* *I* WILL BE THE STRONGER ONE IN THIS BATTLE.

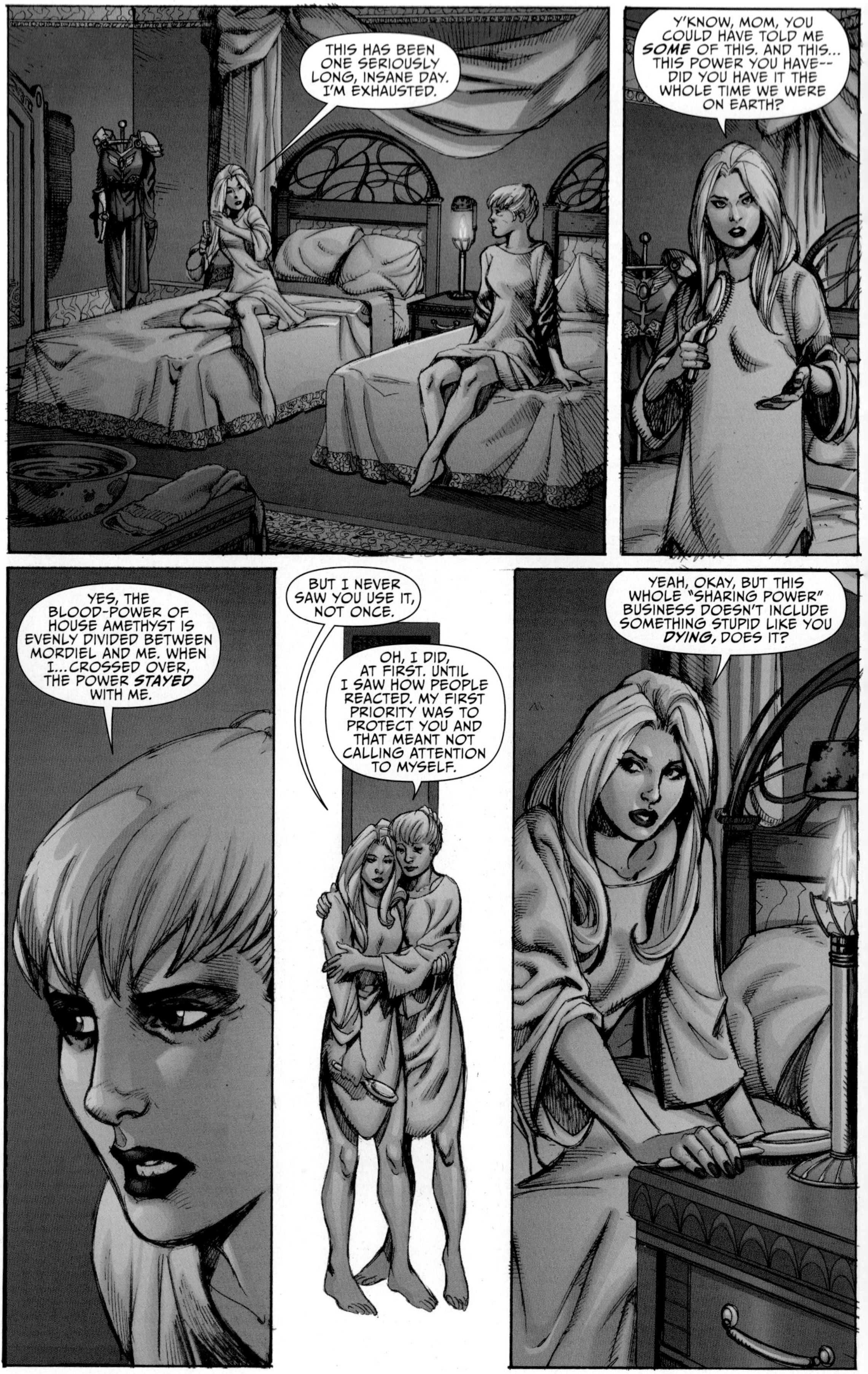
THIS HAS BEEN ONE SERIOUSLY LONG, INSANE DAY. I'M EXHAUSTED.
Y'KNOW, MOM, YOU COULD HAVE TOLD ME SOME OF THIS. AND THIS... THIS POWER YOU HAVE-- DID YOU HAVE IT THE WHOLE TIME WE WERE ON EARTH?
YES, THE BLOOD-POWER OF HOUSE AMETHYST IS EVENLY DIVIDED BETWEEN MORDIEL AND ME. WHEN I...CROSSED OVER, THE POWER STAYED WITH ME.
BUT I NEVER SAW YOU USE IT, NOT ONCE.
OH, I DID, AT FIRST. UNTIL I SAW HOW PEOPLE REACTED. MY FIRST PRIORITY WAS TO PROTECT YOU AND THAT MEANT NOT CALLING ATTENTION TO MYSELF.
YEAH, OKAY, BUT THIS WHOLE "SHARING POWER" BUSINESS DOESN'T INCLUDE SOMETHING STUPID LIKE YOU DYING, DOES IT?

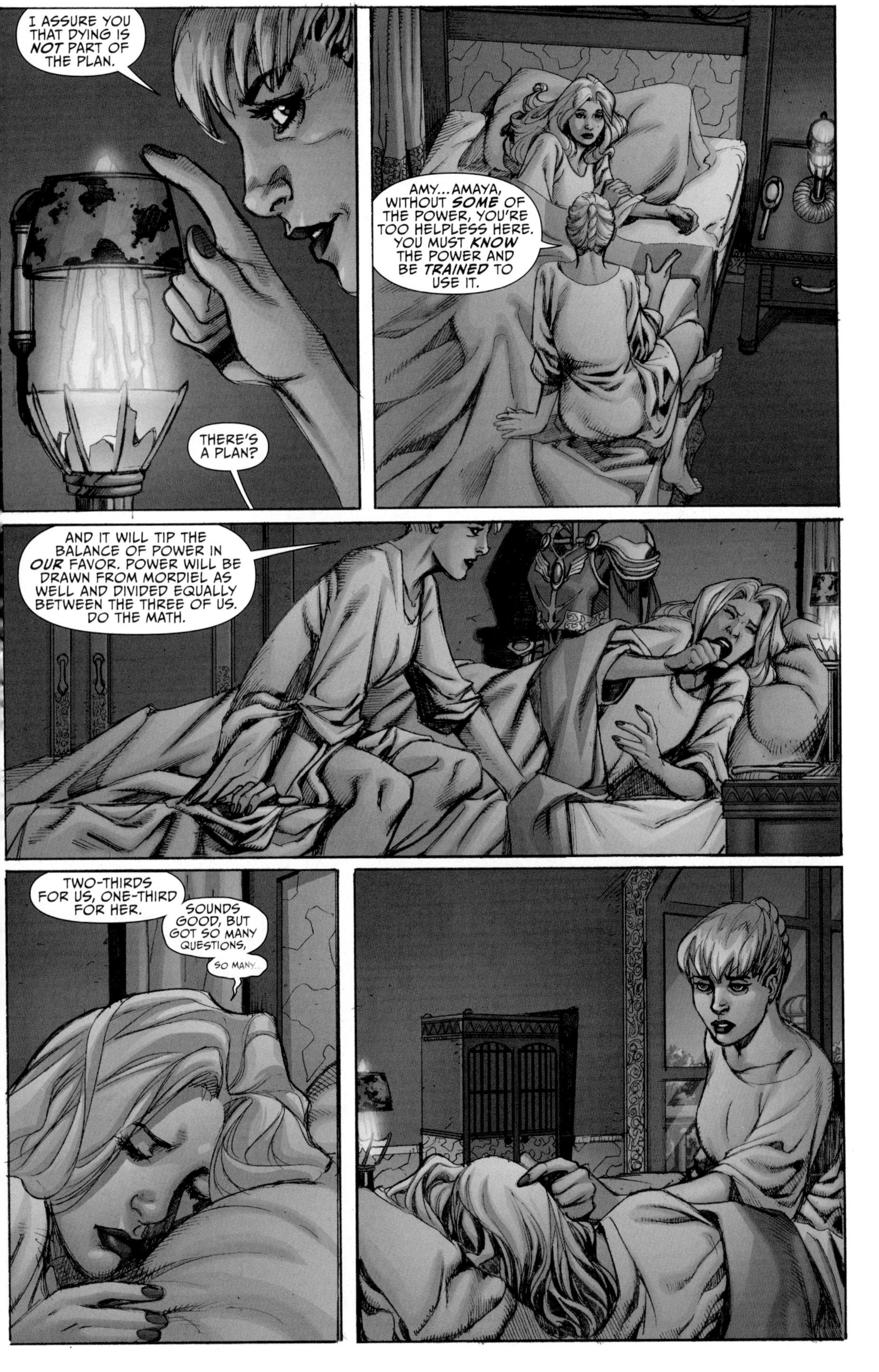
I ASSURE YOU THAT DYING IS NOT PART OF THE PLAN.
THERE'S A PLAN?
AMY...AMAYA, WITHOUT SOME OF THE POWER, YOU'RE TOO HELPLESS HERE. YOU MUST KNOW THE POWER AND BE TRAINED TO USE IT.
AND IT WILL TIP THE BALANCE OF POWER IN OUR FAVOR. POWER WILL BE DRAWN FROM MORDIEL AS WELL AND DIVIDED EQUALLY BETWEEN THE THREE OF US. DO THE MATH.
TWO-THIRDS FOR US, ONE-THIRD FOR HER.
SOUNDS GOOD, BUT GOT SO MANY QUESTIONS,
SO MANY..

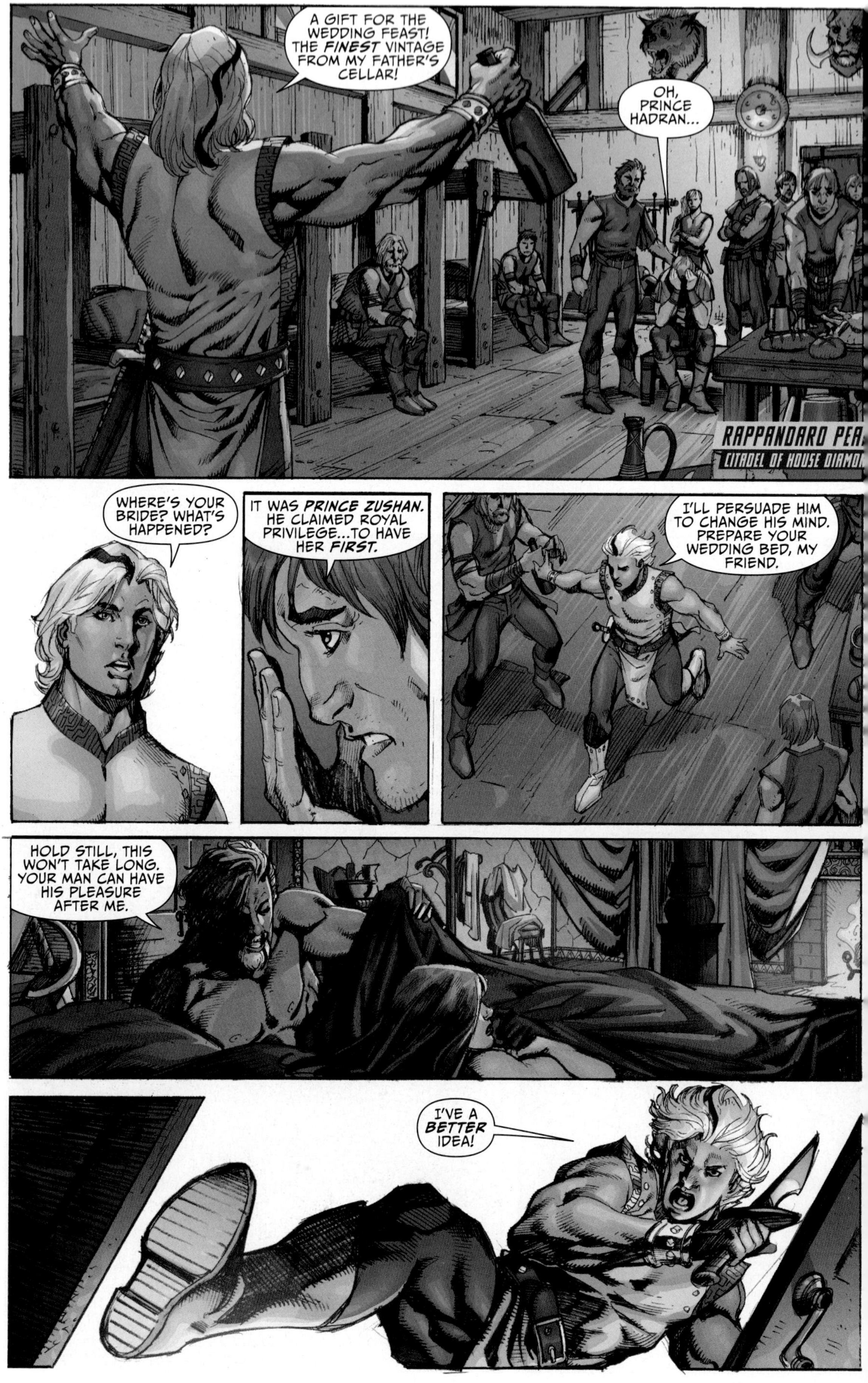
A GIFT FOR THE WEDDING FEAST! THE FINEST VINTAGE FROM MY FATHER'S CELLAR!
OH, PRINCE HADRAN...
RAPPANDARD PEA
CITADEL OF HOUSE DIAMO
WHERE'S YOUR BRIDE? WHAT'S HAPPENED?
IT WAS PRINCE ZUSHAN. HE CLAIMED ROYAL PRIVILEGE...TO HAVE HER FIRST.
I'LL PERSUADE HIM TO CHANGE HIS MIND. PREPARE YOUR WEDDING BED, MY FRIEND.
HOLD STILL, THIS WON'T TAKE LONG. YOUR MAN CAN HAVE HIS PLEASURE AFTER ME.
I'VE A BETTER IDEA!

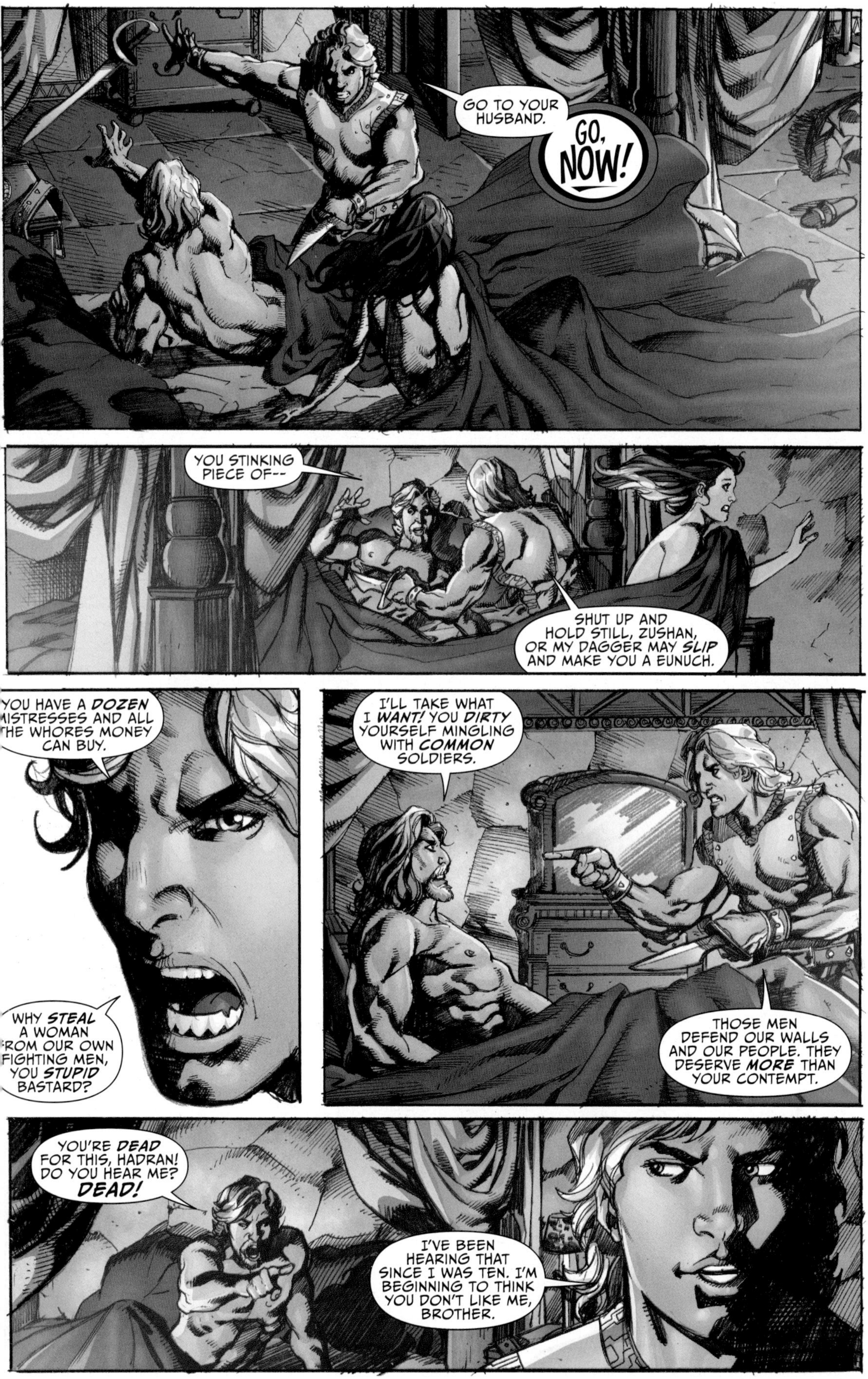
GO TO YOUR HUSBAND.
GO, NOW!
YOU STINKING PIECE OF--
SHUT UP AND HOLD STILL, ZUSHAN, OR MY DAGGER MAY SLIP AND MAKE YOU A EUNUCH.
YOU HAVE A DOZEN MISTRESSES AND ALL THE WHORES MONEY CAN BUY.
WHY STEAL A WOMAN FROM OUR OWN FIGHTING MEN, YOU STUPID BASTARD?
I'LL TAKE WHAT I WANT! YOU DIRTY YOURSELF MINGLING WITH COMMON SOLDIERS.
THOSE MEN DEFEND OUR WALLS AND OUR PEOPLE. THEY DESERVE MORE THAN YOUR CONTEMPT.
YOU'RE DEAD FOR THIS, HADRAN! DO YOU HEAR ME? DEAD!
I'VE BEEN HEARING THAT SINCE I WAS TEN. I'M BEGINNING TO THINK YOU DON'T LIKE ME, BROTHER.

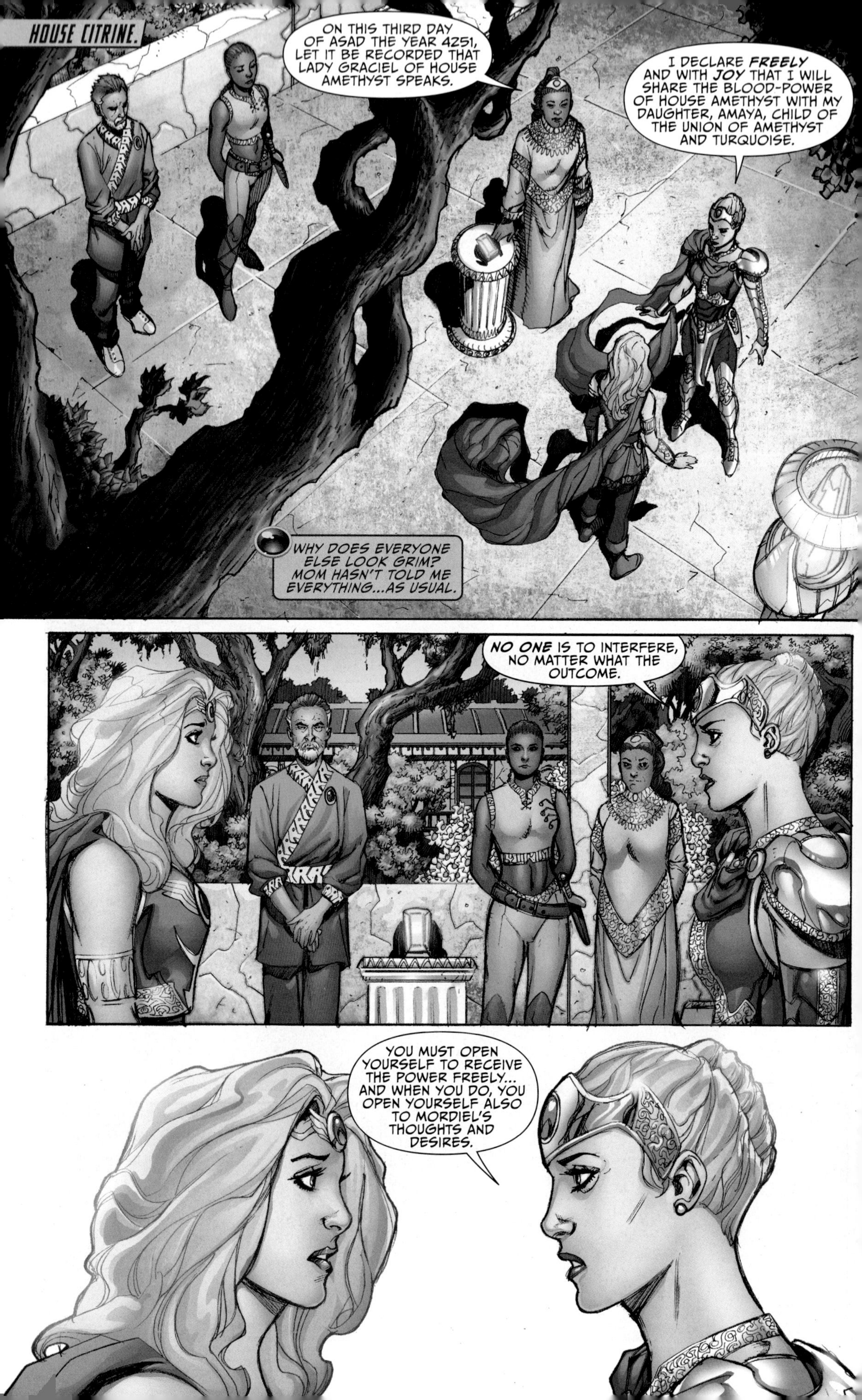
HOUSE CITRINE.
ON THIS THIRD DAY OF ASAD THE YEAR 4251, LET IT BE RECORDED THAT LADY GRACIEL OF HOUSE AMETHYST SPEAKS.
I DECLARE FREELY AND WITH JOY THAT I WILL SHARE THE BLOOD-POWER OF HOUSE AMETHYST WITH MY DAUGHTER, AMAYA, CHILD OF THE UNION OF AMETHYST AND TURQUOISE.
WHY DOES EVERYONE ELSE LOOK GRIM? MOM HASN'T TOLD ME EVERYTHING...AS USUAL.
NO ONE IS TO INTERFERE, NO MATTER WHAT THE OUTCOME.
YOU MUST OPEN YOURSELF TO RECEIVE THE POWER FREELY... AND WHEN YOU DO, YOU OPEN YOURSELF ALSO TO MORDIEL'S THOUGHTS AND DESIRES.

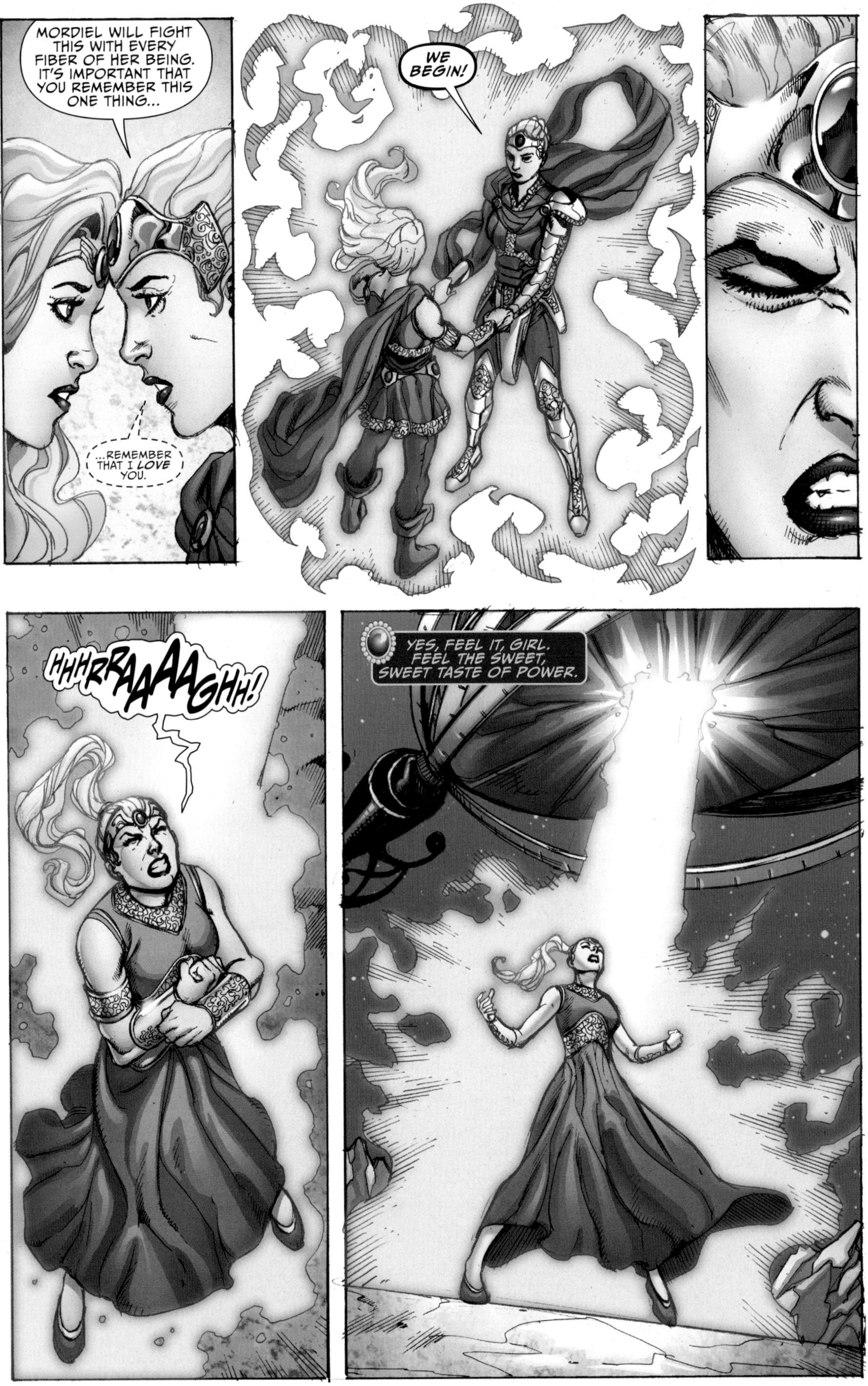
MORDIEL WILL FIGHT THIS WITH EVERY FIBER OF HER BEING. IT'S IMPORTANT THAT YOU REMEMBER THIS ONE THING...
...REMEMBER THAT I LOVE YOU.
WE BEGIN!
HHHRRAAAAGHH!
YES, FEEL IT, GIRL. FEEL THE SWEET, SWEET TASTE OF POWER.

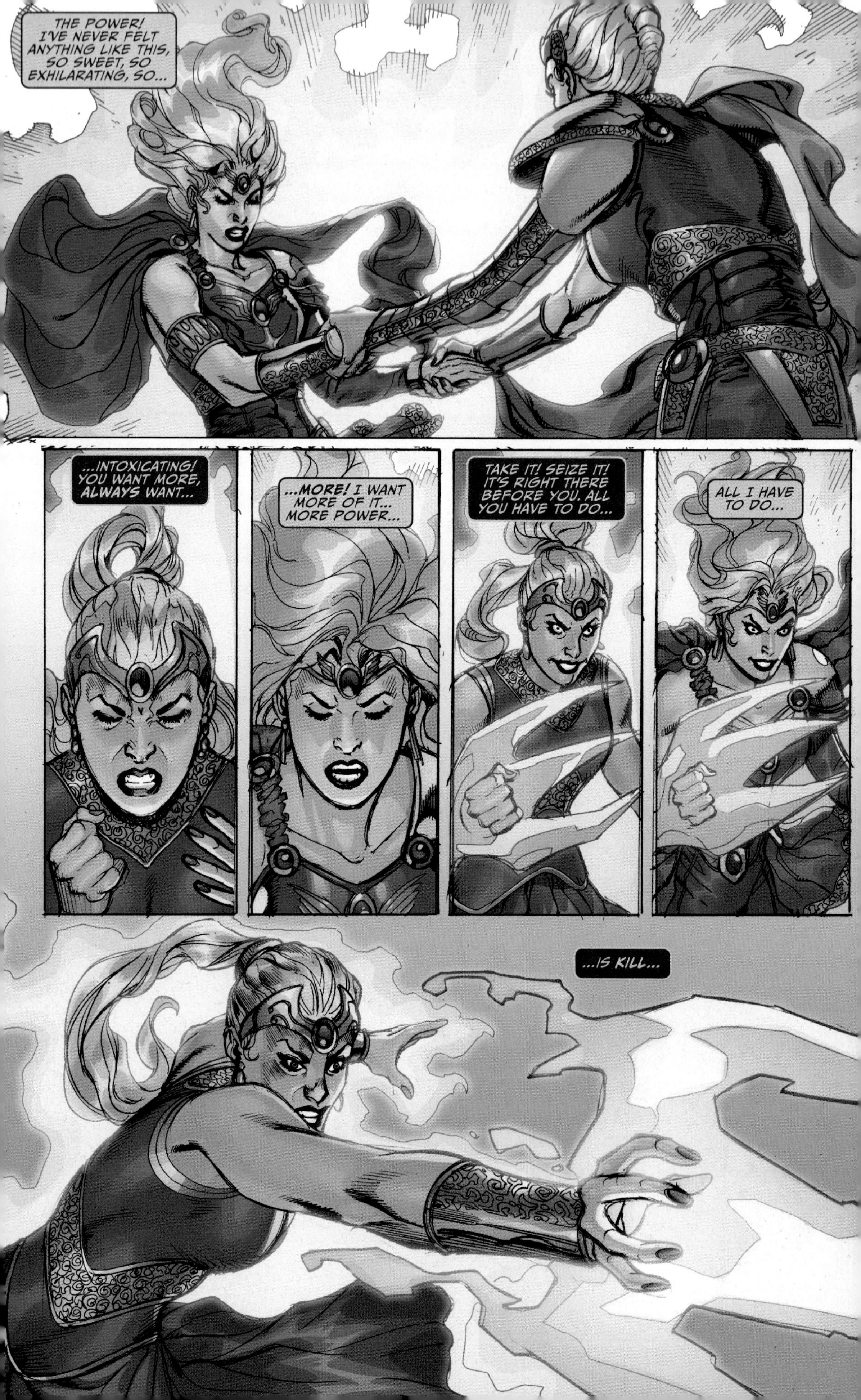
THE POWER! I'VE NEVER FELT ANYTHING LIKE THIS, SO SWEET, SO EXHILARATING, SO...
...INTOXICATING! YOU WANT MORE, ALWAYS WANT...
...MORE! I WANT MORE OF IT... MORE POWER...
TAKE IT! SEIZE IT! IT'S RIGHT THERE BEFORE YOU. ALL YOU HAVE TO DO...
ALL I HAVE TO DO...
...IS KILL...

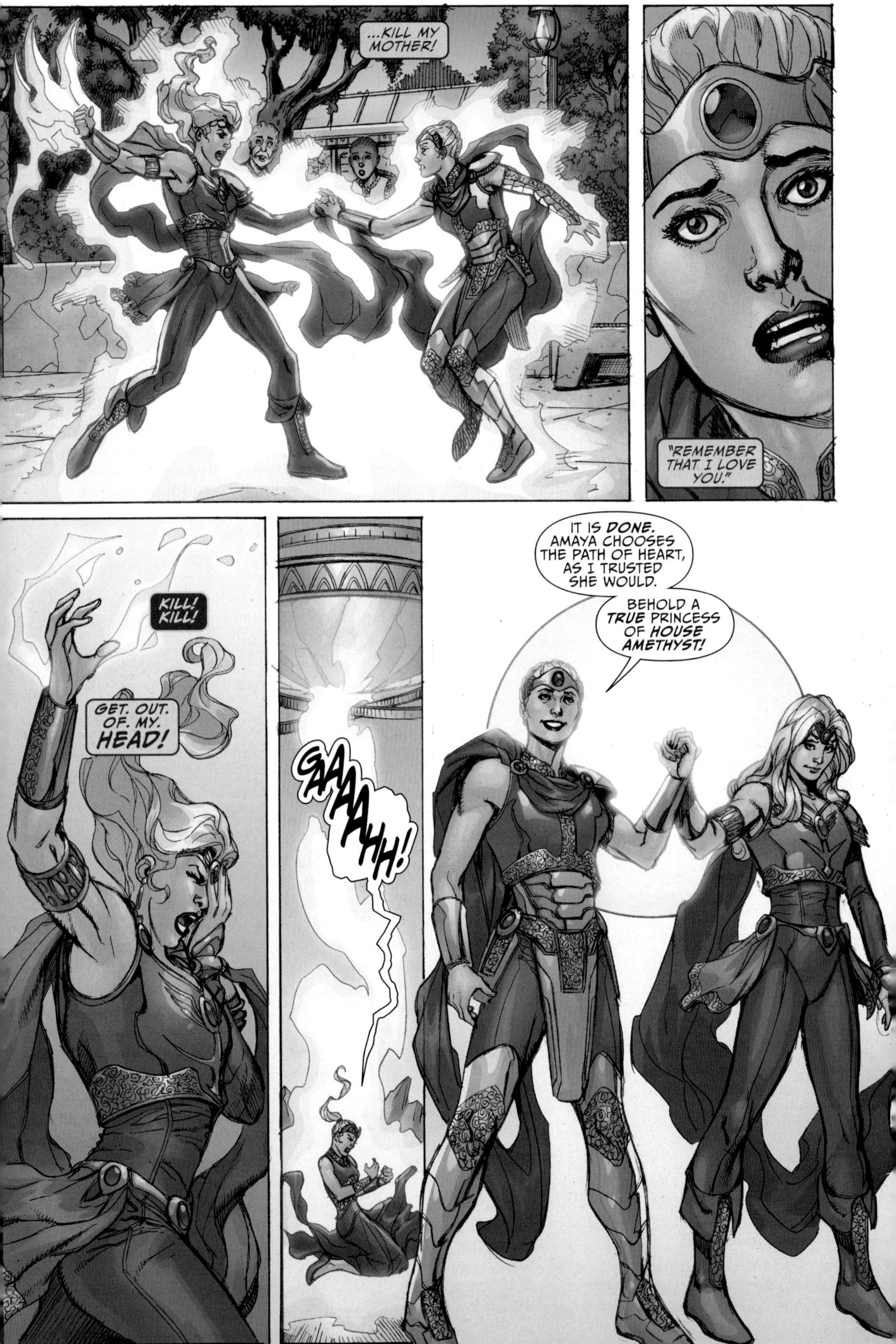
...KILL MY MOTHER!
"REMEMBER THAT I LOVE YOU."
KILL! KILL!
GET. OUT. OF. MY. HEAD!
GAAAAAHH!
IT IS DONE. AMAYA CHOOSES THE PATH OF HEART, AS I TRUSTED SHE WOULD.
BEHOLD A TRUE PRINCESS OF HOUSE AMETHYST!

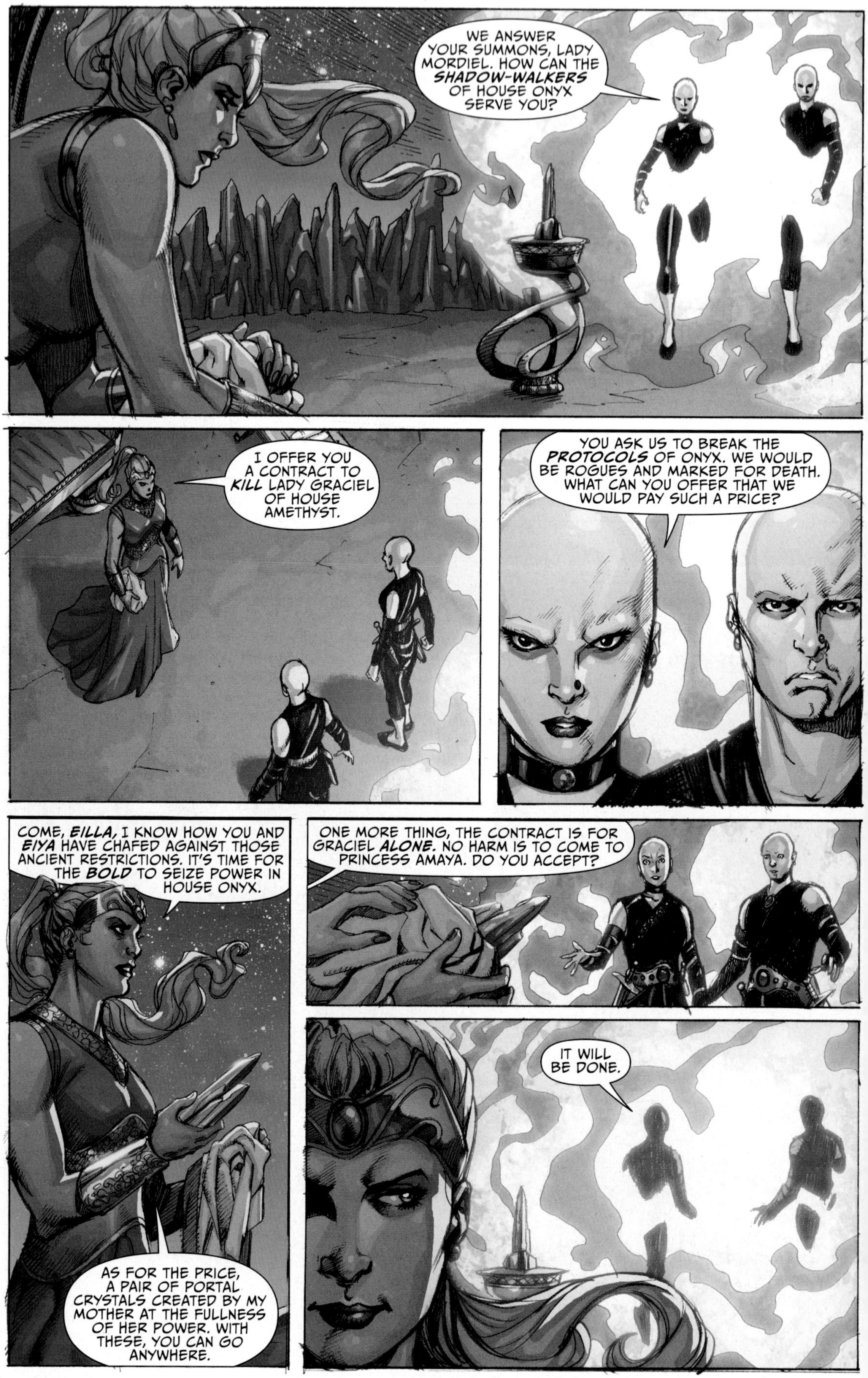
WE ANSWER YOUR SUMMONS, LADY MORDIEL. HOW CAN THE SHADOW-WALKERS OF HOUSE ONYX SERVE YOU?
I OFFER YOU A CONTRACT TO KILL LADY GRACIEL OF HOUSE AMETHYST.
YOU ASK US TO BREAK THE PROTOCOLS OF ONYX. WE WOULD BE ROGUES AND MARKED FOR DEATH. WHAT CAN YOU OFFER THAT WE WOULD PAY SUCH A PRICE?
COME, EILLA, I KNOW HOW YOU AND EIYA HAVE CHAFED AGAINST THOSE ANCIENT RESTRICTIONS. IT'S TIME FOR THE BOLD TO SEIZE POWER IN HOUSE ONYX.
AS FOR THE PRICE, A PAIR OF PORTAL CRYSTALS CREATED BY MY MOTHER AT THE FULLNESS OF HER POWER. WITH THESE, YOU CAN GO ANYWHERE.
ONE MORE THING, THE CONTRACT IS FOR GRACIEL ALONE. NO HARM IS TO COME TO PRINCESS AMAYA. DO YOU ACCEPT?
IT WILL BE DONE.

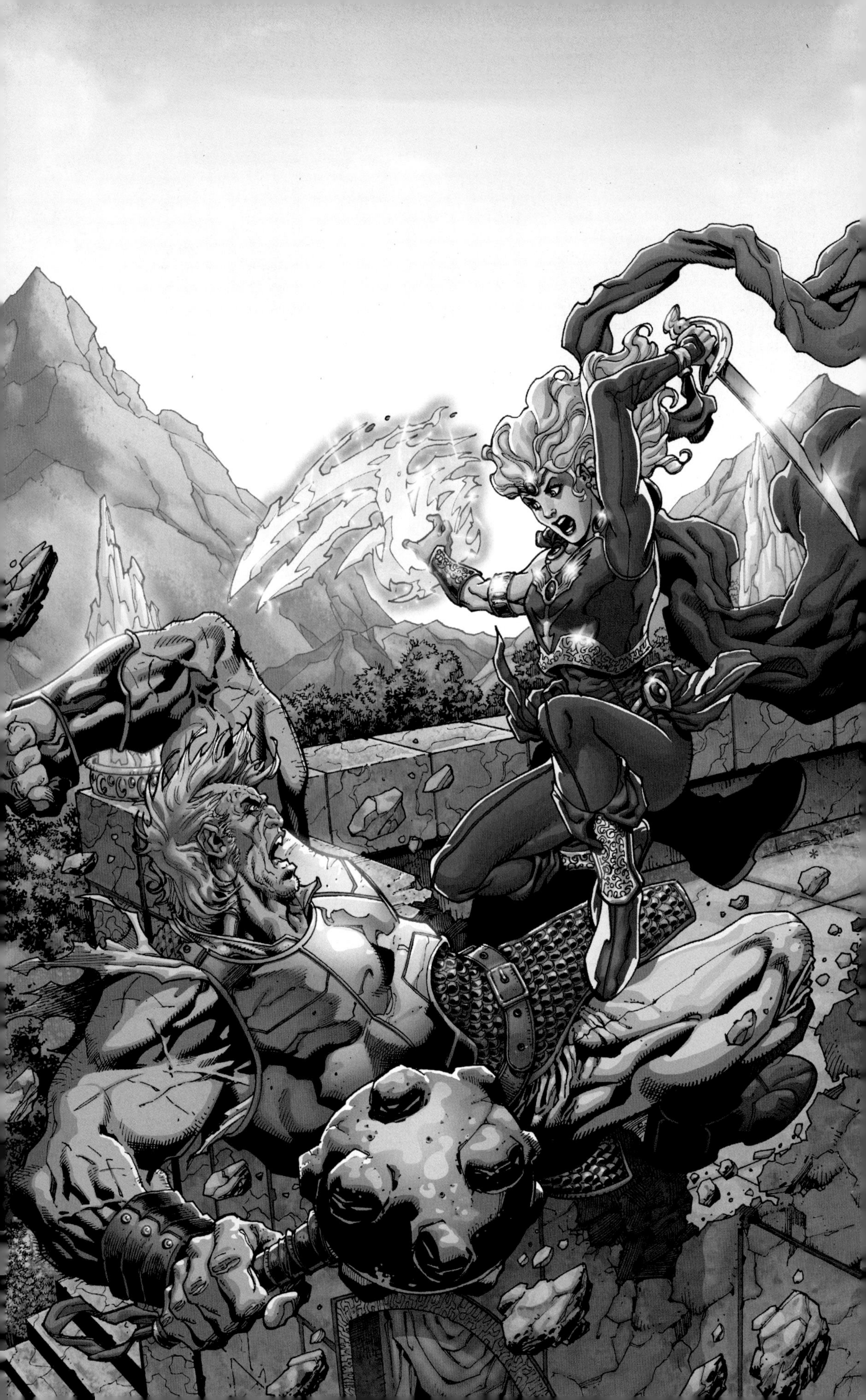

AMETHYST part four FAMILY REUNION

CHRISTY MARX writer **AARON LOPRESTI CLAUDE St. AUBIN** artists cover by **AARON LOPRESTI & HI-FI**

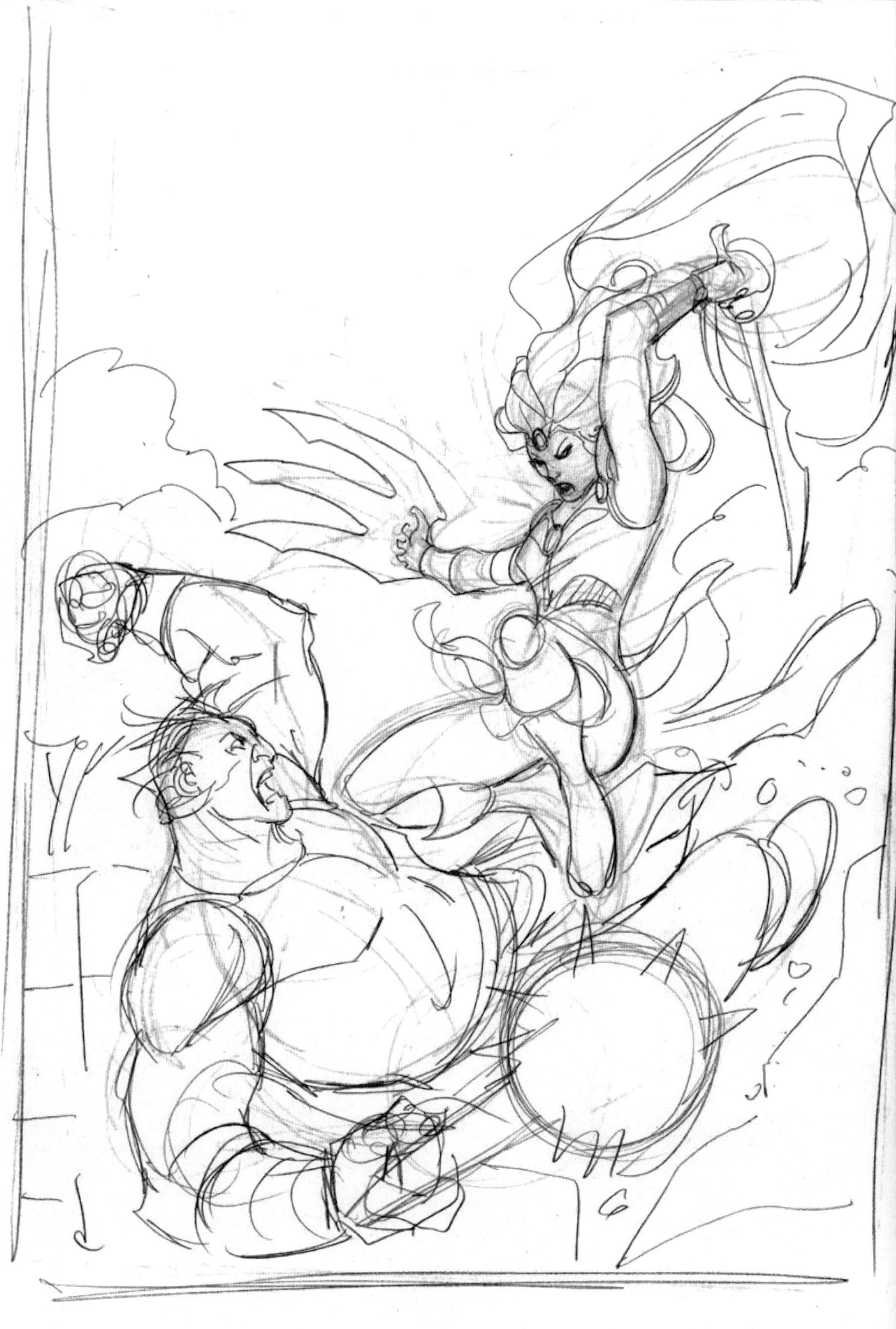

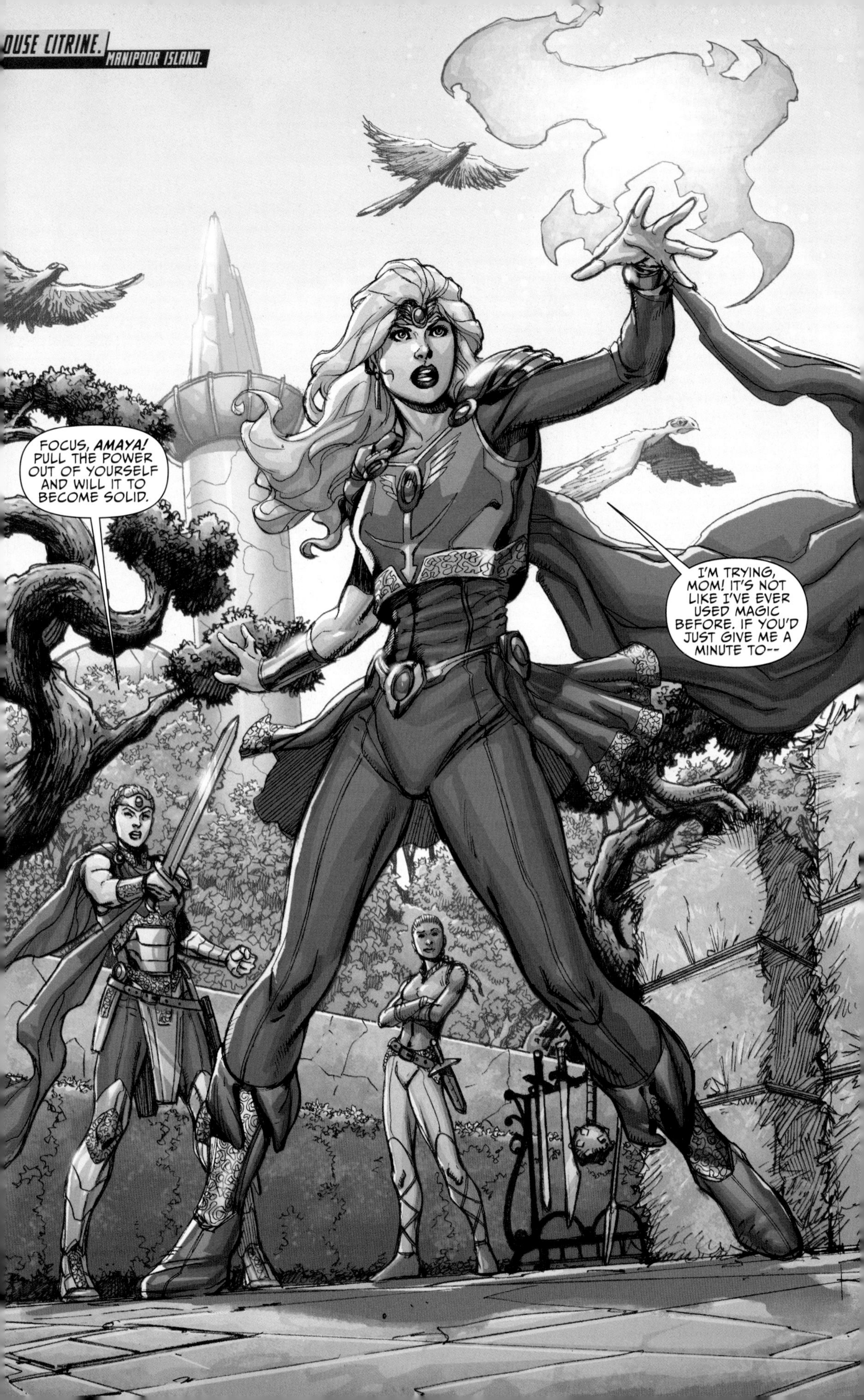
OUSE CITRINE.
MANIPOOR ISLAND.
FOCUS, AMAYA! PULL THE POWER OUT OF YOURSELF AND WILL IT TO BECOME SOLID.
I'M TRYING, MOM! IT'S NOT LIKE I'VE EVER USED MAGIC BEFORE. IF YOU'D JUST GIVE ME A MINUTE TO--

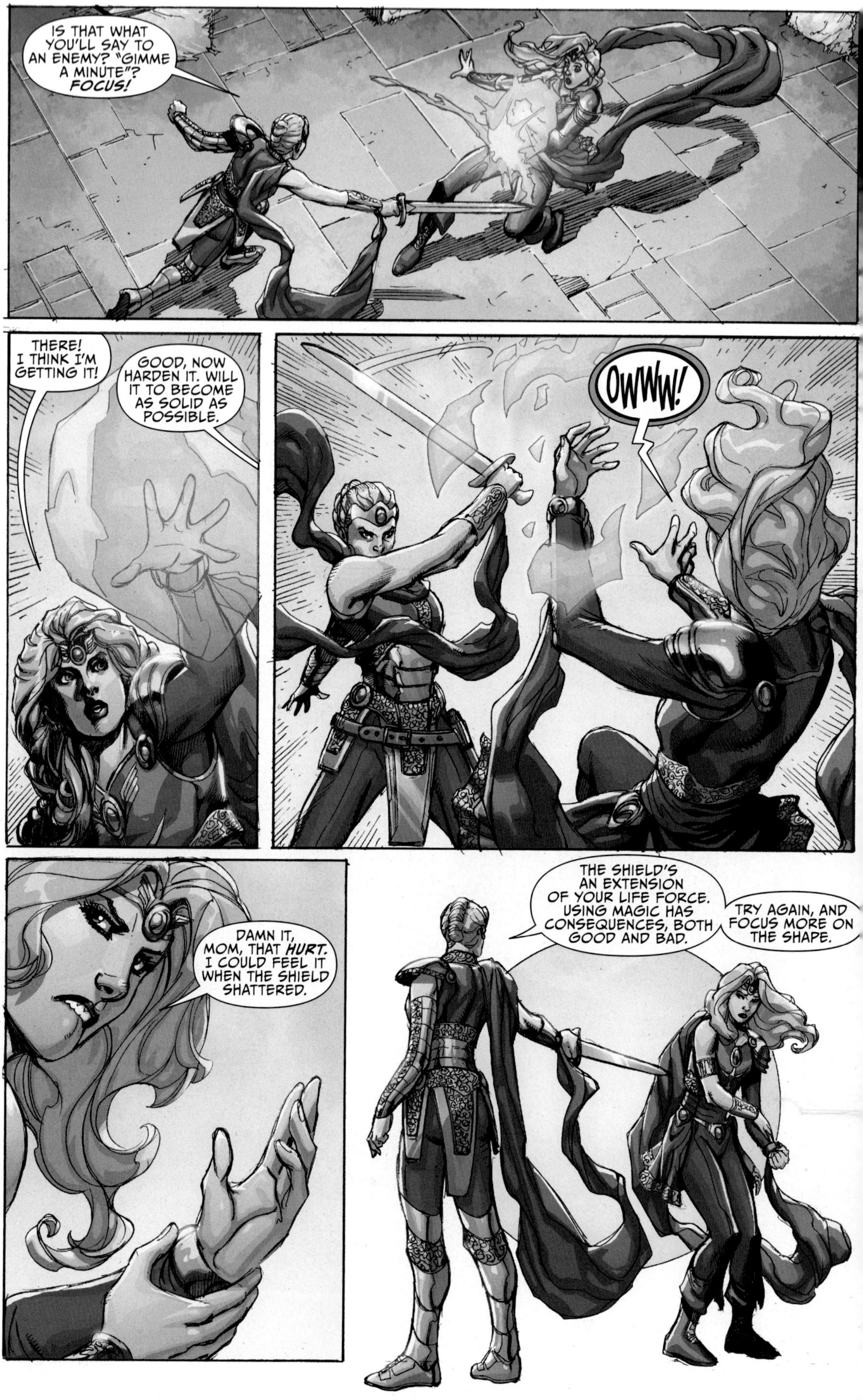
IS THAT WHAT YOU'LL SAY TO AN ENEMY? "GIMME A MINUTE"? FOCUS!
THERE! I THINK I'M GETTING IT!
GOOD, NOW HARDEN IT. WILL IT TO BECOME AS SOLID AS POSSIBLE.
OWWW!
DAMN IT, MOM, THAT HURT. I COULD FEEL IT WHEN THE SHIELD SHATTERED.
THE SHIELD'S AN EXTENSION OF YOUR LIFE FORCE. USING MAGIC HAS CONSEQUENCES, BOTH GOOD AND BAD.
TRY AGAIN, AND FOCUS MORE ON THE SHAPE.

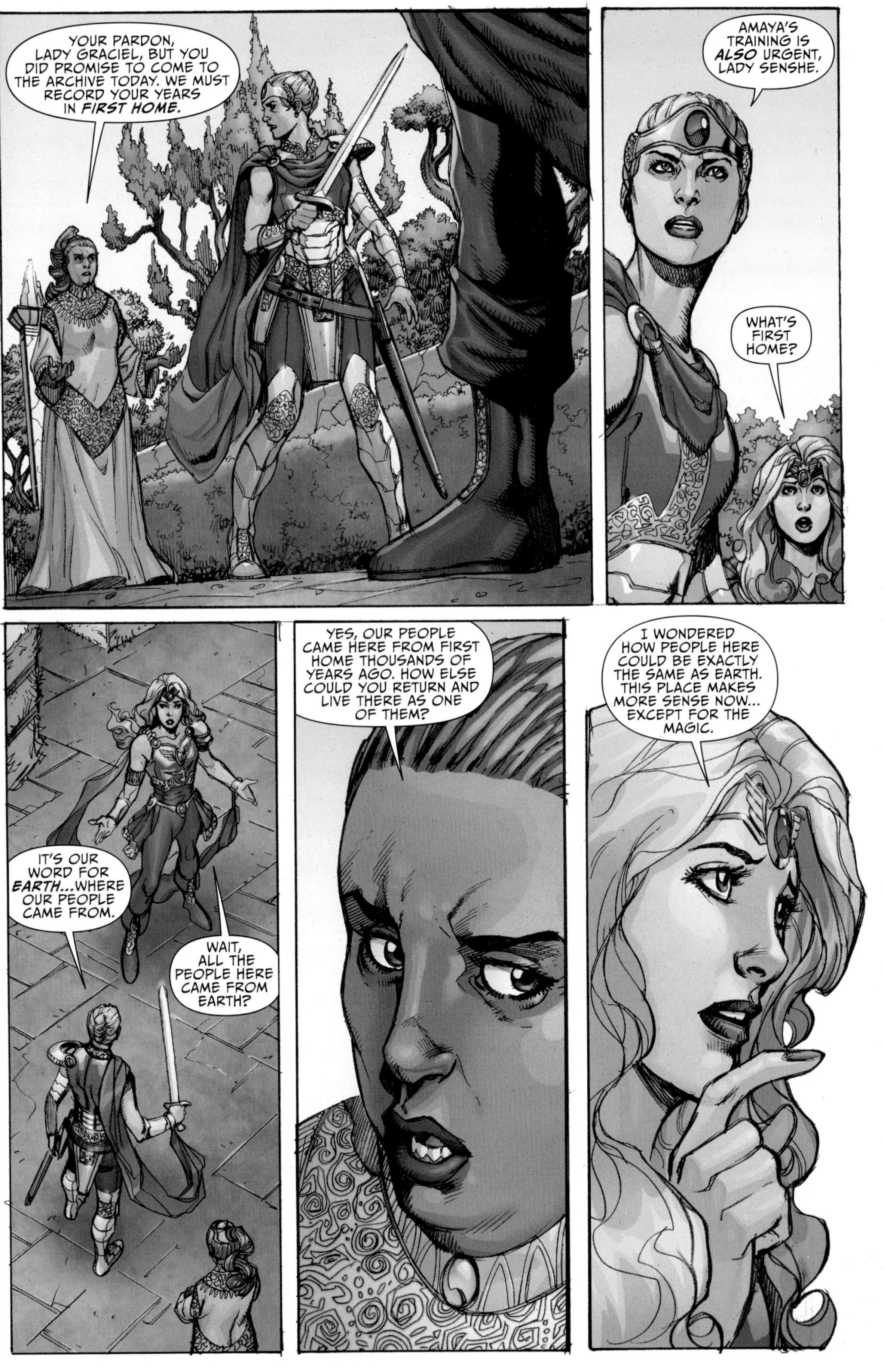
YOUR PARDON, LADY GRACIEL, BUT YOU DID PROMISE TO COME TO THE ARCHIVE TODAY. WE MUST RECORD YOUR YEARS IN *FIRST HOME.*
AMAYA'S TRAINING IS *ALSO* URGENT, LADY SENSHE.
WHAT'S FIRST HOME?
IT'S OUR WORD FOR *EARTH*...WHERE OUR PEOPLE CAME FROM.
WAIT, ALL THE PEOPLE HERE CAME FROM EARTH?
YES, OUR PEOPLE CAME HERE FROM FIRST HOME THOUSANDS OF YEARS AGO. HOW ELSE COULD YOU RETURN AND LIVE THERE AS ONE OF THEM?
I WONDERED HOW PEOPLE HERE COULD BE EXACTLY THE SAME AS EARTH. THIS PLACE MAKES MORE SENSE NOW... EXCEPT FOR THE MAGIC.

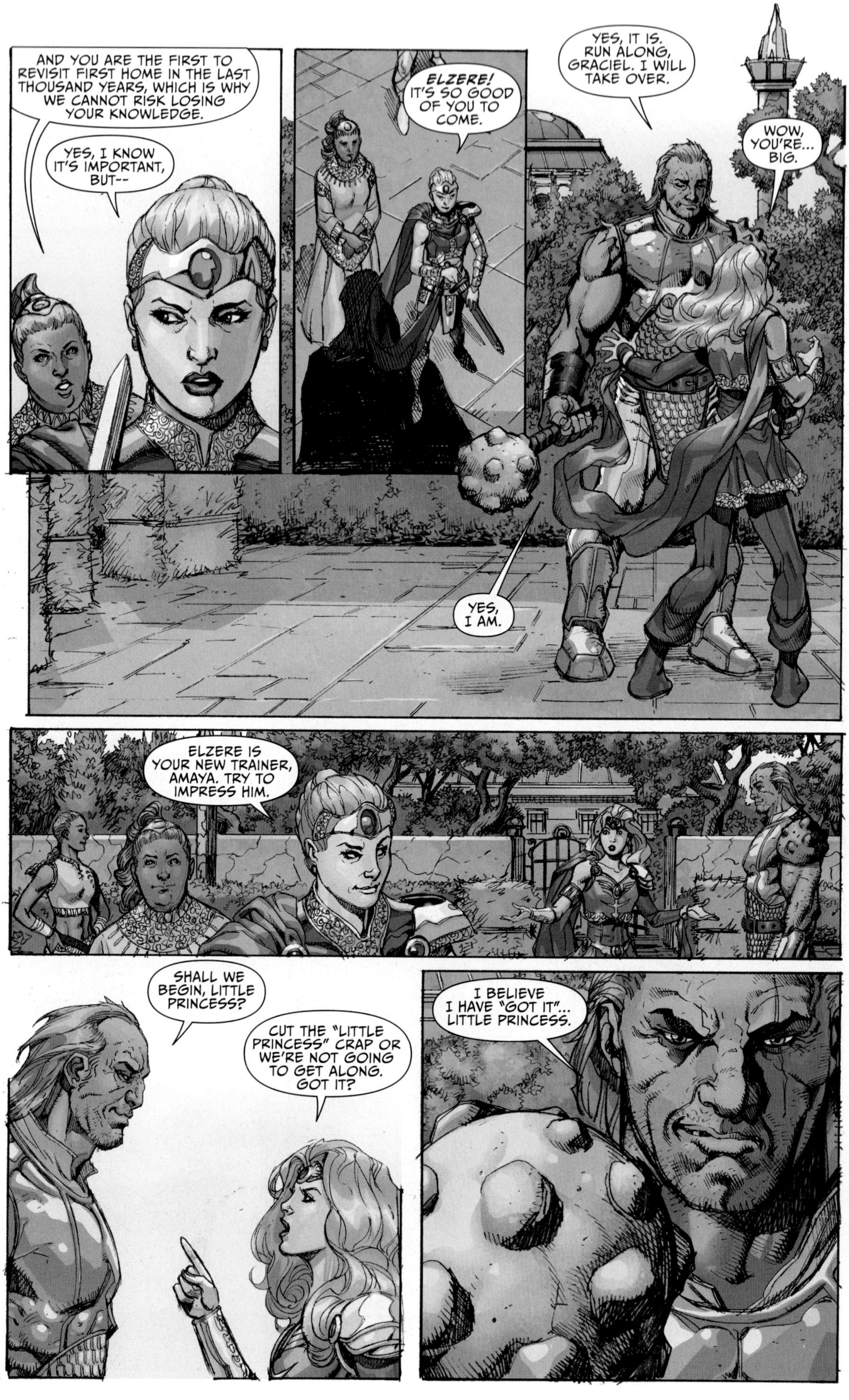
AND YOU ARE THE FIRST TO REVISIT FIRST HOME IN THE LAST THOUSAND YEARS, WHICH IS WHY WE CANNOT RISK LOSING YOUR KNOWLEDGE.
YES, I KNOW IT'S IMPORTANT, BUT--
ELZERE! IT'S SO GOOD OF YOU TO COME.
YES, IT IS. RUN ALONG, GRACIEL. I WILL TAKE OVER.
WOW, YOU'RE... BIG.
YES, I AM.
ELZERE IS YOUR NEW TRAINER, AMAYA. TRY TO IMPRESS HIM.
SHALL WE BEGIN, LITTLE PRINCESS?
CUT THE "LITTLE PRINCESS" CRAP OR WE'RE NOT GOING TO GET ALONG. GOT IT?
I BELIEVE I HAVE "GOT IT"... LITTLE PRINCESS.

MY CHIEFTAIN, I ASK PERMISSION TO AVENGE THE DEATH OF MY MATE.

EVERY DAY I SAY *NO.* YESTERDAY I SAID NO. *TODAY* I SAY NO. *TOMORROW* I WILL SAY NO.

HE HUNTER CAMP OF HE GHAGGRA CLAN. *BEYOND THE SETTLED LANDS.*

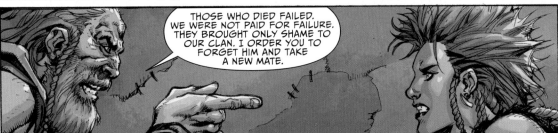

THOSE WHO DIED FAILED. WE WERE NOT PAID FOR FAILURE. THEY BROUGHT ONLY SHAME TO OUR CLAN. I ORDER YOU TO FORGET HIM AND TAKE A NEW MATE.

NO. I WILL HUNT THOSE WHO KILLED HIM AND TAKE THEIR SKINS.

NIYATI, IF YOU DEFY ME, YOU ARE OUTCAST! THE FATE OF AN OUTCAST IS *DEATH.*

DEATH IS THE ONLY FATE I SEEK.

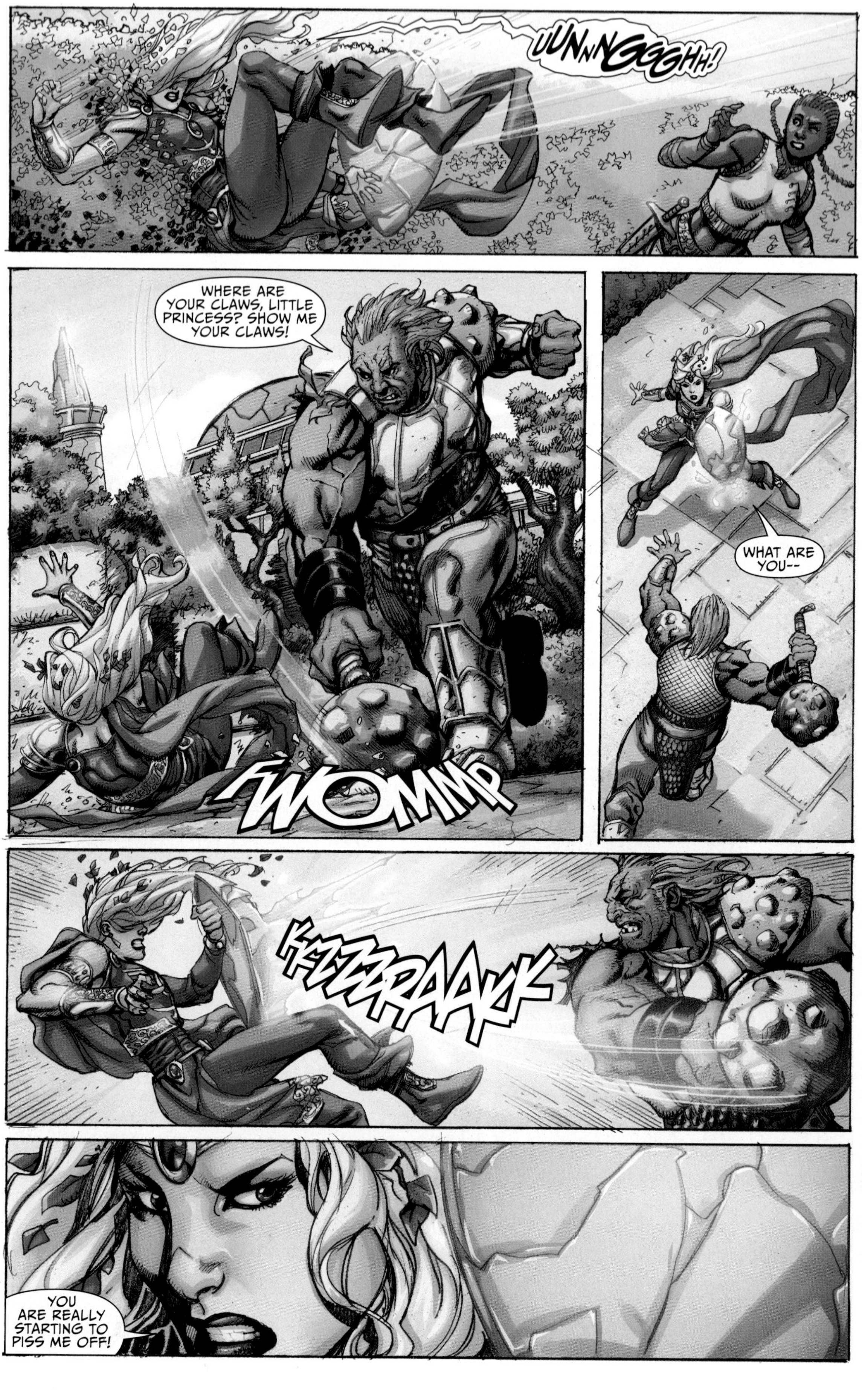
UUNNNGGGHH!
WHERE ARE YOUR CLAWS, LITTLE PRINCESS? SHOW ME YOUR CLAWS!
FWOMMP
WHAT ARE YOU--
KRZZRAAKK
YOU ARE REALLY STARTING TO PISS ME OFF!

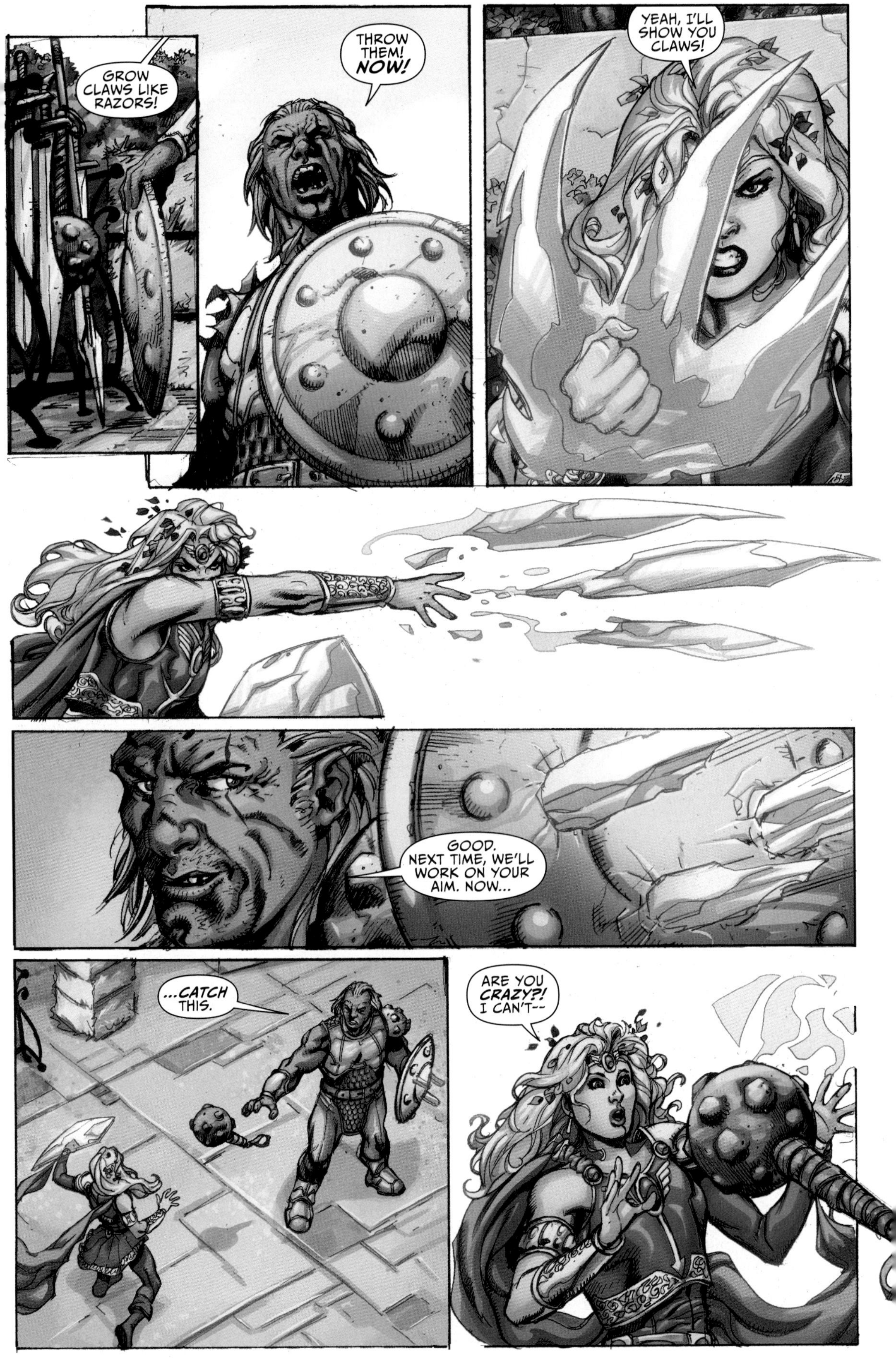
GROW CLAWS LIKE RAZORS!
THROW THEM! NOW!
YEAH, I'LL SHOW YOU CLAWS!
GOOD. NEXT TIME, WE'LL WORK ON YOUR AIM. NOW...
...CATCH THIS.
ARE YOU CRAZY?! I CAN'T--

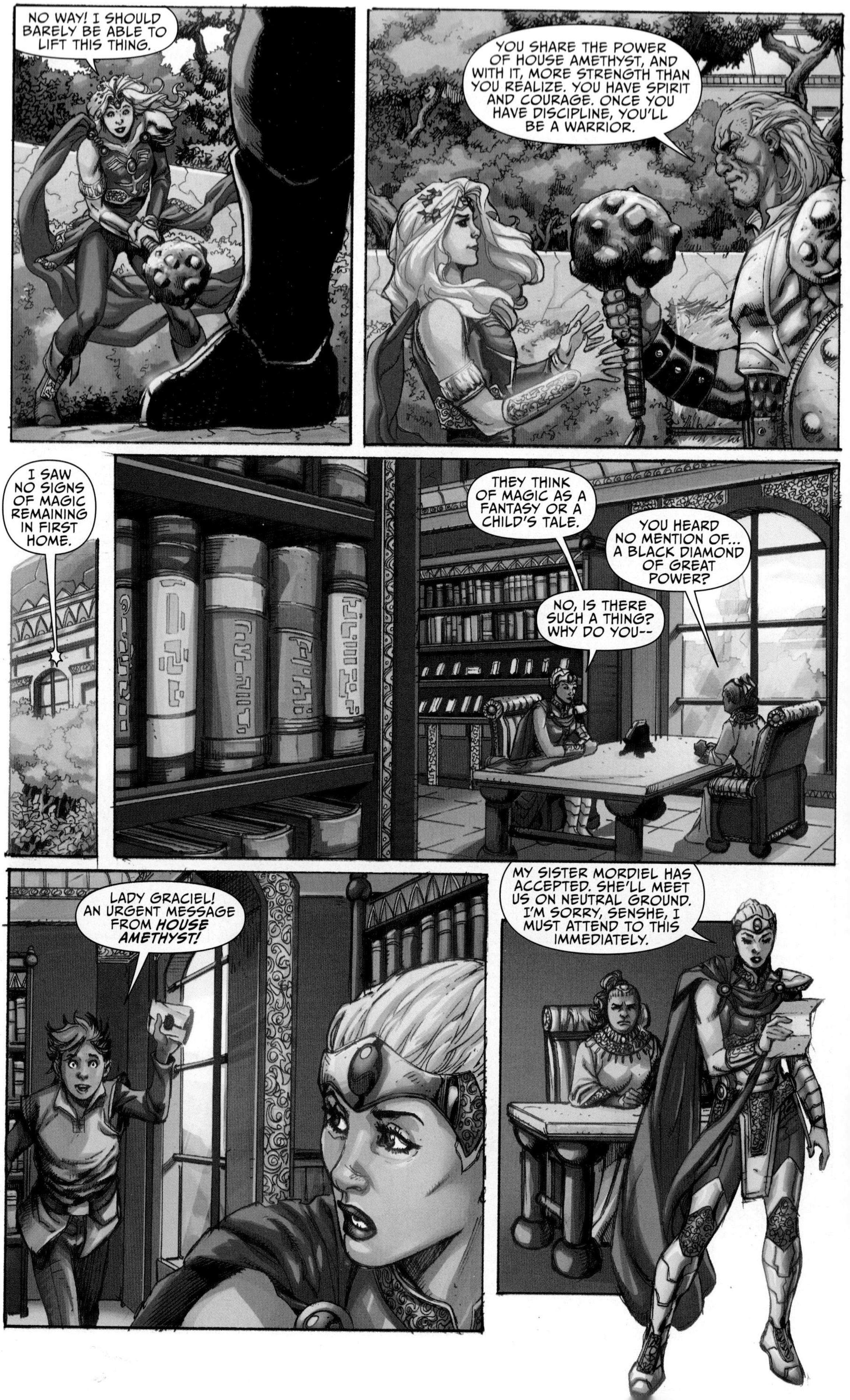

NO WAY! I SHOULD BARELY BE ABLE TO LIFT THIS THING.
YOU SHARE THE POWER OF HOUSE AMETHYST, AND WITH IT, MORE STRENGTH THAN YOU REALIZE. YOU HAVE SPIRIT AND COURAGE. ONCE YOU HAVE DISCIPLINE, YOU'LL BE A WARRIOR.
I SAW NO SIGNS OF MAGIC REMAINING IN FIRST HOME.
THEY THINK OF MAGIC AS A FANTASY OR A CHILD'S TALE.
YOU HEARD NO MENTION OF... A BLACK DIAMOND OF GREAT POWER?
NO, IS THERE SUCH A THING? WHY DO YOU--
LADY GRACIEL! AN URGENT MESSAGE FROM *HOUSE AMETHYST!*
MY SISTER MORDIEL HAS ACCEPTED. SHE'LL MEET US ON NEUTRAL GROUND. I'M SORRY, SENSHE, I MUST ATTEND TO THIS IMMEDIATELY.

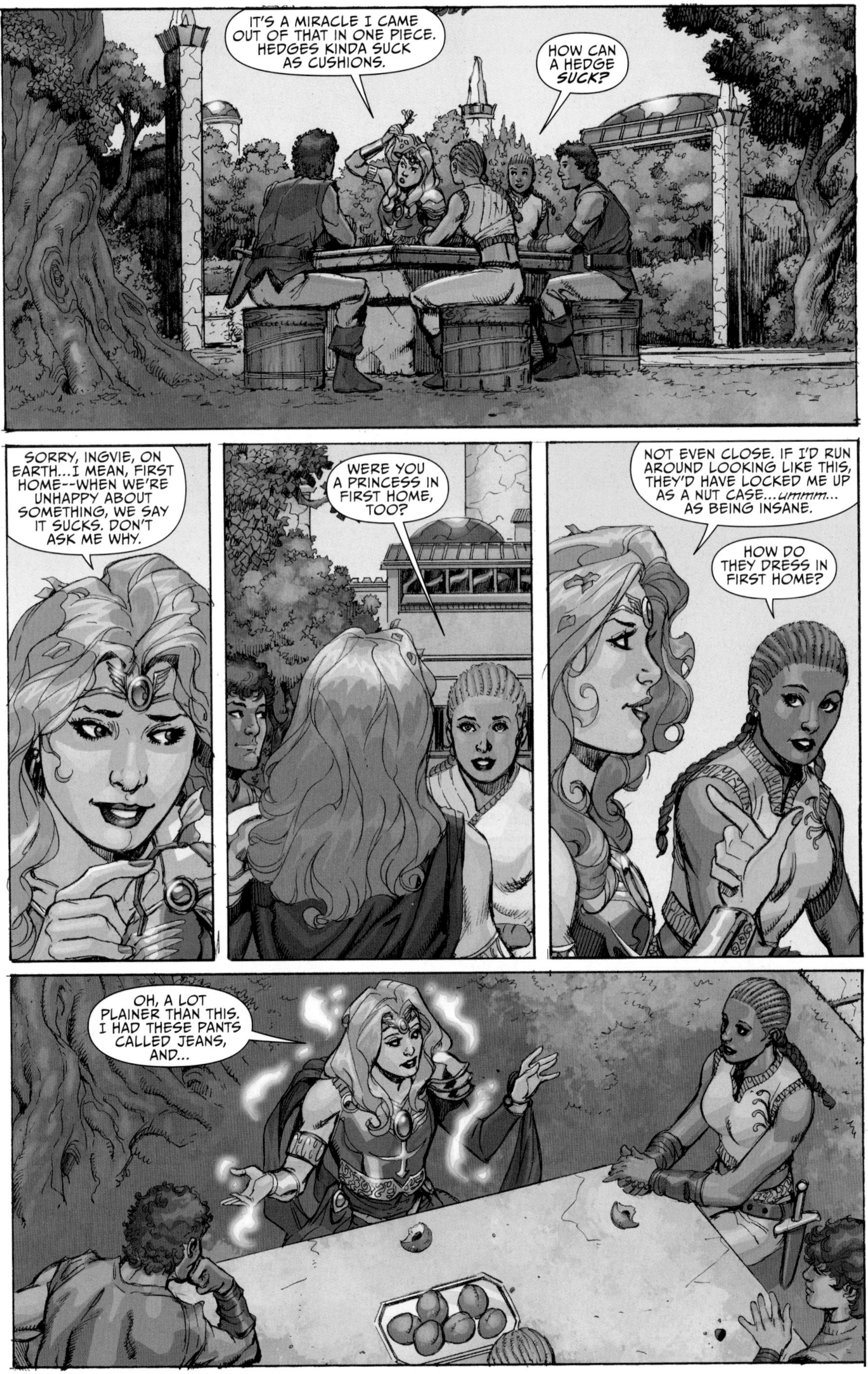
IT'S A MIRACLE I CAME OUT OF THAT IN ONE PIECE. HEDGES KINDA SUCK AS CUSHIONS.
HOW CAN A HEDGE SUCK?
SORRY, INGVIE, ON EARTH...I MEAN, FIRST HOME--WHEN WE'RE UNHAPPY ABOUT SOMETHING, WE SAY IT SUCKS. DON'T ASK ME WHY.
WERE YOU A PRINCESS IN FIRST HOME, TOO?
NOT EVEN CLOSE. IF I'D RUN AROUND LOOKING LIKE THIS, THEY'D HAVE LOCKED ME UP AS A NUT CASE...ummm... AS BEING INSANE.
HOW DO THEY DRESS IN FIRST HOME?
OH, A LOT PLAINER THAN THIS. I HAD THESE PANTS CALLED JEANS, AND...

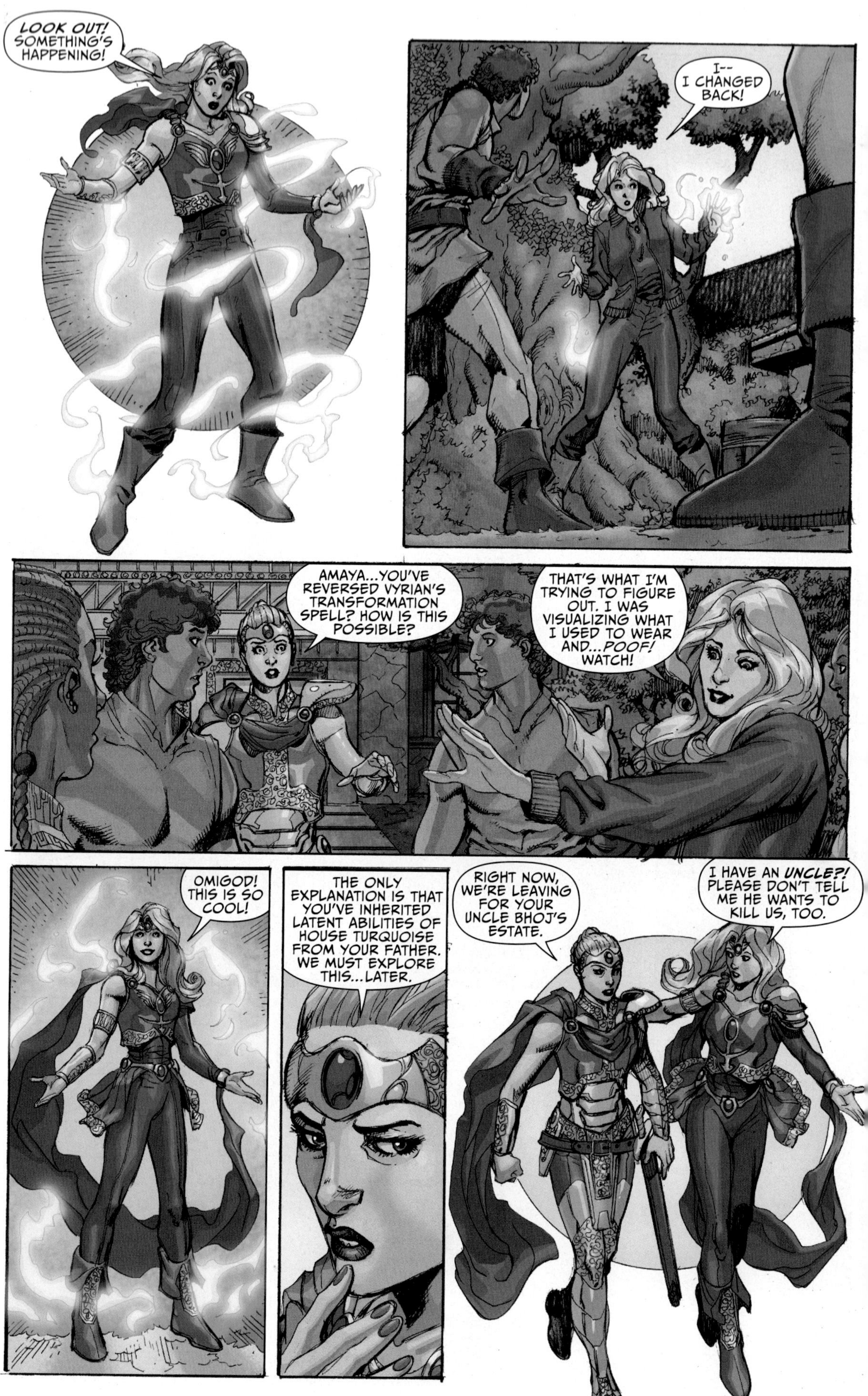
LOOK OUT! SOMETHING'S HAPPENING!
I-- I CHANGED BACK!
AMAYA...YOU'VE REVERSED VYRIAN'S TRANSFORMATION SPELL? HOW IS THIS POSSIBLE?
THAT'S WHAT I'M TRYING TO FIGURE OUT. I WAS VISUALIZING WHAT I USED TO WEAR AND...POOF! WATCH!
OMIGOD! THIS IS SO COOL!
THE ONLY EXPLANATION IS THAT YOU'VE INHERITED LATENT ABILITIES OF HOUSE TURQUOISE FROM YOUR FATHER. WE MUST EXPLORE THIS...LATER.
RIGHT NOW, WE'RE LEAVING FOR YOUR UNCLE BHOJ'S ESTATE.
I HAVE AN UNCLE?! PLEASE DON'T TELL ME HE WANTS TO KILL US, TOO.

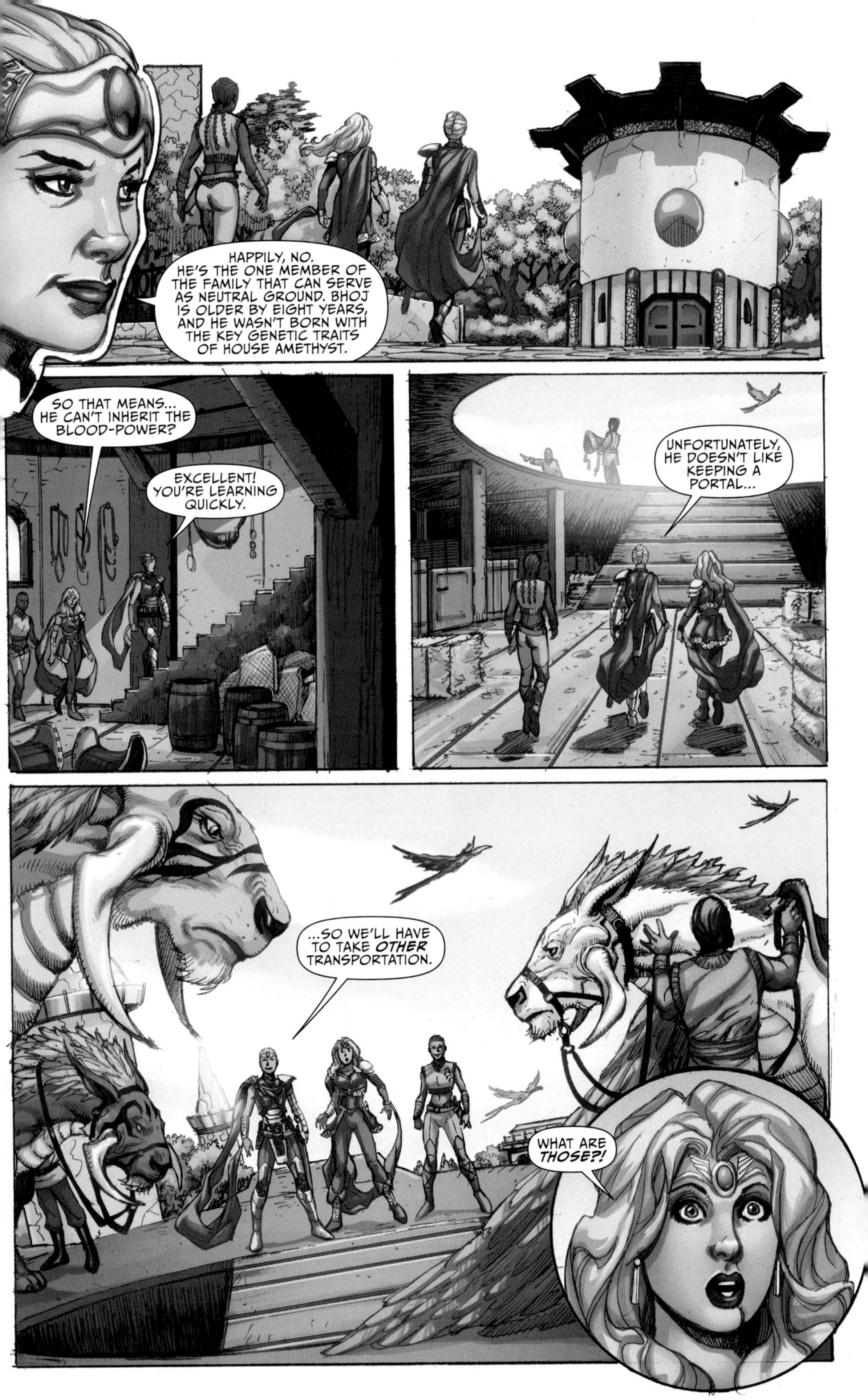

HAPPILY, NO. HE'S THE ONE MEMBER OF THE FAMILY THAT CAN SERVE AS NEUTRAL GROUND. BHOJ IS OLDER BY EIGHT YEARS, AND HE WASN'T BORN WITH THE KEY GENETIC TRAITS OF HOUSE AMETHYST.
SO THAT MEANS... HE CAN'T INHERIT THE BLOOD-POWER?
EXCELLENT! YOU'RE LEARNING QUICKLY.
UNFORTUNATELY, HE DOESN'T LIKE KEEPING A PORTAL...
...SO WE'LL HAVE TO TAKE *OTHER* TRANSPORTATION.
WHAT ARE *THOSE?!*

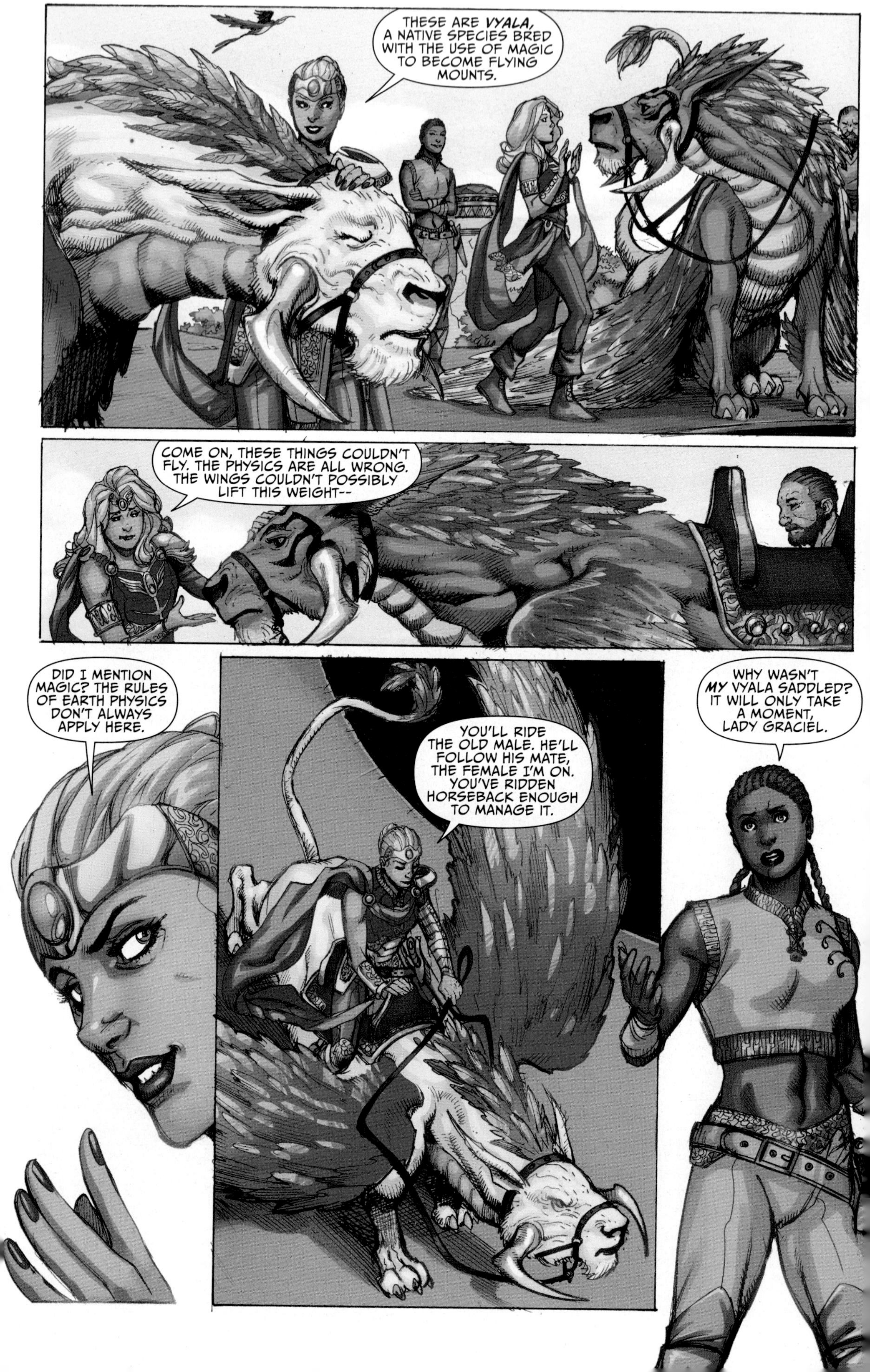
THESE ARE VYALA, A NATIVE SPECIES BRED WITH THE USE OF MAGIC TO BECOME FLYING MOUNTS.
COME ON, THESE THINGS COULDN'T FLY. THE PHYSICS ARE ALL WRONG. THE WINGS COULDN'T POSSIBLY LIFT THIS WEIGHT--
DID I MENTION MAGIC? THE RULES OF EARTH PHYSICS DON'T ALWAYS APPLY HERE.
YOU'LL RIDE THE OLD MALE. HE'LL FOLLOW HIS MATE, THE FEMALE I'M ON. YOU'VE RIDDEN HORSEBACK ENOUGH TO MANAGE IT.
WHY WASN'T MY VYALA SADDLED? IT WILL ONLY TAKE A MOMENT, LADY GRACIEL.

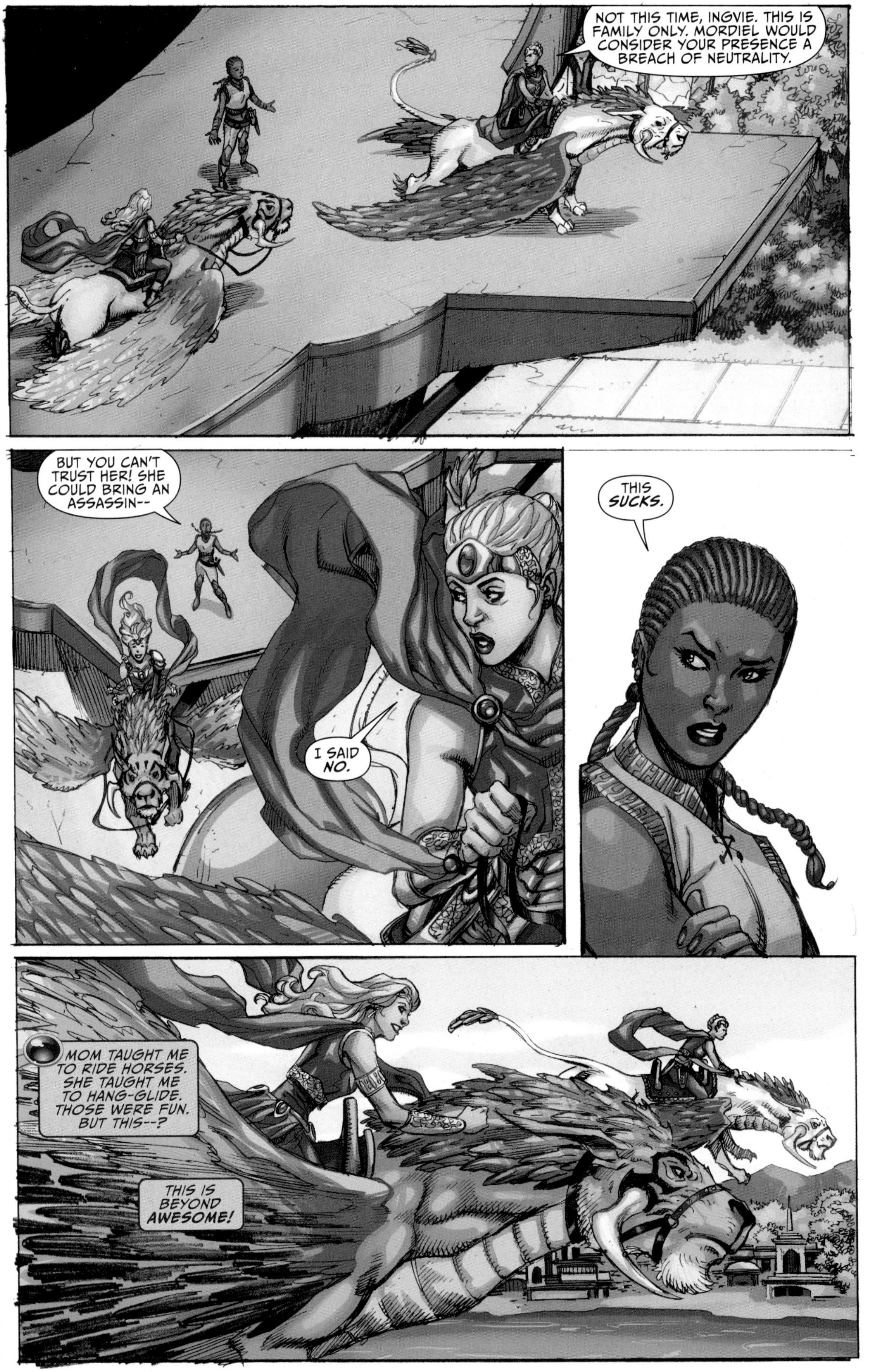
NOT THIS TIME, INGVIE. THIS IS FAMILY ONLY. MORDIEL WOULD CONSIDER YOUR PRESENCE A BREACH OF NEUTRALITY.
BUT YOU CAN'T TRUST HER! SHE COULD BRING AN ASSASSIN--
I SAID NO.
THIS SUCKS.
MOM TAUGHT ME TO RIDE HORSES. SHE TAUGHT ME TO HANG-GLIDE. THOSE WERE FUN. BUT THIS--?
THIS IS BEYOND AWESOME!

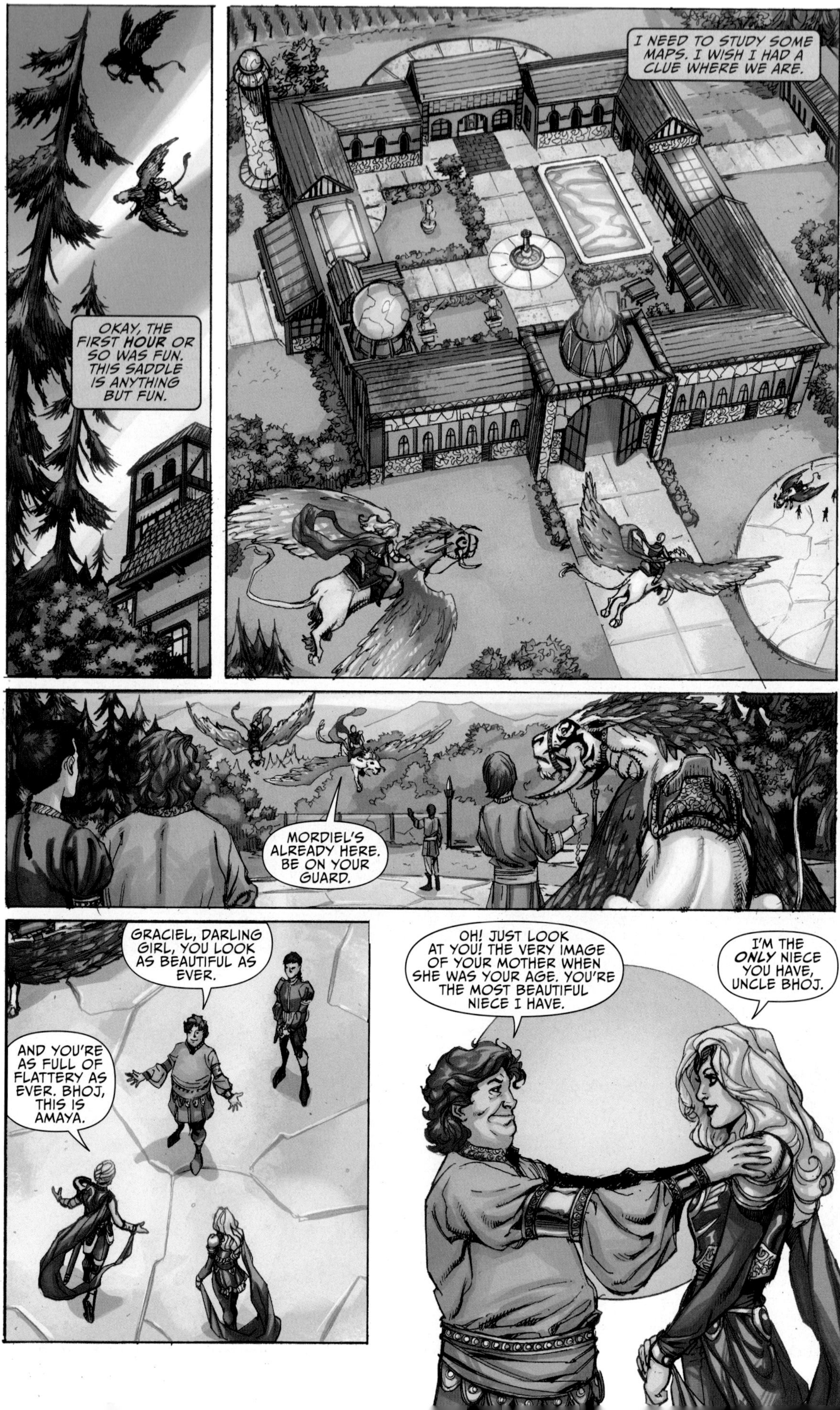
OKAY, THE FIRST HOUR OR SO WAS FUN. THIS SADDLE IS ANYTHING BUT FUN.
I NEED TO STUDY SOME MAPS. I WISH I HAD A CLUE WHERE WE ARE.
MORDIEL'S ALREADY HERE. BE ON YOUR GUARD.
GRACIEL, DARLING GIRL, YOU LOOK AS BEAUTIFUL AS EVER.
AND YOU'RE AS FULL OF FLATTERY AS EVER. BHOJ, THIS IS AMAYA.
OH! JUST LOOK AT YOU! THE VERY IMAGE OF YOUR MOTHER WHEN SHE WAS YOUR AGE. YOU'RE THE MOST BEAUTIFUL NIECE I HAVE.
I'M THE ONLY NIECE YOU HAVE, UNCLE BHOJ.

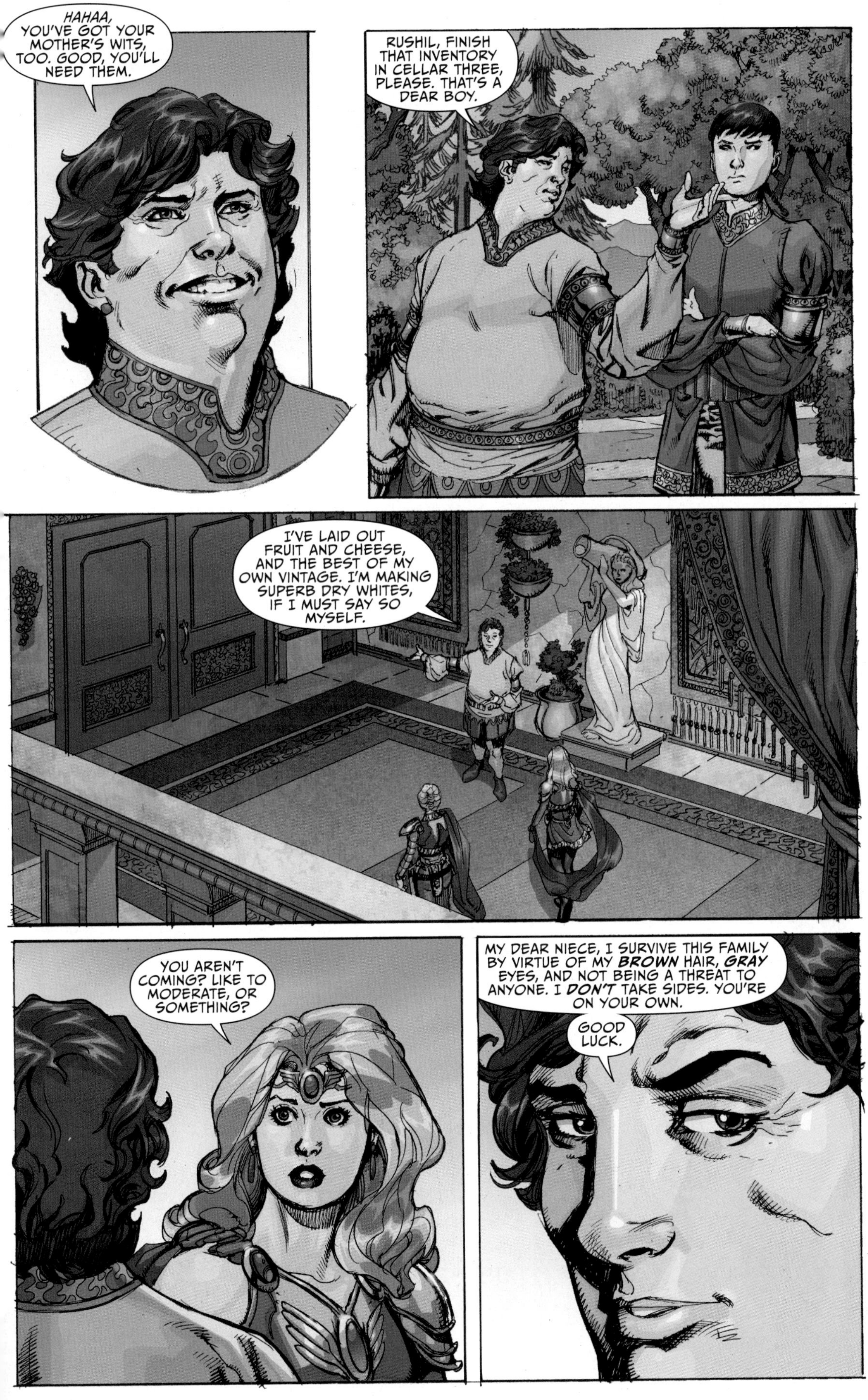
HAHAA, YOU'VE GOT YOUR MOTHER'S WITS, TOO. GOOD, YOU'LL NEED THEM.
RUSHIL, FINISH THAT INVENTORY IN CELLAR THREE, PLEASE. THAT'S A DEAR BOY.
I'VE LAID OUT FRUIT AND CHEESE, AND THE BEST OF MY OWN VINTAGE. I'M MAKING SUPERB DRY WHITES, IF I MUST SAY SO MYSELF.
YOU AREN'T COMING? LIKE TO MODERATE, OR SOMETHING?
MY DEAR NIECE, I SURVIVE THIS FAMILY BY VIRTUE OF MY BROWN HAIR, GRAY EYES, AND NOT BEING A THREAT TO ANYONE. I DON'T TAKE SIDES. YOU'RE ON YOUR OWN.
GOOD LUCK.

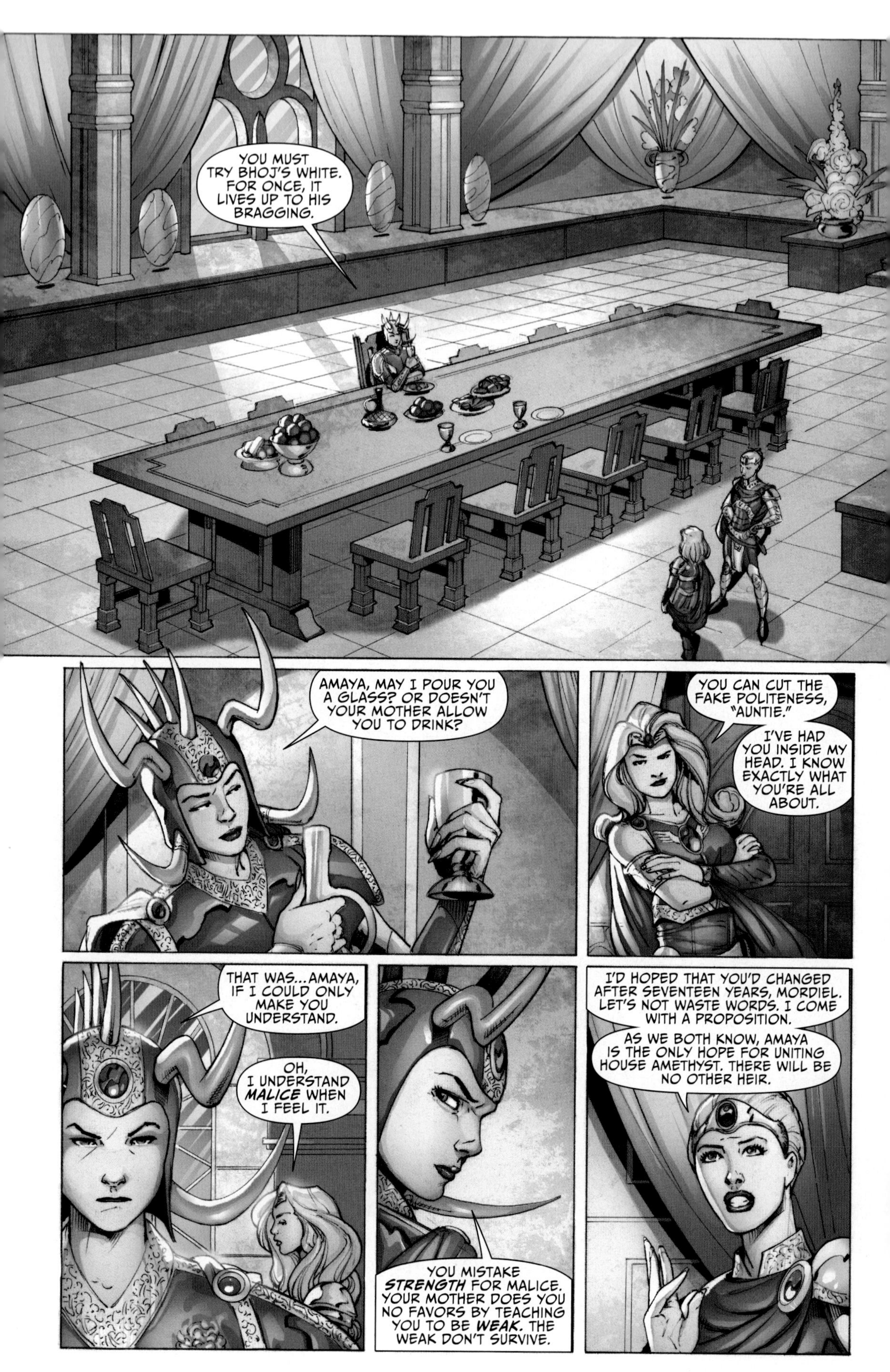
YOU MUST TRY BHOJ'S WHITE. FOR ONCE, IT LIVES UP TO HIS BRAGGING.
AMAYA, MAY I POUR YOU A GLASS? OR DOESN'T YOUR MOTHER ALLOW YOU TO DRINK?
YOU CAN CUT THE FAKE POLITENESS, "AUNTIE."
I'VE HAD YOU INSIDE MY HEAD. I KNOW EXACTLY WHAT YOU'RE ALL ABOUT.
THAT WAS...AMAYA, IF I COULD ONLY MAKE YOU UNDERSTAND.
OH, I UNDERSTAND *MALICE* WHEN I FEEL IT.
YOU MISTAKE ***STRENGTH*** FOR MALICE. YOUR MOTHER DOES YOU NO FAVORS BY TEACHING YOU TO BE ***WEAK.*** THE WEAK DON'T SURVIVE.
I'D HOPED THAT YOU'D CHANGED AFTER SEVENTEEN YEARS, MORDIEL. LET'S NOT WASTE WORDS. I COME WITH A PROPOSITION.
AS WE BOTH KNOW, AMAYA IS THE ONLY HOPE FOR UNITING HOUSE AMETHYST. THERE WILL BE NO OTHER HEIR.

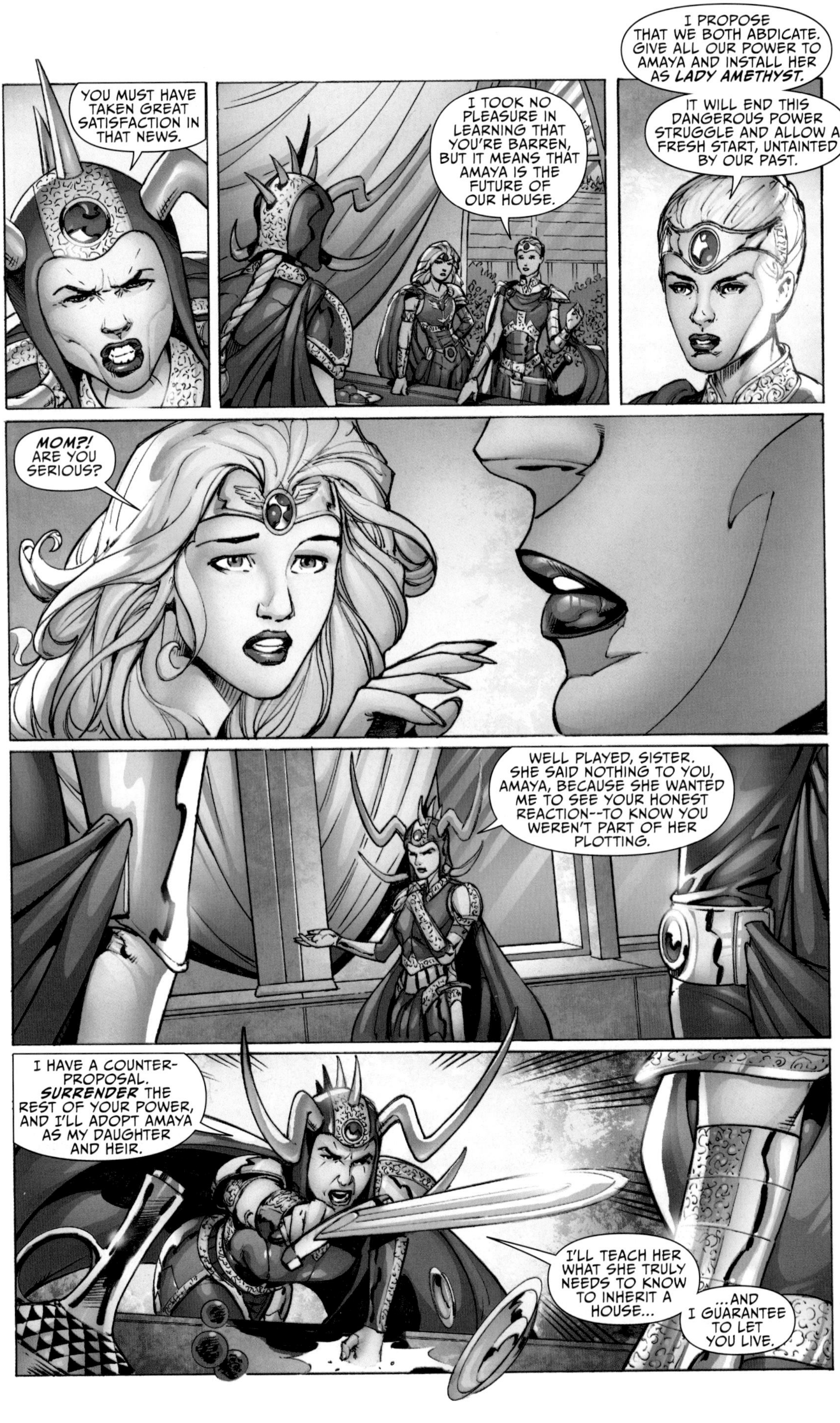
YOU MUST HAVE TAKEN GREAT SATISFACTION IN THAT NEWS.
I TOOK NO PLEASURE IN LEARNING THAT YOU'RE BARREN, BUT IT MEANS THAT AMAYA IS THE FUTURE OF OUR HOUSE.
I PROPOSE THAT WE BOTH ABDICATE. GIVE ALL OUR POWER TO AMAYA AND INSTALL HER AS *LADY AMETHYST.*
IT WILL END THIS DANGEROUS POWER STRUGGLE AND ALLOW A FRESH START, UNTAINTED BY OUR PAST.
MOM?! ARE YOU SERIOUS?
WELL PLAYED, SISTER. SHE SAID NOTHING TO YOU, AMAYA, BECAUSE SHE WANTED ME TO SEE YOUR HONEST REACTION--TO KNOW YOU WEREN'T PART OF HER PLOTTING.
I HAVE A COUNTER-PROPOSAL. *SURRENDER* THE REST OF YOUR POWER, AND I'LL ADOPT AMAYA AS MY DAUGHTER AND HEIR.
I'LL TEACH HER WHAT SHE TRULY NEEDS TO KNOW TO INHERIT A HOUSE...
...AND I GUARANTEE TO LET YOU LIVE.

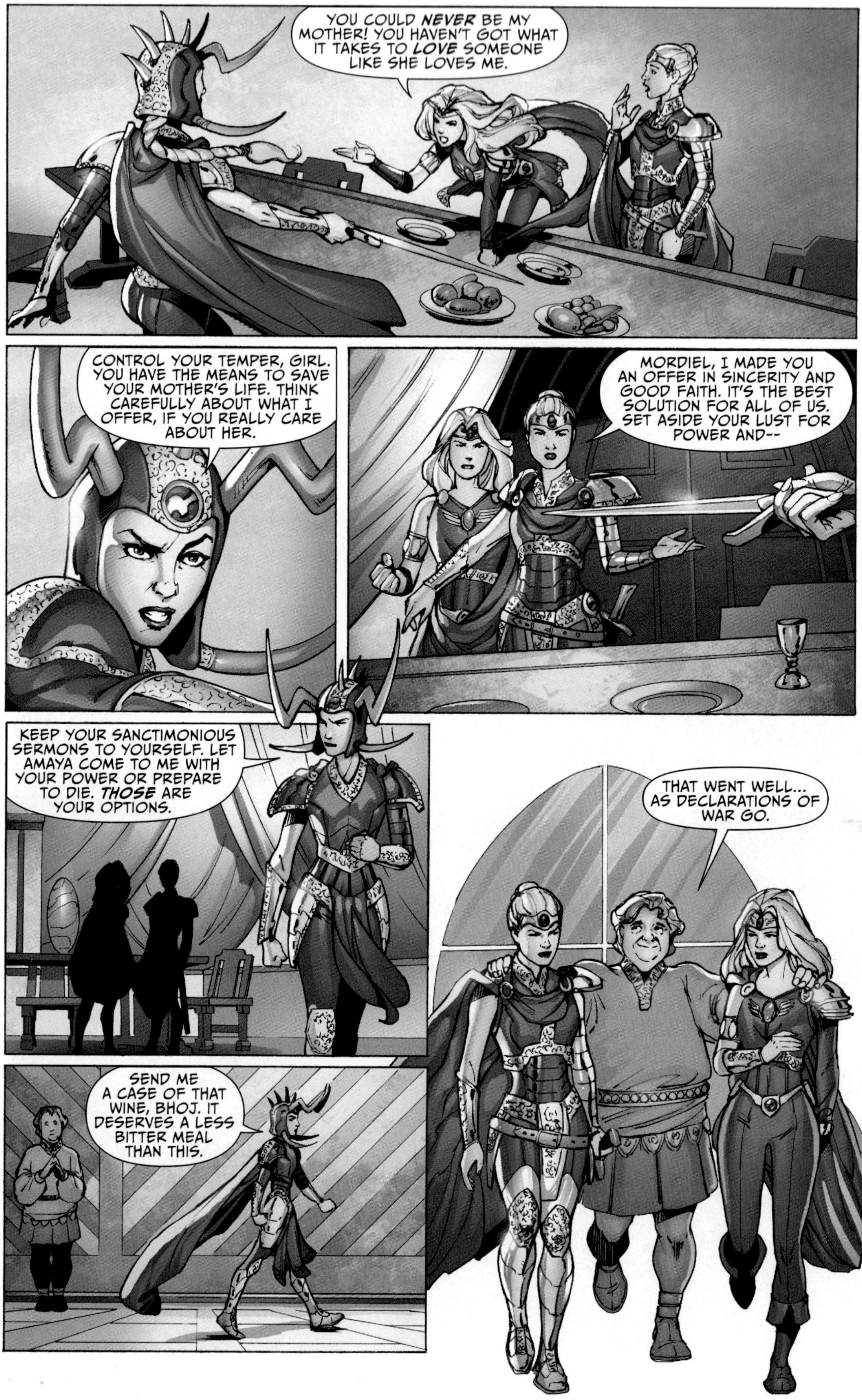
YOU COULD NEVER BE MY MOTHER! YOU HAVEN'T GOT WHAT IT TAKES TO LOVE SOMEONE LIKE SHE LOVES ME.
CONTROL YOUR TEMPER, GIRL. YOU HAVE THE MEANS TO SAVE YOUR MOTHER'S LIFE. THINK CAREFULLY ABOUT WHAT I OFFER, IF YOU REALLY CARE ABOUT HER.
MORDIEL, I MADE YOU AN OFFER IN SINCERITY AND GOOD FAITH. IT'S THE BEST SOLUTION FOR ALL OF US. SET ASIDE YOUR LUST FOR POWER AND--
KEEP YOUR SANCTIMONIOUS SERMONS TO YOURSELF. LET AMAYA COME TO ME WITH YOUR POWER OR PREPARE TO DIE. THOSE ARE YOUR OPTIONS.
SEND ME A CASE OF THAT WINE, BHOJ. IT DESERVES A LESS BITTER MEAL THAN THIS.
THAT WENT WELL... AS DECLARATIONS OF WAR GO.

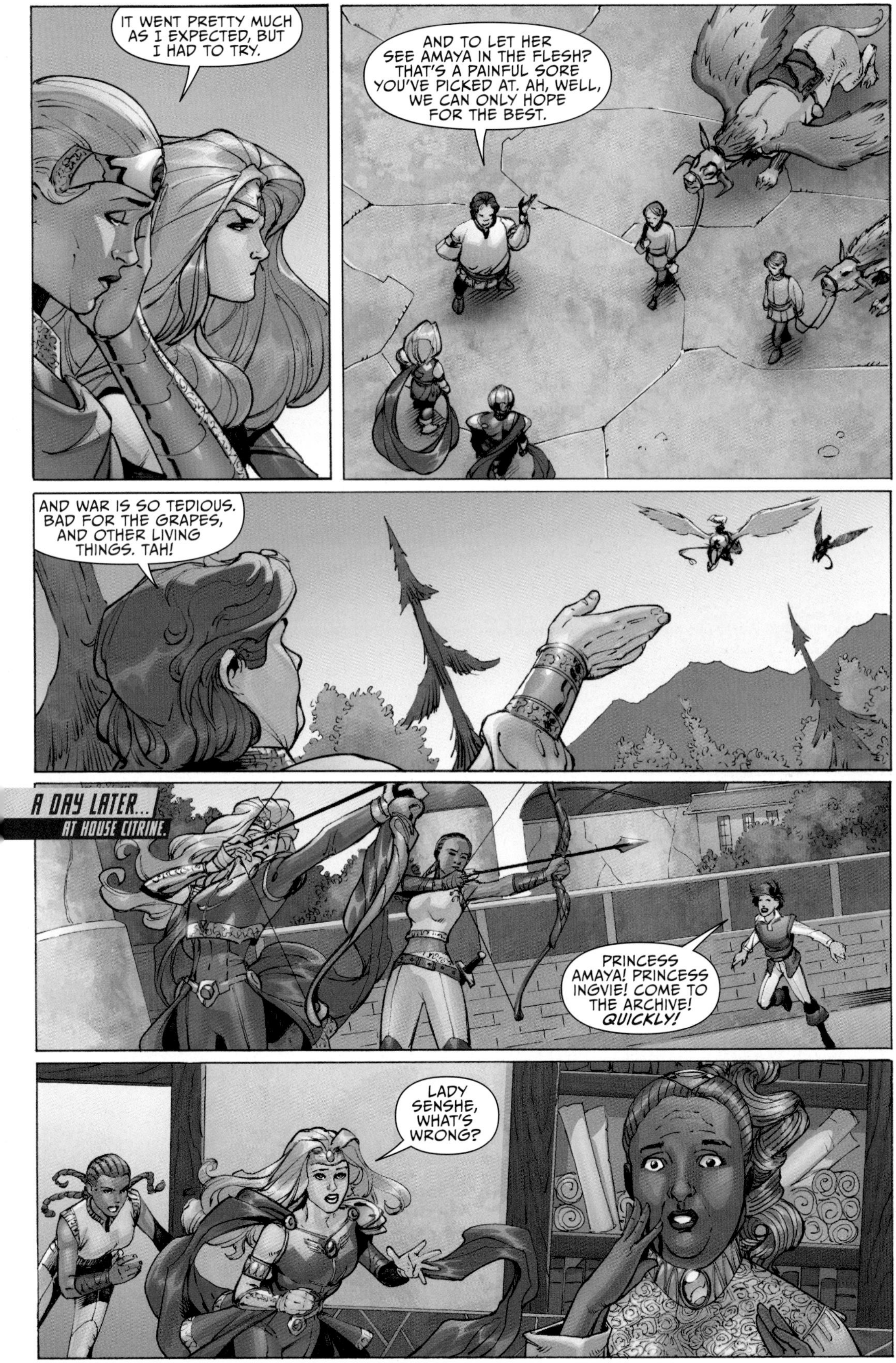
IT WENT PRETTY MUCH AS I EXPECTED, BUT I HAD TO TRY.
AND TO LET HER SEE AMAYA IN THE FLESH? THAT'S A PAINFUL SORE YOU'VE PICKED AT. AH, WELL, WE CAN ONLY HOPE FOR THE BEST.
AND WAR IS SO TEDIOUS. BAD FOR THE GRAPES, AND OTHER LIVING THINGS. TAH!
A DAY LATER...
AT HOUSE CITRINE.
PRINCESS AMAYA! PRINCESS INGVIE! COME TO THE ARCHIVE! QUICKLY!
LADY SENSHE, WHAT'S WRONG?

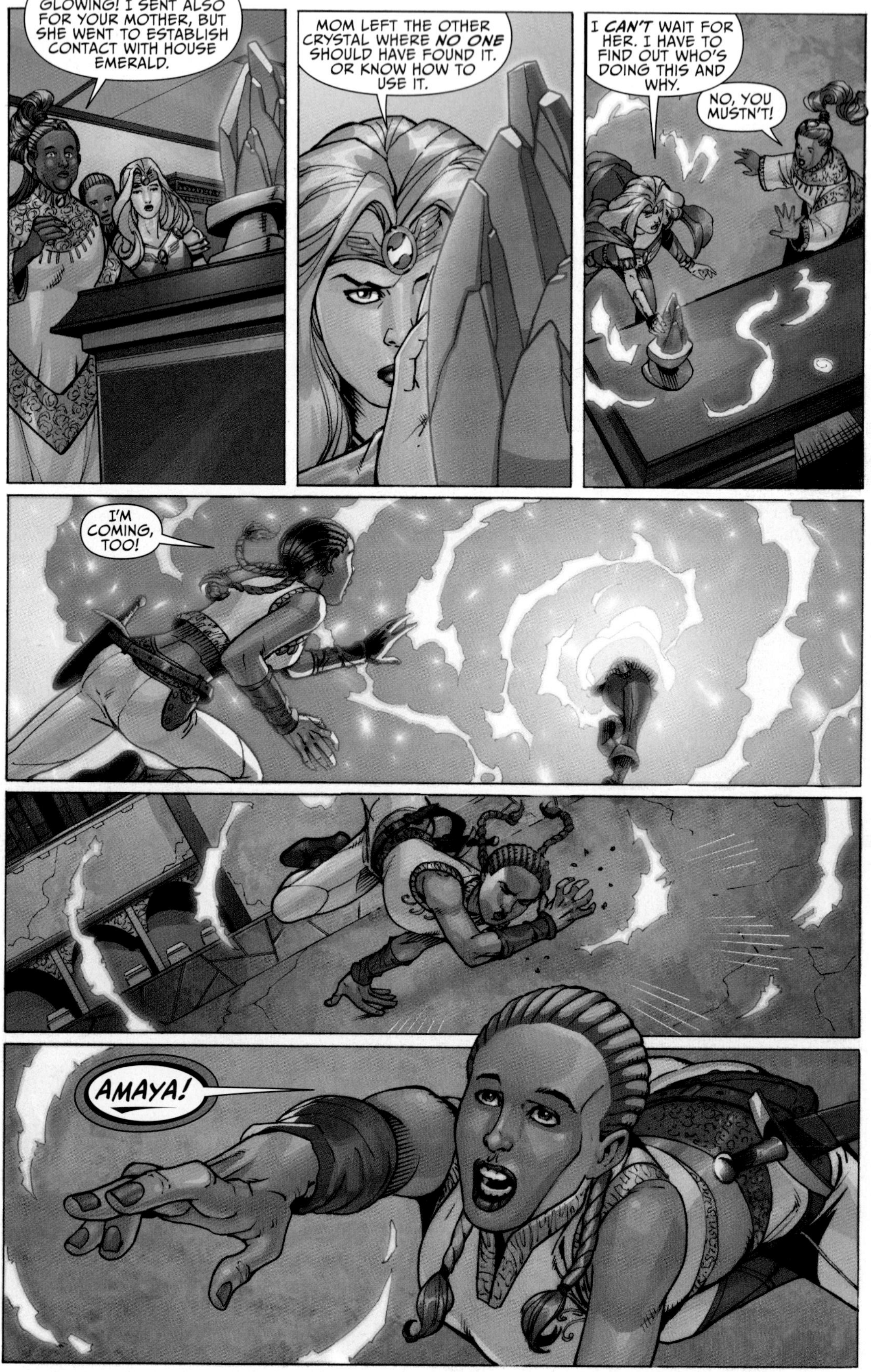
THE PORTAL CRYSTAL HAS BEEN GLOWING! I SENT ALSO FOR YOUR MOTHER, BUT SHE WENT TO ESTABLISH CONTACT WITH HOUSE EMERALD.
MOM LEFT THE OTHER CRYSTAL WHERE NO ONE SHOULD HAVE FOUND IT. OR KNOW HOW TO USE IT.
I CAN'T WAIT FOR HER. I HAVE TO FIND OUT WHO'S DOING THIS AND WHY.
NO, YOU MUSTN'T!
I'M COMING, TOO!
AMAYA!

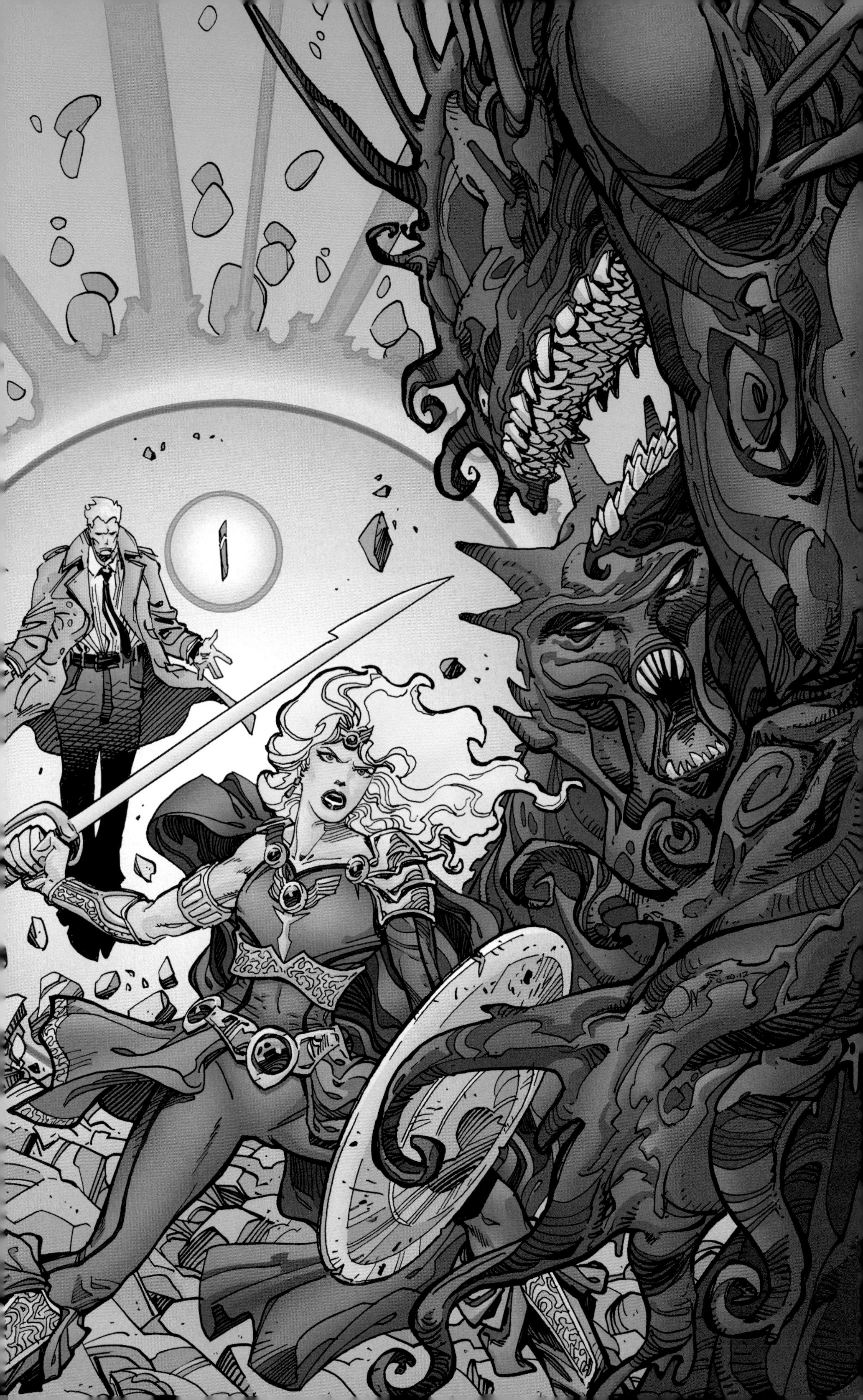

AMETHYST part five HOSTILE TAKEOVER

CHRISTY MARX writer **TRAVIS MOORE** penciller **KARL STORY** inker cover by **WALTER SIMONSON & LOVERN KINDZIERSKI**

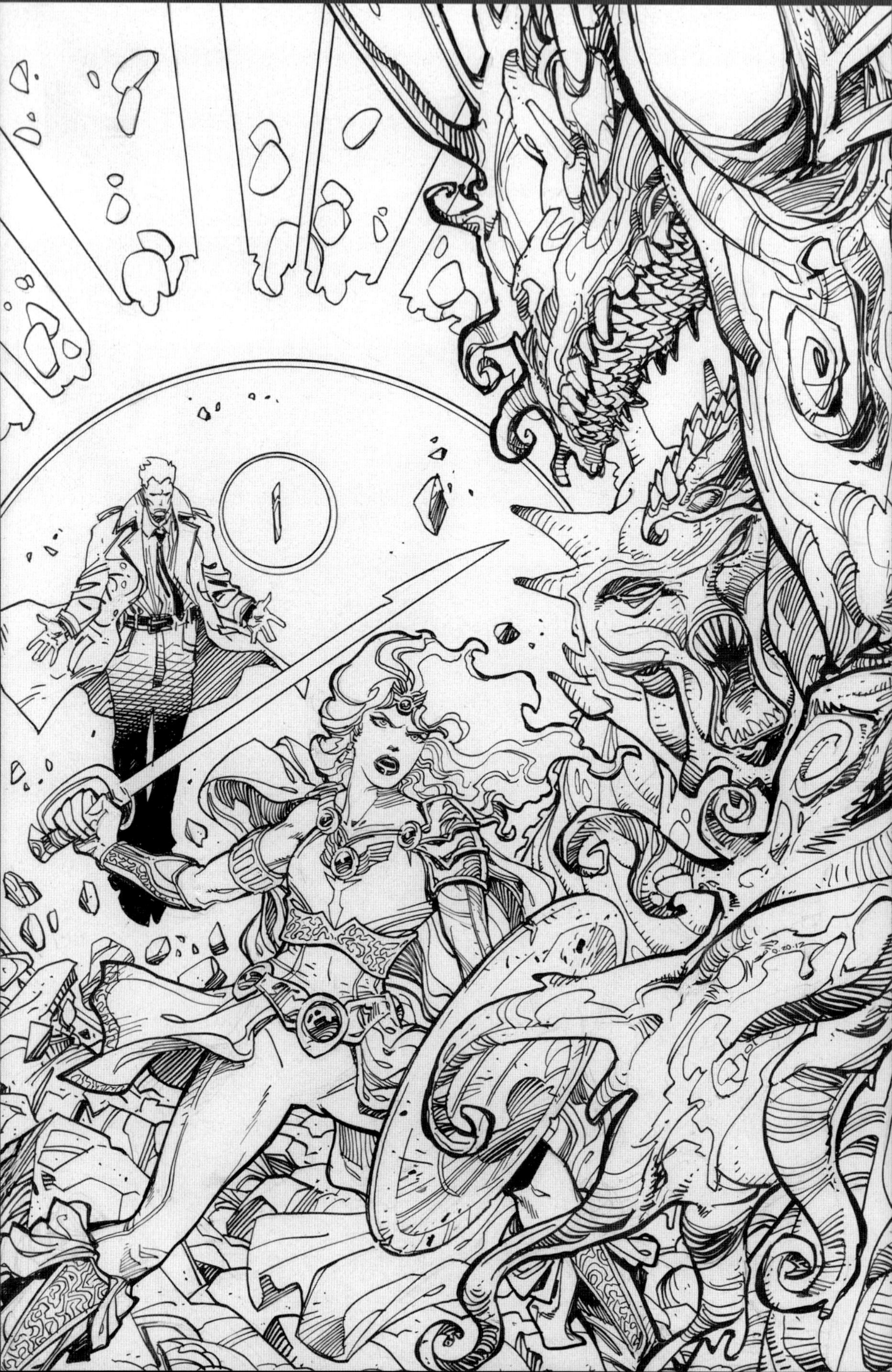

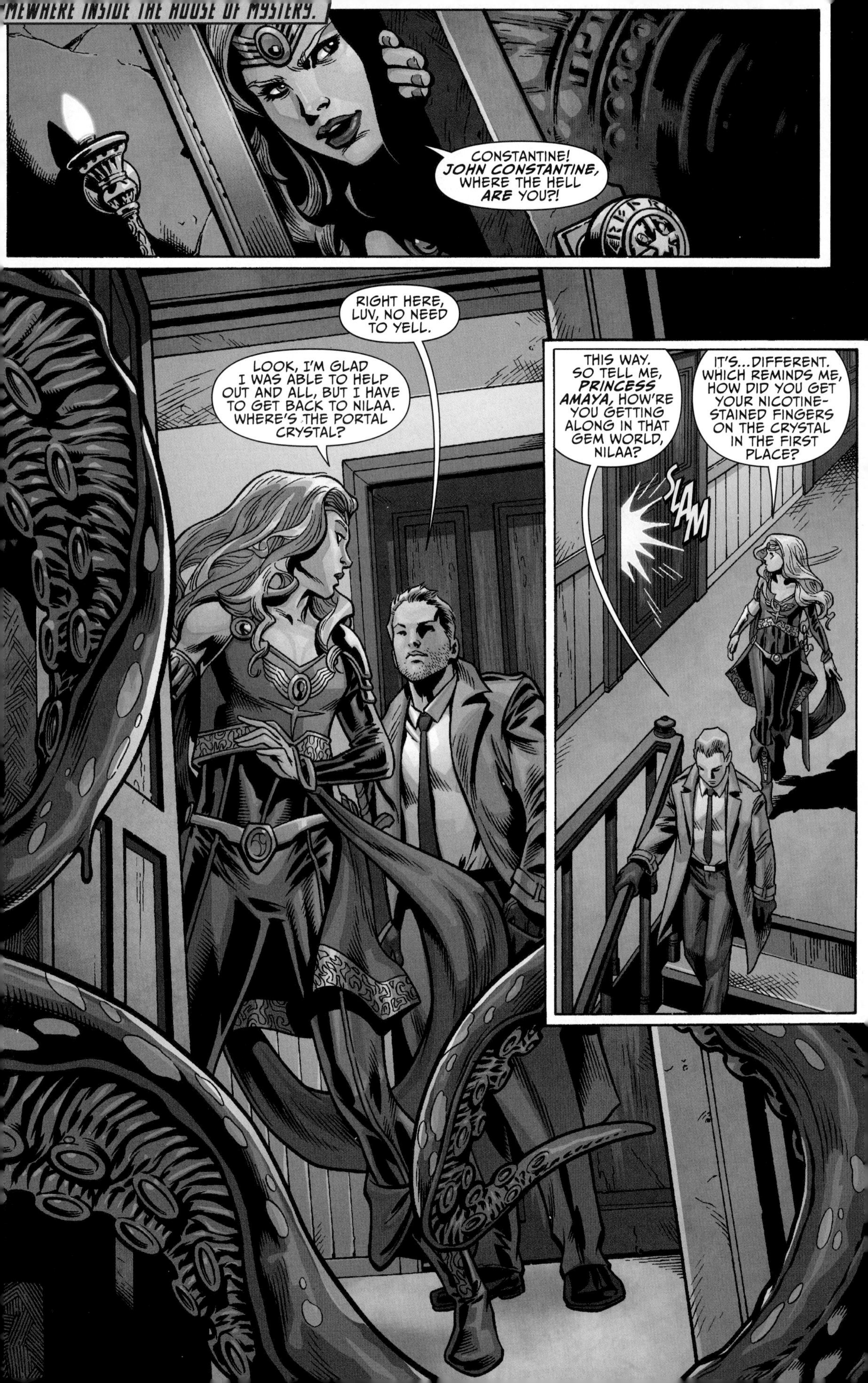
MEWHERE INSIDE THE HOUSE OF MYSTERY.
CONSTANTINE! JOHN CONSTANTINE, WHERE THE HELL ARE YOU?!
LOOK, I'M GLAD I WAS ABLE TO HELP OUT AND ALL, BUT I HAVE TO GET BACK TO NILAA. WHERE'S THE PORTAL CRYSTAL?
RIGHT HERE, LUV, NO NEED TO YELL.
THIS WAY. SO TELL ME, PRINCESS AMAYA, HOW'RE YOU GETTING ALONG IN THAT GEM WORLD, NILAA?
IT'S...DIFFERENT. WHICH REMINDS ME, HOW DID YOU GET YOUR NICOTINE-STAINED FINGERS ON THE CRYSTAL IN THE FIRST PLACE?
SLAM

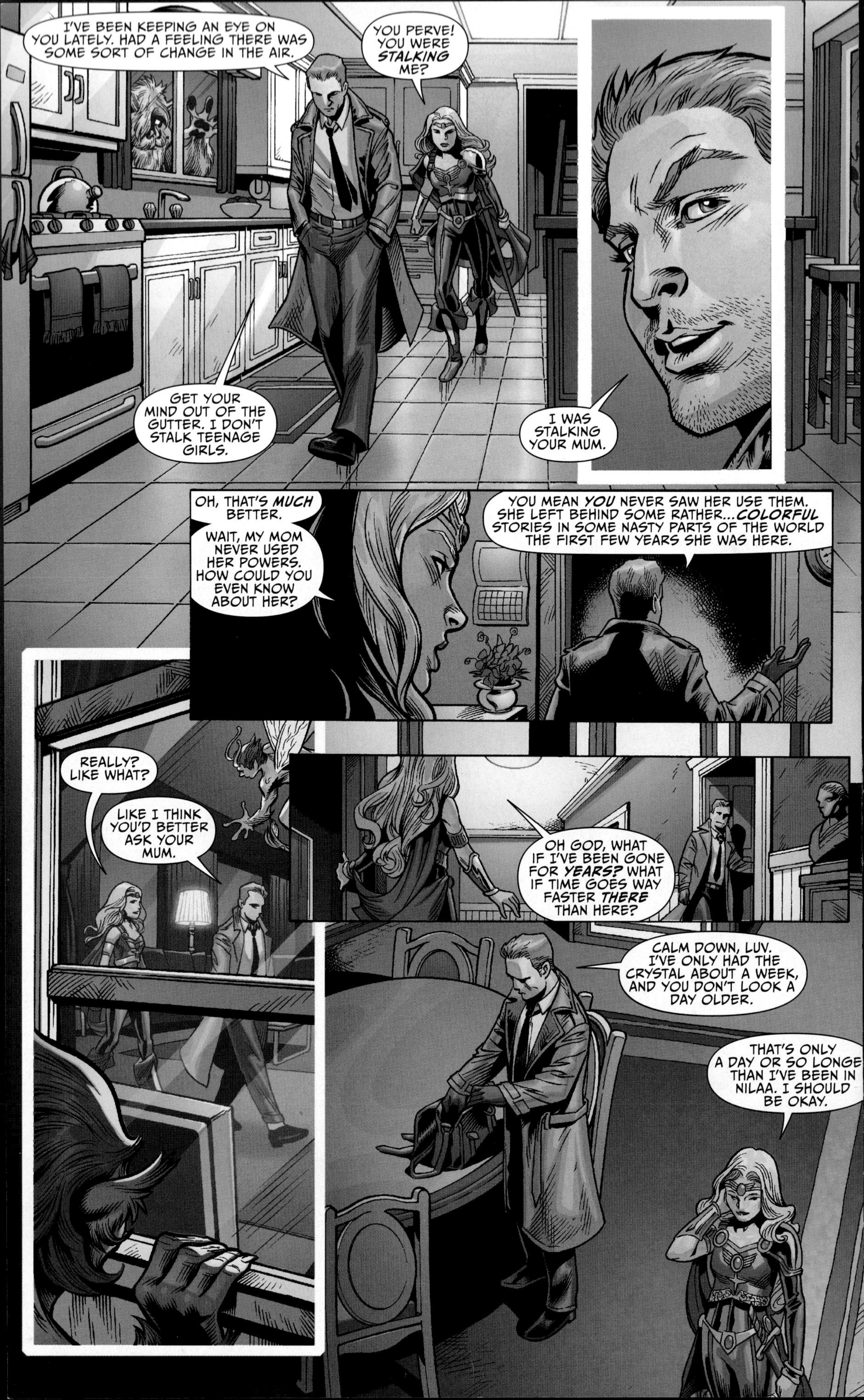

I'VE BEEN KEEPING AN EYE ON YOU LATELY. HAD A FEELING THERE WAS SOME SORT OF CHANGE IN THE AIR.
YOU PERVE! YOU WERE STALKING ME?
GET YOUR MIND OUT OF THE GUTTER. I DON'T STALK TEENAGE GIRLS.
I WAS STALKING YOUR MUM.
OH, THAT'S MUCH BETTER.
WAIT, MY MOM NEVER USED HER POWERS. HOW COULD YOU EVEN KNOW ABOUT HER?
YOU MEAN YOU NEVER SAW HER USE THEM. SHE LEFT BEHIND SOME RATHER...COLORFUL STORIES IN SOME NASTY PARTS OF THE WORLD THE FIRST FEW YEARS SHE WAS HERE.
REALLY? LIKE WHAT?
LIKE I THINK YOU'D BETTER ASK YOUR MUM.
OH GOD, WHAT IF I'VE BEEN GONE FOR YEARS? WHAT IF TIME GOES WAY FASTER THERE THAN HERE?
CALM DOWN, LUV. I'VE ONLY HAD THE CRYSTAL ABOUT A WEEK, AND YOU DON'T LOOK A DAY OLDER.
THAT'S ONLY A DAY OR SO LONGE THAN I'VE BEEN IN NILAA. I SHOULD BE OKAY.

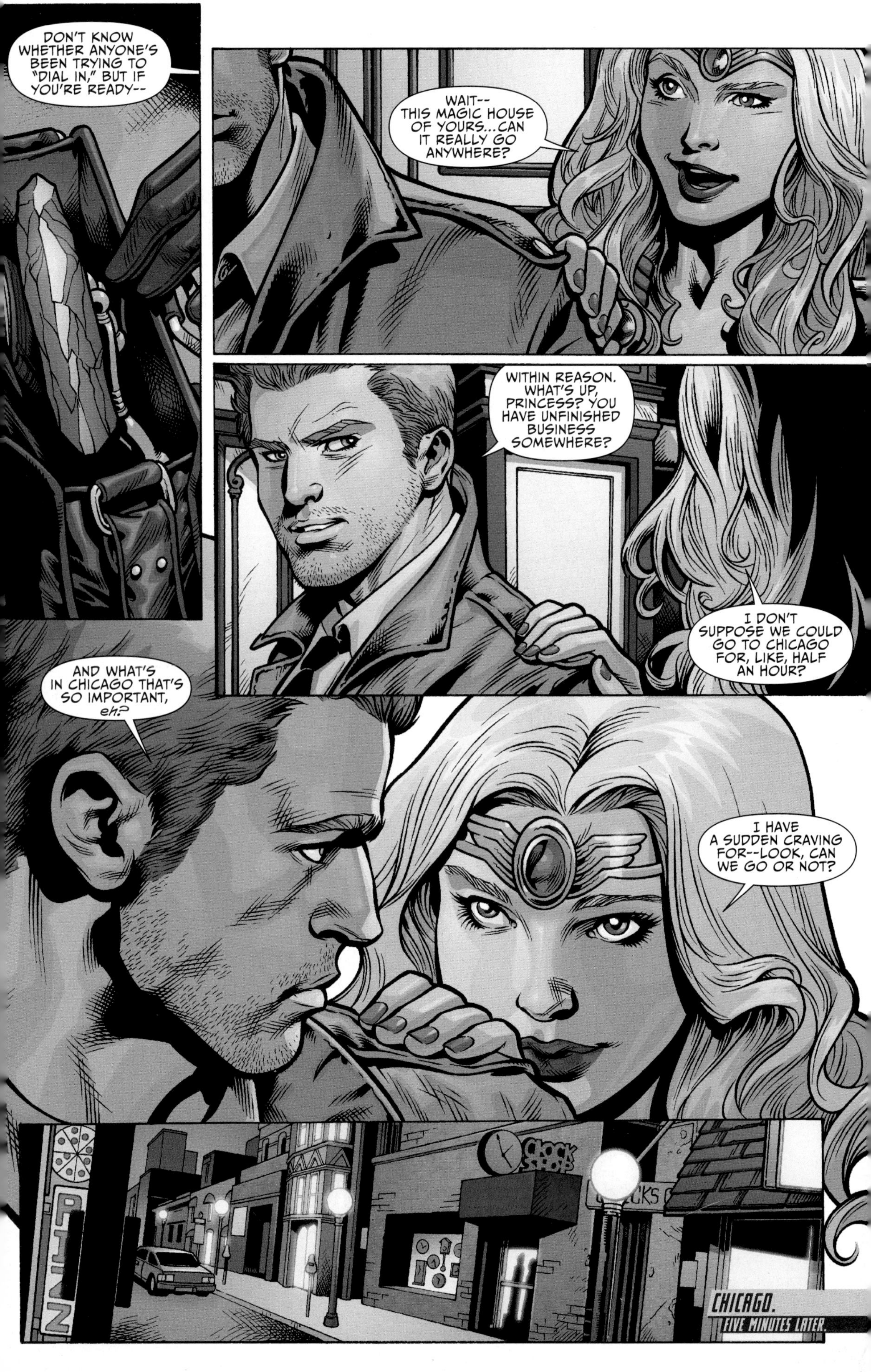
DON'T KNOW WHETHER ANYONE'S BEEN TRYING TO "DIAL IN," BUT IF YOU'RE READY--
WAIT-- THIS MAGIC HOUSE OF YOURS...CAN IT REALLY GO ANYWHERE?
WITHIN REASON. WHAT'S UP, PRINCESS? YOU HAVE UNFINISHED BUSINESS SOMEWHERE?
I DON'T SUPPOSE WE COULD GO TO CHICAGO FOR, LIKE, HALF AN HOUR?
AND WHAT'S IN CHICAGO THAT'S SO IMPORTANT, *eh?*
I HAVE A SUDDEN CRAVING FOR--LOOK, CAN WE GO OR NOT?
CLOCK SHOP
CHICAGO.
FIVE MINUTES LATER.

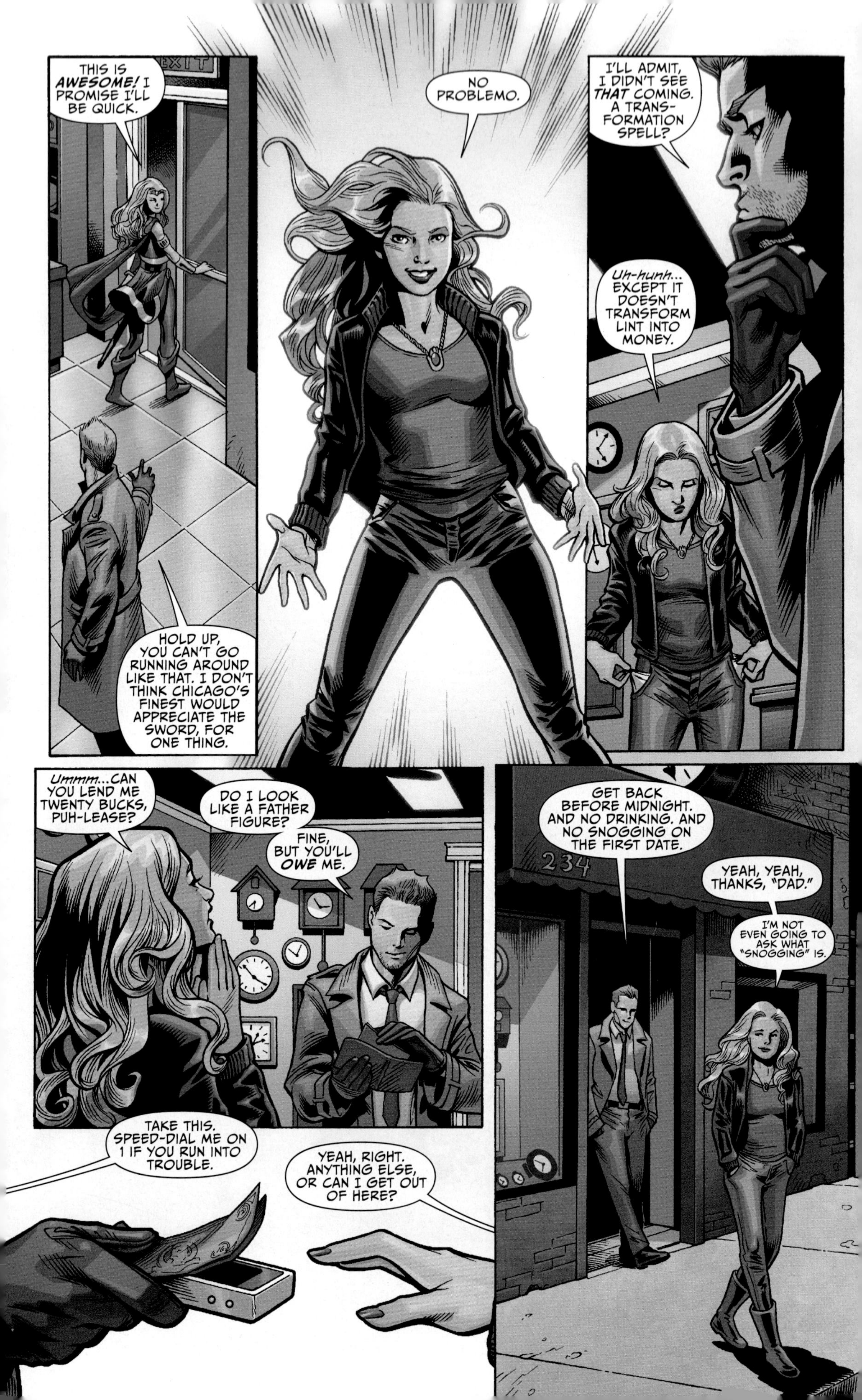
THIS IS *AWESOME!* I PROMISE I'LL BE QUICK.
HOLD UP, YOU CAN'T GO RUNNING AROUND LIKE THAT. I DON'T THINK CHICAGO'S FINEST WOULD APPRECIATE THE SWORD, FOR ONE THING.
NO PROBLEMO.
I'LL ADMIT, I DIDN'T SEE *THAT* COMING. A TRANS-FORMATION SPELL?
Uh-hunh... EXCEPT IT DOESN'T TRANSFORM LINT INTO MONEY.
Ummm...CAN YOU LEND ME TWENTY BUCKS, PUH-LEASE?
DO I LOOK LIKE A FATHER FIGURE?
FINE, BUT YOU'LL *OWE* ME.
TAKE THIS. SPEED-DIAL ME ON 1 IF YOU RUN INTO TROUBLE.
YEAH, RIGHT. ANYTHING ELSE, OR CAN I GET OUT OF HERE?
GET BACK BEFORE MIDNIGHT. AND NO DRINKING. AND NO SNOGGING ON THE FIRST DATE.
234
YEAH, YEAH, THANKS, "DAD."
I'M NOT EVEN GOING TO ASK WHAT "SNOGGING" IS.

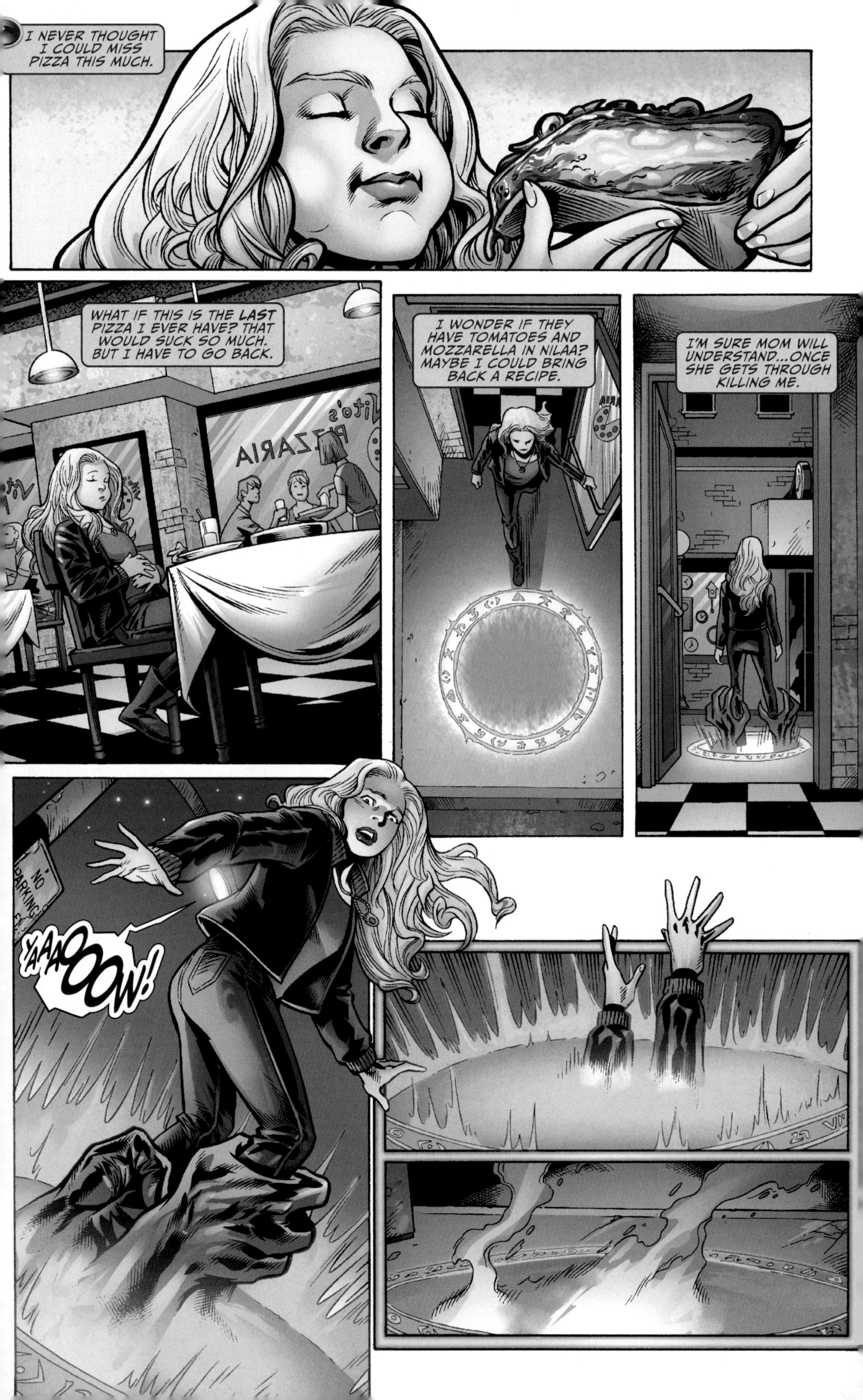
I NEVER THOUGHT I COULD MISS PIZZA THIS MUCH.
WHAT IF THIS IS THE LAST PIZZA I EVER HAVE? THAT WOULD SUCK SO MUCH. BUT I HAVE TO GO BACK.
VITO'S PIZZARIA
I WONDER IF THEY HAVE TOMATOES AND MOZZARELLA IN NILAA? MAYBE I COULD BRING BACK A RECIPE.
I'M SURE MOM WILL UNDERSTAND...ONCE SHE GETS THROUGH KILLING ME.
NO PARKING
YAAAOOOW!

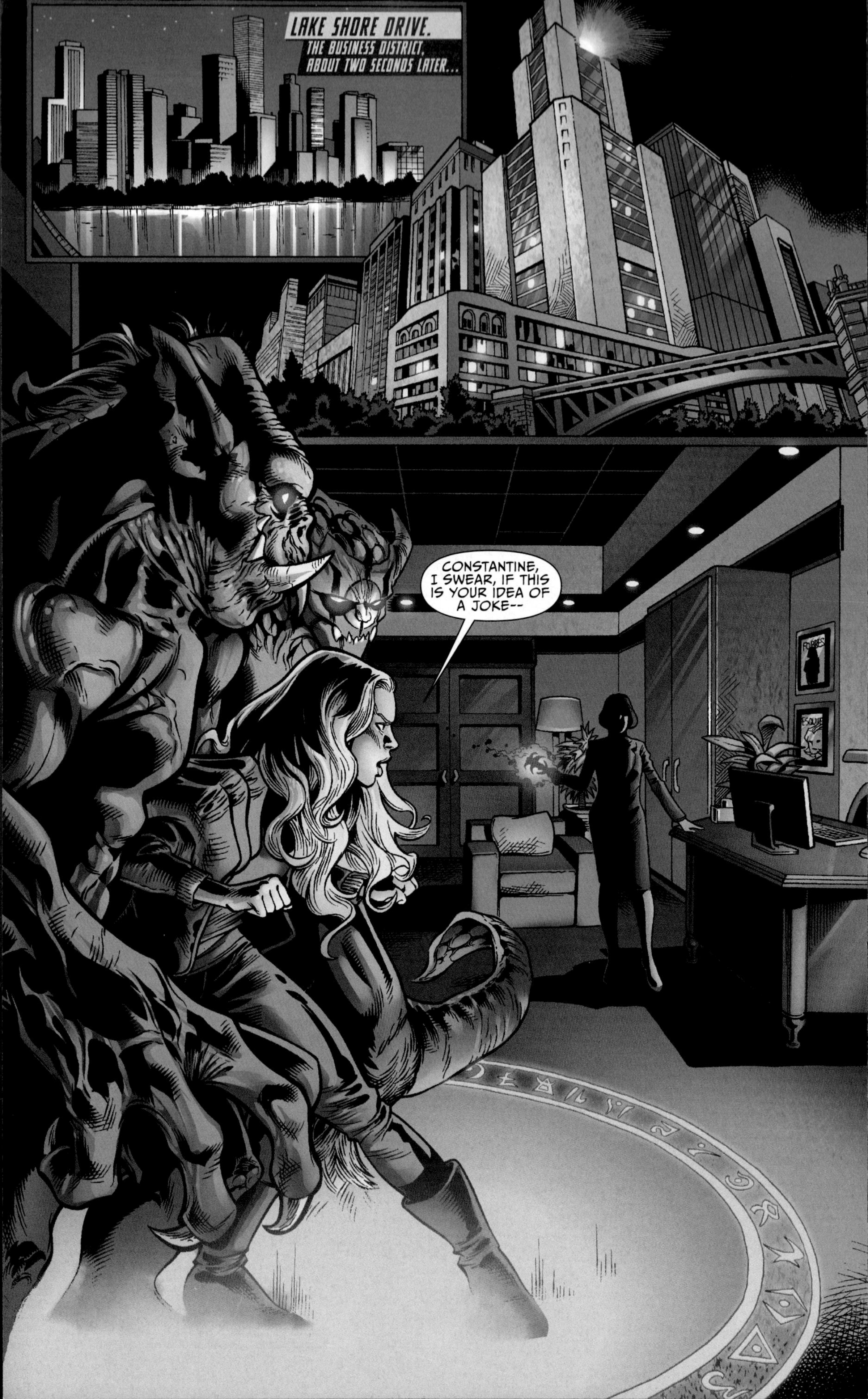
LAKE SHORE DRIVE.
THE BUSINESS DISTRICT, ABOUT TWO SECONDS LATER...
CONSTANTINE, I SWEAR, IF THIS IS YOUR IDEA OF A JOKE--

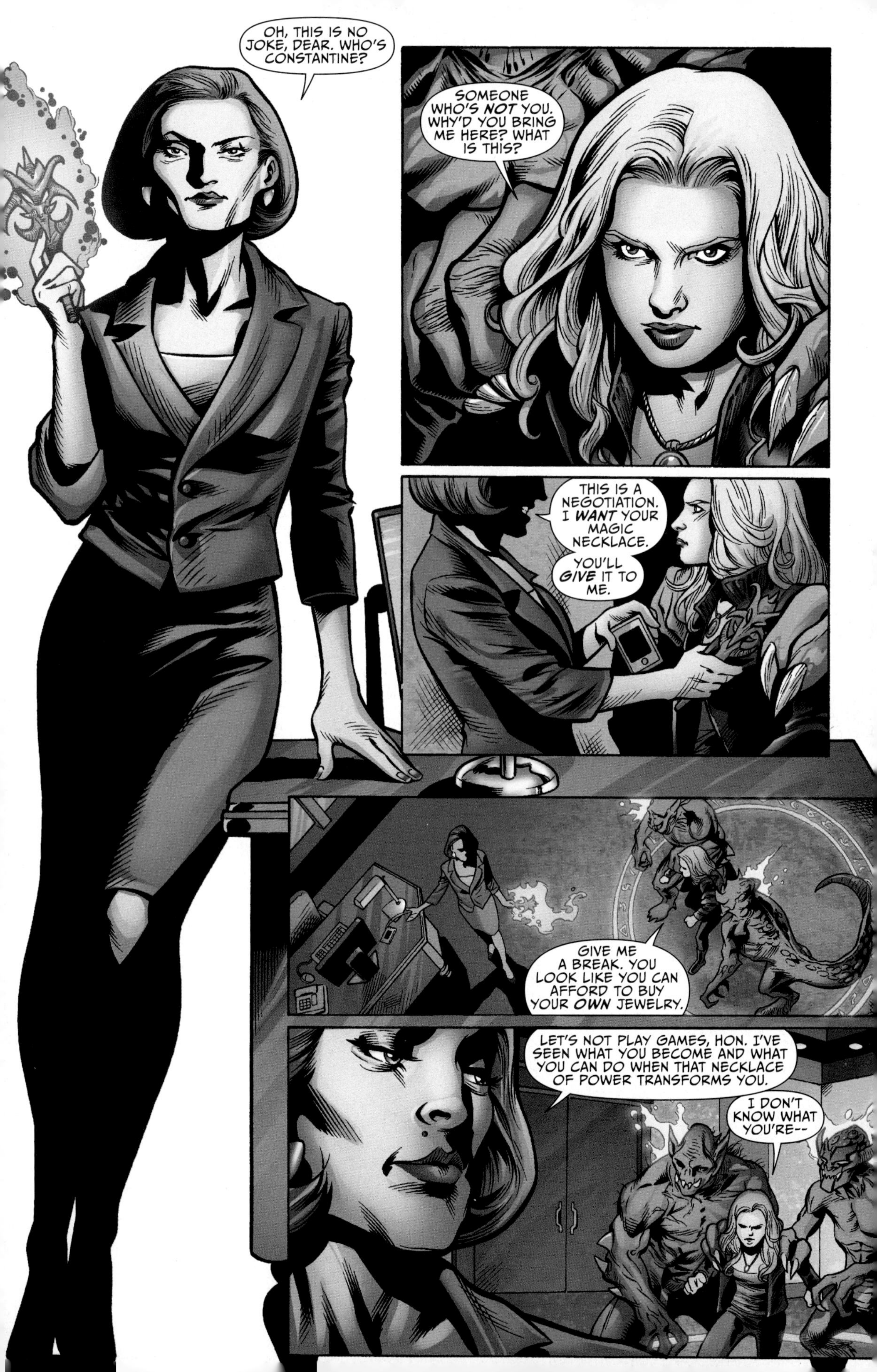
OH, THIS IS NO JOKE, DEAR. WHO'S CONSTANTINE?
SOMEONE WHO'S **NOT** YOU. WHY'D YOU BRING ME HERE? WHAT IS THIS?
THIS IS A NEGOTIATION. I **WANT** YOUR MAGIC NECKLACE.
YOU'LL **GIVE** IT TO ME.
GIVE ME A BREAK. YOU LOOK LIKE YOU CAN AFFORD TO BUY YOUR **OWN** JEWELRY.
LET'S NOT PLAY GAMES, HON. I'VE SEEN WHAT YOU BECOME AND WHAT YOU CAN DO WHEN THAT NECKLACE OF POWER TRANSFORMS YOU.
I DON'T KNOW WHAT YOU'RE--

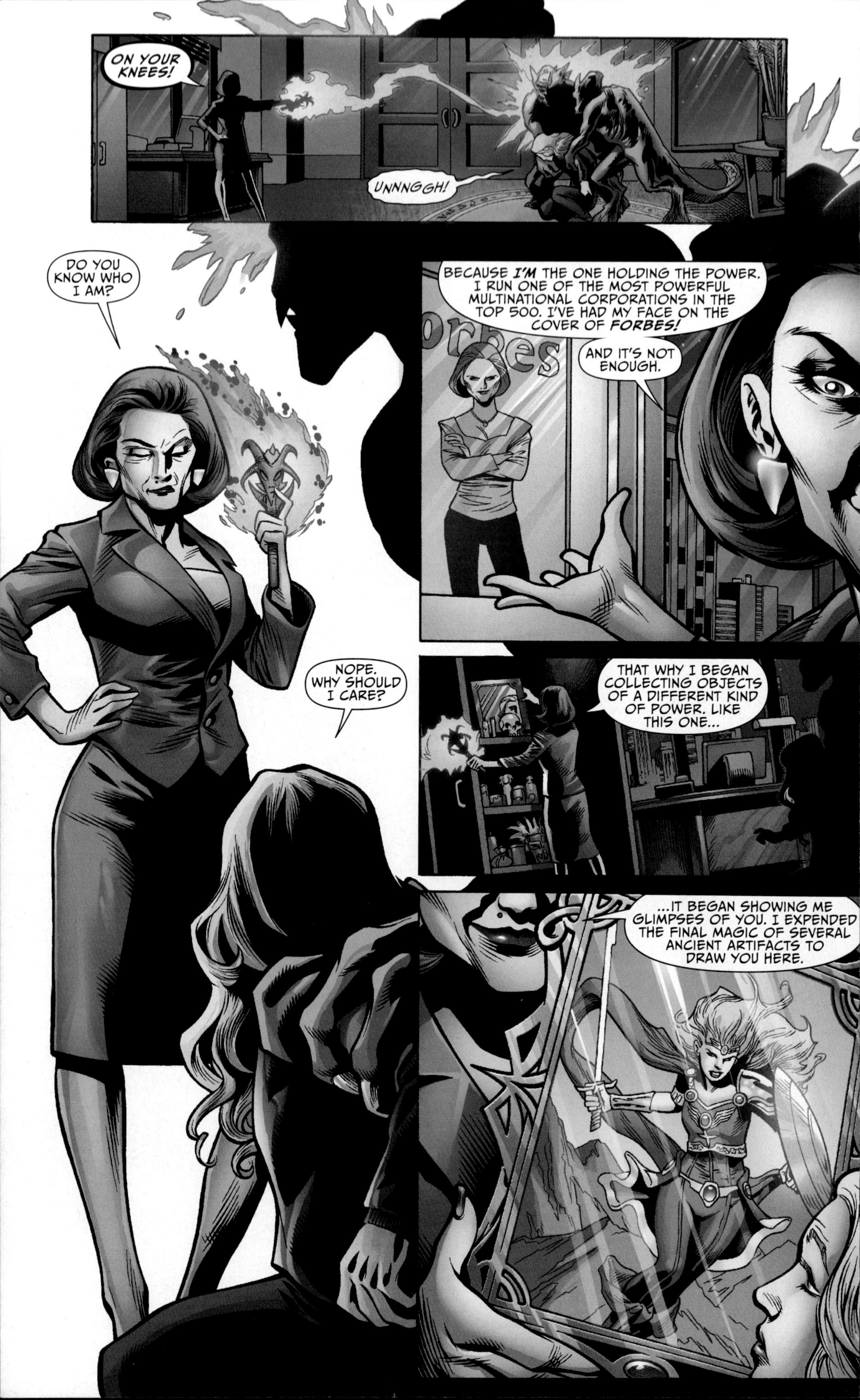
ON YOUR KNEES!
UNNNGGH!
DO YOU KNOW WHO I AM?
BECAUSE I'M THE ONE HOLDING THE POWER. I RUN ONE OF THE MOST POWERFUL MULTINATIONAL CORPORATIONS IN THE TOP 500. I'VE HAD MY FACE ON THE COVER OF FORBES!
AND IT'S NOT ENOUGH.
NOPE. WHY SHOULD I CARE?
THAT WHY I BEGAN COLLECTING OBJECTS OF A DIFFERENT KIND OF POWER. LIKE THIS ONE...
...IT BEGAN SHOWING ME GLIMPSES OF YOU. I EXPENDED THE FINAL MAGIC OF SEVERAL ANCIENT ARTIFACTS TO DRAW YOU HERE.

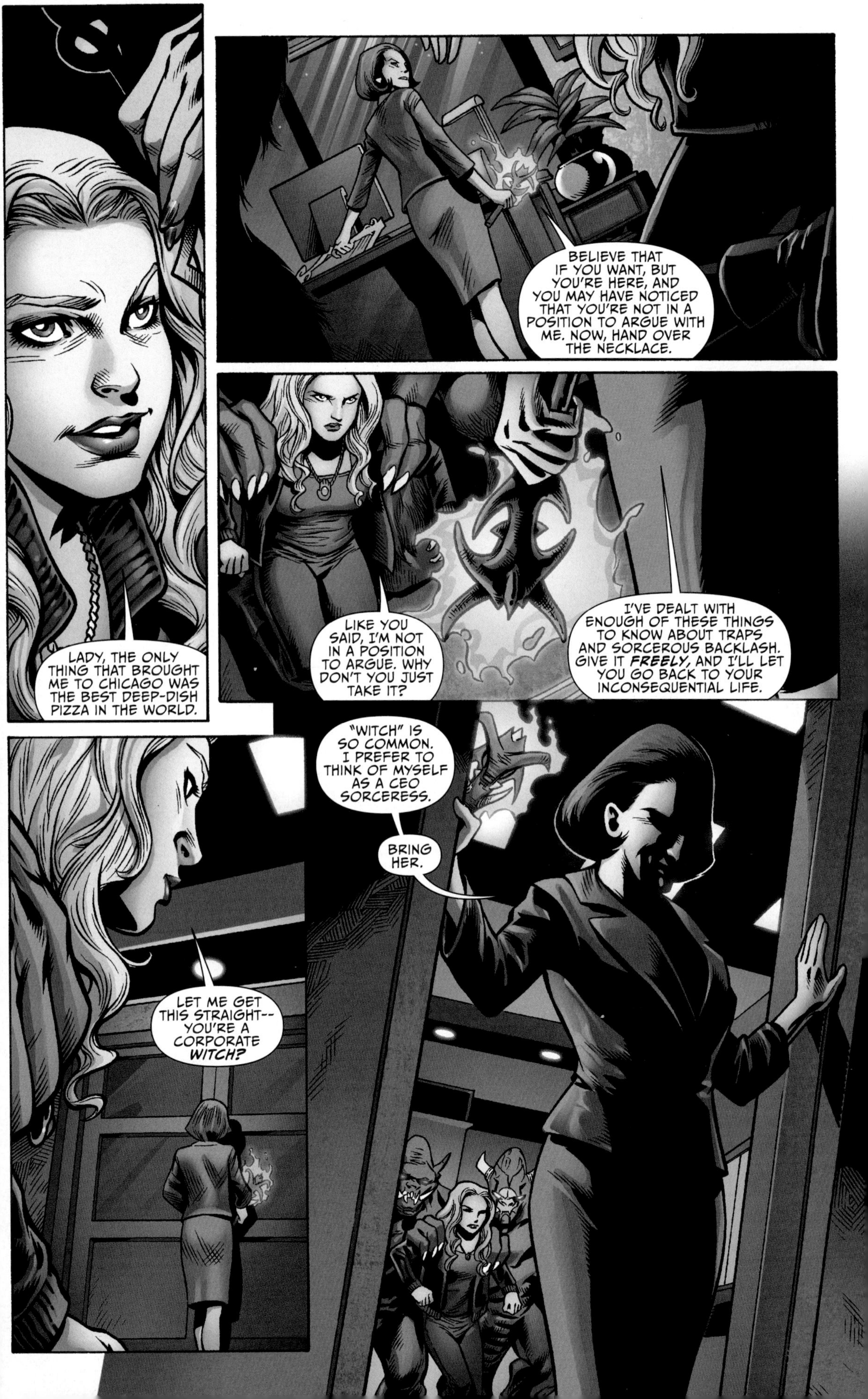

BELIEVE THAT IF YOU WANT, BUT YOU'RE HERE, AND YOU MAY HAVE NOTICED THAT YOU'RE NOT IN A POSITION TO ARGUE WITH ME. NOW, HAND OVER THE NECKLACE.
LADY, THE ONLY THING THAT BROUGHT ME TO CHICAGO WAS THE BEST DEEP-DISH PIZZA IN THE WORLD.
LIKE YOU SAID, I'M NOT IN A POSITION TO ARGUE. WHY DON'T YOU JUST TAKE IT?
I'VE DEALT WITH ENOUGH OF THESE THINGS TO KNOW ABOUT TRAPS AND SORCEROUS BACKLASH. GIVE IT FREELY, AND I'LL LET YOU GO BACK TO YOUR INCONSEQUENTIAL LIFE.
LET ME GET THIS STRAIGHT-- YOU'RE A CORPORATE WITCH?
"WITCH" IS SO COMMON. I PREFER TO THINK OF MYSELF AS A CEO SORCERESS.
BRING HER.

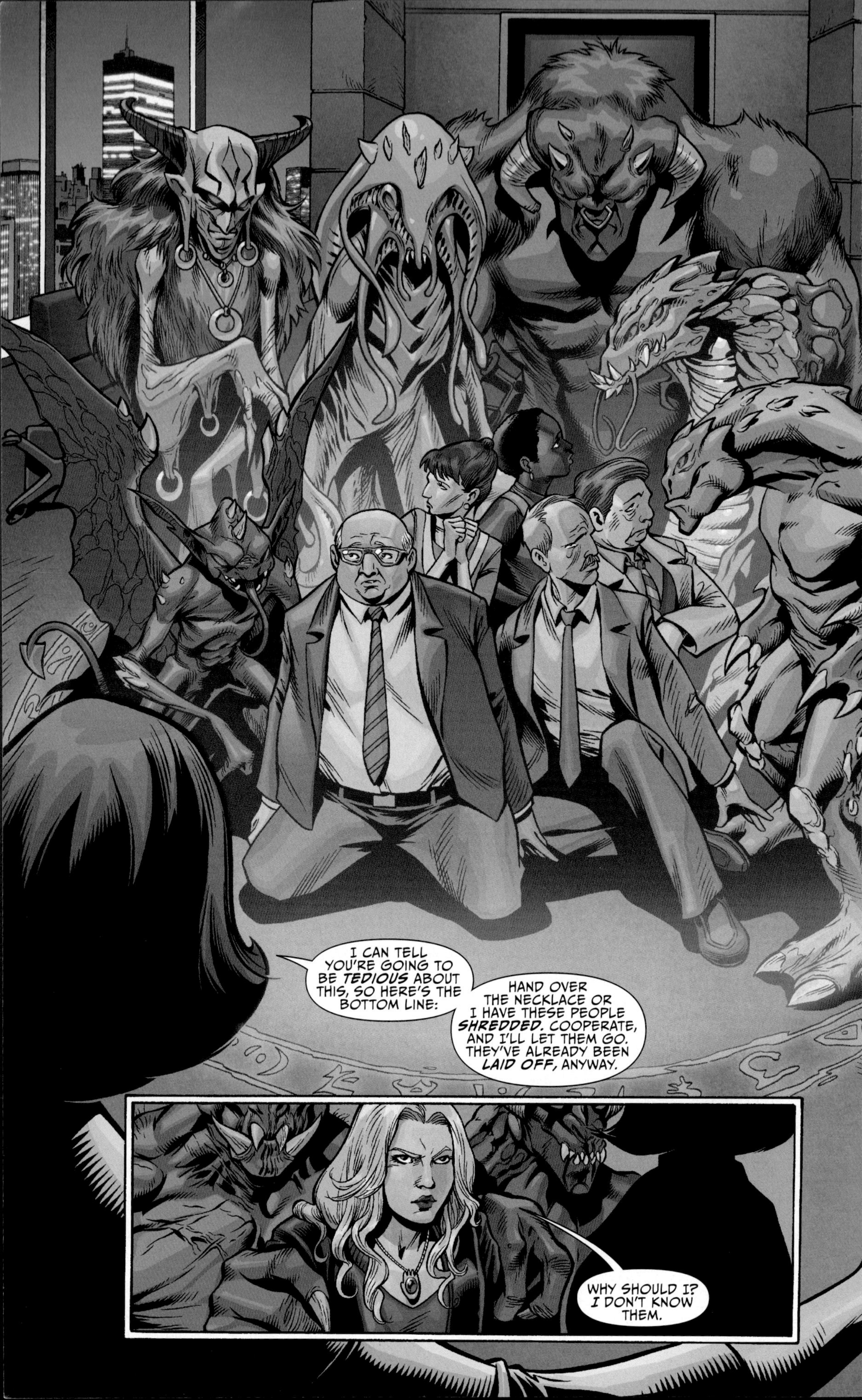
I CAN TELL YOU'RE GOING TO BE *TEDIOUS* ABOUT THIS, SO HERE'S THE BOTTOM LINE:
HAND OVER THE NECKLACE OR I HAVE THESE PEOPLE *SHREDDED.* COOPERATE, AND I'LL LET THEM GO. THEY'VE ALREADY BEEN *LAID OFF,* ANYWAY.
WHY SHOULD I? *I* DON'T KNOW THEM.

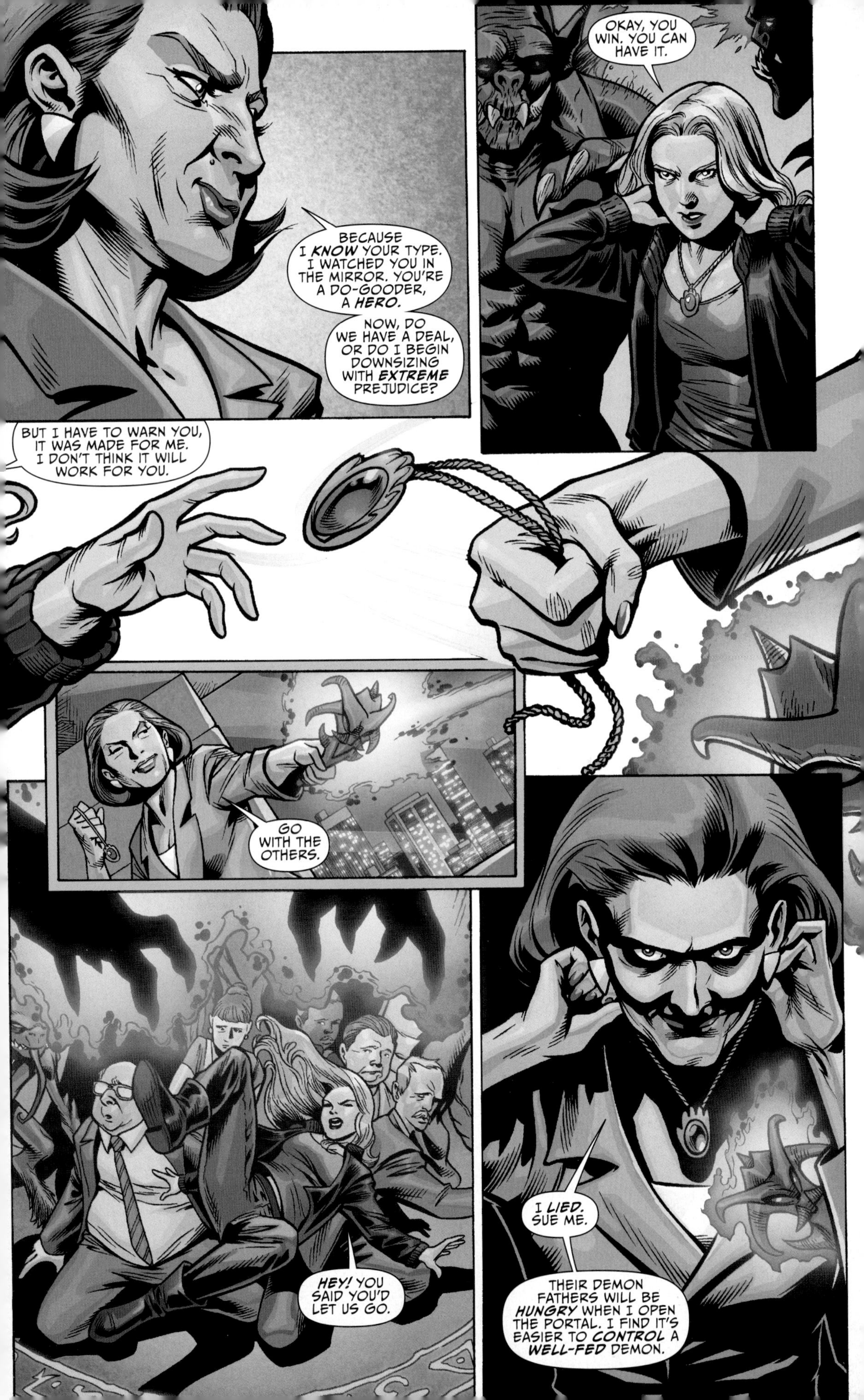

BECAUSE I *KNOW* YOUR TYPE. I WATCHED YOU IN THE MIRROR. YOU'RE A DO-GOODER, A *HERO.*
NOW, DO WE HAVE A DEAL, OR DO I BEGIN DOWNSIZING WITH *EXTREME* PREJUDICE?
OKAY, YOU WIN. YOU CAN HAVE IT.
BUT I HAVE TO WARN YOU, IT WAS MADE FOR ME. I DON'T THINK IT WILL WORK FOR YOU.
GO WITH THE OTHERS.
HEY! YOU SAID YOU'D LET US GO.
I *LIED.* SUE ME.
THEIR DEMON FATHERS WILL BE *HUNGRY* WHEN I OPEN THE PORTAL. I FIND IT'S EASIER TO *CONTROL* A *WELL-FED* DEMON.

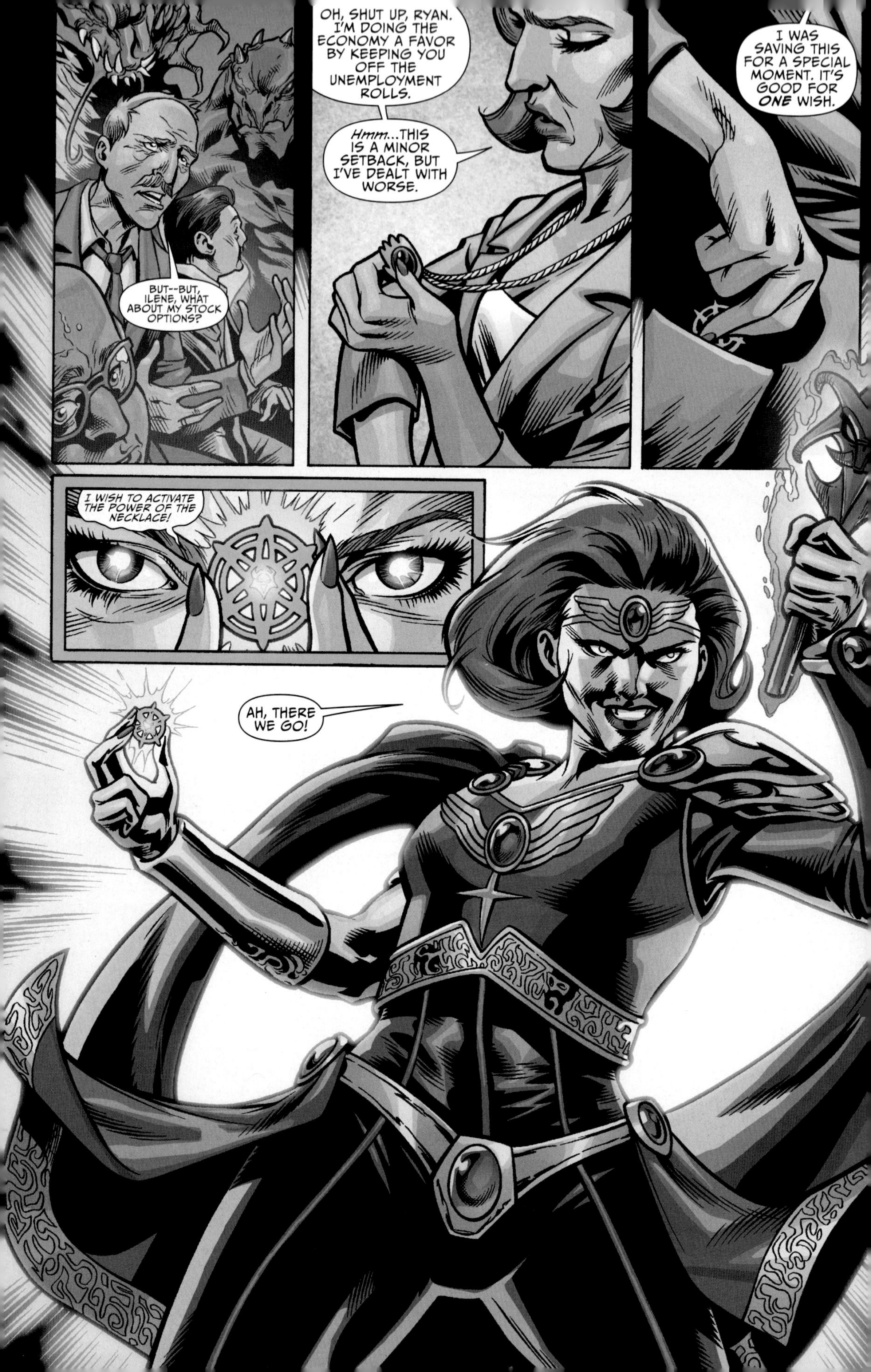
BUT--BUT, ILENE, WHAT ABOUT MY STOCK OPTIONS?
OH, SHUT UP, RYAN. I'M DOING THE ECONOMY A FAVOR BY KEEPING YOU OFF THE UNEMPLOYMENT ROLLS.
Hmm...THIS IS A MINOR SETBACK, BUT I'VE DEALT WITH WORSE.
I WAS SAVING THIS FOR A SPECIAL MOMENT. IT'S GOOD FOR ***ONE*** WISH.
I WISH TO ACTIVATE THE POWER OF THE NECKLACE!
AH, THERE WE GO!

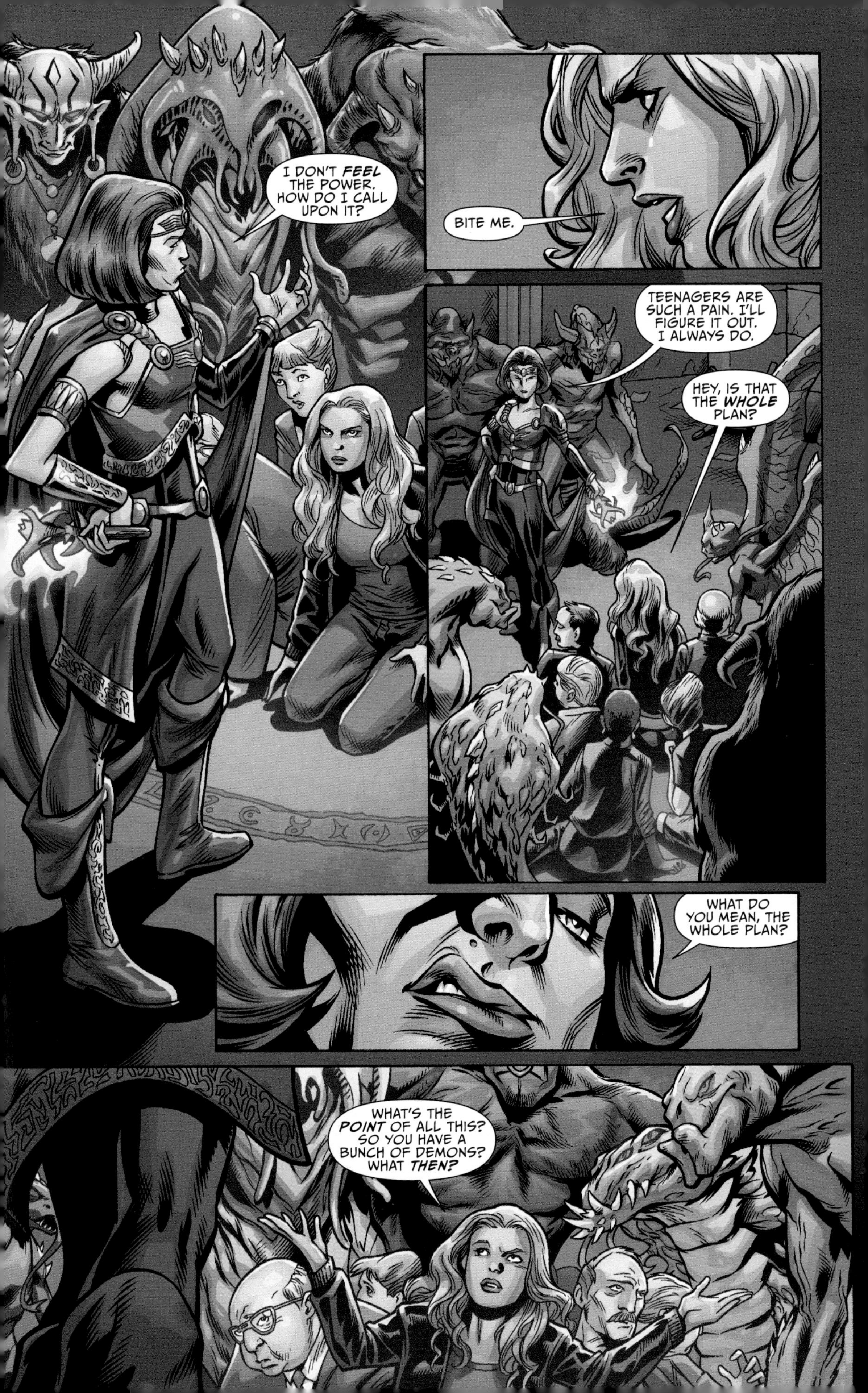
I DON'T *FEEL* THE POWER. HOW DO I CALL UPON IT?
BITE ME.
TEENAGERS ARE SUCH A PAIN. I'LL FIGURE IT OUT. I ALWAYS DO.
HEY, IS THAT THE *WHOLE* PLAN?
WHAT DO YOU MEAN, THE WHOLE PLAN?
WHAT'S THE *POINT* OF ALL THIS? SO YOU HAVE A BUNCH OF DEMONS? WHAT *THEN?*

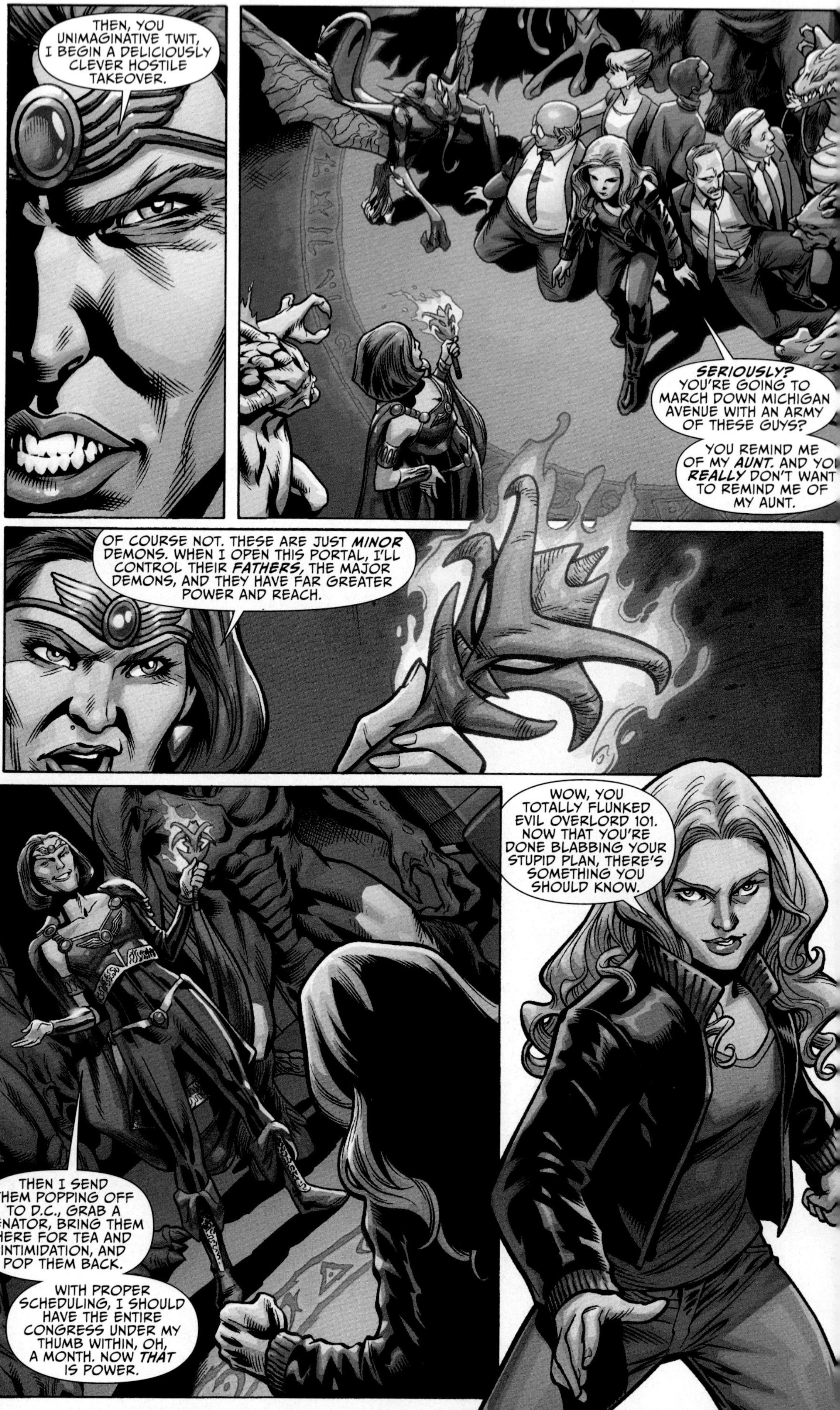
THEN, YOU UNIMAGINATIVE TWIT, I BEGIN A DELICIOUSLY CLEVER HOSTILE TAKEOVER.
SERIOUSLY? YOU'RE GOING TO MARCH DOWN MICHIGAN AVENUE WITH AN ARMY OF THESE GUYS?
YOU REMIND ME OF MY AUNT. AND YOU REALLY DON'T WANT TO REMIND ME OF MY AUNT.
OF COURSE NOT. THESE ARE JUST MINOR DEMONS. WHEN I OPEN THIS PORTAL, I'LL CONTROL THEIR FATHERS, THE MAJOR DEMONS, AND THEY HAVE FAR GREATER POWER AND REACH.
THEN I SEND THEM POPPING OFF TO D.C., GRAB A SENATOR, BRING THEM HERE FOR TEA AND INTIMIDATION, AND POP THEM BACK.
WITH PROPER SCHEDULING, I SHOULD HAVE THE ENTIRE CONGRESS UNDER MY THUMB WITHIN, OH, A MONTH. NOW THAT IS POWER.
WOW, YOU TOTALLY FLUNKED EVIL OVERLORD 101. NOW THAT YOU'RE DONE BLABBING YOUR STUPID PLAN, THERE'S SOMETHING YOU SHOULD KNOW.

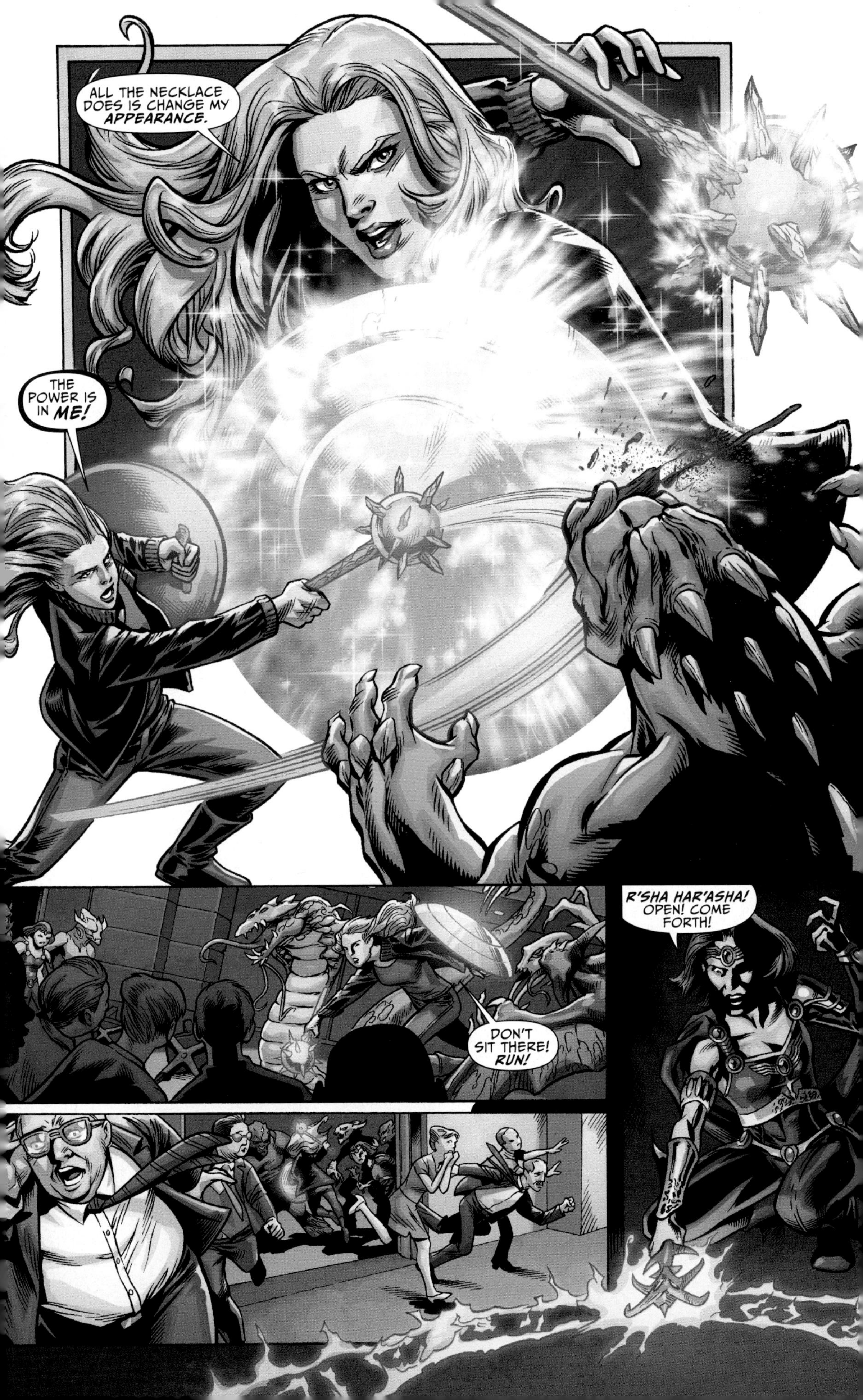
ALL THE NECKLACE DOES IS CHANGE MY APPEARANCE.
THE POWER IS IN ME!
DON'T SIT THERE! RUN!
R'SHA HAR'ASHA! OPEN! COME FORTH!

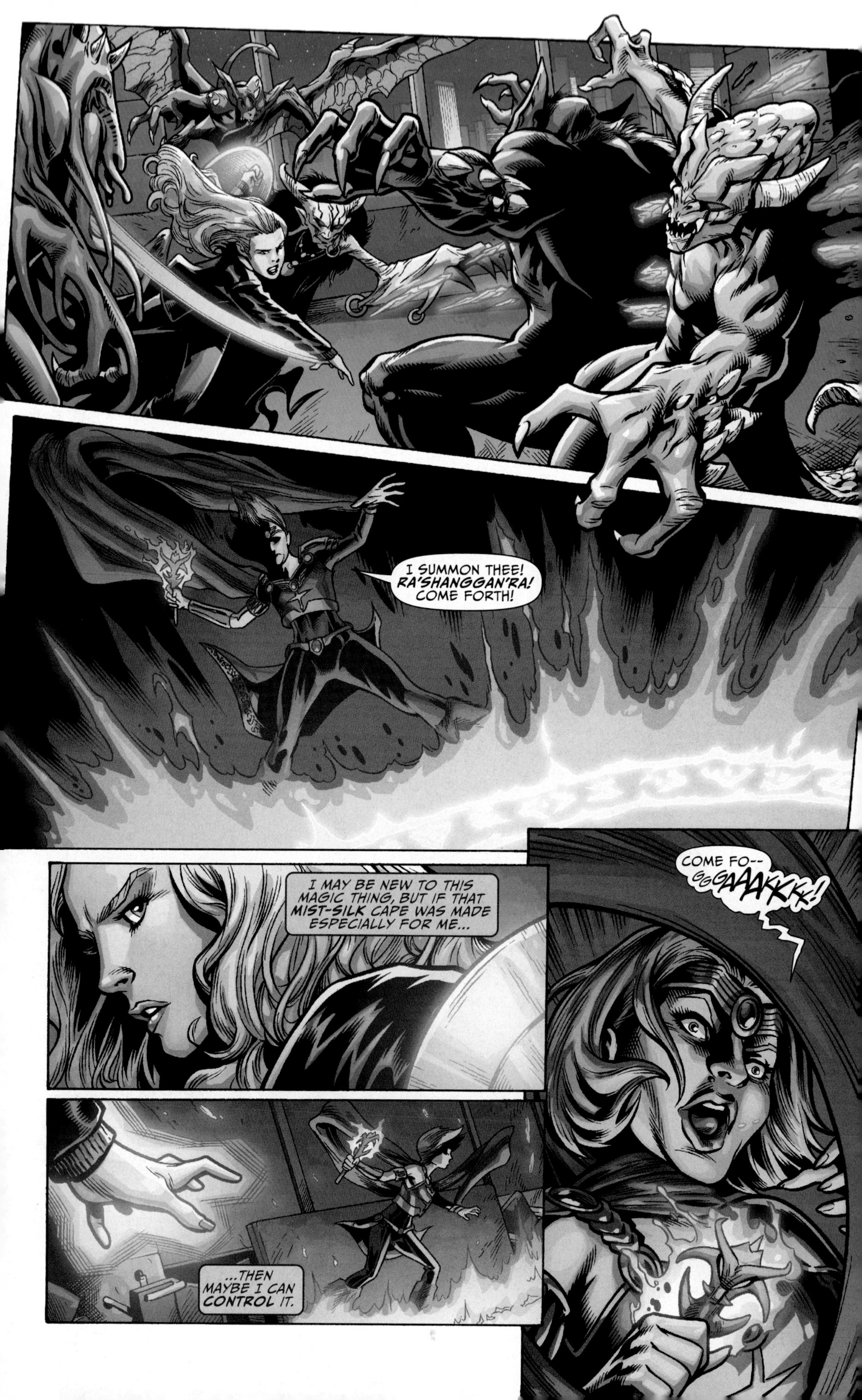
I SUMMON THEE! RA'SHANGGAN'RA! COME FORTH!
I MAY BE NEW TO THIS MAGIC THING, BUT IF THAT MIST-SILK CAPE WAS MADE ESPECIALLY FOR ME...
COME FO-- GGGAAAKKK!
...THEN MAYBE I CAN CONTROL IT.

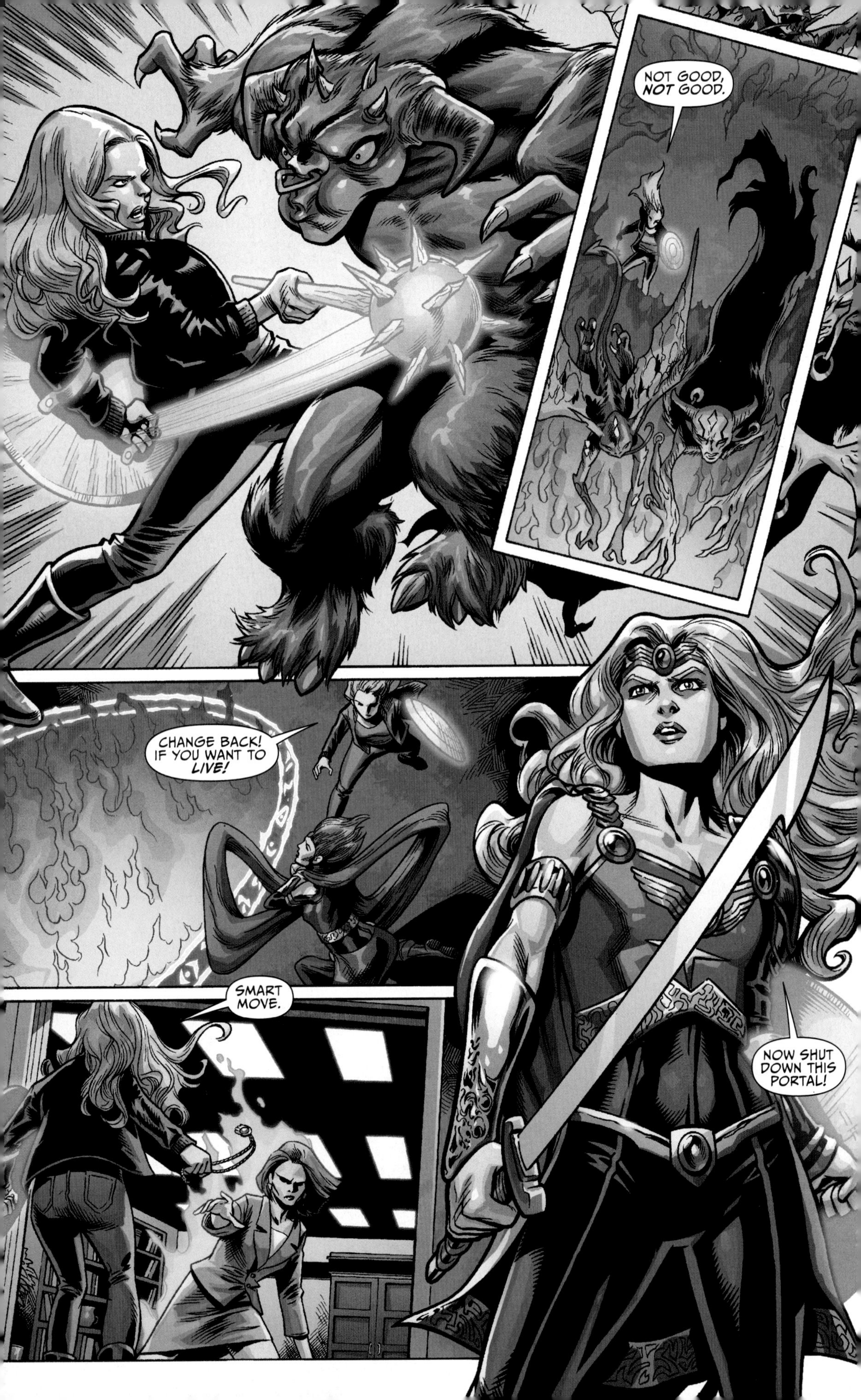
NOT GOOD, NOT GOOD.
CHANGE BACK! IF YOU WANT TO LIVE!
SMART MOVE.
NOW SHUT DOWN THIS PORTAL!

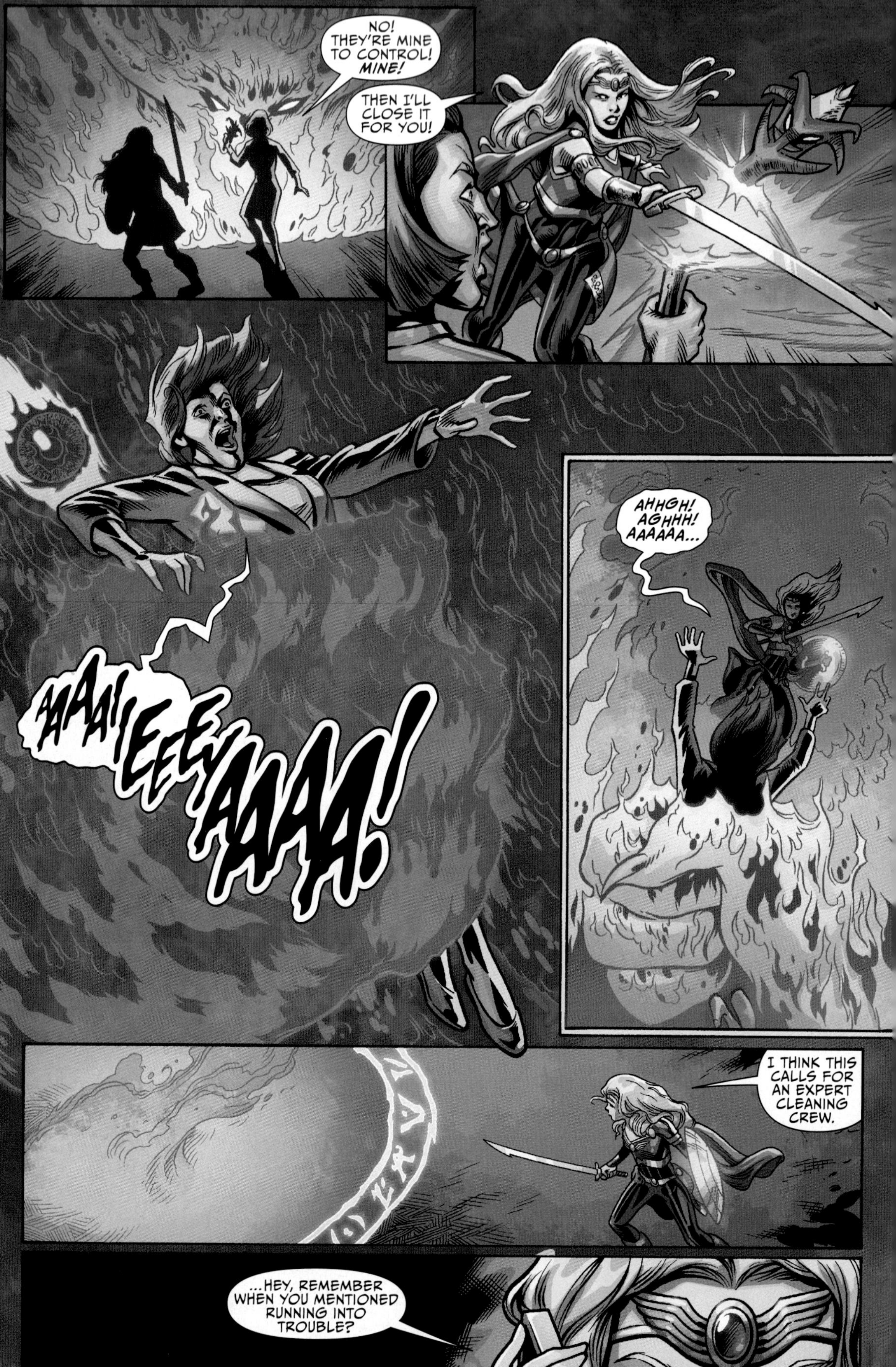
NO! THEY'RE MINE TO CONTROL! MINE!
THEN I'LL CLOSE IT FOR YOU!
AHHGH! AGHHH! AAAAAA...
I THINK THIS CALLS FOR AN EXPERT CLEANING CREW.
...HEY, REMEMBER WHEN YOU MENTIONED RUNNING INTO TROUBLE?

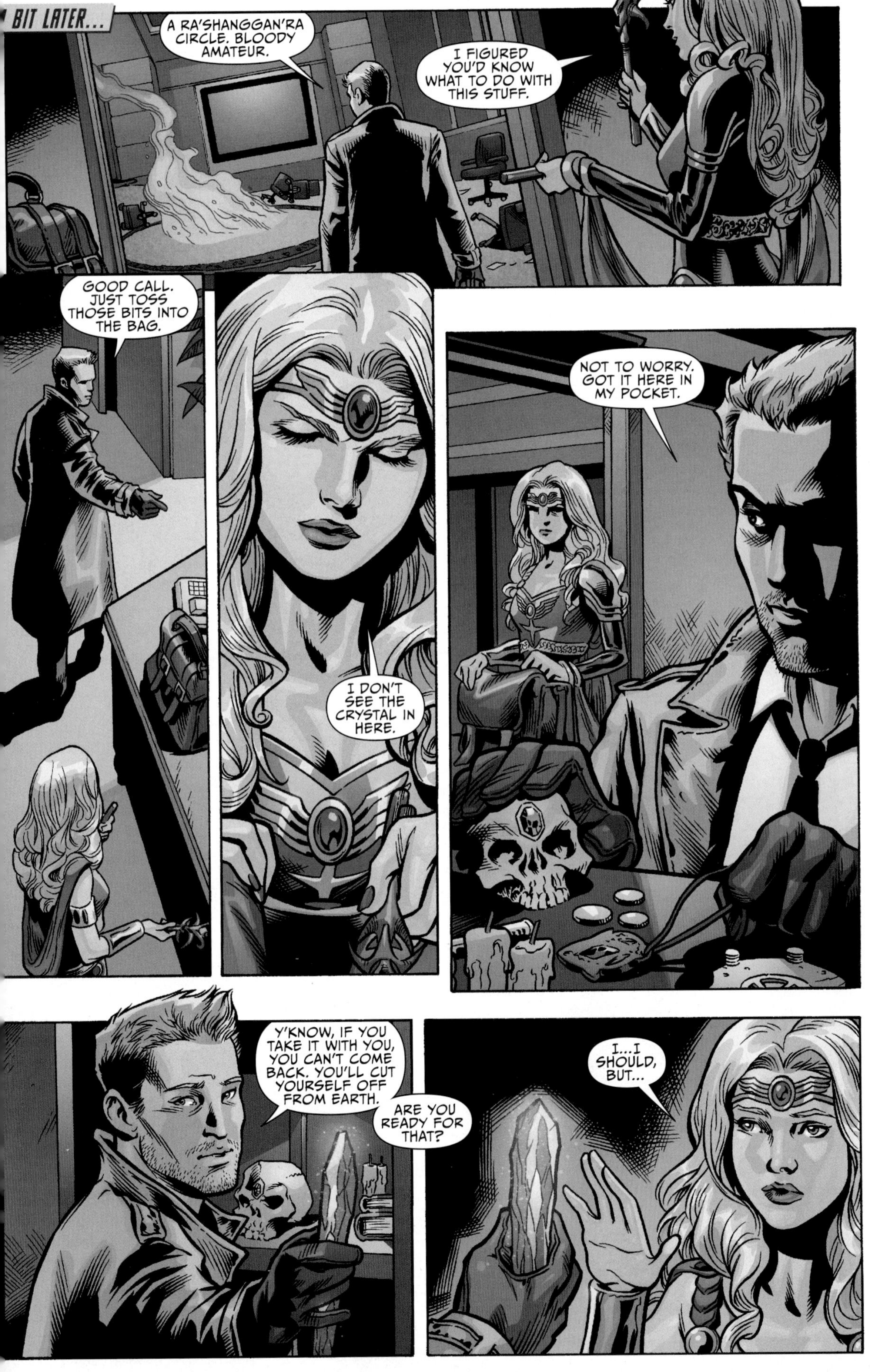
BIT LATER...
A RA'SHANGGAN'RA CIRCLE. BLOODY AMATEUR.
I FIGURED YOU'D KNOW WHAT TO DO WITH THIS STUFF.
GOOD CALL. JUST TOSS THOSE BITS INTO THE BAG.
I DON'T SEE THE CRYSTAL IN HERE.
NOT TO WORRY. GOT IT HERE IN MY POCKET.
Y'KNOW, IF YOU TAKE IT WITH YOU, YOU CAN'T COME BACK. YOU'LL CUT YOURSELF OFF FROM EARTH.
ARE YOU READY FOR THAT?
I...I SHOULD, BUT...

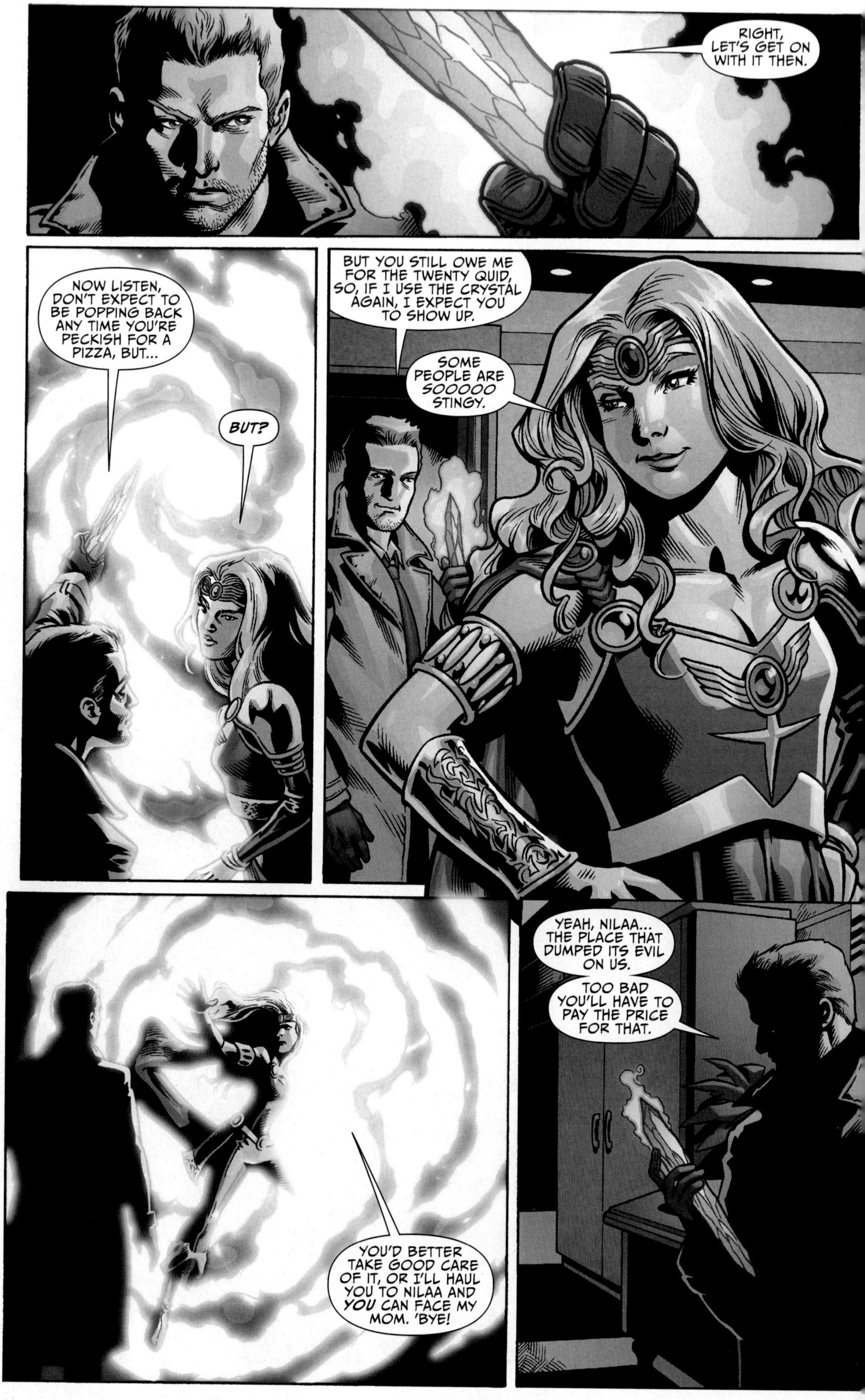
RIGHT, LET'S GET ON WITH IT THEN.
NOW LISTEN, DON'T EXPECT TO BE POPPING BACK ANY TIME YOU'RE PECKISH FOR A PIZZA, BUT...
BUT?
BUT YOU STILL OWE ME FOR THE TWENTY QUID, SO, IF I USE THE CRYSTAL AGAIN, I EXPECT YOU TO SHOW UP.
SOME PEOPLE ARE SOOOOO STINGY.
YOU'D BETTER TAKE GOOD CARE OF IT, OR I'LL HAUL YOU TO NILAA AND *YOU* CAN FACE MY MOM. 'BYE!
YEAH, NILAA... THE PLACE THAT DUMPED ITS EVIL ON US.
TOO BAD YOU'LL HAVE TO PAY THE PRICE FOR THAT.

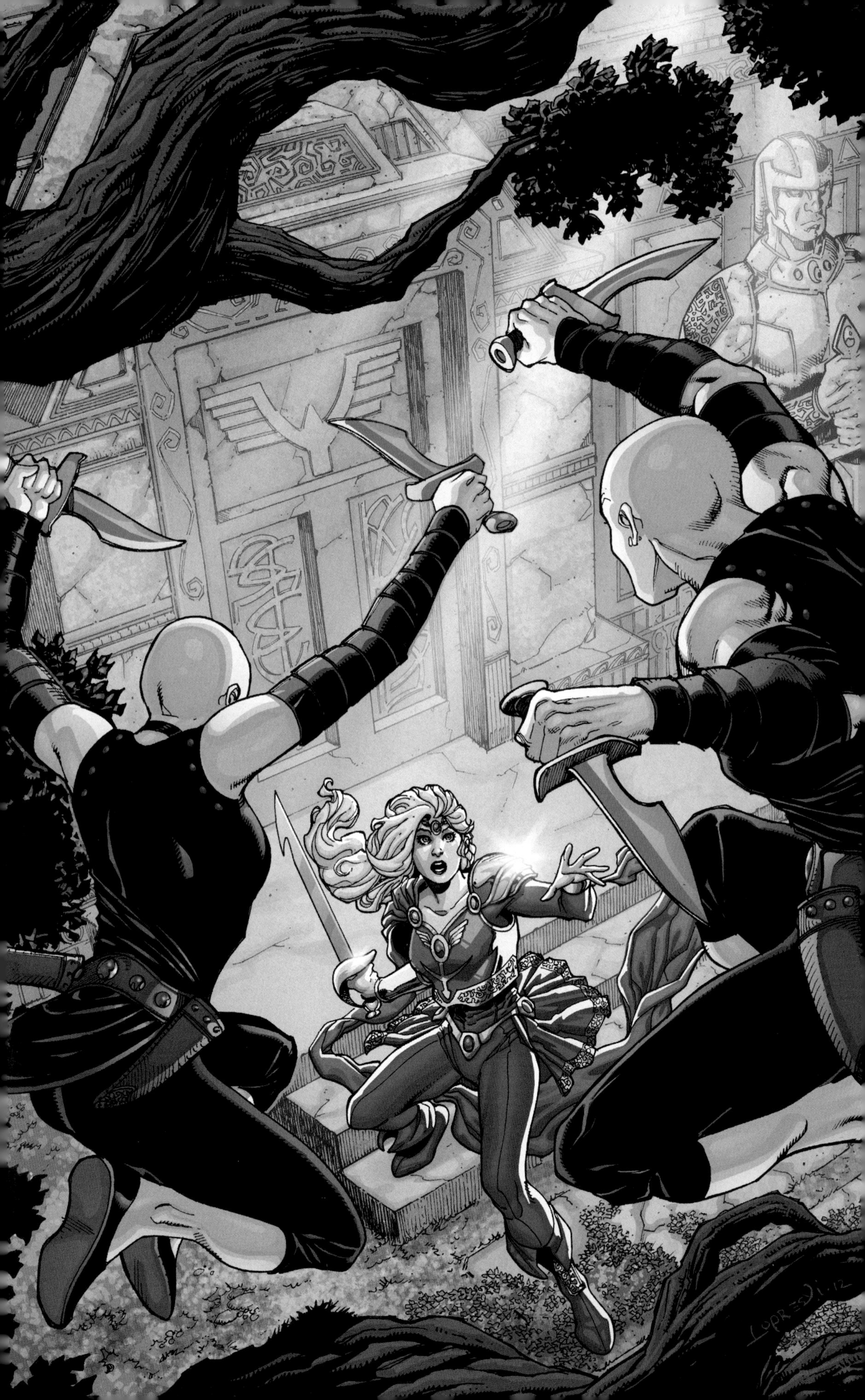

AMETHYST part six VYRIAN'S TOMB

CHRISTY MARX writer AARON LOPRESTI artist cover by AARON LOPRESTI & HI-FI

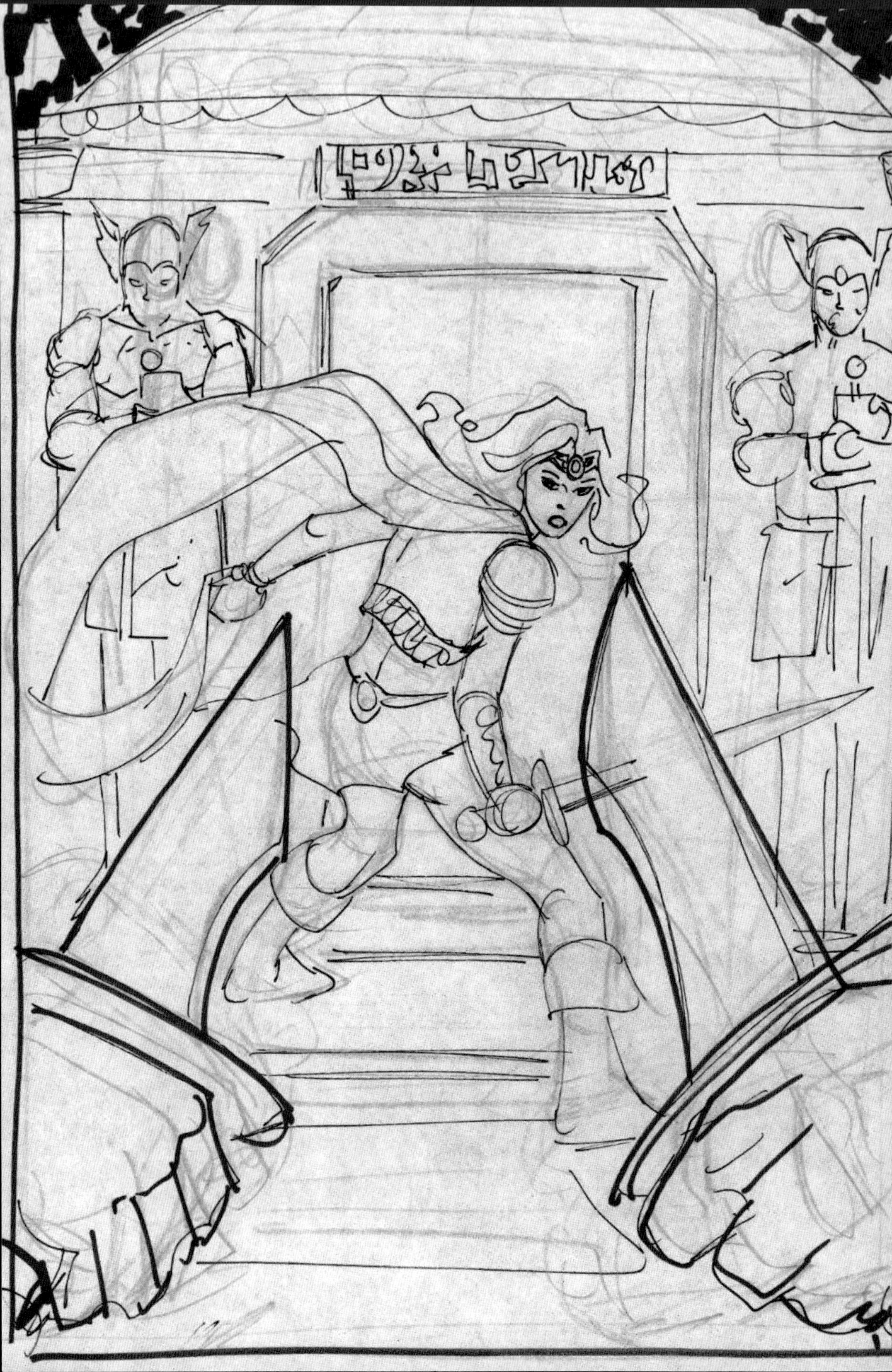

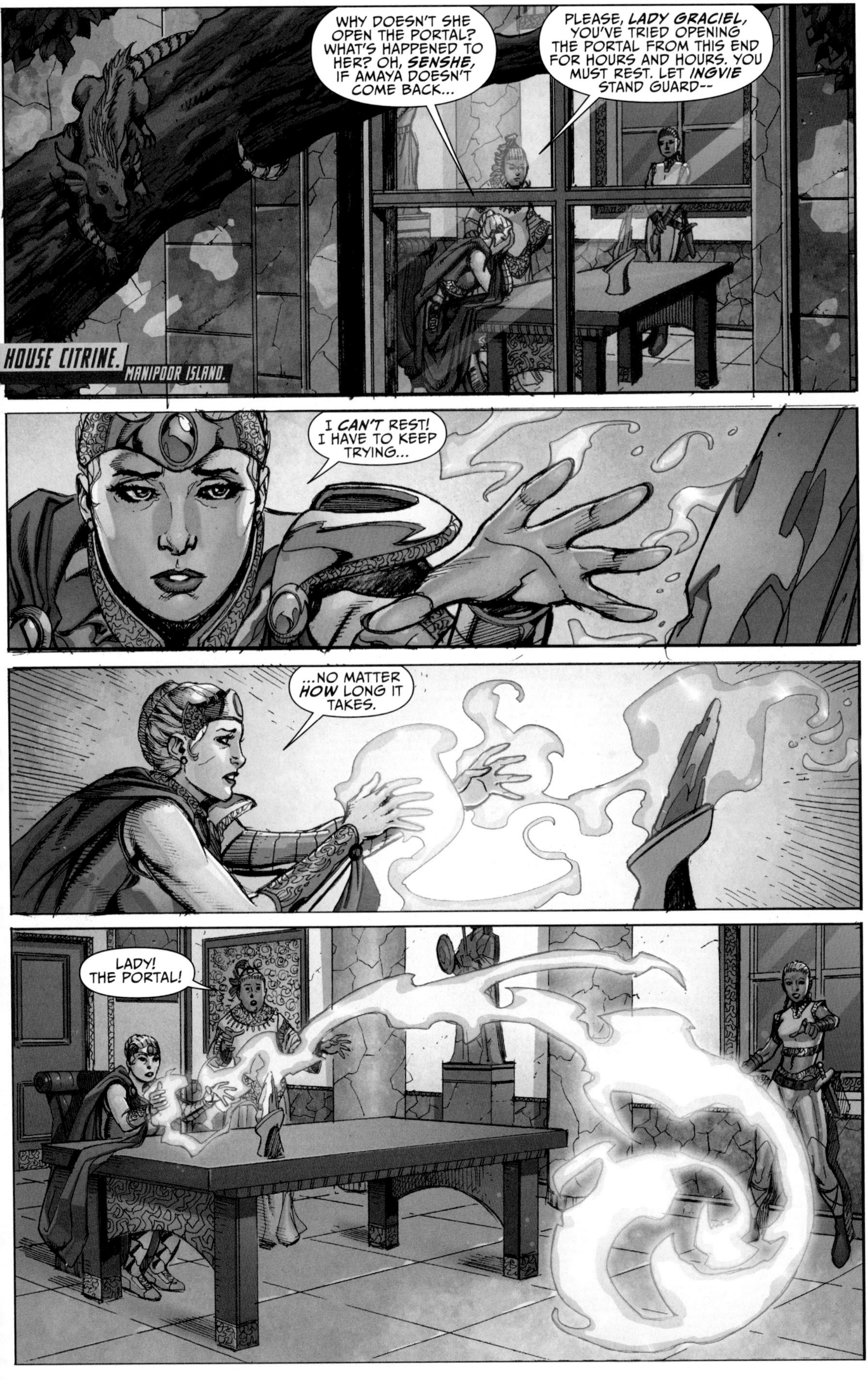
WHY DOESN'T SHE OPEN THE PORTAL? WHAT'S HAPPENED TO HER? OH, SENSHE, IF AMAYA DOESN'T COME BACK...
PLEASE, LADY GRACIEL, YOU'VE TRIED OPENING THE PORTAL FROM THIS END FOR HOURS AND HOURS. YOU MUST REST. LET INGVIE STAND GUARD--
HOUSE CITRINE.
MANIPOOR ISLAND.
I CAN'T REST! I HAVE TO KEEP TRYING...
...NO MATTER HOW LONG IT TAKES.
LADY! THE PORTAL!

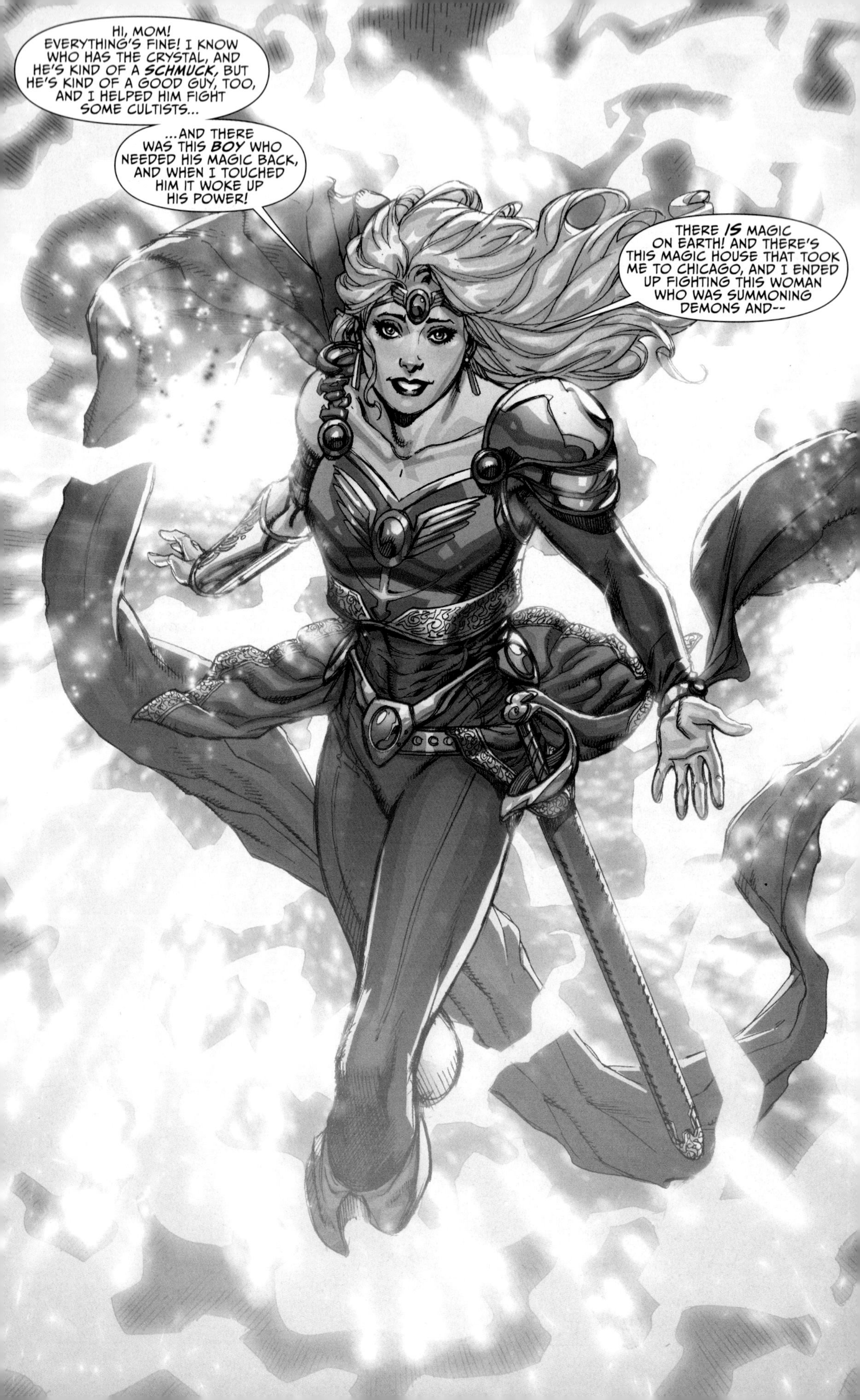
HI, MOM! EVERYTHING'S FINE! I KNOW WHO HAS THE CRYSTAL, AND HE'S KIND OF A SCHMUCK, BUT HE'S KIND OF A GOOD GUY, TOO, AND I HELPED HIM FIGHT SOME CULTISTS...
...AND THERE WAS THIS BOY WHO NEEDED HIS MAGIC BACK, AND WHEN I TOUCHED HIM IT WOKE UP HIS POWER!
THERE IS MAGIC ON EARTH! AND THERE'S THIS MAGIC HOUSE THAT TOOK ME TO CHICAGO, AND I ENDED UP FIGHTING THIS WOMAN WHO WAS SUMMONING DEMONS AND--

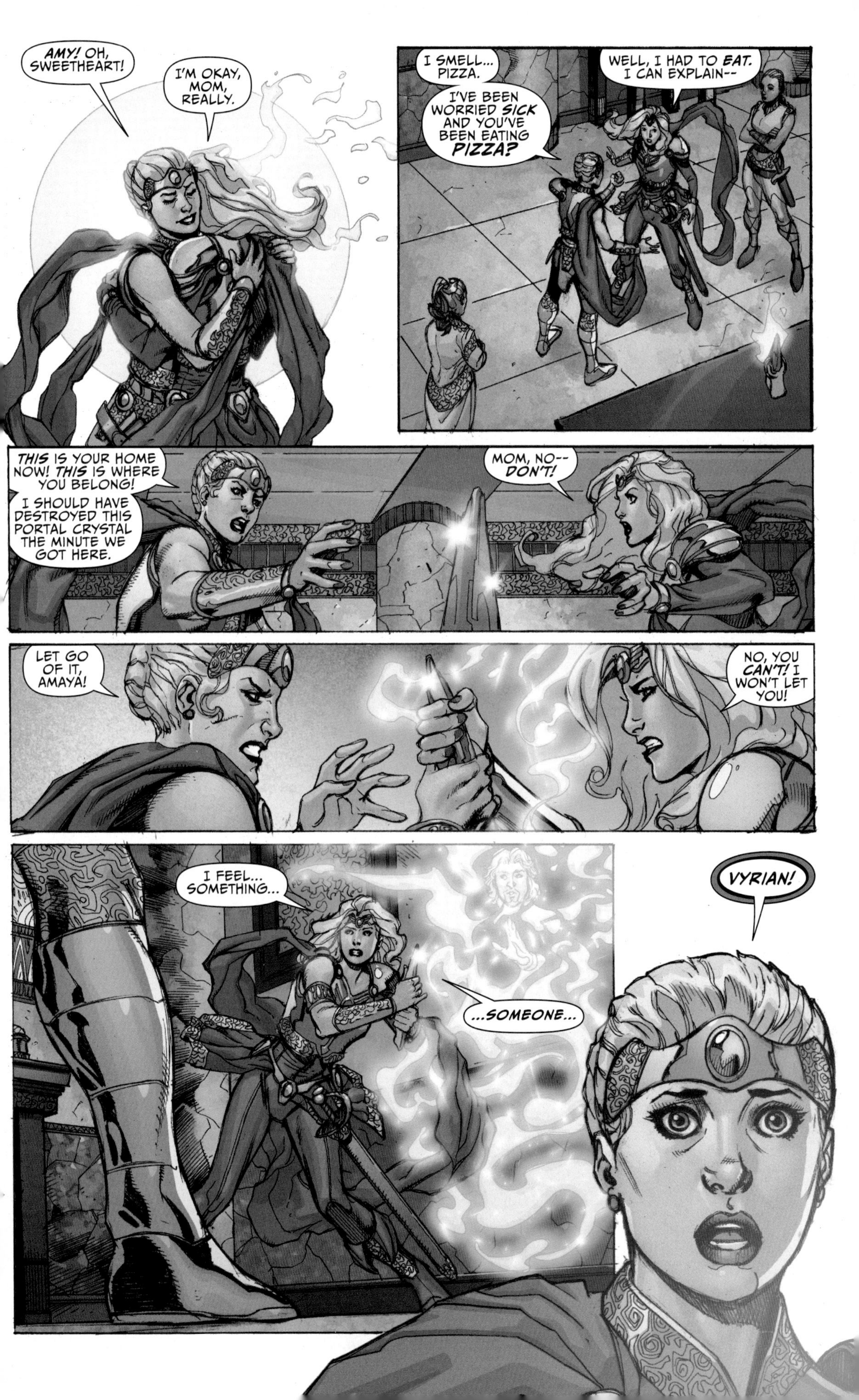

AMY! OH, SWEETHEART!
I'M OKAY, MOM, REALLY.
I SMELL... PIZZA.
I'VE BEEN WORRIED SICK AND YOU'VE BEEN EATING PIZZA?
WELL, I HAD TO EAT. I CAN EXPLAIN--
THIS IS YOUR HOME NOW! THIS IS WHERE YOU BELONG!
I SHOULD HAVE DESTROYED THIS PORTAL CRYSTAL THE MINUTE WE GOT HERE.
MOM, NO-- DON'T!
LET GO OF IT, AMAYA!
NO, YOU CAN'T! I WON'T LET YOU!
I FEEL... SOMETHING...
...SOMEONE...
VYRIAN!

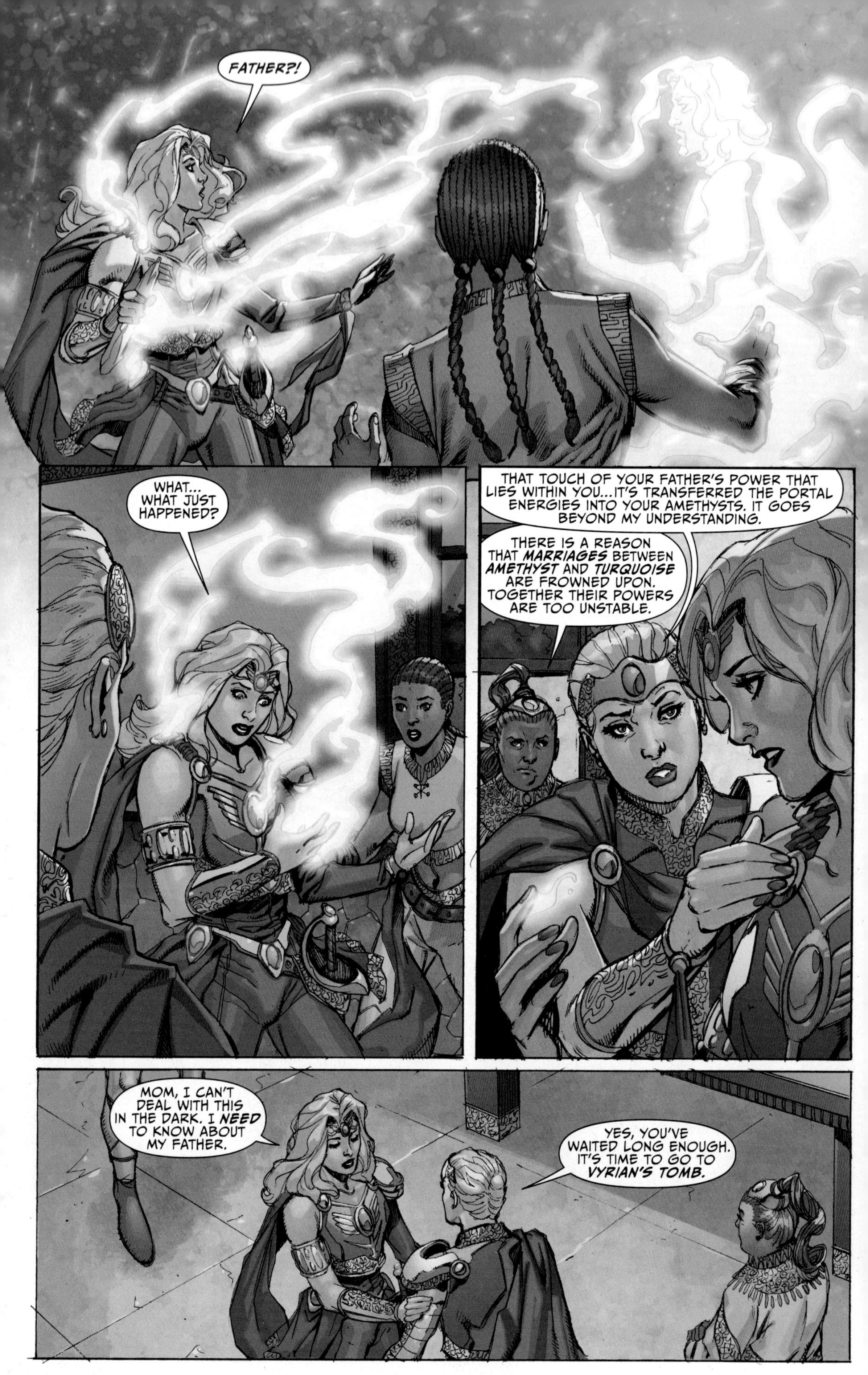
FATHER?!
WHAT... WHAT JUST HAPPENED?
THAT TOUCH OF YOUR FATHER'S POWER THAT LIES WITHIN YOU...IT'S TRANSFERRED THE PORTAL ENERGIES INTO YOUR AMETHYSTS. IT GOES BEYOND MY UNDERSTANDING.
THERE IS A REASON THAT ***MARRIAGES*** BETWEEN ***AMETHYST*** AND ***TURQUOISE*** ARE FROWNED UPON. TOGETHER THEIR POWERS ARE TOO UNSTABLE.
MOM, I CAN'T DEAL WITH THIS IN THE DARK. I ***NEED*** TO KNOW ABOUT MY FATHER.
YES, YOU'VE WAITED LONG ENOUGH. IT'S TIME TO GO TO ***VYRIAN'S TOMB.***

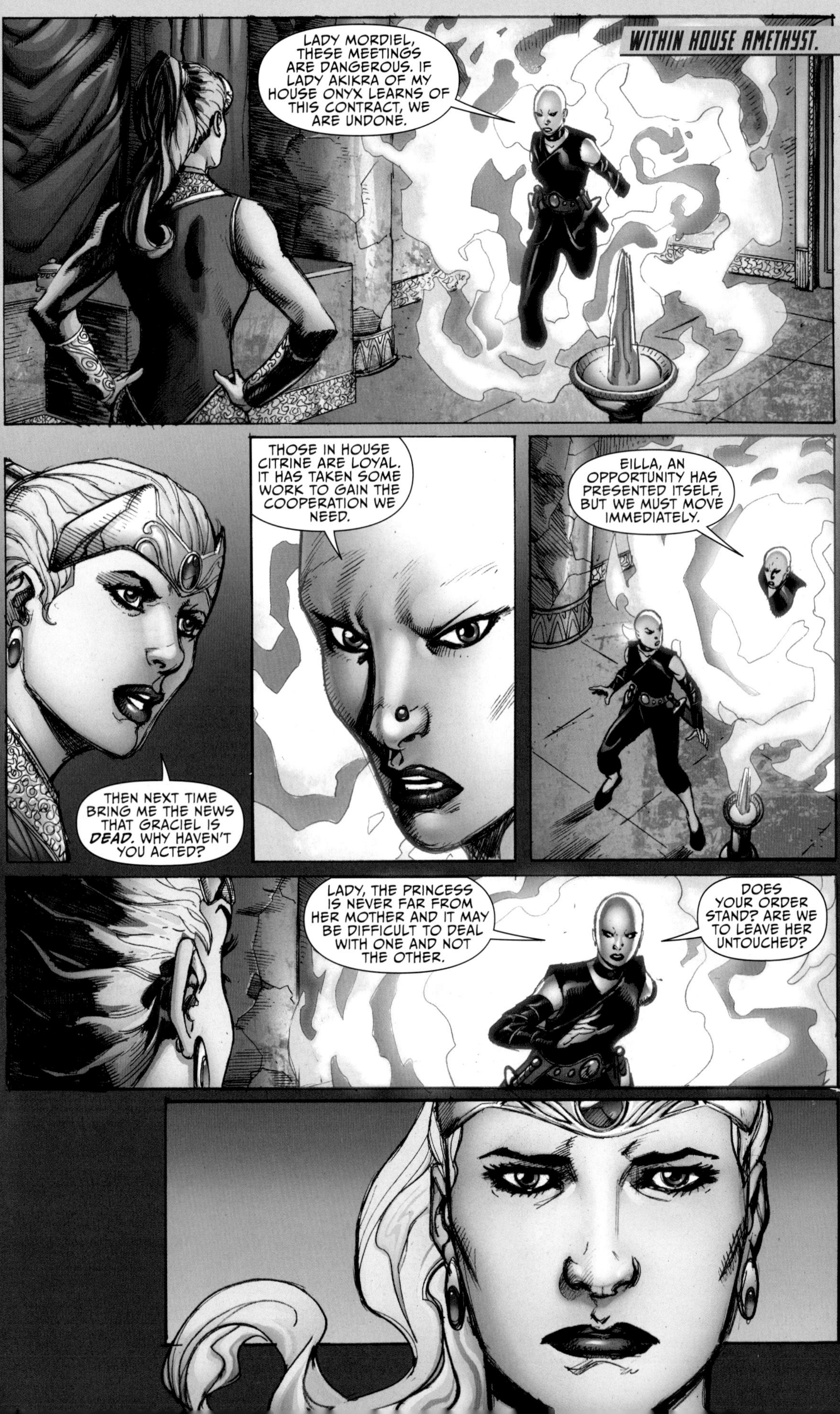
WITHIN HOUSE AMETHYST.
LADY MORDIEL, THESE MEETINGS ARE DANGEROUS. IF LADY AKIKRA OF MY HOUSE ONYX LEARNS OF THIS CONTRACT, WE ARE UNDONE.
THOSE IN HOUSE CITRINE ARE LOYAL. IT HAS TAKEN SOME WORK TO GAIN THE COOPERATION WE NEED.
THEN NEXT TIME BRING ME THE NEWS THAT GRACIEL IS DEAD. WHY HAVEN'T YOU ACTED?
EILLA, AN OPPORTUNITY HAS PRESENTED ITSELF, BUT WE MUST MOVE IMMEDIATELY.
LADY, THE PRINCESS IS NEVER FAR FROM HER MOTHER AND IT MAY BE DIFFICULT TO DEAL WITH ONE AND NOT THE OTHER.
DOES YOUR ORDER STAND? ARE WE TO LEAVE HER UNTOUCHED?

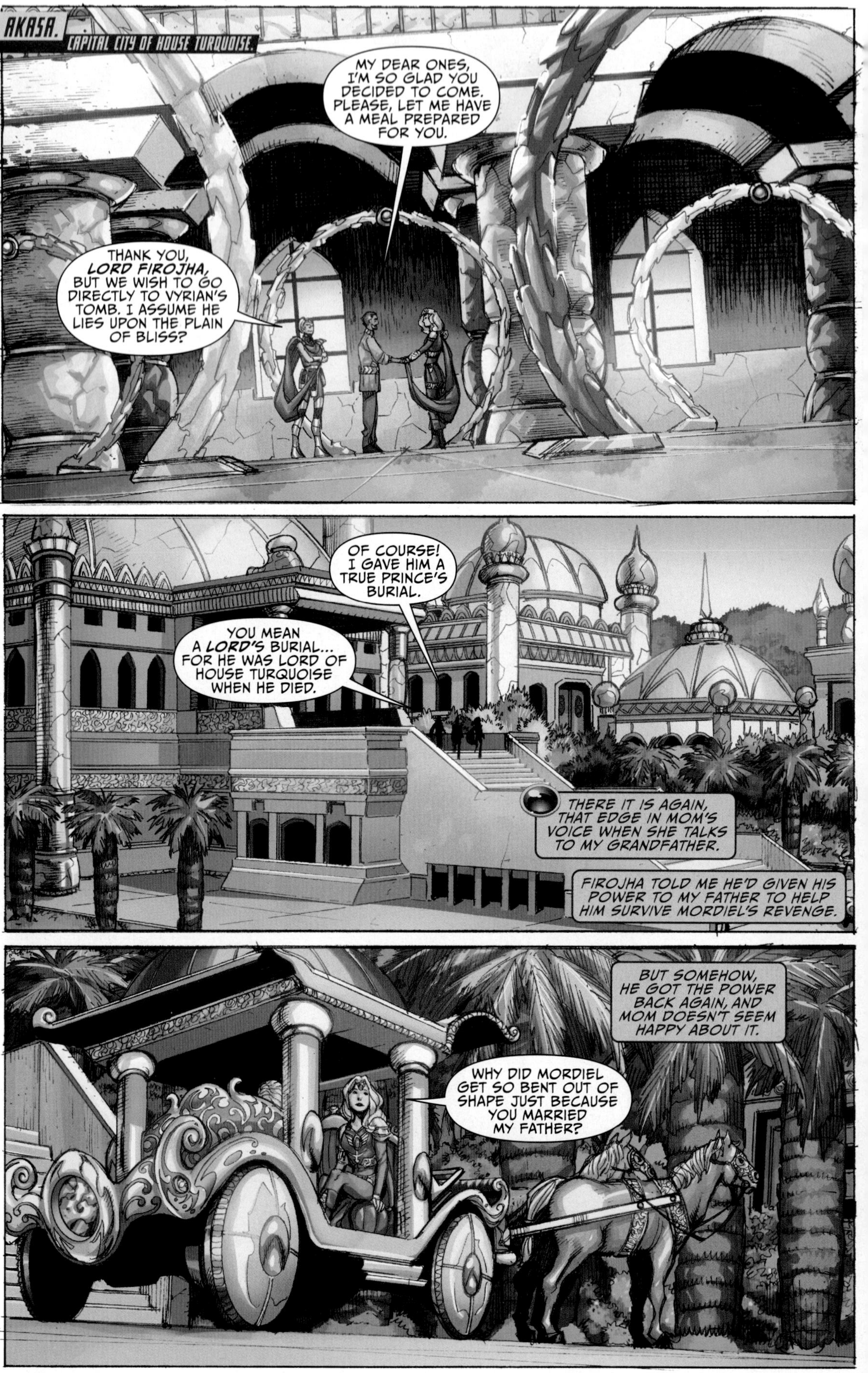
AKASA.
CAPITAL CITY OF HOUSE TURQUOISE.
MY DEAR ONES, I'M SO GLAD YOU DECIDED TO COME. PLEASE, LET ME HAVE A MEAL PREPARED FOR YOU.
THANK YOU, LORD FIROJHA, BUT WE WISH TO GO DIRECTLY TO VYRIAN'S TOMB. I ASSUME HE LIES UPON THE PLAIN OF BLISS?
OF COURSE! I GAVE HIM A TRUE PRINCE'S BURIAL.
YOU MEAN A LORD'S BURIAL... FOR HE WAS LORD OF HOUSE TURQUOISE WHEN HE DIED.
THERE IT IS AGAIN, THAT EDGE IN MOM'S VOICE WHEN SHE TALKS TO MY GRANDFATHER.
FIROJHA TOLD ME HE'D GIVEN HIS POWER TO MY FATHER TO HELP HIM SURVIVE MORDIEL'S REVENGE.
BUT SOMEHOW, HE GOT THE POWER BACK AGAIN, AND MOM DOESN'T SEEM HAPPY ABOUT IT.
WHY DID MORDIEL GET SO BENT OUT OF SHAPE JUST BECAUSE YOU MARRIED MY FATHER?

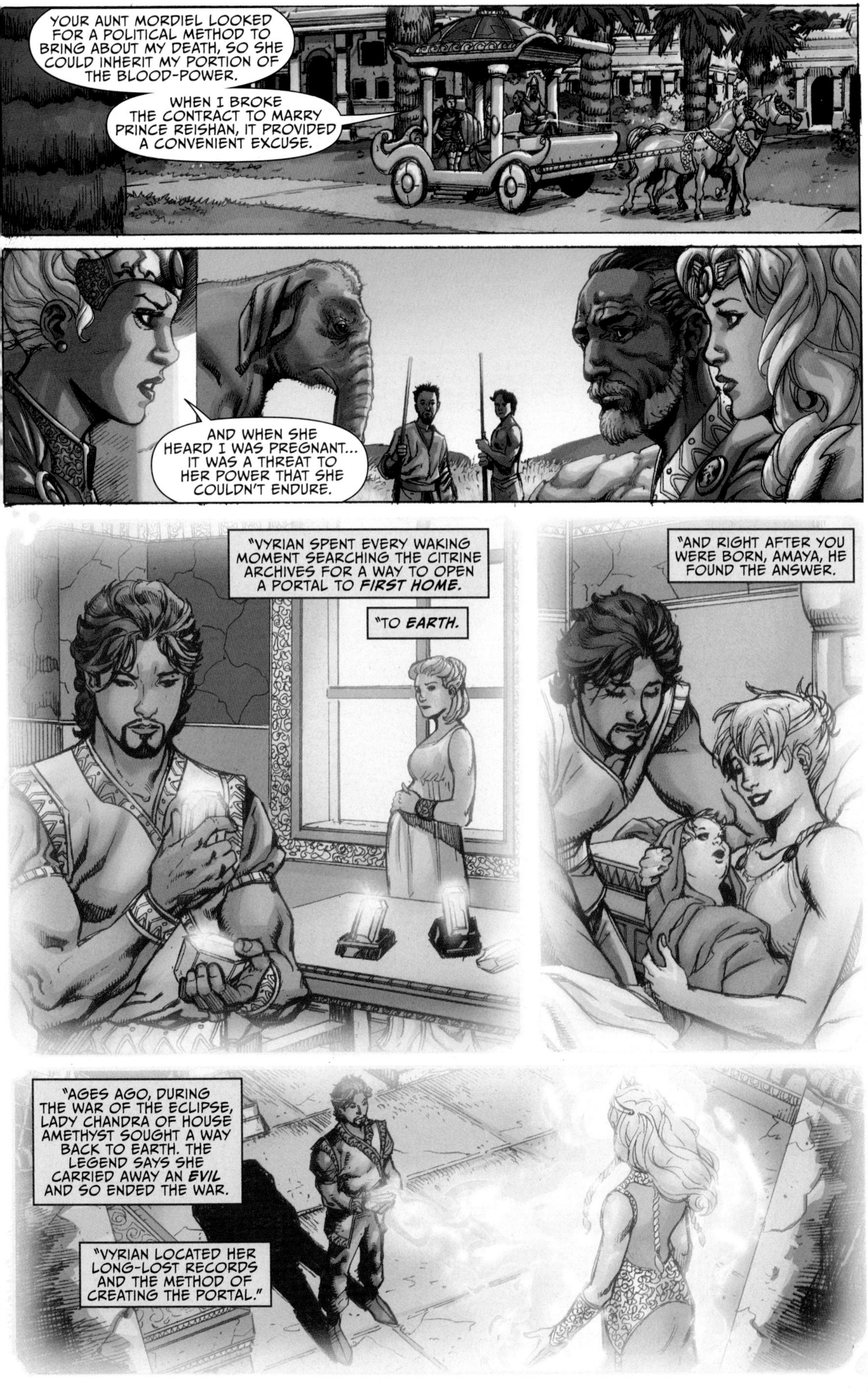
YOUR AUNT MORDIEL LOOKED FOR A POLITICAL METHOD TO BRING ABOUT MY DEATH, SO SHE COULD INHERIT MY PORTION OF THE BLOOD-POWER.
WHEN I BROKE THE CONTRACT TO MARRY PRINCE REISHAN, IT PROVIDED A CONVENIENT EXCUSE.
AND WHEN SHE HEARD I WAS PREGNANT... IT WAS A THREAT TO HER POWER THAT SHE COULDN'T ENDURE.
"VYRIAN SPENT EVERY WAKING MOMENT SEARCHING THE CITRINE ARCHIVES FOR A WAY TO OPEN A PORTAL TO *FIRST HOME.*
"TO *EARTH.*
"AND RIGHT AFTER YOU WERE BORN, AMAYA, HE FOUND THE ANSWER.
"AGES AGO, DURING THE WAR OF THE ECLIPSE, LADY CHANDRA OF HOUSE AMETHYST SOUGHT A WAY BACK TO EARTH. THE LEGEND SAYS SHE CARRIED AWAY AN *EVIL* AND SO ENDED THE WAR.
"VYRIAN LOCATED HER LONG-LOST RECORDS AND THE METHOD OF CREATING THE PORTAL."

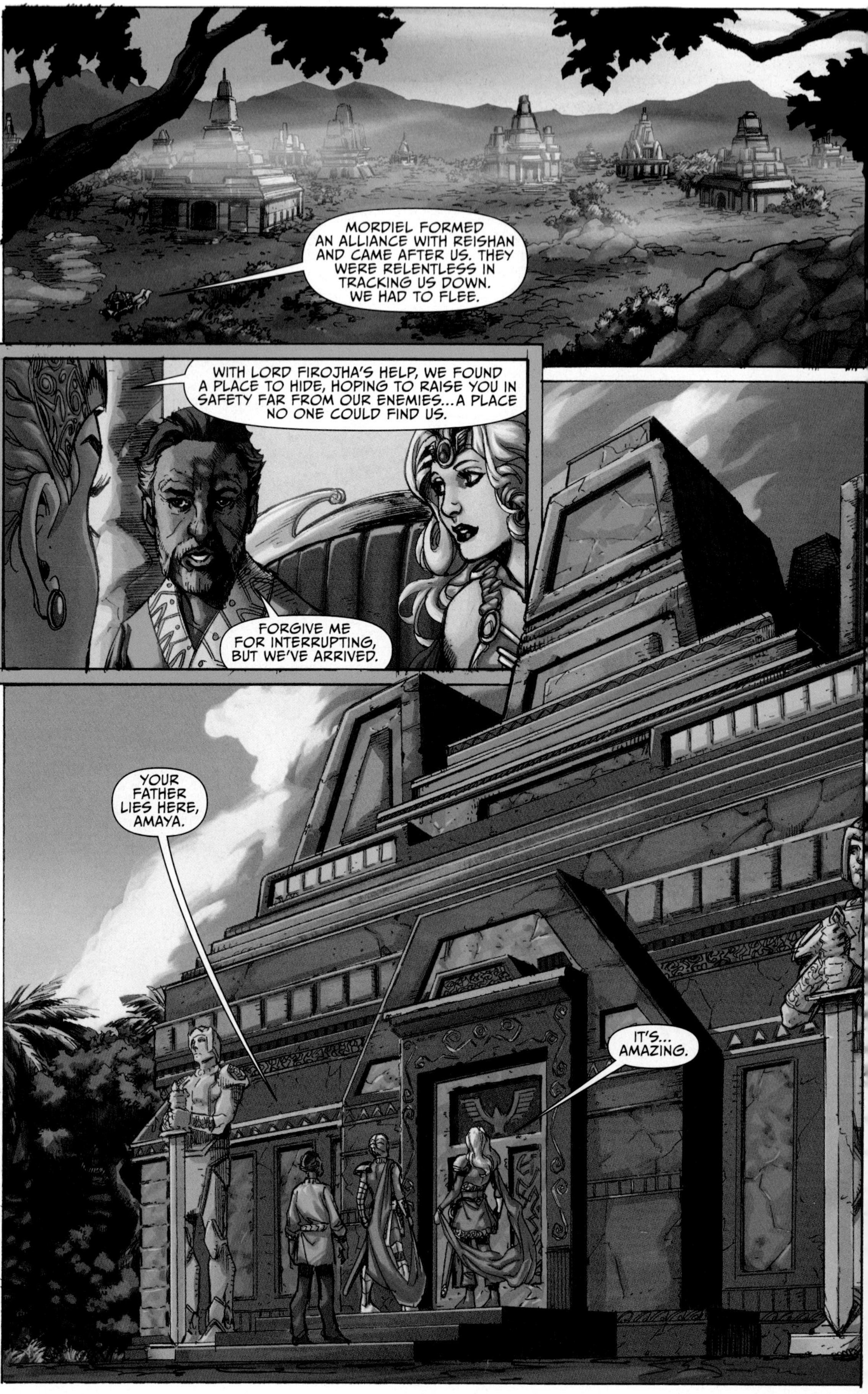
MORDIEL FORMED AN ALLIANCE WITH REISHAN AND CAME AFTER US. THEY WERE RELENTLESS IN TRACKING US DOWN. WE HAD TO FLEE.
WITH LORD FIROJHA'S HELP, WE FOUND A PLACE TO HIDE, HOPING TO RAISE YOU IN SAFETY FAR FROM OUR ENEMIES...A PLACE NO ONE COULD FIND US.
FORGIVE ME FOR INTERRUPTING, BUT WE'VE ARRIVED.
YOUR FATHER LIES HERE, AMAYA.
IT'S... AMAZING.

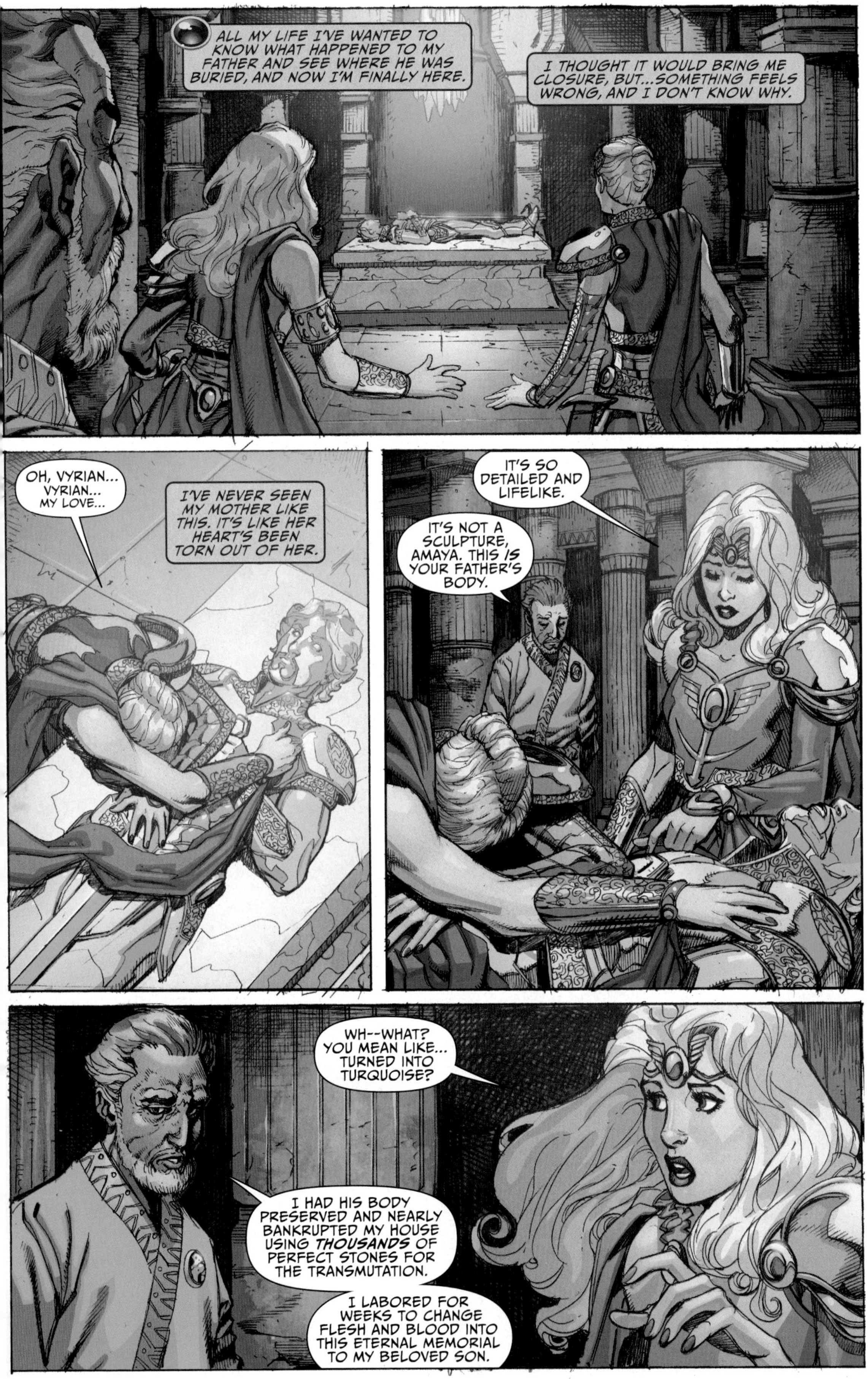
ALL MY LIFE I'VE WANTED TO KNOW WHAT HAPPENED TO MY FATHER AND SEE WHERE HE WAS BURIED, AND NOW I'M FINALLY HERE.
I THOUGHT IT WOULD BRING ME CLOSURE, BUT...SOMETHING FEELS WRONG, AND I DON'T KNOW WHY.
OH, VYRIAN... VYRIAN... MY LOVE...
I'VE NEVER SEEN MY MOTHER LIKE THIS. IT'S LIKE HER HEART'S BEEN TORN OUT OF HER.
IT'S SO DETAILED AND LIFELIKE.
IT'S NOT A SCULPTURE, AMAYA. THIS IS YOUR FATHER'S BODY.
WH--WHAT? YOU MEAN LIKE... TURNED INTO TURQUOISE?
I HAD HIS BODY PRESERVED AND NEARLY BANKRUPTED MY HOUSE USING THOUSANDS OF PERFECT STONES FOR THE TRANSMUTATION.
I LABORED FOR WEEKS TO CHANGE FLESH AND BLOOD INTO THIS ETERNAL MEMORIAL TO MY BELOVED SON.

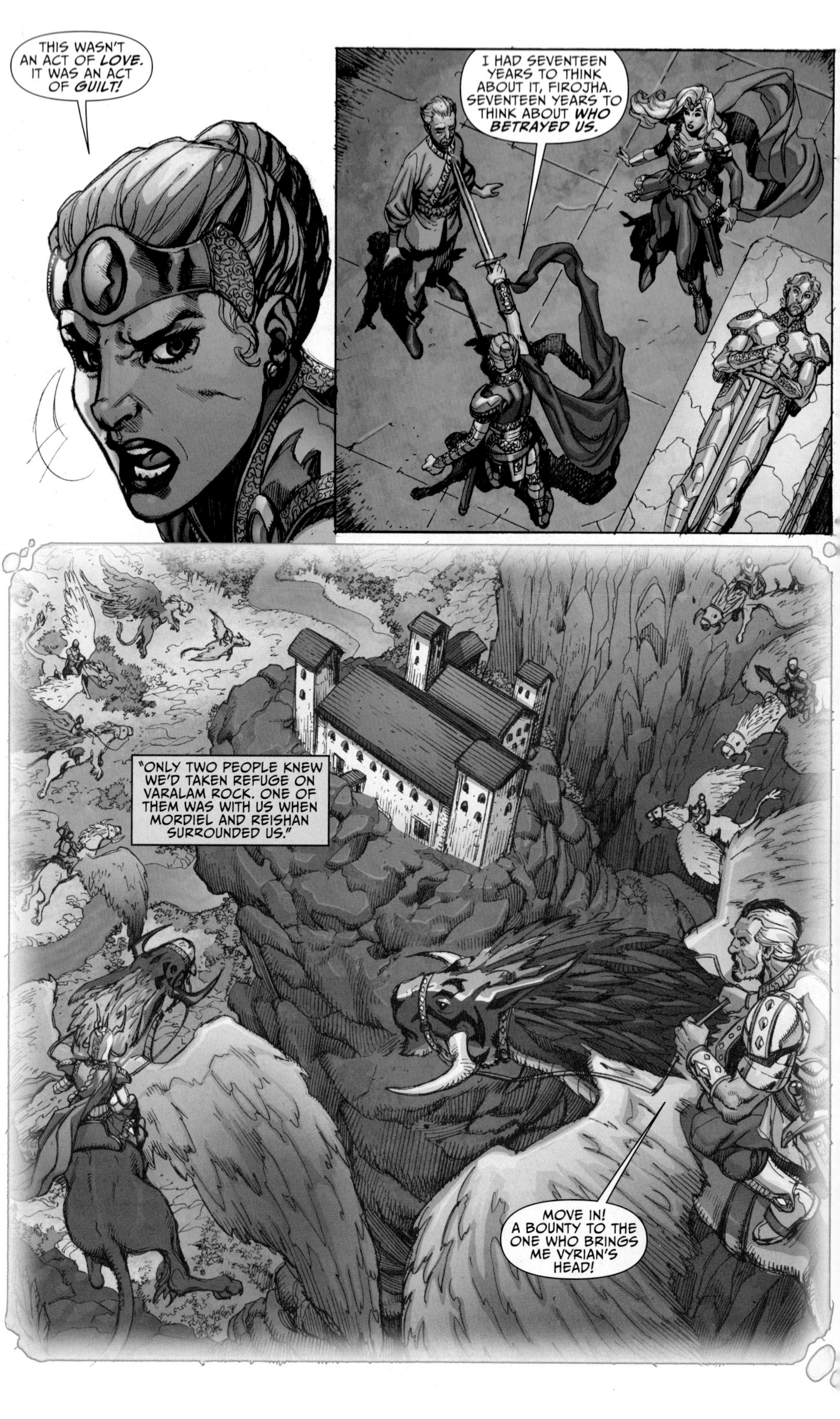
THIS WASN'T AN ACT OF LOVE. IT WAS AN ACT OF GUILT!
I HAD SEVENTEEN YEARS TO THINK ABOUT IT, FIROJHA. SEVENTEEN YEARS TO THINK ABOUT WHO BETRAYED US.
"ONLY TWO PEOPLE KNEW WE'D TAKEN REFUGE ON VARALAM ROCK. ONE OF THEM WAS WITH US WHEN MORDIEL AND REISHAN SURROUNDED US."
MOVE IN! A BOUNTY TO THE ONE WHO BRINGS ME VYRIAN'S HEAD!

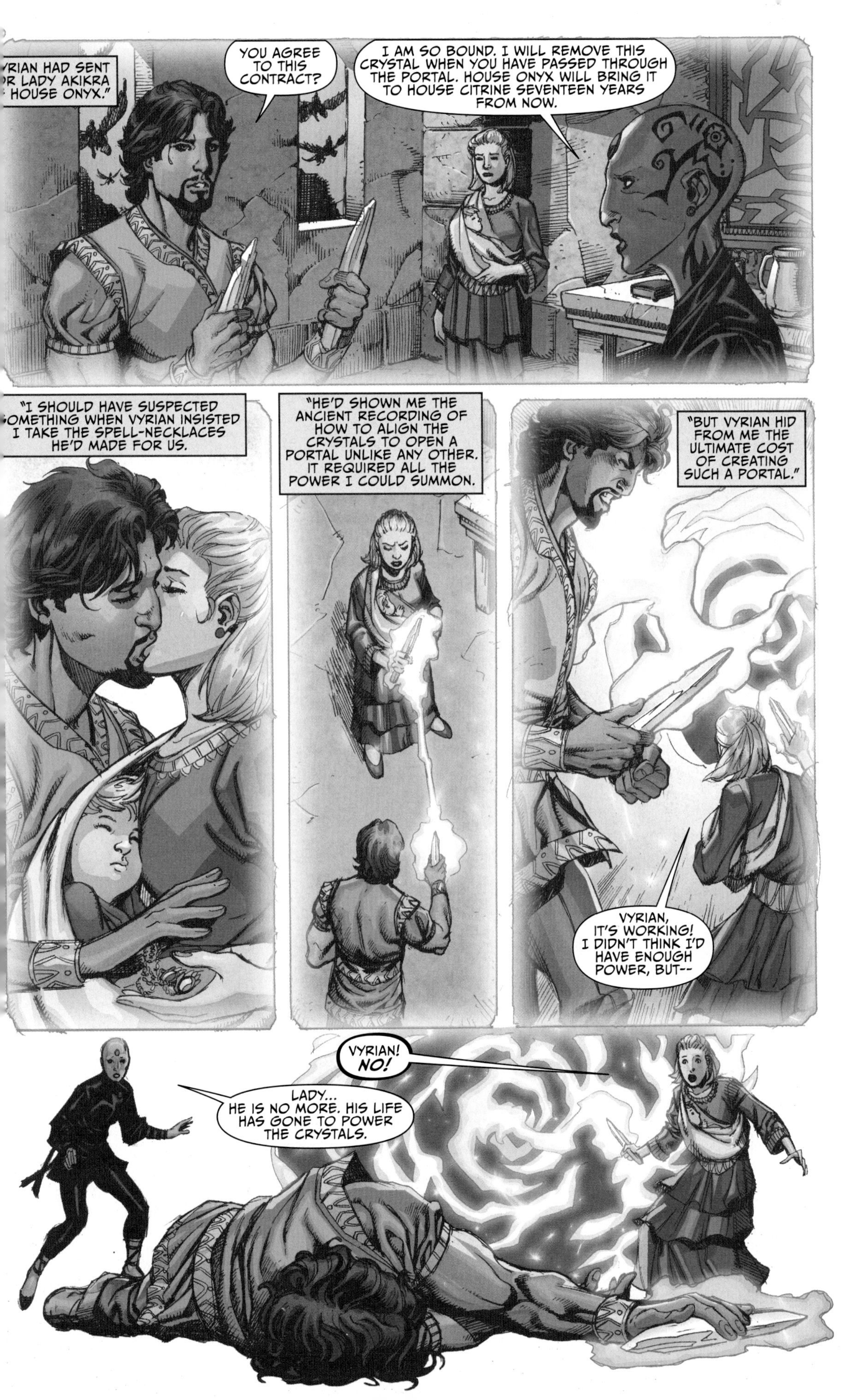

VYRIAN HAD SENT FOR LADY AKIKRA OF HOUSE ONYX."
YOU AGREE TO THIS CONTRACT?
I AM SO BOUND. I WILL REMOVE THIS CRYSTAL WHEN YOU HAVE PASSED THROUGH THE PORTAL. HOUSE ONYX WILL BRING IT TO HOUSE CITRINE SEVENTEEN YEARS FROM NOW.
"I SHOULD HAVE SUSPECTED SOMETHING WHEN VYRIAN INSISTED I TAKE THE SPELL-NECKLACES HE'D MADE FOR US.
"HE'D SHOWN ME THE ANCIENT RECORDING OF HOW TO ALIGN THE CRYSTALS TO OPEN A PORTAL UNLIKE ANY OTHER. IT REQUIRED ALL THE POWER I COULD SUMMON.
"BUT VYRIAN HID FROM ME THE ULTIMATE COST OF CREATING SUCH A PORTAL."
VYRIAN, IT'S WORKING! I DIDN'T THINK I'D HAVE ENOUGH POWER, BUT--
VYRIAN! NO!
LADY... HE IS NO MORE. HIS LIFE HAS GONE TO POWER THE CRYSTALS.

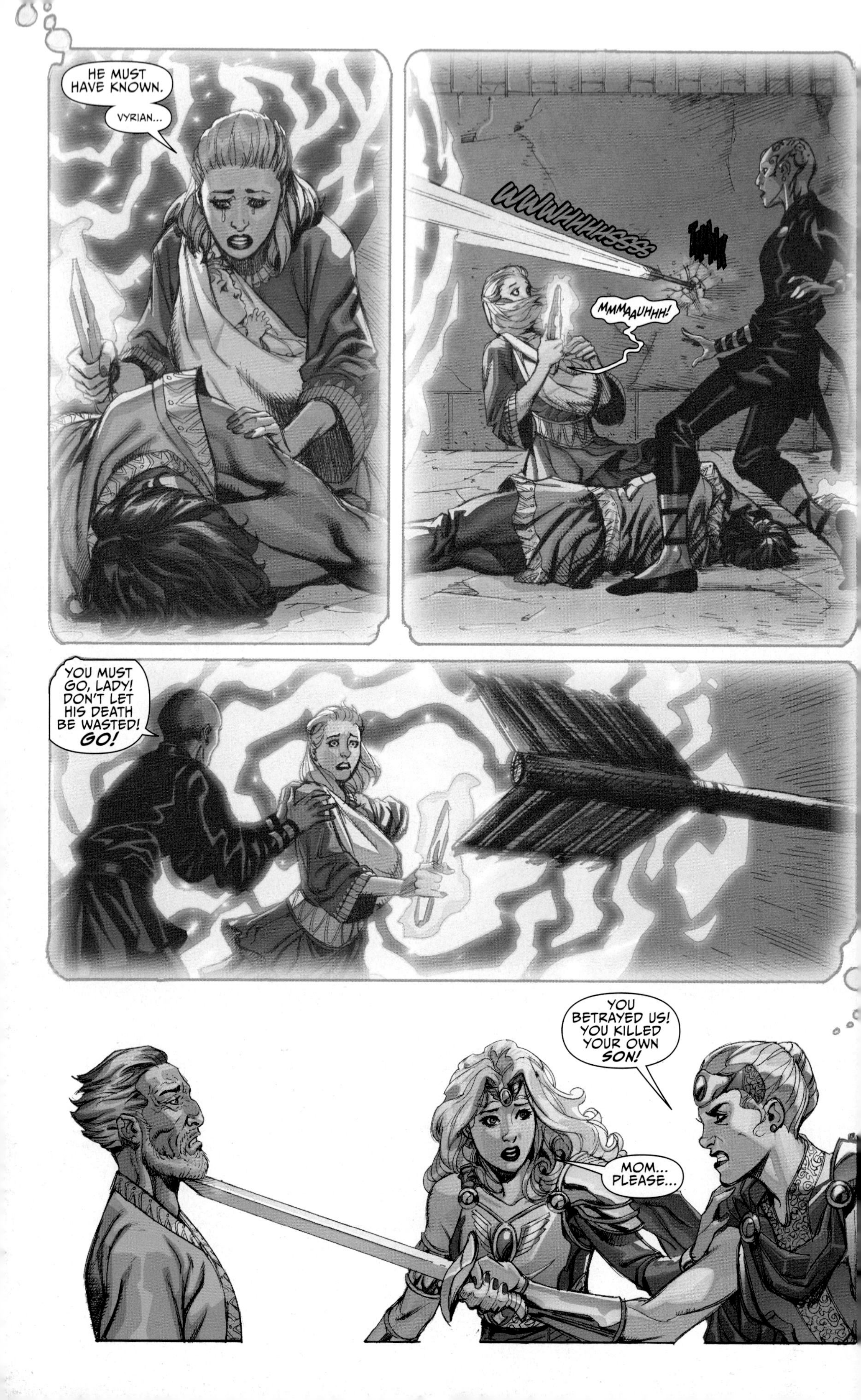
HE MUST HAVE KNOWN.
VYRIAN...
MMMAAUHHH!
YOU MUST GO, LADY! DON'T LET HIS DEATH BE WASTED! GO!
YOU BETRAYED US! YOU KILLED YOUR OWN SON!
MOM... PLEASE...

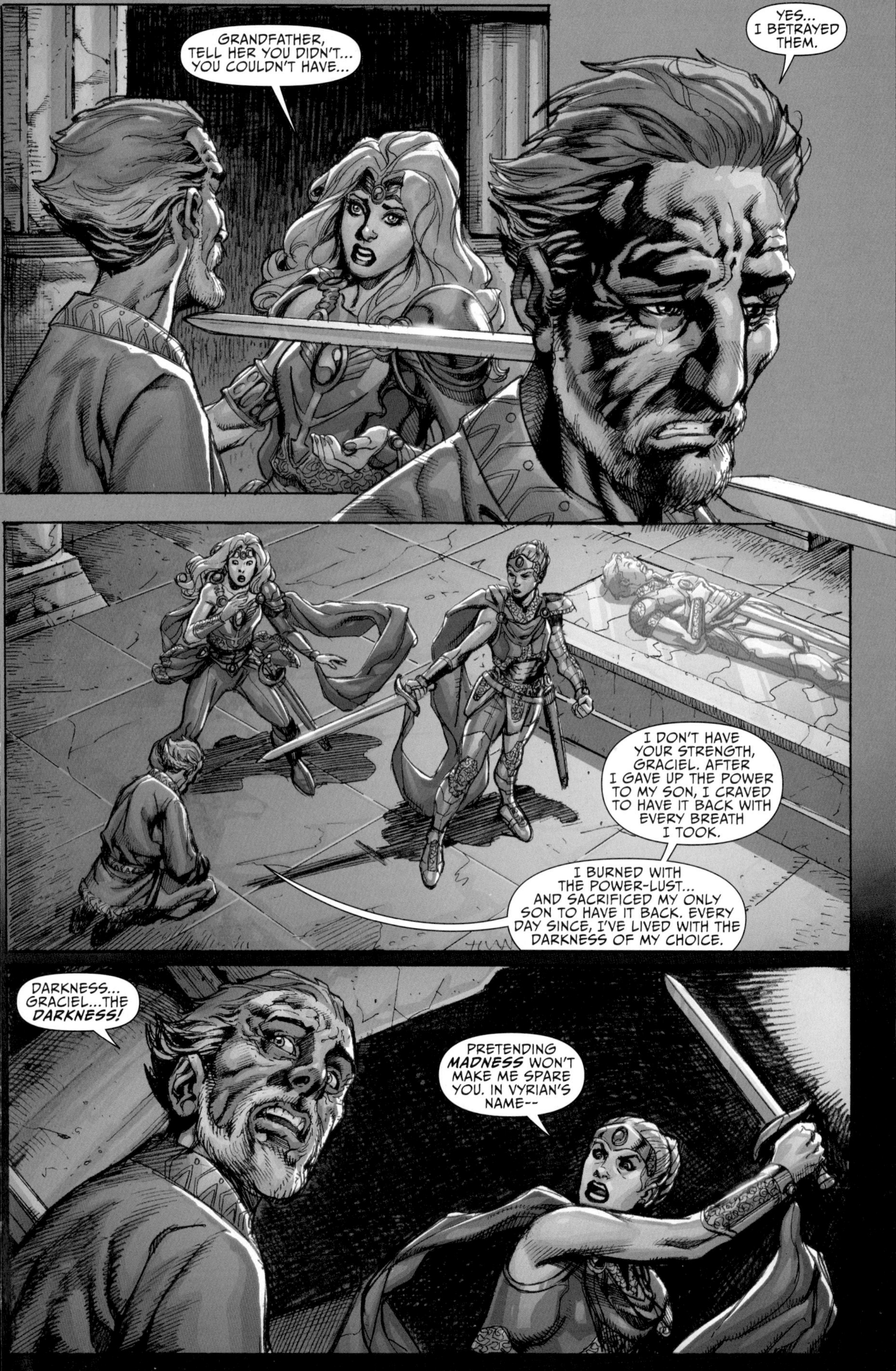
GRANDFATHER, TELL HER YOU DIDN'T... YOU COULDN'T HAVE...
YES... I BETRAYED THEM.
I DON'T HAVE YOUR STRENGTH, GRACIEL. AFTER I GAVE UP THE POWER TO MY SON, I CRAVED TO HAVE IT BACK WITH EVERY BREATH I TOOK.
I BURNED WITH THE POWER-LUST... AND SACRIFICED MY ONLY SON TO HAVE IT BACK. EVERY DAY SINCE, I'VE LIVED WITH THE DARKNESS OF MY CHOICE.
DARKNESS... GRACIEL...THE *DARKNESS!*
PRETENDING *MADNESS* WON'T MAKE ME SPARE YOU. IN VYRIAN'S NAME--

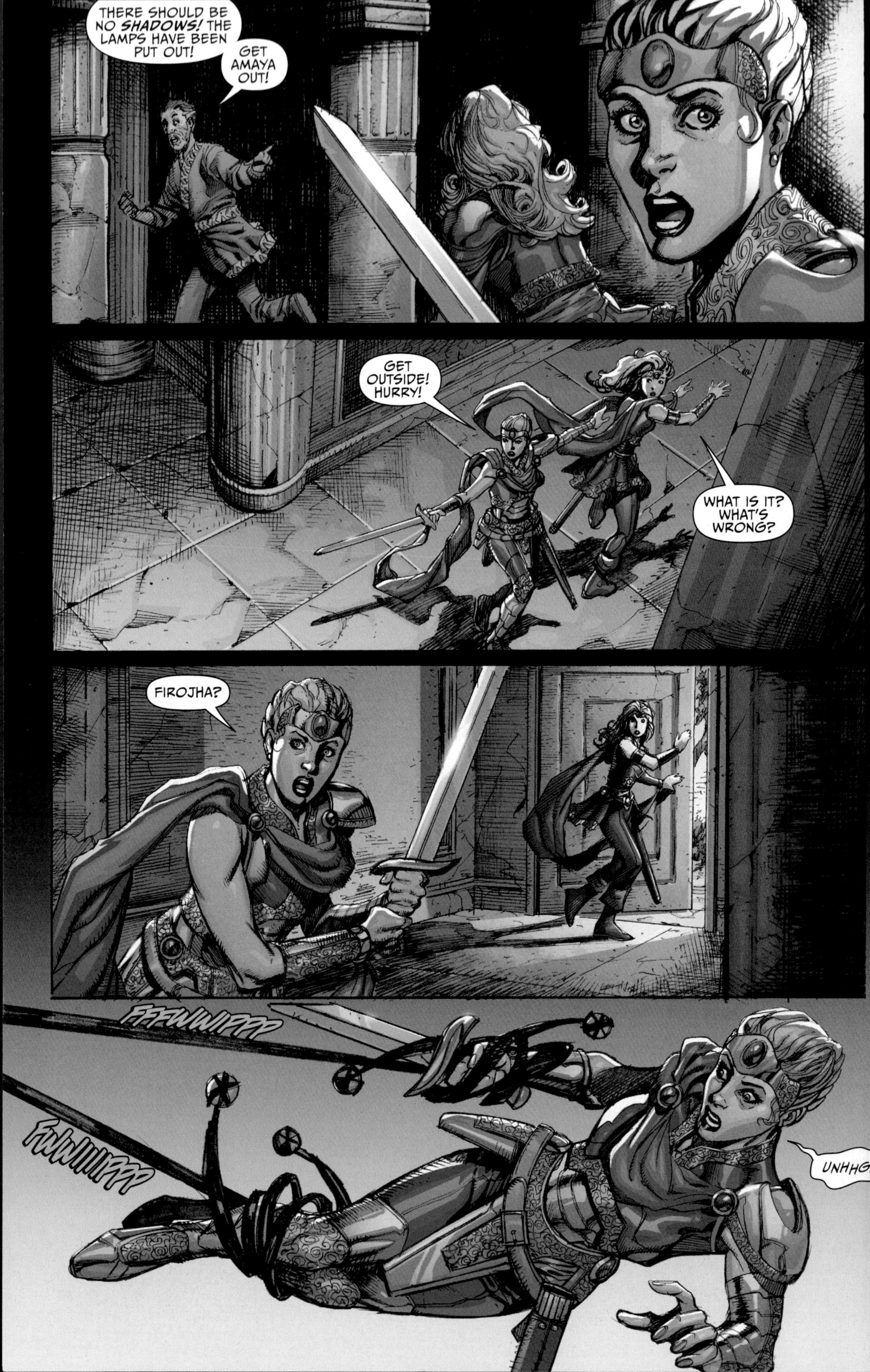
THERE SHOULD BE NO SHADOWS! THE LAMPS HAVE BEEN PUT OUT!
GET AMAYA OUT!
GET OUTSIDE! HURRY!
WHAT IS IT? WHAT'S WRONG?
FIROJHA?
FFFWWIIPPP
FWWIIIIPPP
UNHHG

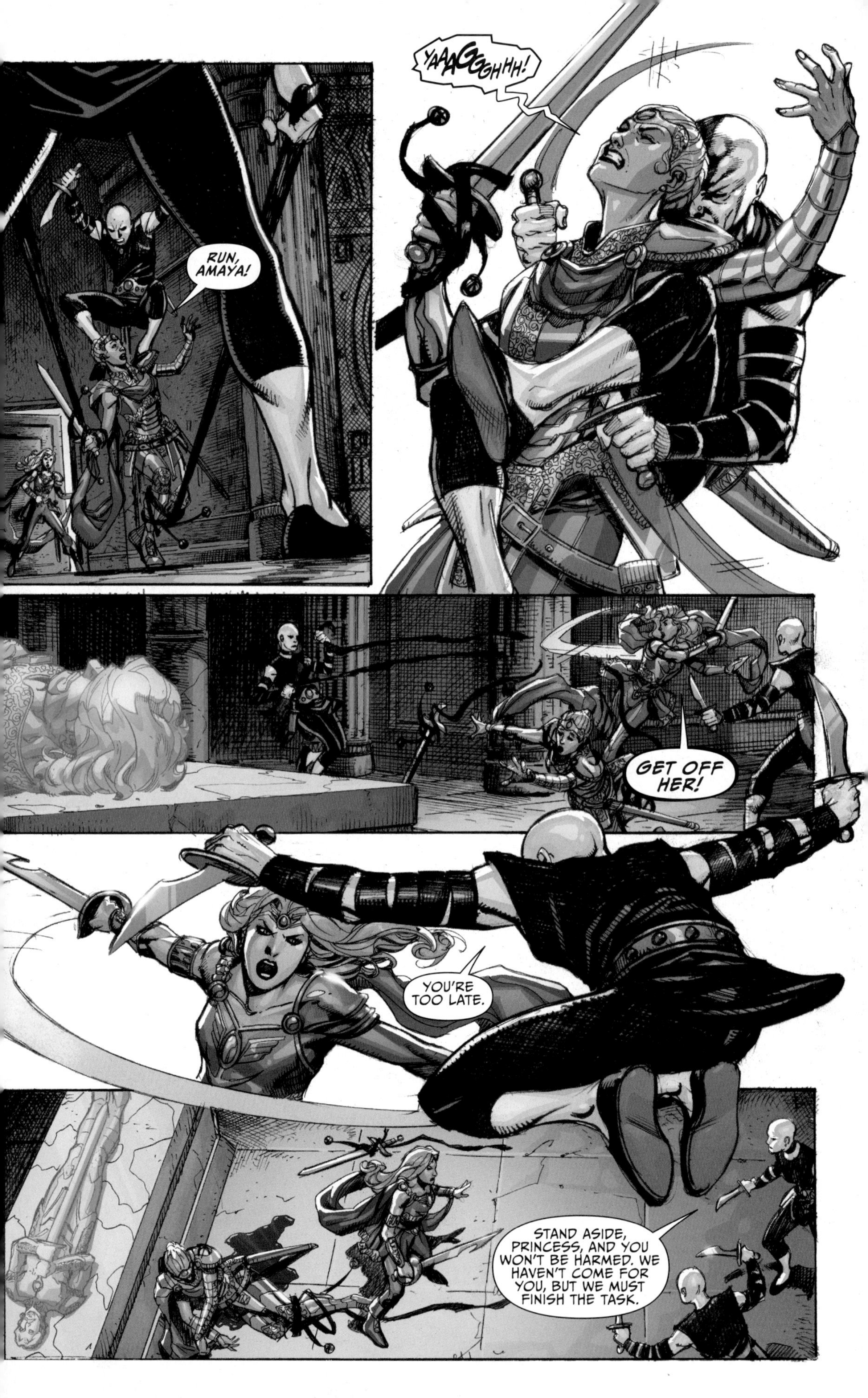
RUN, AMAYA!
YAAAGGGHHH!
GET OFF HER!
YOU'RE TOO LATE.
STAND ASIDE, PRINCESS, AND YOU WON'T BE HARMED. WE HAVEN'T COME FOR YOU, BUT WE MUST FINISH THE TASK.

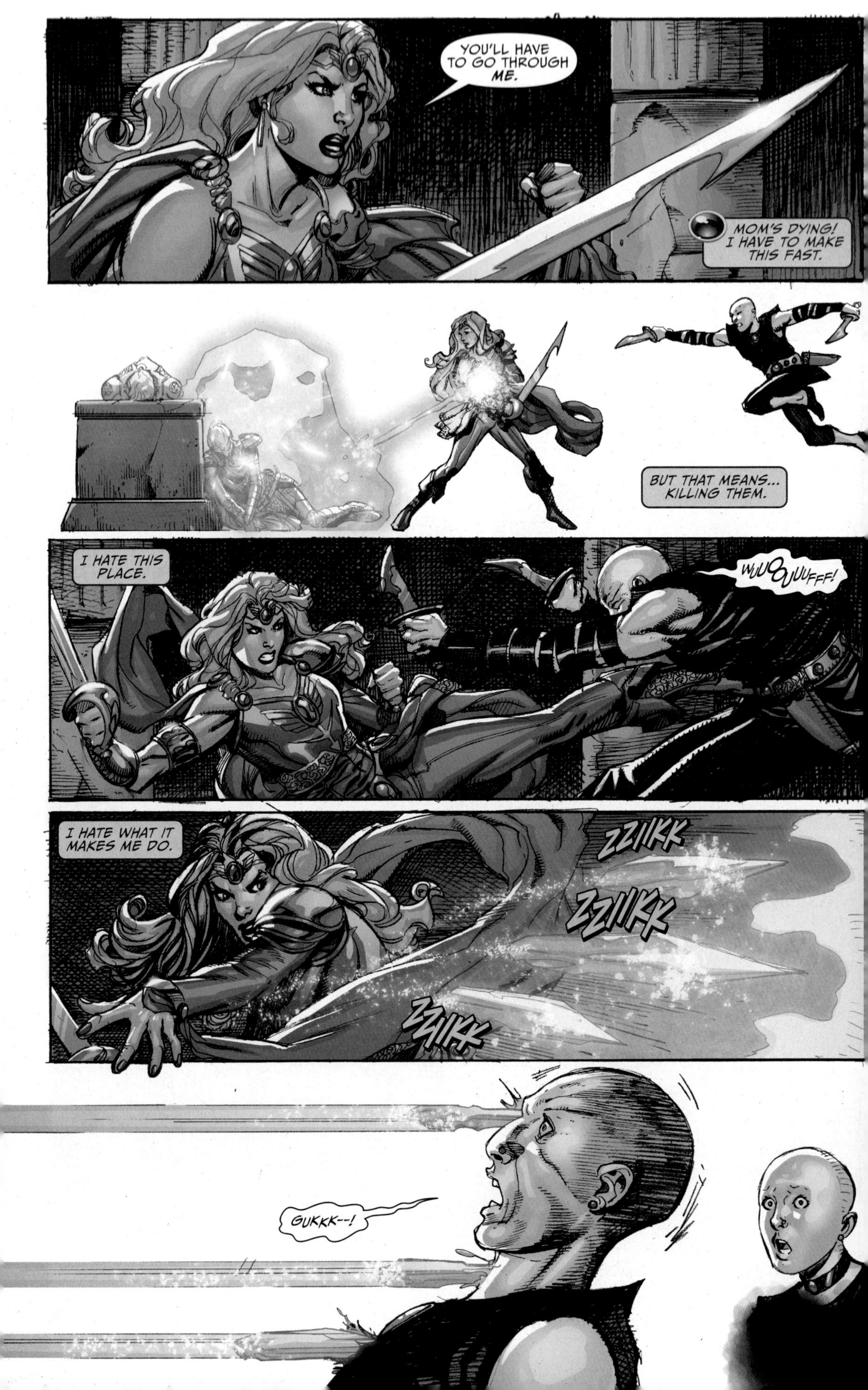

YOU'LL HAVE TO GO THROUGH ME.
MOM'S DYING! I HAVE TO MAKE THIS FAST.
BUT THAT MEANS... KILLING THEM.
I HATE THIS PLACE.
WUUOOUUUFFF!
I HATE WHAT IT MAKES ME DO.
ZZIIKK
ZZIIKK
ZZIIKK
GUKKK--!

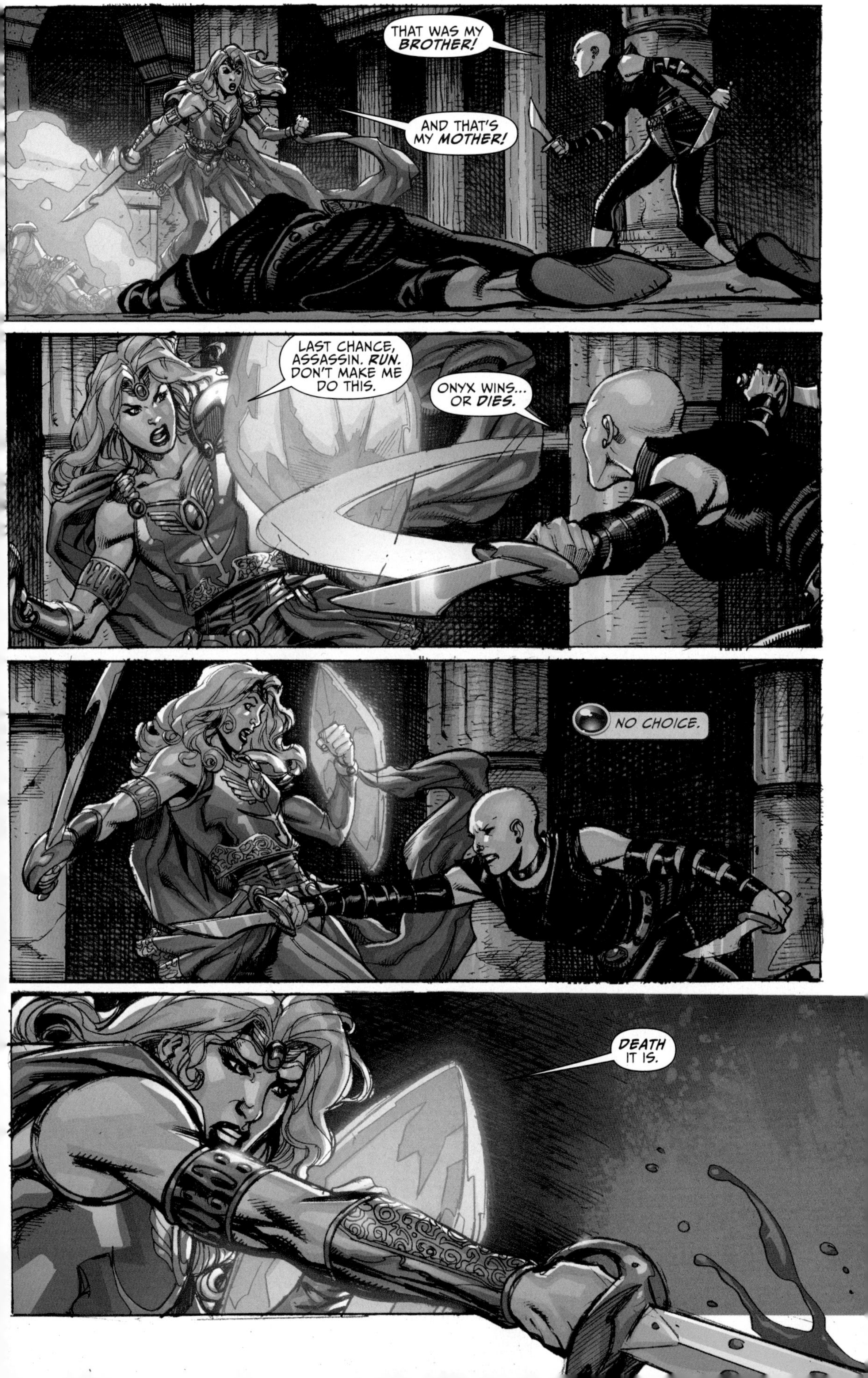
THAT WAS MY BROTHER!
AND THAT'S MY MOTHER!
LAST CHANCE, ASSASSIN. RUN. DON'T MAKE ME DO THIS.
ONYX WINS... OR DIES.
NO CHOICE.
DEATH IT IS.

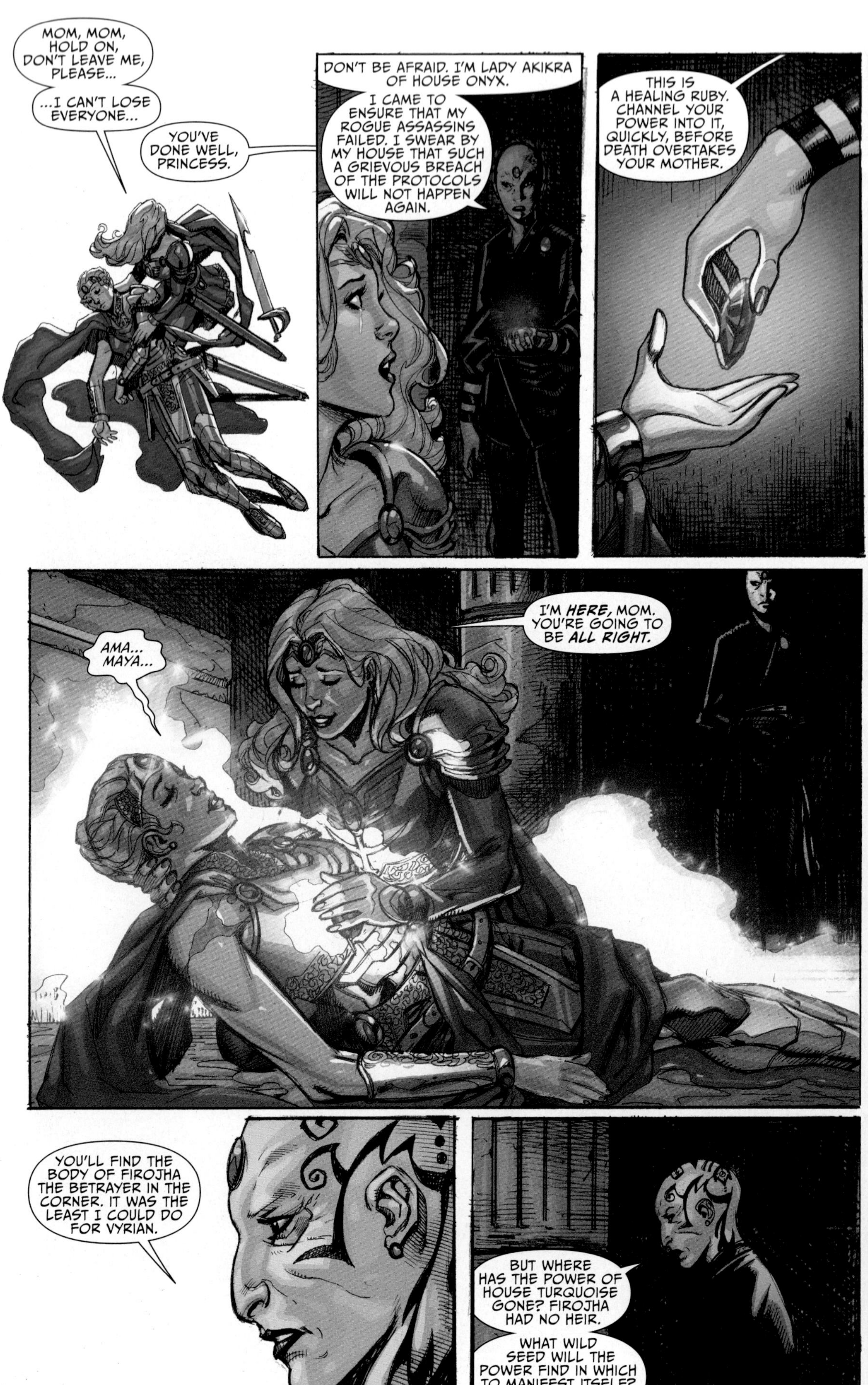
MOM, MOM, HOLD ON, DON'T LEAVE ME, PLEASE...
...I CAN'T LOSE EVERYONE...
YOU'VE DONE WELL, PRINCESS.
DON'T BE AFRAID. I'M LADY AKIKRA OF HOUSE ONYX.
I CAME TO ENSURE THAT MY ROGUE ASSASSINS FAILED. I SWEAR BY MY HOUSE THAT SUCH A GRIEVOUS BREACH OF THE PROTOCOLS WILL NOT HAPPEN AGAIN.
THIS IS A HEALING RUBY. CHANNEL YOUR POWER INTO IT, QUICKLY, BEFORE DEATH OVERTAKES YOUR MOTHER.
AMA... MAYA...
I'M HERE, MOM. YOU'RE GOING TO BE ALL RIGHT.
YOU'LL FIND THE BODY OF FIROJHA THE BETRAYER IN THE CORNER. IT WAS THE LEAST I COULD DO FOR VYRIAN.
BUT WHERE HAS THE POWER OF HOUSE TURQUOISE GONE? FIROJHA HAD NO HEIR.
WHAT WILD SEED WILL THE POWER FIND IN WHICH TO MANIFEST ITSELF?

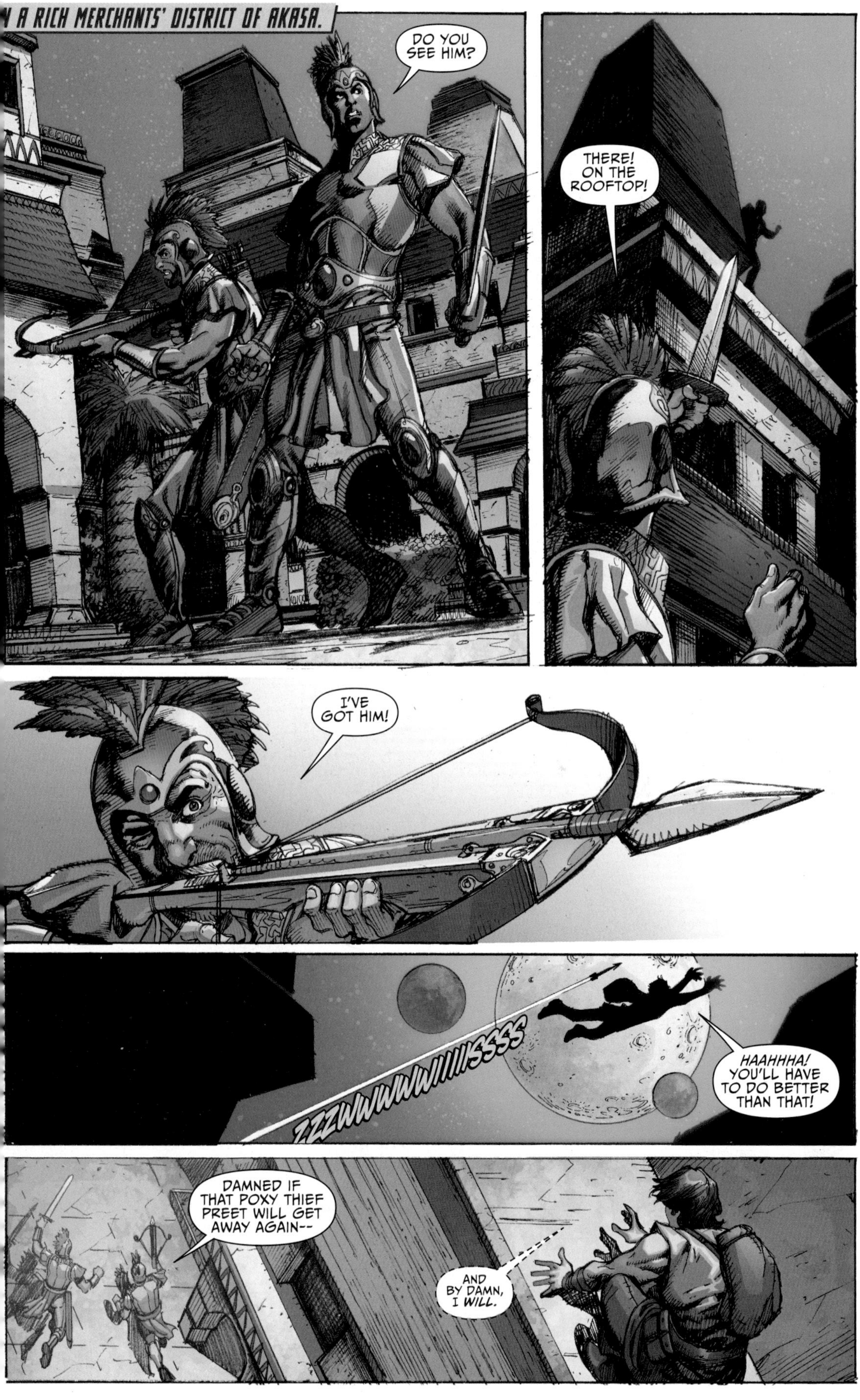

...N A RICH MERCHANTS' DISTRICT OF AKASA.
DO YOU SEE HIM?
THERE! ON THE ROOFTOP!
I'VE GOT HIM!
ZZZWWWWWWIIIIISSSSS
HAAHHHA! YOU'LL HAVE TO DO BETTER THAN THAT!
DAMNED IF THAT POXY THIEF PREET WILL GET AWAY AGAIN--
AND BY DAMN, I WILL.

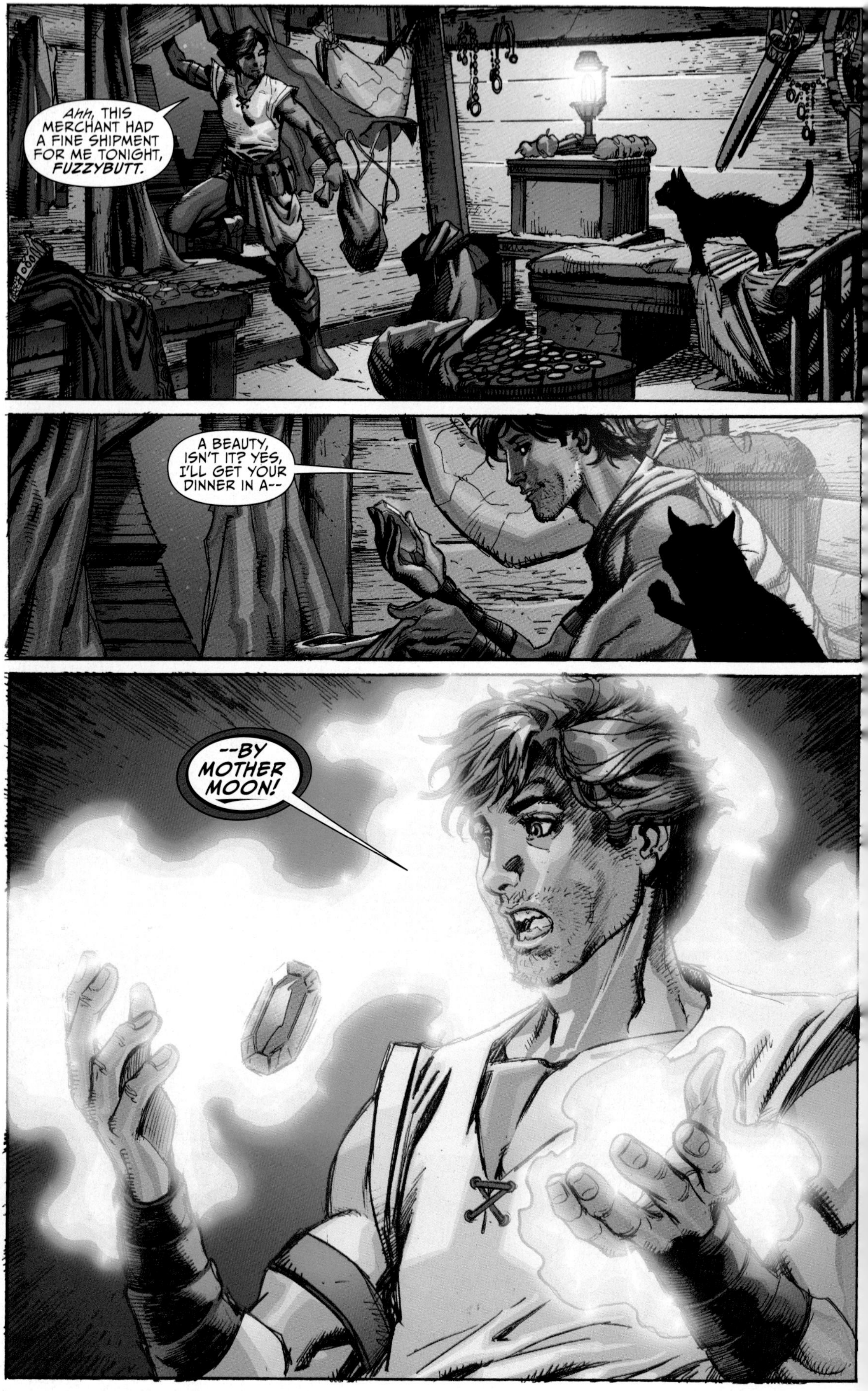
AHH, THIS MERCHANT HAD A FINE SHIPMENT FOR ME TONIGHT, FUZZYBUTT.
A BEAUTY, ISN'T IT? YES, I'LL GET YOUR DINNER IN A--
--BY MOTHER MOON!

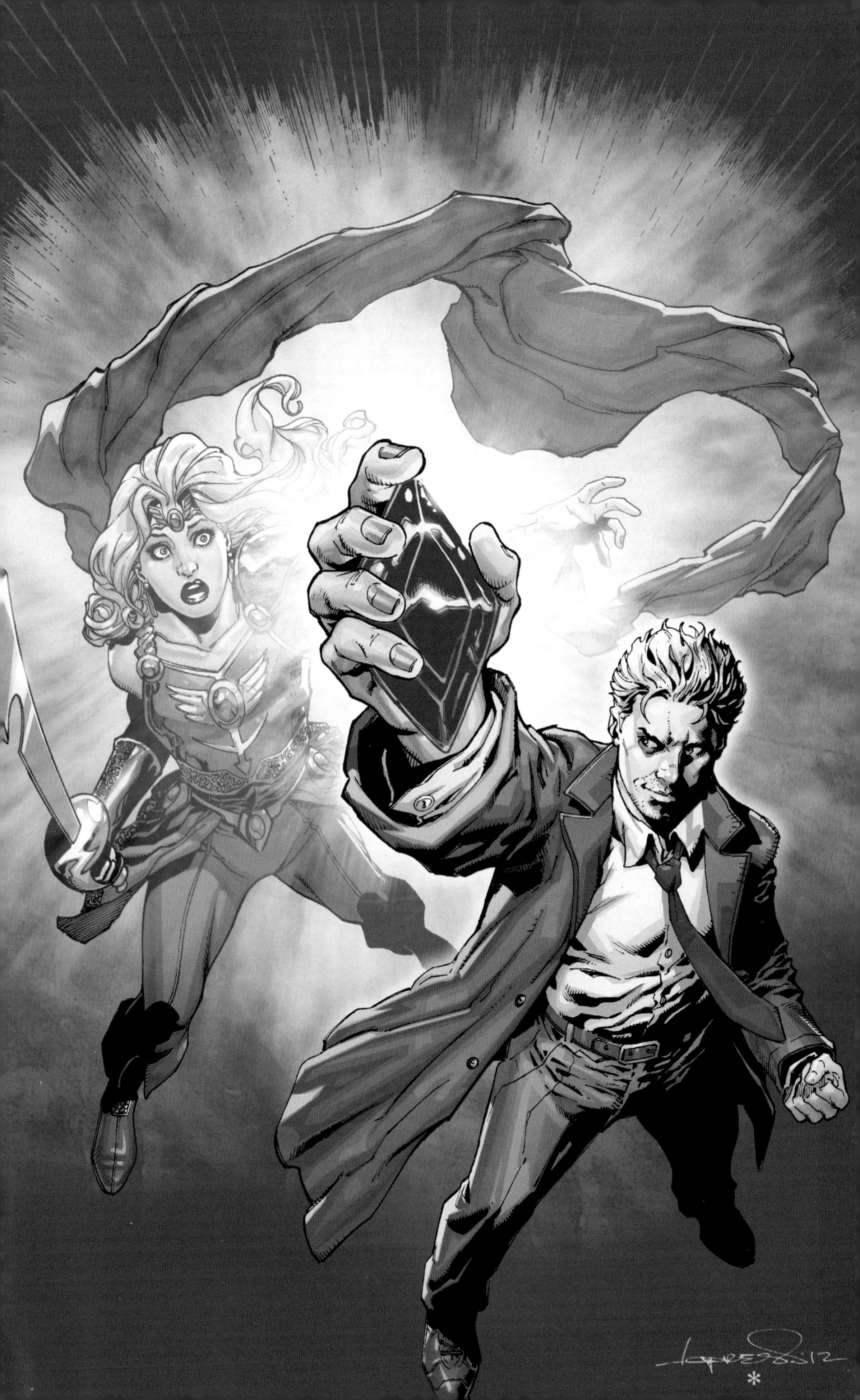

AMETHYST part seven DEVIL'S BARGAIN

CHRISTY MARX writer **AARON LOPRESTI** artist cover by **AARON LOPRESTI & HI-FI**

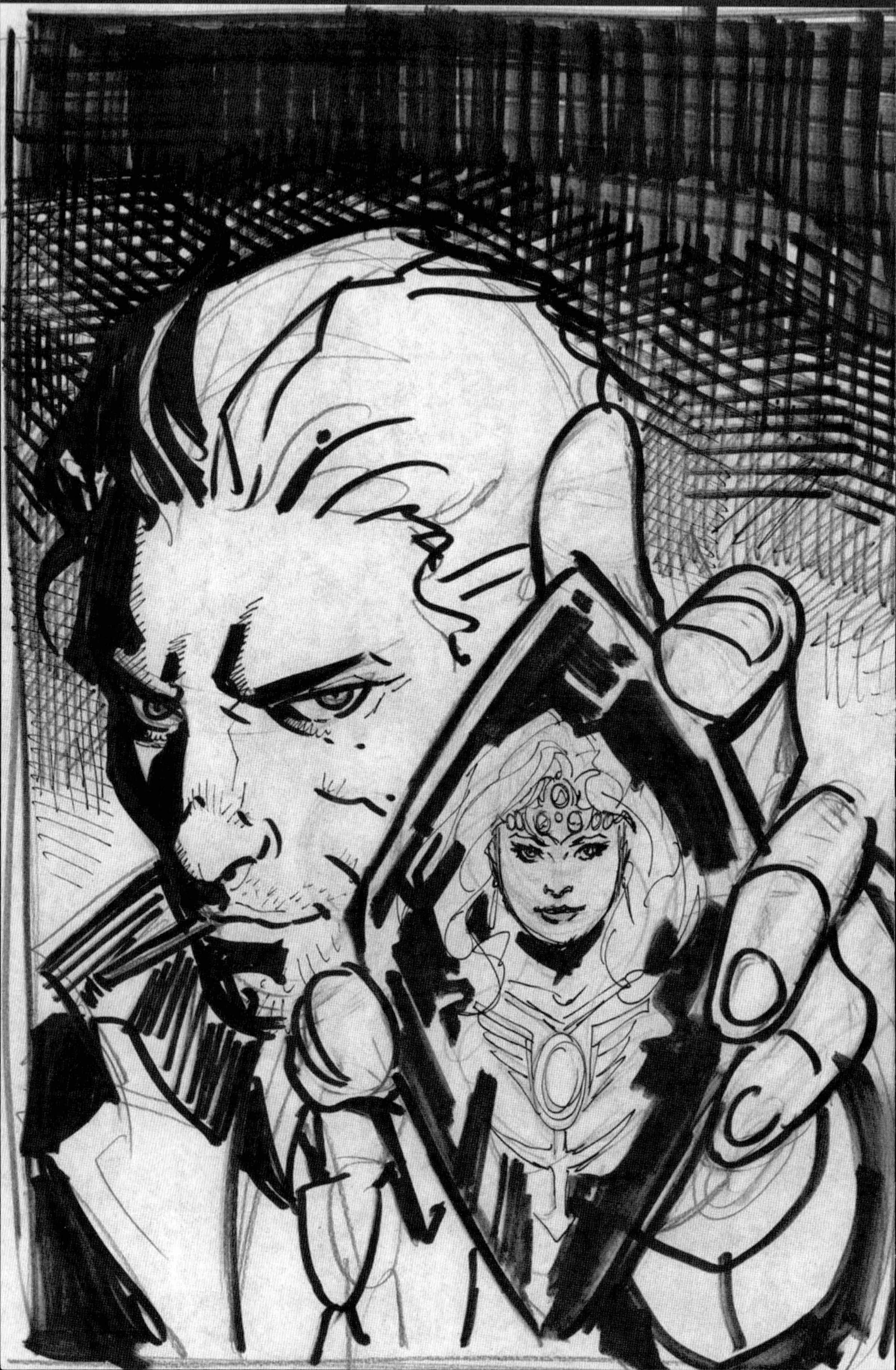

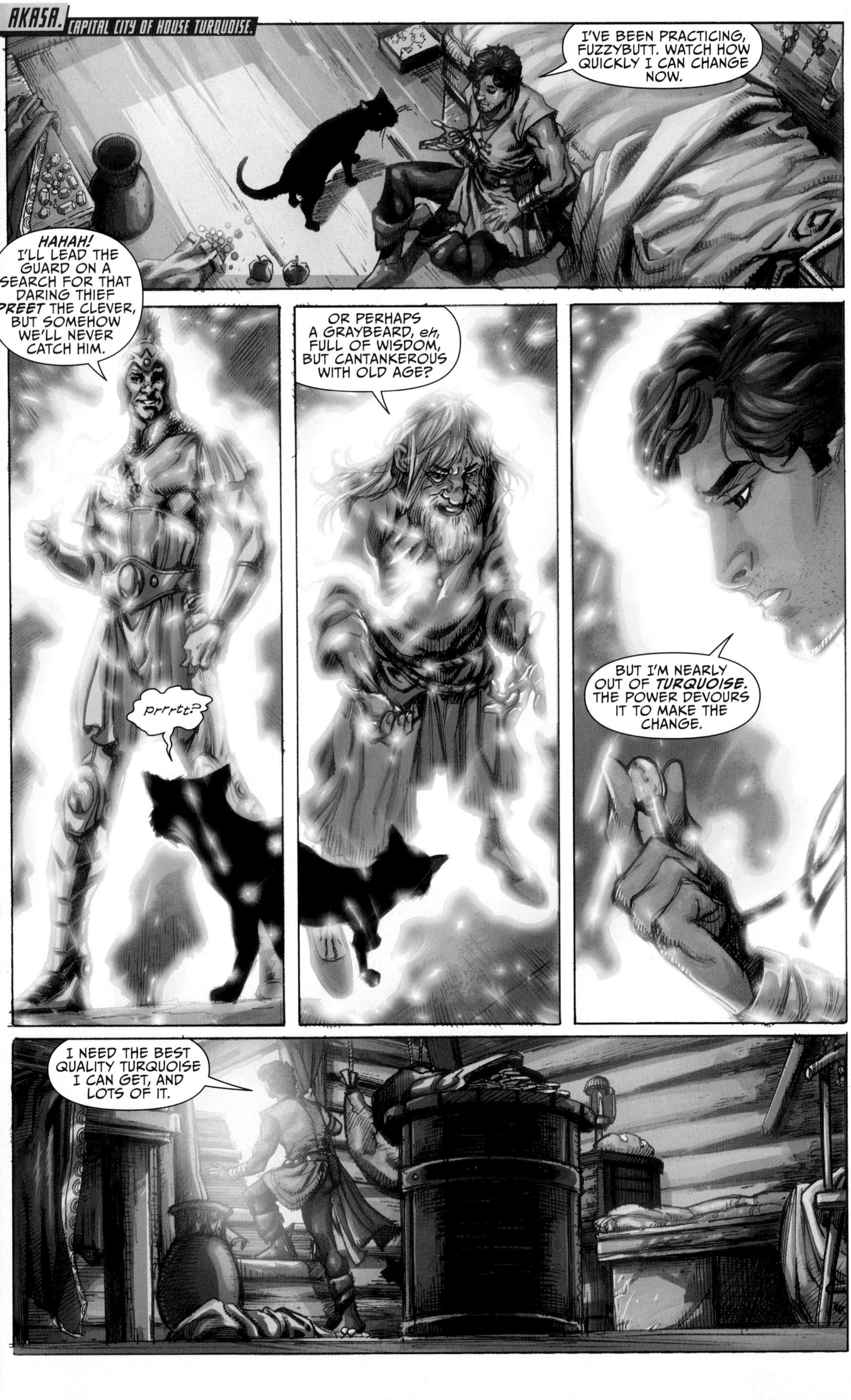
AKASA. CAPITAL CITY OF HOUSE TURQUOISE.
I'VE BEEN PRACTICING, FUZZYBUTT. WATCH HOW QUICKLY I CAN CHANGE NOW.
HAHAH! I'LL LEAD THE GUARD ON A SEARCH FOR THAT DARING THIEF PREET THE CLEVER, BUT SOMEHOW WE'LL NEVER CATCH HIM.
prrrtt?
OR PERHAPS A GRAYBEARD, eh, FULL OF WISDOM, BUT CANTANKEROUS WITH OLD AGE?
BUT I'M NEARLY OUT OF TURQUOISE. THE POWER DEVOURS IT TO MAKE THE CHANGE.
I NEED THE BEST QUALITY TURQUOISE I CAN GET, AND LOTS OF IT.

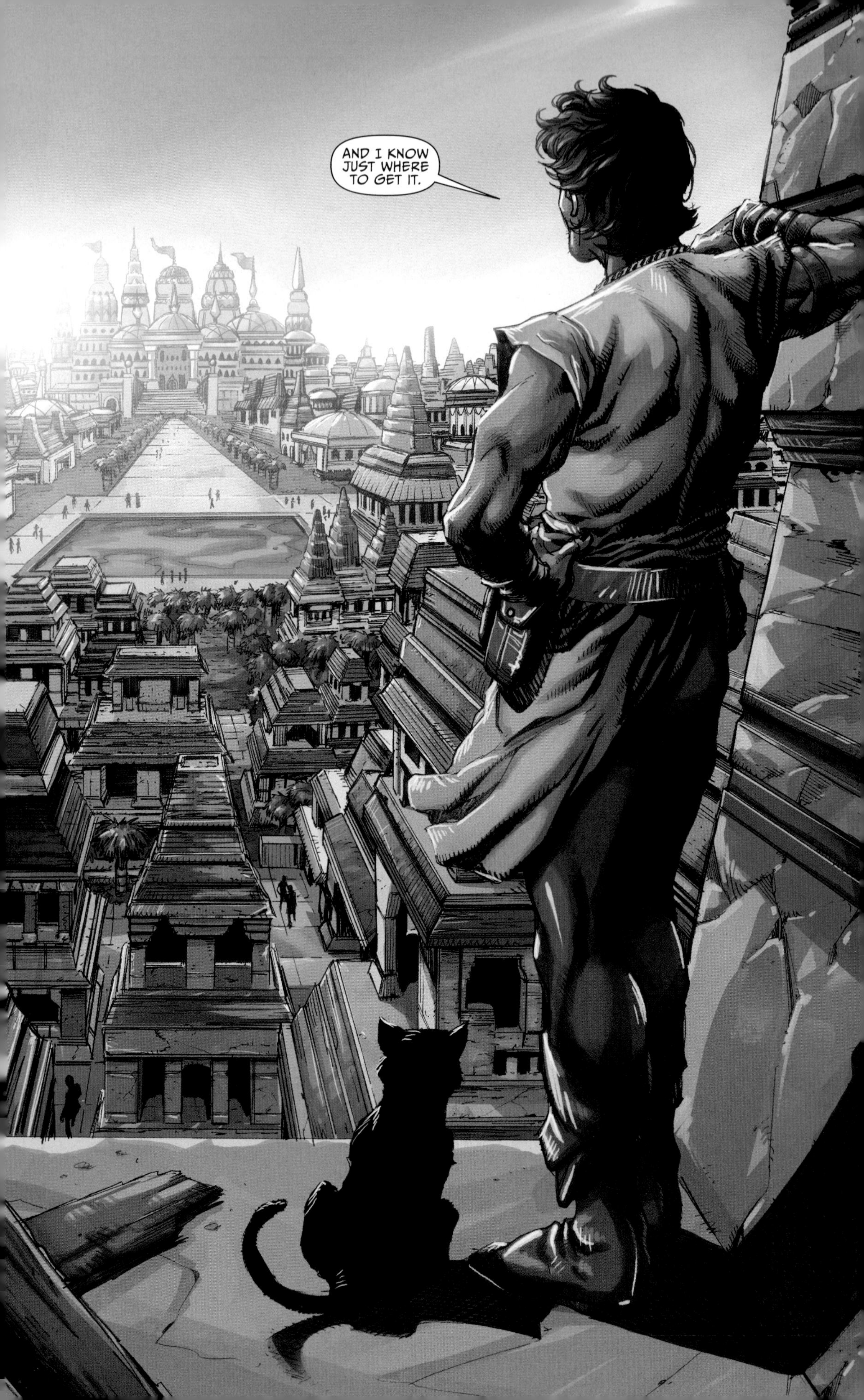
AND I KNOW JUST WHERE TO GET IT.

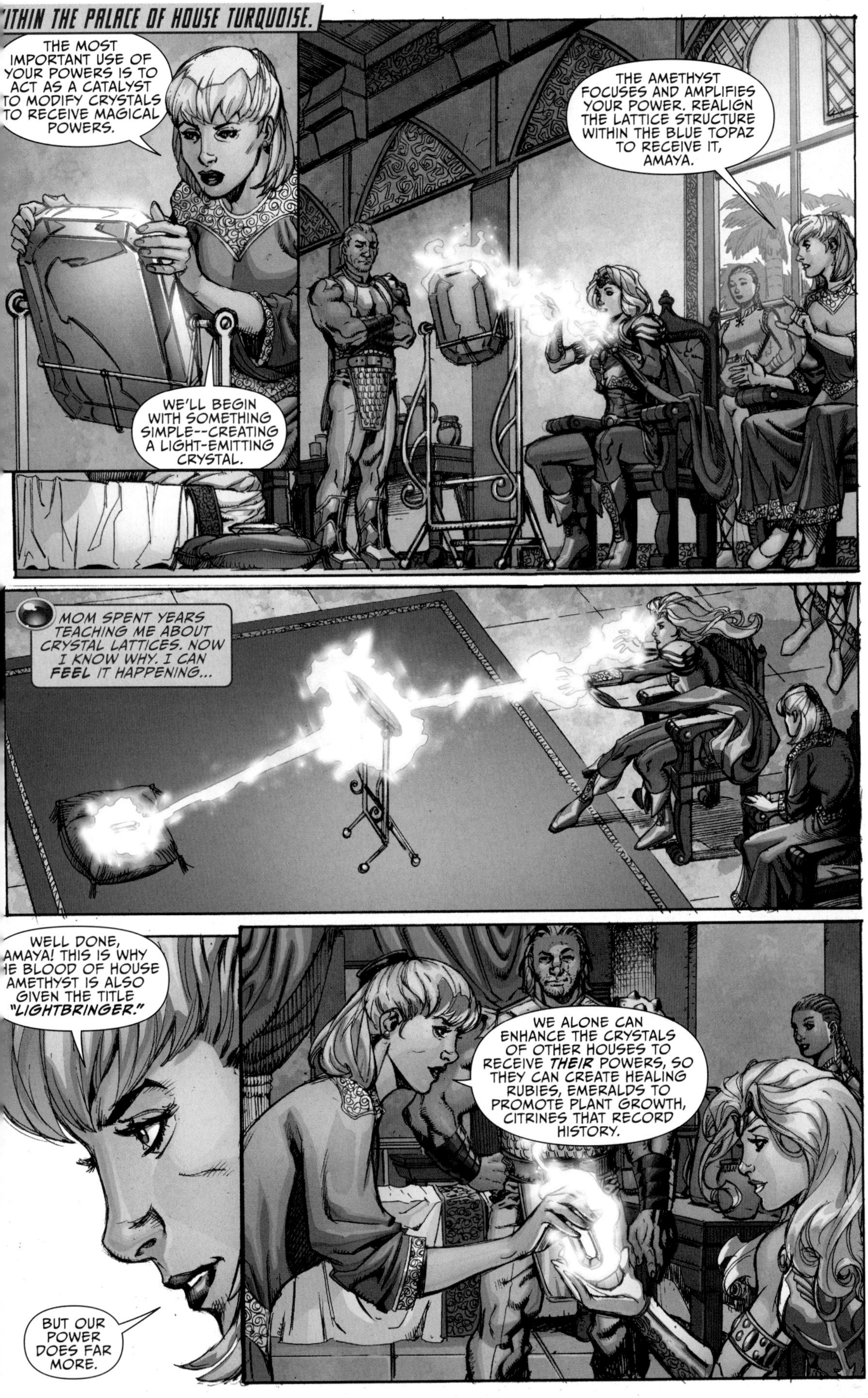
ITHIN THE PALACE OF HOUSE TURQUOISE.
THE MOST IMPORTANT USE OF YOUR POWERS IS TO ACT AS A CATALYST TO MODIFY CRYSTALS TO RECEIVE MAGICAL POWERS.
WE'LL BEGIN WITH SOMETHING SIMPLE--CREATING A LIGHT-EMITTING CRYSTAL.
THE AMETHYST FOCUSES AND AMPLIFIES YOUR POWER. REALIGN THE LATTICE STRUCTURE WITHIN THE BLUE TOPAZ TO RECEIVE IT, AMAYA.
MOM SPENT YEARS TEACHING ME ABOUT CRYSTAL LATTICES. NOW I KNOW WHY. I CAN FEEL IT HAPPENING...
WELL DONE, AMAYA! THIS IS WHY IE BLOOD OF HOUSE AMETHYST IS ALSO GIVEN THE TITLE "LIGHTBRINGER."
WE ALONE CAN ENHANCE THE CRYSTALS OF OTHER HOUSES TO RECEIVE THEIR POWERS, SO THEY CAN CREATE HEALING RUBIES, EMERALDS TO PROMOTE PLANT GROWTH, CITRINES THAT RECORD HISTORY.
BUT OUR POWER DOES FAR MORE.

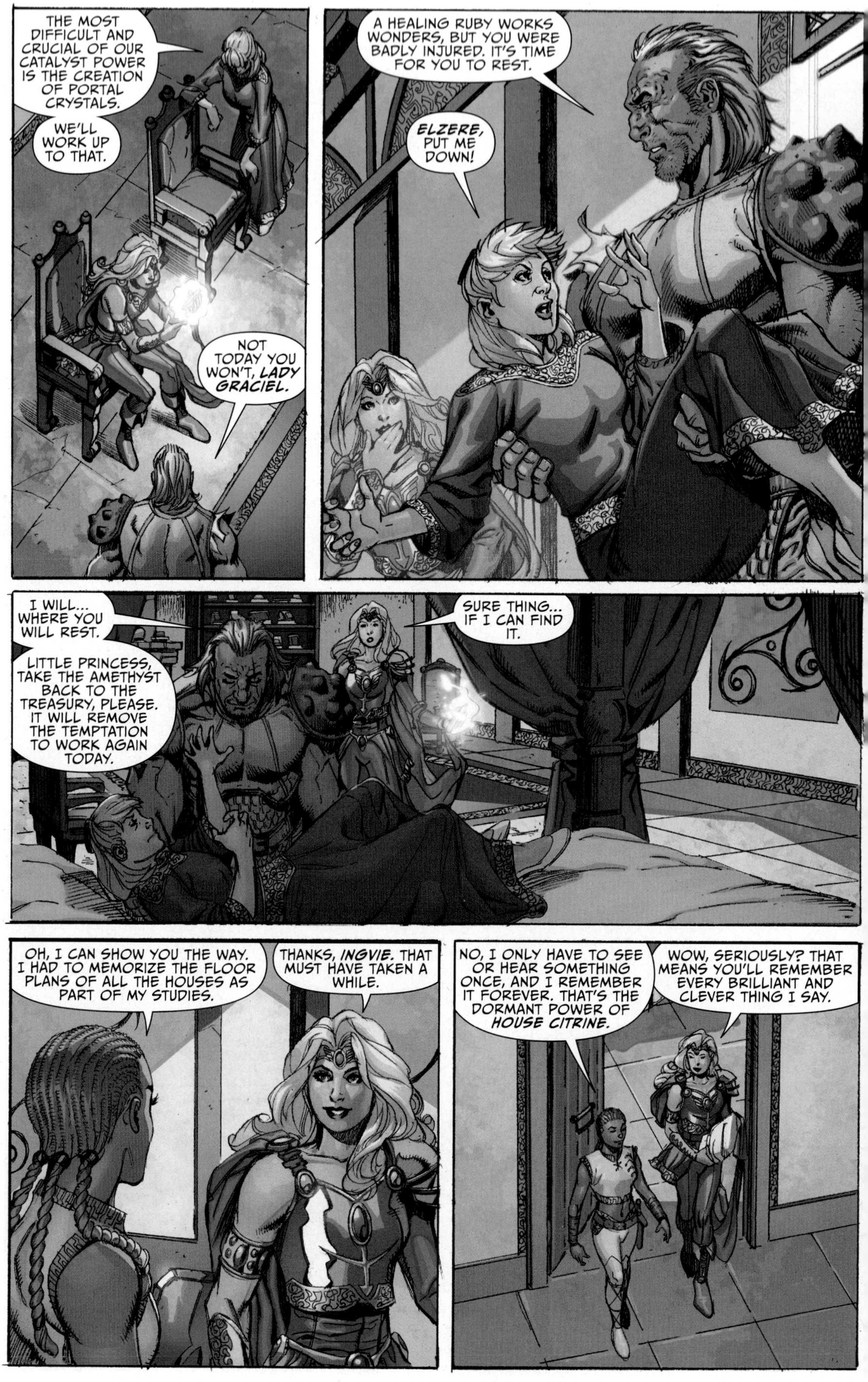
THE MOST DIFFICULT AND CRUCIAL OF OUR CATALYST POWER IS THE CREATION OF PORTAL CRYSTALS.
WE'LL WORK UP TO THAT.
NOT TODAY YOU WON'T, LADY GRACIEL.
A HEALING RUBY WORKS WONDERS, BUT YOU WERE BADLY INJURED. IT'S TIME FOR YOU TO REST.
ELZERE, PUT ME DOWN!
I WILL... WHERE YOU WILL REST.
LITTLE PRINCESS, TAKE THE AMETHYST BACK TO THE TREASURY, PLEASE. IT WILL REMOVE THE TEMPTATION TO WORK AGAIN TODAY.
SURE THING... IF I CAN FIND IT.
OH, I CAN SHOW YOU THE WAY. I HAD TO MEMORIZE THE FLOOR PLANS OF ALL THE HOUSES AS PART OF MY STUDIES.
THANKS, INGVIE. THAT MUST HAVE TAKEN A WHILE.
NO, I ONLY HAVE TO SEE OR HEAR SOMETHING ONCE, AND I REMEMBER IT FOREVER. THAT'S THE DORMANT POWER OF HOUSE CITRINE.
WOW, SERIOUSLY? THAT MEANS YOU'LL REMEMBER EVERY BRILLIANT AND CLEVER THING I SAY.

IF YOU EVER SAY ANYTHING BRILLIANT OR CLEVER, I'LL LET YOU KNOW.

SNRRFFF! GOOD ONE.

THEN...WOULD YOU KNOW ABOUT THE PROTOCOLS OF ONYX?

OF COURSE. THEY'RE RATHER IMPORTANT. I KNOW EVERY WORD OF THEM. WHY?

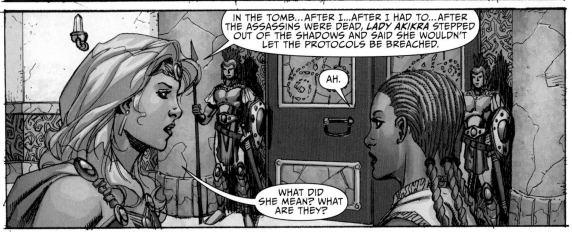

IN THE TOMB...AFTER I...AFTER I HAD TO...AFTER THE ASSASSINS WERE DEAD, *LADY AKIKRA* STEPPED OUT OF THE SHADOWS AND SAID SHE WOULDN'T LET THE PROTOCOLS BE BREACHED.

AH.

WHAT DID SHE MEAN? WHAT ARE THEY?

THEN THEY FORBID HOUSE ONYX FROM CONTRACTING TO ASSASSINATE ANYONE OF HIGH BLOOD IN THE FIVE CARDINAL HOUSES. IN EXCHANGE, ONYX RECEIVES A REGULAR "TRIBUTE" PAYMENT.

THE POWER OF ONYX NEUTRALIZES OTHER BLOOD-POWERS, MAKING THEM DEADLY ASSASSINS. IF THEY HADN'T SIGNED THE PROTOCOLS, THE OTHER HOUSES WOULD HAVE DESTROYED THEIR BLOODLINE.

THE PROTOCOLS WERE PUT IN PLACE AFTER *THE WAR OF THE ECLIPSE.*

MOTHER WANTED ME TO STUDY THE WAR, BUT THAT'S ANCIENT HISTORY, SO I DIDN'T BOTHER.

BUT I HAD TO LEARN THE PROTOCOLS. FIRST, THEY STRICTLY FORBID HOUSE ONYX FROM MARRYING *ANYONE* WITH BLOOD-POWER.

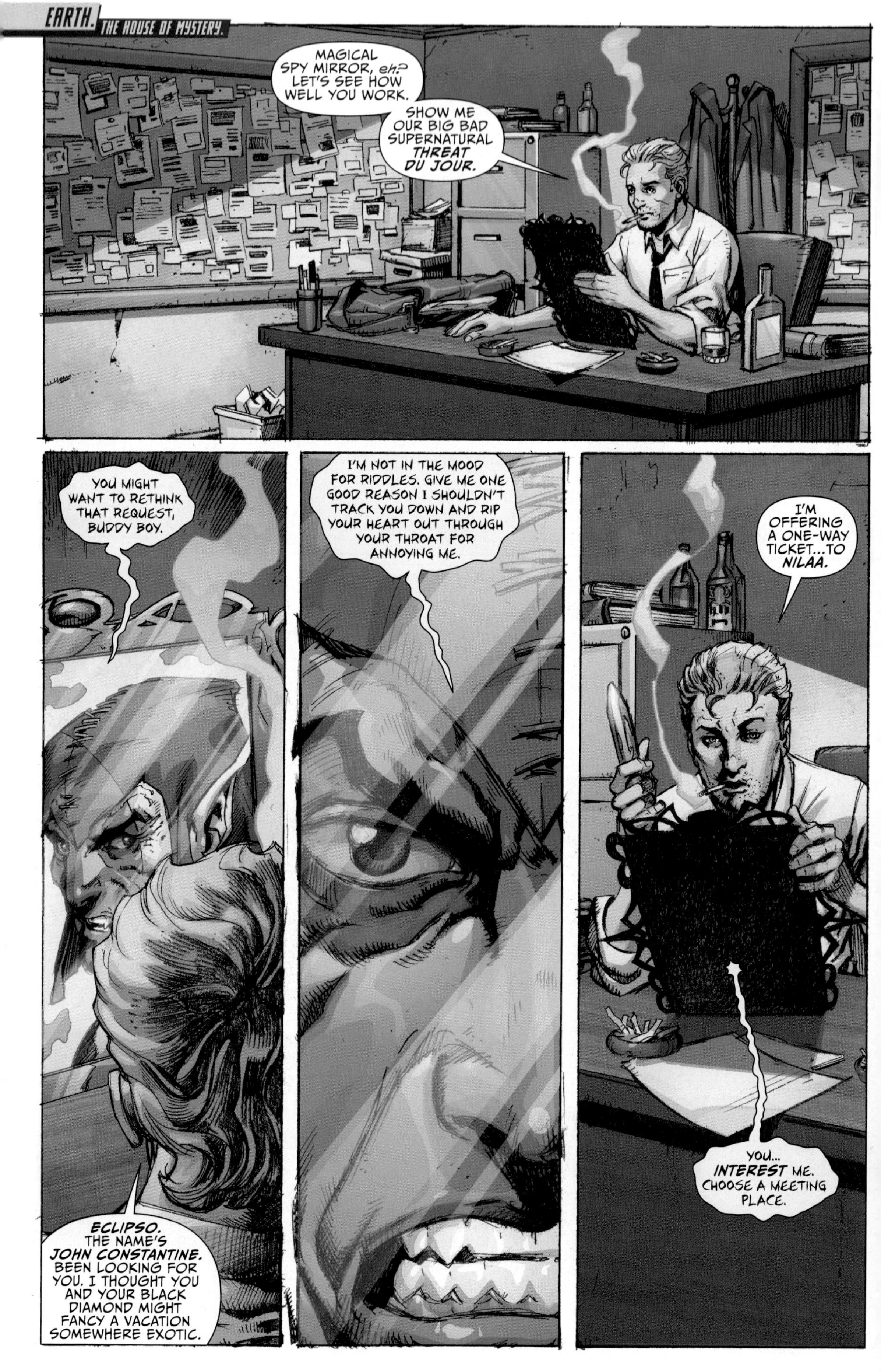
EARTH.
THE HOUSE OF MYSTERY.
MAGICAL SPY MIRROR, eh? LET'S SEE HOW WELL YOU WORK.
SHOW ME OUR BIG BAD SUPERNATURAL THREAT DU JOUR.
YOU MIGHT WANT TO RETHINK THAT REQUEST, BUDDY BOY.
ECLIPSO. THE NAME'S JOHN CONSTANTINE. BEEN LOOKING FOR YOU. I THOUGHT YOU AND YOUR BLACK DIAMOND MIGHT FANCY A VACATION SOMEWHERE EXOTIC.
I'M NOT IN THE MOOD FOR RIDDLES. GIVE ME ONE GOOD REASON I SHOULDN'T TRACK YOU DOWN AND RIP YOUR HEART OUT THROUGH YOUR THROAT FOR ANNOYING ME.
I'M OFFERING A ONE-WAY TICKET...TO NILAA.
YOU... INTEREST ME. CHOOSE A MEETING PLACE.

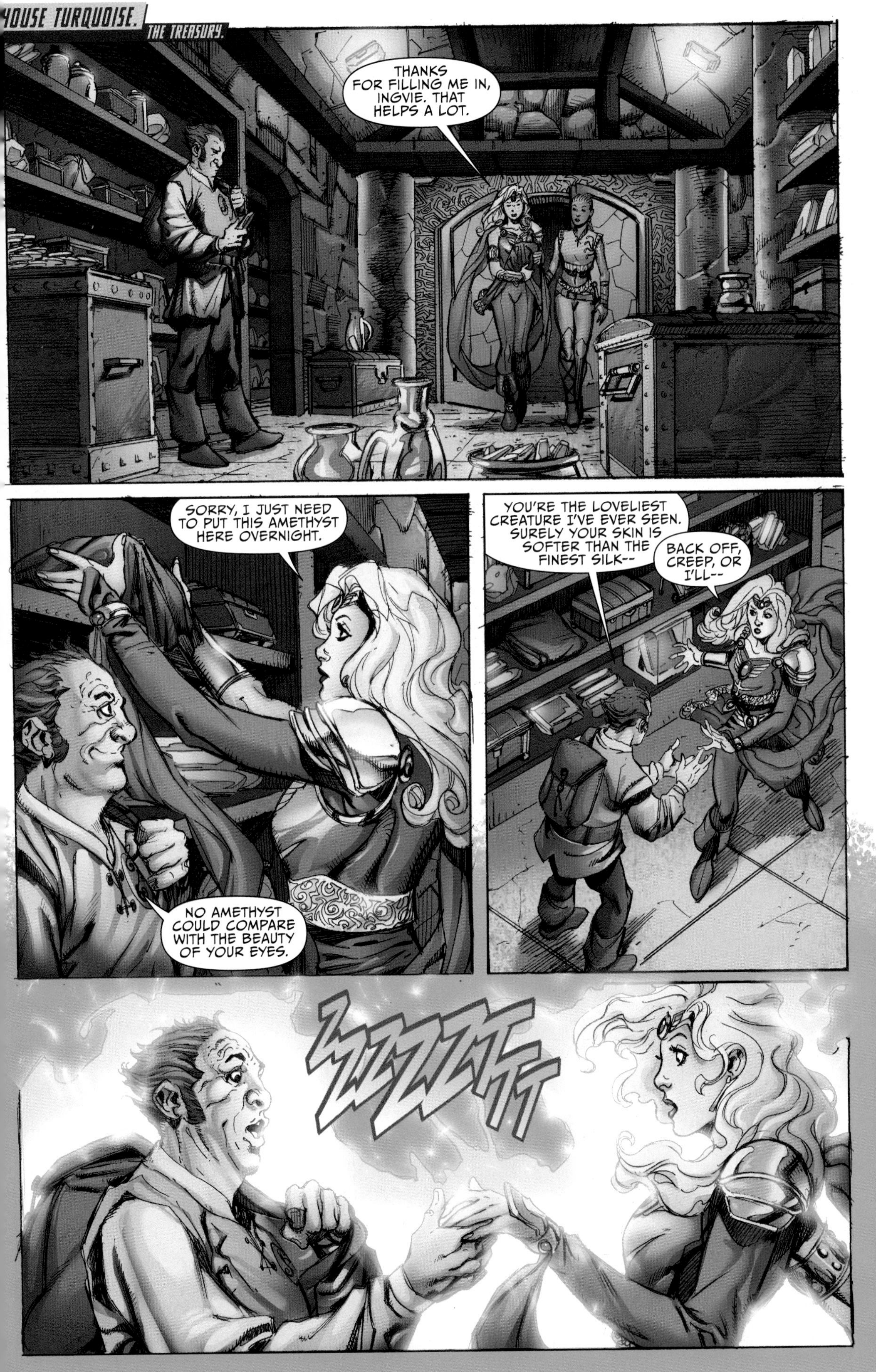
HOUSE TURQUOISE.
THE TREASURY.
THANKS FOR FILLING ME IN, INGVIE. THAT HELPS A LOT.
SORRY, I JUST NEED TO PUT THIS AMETHYST HERE OVERNIGHT.
NO AMETHYST COULD COMPARE WITH THE BEAUTY OF YOUR EYES.
YOU'RE THE LOVELIEST CREATURE I'VE EVER SEEN. SURELY YOUR SKIN IS SOFTER THAN THE FINEST SILK--
BACK OFF, CREEP, OR I'LL--
ZZZZTTT

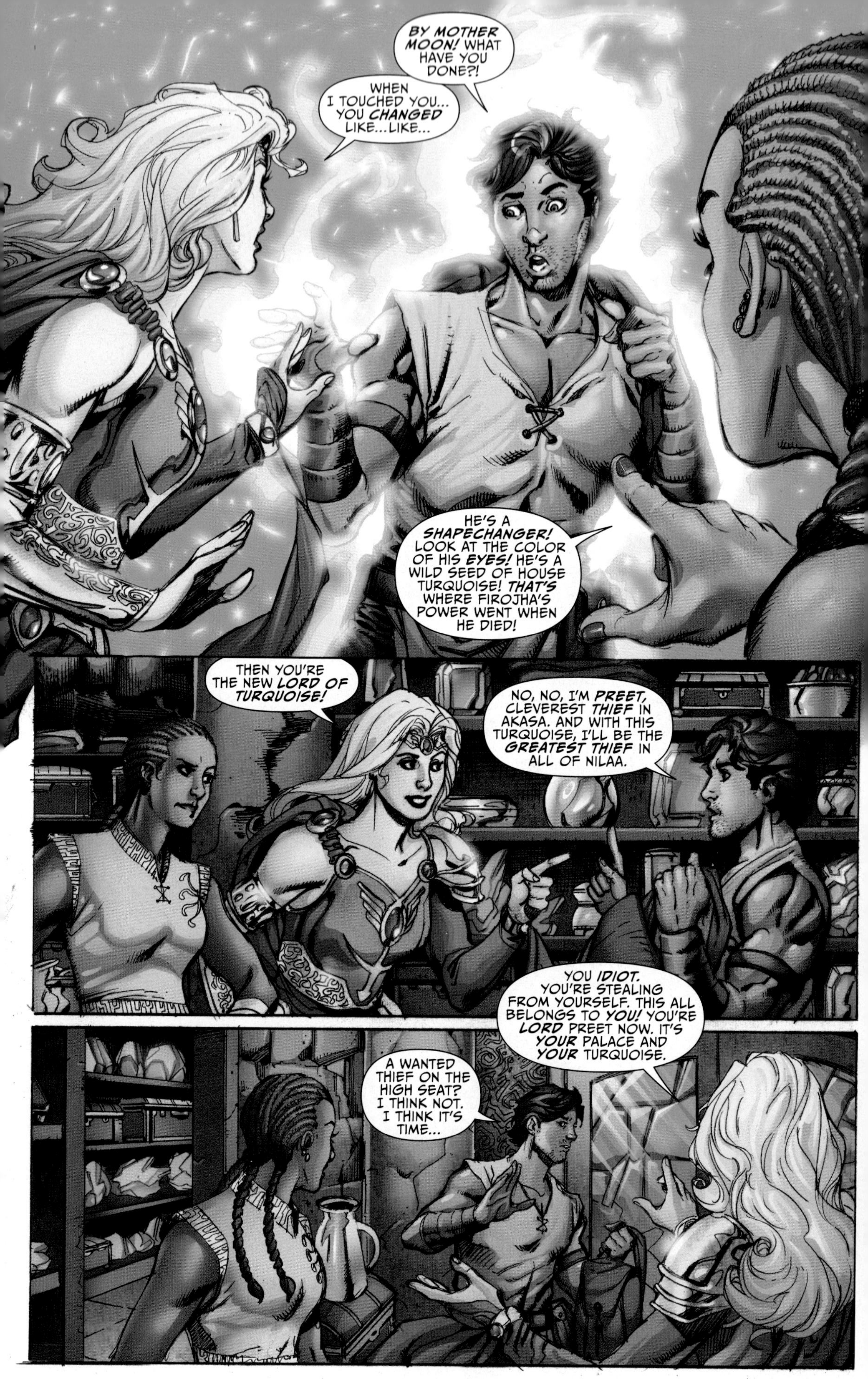
BY MOTHER MOON! WHAT HAVE YOU DONE?!
WHEN I TOUCHED YOU... YOU CHANGED LIKE...LIKE...
HE'S A SHAPECHANGER! LOOK AT THE COLOR OF HIS EYES! HE'S A WILD SEED OF HOUSE TURQUOISE! THAT'S WHERE FIROJHA'S POWER WENT WHEN HE DIED!
THEN YOU'RE THE NEW LORD OF TURQUOISE!
NO, NO, I'M PREET, CLEVEREST THIEF IN AKASA. AND WITH THIS TURQUOISE, I'LL BE THE GREATEST THIEF IN ALL OF NILAA.
YOU IDIOT. YOU'RE STEALING FROM YOURSELF. THIS ALL BELONGS TO YOU! YOU'RE LORD PREET NOW. IT'S YOUR PALACE AND YOUR TURQUOISE.
A WANTED THIEF ON THE HIGH SEAT? I THINK NOT. I THINK IT'S TIME...

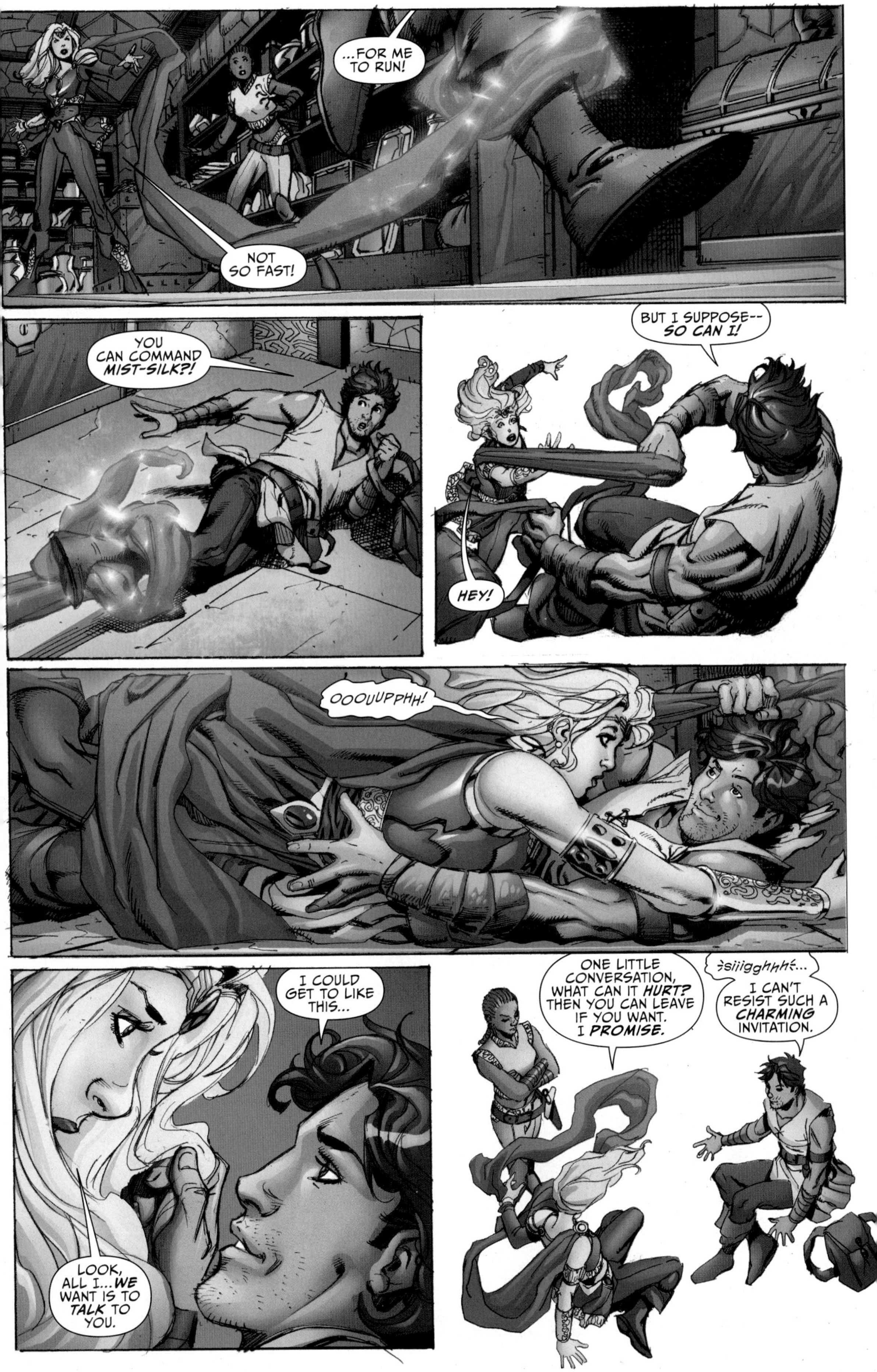
...FOR ME TO RUN!
NOT SO FAST!
YOU CAN COMMAND *MIST-SILK?!*
BUT I SUPPOSE-- *SO CAN I!*
HEY!
OOOUUPPHH!
I COULD GET TO LIKE THIS...
LOOK, ALL I...*WE* WANT IS TO *TALK* TO YOU.
ONE LITTLE CONVERSATION, WHAT CAN IT *HURT?* THEN YOU CAN LEAVE IF YOU WANT. I *PROMISE.*
siiigghhh...
I CAN'T RESIST SUCH A *CHARMING* INVITATION.

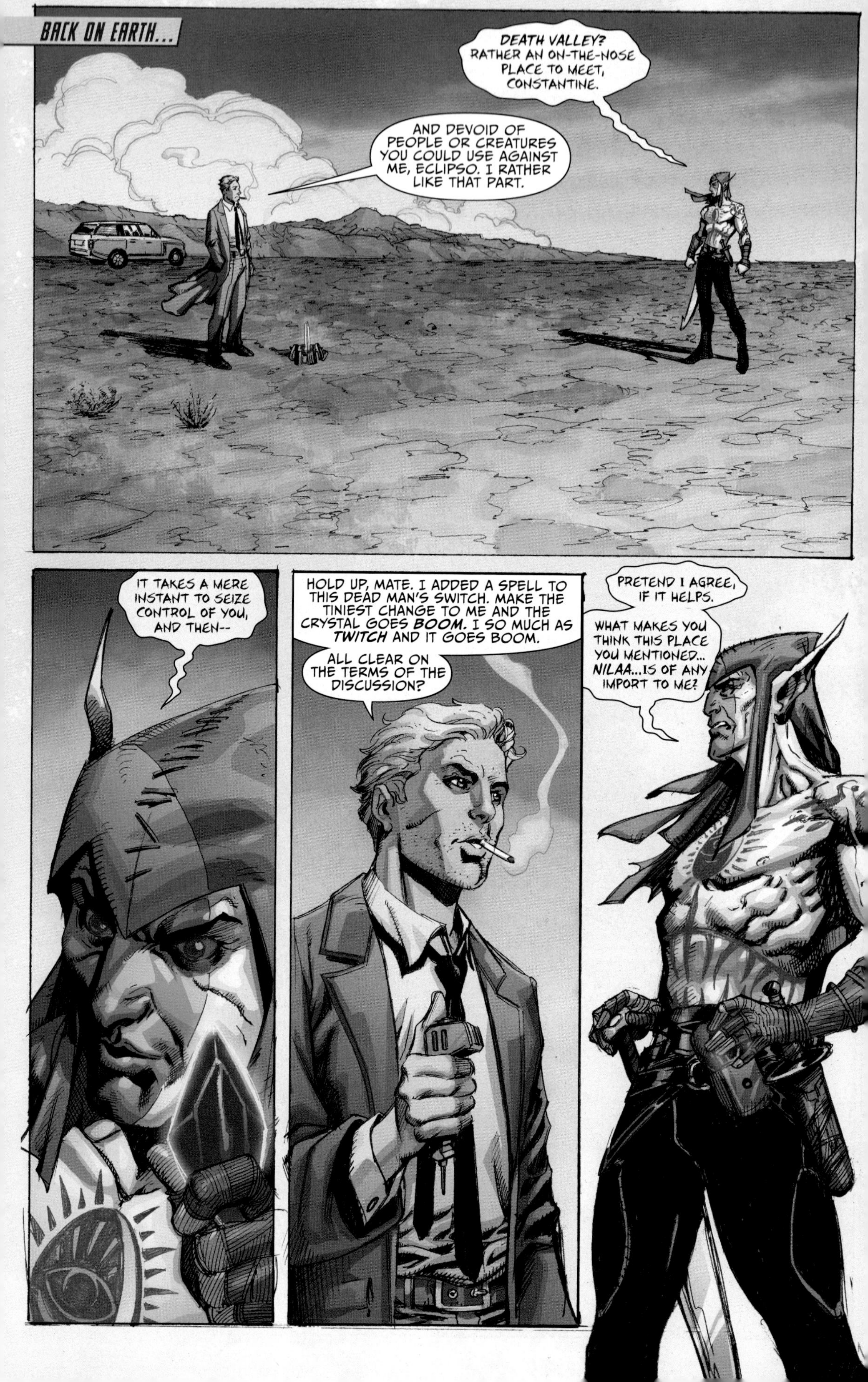
BACK ON EARTH...
DEATH VALLEY? RATHER AN ON-THE-NOSE PLACE TO MEET, CONSTANTINE.
AND DEVOID OF PEOPLE OR CREATURES YOU COULD USE AGAINST ME, ECLIPSO. I RATHER LIKE THAT PART.
IT TAKES A MERE INSTANT TO SEIZE CONTROL OF YOU, AND THEN--
HOLD UP, MATE. I ADDED A SPELL TO THIS DEAD MAN'S SWITCH. MAKE THE TINIEST CHANGE TO ME AND THE CRYSTAL GOES BOOM. I SO MUCH AS TWITCH AND IT GOES BOOM.
ALL CLEAR ON THE TERMS OF THE DISCUSSION?
PRETEND I AGREE, IF IT HELPS.
WHAT MAKES YOU THINK THIS PLACE YOU MENTIONED... NILAA...IS OF ANY IMPORT TO ME?

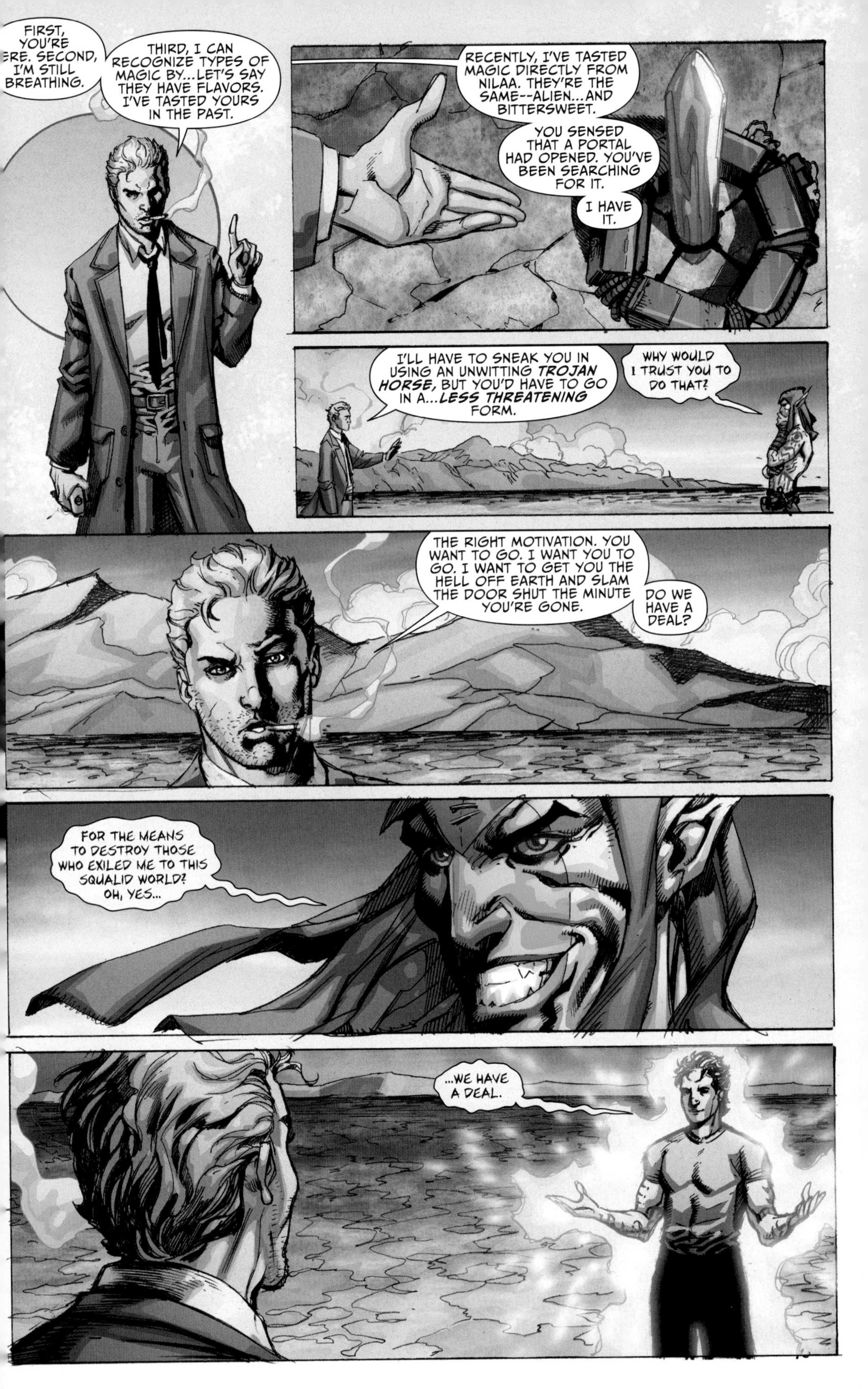

FIRST, YOU'RE ERE. SECOND, I'M STILL BREATHING.
THIRD, I CAN RECOGNIZE TYPES OF MAGIC BY...LET'S SAY THEY HAVE FLAVORS. I'VE TASTED YOURS IN THE PAST.
RECENTLY, I'VE TASTED MAGIC DIRECTLY FROM NILAA. THEY'RE THE SAME--ALIEN...AND BITTERSWEET.
YOU SENSED THAT A PORTAL HAD OPENED. YOU'VE BEEN SEARCHING FOR IT.
I HAVE IT.
I'LL HAVE TO SNEAK YOU IN USING AN UNWITTING TROJAN HORSE, BUT YOU'D HAVE TO GO IN A...LESS THREATENING FORM.
WHY WOULD I TRUST YOU TO DO THAT?
THE RIGHT MOTIVATION. YOU WANT TO GO. I WANT YOU TO GO. I WANT TO GET YOU THE HELL OFF EARTH AND SLAM THE DOOR SHUT THE MINUTE YOU'RE GONE.
DO WE HAVE A DEAL?
FOR THE MEANS TO DESTROY THOSE WHO EXILED ME TO THIS SQUALID WORLD? OH, YES...
...WE HAVE A DEAL.

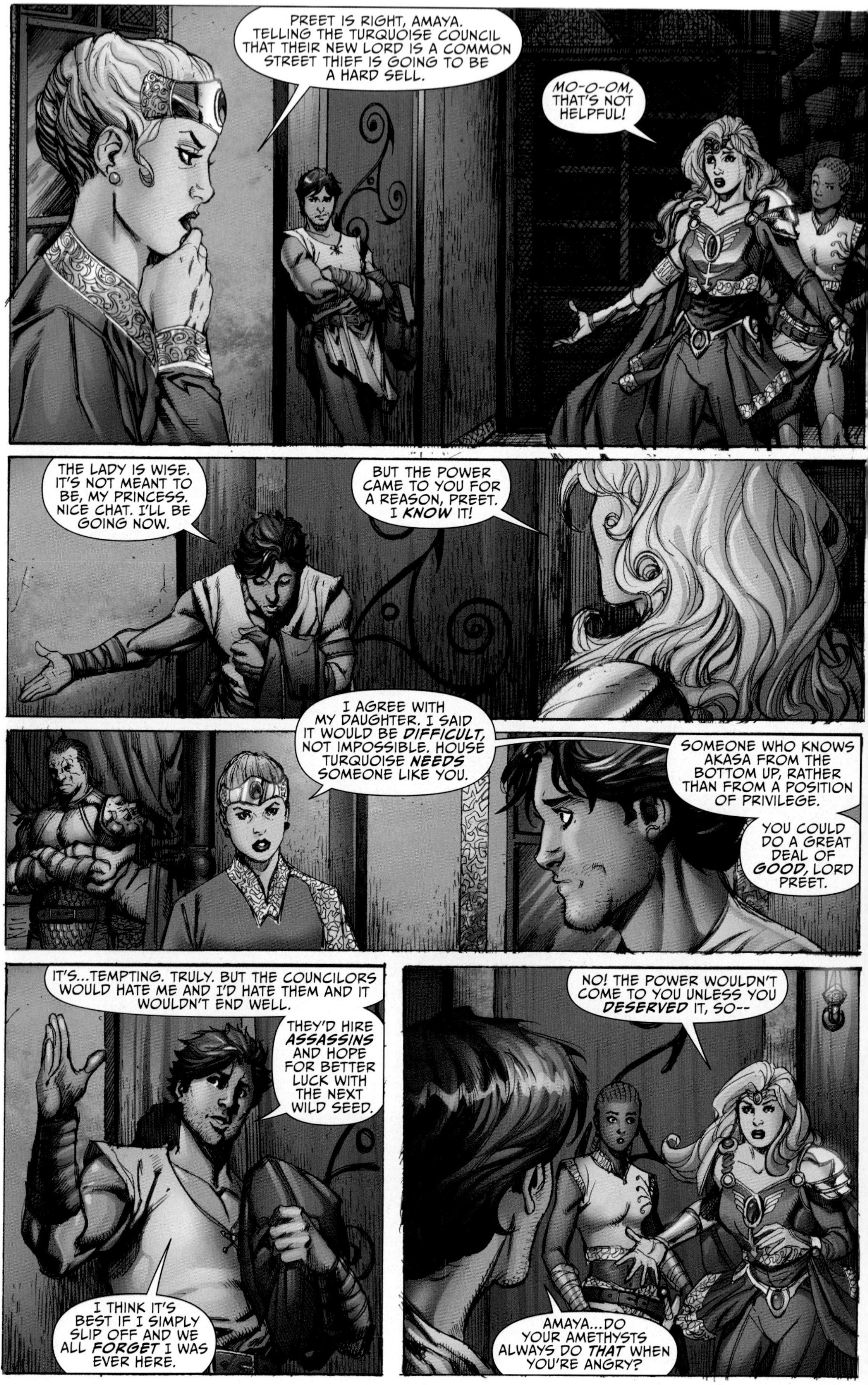
PREET IS RIGHT, AMAYA. TELLING THE TURQUOISE COUNCIL THAT THEIR NEW LORD IS A COMMON STREET THIEF IS GOING TO BE A HARD SELL.
MO-O-OM, THAT'S NOT HELPFUL!
THE LADY IS WISE. IT'S NOT MEANT TO BE, MY PRINCESS. NICE CHAT. I'LL BE GOING NOW.
BUT THE POWER CAME TO YOU FOR A REASON, PREET. I KNOW IT!
I AGREE WITH MY DAUGHTER. I SAID IT WOULD BE DIFFICULT, NOT IMPOSSIBLE. HOUSE TURQUOISE NEEDS SOMEONE LIKE YOU.
SOMEONE WHO KNOWS AKASA FROM THE BOTTOM UP, RATHER THAN FROM A POSITION OF PRIVILEGE.
YOU COULD DO A GREAT DEAL OF GOOD, LORD PREET.
IT'S...TEMPTING. TRULY. BUT THE COUNCILORS WOULD HATE ME AND I'D HATE THEM AND IT WOULDN'T END WELL.
THEY'D HIRE ASSASSINS AND HOPE FOR BETTER LUCK WITH THE NEXT WILD SEED.
I THINK IT'S BEST IF I SIMPLY SLIP OFF AND WE ALL FORGET I WAS EVER HERE.
NO! THE POWER WOULDN'T COME TO YOU UNLESS YOU DESERVED IT, SO--
AMAYA...DO YOUR AMETHYSTS ALWAYS DO THAT WHEN YOU'RE ANGRY?

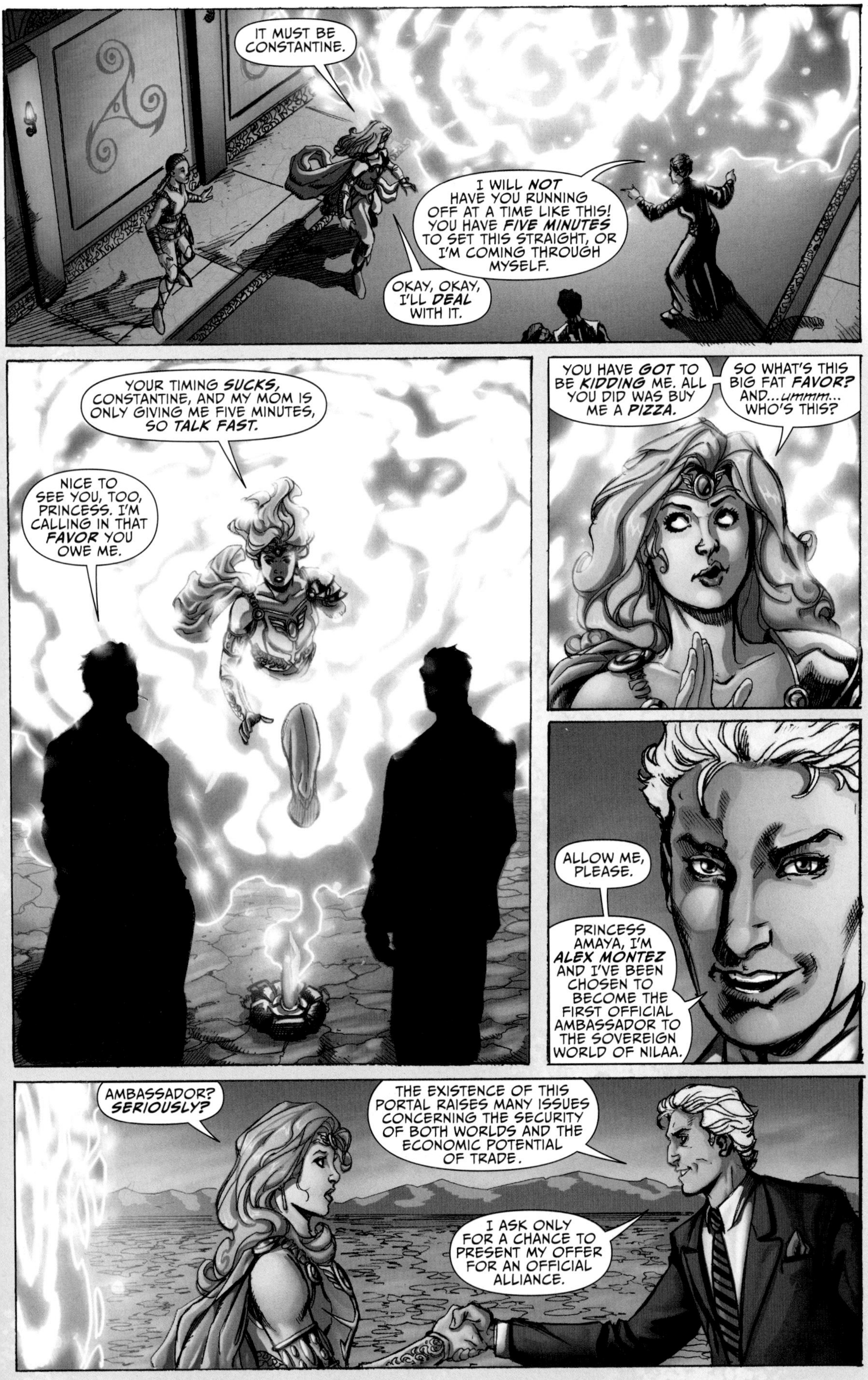
IT MUST BE CONSTANTINE.
I WILL NOT HAVE YOU RUNNING OFF AT A TIME LIKE THIS! YOU HAVE FIVE MINUTES TO SET THIS STRAIGHT, OR I'M COMING THROUGH MYSELF.
OKAY, OKAY, I'LL DEAL WITH IT.
YOUR TIMING SUCKS, CONSTANTINE, AND MY MOM IS ONLY GIVING ME FIVE MINUTES, SO TALK FAST.
NICE TO SEE YOU, TOO, PRINCESS. I'M CALLING IN THAT FAVOR YOU OWE ME.
YOU HAVE GOT TO BE KIDDING ME. ALL YOU DID WAS BUY ME A PIZZA.
SO WHAT'S THIS BIG FAT FAVOR? AND...ummm... WHO'S THIS?
ALLOW ME, PLEASE.
PRINCESS AMAYA, I'M ALEX MONTEZ AND I'VE BEEN CHOSEN TO BECOME THE FIRST OFFICIAL AMBASSADOR TO THE SOVEREIGN WORLD OF NILAA.
AMBASSADOR? SERIOUSLY?
THE EXISTENCE OF THIS PORTAL RAISES MANY ISSUES CONCERNING THE SECURITY OF BOTH WORLDS AND THE ECONOMIC POTENTIAL OF TRADE.
I ASK ONLY FOR A CHANCE TO PRESENT MY OFFER FOR AN OFFICIAL ALLIANCE.

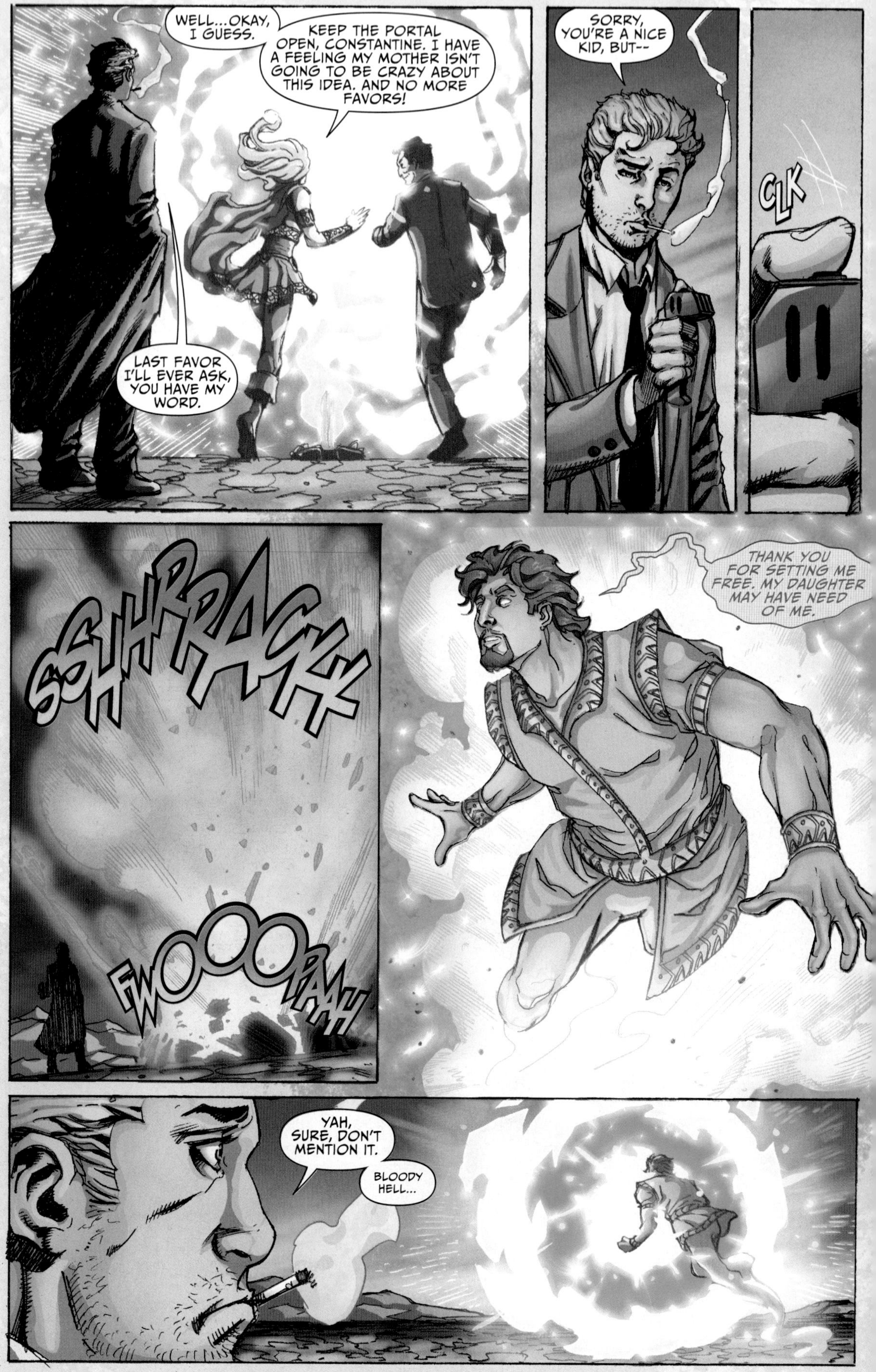
WELL...OKAY, I GUESS.
KEEP THE PORTAL OPEN, CONSTANTINE. I HAVE A FEELING MY MOTHER ISN'T GOING TO BE CRAZY ABOUT THIS IDEA. AND NO MORE FAVORS!
LAST FAVOR I'LL EVER ASK, YOU HAVE MY WORD.
SORRY, YOU'RE A NICE KID, BUT--
CLK
SSHHRACKK
FWOOOPAAH
THANK YOU FOR SETTING ME FREE. MY DAUGHTER MAY HAVE NEED OF ME.
YAH, SURE, DON'T MENTION IT.
BLOODY HELL...

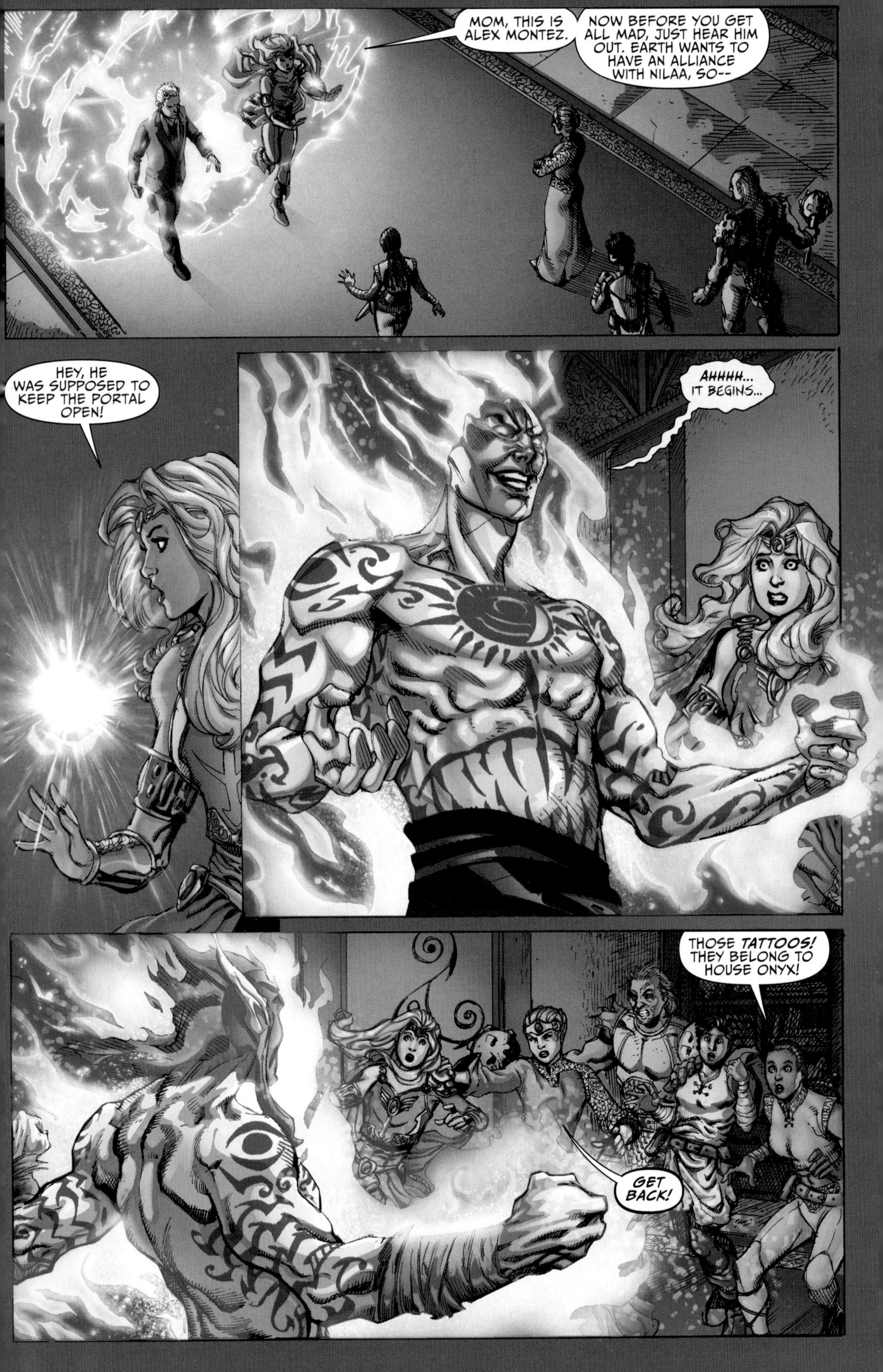
MOM, THIS IS ALEX MONTEZ.
NOW BEFORE YOU GET ALL MAD, JUST HEAR HIM OUT. EARTH WANTS TO HAVE AN ALLIANCE WITH NILAA, SO--
HEY, HE WAS SUPPOSED TO KEEP THE PORTAL OPEN!
AHHHH... IT BEGINS...
THOSE TATTOOS! THEY BELONG TO HOUSE ONYX!
GET BACK!

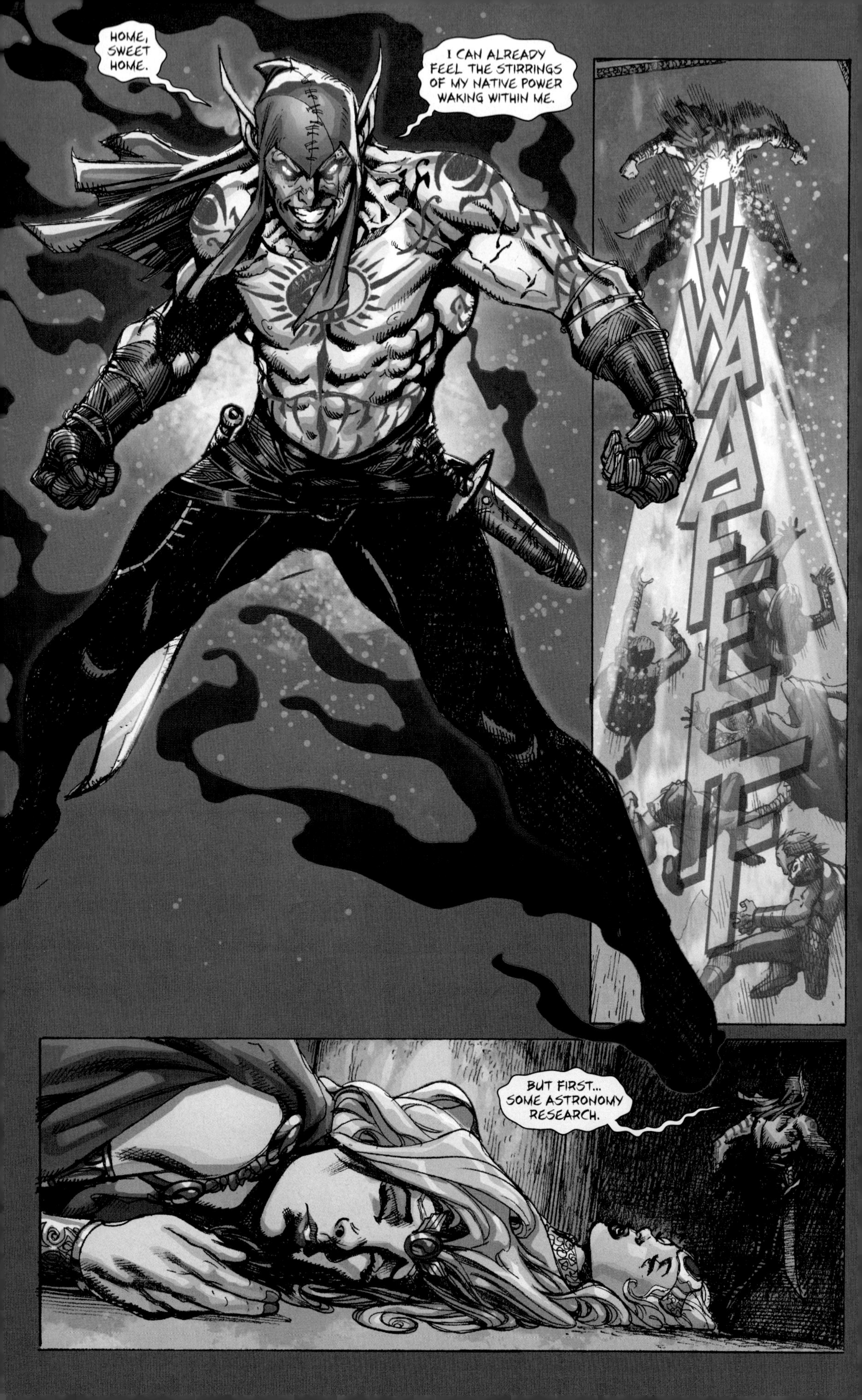
HOME, SWEET HOME.
I CAN ALREADY FEEL THE STIRRINGS OF MY NATIVE POWER WAKING WITHIN ME.
HWAAFEEEEEEH
BUT FIRST... SOME ASTRONOMY RESEARCH.

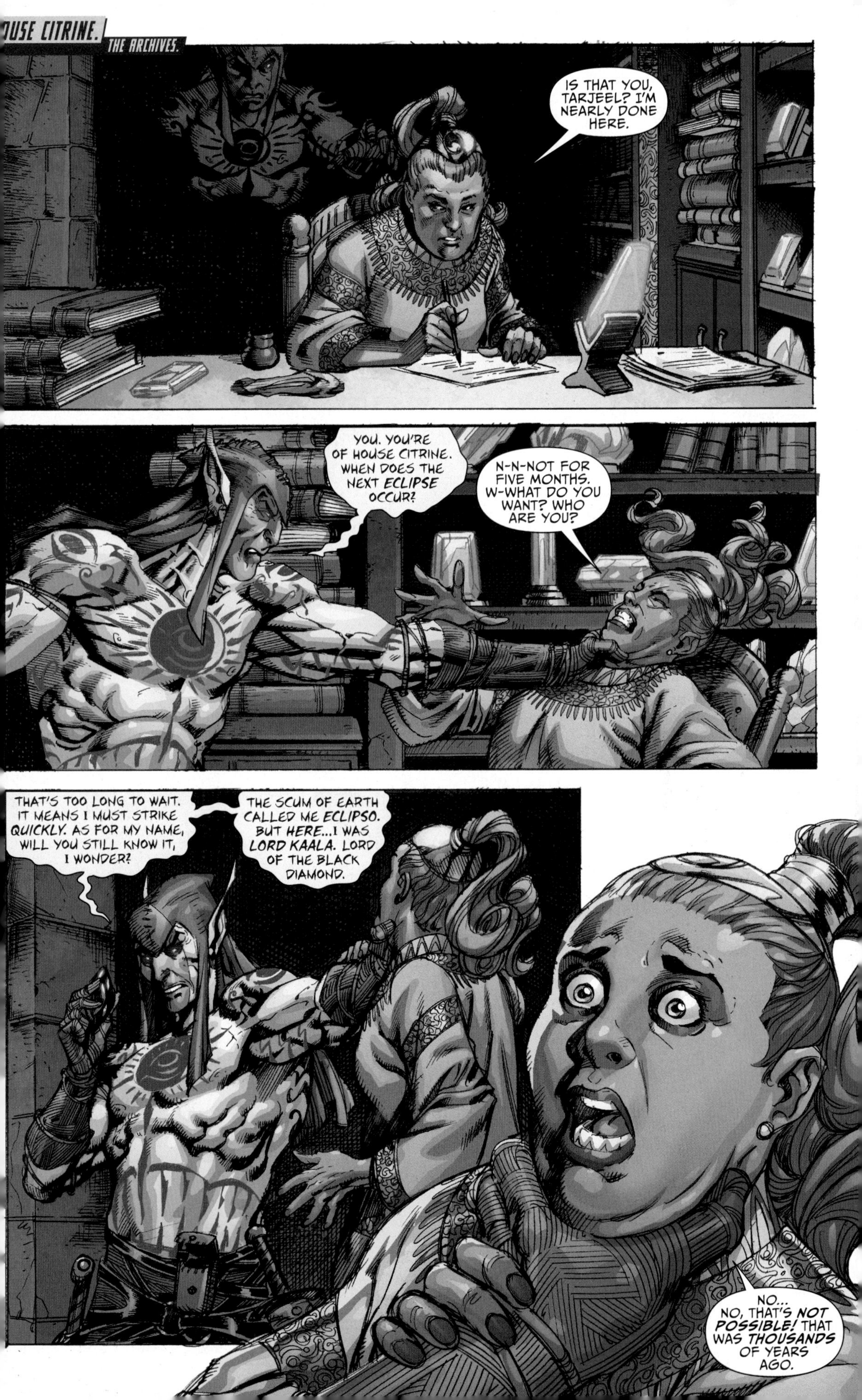
OUSE CITRINE.
THE ARCHIVES.
IS THAT YOU, TARJEEL? I'M NEARLY DONE HERE.
YOU. YOU'RE OF HOUSE CITRINE. WHEN DOES THE NEXT ECLIPSE OCCUR?
N-N-NOT FOR FIVE MONTHS. W-WHAT DO YOU WANT? WHO ARE YOU?
THAT'S TOO LONG TO WAIT. IT MEANS I MUST STRIKE QUICKLY. AS FOR MY NAME, WILL YOU STILL KNOW IT, I WONDER?
THE SCUM OF EARTH CALLED ME ECLIPSO. BUT HERE...I WAS LORD KAALA. LORD OF THE BLACK DIAMOND.
NO... NO, THAT'S NOT POSSIBLE! THAT WAS THOUSANDS OF YEARS AGO.

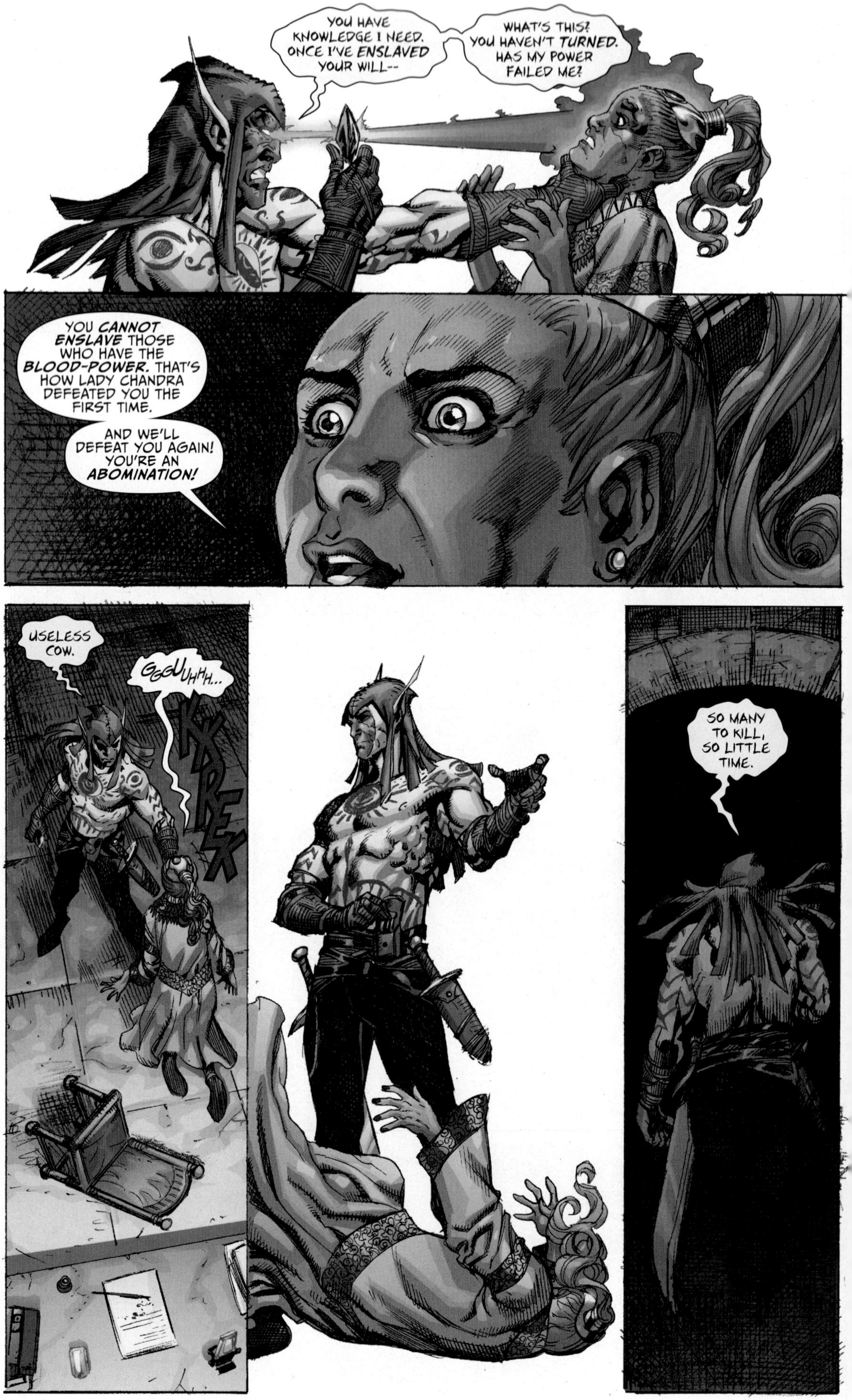
YOU HAVE KNOWLEDGE I NEED. ONCE I'VE ENSLAVED YOUR WILL--
WHAT'S THIS? YOU HAVEN'T TURNED. HAS MY POWER FAILED ME?
YOU CANNOT ENSLAVE THOSE WHO HAVE THE BLOOD-POWER. THAT'S HOW LADY CHANDRA DEFEATED YOU THE FIRST TIME.
AND WE'LL DEFEAT YOU AGAIN! YOU'RE AN ABOMINATION!
USELESS COW.
GGGUHHH...
KKREK
SO MANY TO KILL, SO LITTLE TIME.

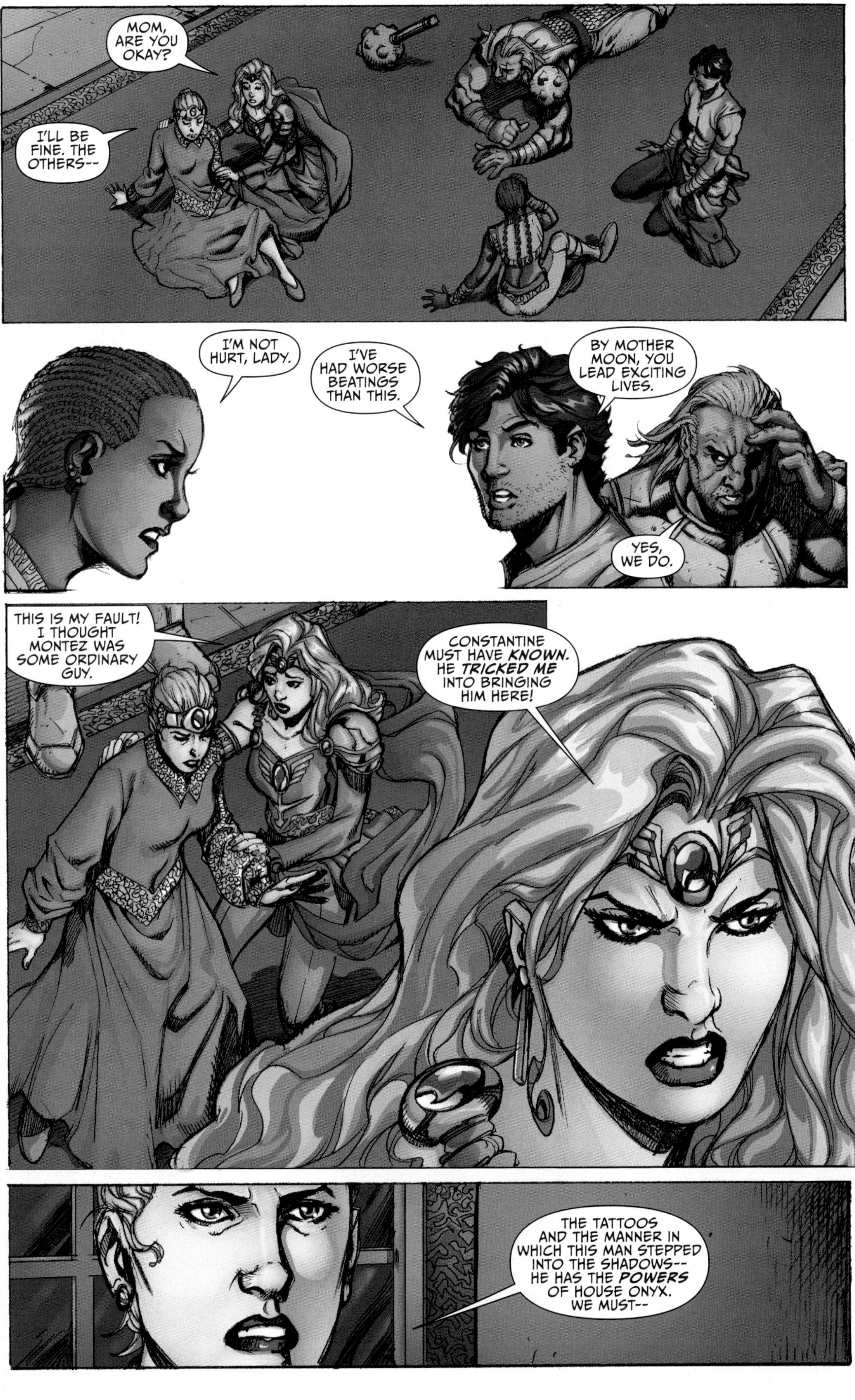

MOM, ARE YOU OKAY?
I'LL BE FINE. THE OTHERS--
I'M NOT HURT, LADY.
I'VE HAD WORSE BEATINGS THAN THIS.
BY MOTHER MOON, YOU LEAD EXCITING LIVES.
YES, WE DO.
THIS IS MY FAULT! I THOUGHT MONTEZ WAS SOME ORDINARY GUY.
CONSTANTINE MUST HAVE ***KNOWN.*** HE ***TRICKED ME*** INTO BRINGING HIM HERE!
THE TATTOOS AND THE MANNER IN WHICH THIS MAN STEPPED INTO THE SHADOWS-- HE HAS THE ***POWERS*** OF HOUSE ONYX. WE MUST--

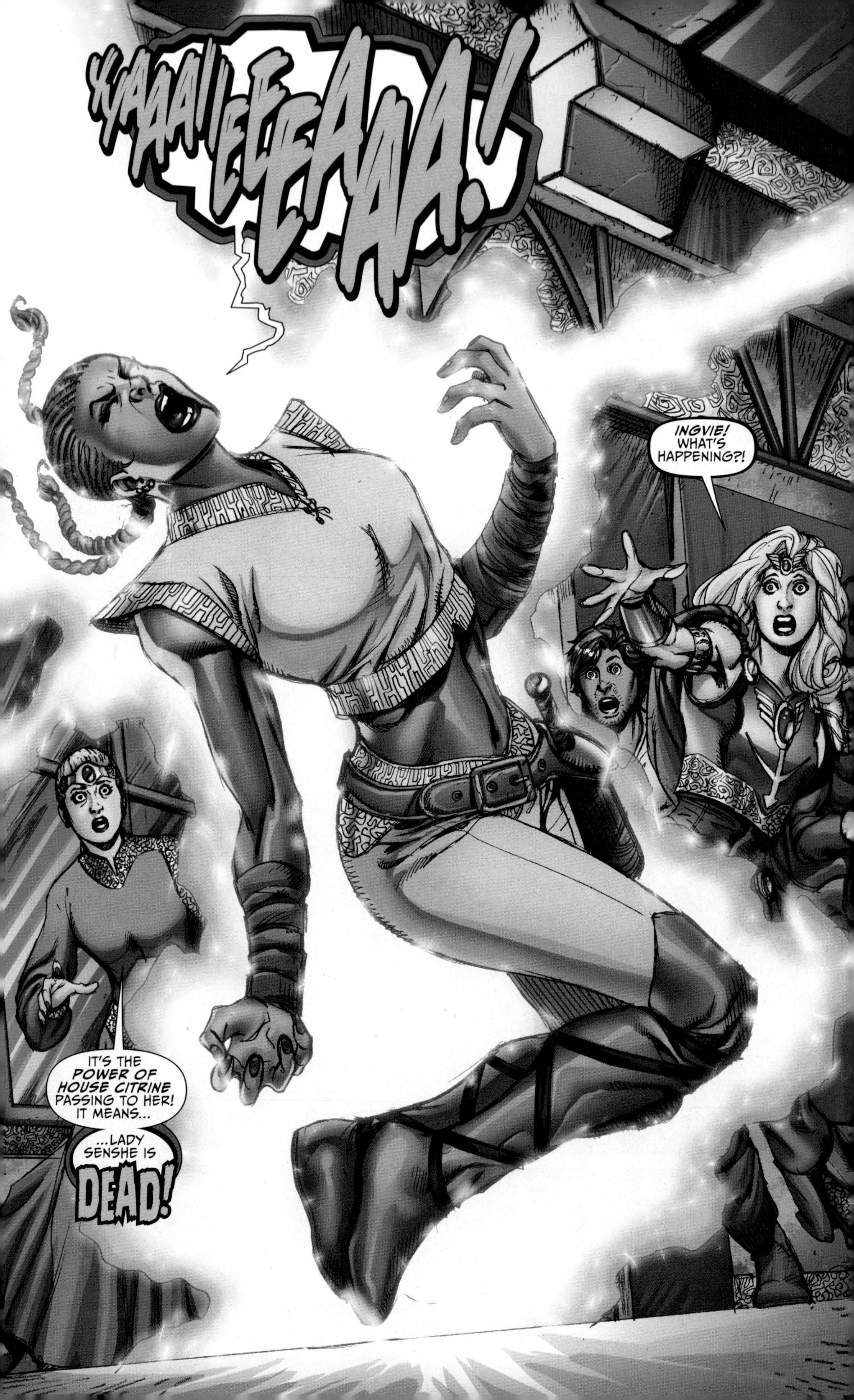
KYAAAIIIEEEEAAAA!
INGVIE! WHAT'S HAPPENING?!
IT'S THE POWER OF HOUSE CITRINE PASSING TO HER! IT MEANS...
...LADY SENSHE IS DEAD!

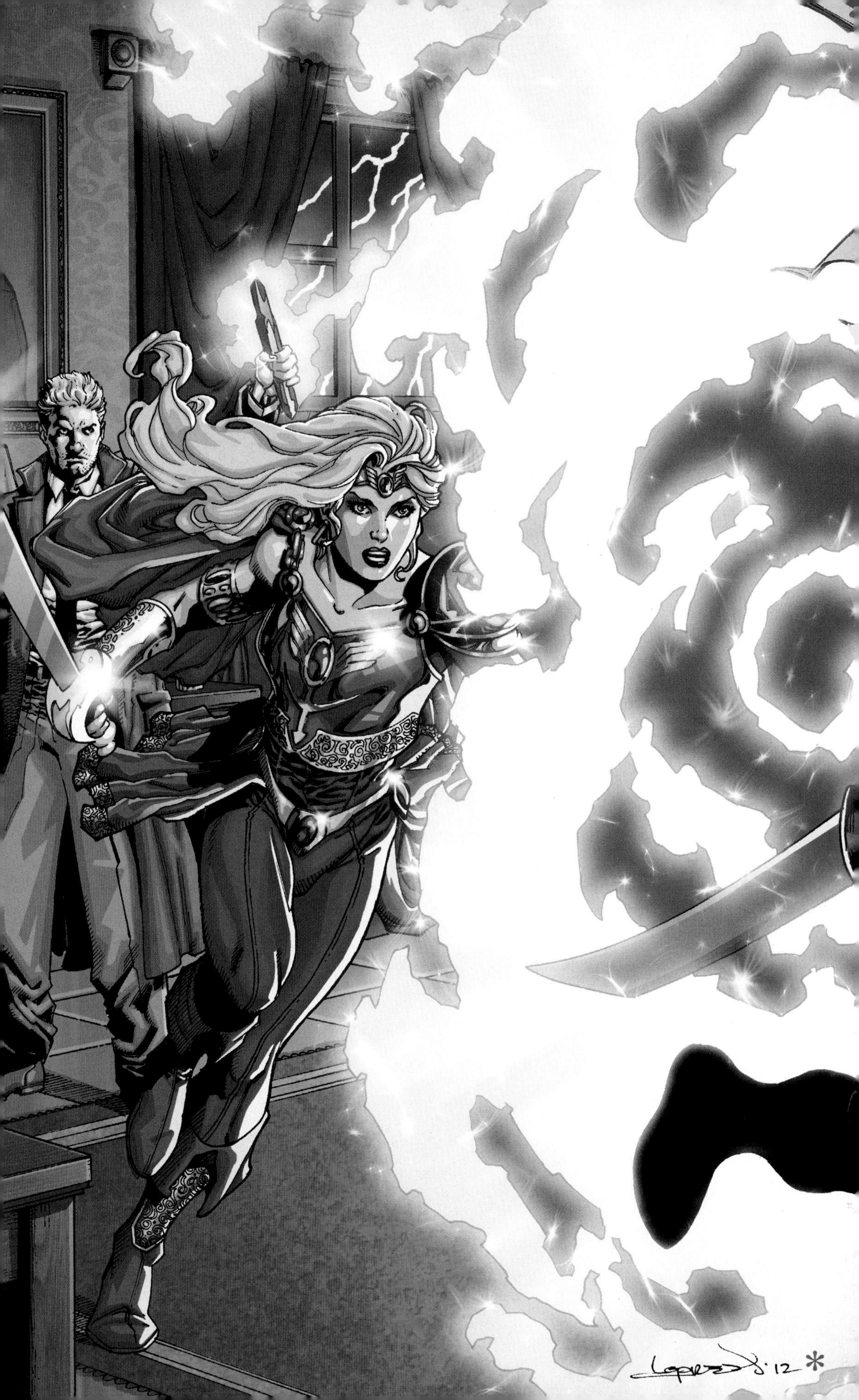

AMETHYST part eight ECLIPSO UNLEASHED

CHRISTY MARX writer **AARON LOPRESTI** artist cover by **AARON LOPRESTI & HI-FI**

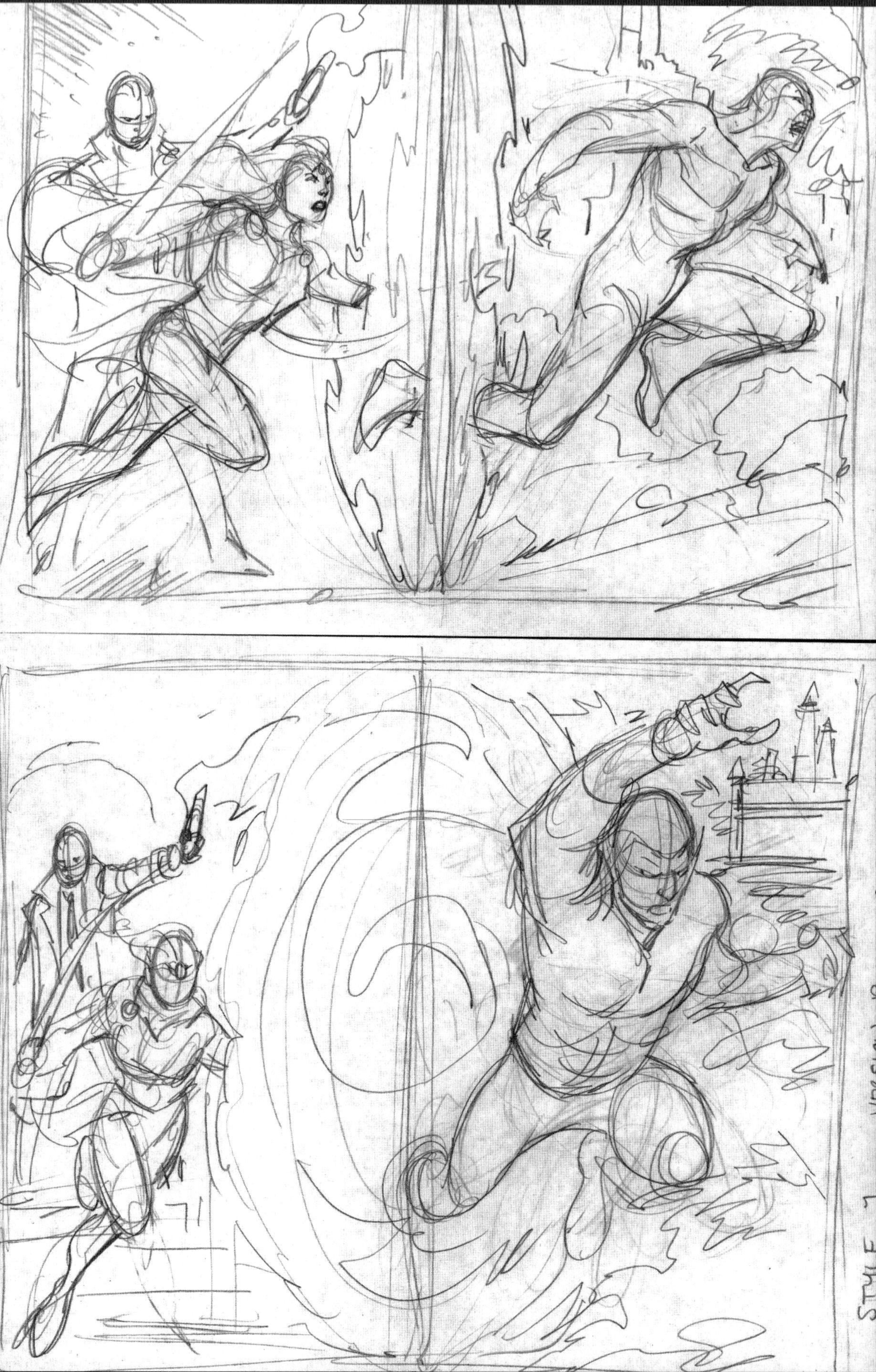

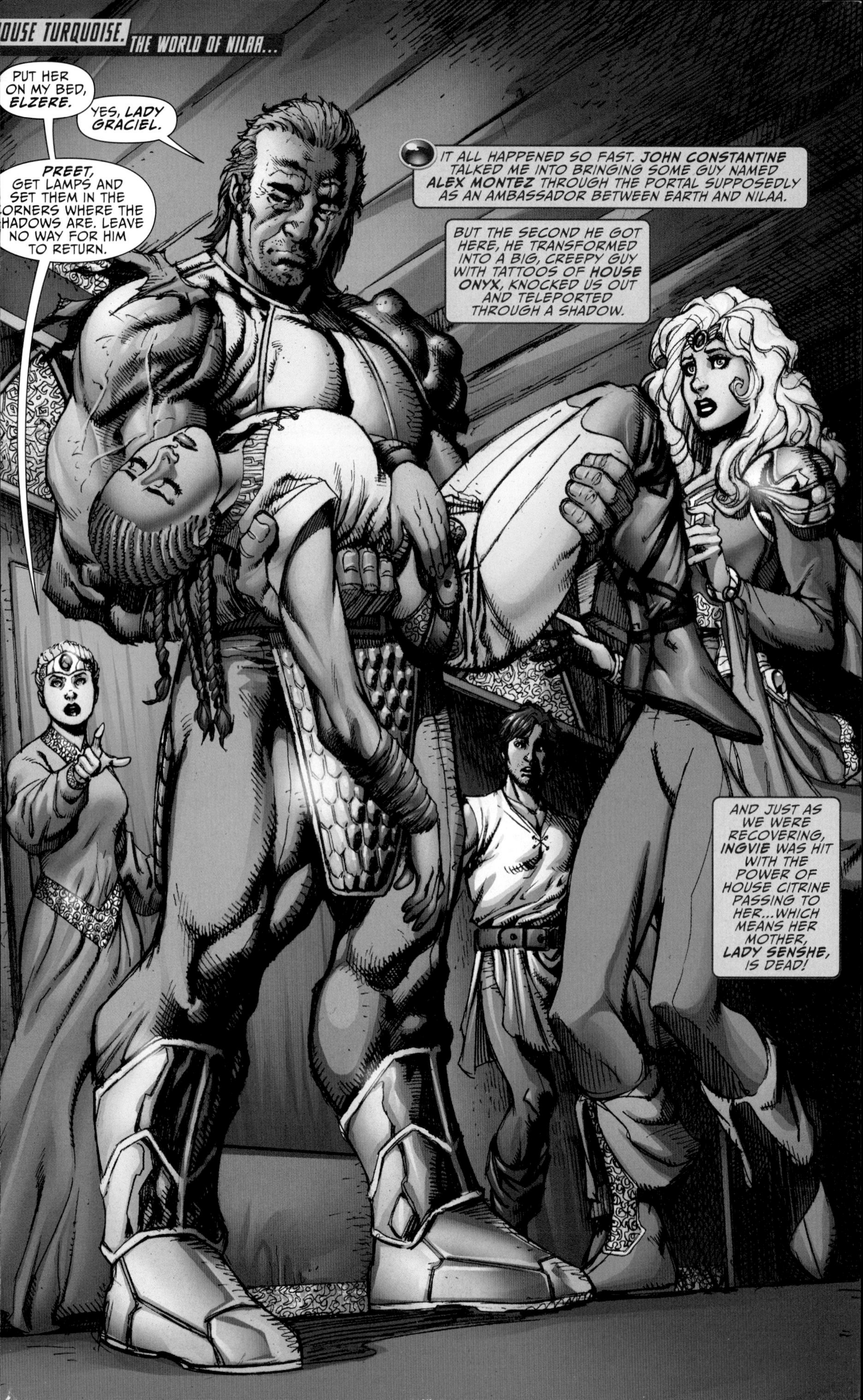
OUSE TURQUOISE.
THE WORLD OF NILAA...
PUT HER ON MY BED, ELZERE.
YES, LADY GRACIEL.
PREET, GET LAMPS AND SET THEM IN THE CORNERS WHERE THE SHADOWS ARE. LEAVE NO WAY FOR HIM TO RETURN.
IT ALL HAPPENED SO FAST. JOHN CONSTANTINE TALKED ME INTO BRINGING SOME GUY NAMED ALEX MONTEZ THROUGH THE PORTAL SUPPOSEDLY AS AN AMBASSADOR BETWEEN EARTH AND NILAA.
BUT THE SECOND HE GOT HERE, HE TRANSFORMED INTO A BIG, CREEPY GUY WITH TATTOOS OF HOUSE ONYX, KNOCKED US OUT AND TELEPORTED THROUGH A SHADOW.
AND JUST AS WE WERE RECOVERING, INGVIE WAS HIT WITH THE POWER OF HOUSE CITRINE PASSING TO HER...WHICH MEANS HER MOTHER, LADY SENSHE, IS DEAD!

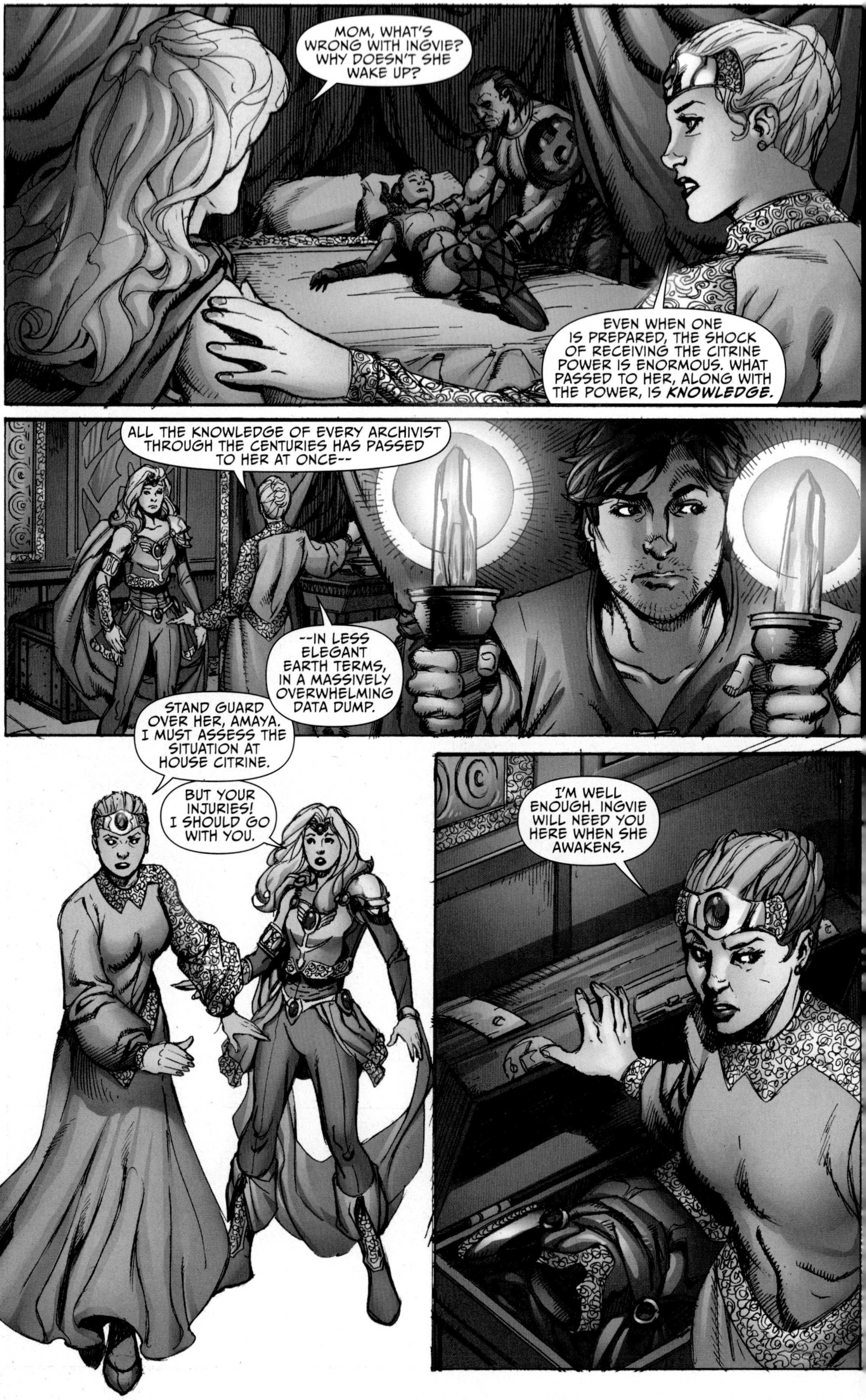
MOM, WHAT'S WRONG WITH INGVIE? WHY DOESN'T SHE WAKE UP?
EVEN WHEN ONE IS PREPARED, THE SHOCK OF RECEIVING THE CITRINE POWER IS ENORMOUS. WHAT PASSED TO HER, ALONG WITH THE POWER, IS *KNOWLEDGE.*
ALL THE KNOWLEDGE OF EVERY ARCHIVIST THROUGH THE CENTURIES HAS PASSED TO HER AT ONCE--
--IN LESS ELEGANT EARTH TERMS, IN A MASSIVELY OVERWHELMING DATA DUMP.
STAND GUARD OVER HER, AMAYA. I MUST ASSESS THE SITUATION AT HOUSE CITRINE.
BUT YOUR INJURIES! I SHOULD GO WITH YOU.
I'M WELL ENOUGH. INGVIE WILL NEED YOU HERE WHEN SHE AWAKENS.

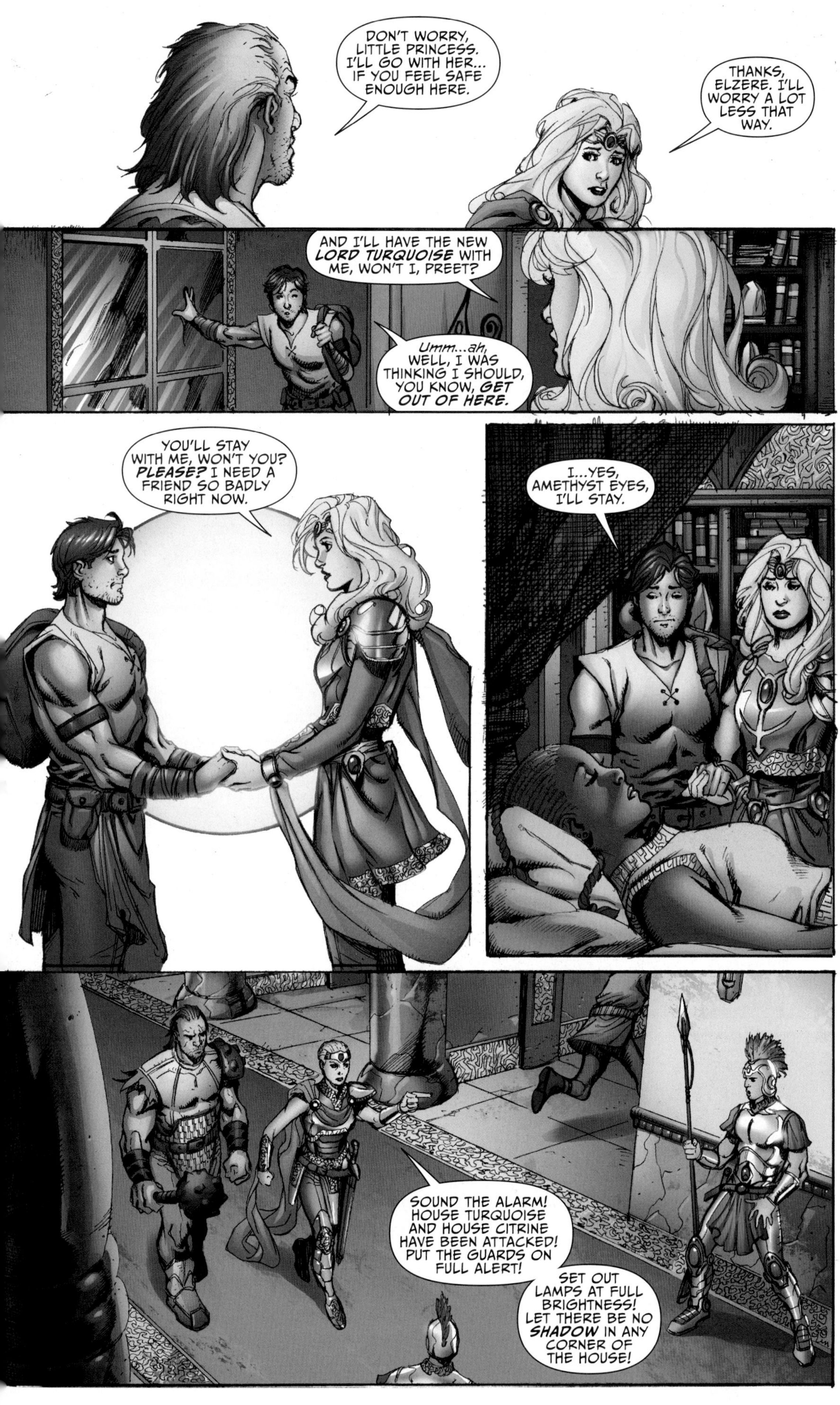
DON'T WORRY, LITTLE PRINCESS. I'LL GO WITH HER... IF YOU FEEL SAFE ENOUGH HERE.
THANKS, ELZERE. I'LL WORRY A LOT LESS THAT WAY.
AND I'LL HAVE THE NEW LORD TURQUOISE WITH ME, WON'T I, PREET?
Umm...ah, WELL, I WAS THINKING I SHOULD, YOU KNOW, GET OUT OF HERE.
YOU'LL STAY WITH ME, WON'T YOU? PLEASE? I NEED A FRIEND SO BADLY RIGHT NOW.
I...YES, AMETHYST EYES, I'LL STAY.
SOUND THE ALARM! HOUSE TURQUOISE AND HOUSE CITRINE HAVE BEEN ATTACKED! PUT THE GUARDS ON FULL ALERT!
SET OUT LAMPS AT FULL BRIGHTNESS! LET THERE BE NO SHADOW IN ANY CORNER OF THE HOUSE!

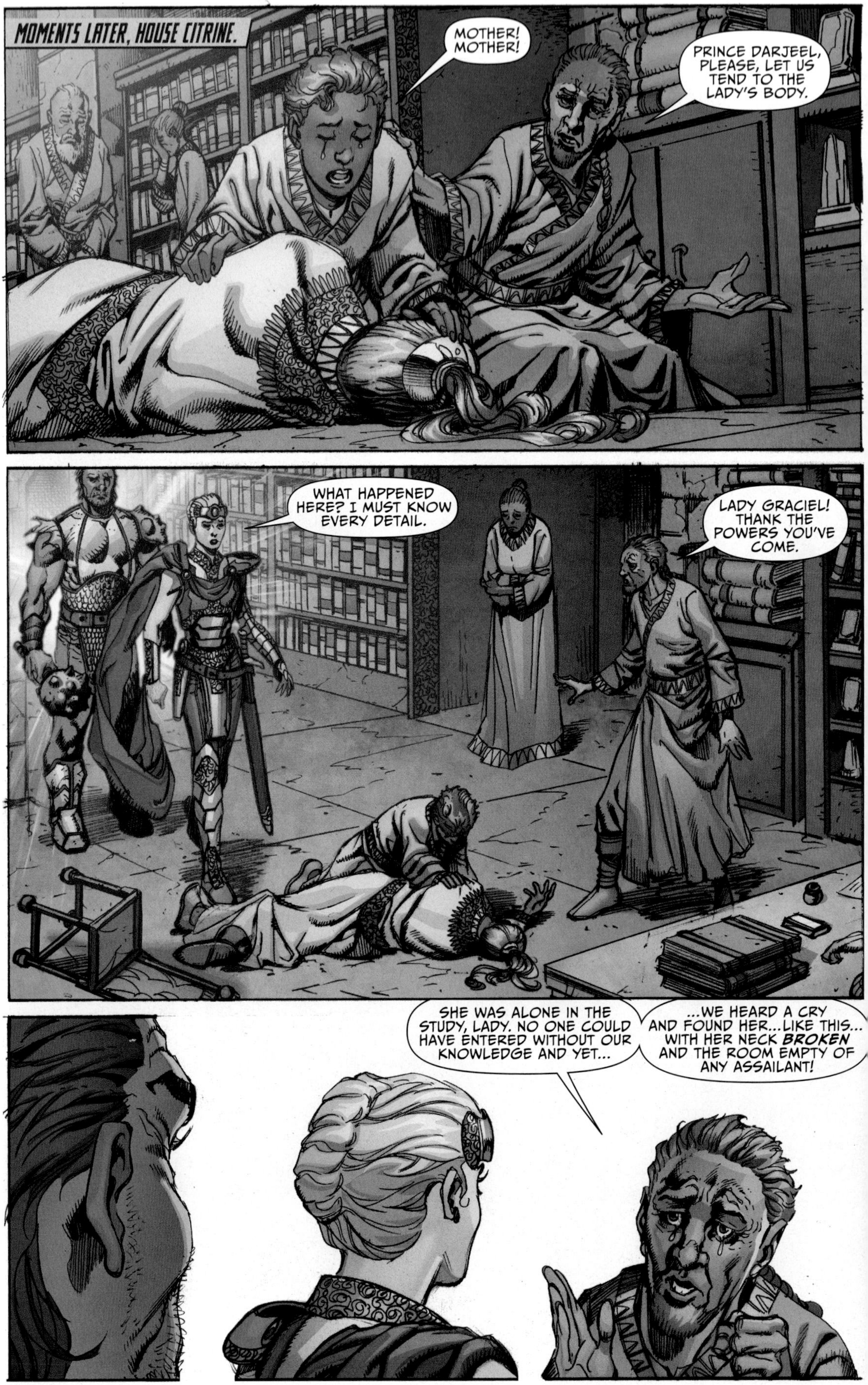

MOMENTS LATER, HOUSE CITRINE.
MOTHER! MOTHER!
PRINCE DARJEEL, PLEASE, LET US TEND TO THE LADY'S BODY.
WHAT HAPPENED HERE? I MUST KNOW EVERY DETAIL.
LADY GRACIEL! THANK THE POWERS YOU'VE COME.
SHE WAS ALONE IN THE STUDY, LADY. NO ONE COULD HAVE ENTERED WITHOUT OUR KNOWLEDGE AND YET...
...WE HEARD A CRY AND FOUND HER...LIKE THIS... WITH HER NECK BROKEN AND THE ROOM EMPTY OF ANY ASSAILANT!

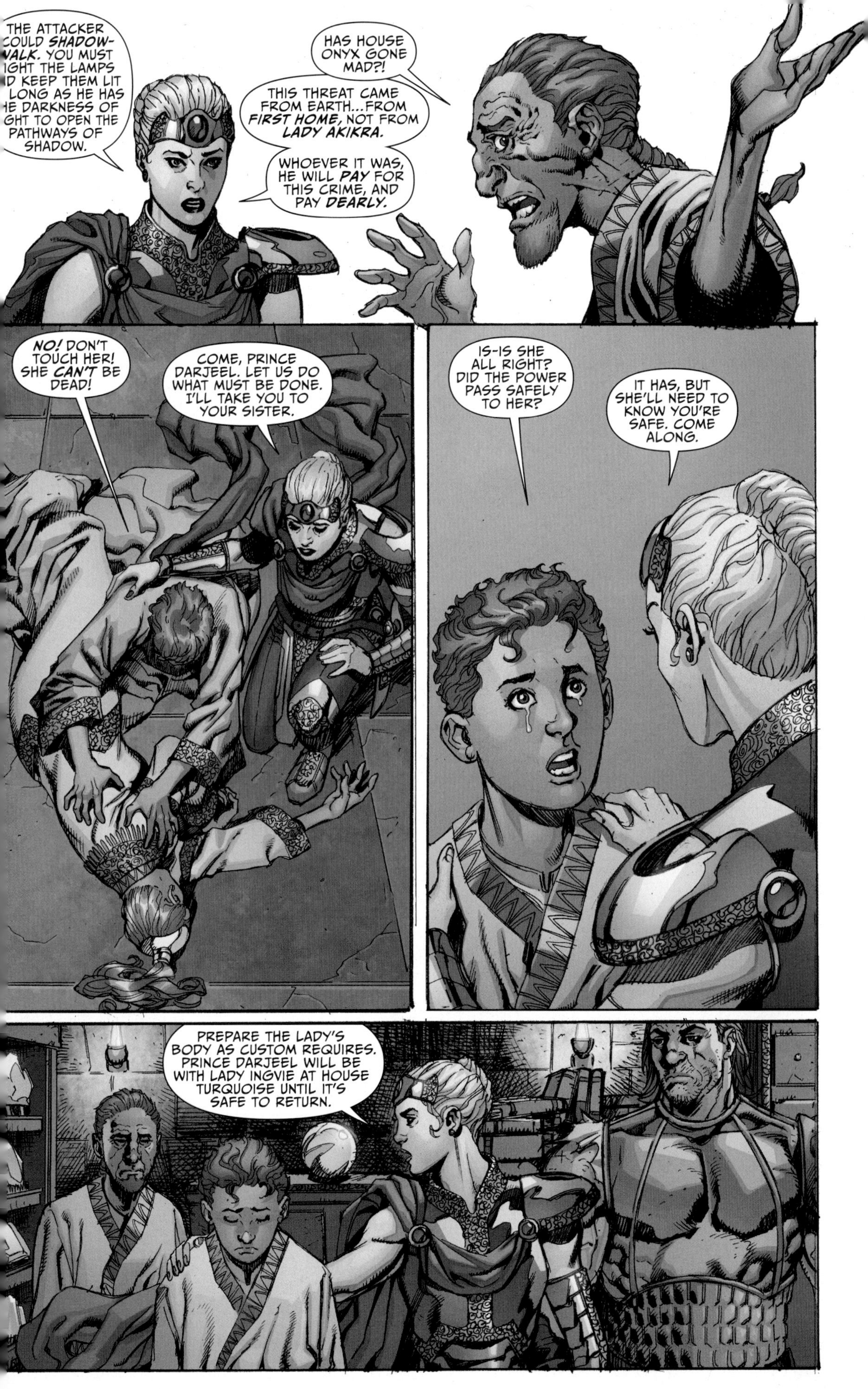
THE ATTACKER COULD SHADOW-WALK. YOU MUST LIGHT THE LAMPS AND KEEP THEM LIT AS LONG AS HE HAS THE DARKNESS OF NIGHT TO OPEN THE PATHWAYS OF SHADOW.
HAS HOUSE ONYX GONE MAD?!
THIS THREAT CAME FROM EARTH...FROM FIRST HOME, NOT FROM LADY AKIKRA.
WHOEVER IT WAS, HE WILL PAY FOR THIS CRIME, AND PAY DEARLY.
NO! DON'T TOUCH HER! SHE CAN'T BE DEAD!
COME, PRINCE DARJEEL. LET US DO WHAT MUST BE DONE. I'LL TAKE YOU TO YOUR SISTER.
IS-IS SHE ALL RIGHT? DID THE POWER PASS SAFELY TO HER?
IT HAS, BUT SHE'LL NEED TO KNOW YOU'RE SAFE. COME ALONG.
PREPARE THE LADY'S BODY AS CUSTOM REQUIRES. PRINCE DARJEEL WILL BE WITH LADY INGVIE AT HOUSE TURQUOISE UNTIL IT'S SAFE TO RETURN.

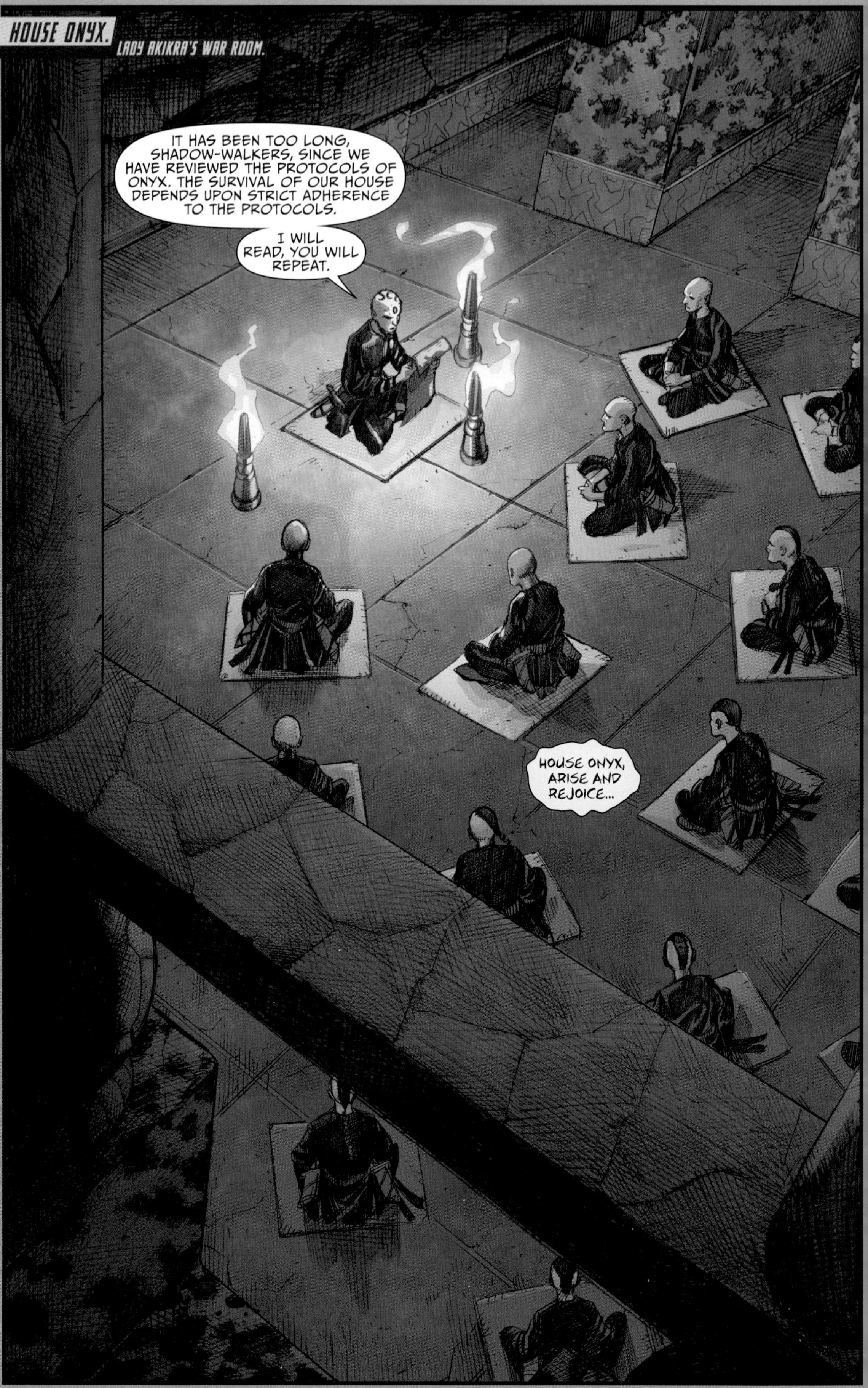
HOUSE ONYX.
LADY AKIKRA'S WAR ROOM.
IT HAS BEEN TOO LONG, SHADOW-WALKERS, SINCE WE HAVE REVIEWED THE PROTOCOLS OF ONYX. THE SURVIVAL OF OUR HOUSE DEPENDS UPON STRICT ADHERENCE TO THE PROTOCOLS.
I WILL READ, YOU WILL REPEAT.
HOUSE ONYX, ARISE AND REJOICE...

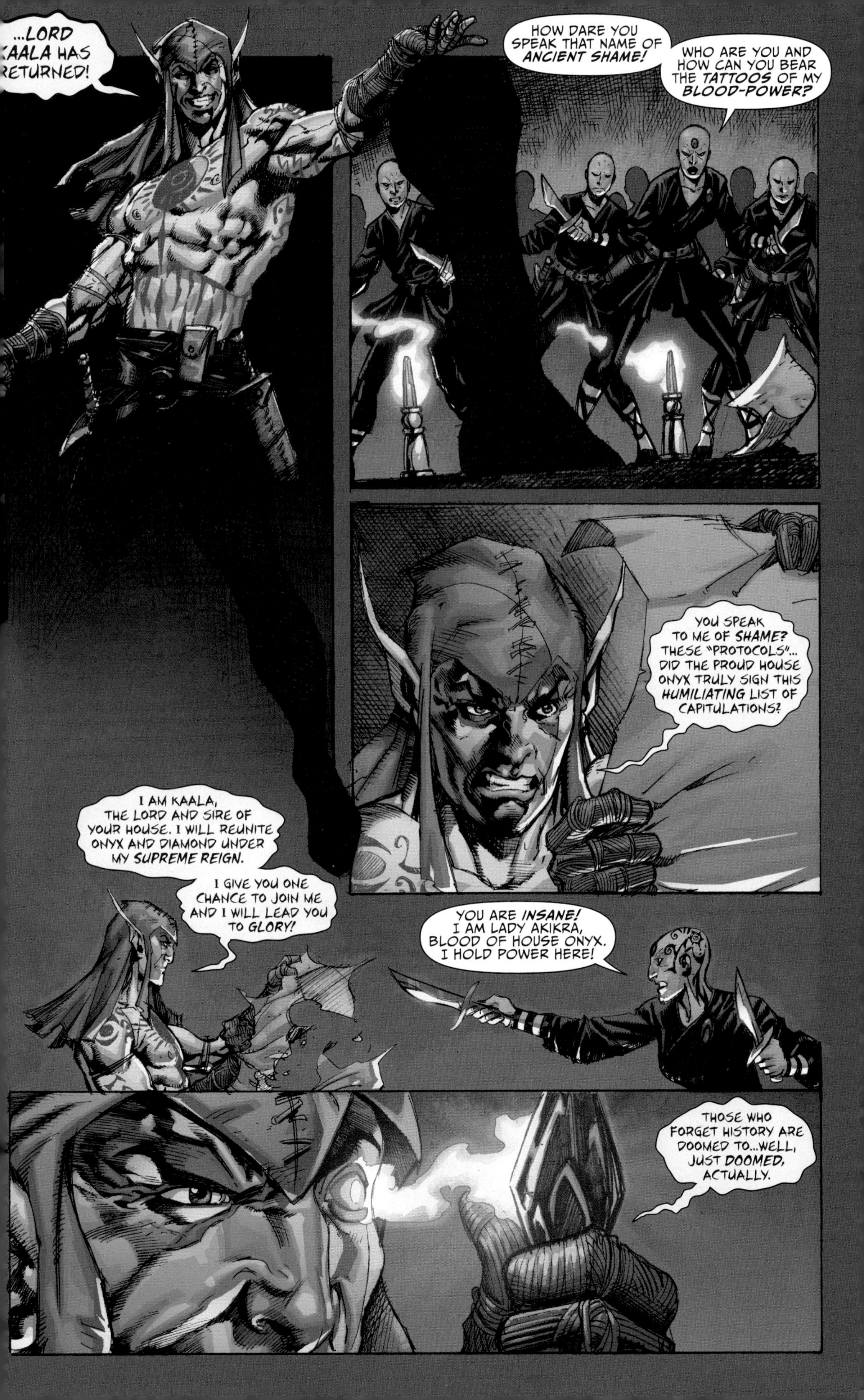
...LORD KAALA HAS RETURNED!
HOW DARE YOU SPEAK THAT NAME OF ANCIENT SHAME!
WHO ARE YOU AND HOW CAN YOU BEAR THE TATTOOS OF MY BLOOD-POWER?
YOU SPEAK TO ME OF SHAME? THESE "PROTOCOLS"... DID THE PROUD HOUSE ONYX TRULY SIGN THIS HUMILIATING LIST OF CAPITULATIONS?
I AM KAALA, THE LORD AND SIRE OF YOUR HOUSE. I WILL REUNITE ONYX AND DIAMOND UNDER MY SUPREME REIGN.
I GIVE YOU ONE CHANCE TO JOIN ME AND I WILL LEAD YOU TO GLORY!
YOU ARE INSANE! I AM LADY AKIKRA, BLOOD OF HOUSE ONYX. I HOLD POWER HERE!
THOSE WHO FORGET HISTORY ARE DOOMED TO...WELL, JUST DOOMED, ACTUALLY.

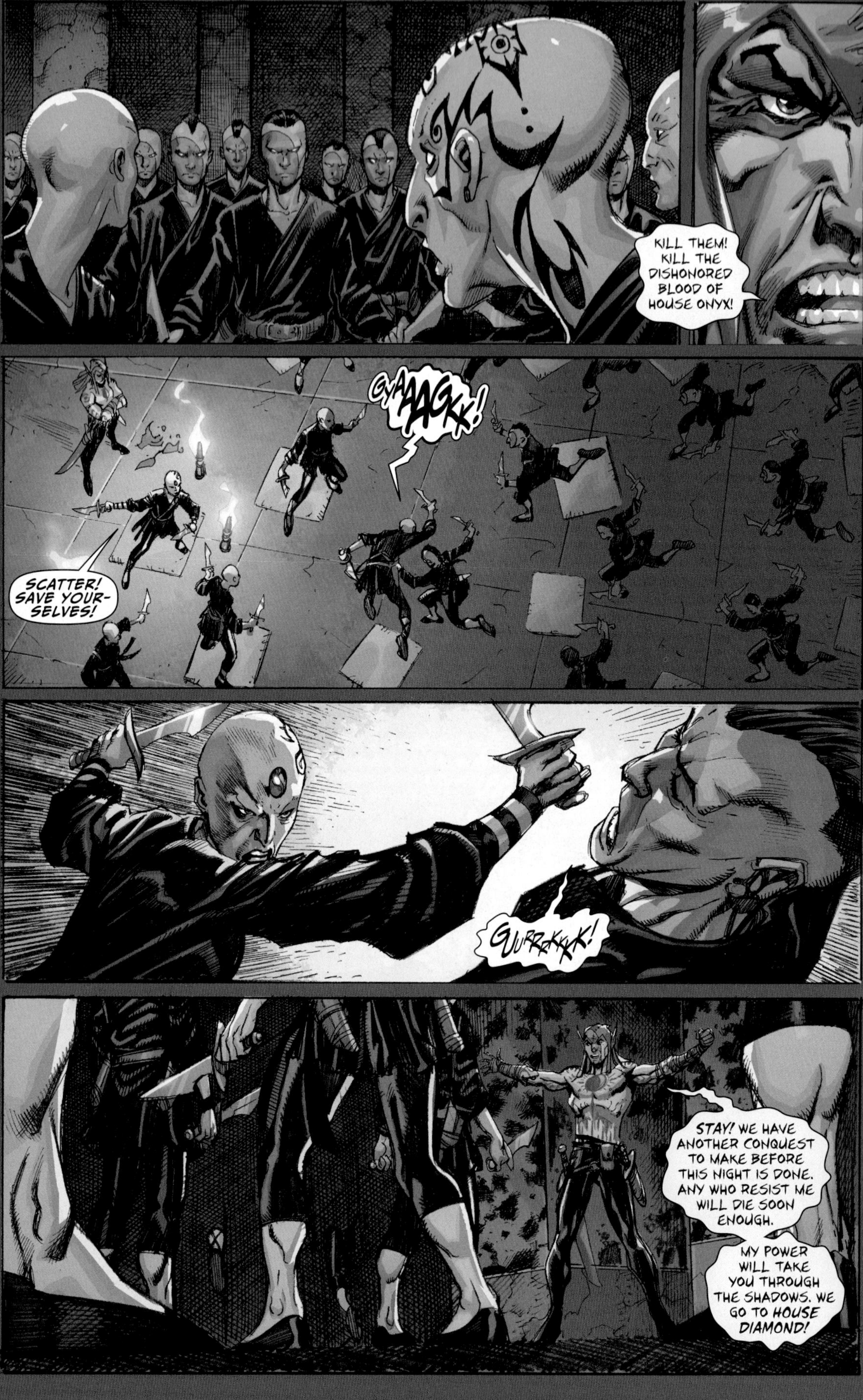
KILL THEM! KILL THE DISHONORED BLOOD OF HOUSE ONYX!
GYAAAGKK!
SCATTER! SAVE YOURSELVES!
GUURRKKKK!
STAY! WE HAVE ANOTHER CONQUEST TO MAKE BEFORE THIS NIGHT IS DONE. ANY WHO RESIST ME WILL DIE SOON ENOUGH.
MY POWER WILL TAKE YOU THROUGH THE SHADOWS. WE GO TO HOUSE DIAMOND!

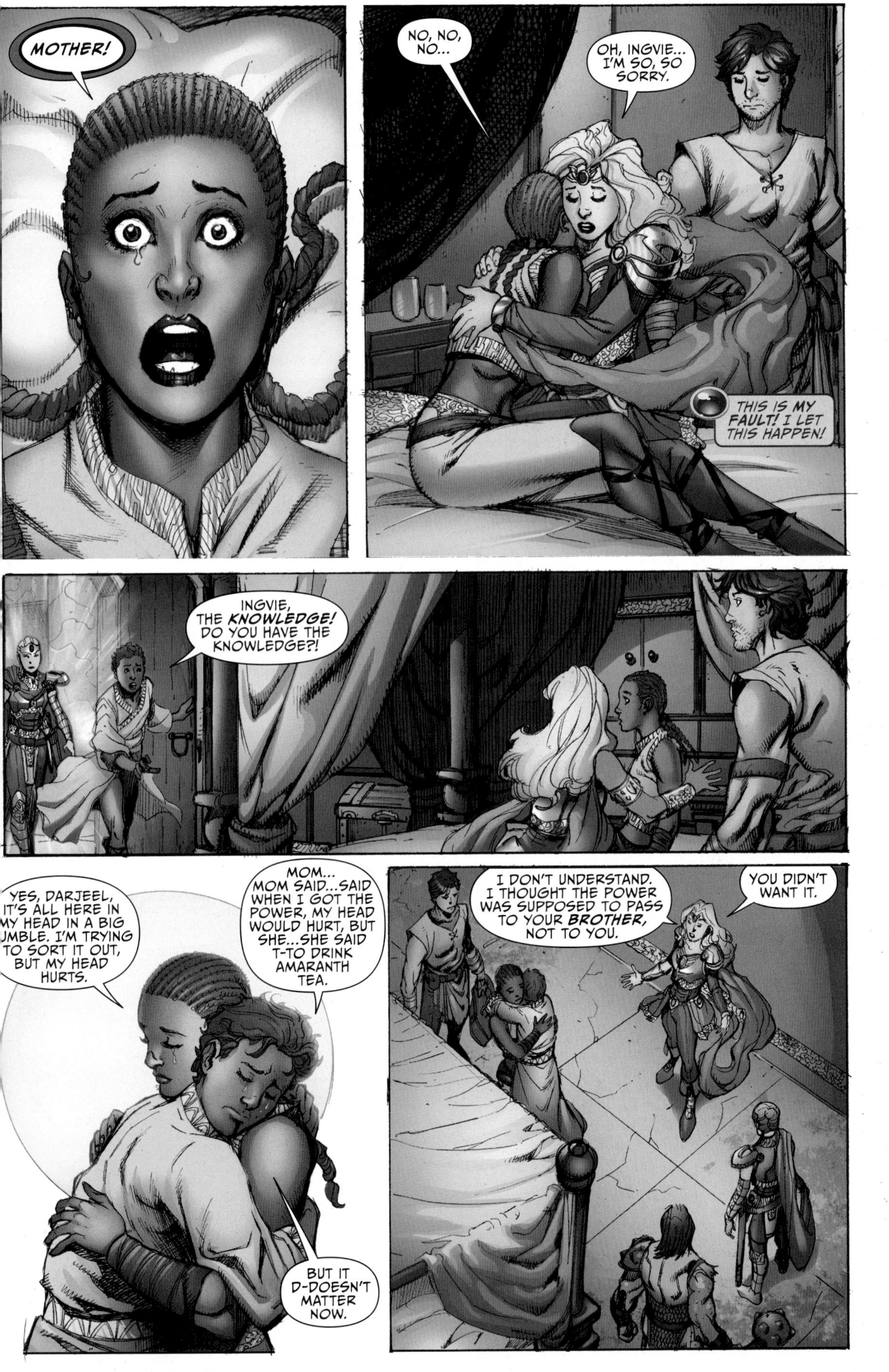
MOTHER!
NO, NO, NO...
OH, INGVIE... I'M SO, SO SORRY.
THIS IS MY FAULT! I LET THIS HAPPEN!
INGVIE, THE KNOWLEDGE! DO YOU HAVE THE KNOWLEDGE?!
YES, DARJEEL, IT'S ALL HERE IN MY HEAD IN A BIG JUMBLE. I'M TRYING TO SORT IT OUT, BUT MY HEAD HURTS.
MOM... MOM SAID...SAID WHEN I GOT THE POWER, MY HEAD WOULD HURT, BUT SHE...SHE SAID T-TO DRINK AMARANTH TEA.
BUT IT D-DOESN'T MATTER NOW.
I DON'T UNDERSTAND. I THOUGHT THE POWER WAS SUPPOSED TO PASS TO YOUR BROTHER, NOT TO YOU.
YOU DIDN'T WANT IT.

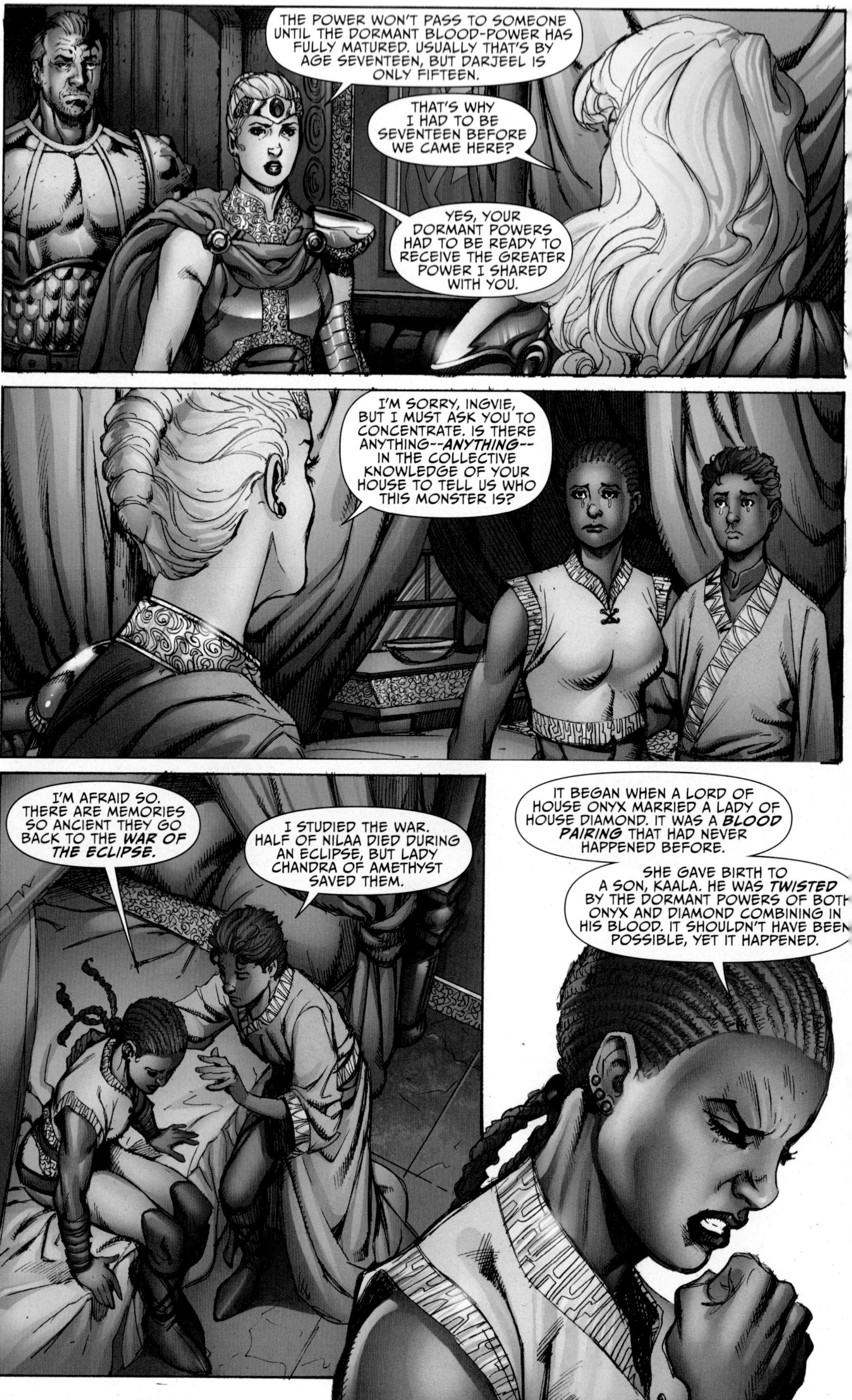
THE POWER WON'T PASS TO SOMEONE UNTIL THE DORMANT BLOOD-POWER HAS FULLY MATURED. USUALLY THAT'S BY AGE SEVENTEEN, BUT DARJEEL IS ONLY FIFTEEN.
THAT'S WHY I HAD TO BE SEVENTEEN BEFORE WE CAME HERE?
YES, YOUR DORMANT POWERS HAD TO BE READY TO RECEIVE THE GREATER POWER I SHARED WITH YOU.
I'M SORRY, INGVIE, BUT I MUST ASK YOU TO CONCENTRATE. IS THERE ANYTHING--*ANYTHING*-- IN THE COLLECTIVE KNOWLEDGE OF YOUR HOUSE TO TELL US WHO THIS MONSTER IS?
I'M AFRAID SO. THERE ARE MEMORIES SO ANCIENT THEY GO BACK TO THE *WAR OF THE ECLIPSE.*
I STUDIED THE WAR. HALF OF NILAA DIED DURING AN ECLIPSE, BUT LADY CHANDRA OF AMETHYST SAVED THEM.
IT BEGAN WHEN A LORD OF HOUSE ONYX MARRIED A LADY OF HOUSE DIAMOND. IT WAS A *BLOOD PAIRING* THAT HAD NEVER HAPPENED BEFORE.
SHE GAVE BIRTH TO A SON, KAALA. HE WAS *TWISTED* BY THE DORMANT POWERS OF BOTH ONYX AND DIAMOND COMBINING IN HIS BLOOD. IT SHOULDN'T HAVE BEEN POSSIBLE, YET IT HAPPENED.

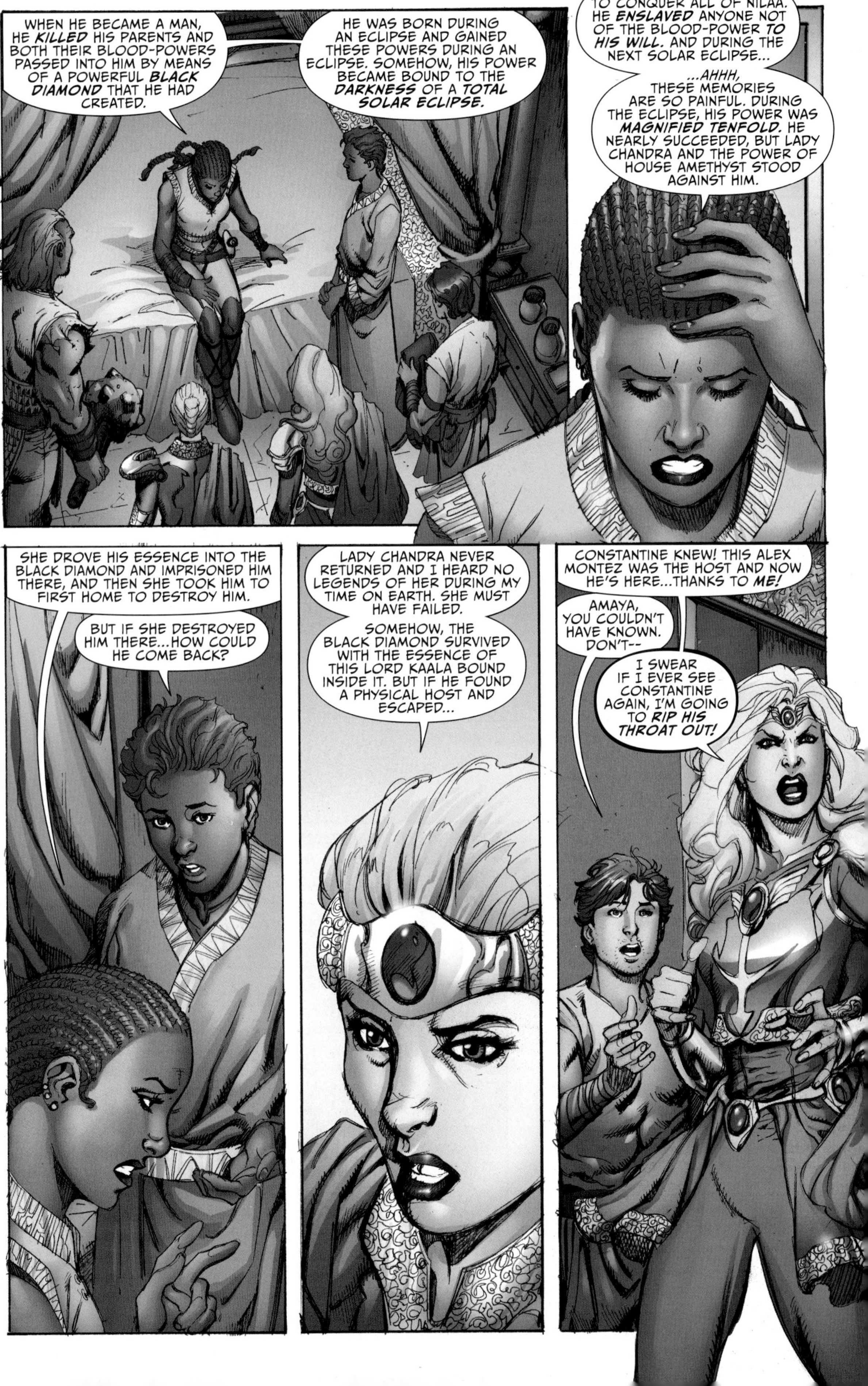
WHEN HE BECAME A MAN, HE KILLED HIS PARENTS AND BOTH THEIR BLOOD-POWERS PASSED INTO HIM BY MEANS OF A POWERFUL BLACK DIAMOND THAT HE HAD CREATED.
HE WAS BORN DURING AN ECLIPSE AND GAINED THESE POWERS DURING AN ECLIPSE. SOMEHOW, HIS POWER BECAME BOUND TO THE DARKNESS OF A TOTAL SOLAR ECLIPSE.
HE WAGED WAR TO CONQUER ALL OF NILAA. HE ENSLAVED ANYONE NOT OF THE BLOOD-POWER TO HIS WILL. AND DURING THE NEXT SOLAR ECLIPSE...
...AHHH, THESE MEMORIES ARE SO PAINFUL. DURING THE ECLIPSE, HIS POWER WAS MAGNIFIED TENFOLD. HE NEARLY SUCCEEDED, BUT LADY CHANDRA AND THE POWER OF HOUSE AMETHYST STOOD AGAINST HIM.
SHE DROVE HIS ESSENCE INTO THE BLACK DIAMOND AND IMPRISONED HIM THERE, AND THEN SHE TOOK HIM TO FIRST HOME TO DESTROY HIM.
BUT IF SHE DESTROYED HIM THERE...HOW COULD HE COME BACK?
LADY CHANDRA NEVER RETURNED AND I HEARD NO LEGENDS OF HER DURING MY TIME ON EARTH. SHE MUST HAVE FAILED.
SOMEHOW, THE BLACK DIAMOND SURVIVED WITH THE ESSENCE OF THIS LORD KAALA BOUND INSIDE IT. BUT IF HE FOUND A PHYSICAL HOST AND ESCAPED...
CONSTANTINE KNEW! THIS ALEX MONTEZ WAS THE HOST AND NOW HE'S HERE...THANKS TO ME!
AMAYA, YOU COULDN'T HAVE KNOWN. DON'T--
I SWEAR IF I EVER SEE CONSTANTINE AGAIN, I'M GOING TO RIP HIS THROAT OUT!

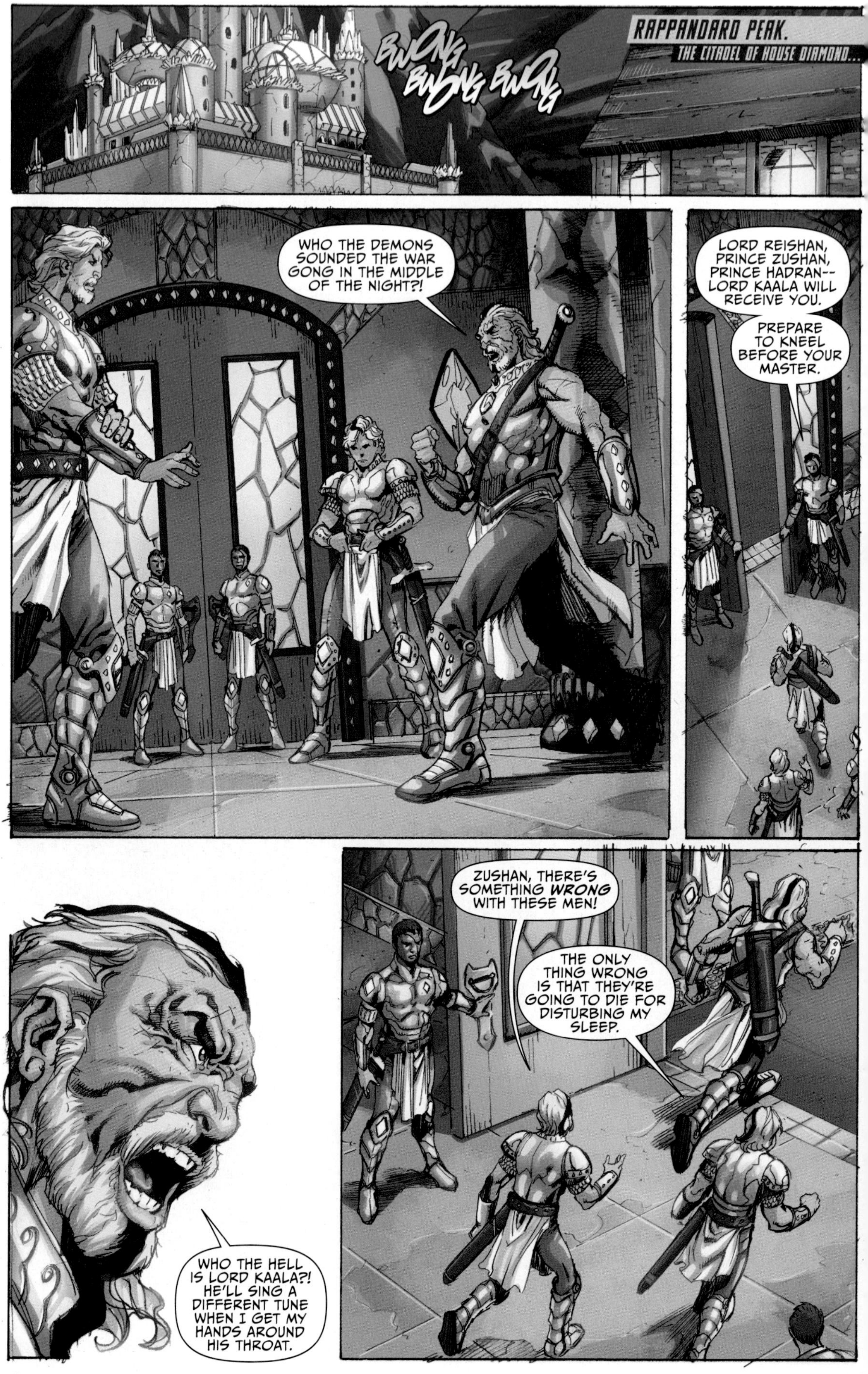
RAPPANDARO PEAK.
THE CITADEL OF HOUSE DIAMOND...
BWONG BWONG BWONG
WHO THE DEMONS SOUNDED THE WAR GONG IN THE MIDDLE OF THE NIGHT?!
LORD REISHAN, PRINCE ZUSHAN, PRINCE HADRAN-- LORD KAALA WILL RECEIVE YOU.
PREPARE TO KNEEL BEFORE YOUR MASTER.
WHO THE HELL IS LORD KAALA?! HE'LL SING A DIFFERENT TUNE WHEN I GET MY HANDS AROUND HIS THROAT.
ZUSHAN, THERE'S SOMETHING WRONG WITH THESE MEN!
THE ONLY THING WRONG IS THAT THEY'RE GOING TO DIE FOR DISTURBING MY SLEEP.

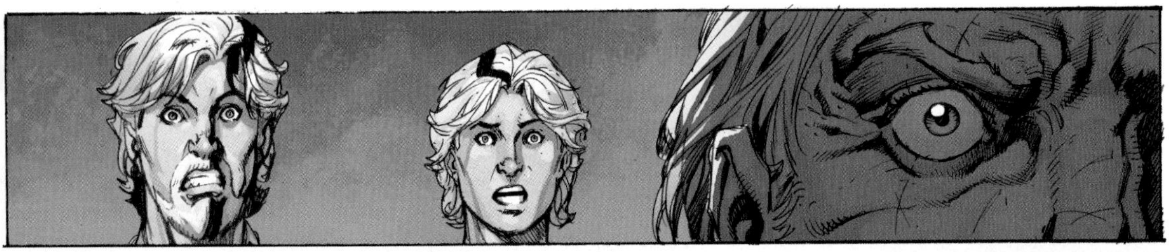

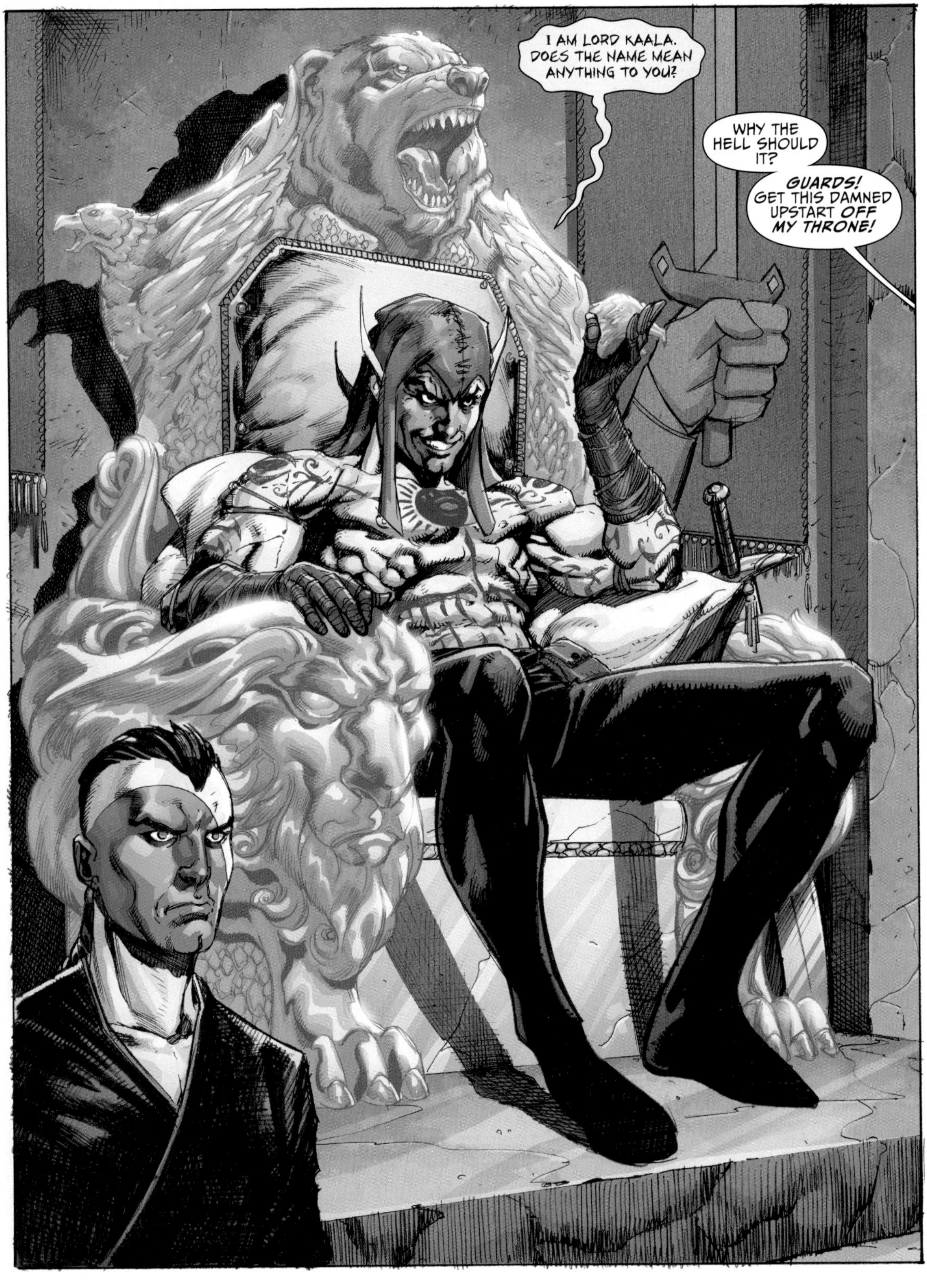
I AM LORD KAALA. DOES THE NAME MEAN ANYTHING TO YOU?
WHY THE HELL SHOULD IT?
GUARDS! GET THIS DAMNED UPSTART OFF MY THRONE!

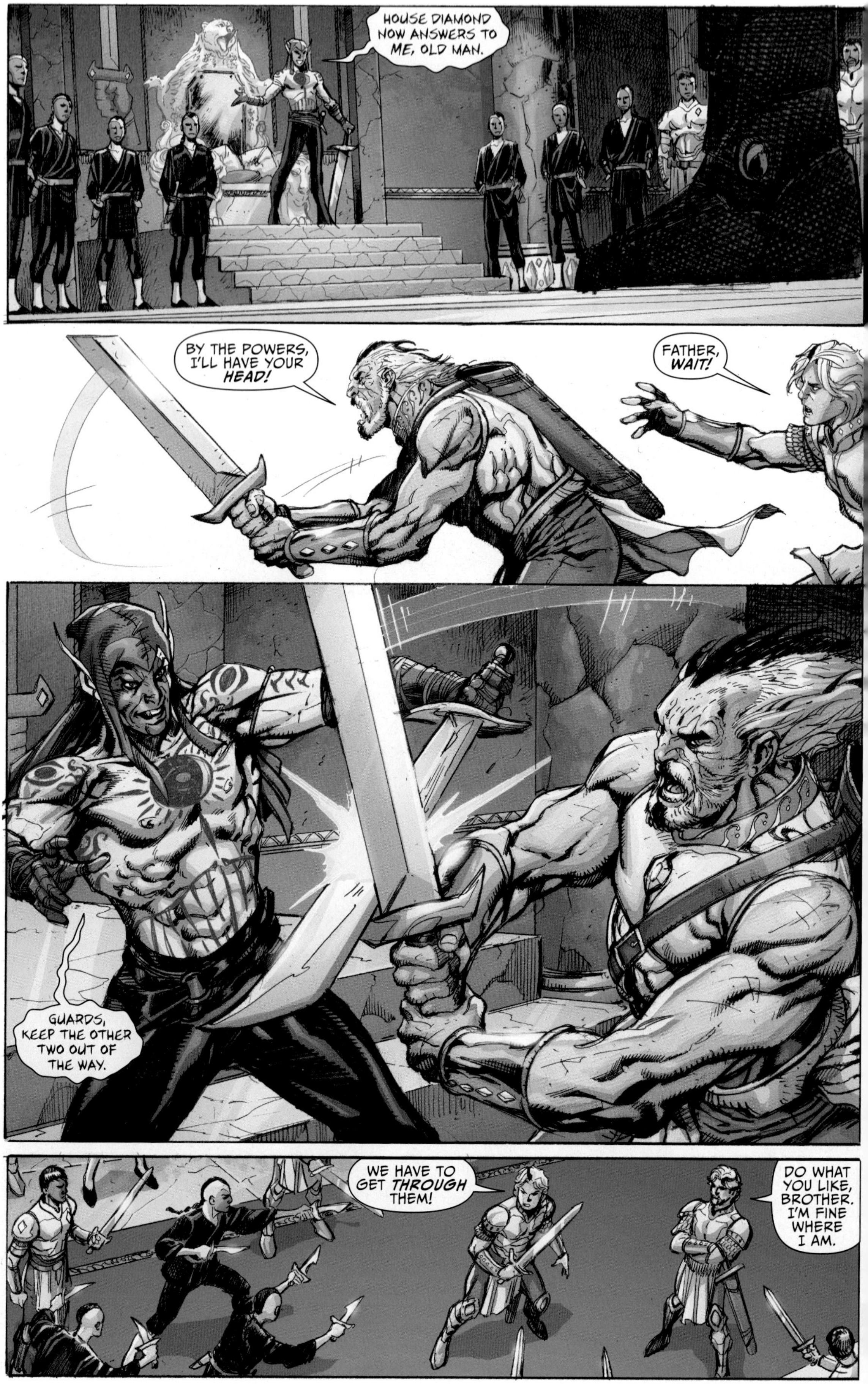
HOUSE DIAMOND NOW ANSWERS TO ME, OLD MAN.
BY THE POWERS, I'LL HAVE YOUR HEAD!
FATHER, WAIT!
GUARDS, KEEP THE OTHER TWO OUT OF THE WAY.
WE HAVE TO GET THROUGH THEM!
DO WHAT YOU LIKE, BROTHER. I'M FINE WHERE I AM.

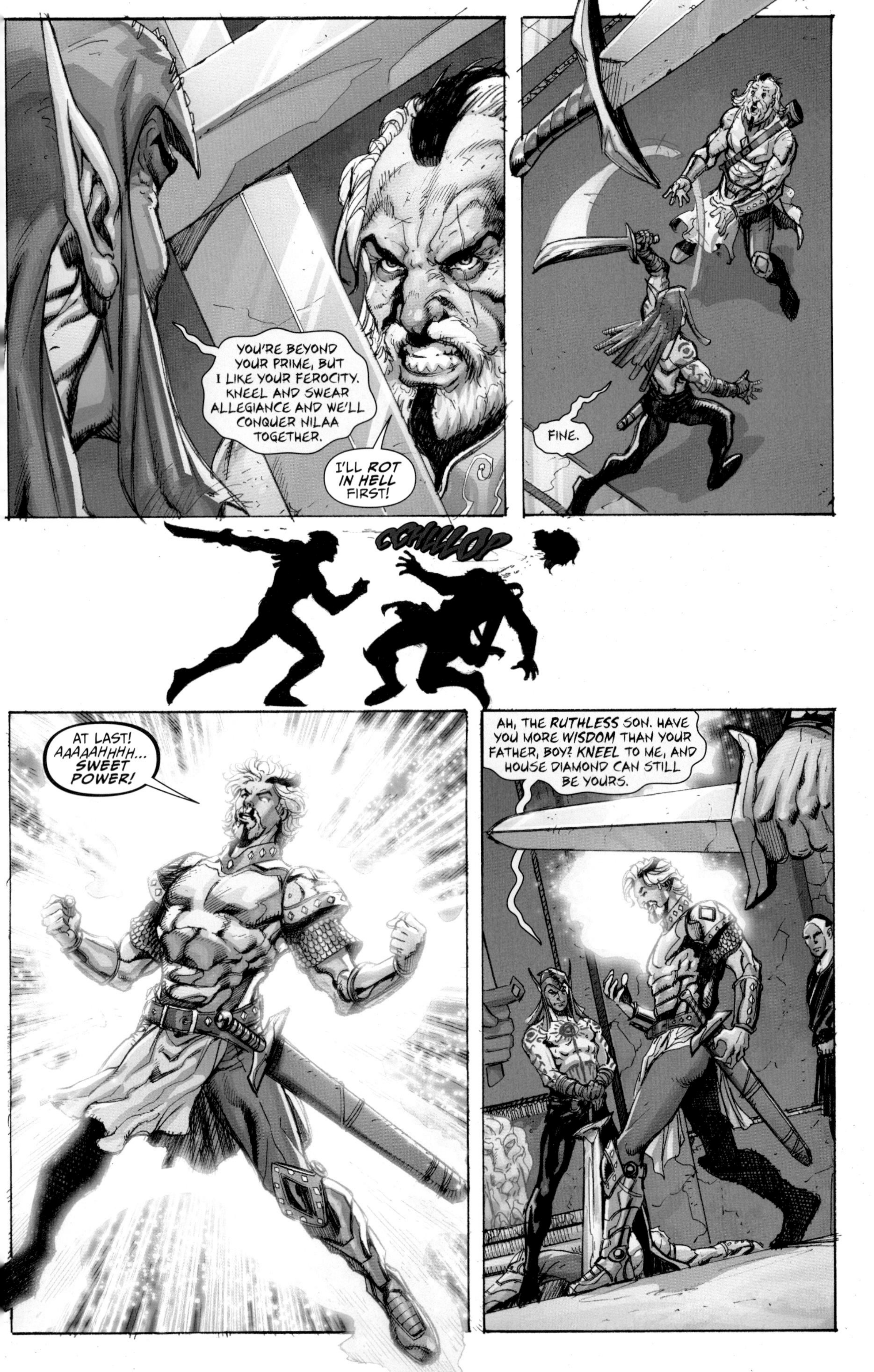
YOU'RE BEYOND YOUR PRIME, BUT I LIKE YOUR FEROCITY. KNEEL AND SWEAR ALLEGIANCE AND WE'LL CONQUER NILAA TOGETHER.
I'LL ROT IN HELL FIRST!
FINE.
CCHHLLOP
AT LAST! AAAAAHHHH... SWEET POWER!
AH, THE RUTHLESS SON. HAVE YOU MORE WISDOM THAN YOUR FATHER, BOY? KNEEL TO ME, AND HOUSE DIAMOND CAN STILL BE YOURS.

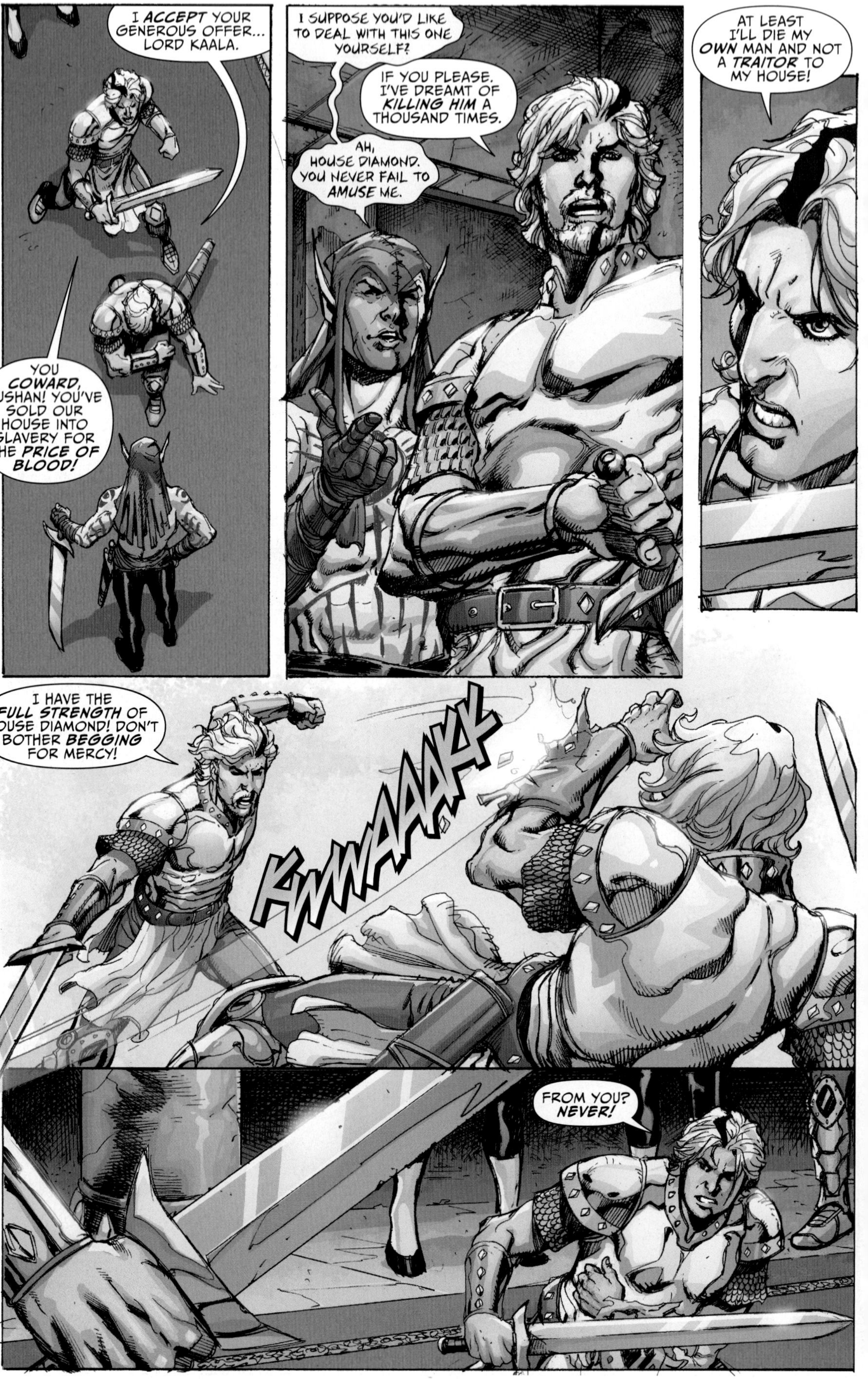
I ACCEPT YOUR GENEROUS OFFER... LORD KAALA.
YOU COWARD, ZUSHAN! YOU'VE SOLD OUR HOUSE INTO SLAVERY FOR THE PRICE OF BLOOD!
I SUPPOSE YOU'D LIKE TO DEAL WITH THIS ONE YOURSELF?
IF YOU PLEASE. I'VE DREAMT OF KILLING HIM A THOUSAND TIMES.
AH, HOUSE DIAMOND. YOU NEVER FAIL TO AMUSE ME.
AT LEAST I'LL DIE MY OWN MAN AND NOT A TRAITOR TO MY HOUSE!
I HAVE THE FULL STRENGTH OF HOUSE DIAMOND! DON'T BOTHER BEGGING FOR MERCY!
KWAAAKK
FROM YOU? NEVER!

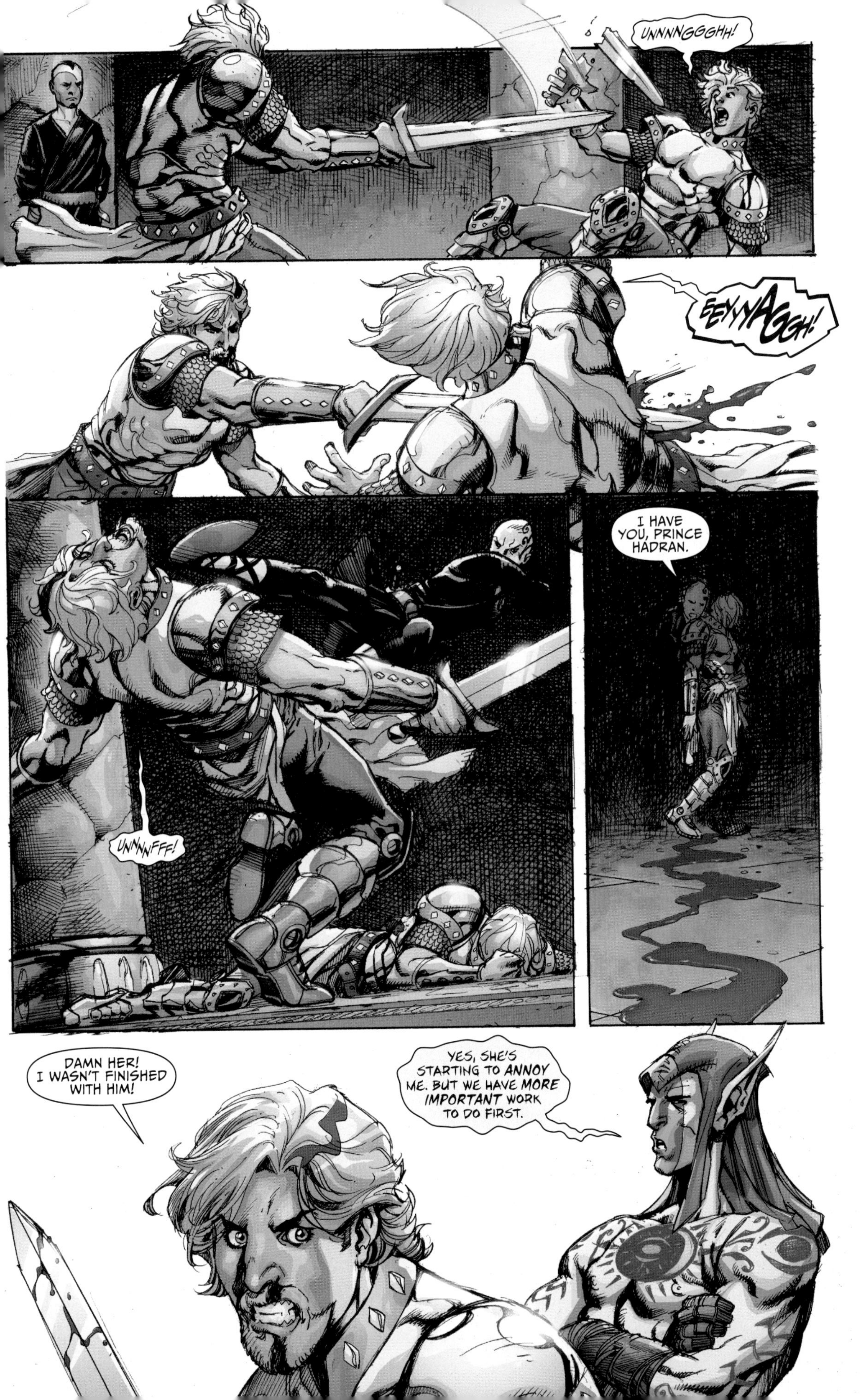
UNNNNGGGHH!
EEYYYAGGH!
UNNNNFFF!
I HAVE YOU, PRINCE HADRAN.
DAMN HER! I WASN'T FINISHED WITH HIM!
YES, SHE'S STARTING TO *ANNOY* ME. BUT WE HAVE *MORE IMPORTANT* WORK TO DO FIRST.

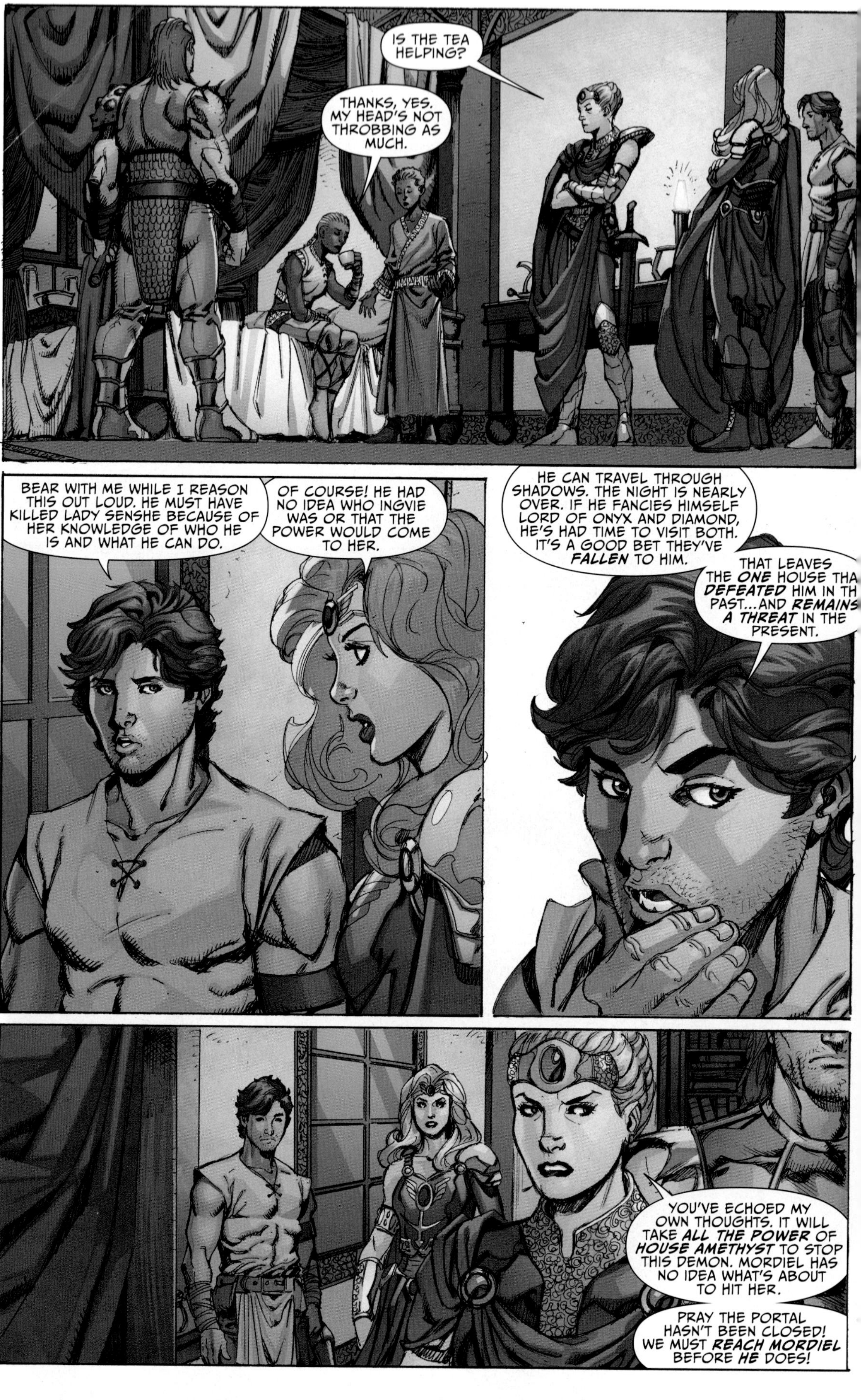
IS THE TEA HELPING?
THANKS, YES. MY HEAD'S NOT THROBBING AS MUCH.
BEAR WITH ME WHILE I REASON THIS OUT LOUD. HE MUST HAVE KILLED LADY SENSHE BECAUSE OF HER KNOWLEDGE OF WHO HE IS AND WHAT HE CAN DO.
OF COURSE! HE HAD NO IDEA WHO INGVIE WAS OR THAT THE POWER WOULD COME TO HER.
HE CAN TRAVEL THROUGH SHADOWS. THE NIGHT IS NEARLY OVER. IF HE FANCIES HIMSELF LORD OF ONYX AND DIAMOND, HE'S HAD TIME TO VISIT BOTH. IT'S A GOOD BET THEY'VE **FALLEN** TO HIM.
THAT LEAVES THE **ONE** HOUSE THA **DEFEATED** HIM IN TH PAST...AND **REMAINS A THREAT** IN THE PRESENT.
YOU'VE ECHOED MY OWN THOUGHTS. IT WILL TAKE **ALL THE POWER** OF **HOUSE AMETHYST** TO STOP THIS DEMON. MORDIEL HAS NO IDEA WHAT'S ABOUT TO HIT HER.
PRAY THE PORTAL HASN'T BEEN CLOSED! WE MUST **REACH MORDIEL** BEFORE **HE** DOES!

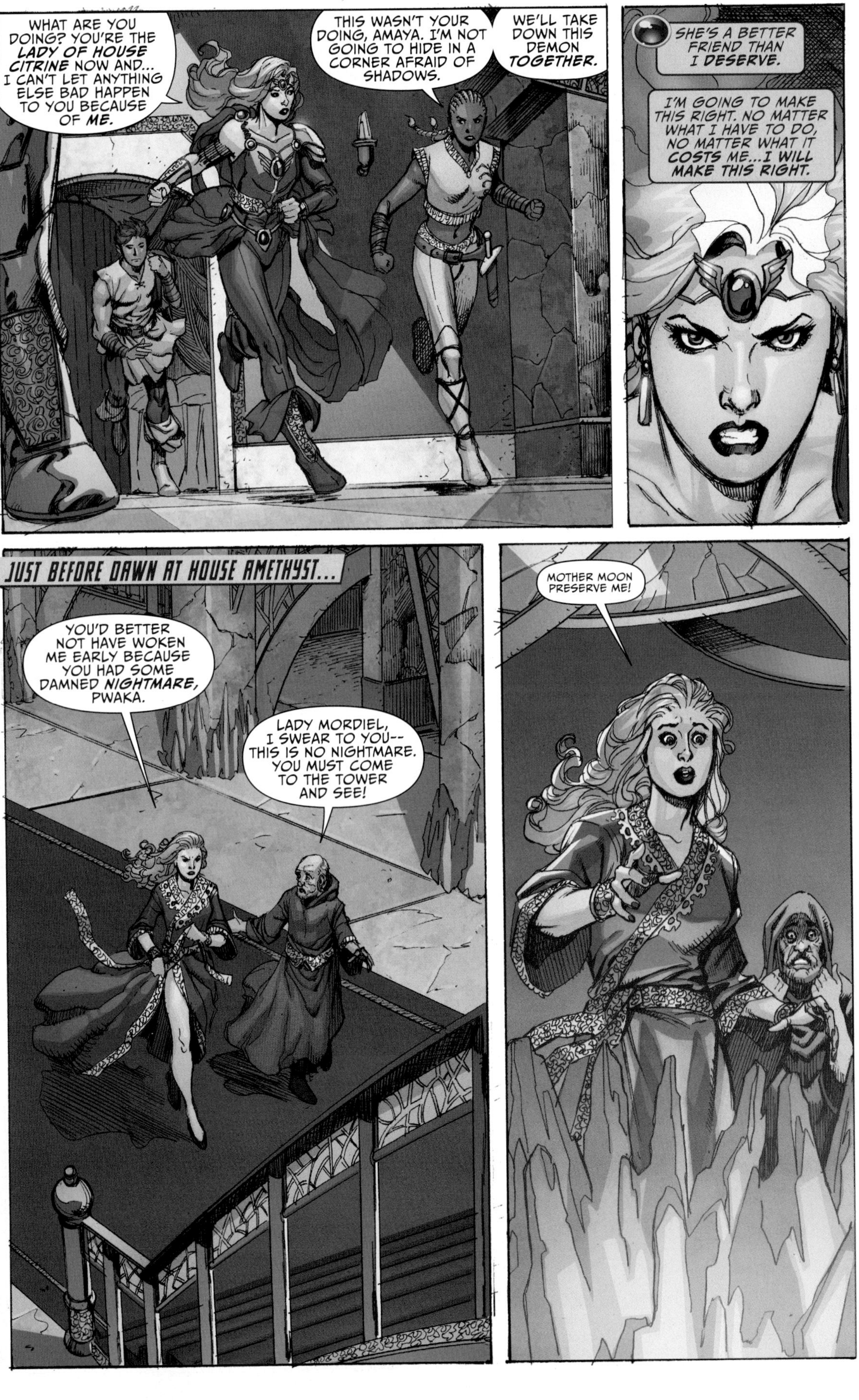
WHAT ARE YOU DOING? YOU'RE THE LADY OF HOUSE CITRINE NOW AND... I CAN'T LET ANYTHING ELSE BAD HAPPEN TO YOU BECAUSE OF ME.
THIS WASN'T YOUR DOING, AMAYA. I'M NOT GOING TO HIDE IN A CORNER AFRAID OF SHADOWS.
WE'LL TAKE DOWN THIS DEMON TOGETHER.
SHE'S A BETTER FRIEND THAN I DESERVE.
I'M GOING TO MAKE THIS RIGHT. NO MATTER WHAT I HAVE TO DO, NO MATTER WHAT IT COSTS ME...I WILL MAKE THIS RIGHT.
JUST BEFORE DAWN AT HOUSE AMETHYST...
YOU'D BETTER NOT HAVE WOKEN ME EARLY BECAUSE YOU HAD SOME DAMNED NIGHTMARE, PWAKA.
LADY MORDIEL, I SWEAR TO YOU-- THIS IS NO NIGHTMARE. YOU MUST COME TO THE TOWER AND SEE!
MOTHER MOON PRESERVE ME!

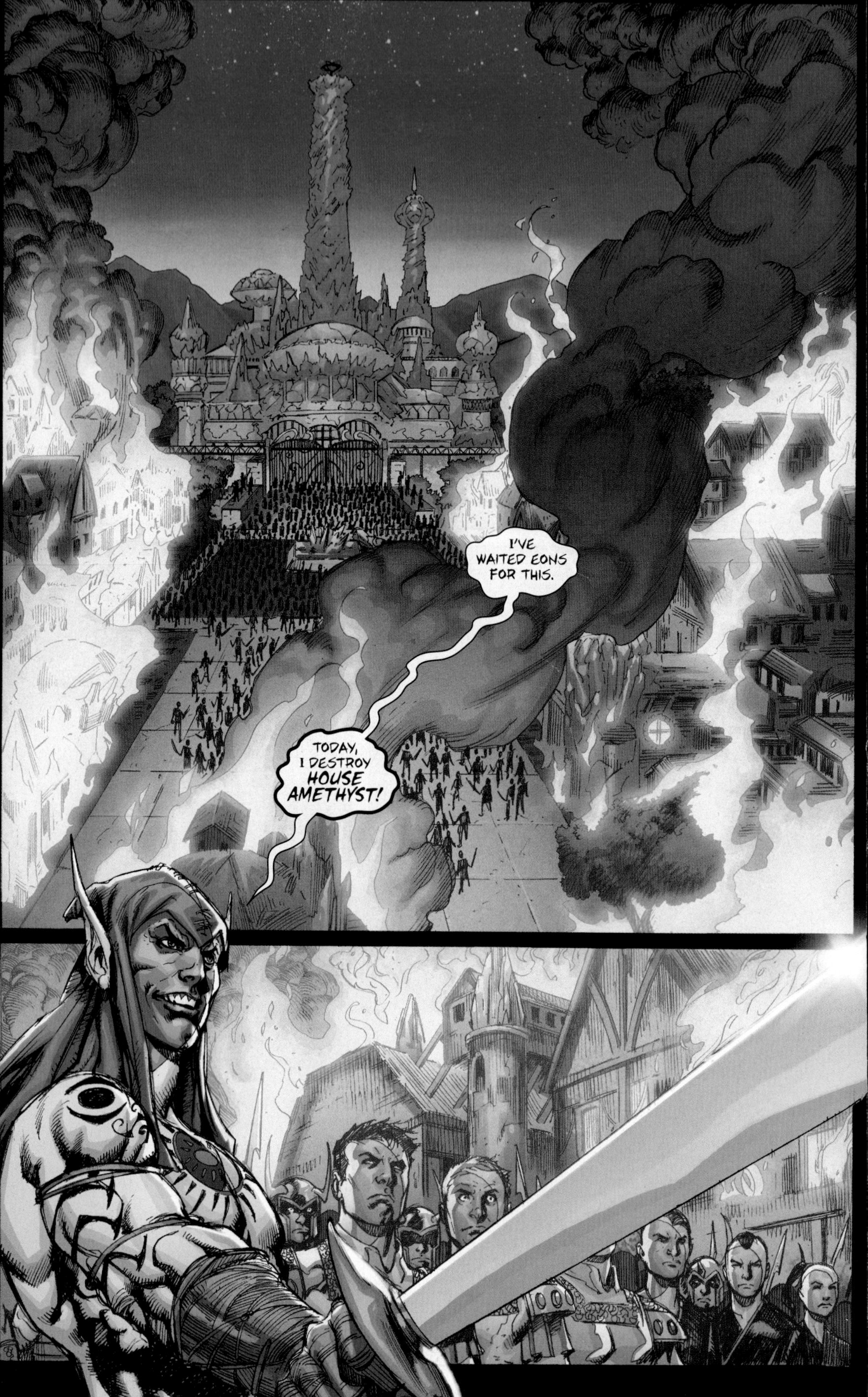
I'VE WAITED EONS FOR THIS.
TODAY, I DESTROY HOUSE AMETHYST!

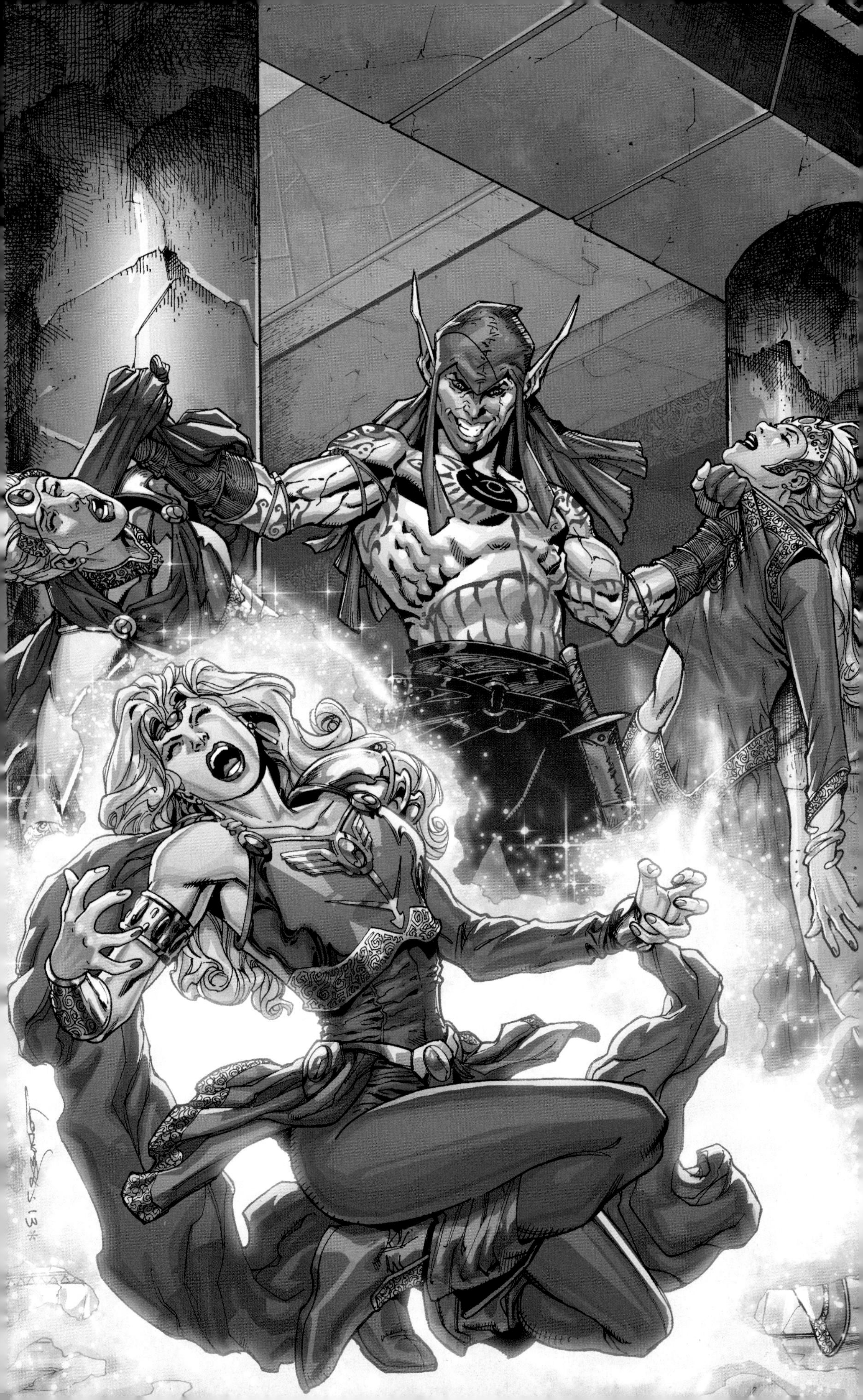

AMETHYST part nine ECLIPSED

CHRISTY MARX writer AARON LOPRESTI artist TRAVIS MOORE & JOHN LIVESAY additional art cover by AARON LOPRESTI & HI-FI

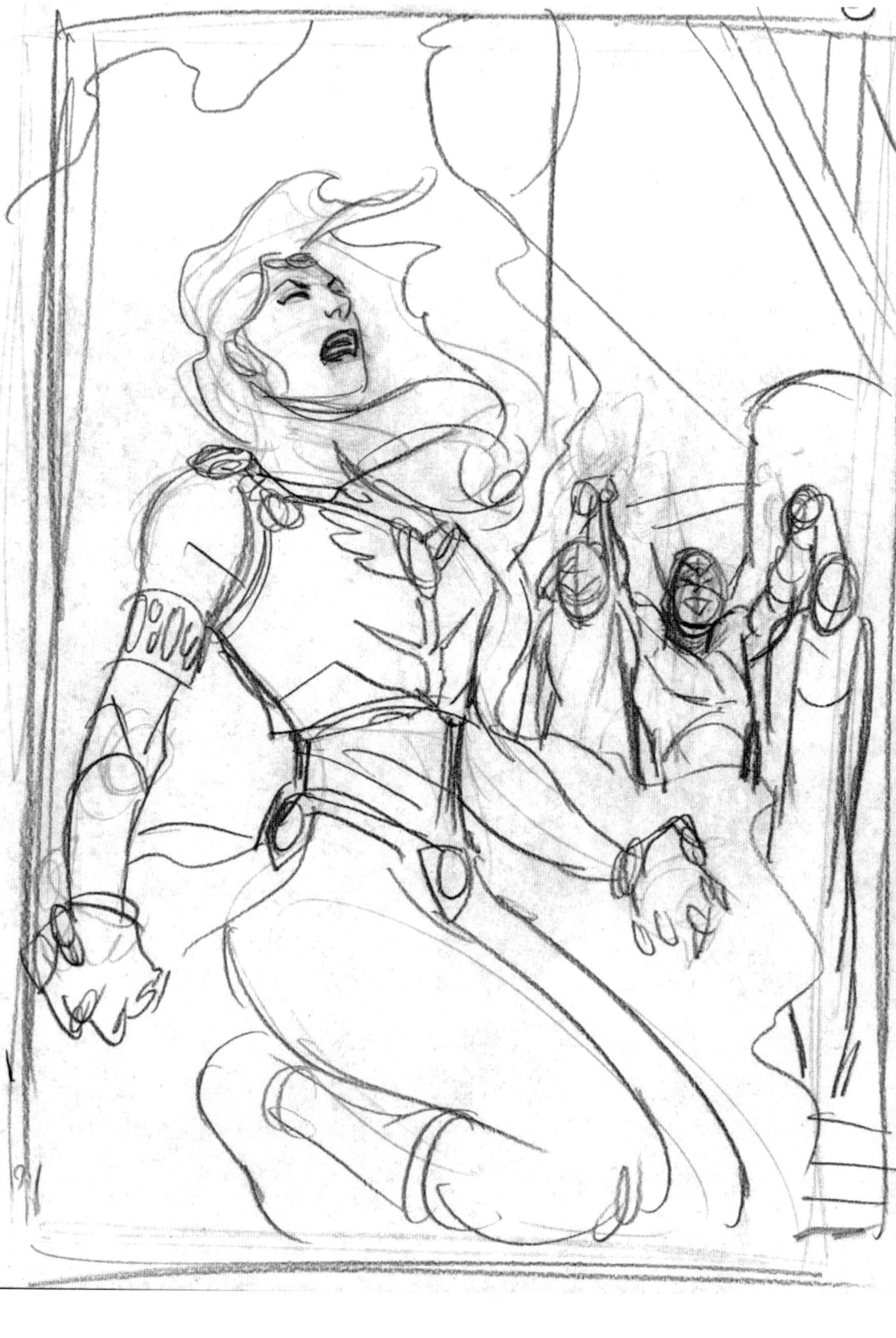

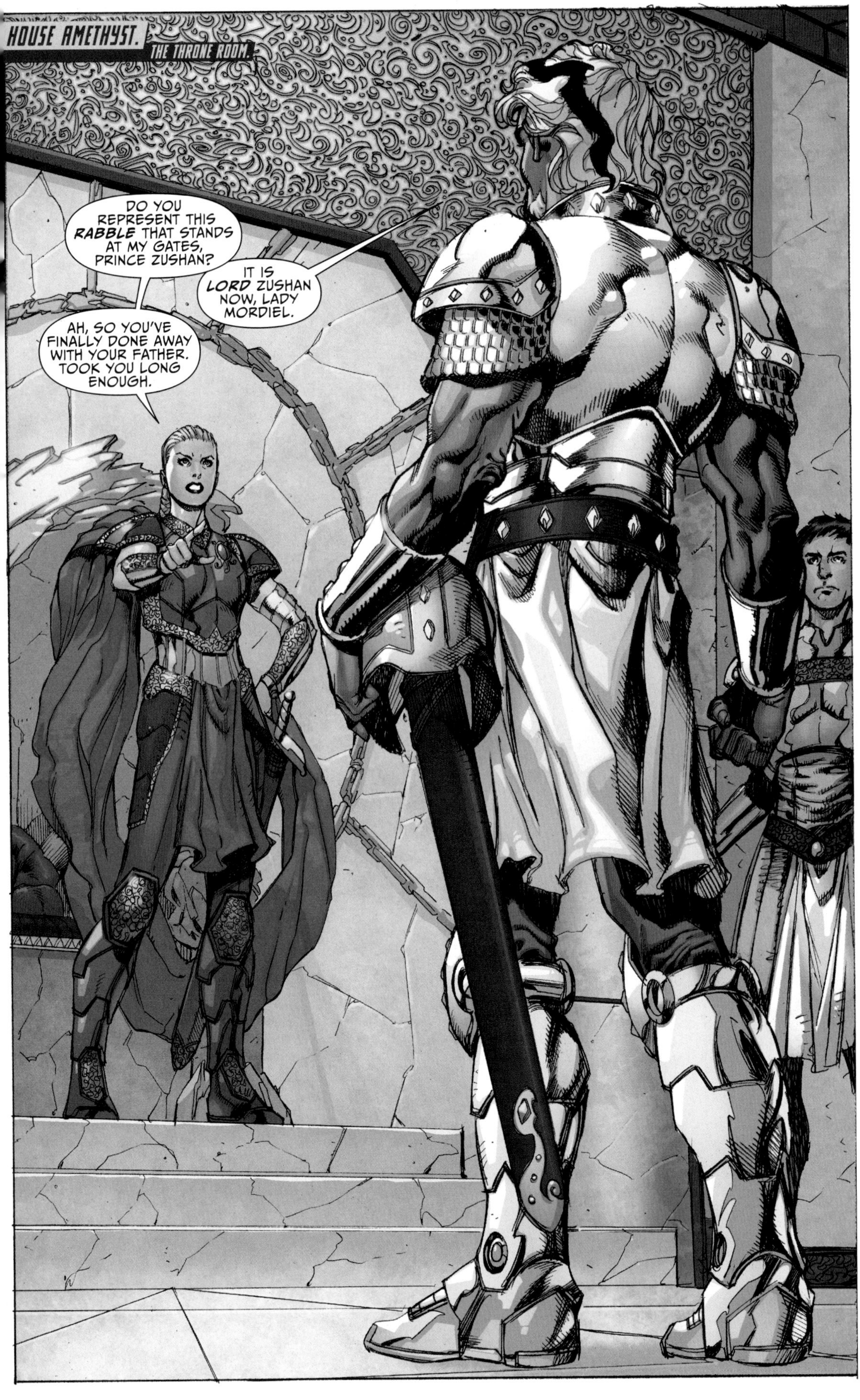
HOUSE AMETHYST.
THE THRONE ROOM.
DO YOU REPRESENT THIS RABBLE THAT STANDS AT MY GATES, PRINCE ZUSHAN?
IT IS LORD ZUSHAN NOW, LADY MORDIEL.
AH, SO YOU'VE FINALLY DONE AWAY WITH YOUR FATHER. TOOK YOU LONG ENOUGH.

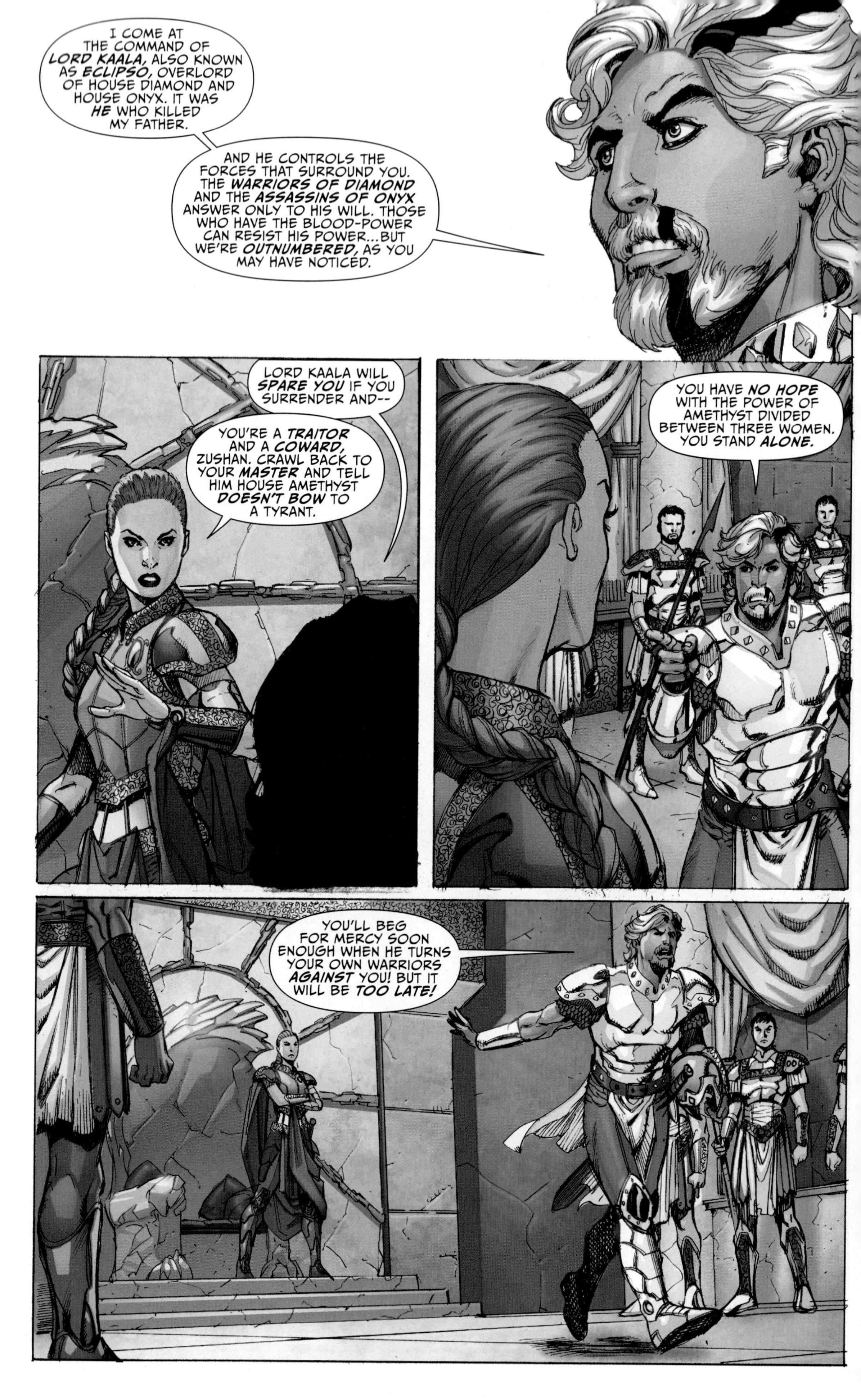
I COME AT THE COMMAND OF LORD KAALA, ALSO KNOWN AS ECLIPSO, OVERLORD OF HOUSE DIAMOND AND HOUSE ONYX. IT WAS HE WHO KILLED MY FATHER.
AND HE CONTROLS THE FORCES THAT SURROUND YOU. THE WARRIORS OF DIAMOND AND THE ASSASSINS OF ONYX ANSWER ONLY TO HIS WILL. THOSE WHO HAVE THE BLOOD-POWER CAN RESIST HIS POWER...BUT WE'RE OUTNUMBERED, AS YOU MAY HAVE NOTICED.
LORD KAALA WILL SPARE YOU IF YOU SURRENDER AND--
YOU'RE A TRAITOR AND A COWARD, ZUSHAN. CRAWL BACK TO YOUR MASTER AND TELL HIM HOUSE AMETHYST DOESN'T BOW TO A TYRANT.
YOU HAVE NO HOPE WITH THE POWER OF AMETHYST DIVIDED BETWEEN THREE WOMEN. YOU STAND ALONE.
YOU'LL BEG FOR MERCY SOON ENOUGH WHEN HE TURNS YOUR OWN WARRIORS AGAINST YOU! BUT IT WILL BE TOO LATE!

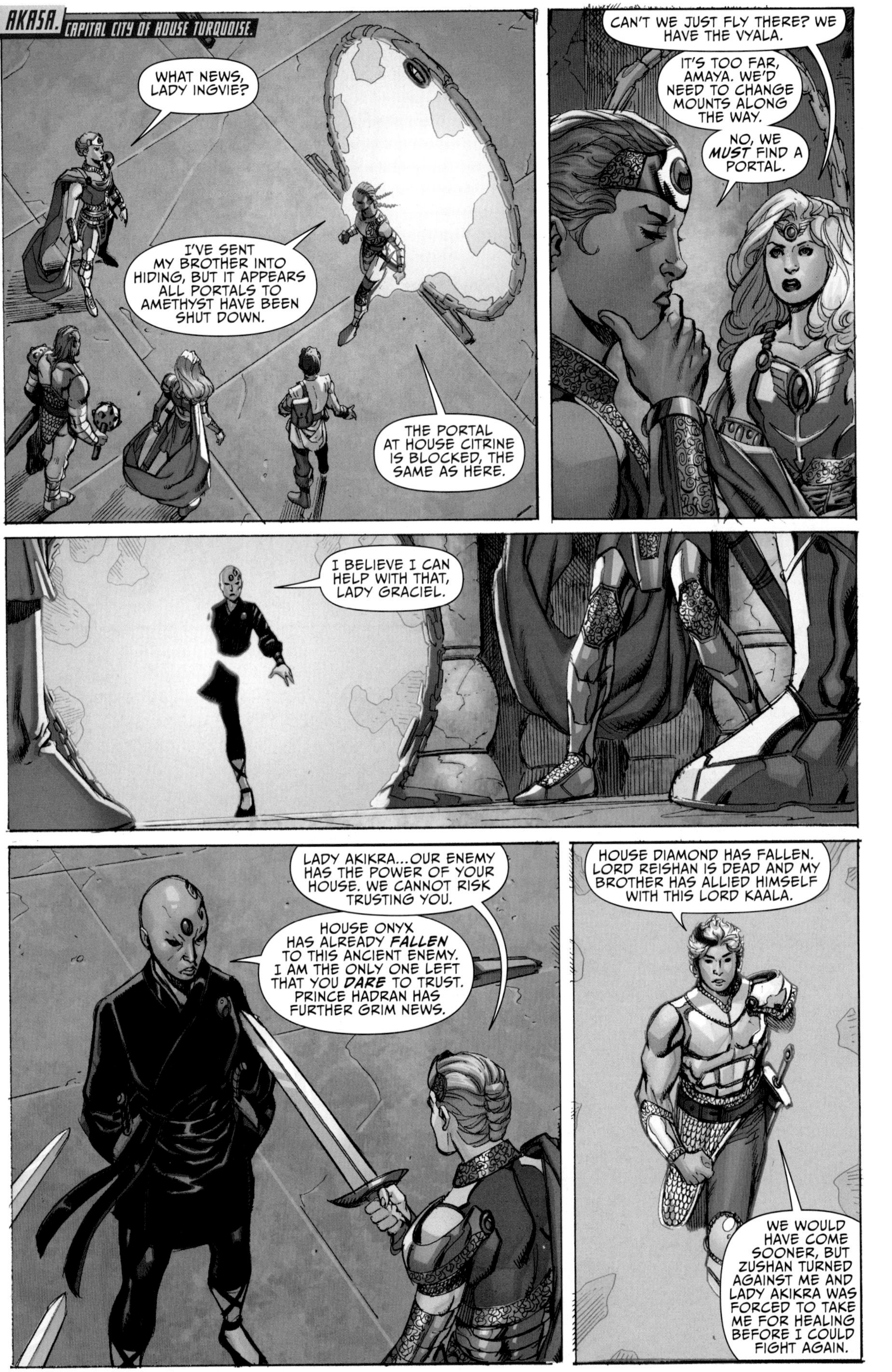
AKASA. CAPITAL CITY OF HOUSE TURQUOISE.
WHAT NEWS, LADY INGVIE?
I'VE SENT MY BROTHER INTO HIDING, BUT IT APPEARS ALL PORTALS TO AMETHYST HAVE BEEN SHUT DOWN.
THE PORTAL AT HOUSE CITRINE IS BLOCKED, THE SAME AS HERE.
CAN'T WE JUST FLY THERE? WE HAVE THE VYALA.
IT'S TOO FAR, AMAYA. WE'D NEED TO CHANGE MOUNTS ALONG THE WAY.
NO, WE MUST FIND A PORTAL.
I BELIEVE I CAN HELP WITH THAT, LADY GRACIEL.
LADY AKIKRA...OUR ENEMY HAS THE POWER OF YOUR HOUSE. WE CANNOT RISK TRUSTING YOU.
HOUSE ONYX HAS ALREADY FALLEN TO THIS ANCIENT ENEMY. I AM THE ONLY ONE LEFT THAT YOU DARE TO TRUST. PRINCE HADRAN HAS FURTHER GRIM NEWS.
HOUSE DIAMOND HAS FALLEN. LORD REISHAN IS DEAD AND MY BROTHER HAS ALLIED HIMSELF WITH THIS LORD KAALA.
WE WOULD HAVE COME SOONER, BUT ZUSHAN TURNED AGAINST ME AND LADY AKIKRA WAS FORCED TO TAKE ME FOR HEALING BEFORE I COULD FIGHT AGAIN.

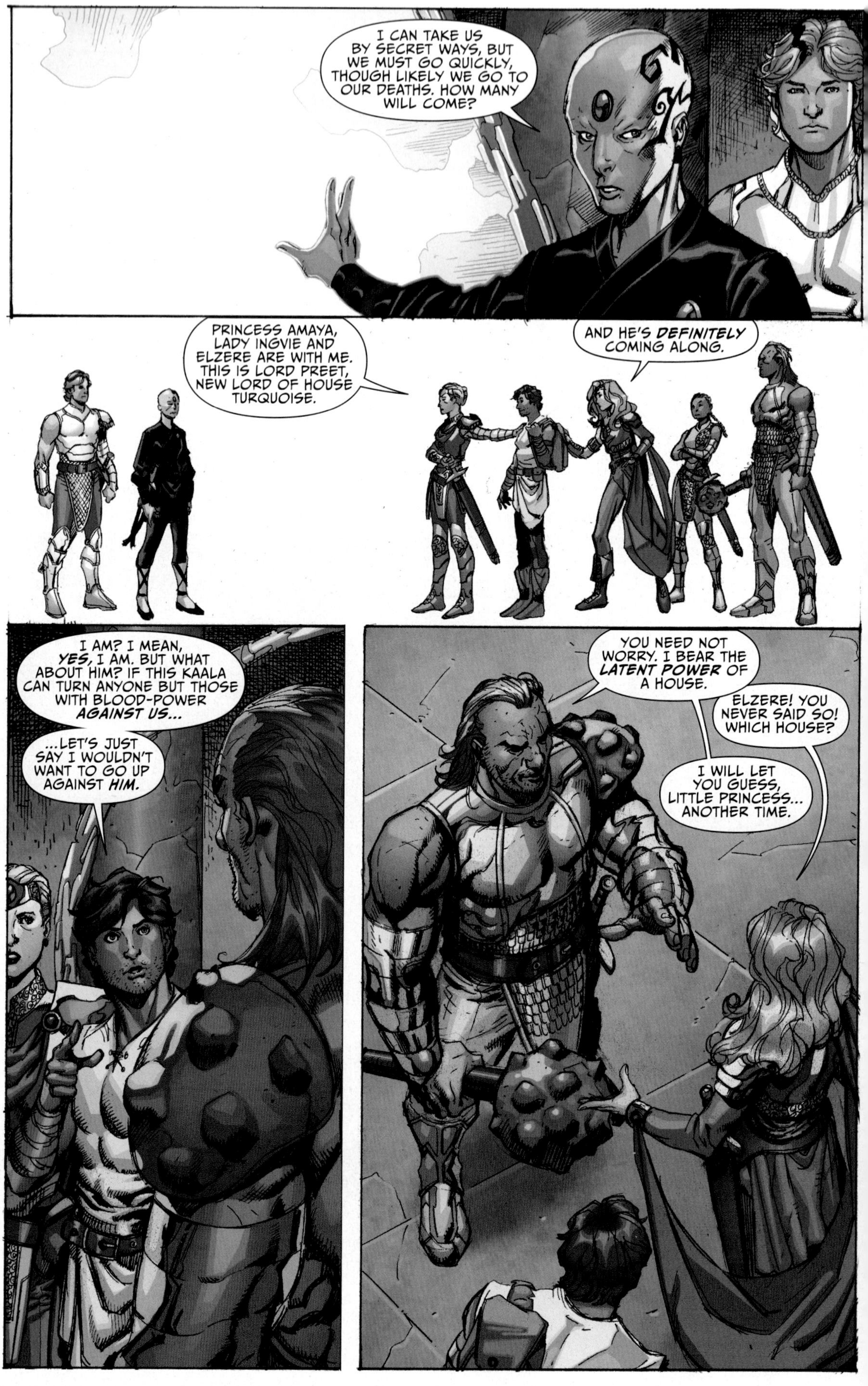
I CAN TAKE US BY SECRET WAYS, BUT WE MUST GO QUICKLY, THOUGH LIKELY WE GO TO OUR DEATHS. HOW MANY WILL COME?
PRINCESS AMAYA, LADY INGVIE AND ELZERE ARE WITH ME. THIS IS LORD PREET, NEW LORD OF HOUSE TURQUOISE.
AND HE'S DEFINITELY COMING ALONG.
I AM? I MEAN, YES, I AM. BUT WHAT ABOUT HIM? IF THIS KAALA CAN TURN ANYONE BUT THOSE WITH BLOOD-POWER AGAINST US...
...LET'S JUST SAY I WOULDN'T WANT TO GO UP AGAINST HIM.
YOU NEED NOT WORRY. I BEAR THE LATENT POWER OF A HOUSE.
ELZERE! YOU NEVER SAID SO! WHICH HOUSE?
I WILL LET YOU GUESS, LITTLE PRINCESS... ANOTHER TIME.

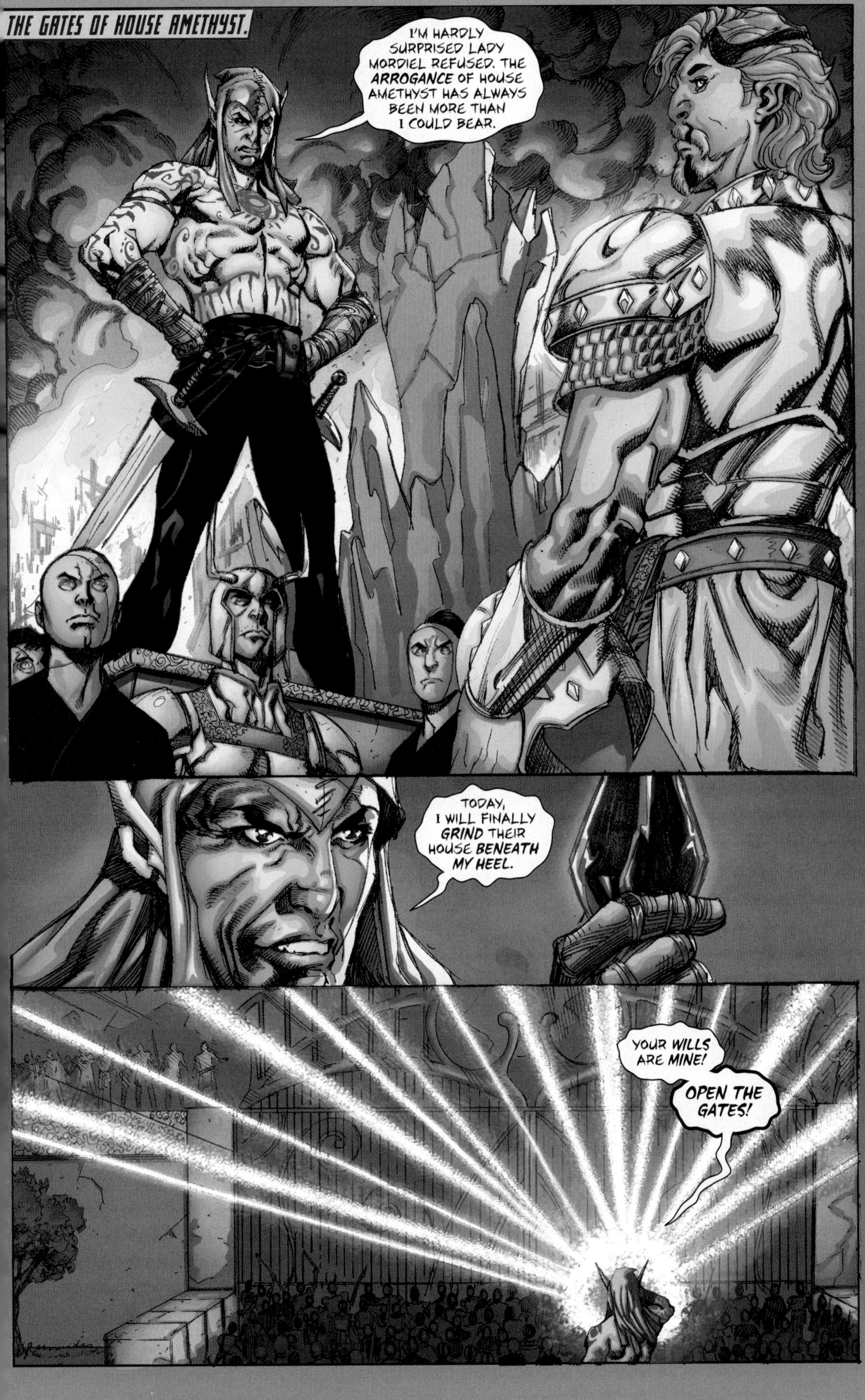
THE GATES OF HOUSE AMETHYST.
I'M HARDLY SURPRISED LADY MORDIEL REFUSED. THE ARROGANCE OF HOUSE AMETHYST HAS ALWAYS BEEN MORE THAN I COULD BEAR.
TODAY, I WILL FINALLY GRIND THEIR HOUSE BENEATH MY HEEL.
YOUR WILLS ARE MINE!
OPEN THE GATES!

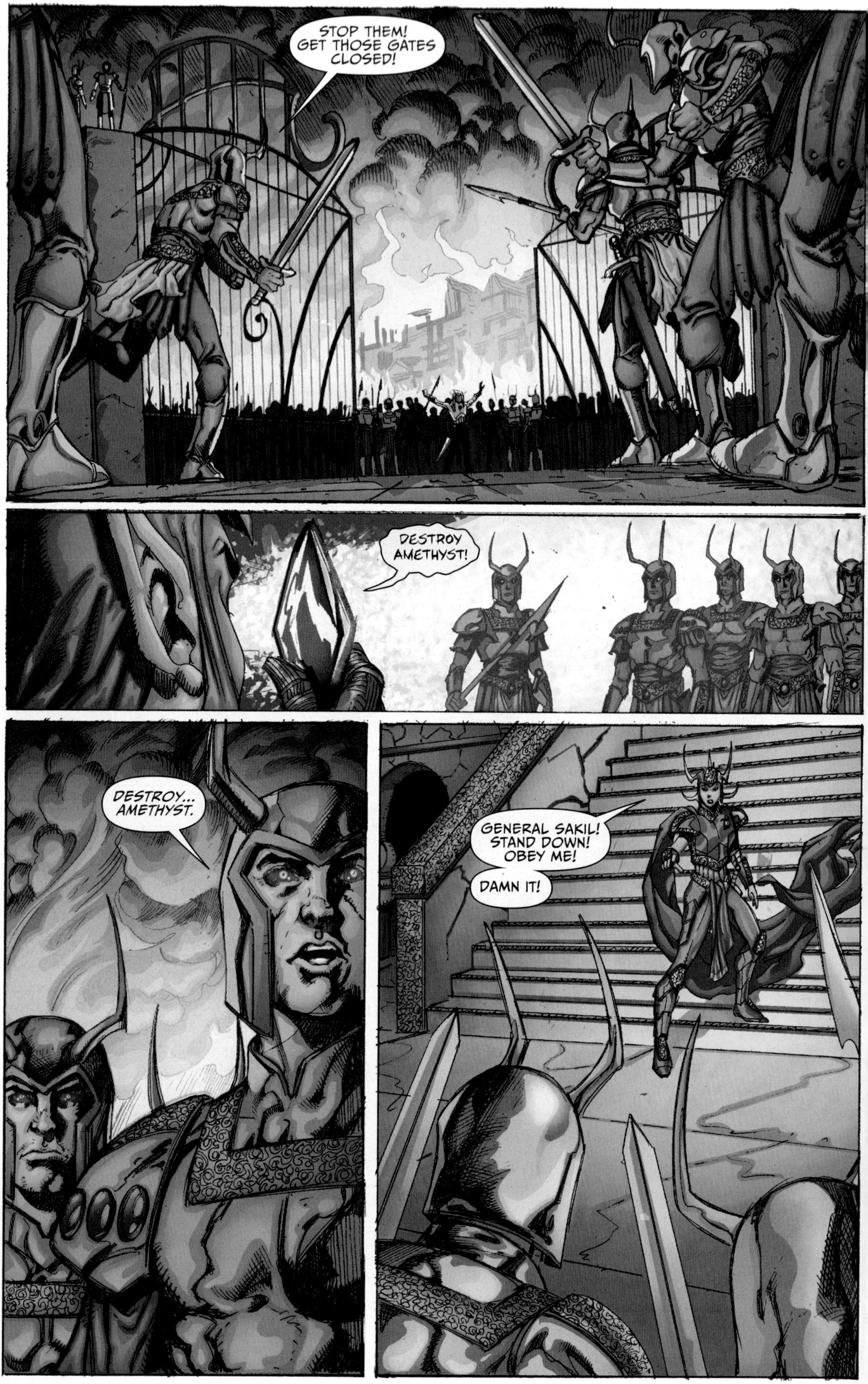
STOP THEM! GET THOSE GATES CLOSED!
DESTROY AMETHYST!
DESTROY... AMETHYST.
GENERAL SAKIL! STAND DOWN! OBEY ME!
DAMN IT!

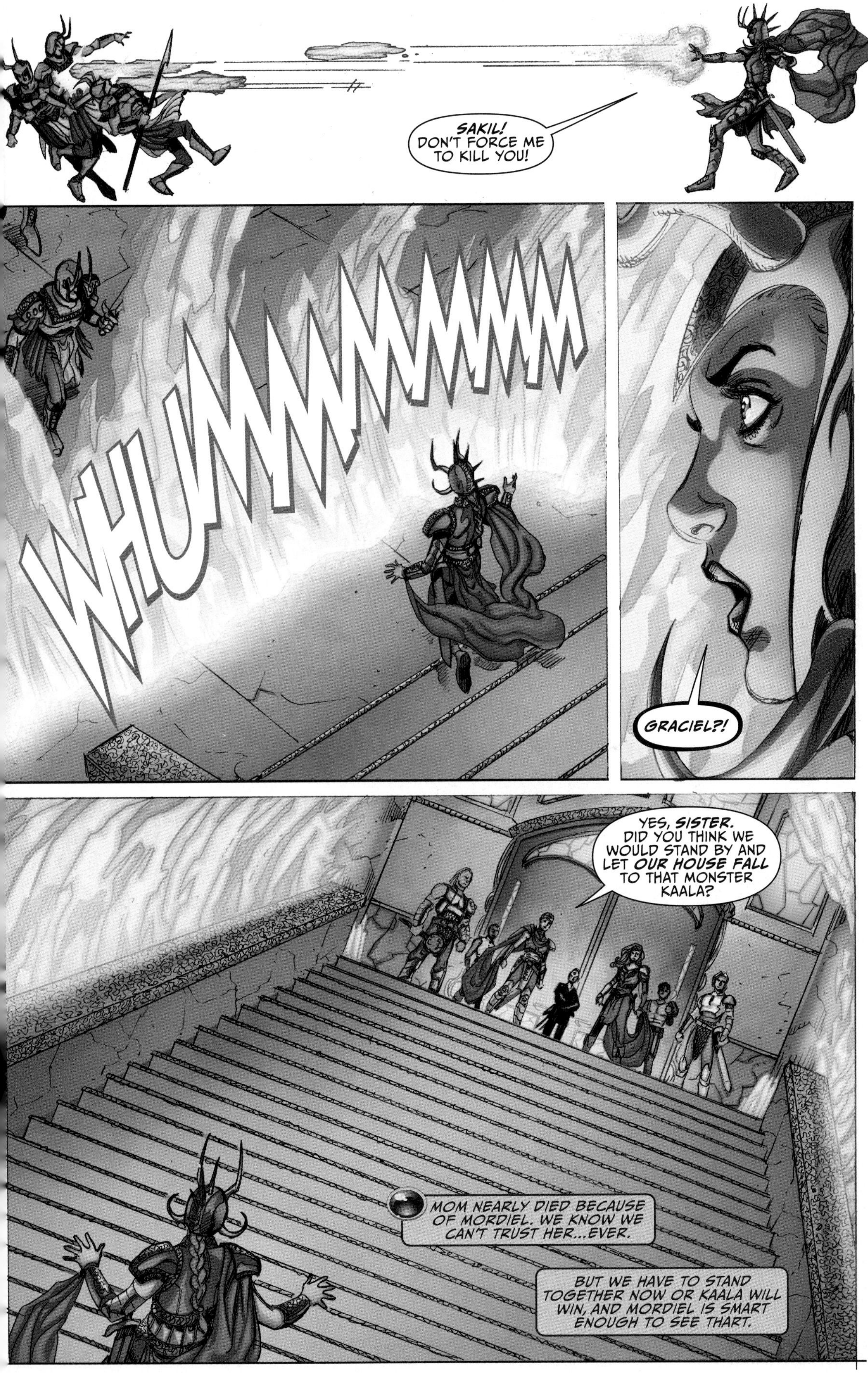
SAKIL! DON'T FORCE ME TO KILL YOU!
WHUMMMMMM
GRACIEL?!
YES, SISTER. DID YOU THINK WE WOULD STAND BY AND LET OUR HOUSE FALL TO THAT MONSTER KAALA?
MOM NEARLY DIED BECAUSE OF MORDIEL. WE KNOW WE CAN'T TRUST HER...EVER.
BUT WE HAVE TO STAND TOGETHER NOW OR KAALA WILL WIN, AND MORDIEL IS SMART ENOUGH TO SEE THART.

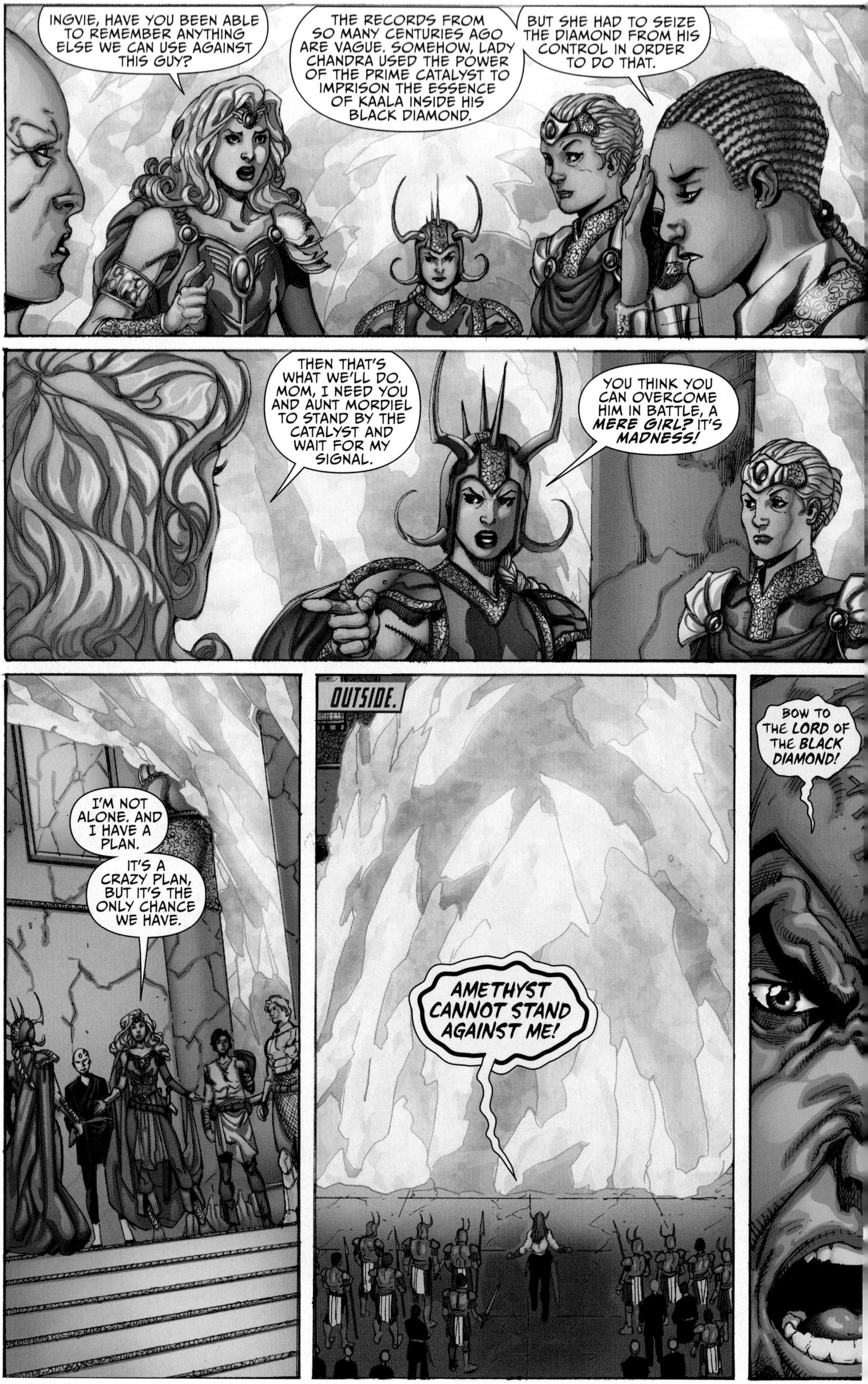
INGVIE, HAVE YOU BEEN ABLE TO REMEMBER ANYTHING ELSE WE CAN USE AGAINST THIS GUY?
THE RECORDS FROM SO MANY CENTURIES AGO ARE VAGUE. SOMEHOW, LADY CHANDRA USED THE POWER OF THE PRIME CATALYST TO IMPRISON THE ESSENCE OF KAALA INSIDE HIS BLACK DIAMOND.
BUT SHE HAD TO SEIZE THE DIAMOND FROM HIS CONTROL IN ORDER TO DO THAT.
THEN THAT'S WHAT WE'LL DO. MOM, I NEED YOU AND AUNT MORDIEL TO STAND BY THE CATALYST AND WAIT FOR MY SIGNAL.
YOU THINK YOU CAN OVERCOME HIM IN BATTLE, A *MERE GIRL?* IT'S *MADNESS!*
I'M NOT ALONE. AND I HAVE A PLAN.
IT'S A CRAZY PLAN, BUT IT'S THE ONLY CHANCE WE HAVE.
OUTSIDE.
AMETHYST CANNOT STAND AGAINST ME!
BOW TO THE *LORD* OF THE *BLACK DIAMOND!*

KRRAAAAAKK

STAND STRONG! WE *WON'T* FAIL YOU!

HE'S BREAKING THROUGH!

I *LOVE* YOU, MOM.

MOM, *GO!* BAR THE DOORS BEHIND YOU!

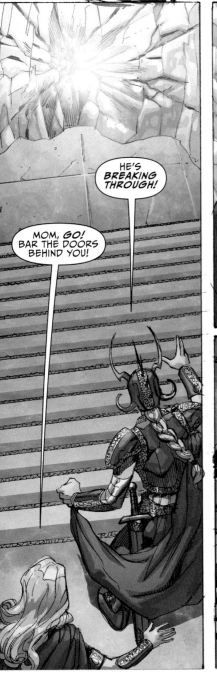

I'LL TACKLE KAALA. I NEED THE REST OF YOU TO KEEP EVERYONE ELSE OFF ME.

LET ME FACE ZUSHAN. HE MAY HAVE THE POWER OF HOUSE DIAMOND, BUT I KNOW HOW HE FIGHTS.

I CAN HOLD HIM OFF...FOR A TIME.

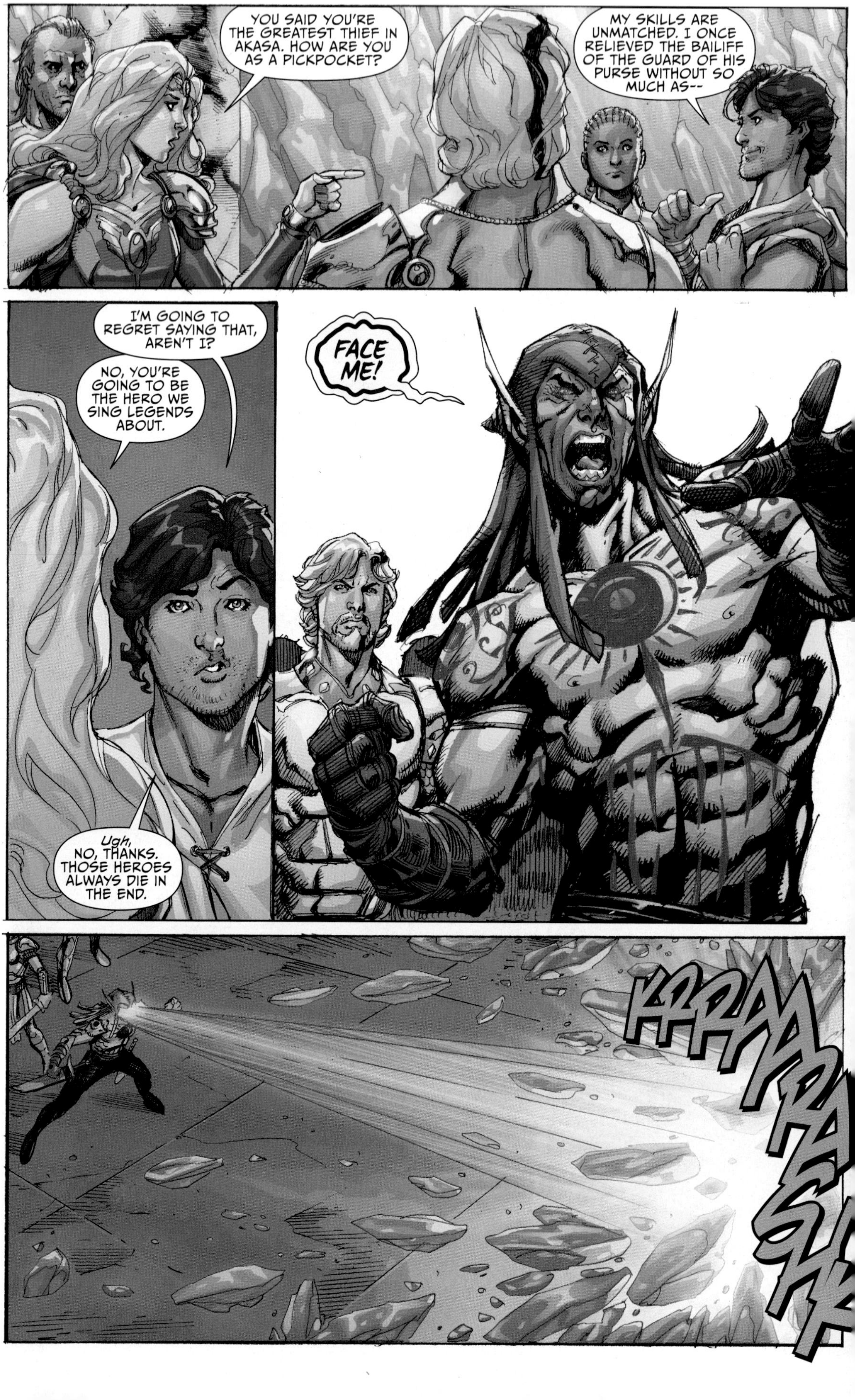
YOU SAID YOU'RE THE GREATEST THIEF IN AKASA. HOW ARE YOU AS A PICKPOCKET?
MY SKILLS ARE UNMATCHED. I ONCE RELIEVED THE BAILIFF OF THE GUARD OF HIS PURSE WITHOUT SO MUCH AS--
I'M GOING TO REGRET SAYING THAT, AREN'T I?
NO, YOU'RE GOING TO BE THE HERO WE SING LEGENDS ABOUT.
Ugh, NO, THANKS. THOSE HEROES ALWAYS DIE IN THE END.
FACE ME!

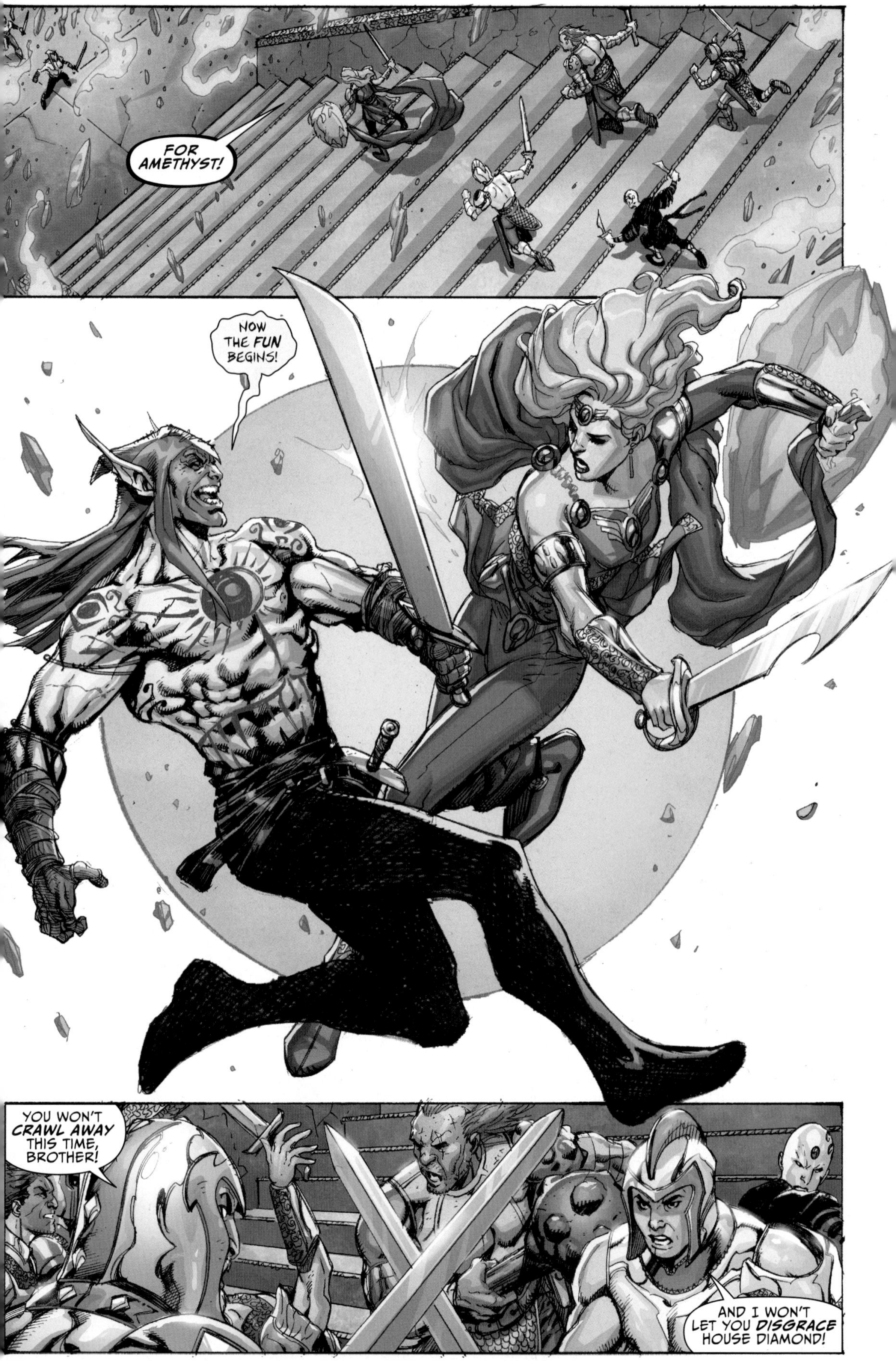
FOR AMETHYST!
NOW THE FUN BEGINS!
YOU WON'T CRAWL AWAY THIS TIME, BROTHER!
AND I WON'T LET YOU DISGRACE HOUSE DIAMOND!

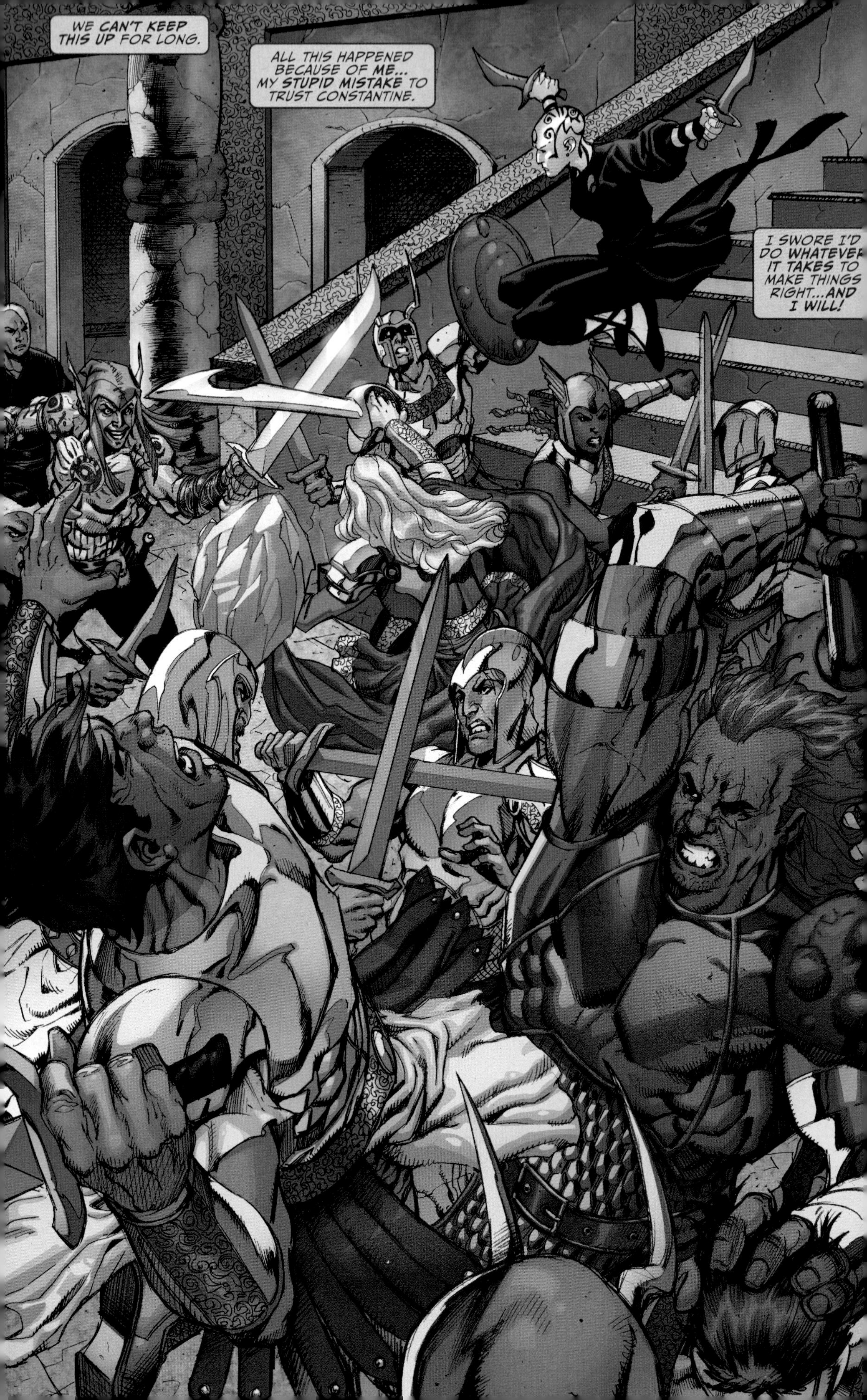
WE CAN'T KEEP THIS UP FOR LONG.
ALL THIS HAPPENED BECAUSE OF ME... MY STUPID MISTAKE TO TRUST CONSTANTINE.
I SWORE I'D DO WHATEVER IT TAKES TO MAKE THINGS RIGHT...AND I WILL!

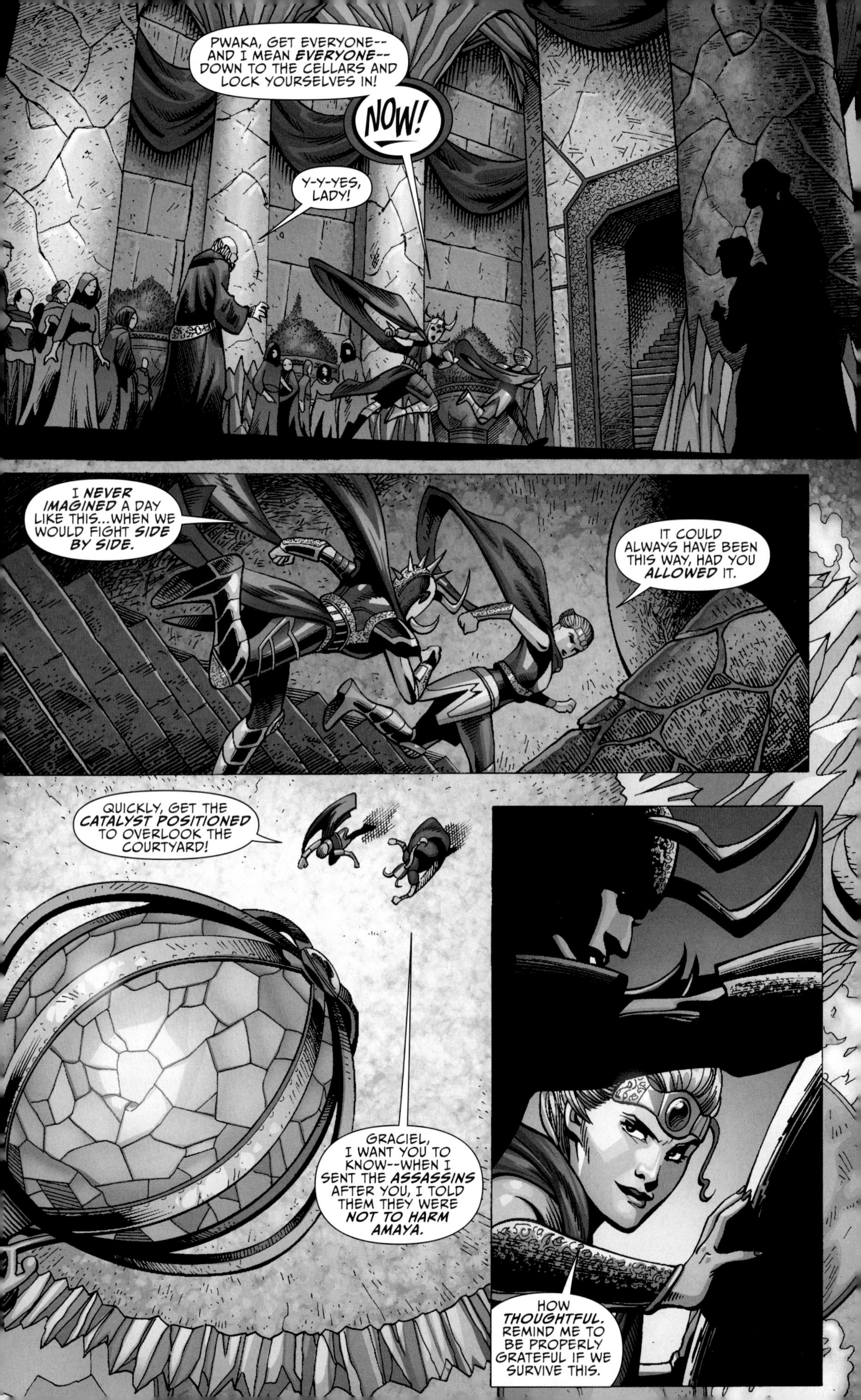
PWAKA, GET EVERYONE-- AND I MEAN EVERYONE-- DOWN TO THE CELLARS AND LOCK YOURSELVES IN!
NOW!
Y-Y-YES, LADY!
I NEVER IMAGINED A DAY LIKE THIS...WHEN WE WOULD FIGHT SIDE BY SIDE.
IT COULD ALWAYS HAVE BEEN THIS WAY, HAD YOU ALLOWED IT.
QUICKLY, GET THE CATALYST POSITIONED TO OVERLOOK THE COURTYARD!
GRACIEL, I WANT YOU TO KNOW--WHEN I SENT THE ASSASSINS AFTER YOU, I TOLD THEM THEY WERE NOT TO HARM AMAYA.
HOW THOUGHTFUL. REMIND ME TO BE PROPERLY GRATEFUL IF WE SURVIVE THIS.

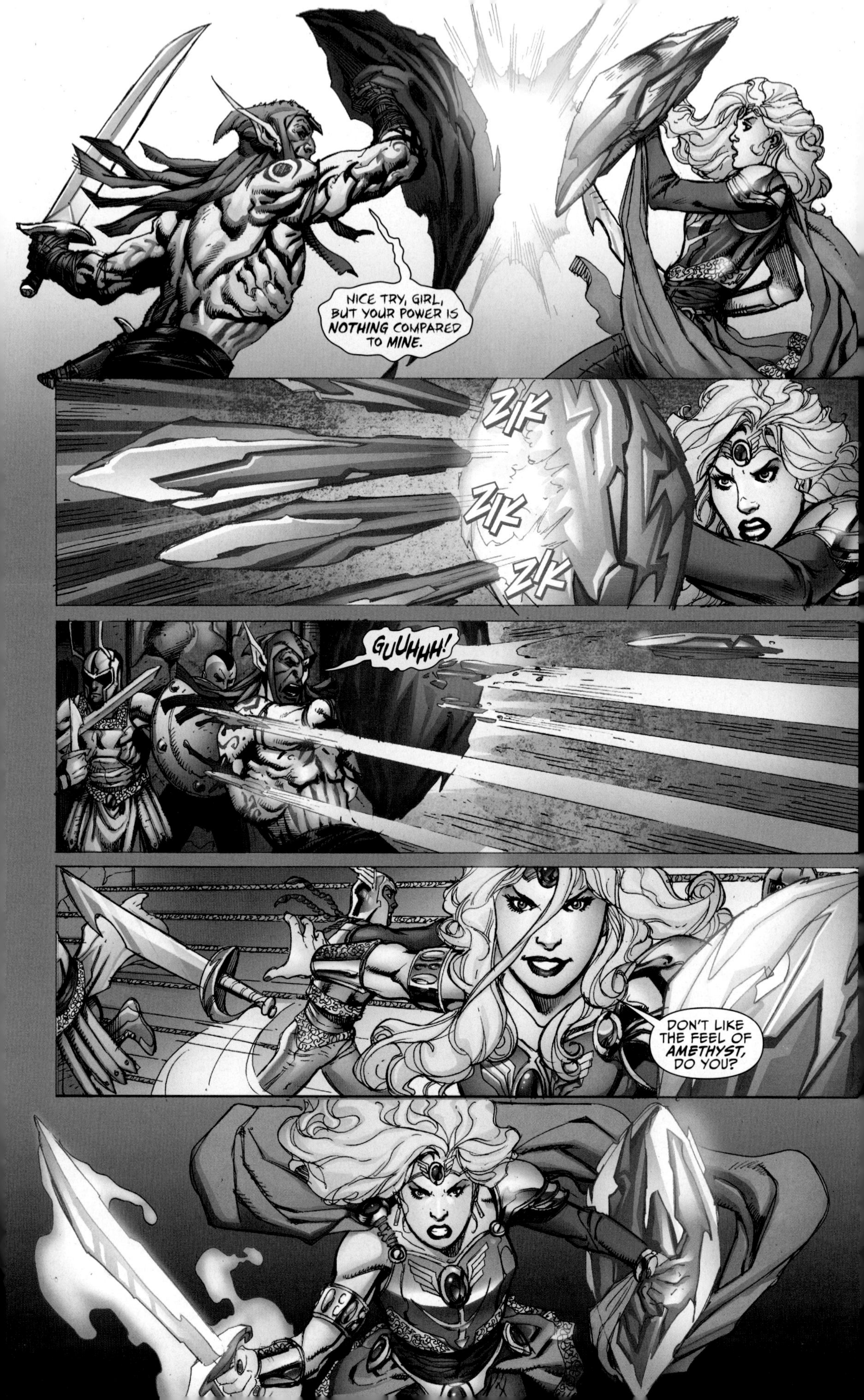
NICE TRY, GIRL, BUT YOUR POWER IS NOTHING COMPARED TO MINE.
ZIK
ZIK
ZIK
GUUHHH!
DON'T LIKE THE FEEL OF AMETHYST, DO YOU?

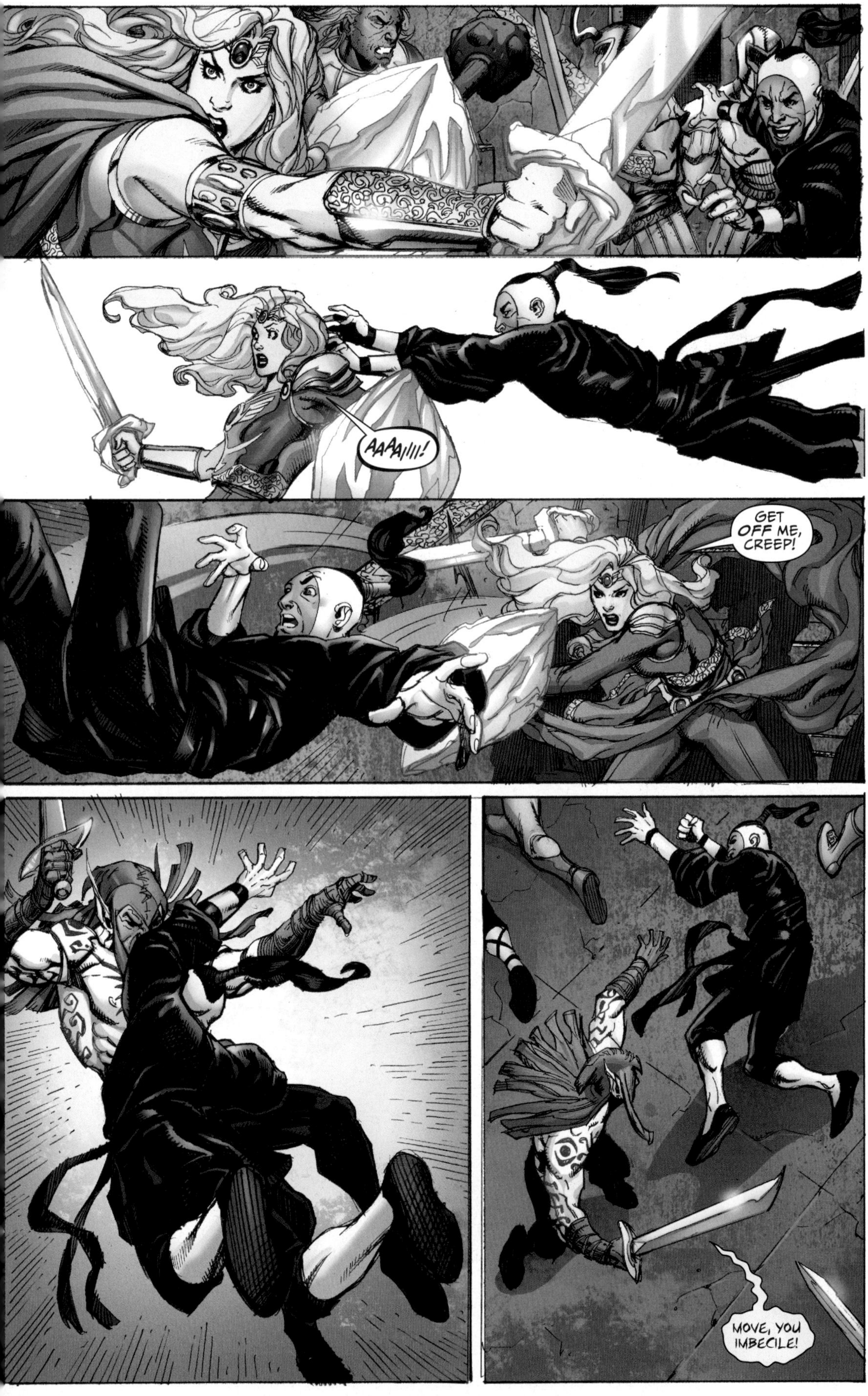
AAAAIIII!
GET OFF ME, CREEP!
MOVE, YOU IMBECILE!

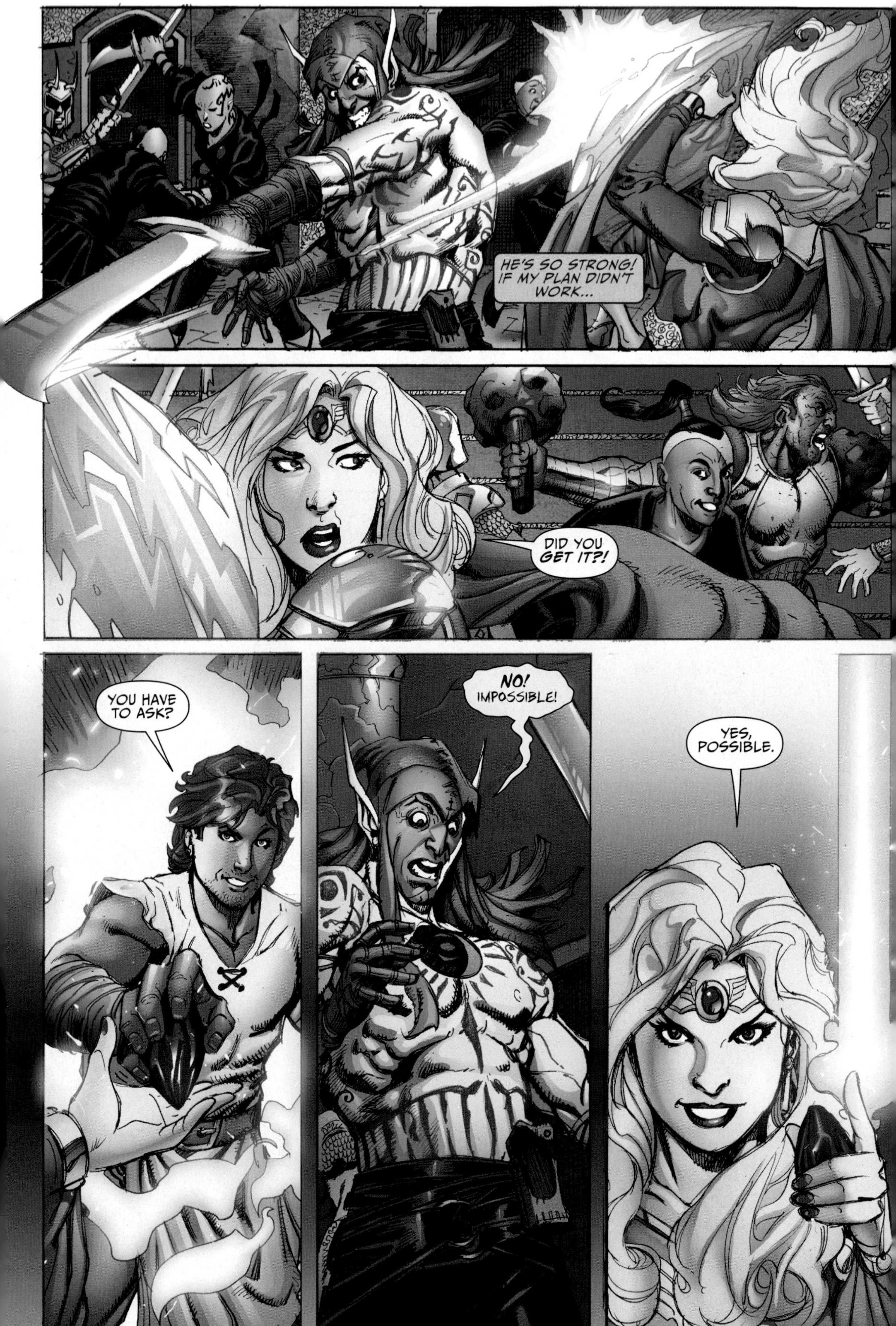
HE'S SO STRONG! IF MY PLAN DIDN'T WORK...
DID YOU GET IT?!
YOU HAVE TO ASK?
NO! IMPOSSIBLE!
YES, POSSIBLE.

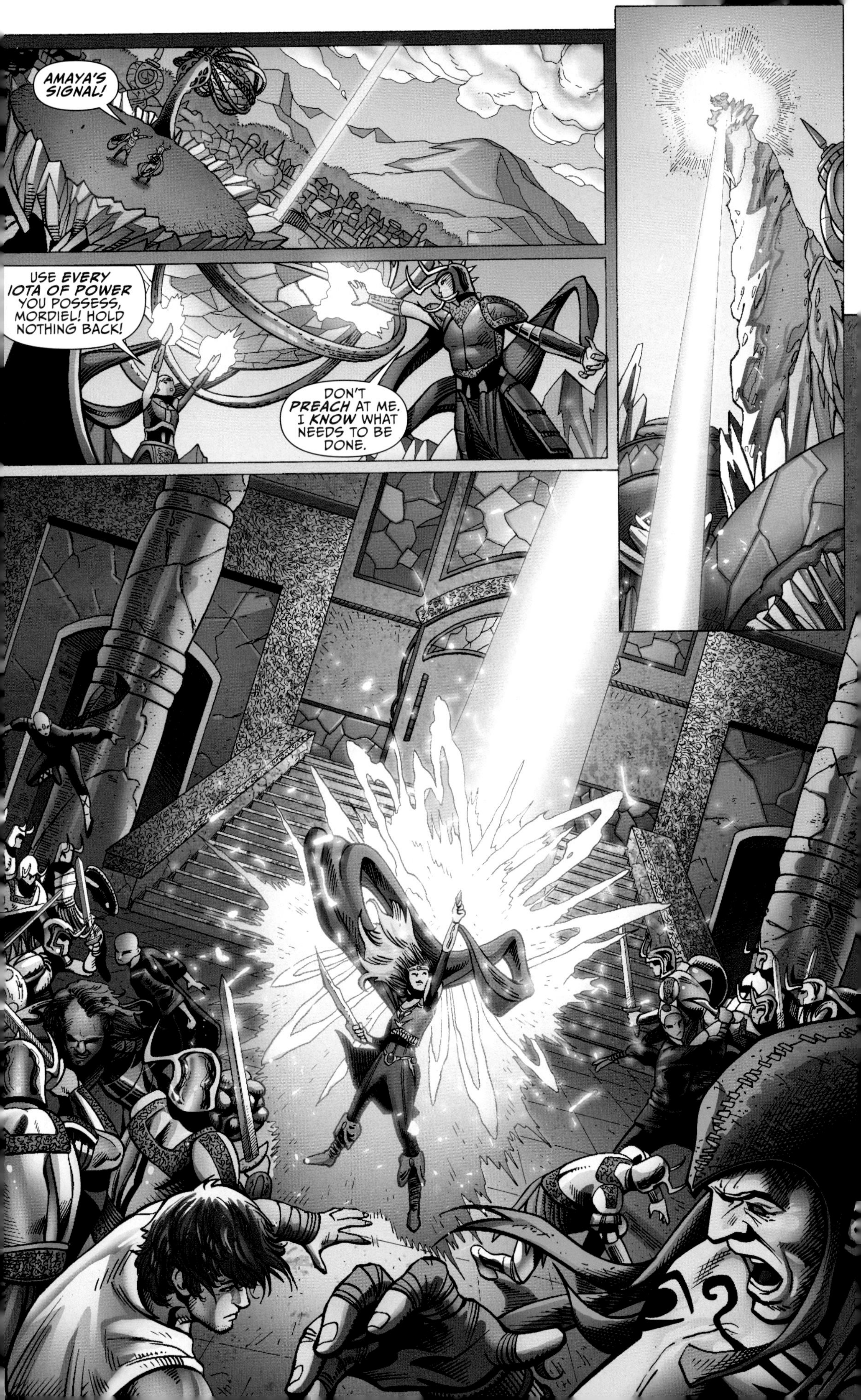
AMAYA'S SIGNAL!
USE EVERY IOTA OF POWER YOU POSSESS, MORDIEL! HOLD NOTHING BACK!
DON'T PREACH AT ME. I KNOW WHAT NEEDS TO BE DONE.

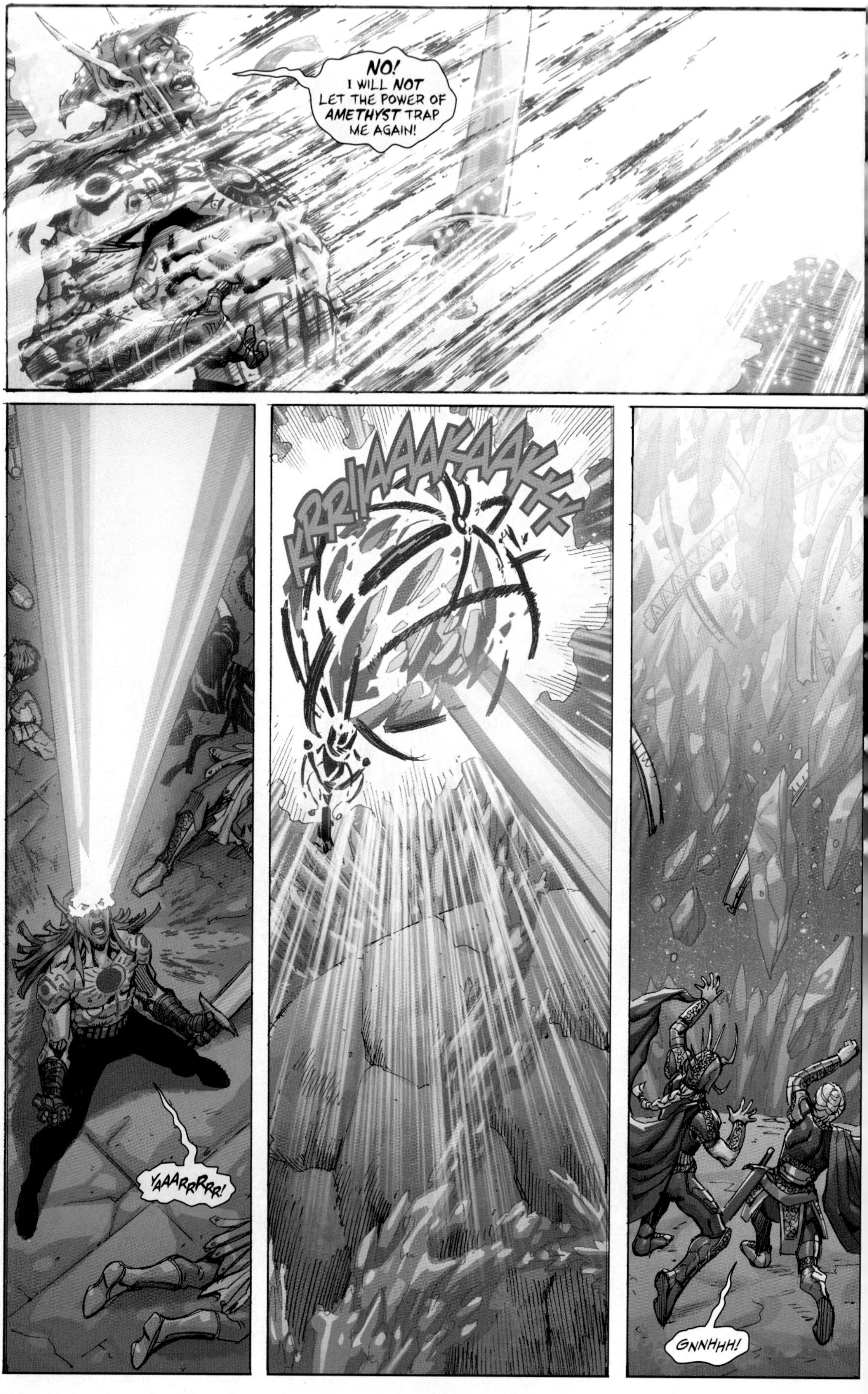
NO! I WILL NOT LET THE POWER OF AMETHYST TRAP ME AGAIN!
YAAARRRRR!
KRRIIAAAKAAKKK
GNNHHH!

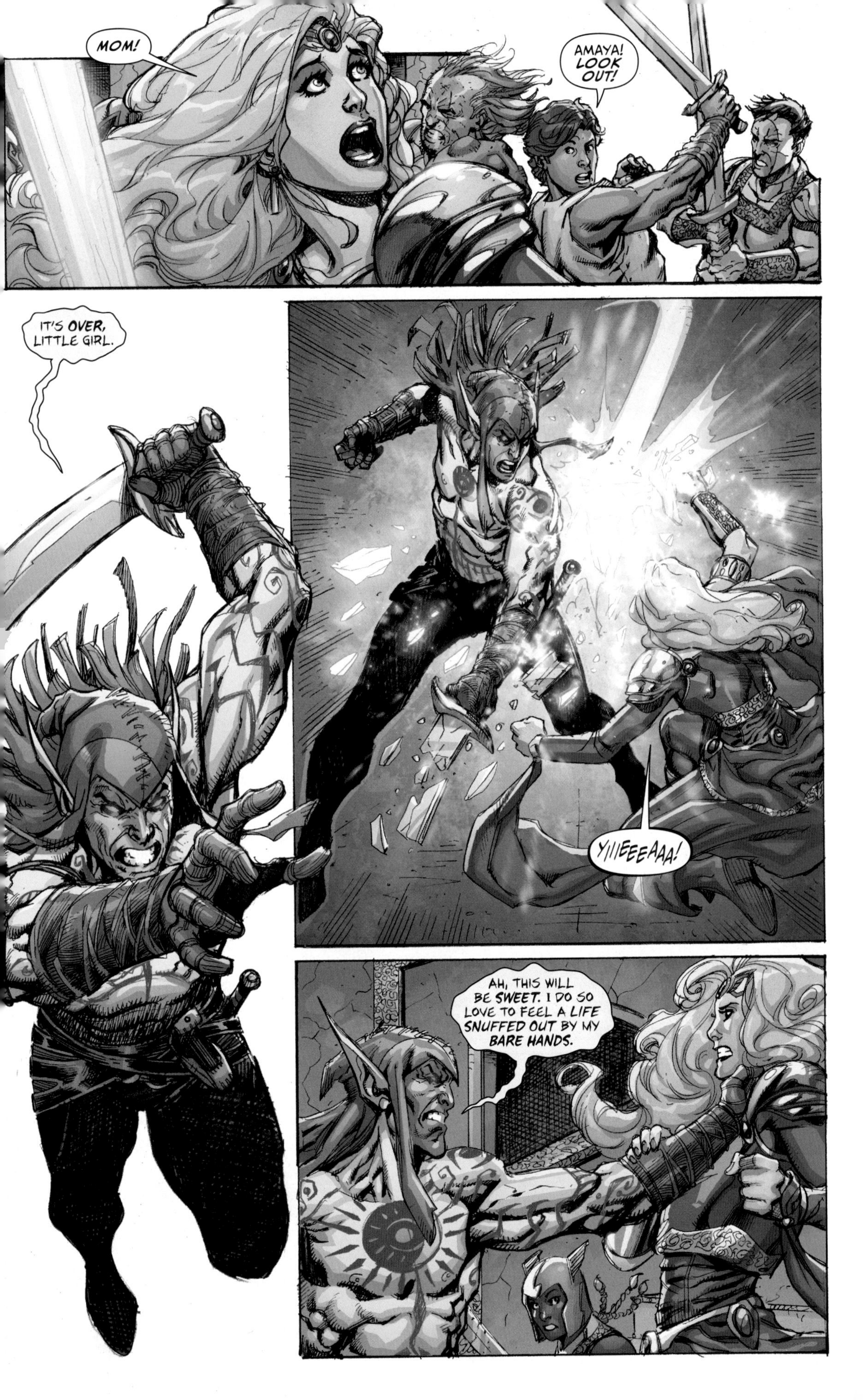
MOM!
AMAYA! LOOK OUT!
IT'S OVER, LITTLE GIRL.
YIIIEEEAAA!
AH, THIS WILL BE SWEET. I DO SO LOVE TO FEEL A LIFE SNUFFED OUT BY MY BARE HANDS.

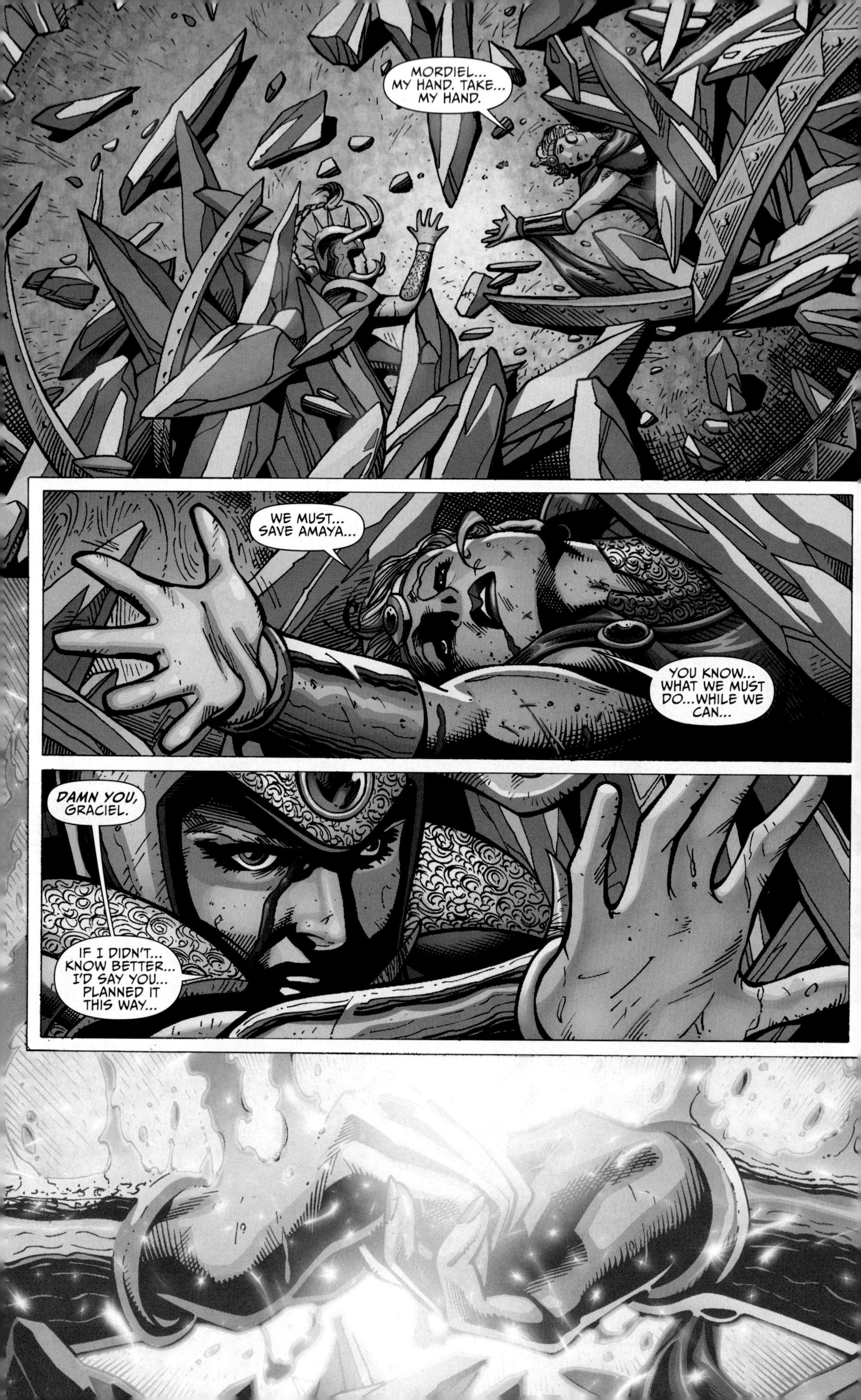
MORDIEL... MY HAND. TAKE... MY HAND.
WE MUST... SAVE AMAYA...
YOU KNOW... WHAT WE MUST DO...WHILE WE CAN...
DAMN YOU, GRACIEL.
IF I DIDN'T... KNOW BETTER... I'D SAY YOU... PLANNED IT THIS WAY...

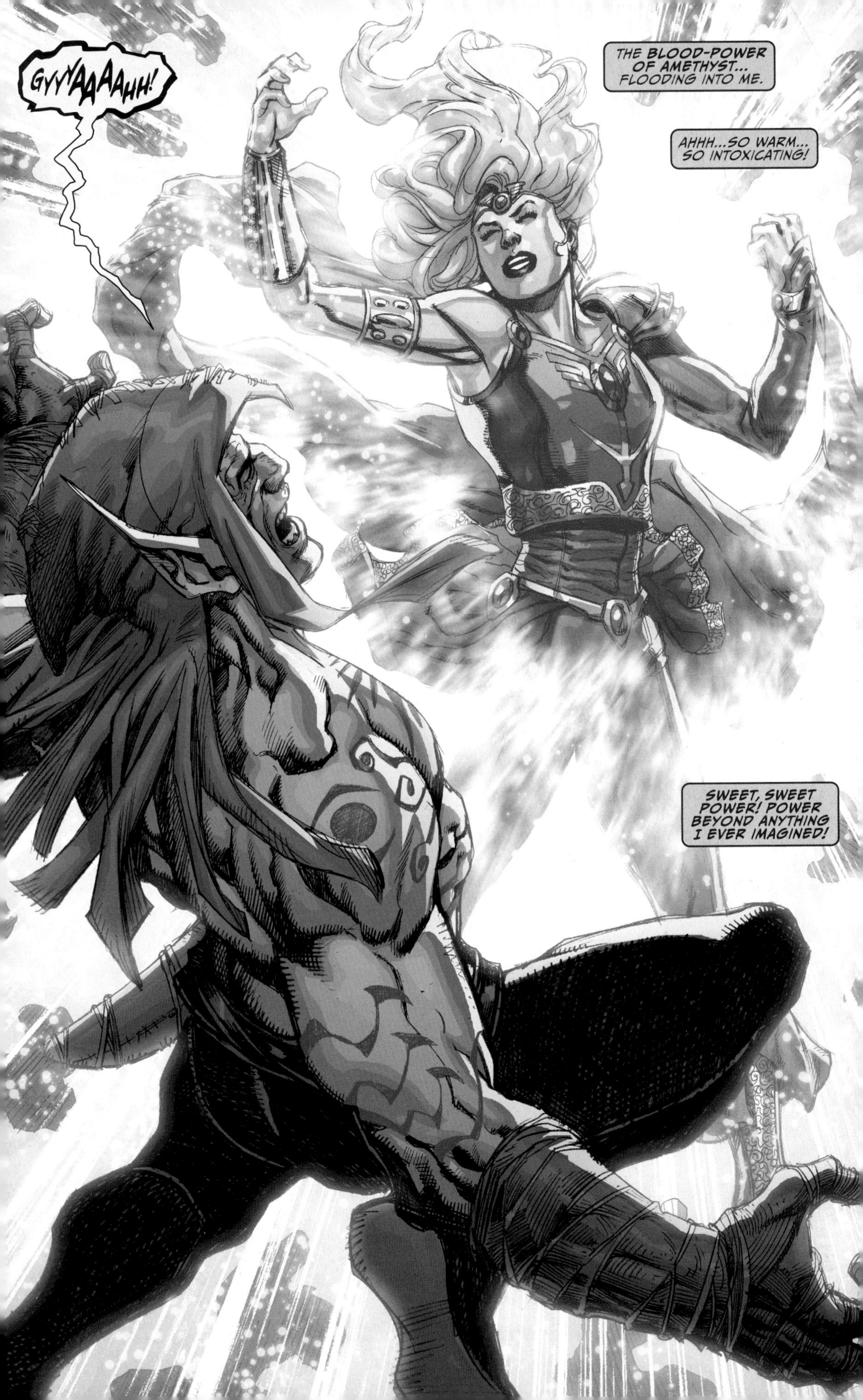
GYYYAAAAAHH!
THE BLOOD-POWER OF AMETHYST... FLOODING INTO ME.
AHHH...SO WARM... SO INTOXICATING!
SWEET, SWEET POWER! POWER BEYOND ANYTHING I EVER IMAGINED!

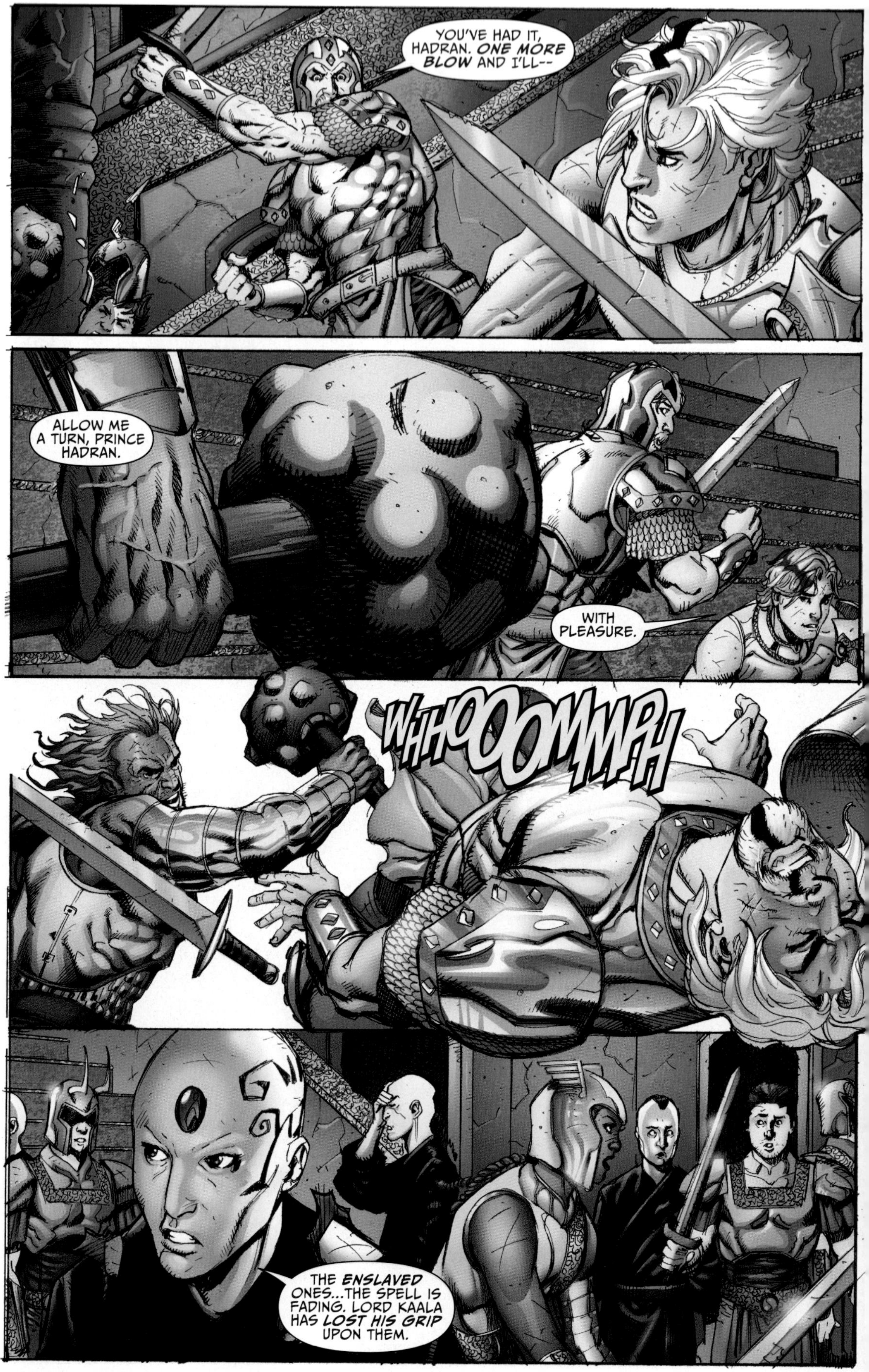
YOU'VE HAD IT, HADRAN. ONE MORE BLOW AND I'LL--
ALLOW ME A TURN, PRINCE HADRAN.
WITH PLEASURE.
WHHOOOOMMPH
THE ENSLAVED ONES...THE SPELL IS FADING. LORD KAALA HAS LOST HIS GRIP UPON THEM.

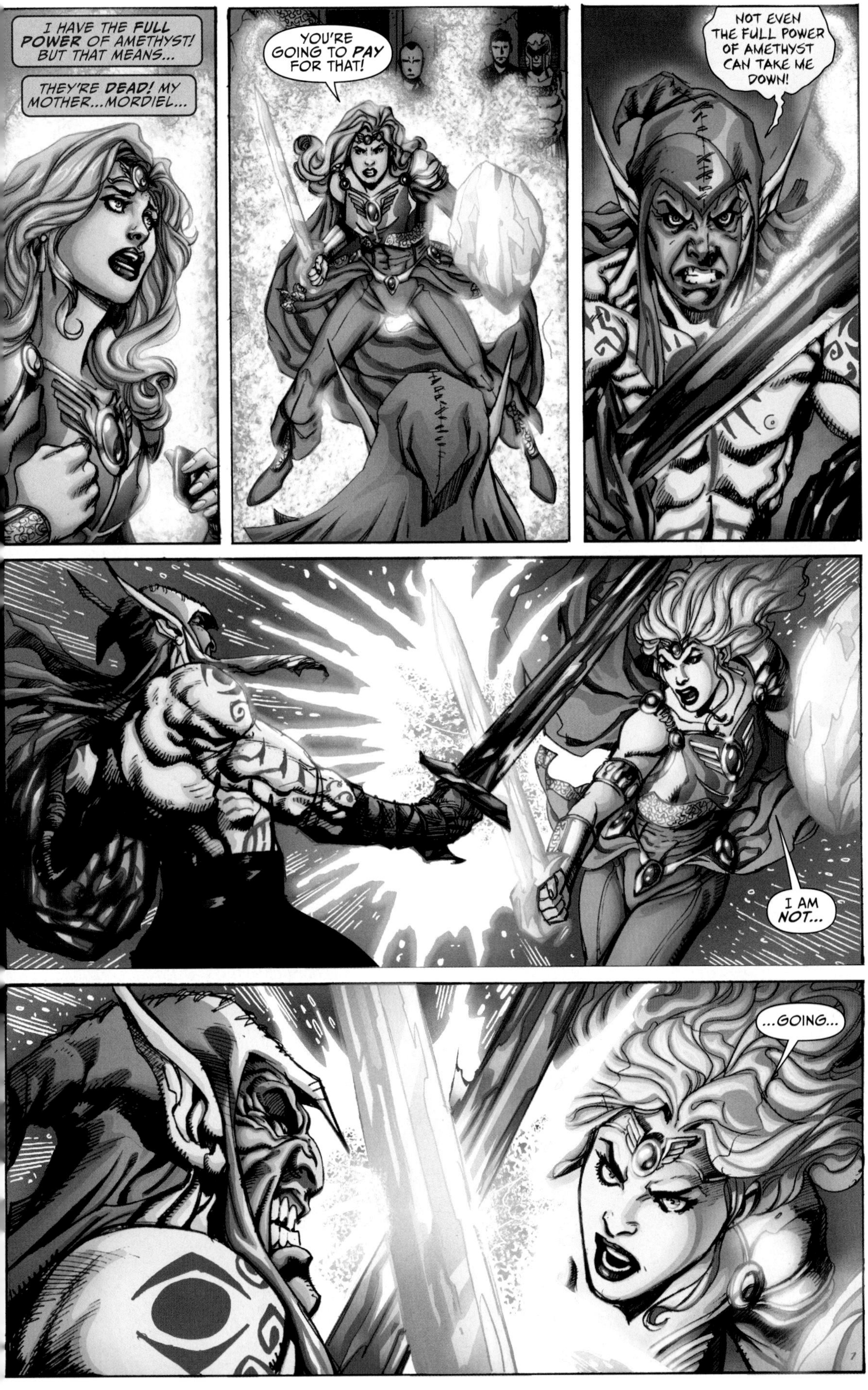

I HAVE THE FULL POWER OF AMETHYST! BUT THAT MEANS...
THEY'RE DEAD! MY MOTHER...MORDIEL...
YOU'RE GOING TO PAY FOR THAT!
NOT EVEN THE FULL POWER OF AMETHYST CAN TAKE ME DOWN!
I AM NOT...
...GOING...

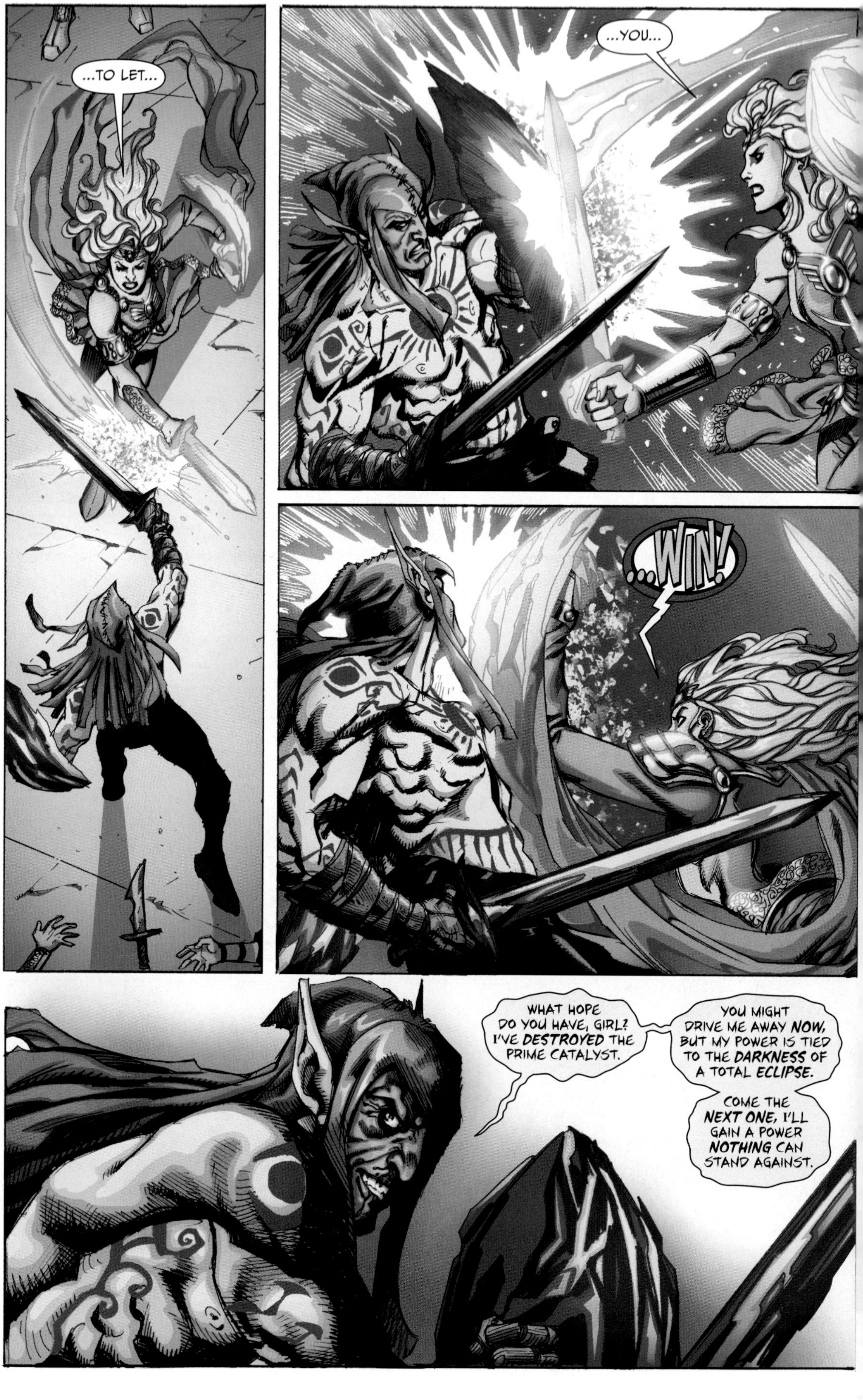
...TO LET...
...YOU...
...WIN!
WHAT HOPE DO YOU HAVE, GIRL? I'VE DESTROYED THE PRIME CATALYST.
YOU MIGHT DRIVE ME AWAY NOW, BUT MY POWER IS TIED TO THE DARKNESS OF A TOTAL ECLIPSE.
COME THE NEXT ONE, I'LL GAIN A POWER NOTHING CAN STAND AGAINST.

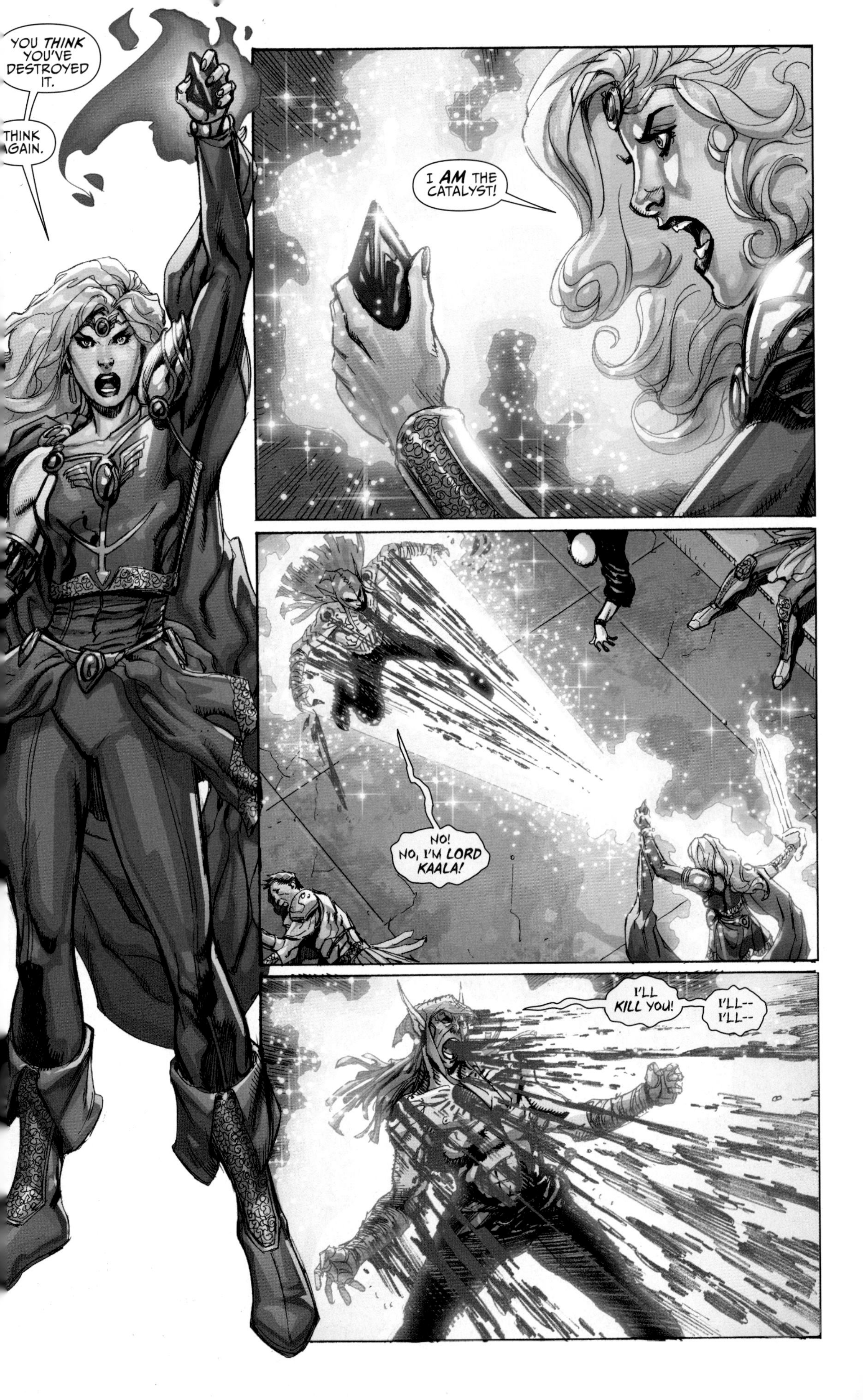
YOU *THINK* YOU'VE DESTROYED IT.
THINK AGAIN.
I *AM* THE CATALYST!
NO! NO, I'M *LORD KAALA!*
I'LL *KILL* YOU!
I'LL-- I'LL--

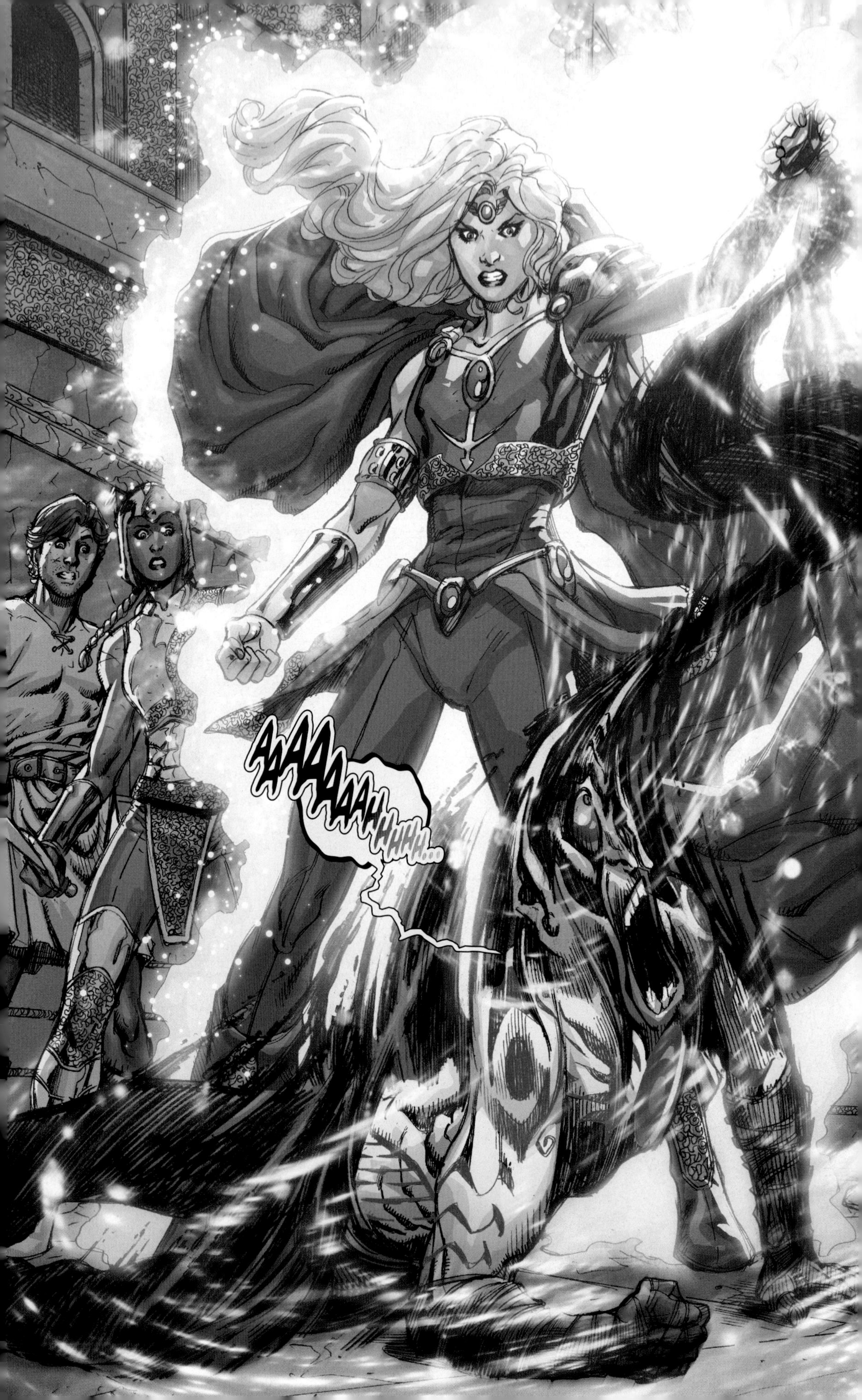
AAAAAAAHHHHH...

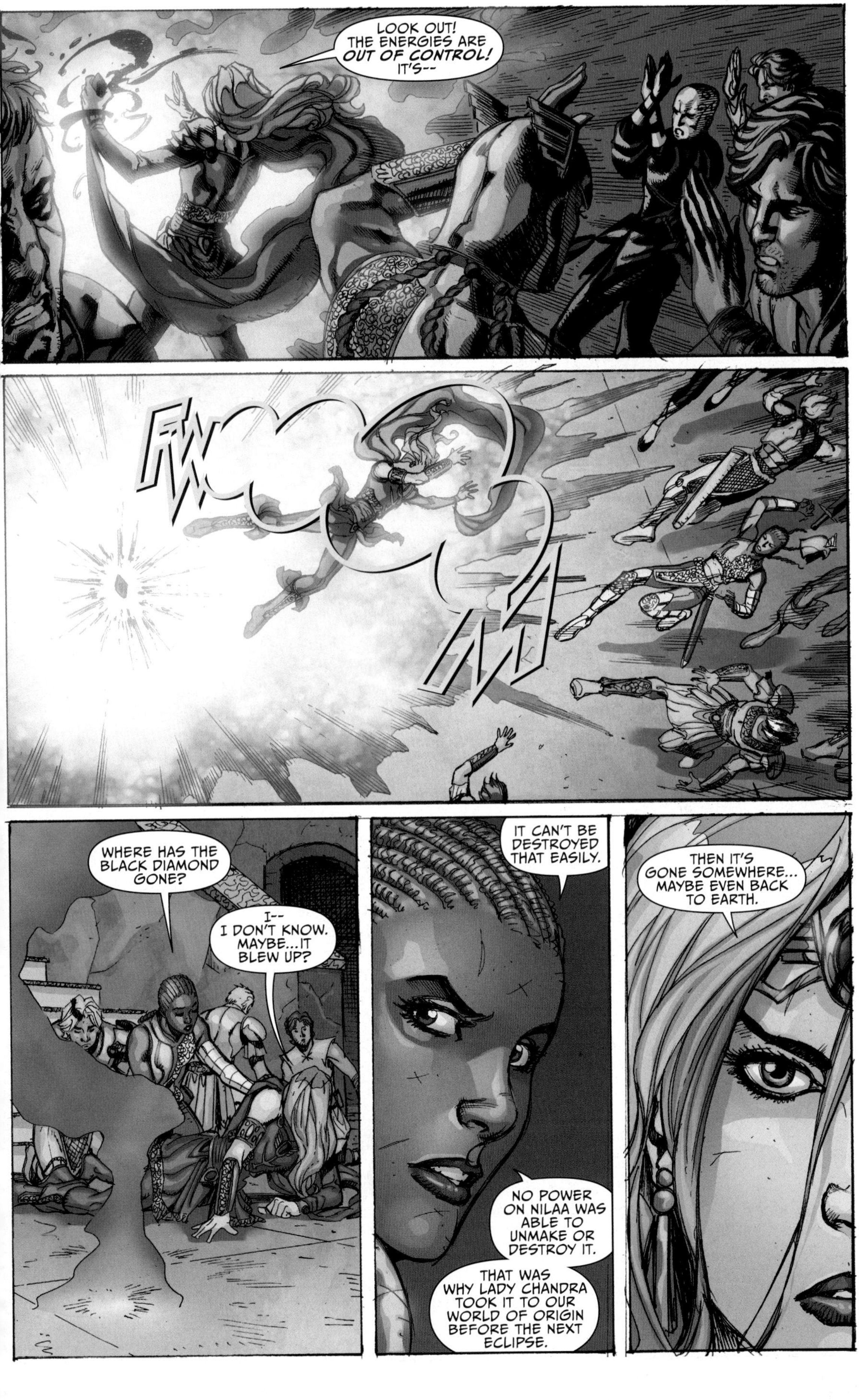
LOOK OUT! THE ENERGIES ARE OUT OF CONTROL! IT'S--
FWOOOM
WHERE HAS THE BLACK DIAMOND GONE?
I-- I DON'T KNOW. MAYBE...IT BLEW UP?
IT CAN'T BE DESTROYED THAT EASILY.
NO POWER ON NILAA WAS ABLE TO UNMAKE OR DESTROY IT.
THAT WAS WHY LADY CHANDRA TOOK IT TO OUR WORLD OF ORIGIN BEFORE THE NEXT ECLIPSE.
THEN IT'S GONE SOMEWHERE... MAYBE EVEN BACK TO EARTH.

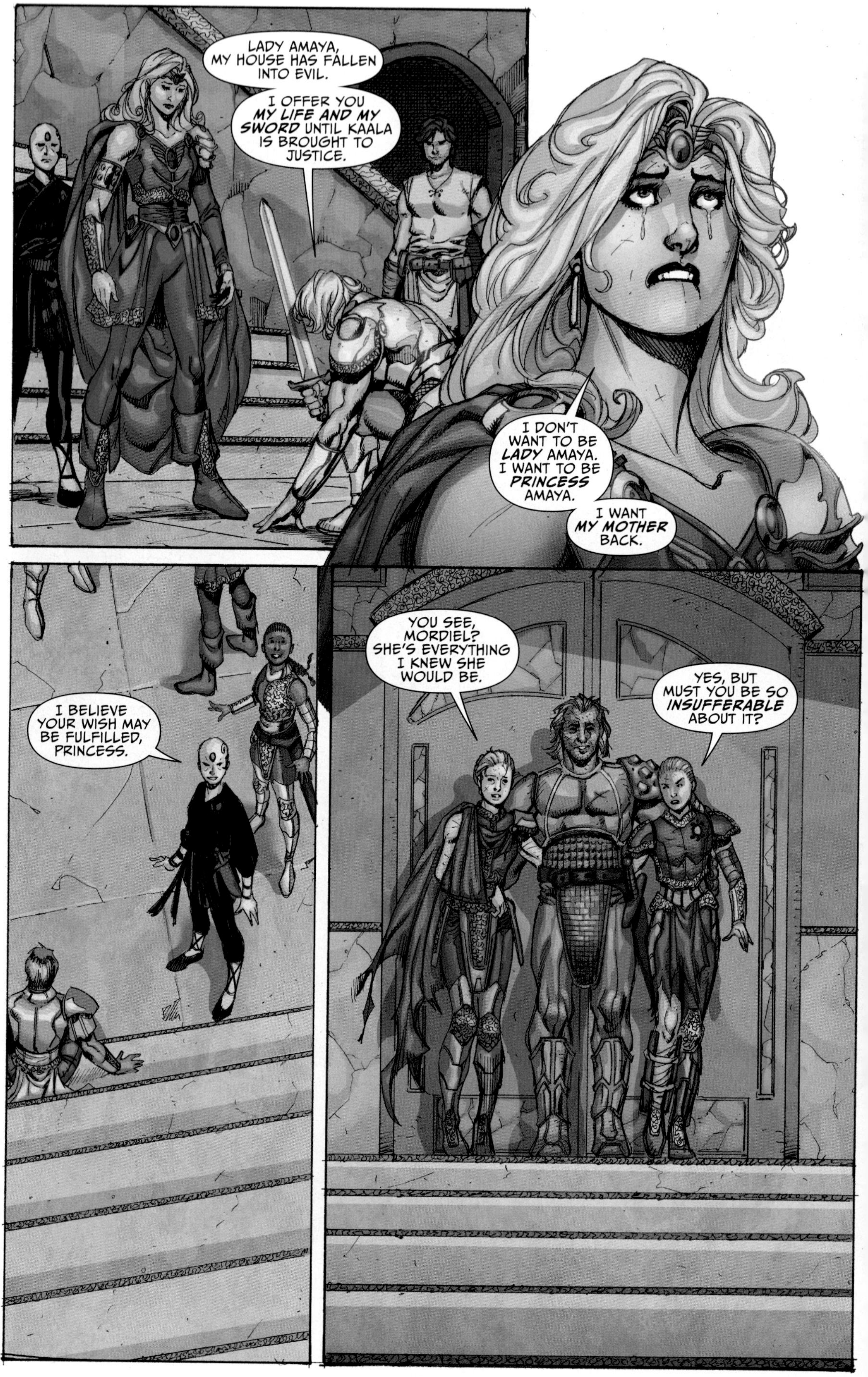
LADY AMAYA, MY HOUSE HAS FALLEN INTO EVIL.
I OFFER YOU MY LIFE AND MY SWORD UNTIL KAALA IS BROUGHT TO JUSTICE.
I DON'T WANT TO BE LADY AMAYA. I WANT TO BE PRINCESS AMAYA.
I WANT MY MOTHER BACK.
I BELIEVE YOUR WISH MAY BE FULFILLED, PRINCESS.
YOU SEE, MORDIEL? SHE'S EVERYTHING I KNEW SHE WOULD BE.
YES, BUT MUST YOU BE SO INSUFFERABLE ABOUT IT?

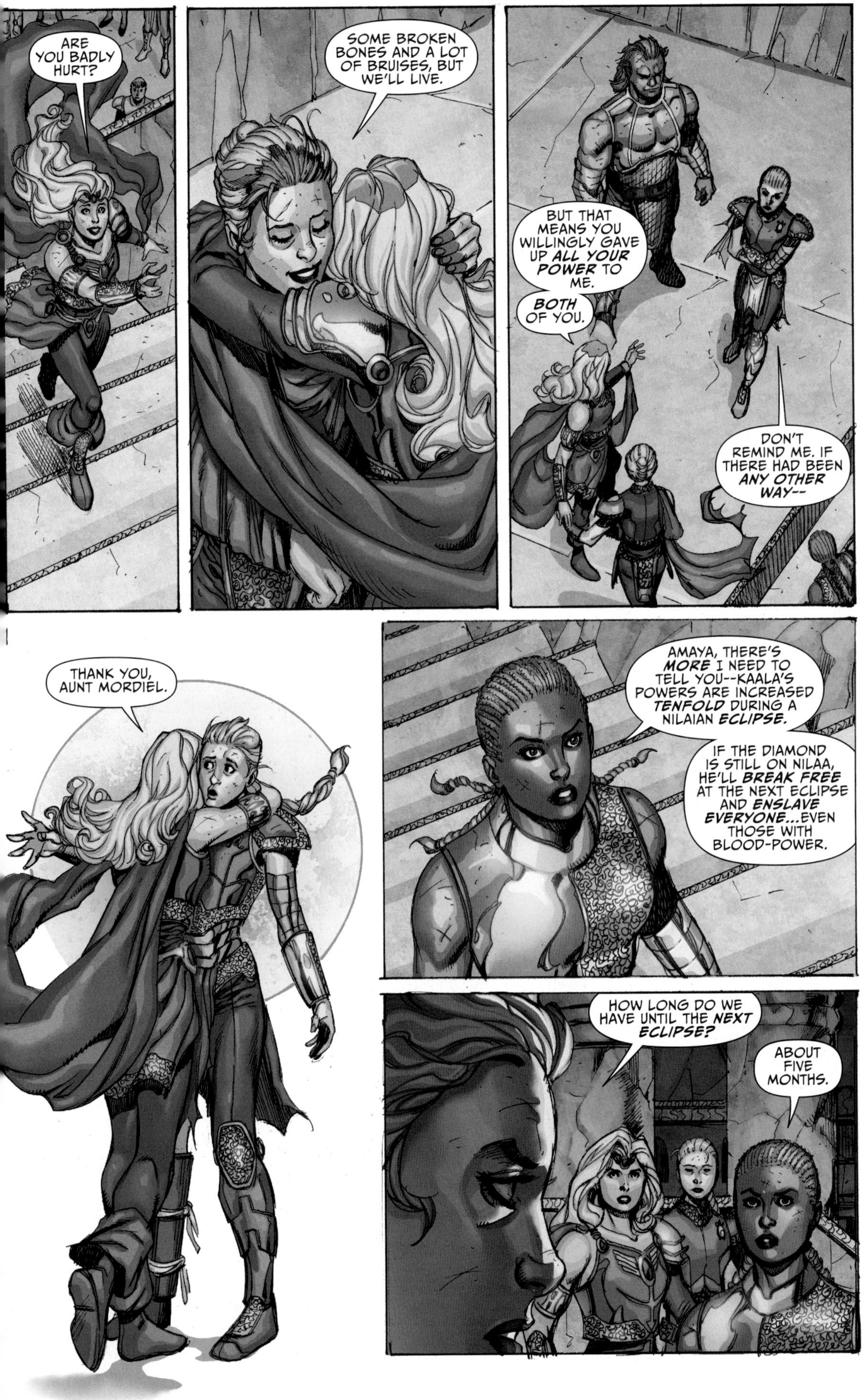
ARE YOU BADLY HURT?
SOME BROKEN BONES AND A LOT OF BRUISES, BUT WE'LL LIVE.
BUT THAT MEANS YOU WILLINGLY GAVE UP ALL YOUR POWER TO ME.
BOTH OF YOU.
DON'T REMIND ME. IF THERE HAD BEEN ANY OTHER WAY--
THANK YOU, AUNT MORDIEL.
AMAYA, THERE'S MORE I NEED TO TELL YOU--KAALA'S POWERS ARE INCREASED TENFOLD DURING A NILAIAN ECLIPSE.
IF THE DIAMOND IS STILL ON NILAA, HE'LL BREAK FREE AT THE NEXT ECLIPSE AND ENSLAVE EVERYONE...EVEN THOSE WITH BLOOD-POWER.
HOW LONG DO WE HAVE UNTIL THE NEXT ECLIPSE?
ABOUT FIVE MONTHS.

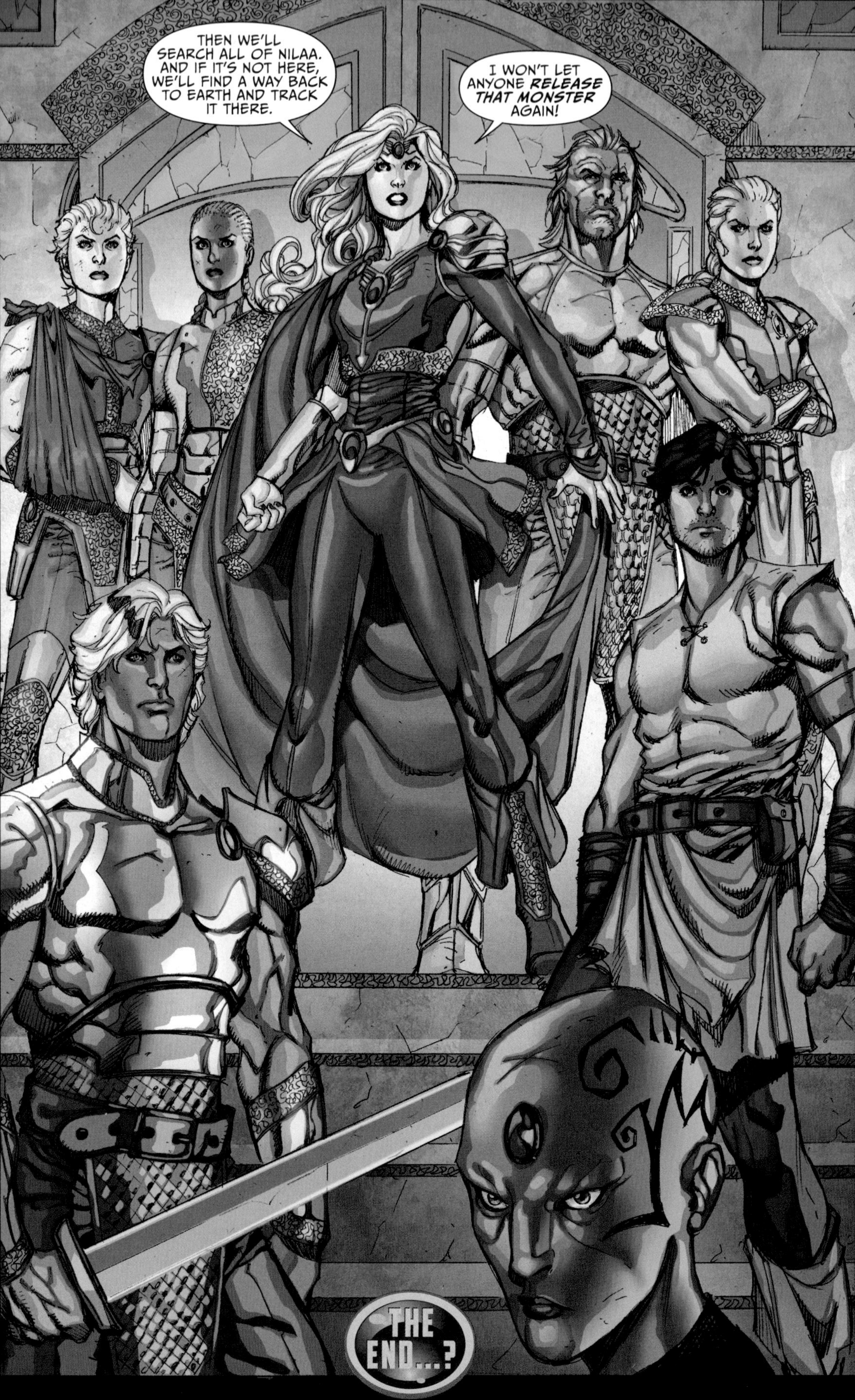
THEN WE'LL SEARCH ALL OF NILAA. AND IF IT'S NOT HERE, WE'LL FIND A WAY BACK TO EARTH AND TRACK IT THERE.
I WON'T LET ANYONE RELEASE THAT MONSTER AGAIN!
THE END...?

BEOWULF

TONY BEDARD
writer

JESÚS SAÍZ
JAVIER PINA
artists

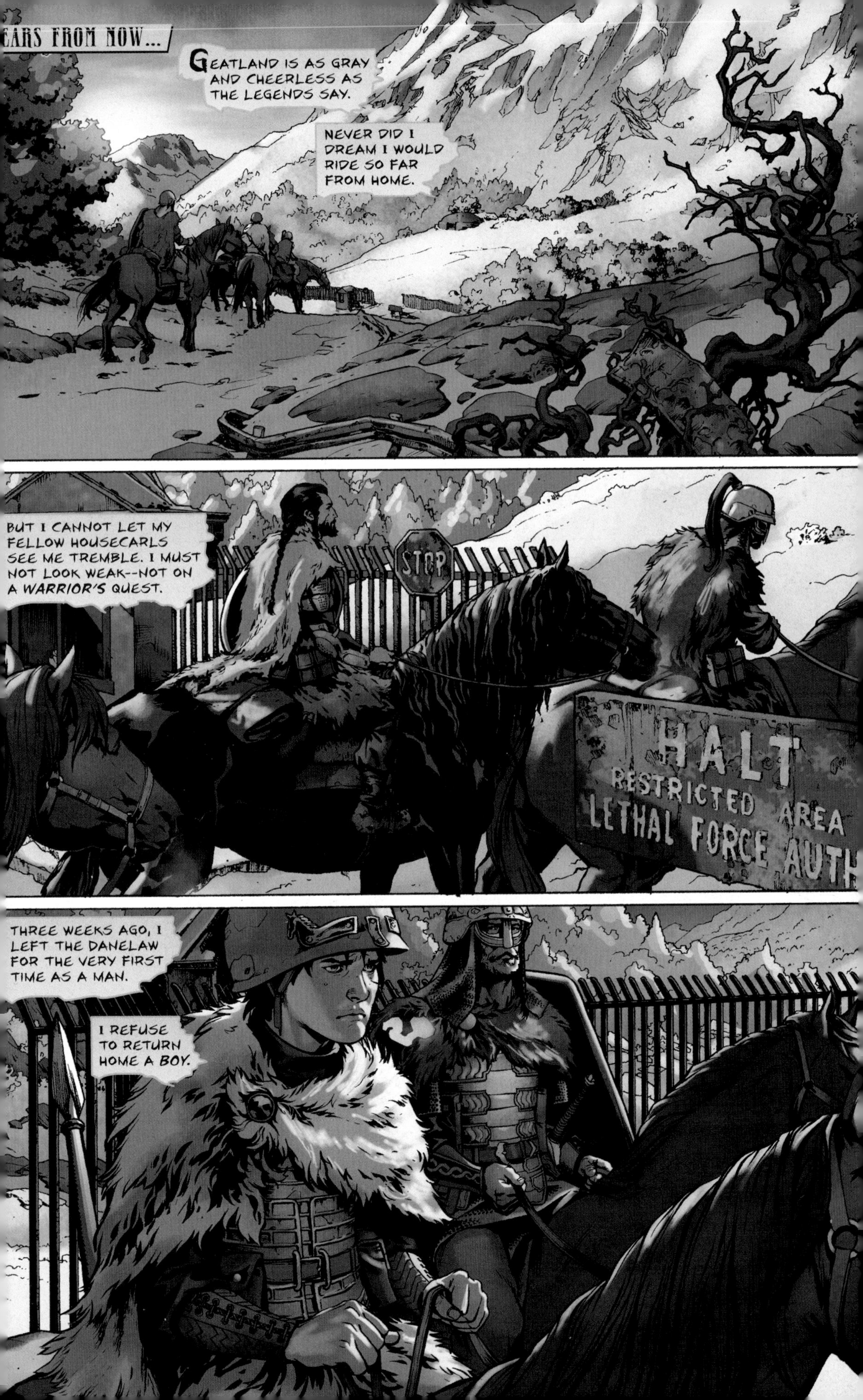

CARS FROM NOW...
GEATLAND IS AS GRAY AND CHEERLESS AS THE LEGENDS SAY.
NEVER DID I DREAM I WOULD RIDE SO FAR FROM HOME.
BUT I CANNOT LET MY FELLOW HOUSECARLS SEE ME TREMBLE. I MUST NOT LOOK WEAK--NOT ON A *WARRIOR'S* QUEST.
STOP
HALT
RESTRICTED AREA
LETHAL FORCE AUTH
THREE WEEKS AGO, I LEFT THE DANELAW FOR THE VERY FIRST TIME AS A MAN.
I REFUSE TO RETURN HOME A BOY.

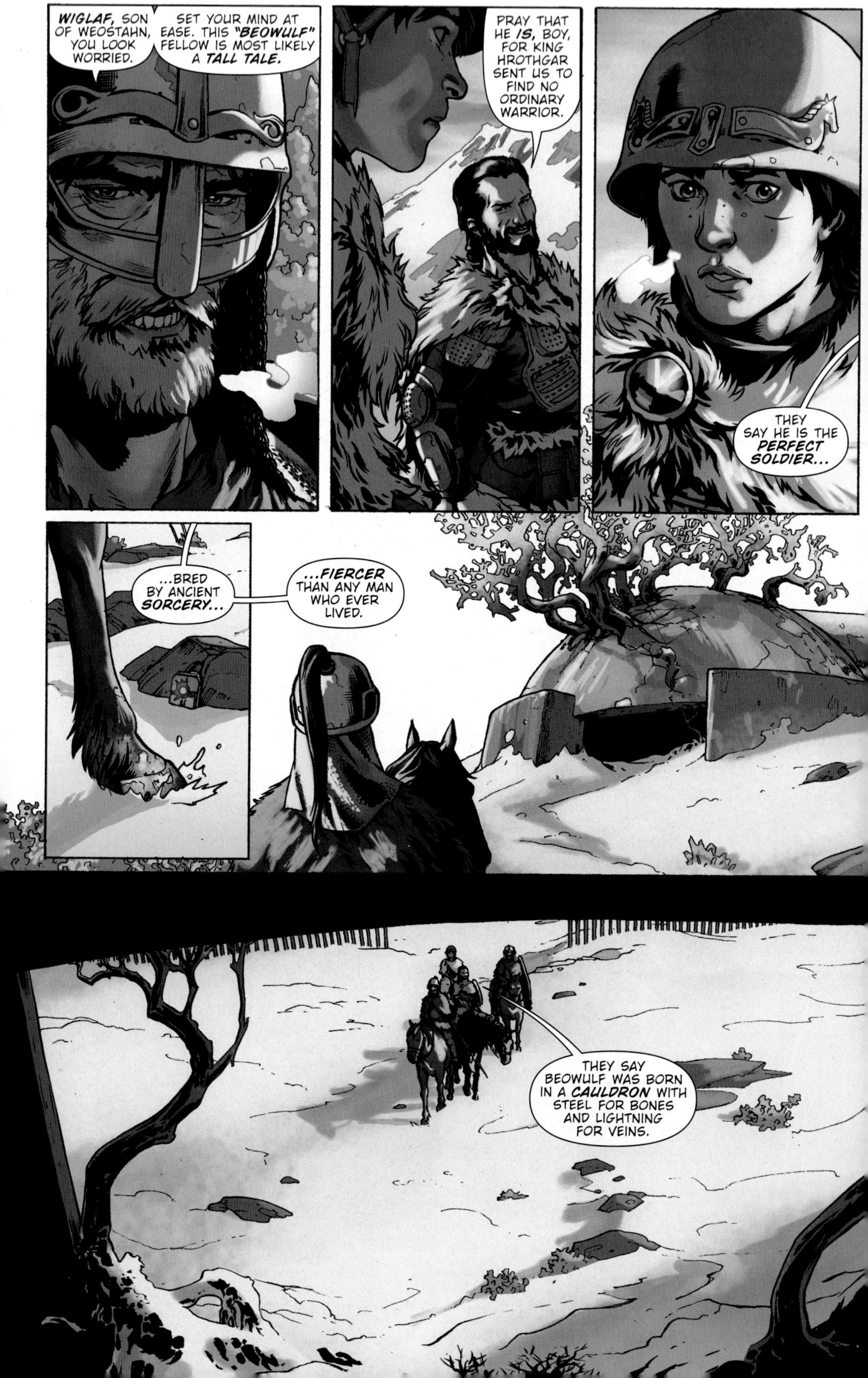
WIGLAF, SON OF WEOSTAHN, YOU LOOK WORRIED.
SET YOUR MIND AT EASE. THIS "BEOWULF" FELLOW IS MOST LIKELY A TALL TALE.
PRAY THAT HE IS, BOY, FOR KING HROTHGAR SENT US TO FIND NO ORDINARY WARRIOR.
THEY SAY HE IS THE PERFECT SOLDIER...
...BRED BY ANCIENT SORCERY...
...FIERCER THAN ANY MAN WHO EVER LIVED.
THEY SAY BEOWULF WAS BORN IN A CAULDRON WITH STEEL FOR BONES AND LIGHTNING FOR VEINS.

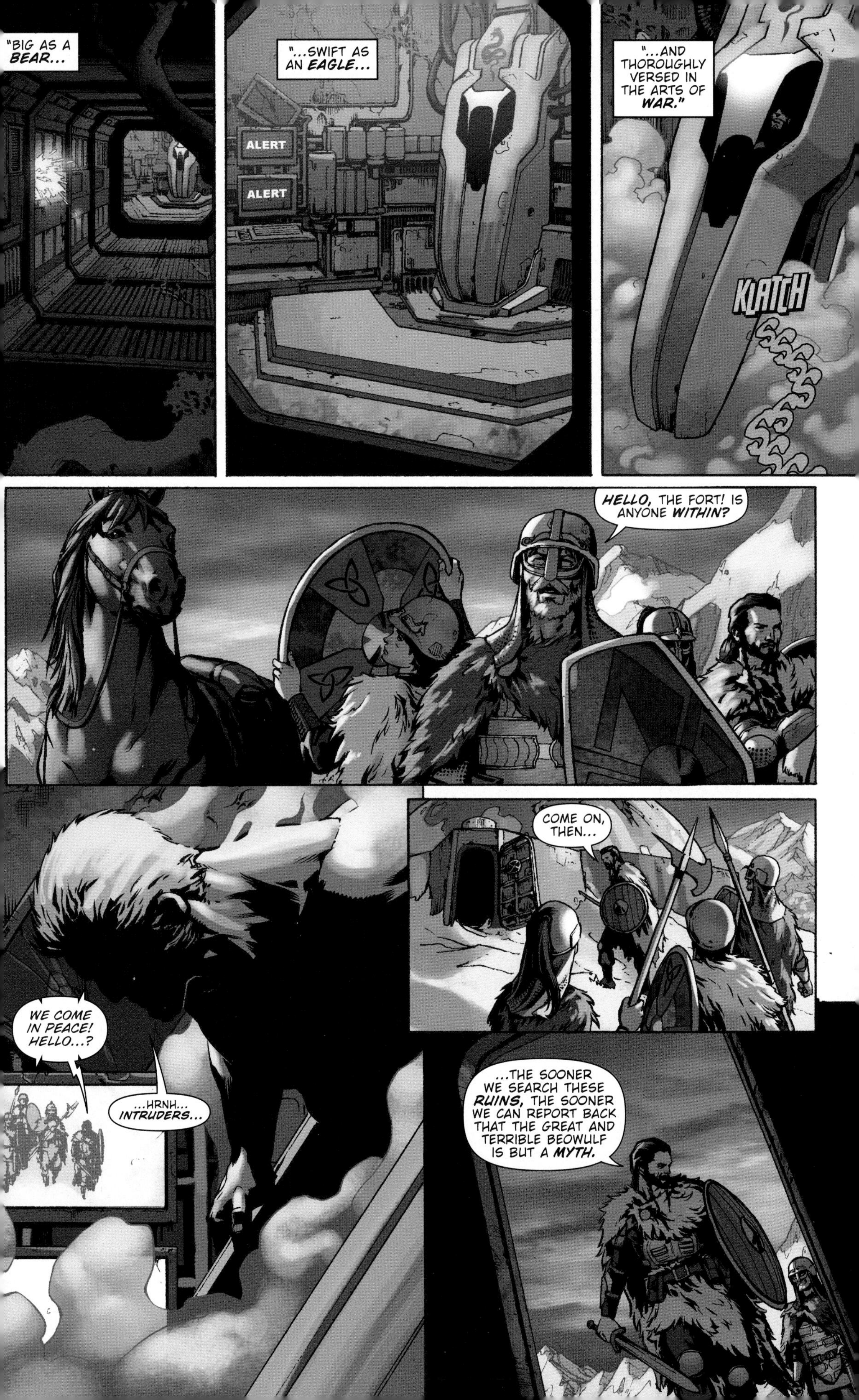
"BIG AS A BEAR...
"...SWIFT AS AN EAGLE...
ALERT
ALERT
"...AND THOROUGHLY VERSED IN THE ARTS OF WAR."
KLATCH
SSS
HELLO, THE FORT! IS ANYONE WITHIN?
WE COME IN PEACE! HELLO...?
...HRNH... INTRUDERS...
COME ON, THEN...
...THE SOONER WE SEARCH THESE RUINS, THE SOONER WE CAN REPORT BACK THAT THE GREAT AND TERRIBLE BEOWULF IS BUT A MYTH.

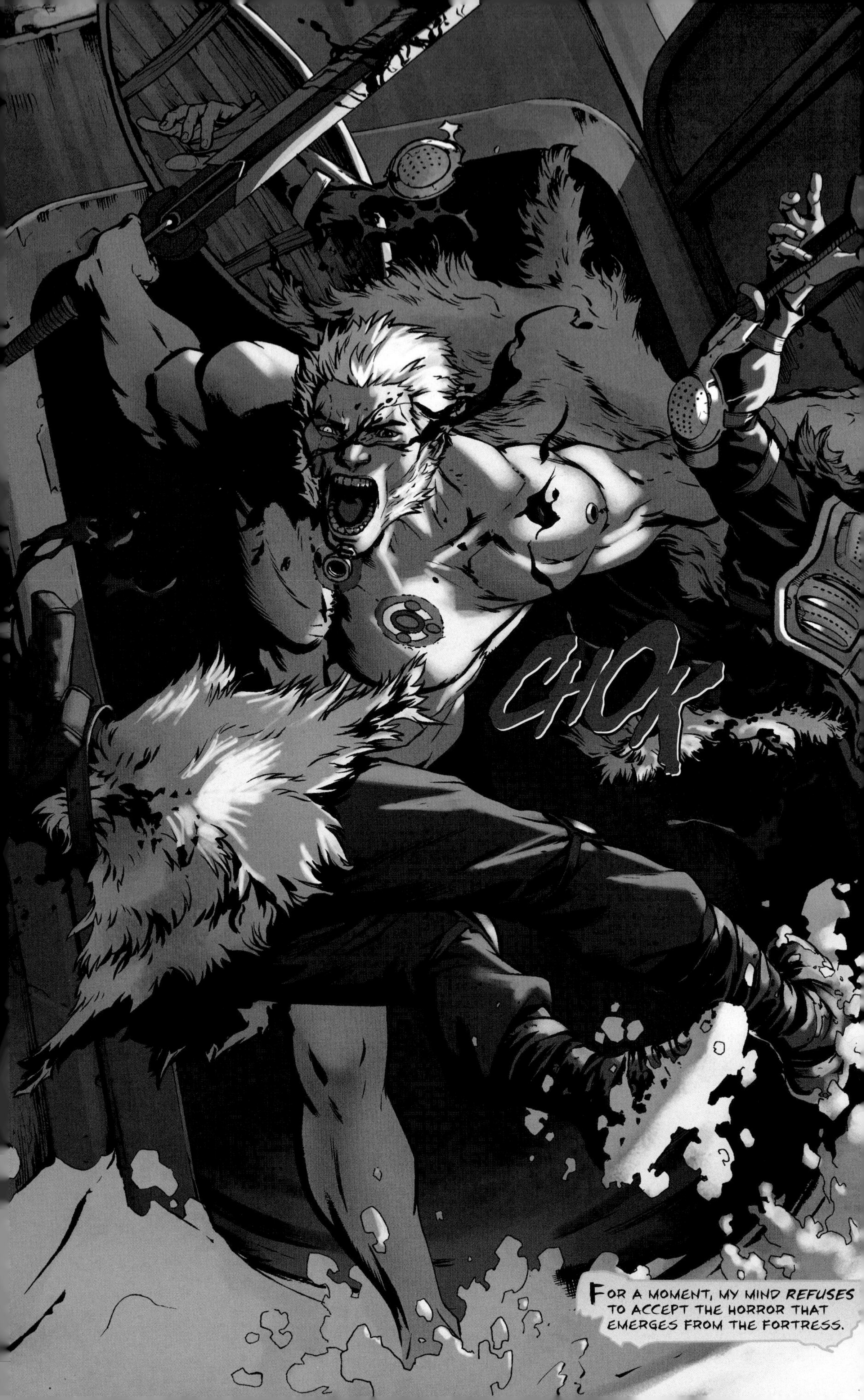
CHOK
FOR A MOMENT, MY MIND REFUSES TO ACCEPT THE HORROR THAT EMERGES FROM THE FORTRESS.

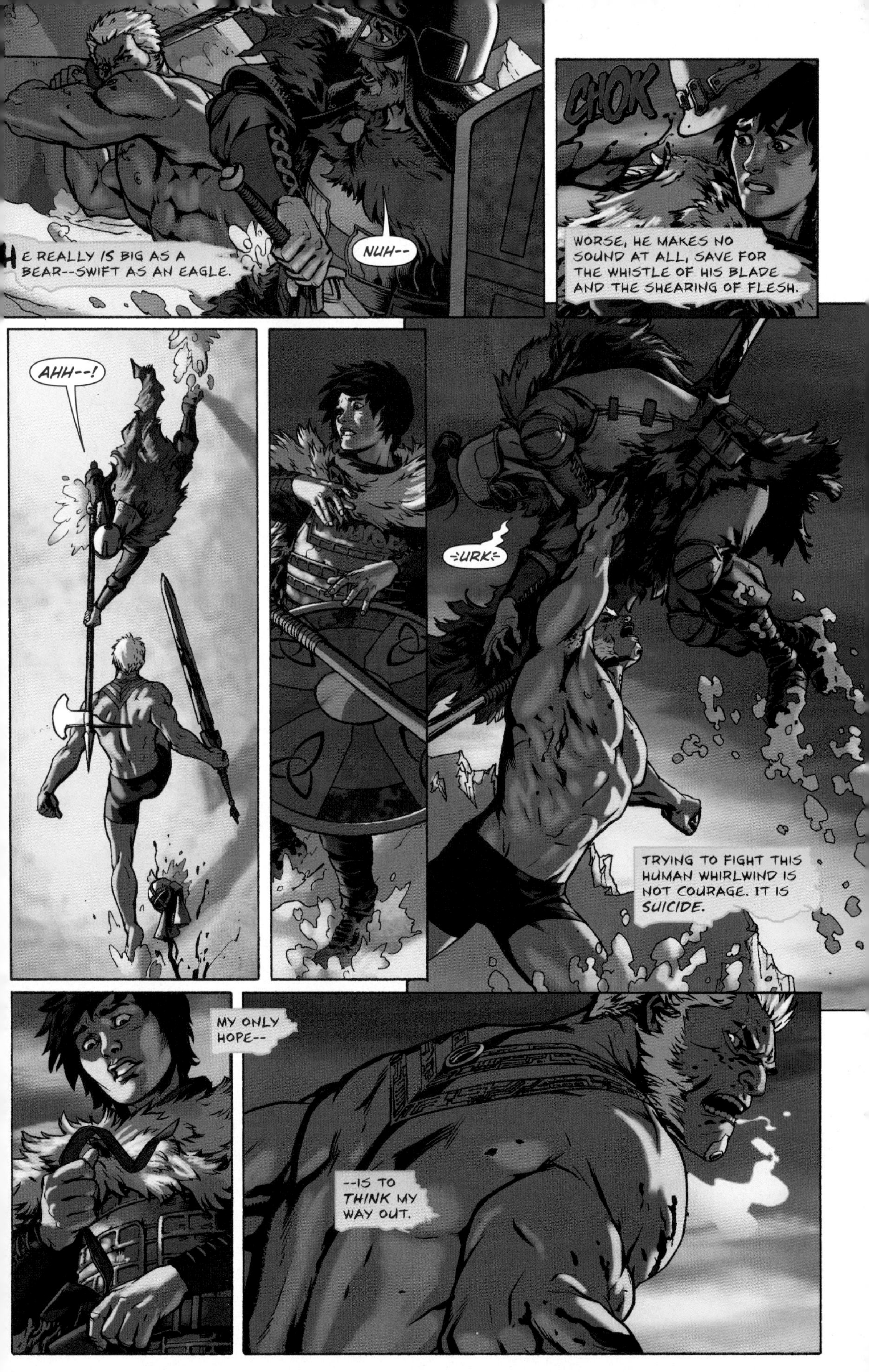
HE REALLY IS BIG AS A BEAR--SWIFT AS AN EAGLE.
NUH--
CHOK
WORSE, HE MAKES NO SOUND AT ALL, SAVE FOR THE WHISTLE OF HIS BLADE AND THE SHEARING OF FLESH.
AHH--!
URK
TRYING TO FIGHT THIS HUMAN WHIRLWIND IS NOT COURAGE. IT IS SUICIDE.
MY ONLY HOPE--
--IS TO THINK MY WAY OUT.

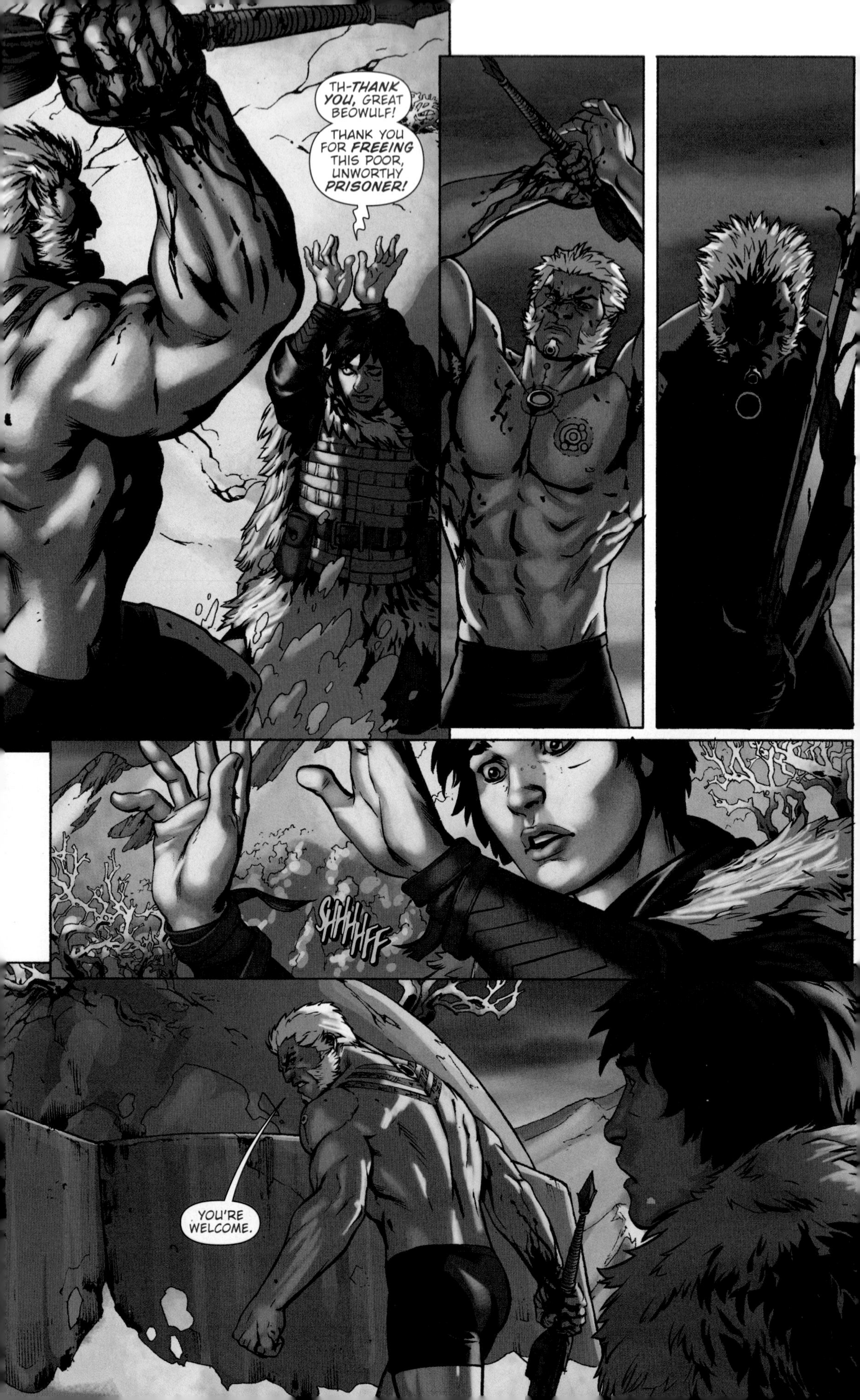
TH-THANK YOU, GREAT BEOWULF!
THANK YOU FOR FREEING THIS POOR, UNWORTHY PRISONER!
SHHHHFF
YOU'RE WELCOME.

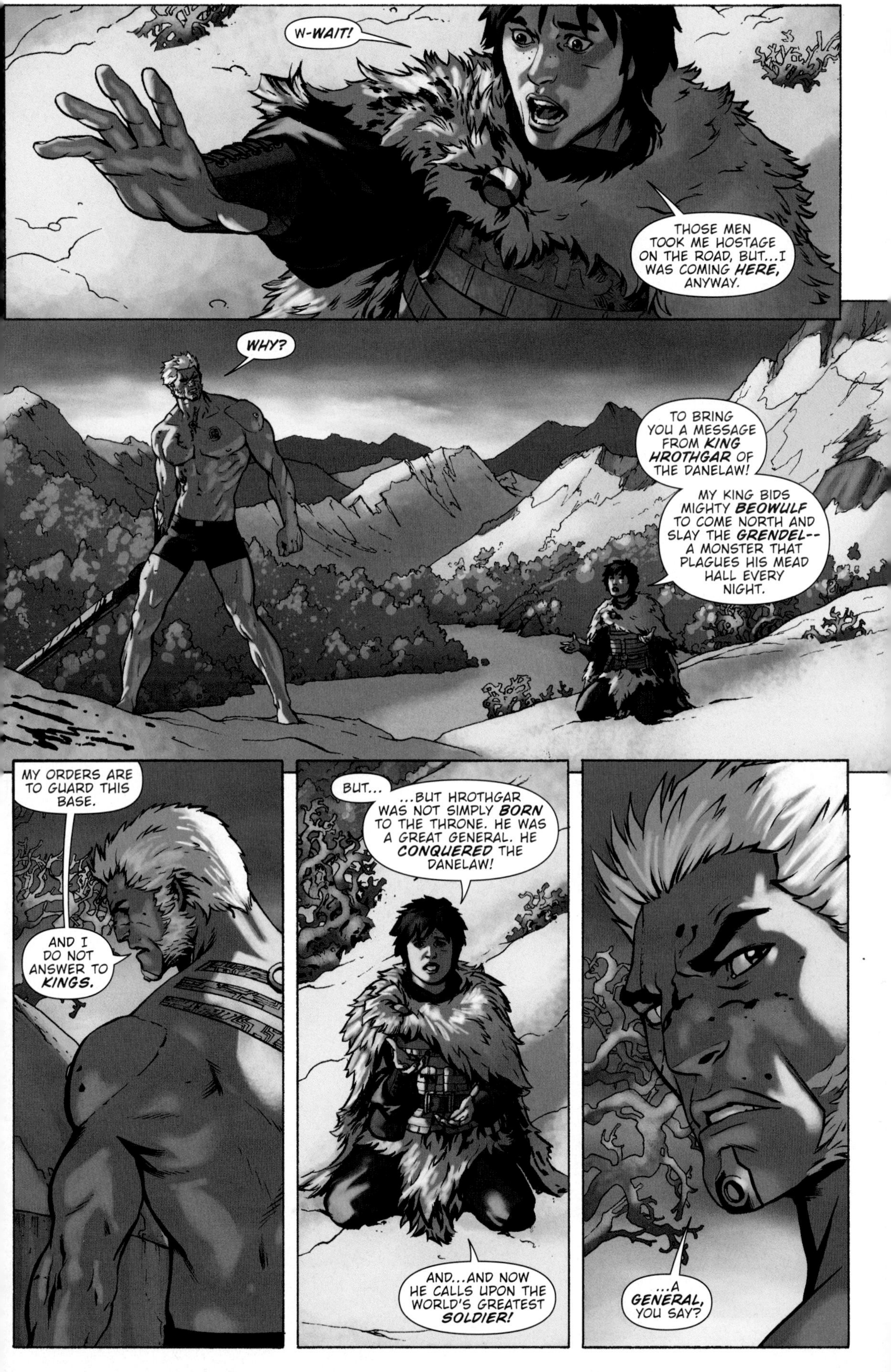
W-WAIT!
THOSE MEN TOOK ME HOSTAGE ON THE ROAD, BUT...I WAS COMING HERE, ANYWAY.
WHY?
TO BRING YOU A MESSAGE FROM KING HROTHGAR OF THE DANELAW!
MY KING BIDS MIGHTY BEOWULF TO COME NORTH AND SLAY THE GRENDEL-- A MONSTER THAT PLAGUES HIS MEAD HALL EVERY NIGHT.
MY ORDERS ARE TO GUARD THIS BASE.
AND I DO NOT ANSWER TO KINGS.
BUT...
...BUT HROTHGAR WAS NOT SIMPLY BORN TO THE THRONE. HE WAS A GREAT GENERAL. HE CONQUERED THE DANELAW!
AND...AND NOW HE CALLS UPON THE WORLD'S GREATEST SOLDIER!
...A GENERAL, YOU SAY?

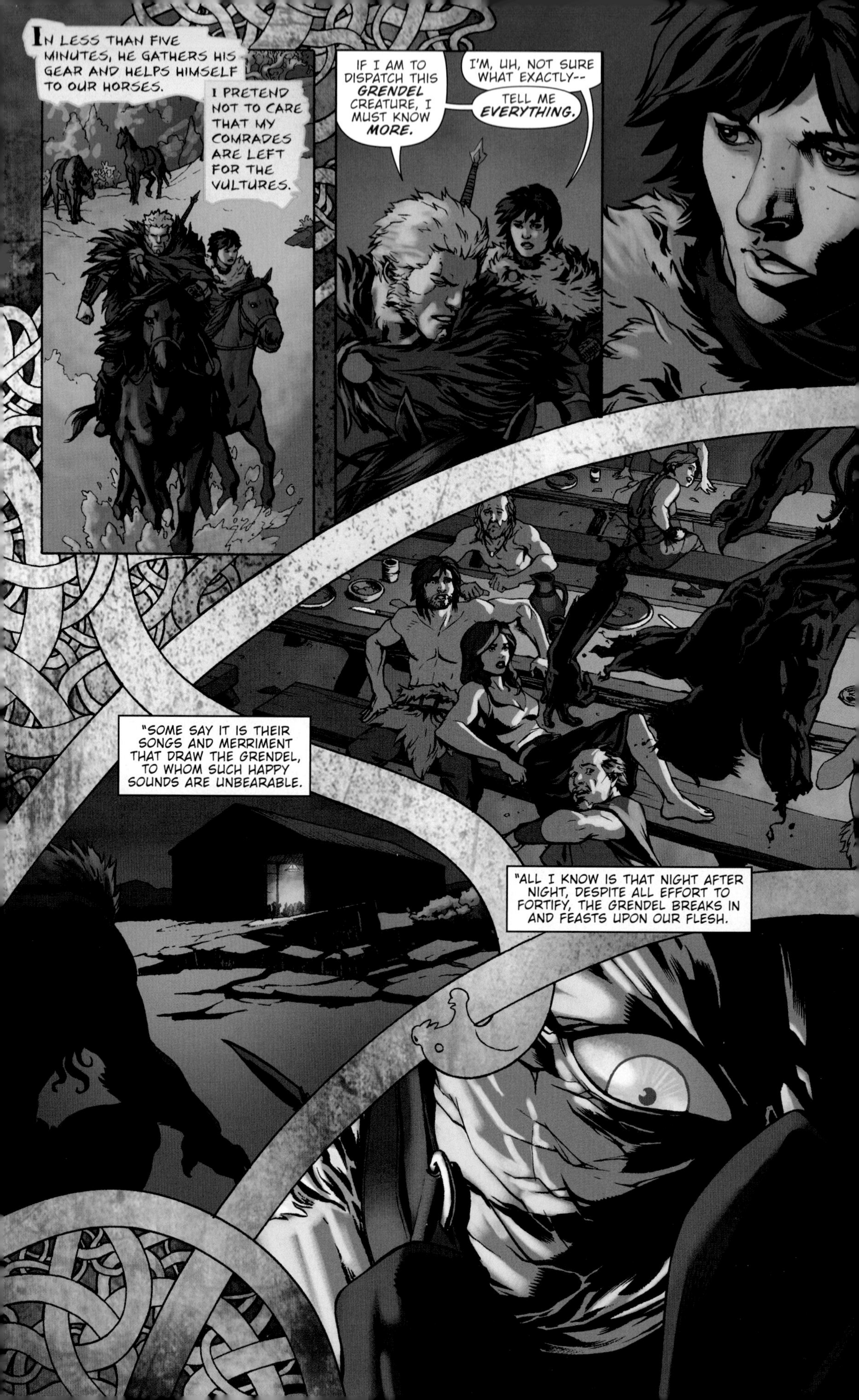
IN LESS THAN FIVE MINUTES, HE GATHERS HIS GEAR AND HELPS HIMSELF TO OUR HORSES.
I PRETEND NOT TO CARE THAT MY COMRADES ARE LEFT FOR THE VULTURES.
IF I AM TO DISPATCH THIS GRENDEL CREATURE, I MUST KNOW MORE.
I'M, UH, NOT SURE WHAT EXACTLY--
TELL ME EVERYTHING.
"SOME SAY IT IS THEIR SONGS AND MERRIMENT THAT DRAW THE GRENDEL, TO WHOM SUCH HAPPY SOUNDS ARE UNBEARABLE.
"ALL I KNOW IS THAT NIGHT AFTER NIGHT, DESPITE ALL EFFORT TO FORTIFY, THE GRENDEL BREAKS IN AND FEASTS UPON OUR FLESH.

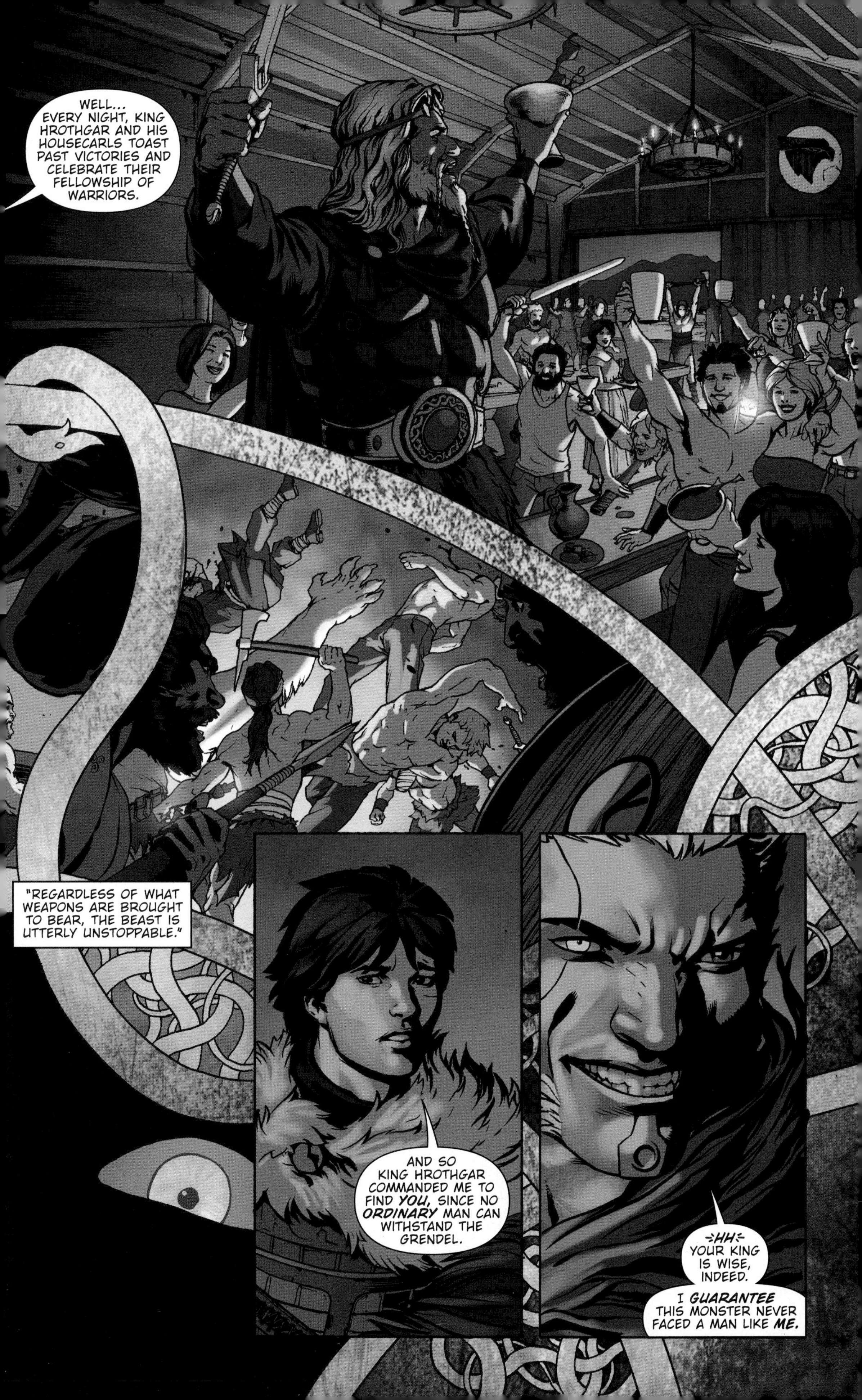
WELL... EVERY NIGHT, KING HROTHGAR AND HIS HOUSECARLS TOAST PAST VICTORIES AND CELEBRATE THEIR FELLOWSHIP OF WARRIORS.
"REGARDLESS OF WHAT WEAPONS ARE BROUGHT TO BEAR, THE BEAST IS UTTERLY UNSTOPPABLE."
AND SO KING HROTHGAR COMMANDED ME TO FIND *YOU*, SINCE NO *ORDINARY* MAN CAN WITHSTAND THE GRENDEL.
HH
YOUR KING IS WISE, INDEED.
I *GUARANTEE* THIS MONSTER NEVER FACED A MAN LIKE *ME*.

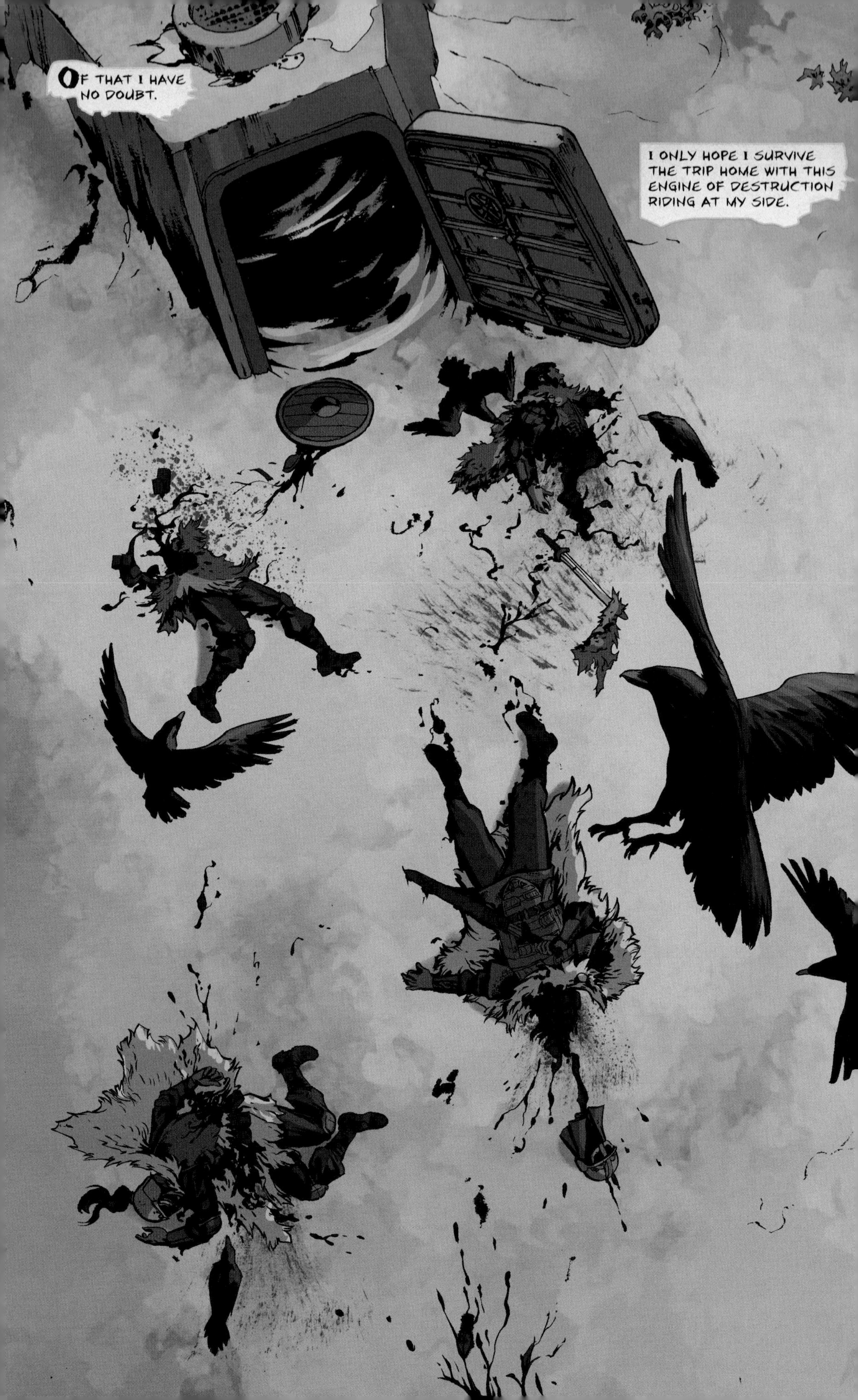
OF THAT I HAVE NO DOUBT.
I ONLY HOPE I SURVIVE THE TRIP HOME WITH THIS ENGINE OF DESTRUCTION RIDING AT MY SIDE.

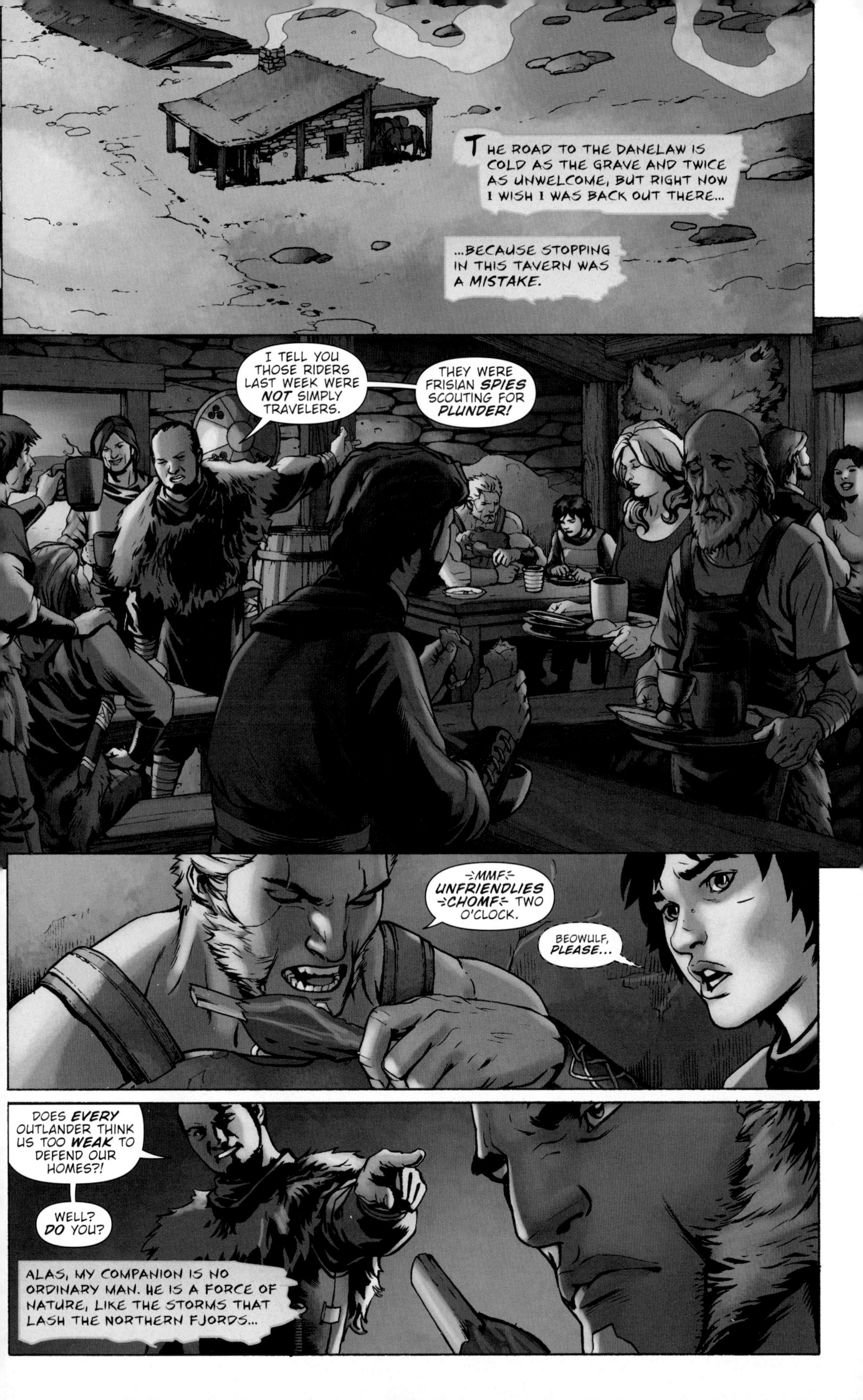
THE ROAD TO THE DANELAW IS COLD AS THE GRAVE AND TWICE AS UNWELCOME, BUT RIGHT NOW I WISH I WAS BACK OUT THERE...
...BECAUSE STOPPING IN THIS TAVERN WAS A *MISTAKE.*
I TELL YOU THOSE RIDERS LAST WEEK WERE ***NOT*** SIMPLY TRAVELERS.
THEY WERE FRISIAN ***SPIES*** SCOUTING FOR ***PLUNDER!***
=MMF=
UNFRIENDLIES =***CHOMF***= TWO O'CLOCK.
BEOWULF, ***PLEASE...***
DOES ***EVERY*** OUTLANDER THINK US TOO ***WEAK*** TO DEFEND OUR HOMES?!
WELL? ***DO*** YOU?
ALAS, MY COMPANION IS NO ORDINARY MAN. HE IS A FORCE OF NATURE, LIKE THE STORMS THAT LASH THE NORTHERN FJORDS...

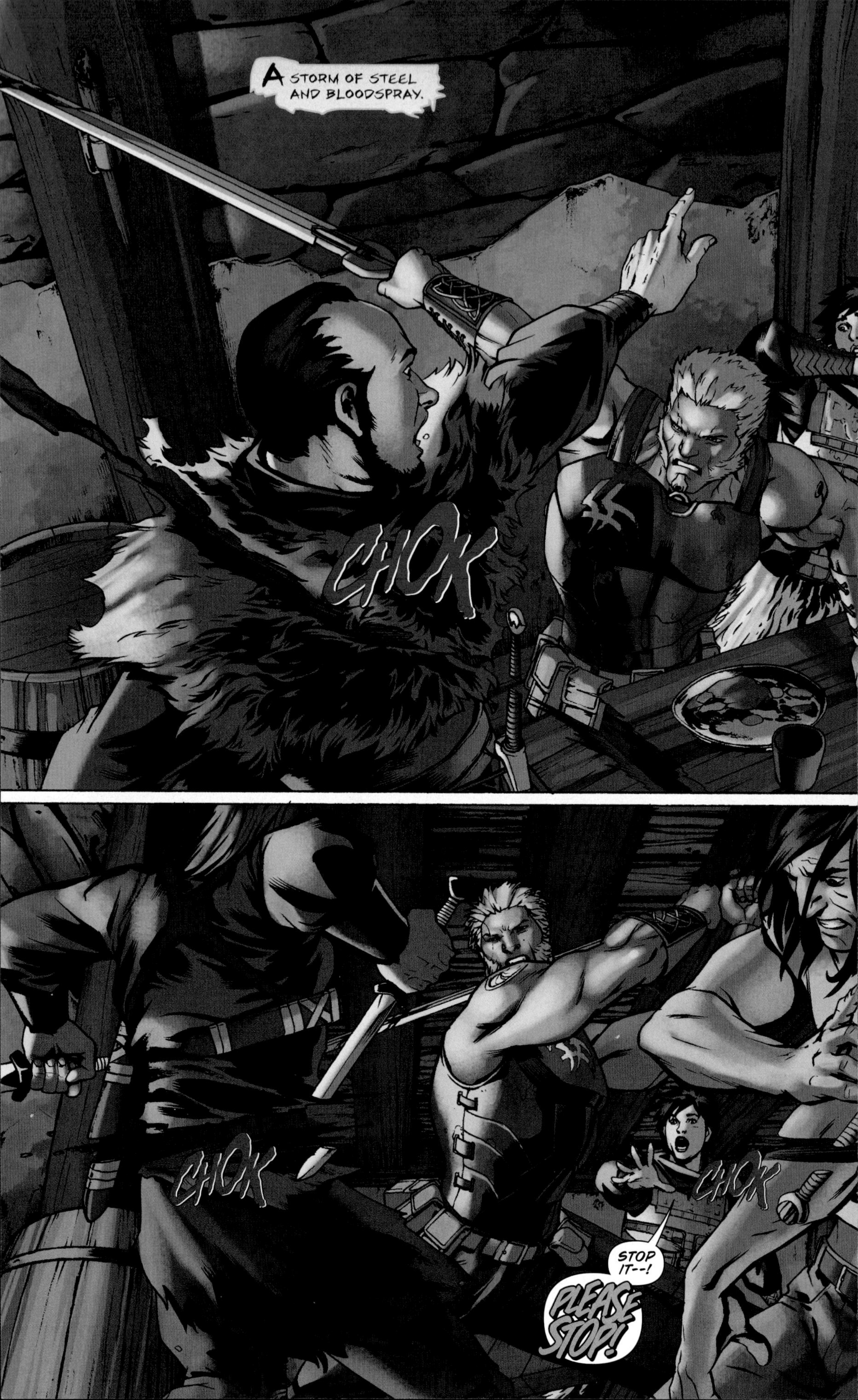
A STORM OF STEEL AND BLOODSPRAY.
CHOK
CHOK
CHOK
STOP IT--!
PLEASE STOP!

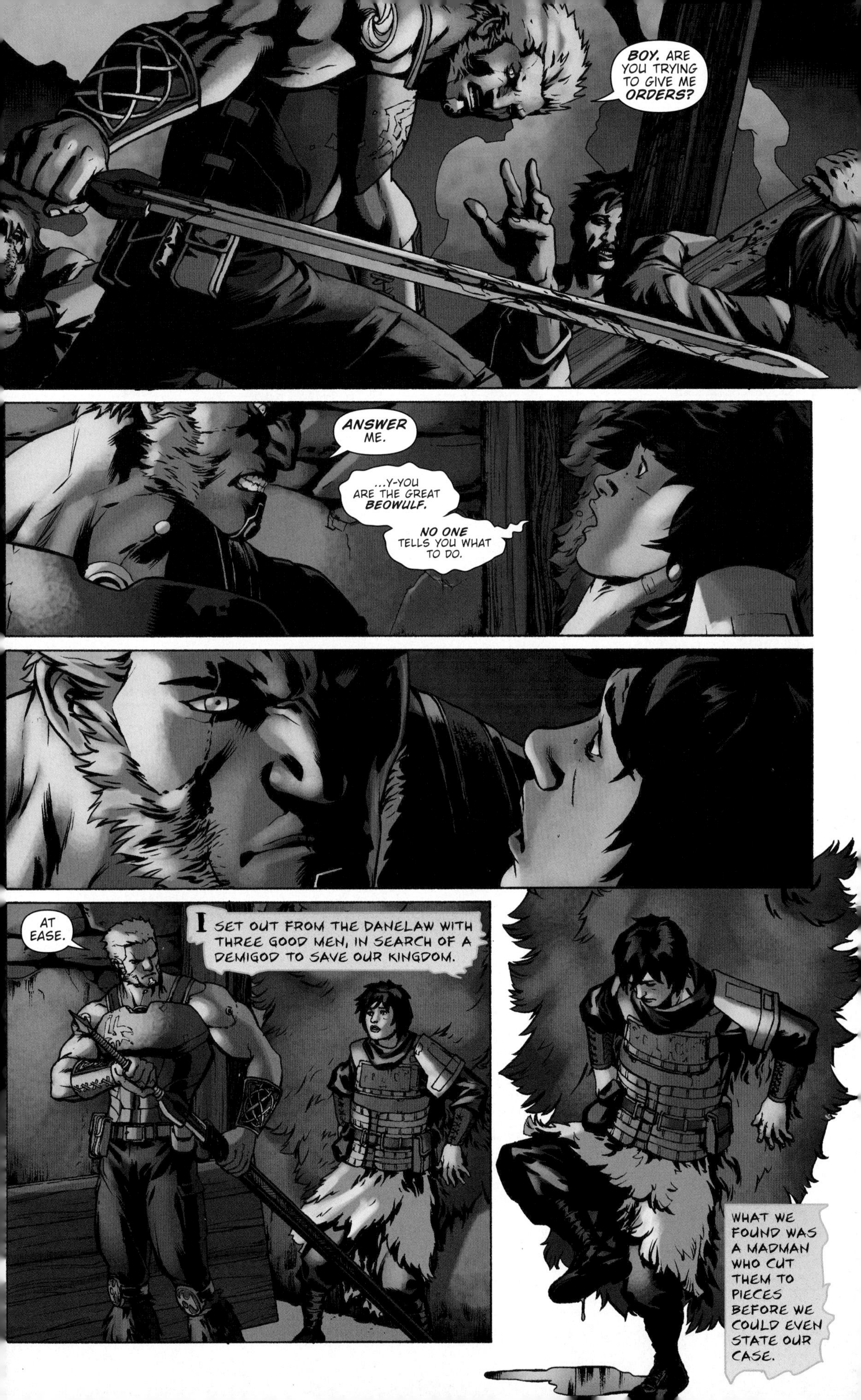
BOY. ARE YOU TRYING TO GIVE ME ORDERS?
ANSWER ME.
...Y-YOU ARE THE GREAT BEOWULF.
NO ONE TELLS YOU WHAT TO DO.
AT EASE.
I SET OUT FROM THE DANELAW WITH THREE GOOD MEN, IN SEARCH OF A DEMIGOD TO SAVE OUR KINGDOM.
WHAT WE FOUND WAS A MADMAN WHO CUT THEM TO PIECES BEFORE WE COULD EVEN STATE OUR CASE.

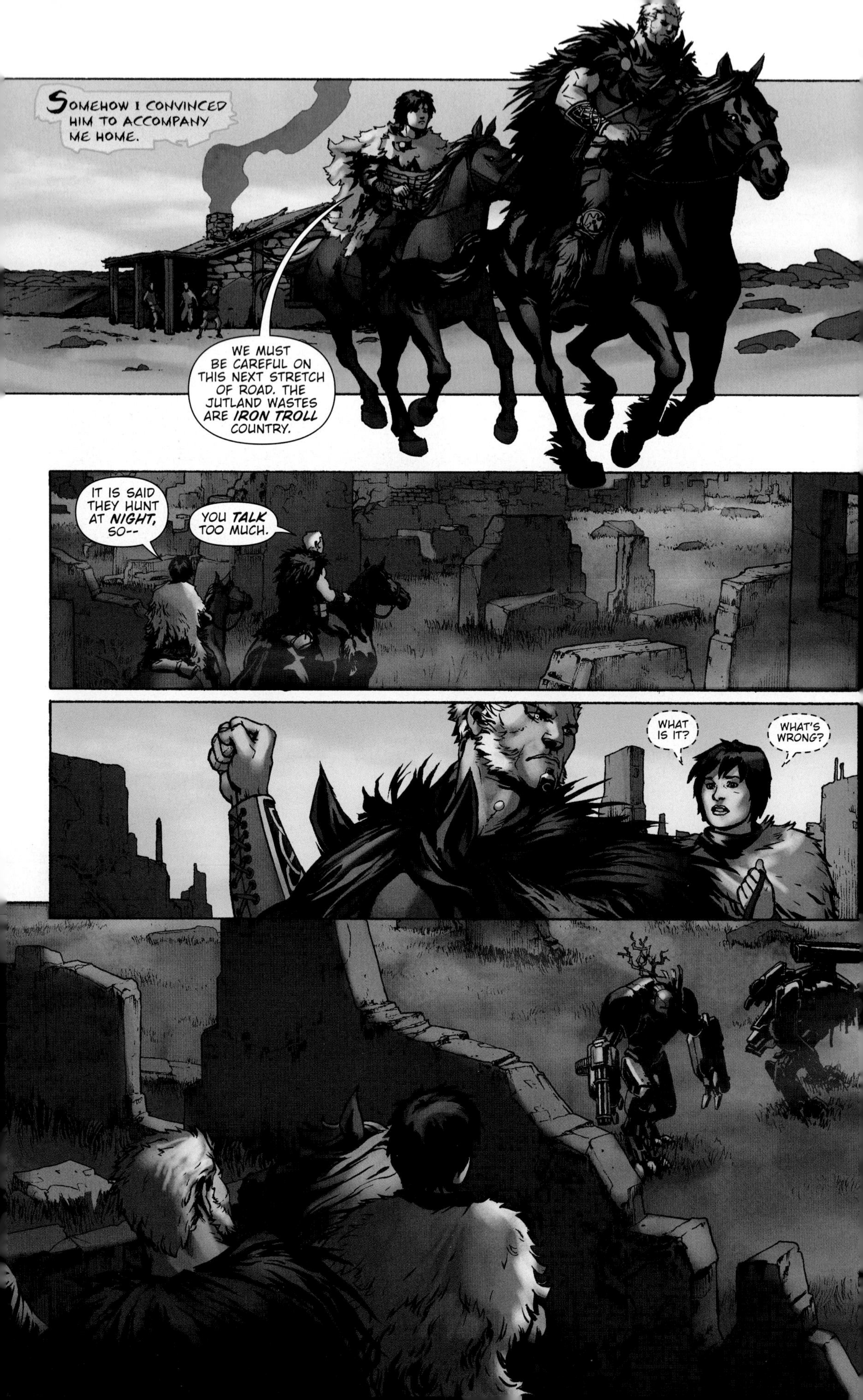
SOMEHOW I CONVINCED HIM TO ACCOMPANY ME HOME.
WE MUST BE CAREFUL ON THIS NEXT STRETCH OF ROAD. THE JUTLAND WASTES ARE IRON TROLL COUNTRY.
IT IS SAID THEY HUNT AT NIGHT, SO--
YOU TALK TOO MUCH.
WHAT IS IT?
WHAT'S WRONG?

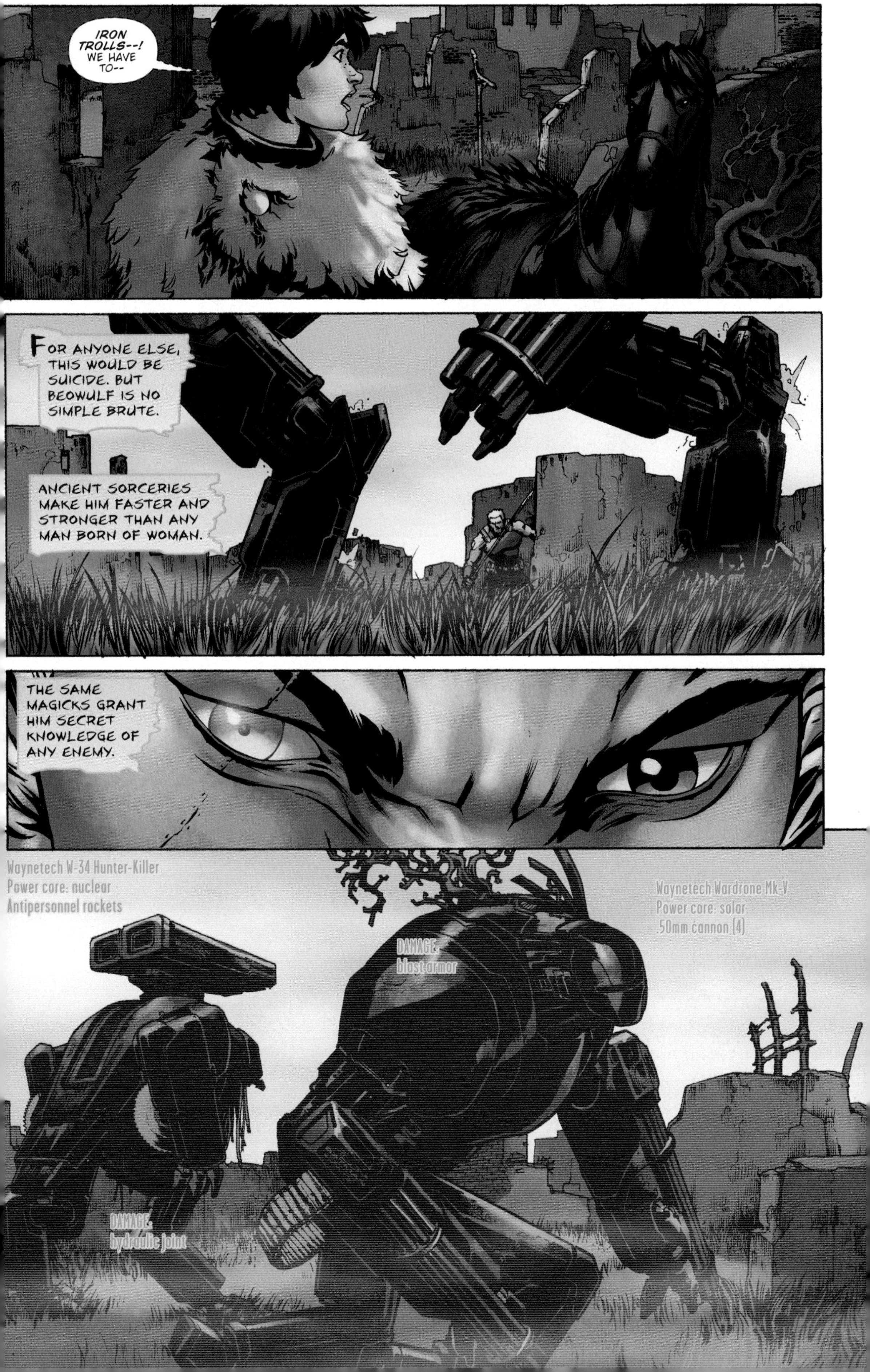
IRON TROLLS--! WE HAVE TO--
FOR ANYONE ELSE, THIS WOULD BE SUICIDE. BUT BEOWULF IS NO SIMPLE BRUTE.
ANCIENT SORCERIES MAKE HIM FASTER AND STRONGER THAN ANY MAN BORN OF WOMAN.
THE SAME MAGICKS GRANT HIM SECRET KNOWLEDGE OF ANY ENEMY.
Waynetech W-34 Hunter-Killer
Power core: nuclear
Antipersonnel rockets
Waynetech Wardrone Mk-V
Power core: solar
.50mm cannon (4)
DAMAGE: blast armor
DAMAGE: hydraulic joint

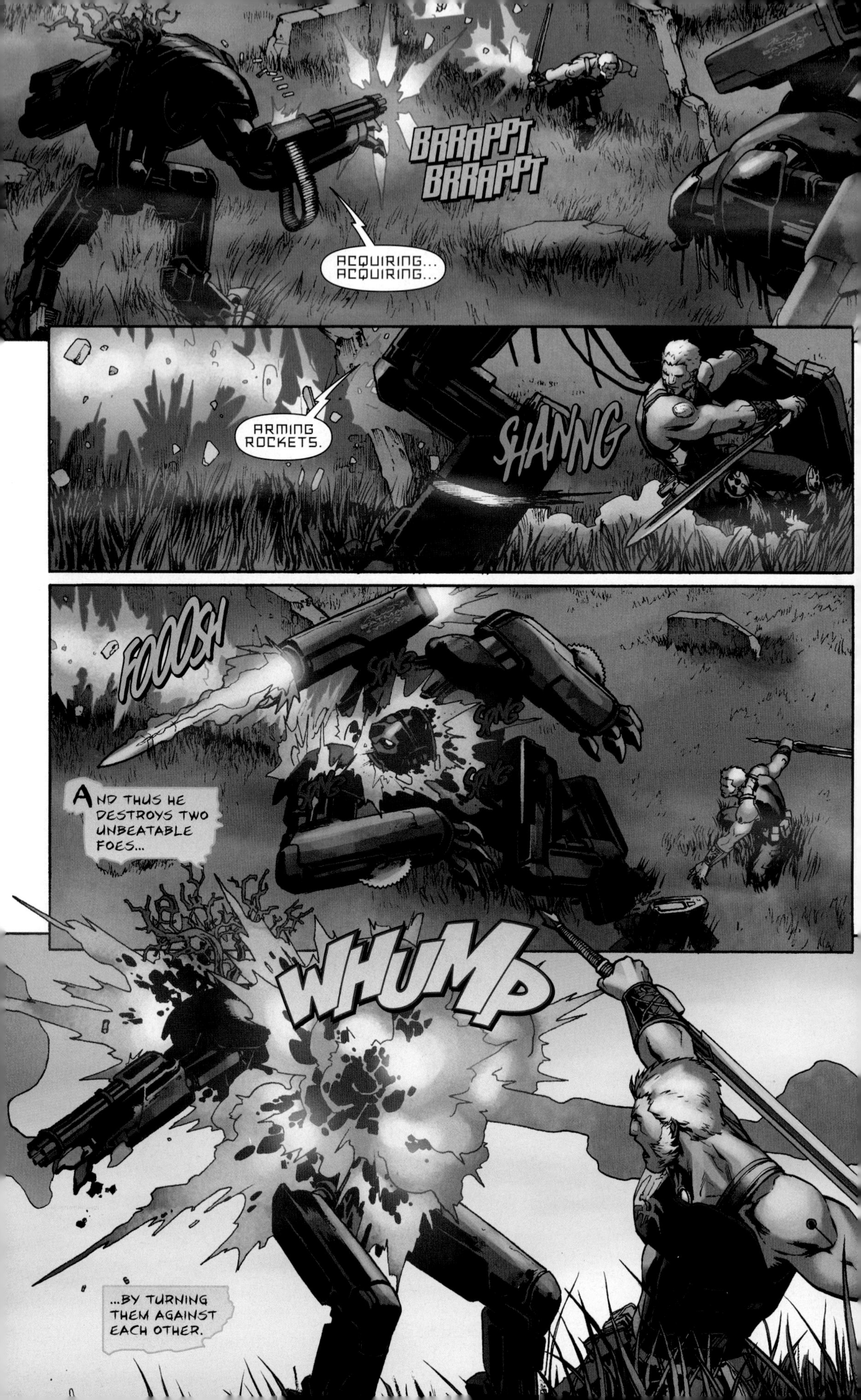
BRRAPPT
BRRAPPT
ACQUIRING... ACQUIRING...
ARMING ROCKETS.
SHANNG
FOOOSH
SPANG
SPANG
SPANG
SPANG
AND THUS HE DESTROYS TWO UNBEATABLE FOES...
WHUMP
...BY TURNING THEM AGAINST EACH OTHER.

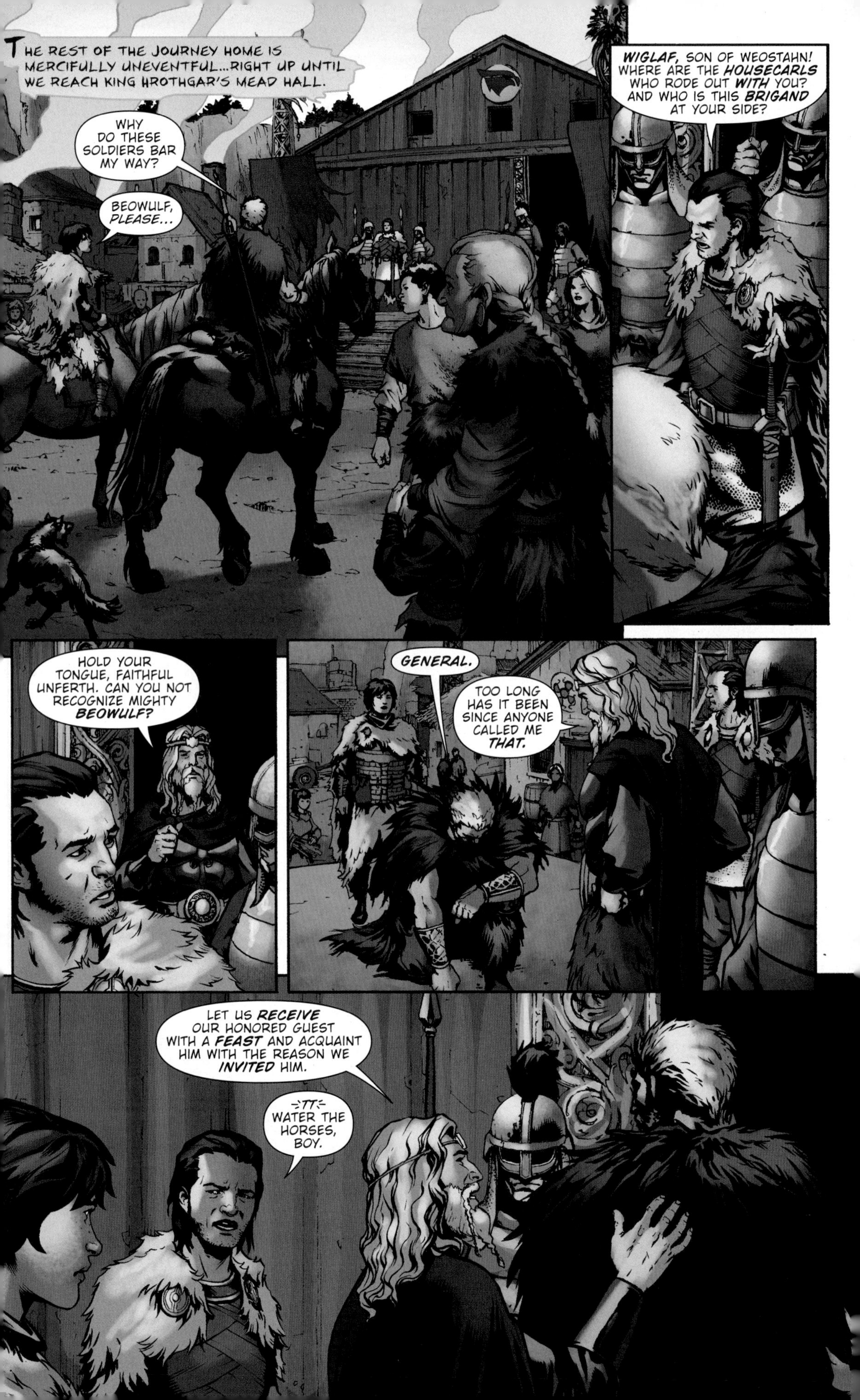
THE REST OF THE JOURNEY HOME IS MERCIFULLY UNEVENTFUL...RIGHT UP UNTIL WE REACH KING HROTHGAR'S MEAD HALL.
WHY DO THESE SOLDIERS BAR MY WAY?
BEOWULF, PLEASE...
WIGLAF, SON OF WEOSTAHN! WHERE ARE THE HOUSECARLS WHO RODE OUT WITH YOU? AND WHO IS THIS BRIGAND AT YOUR SIDE?
HOLD YOUR TONGUE, FAITHFUL UNFERTH. CAN YOU NOT RECOGNIZE MIGHTY BEOWULF?
GENERAL.
TOO LONG HAS IT BEEN SINCE ANYONE CALLED ME THAT.
LET US RECEIVE OUR HONORED GUEST WITH A FEAST AND ACQUAINT HIM WITH THE REASON WE INVITED HIM.
-TT- WATER THE HORSES, BOY.

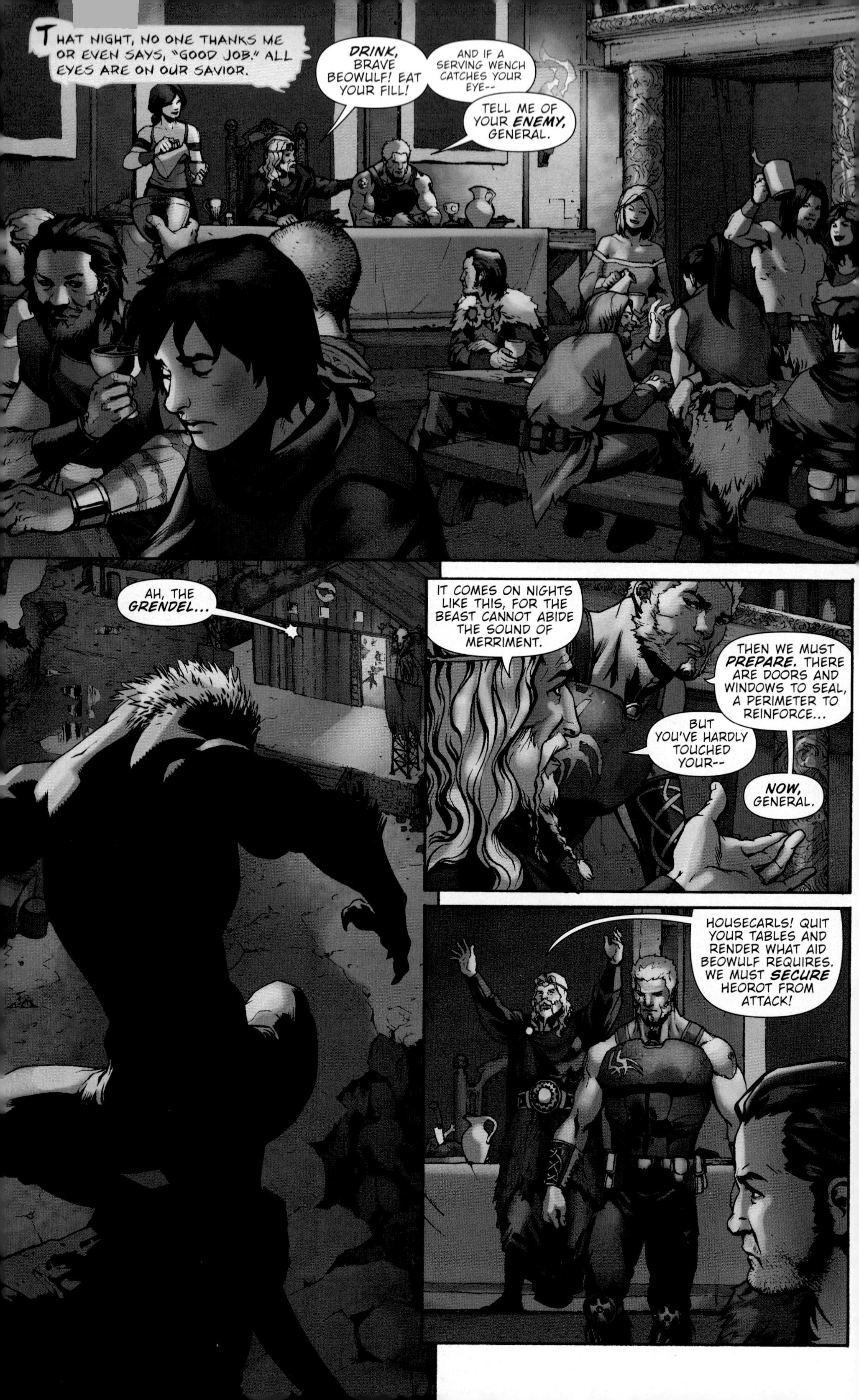
THAT NIGHT, NO ONE THANKS ME OR EVEN SAYS, "GOOD JOB." ALL EYES ARE ON OUR SAVIOR.
DRINK, BRAVE BEOWULF! EAT YOUR FILL!
AND IF A SERVING WENCH CATCHES YOUR EYE--
TELL ME OF YOUR ENEMY, GENERAL.
AH, THE GRENDEL...
IT COMES ON NIGHTS LIKE THIS, FOR THE BEAST CANNOT ABIDE THE SOUND OF MERRIMENT.
THEN WE MUST PREPARE. THERE ARE DOORS AND WINDOWS TO SEAL, A PERIMETER TO REINFORCE...
BUT YOU'VE HARDLY TOUCHED YOUR--
NOW, GENERAL.
HOUSECARLS! QUIT YOUR TABLES AND RENDER WHAT AID BEOWULF REQUIRES. WE MUST SECURE HEOROT FROM ATTACK!

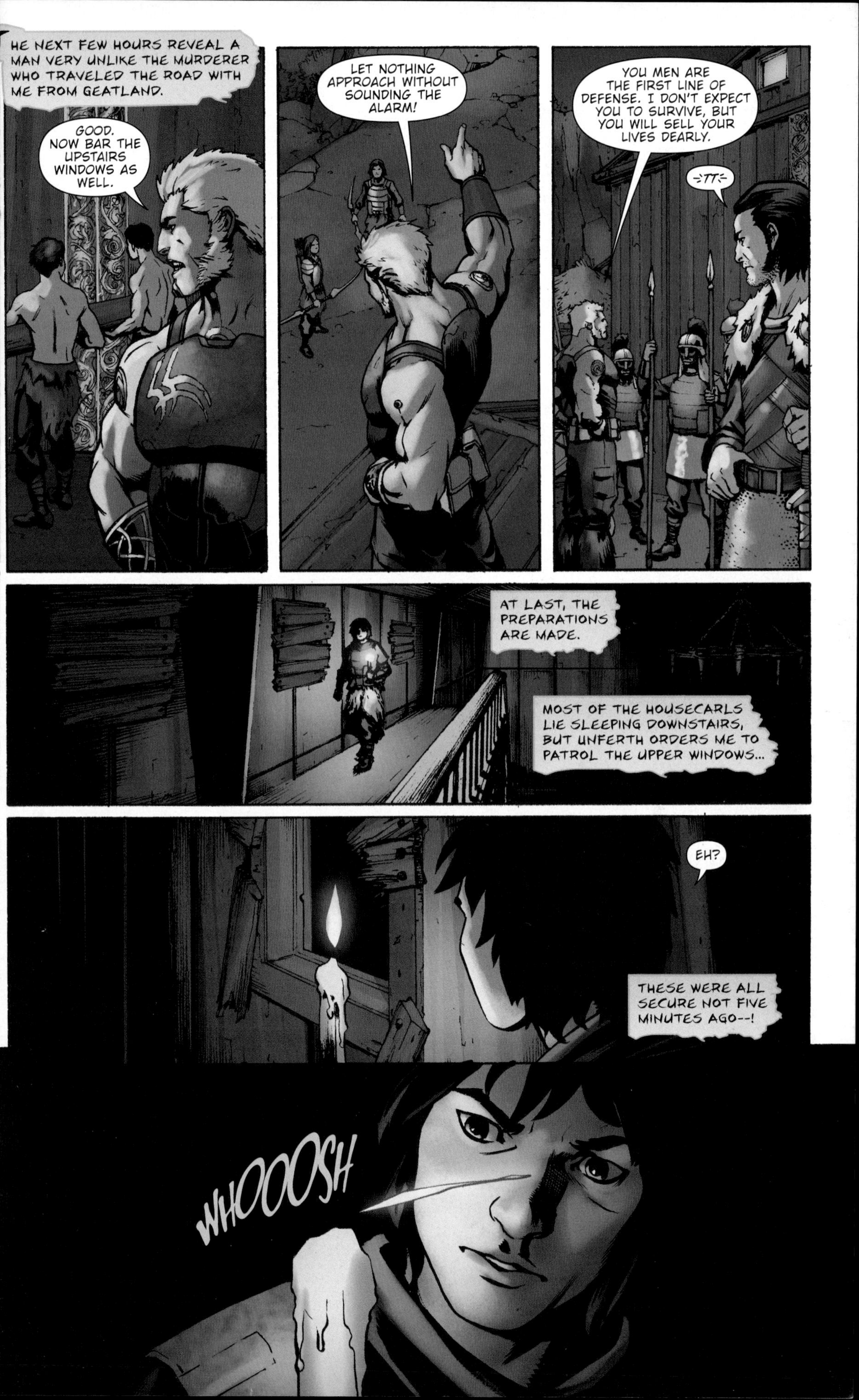

HE NEXT FEW HOURS REVEAL A MAN VERY UNLIKE THE MURDERER WHO TRAVELED THE ROAD WITH ME FROM GEATLAND.
GOOD. NOW BAR THE UPSTAIRS WINDOWS AS WELL.
LET NOTHING APPROACH WITHOUT SOUNDING THE ALARM!
YOU MEN ARE THE FIRST LINE OF DEFENSE. I DON'T EXPECT YOU TO SURVIVE, BUT YOU WILL SELL YOUR LIVES DEARLY.
=TT=
AT LAST, THE PREPARATIONS ARE MADE.
MOST OF THE HOUSECARLS LIE SLEEPING DOWNSTAIRS, BUT UNFERTH ORDERS ME TO PATROL THE UPPER WINDOWS...
EH?
THESE WERE ALL SECURE NOT FIVE MINUTES AGO--!
WHOOOSH

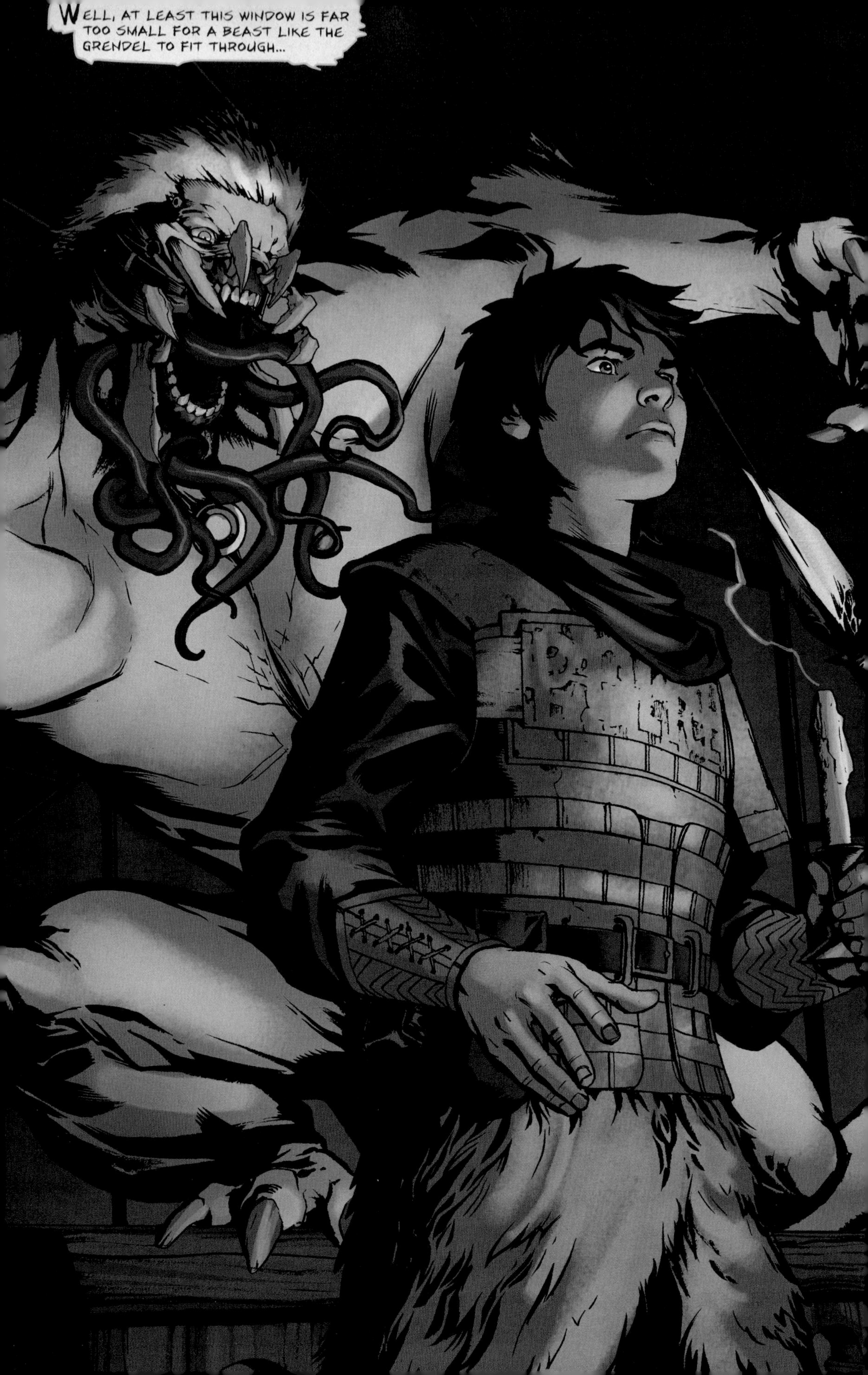
WELL, AT LEAST THIS WINDOW IS FAR TOO SMALL FOR A BEAST LIKE THE GRENDEL TO FIT THROUGH...

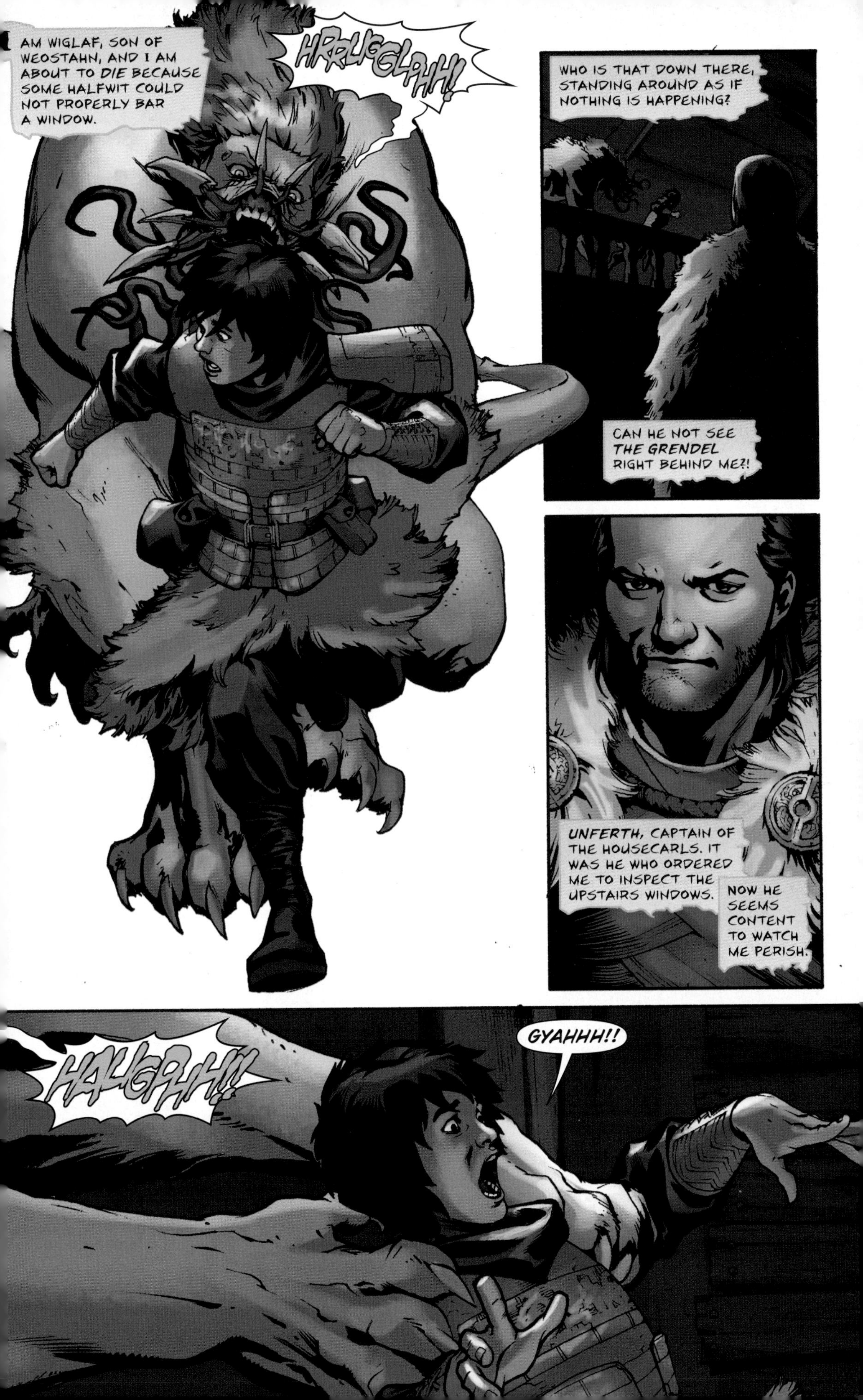
I AM WIGLAF, SON OF WEOSTAHN, AND I AM ABOUT TO *DIE* BECAUSE SOME HALFWIT COULD NOT PROPERLY BAR A WINDOW.
HRRUGGLRHH!
WHO IS THAT DOWN THERE, STANDING AROUND AS IF NOTHING IS HAPPENING?
CAN HE NOT SEE *THE GRENDEL* RIGHT BEHIND ME?!
UNFERTH, CAPTAIN OF THE HOUSECARLS. IT WAS HE WHO ORDERED ME TO INSPECT THE UPSTAIRS WINDOWS.
NOW HE SEEMS CONTENT TO WATCH ME PERISH.
HAUGHH!!
GYAHHH!!

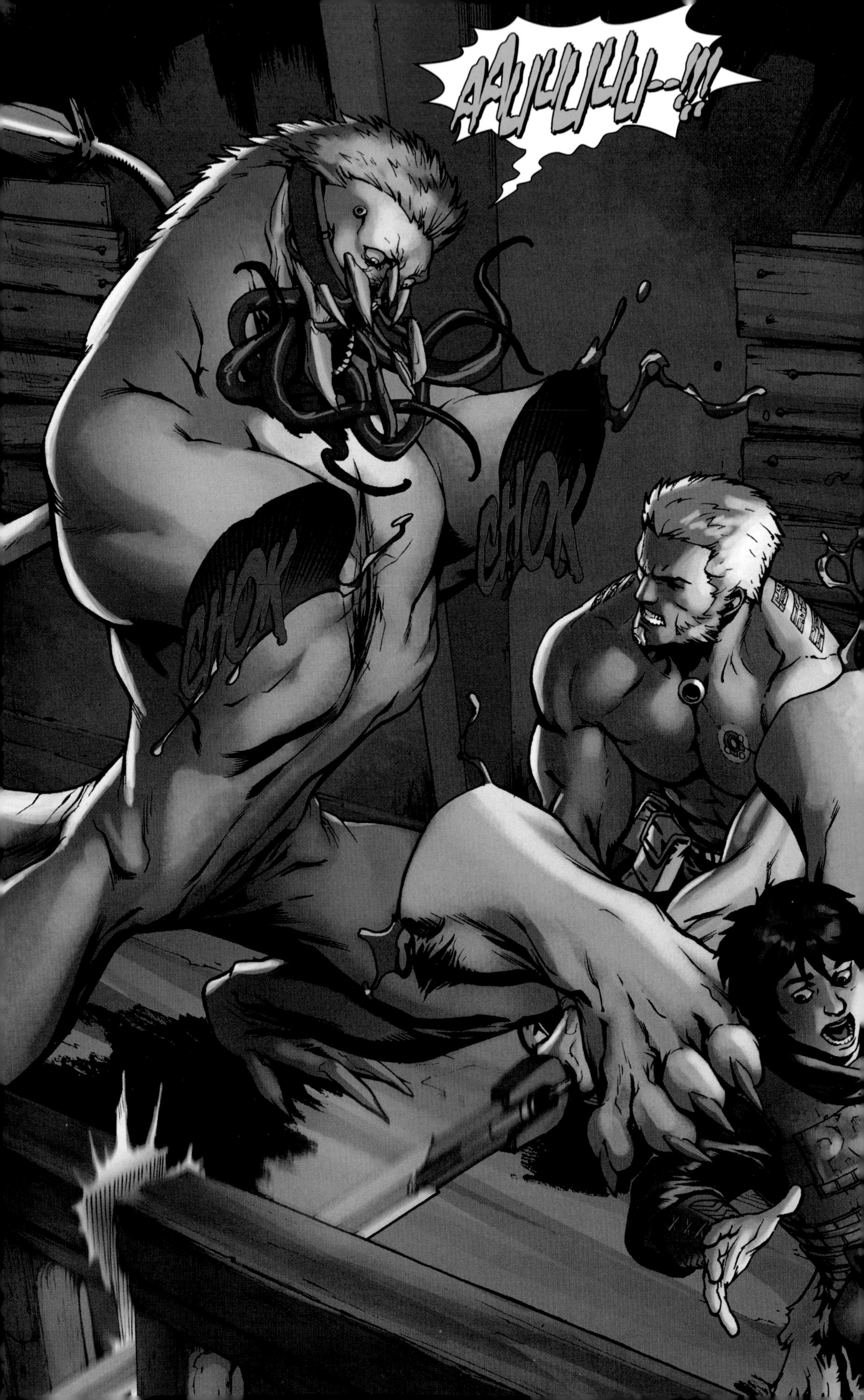
AAUUUUU--!!!
CHOK
CHOK

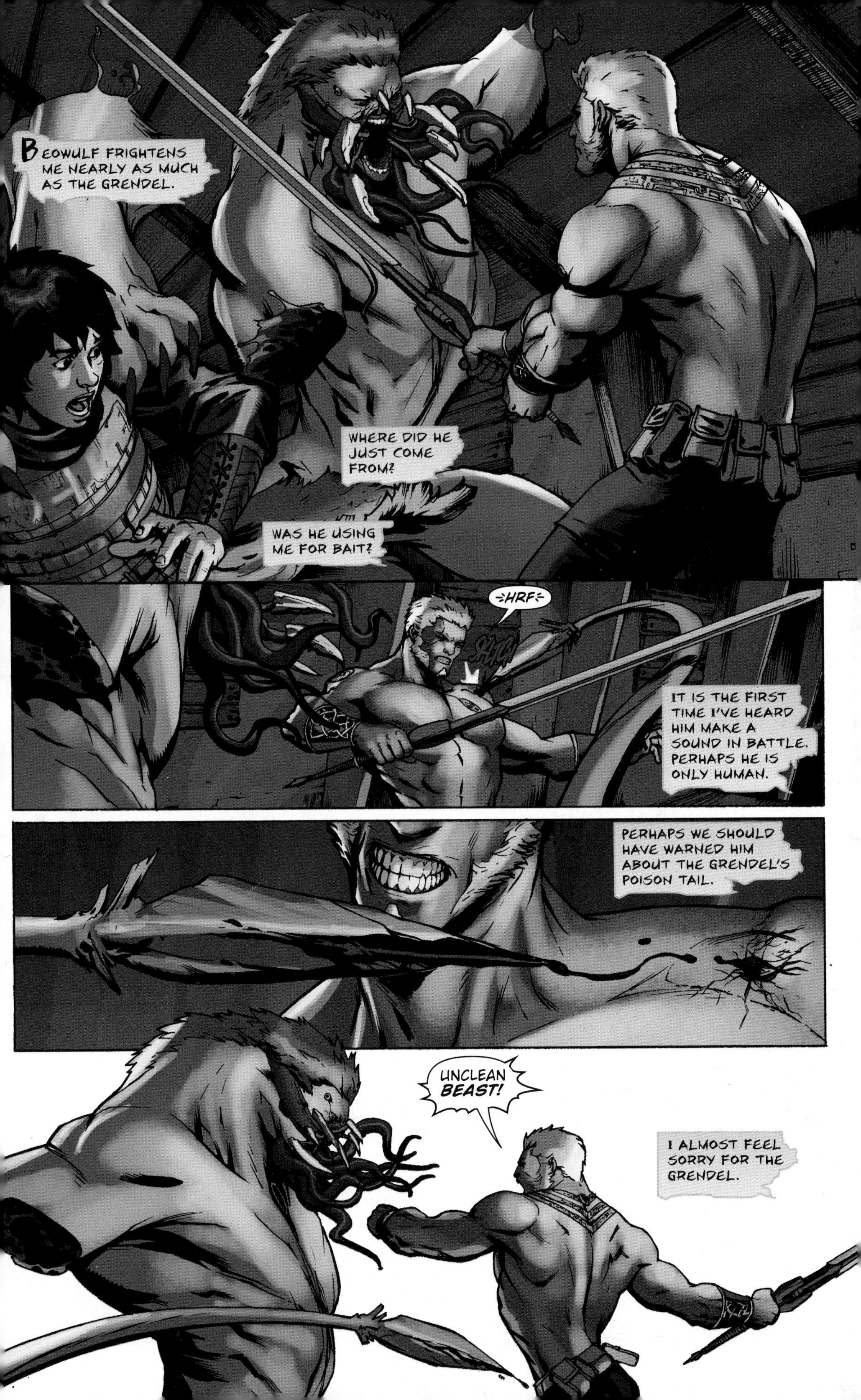
BEOWULF FRIGHTENS ME NEARLY AS MUCH AS THE GRENDEL.
WHERE DID HE JUST COME FROM?
WAS HE USING ME FOR BAIT?
HRF
SHAK
IT IS THE FIRST TIME I'VE HEARD HIM MAKE A SOUND IN BATTLE. PERHAPS HE IS ONLY HUMAN.
PERHAPS WE SHOULD HAVE WARNED HIM ABOUT THE GRENDEL'S POISON TAIL.
UNCLEAN BEAST!
I ALMOST FEEL SORRY FOR THE GRENDEL.

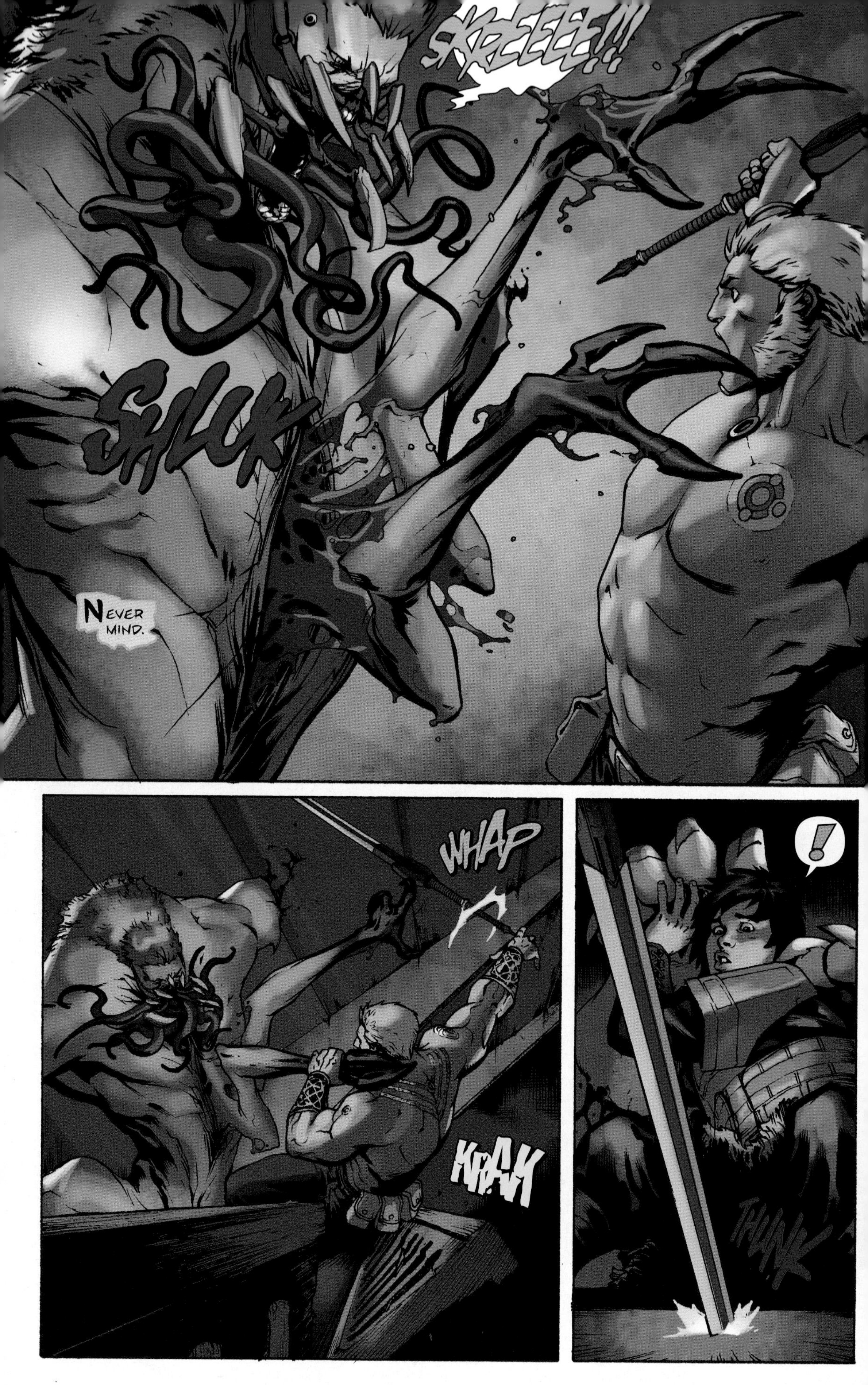
SKREEEE!!!
SHLUK
NEVER MIND.
WHAP
KRAK
!
THUNK

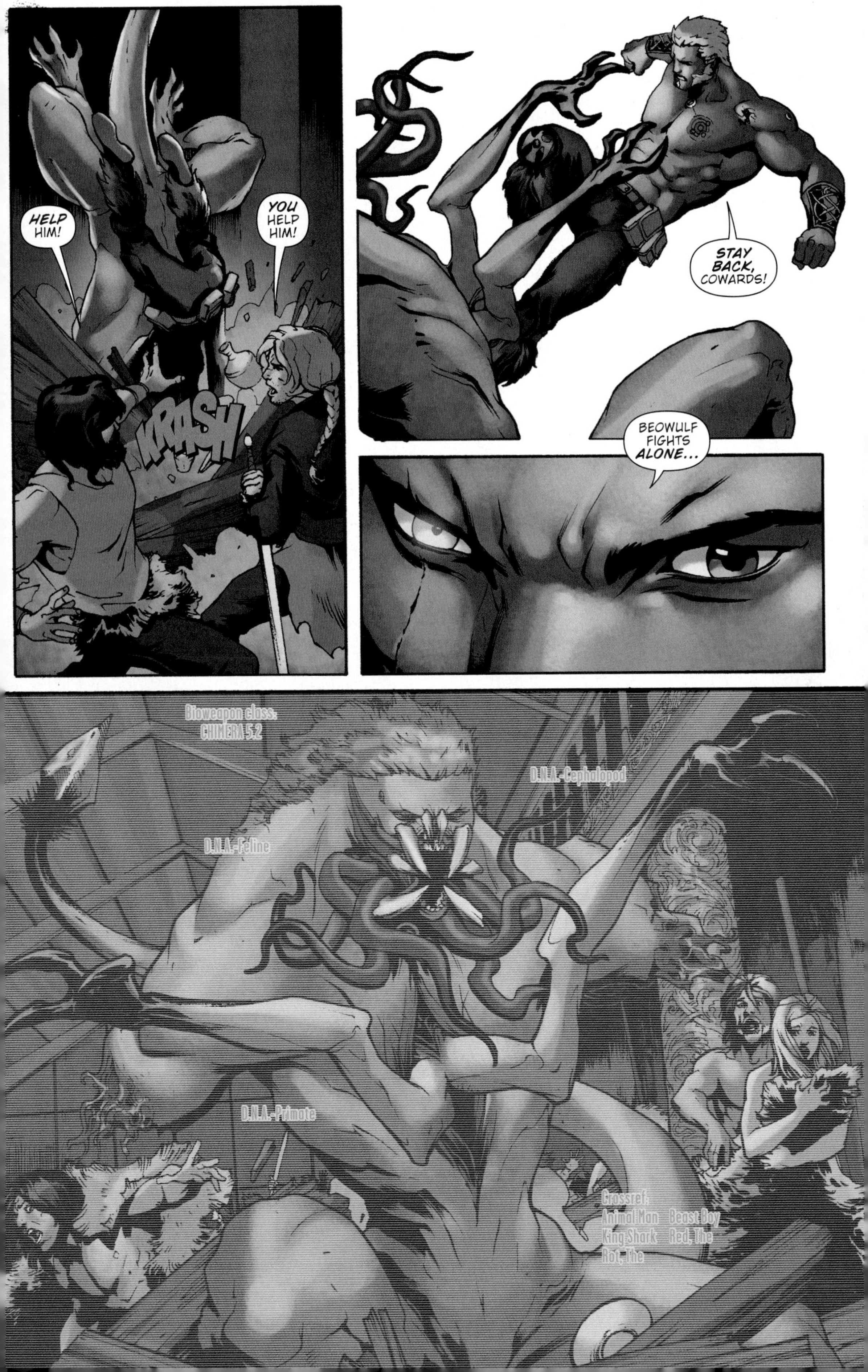
HELP HIM!
YOU HELP HIM!
KRASH
STAY BACK, COWARDS!
BEOWULF FIGHTS ALONE...
Bioweapon class: CHIMERA 5.2
D.N.A.-Cephalopod
D.N.A.-Feline
D.N.A.-Primate
Crossref:
Animal Man
Beast Boy
King Shark
Red, The
Rot, The

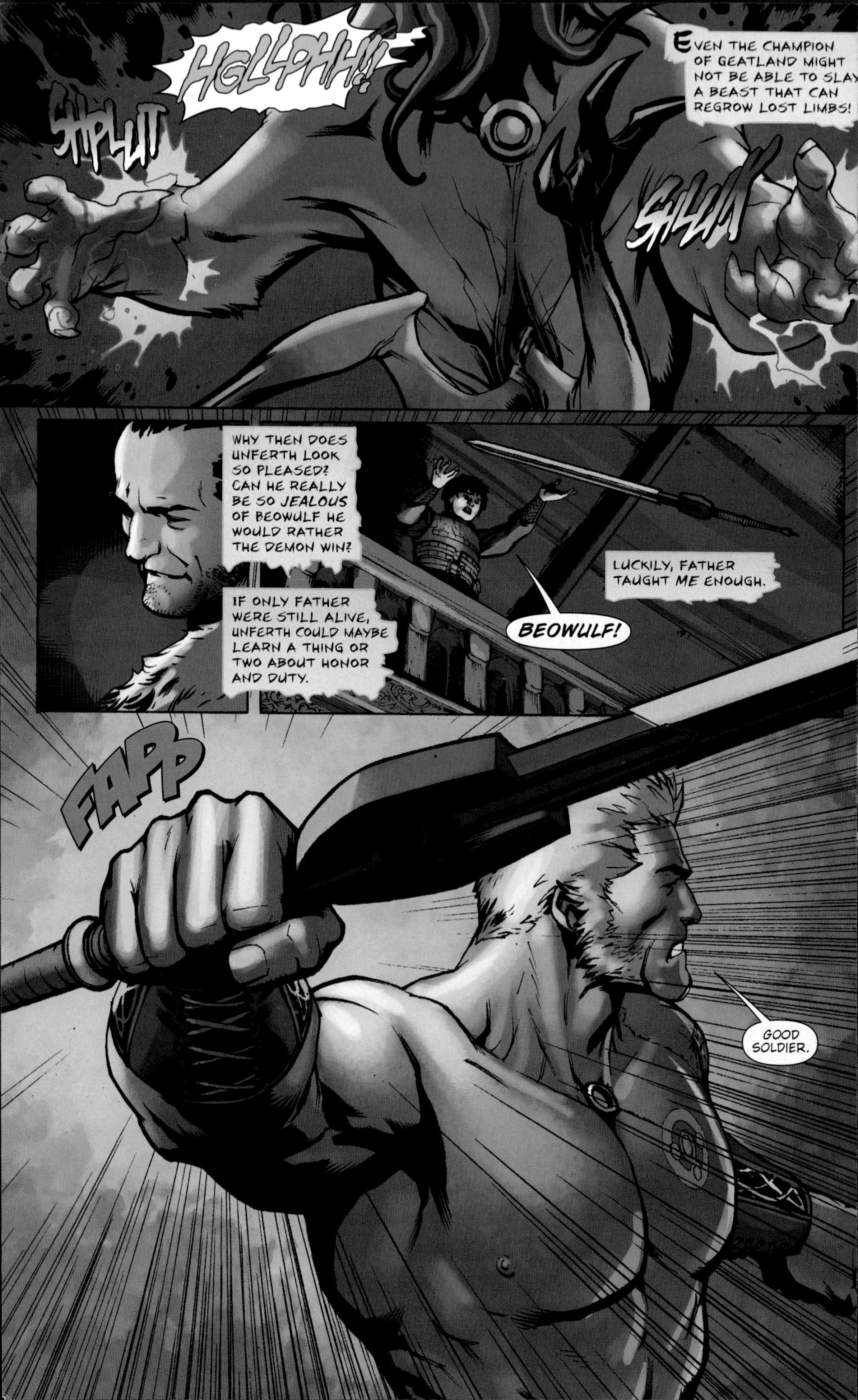
SHPLUT
HGLLPHH!!
EVEN THE CHAMPION OF GEATLAND MIGHT NOT BE ABLE TO SLAY A BEAST THAT CAN REGROW LOST LIMBS!
SHLUK
WHY THEN DOES UNFERTH LOOK SO PLEASED? CAN HE REALLY BE SO JEALOUS OF BEOWULF HE WOULD RATHER THE DEMON WIN?
IF ONLY FATHER WERE STILL ALIVE, UNFERTH COULD MAYBE LEARN A THING OR TWO ABOUT HONOR AND DUTY.
BEOWULF!
LUCKILY, FATHER TAUGHT ME ENOUGH.
FAPP
GOOD SOLDIER.

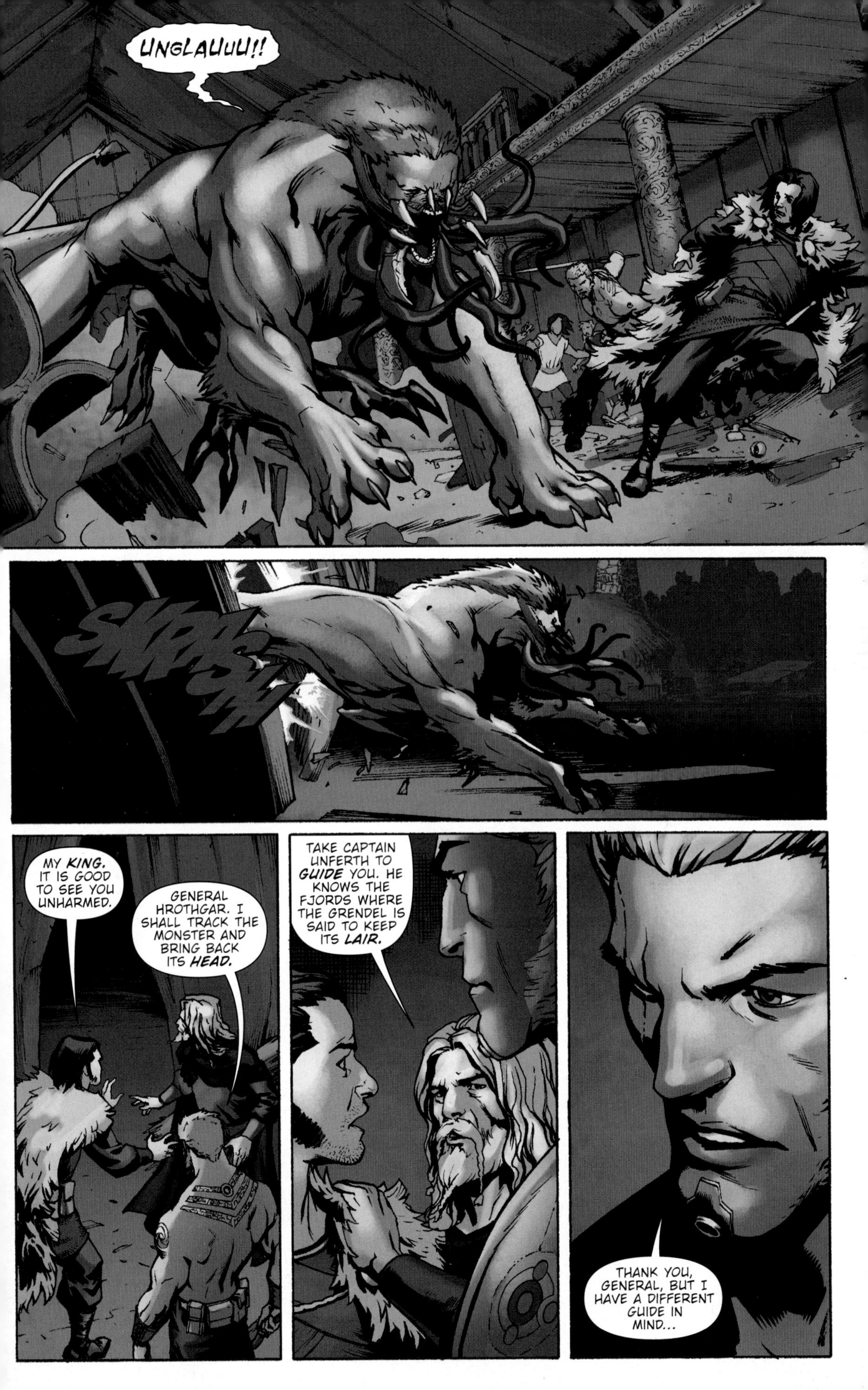
UNGLAUUU!!
MY KING. IT IS GOOD TO SEE YOU UNHARMED.
GENERAL HROTHGAR. I SHALL TRACK THE MONSTER AND BRING BACK ITS HEAD.
TAKE CAPTAIN UNFERTH TO GUIDE YOU. HE KNOWS THE FJORDS WHERE THE GRENDEL IS SAID TO KEEP ITS LAIR.
THANK YOU, GENERAL, BUT I HAVE A DIFFERENT GUIDE IN MIND...

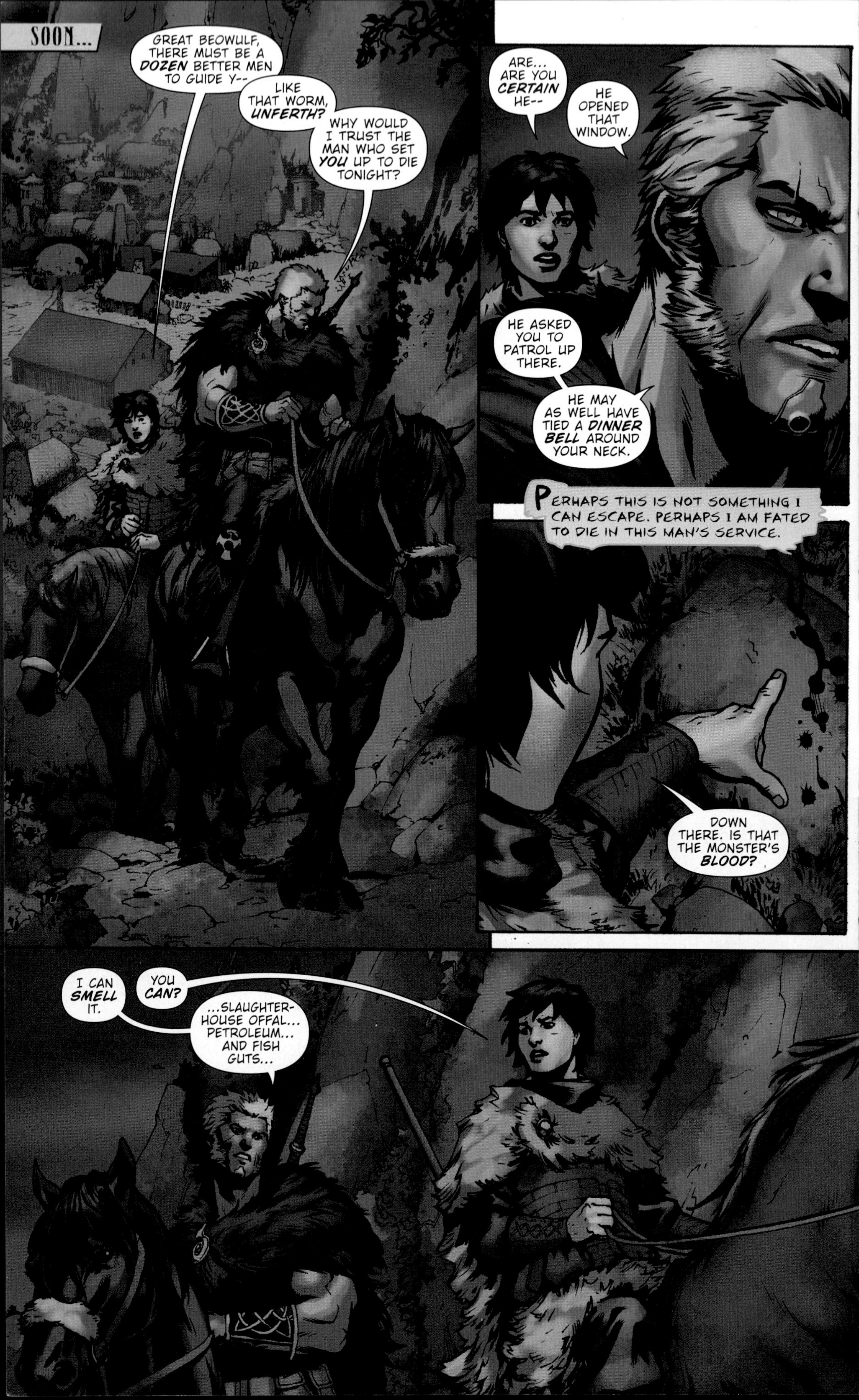
SOON...
GREAT BEOWULF, THERE MUST BE A DOZEN BETTER MEN TO GUIDE Y--
LIKE THAT WORM, UNFERTH?
WHY WOULD I TRUST THE MAN WHO SET YOU UP TO DIE TONIGHT?
ARE... ARE YOU CERTAIN HE--
HE OPENED THAT WINDOW.
HE ASKED YOU TO PATROL UP THERE.
HE MAY AS WELL HAVE TIED A DINNER BELL AROUND YOUR NECK.
PERHAPS THIS IS NOT SOMETHING I CAN ESCAPE. PERHAPS I AM FATED TO DIE IN THIS MAN'S SERVICE.
DOWN THERE. IS THAT THE MONSTER'S BLOOD?
I CAN SMELL IT.
YOU CAN?
...SLAUGHTER-HOUSE OFFAL... PETROLEUM... AND FISH GUTS...

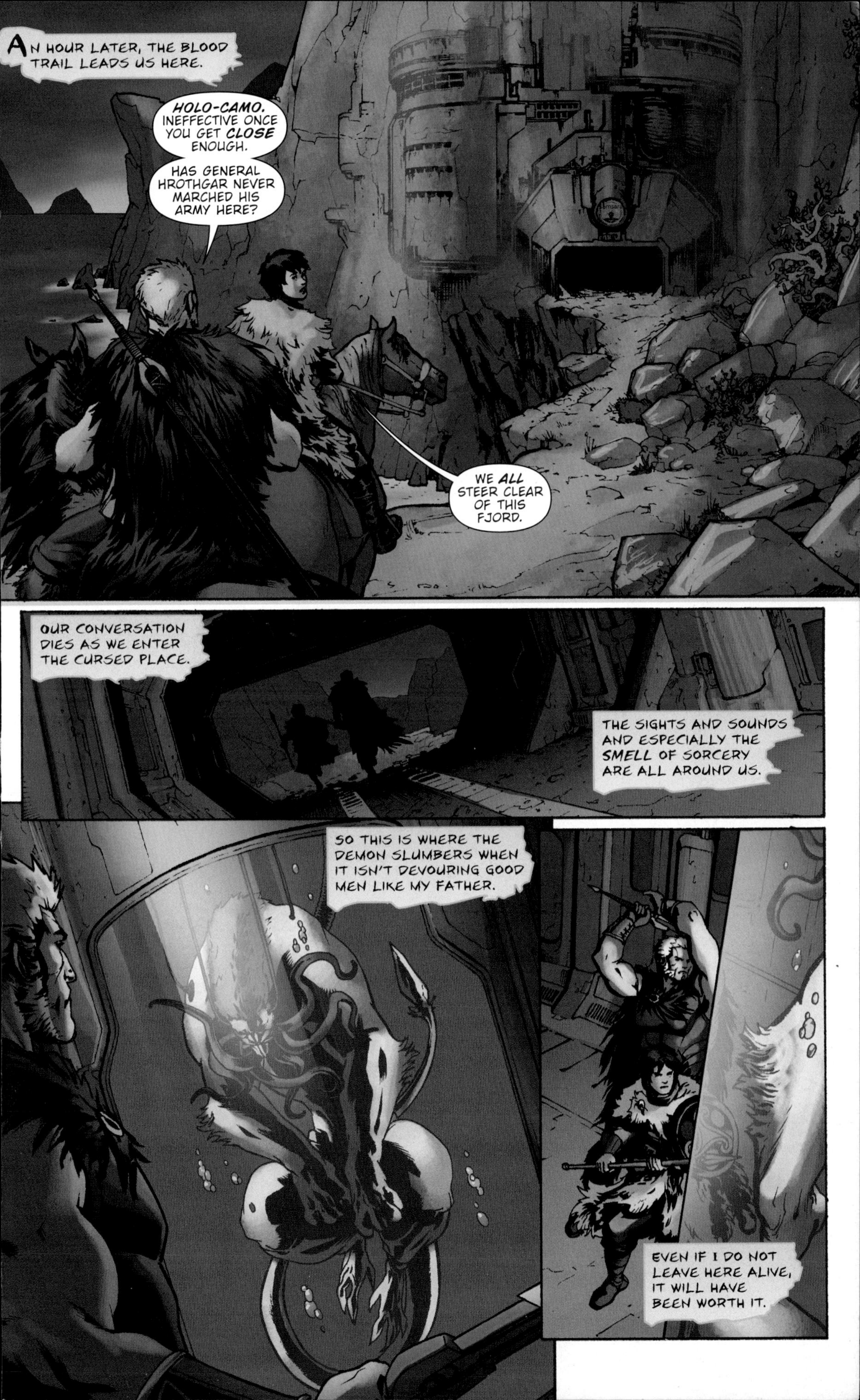

AN HOUR LATER, THE BLOOD TRAIL LEADS US HERE.
HOLO-CAMO. INEFFECTIVE ONCE YOU GET CLOSE ENOUGH.
HAS GENERAL HROTHGAR NEVER MARCHED HIS ARMY HERE?
WE ALL STEER CLEAR OF THIS FJORD.
OUR CONVERSATION DIES AS WE ENTER THE CURSED PLACE.
THE SIGHTS AND SOUNDS AND ESPECIALLY THE SMELL OF SORCERY ARE ALL AROUND US.
SO THIS IS WHERE THE DEMON SLUMBERS WHEN IT ISN'T DEVOURING GOOD MEN LIKE MY FATHER.
EVEN IF I DO NOT LEAVE HERE ALIVE, IT WILL HAVE BEEN WORTH IT.

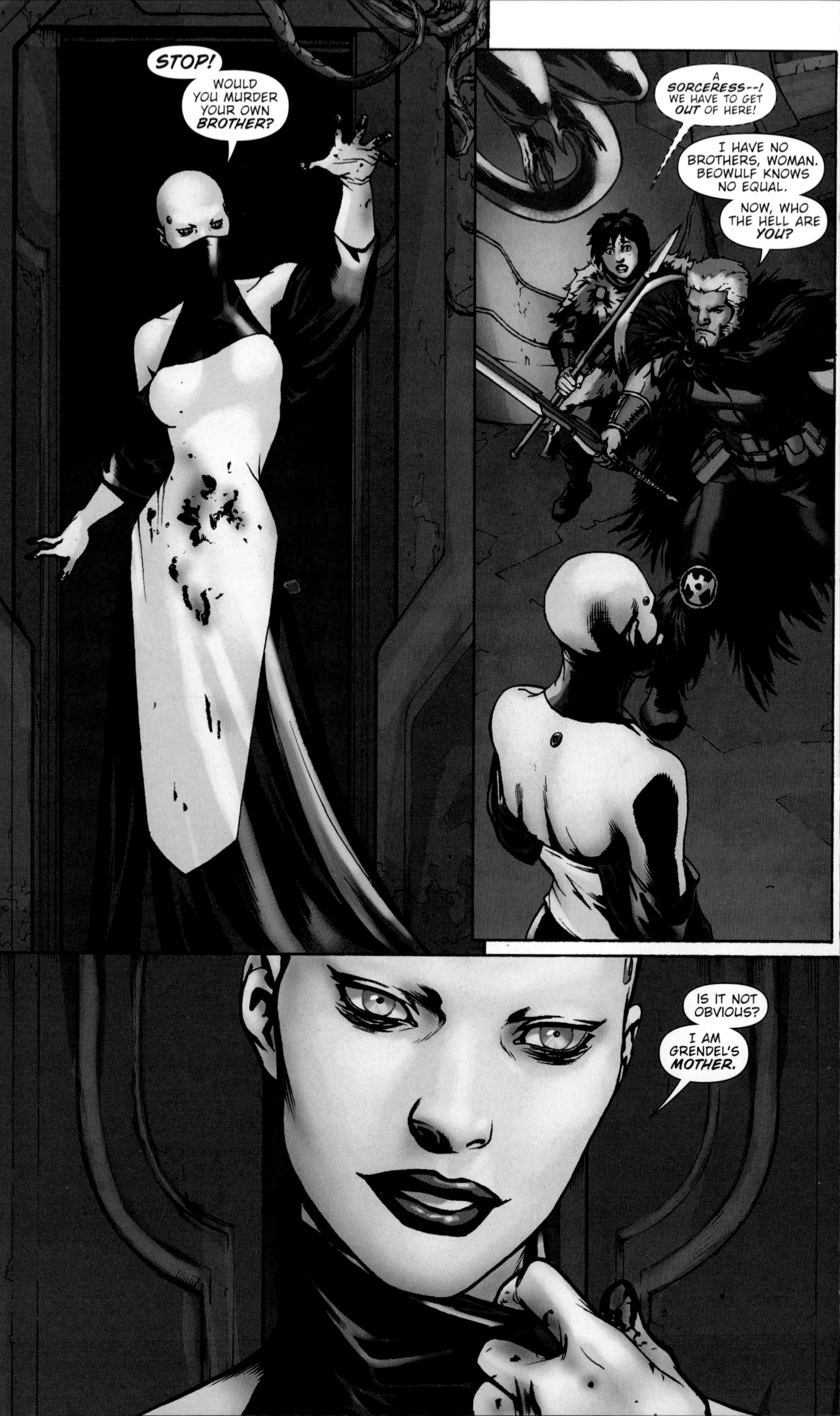
STOP! WOULD YOU MURDER YOUR OWN BROTHER?
A SORCERESS--! WE HAVE TO GET OUT OF HERE!
I HAVE NO BROTHERS, WOMAN. BEOWULF KNOWS NO EQUAL.
NOW, WHO THE HELL ARE YOU?
IS IT NOT OBVIOUS?
I AM GRENDEL'S MOTHER.

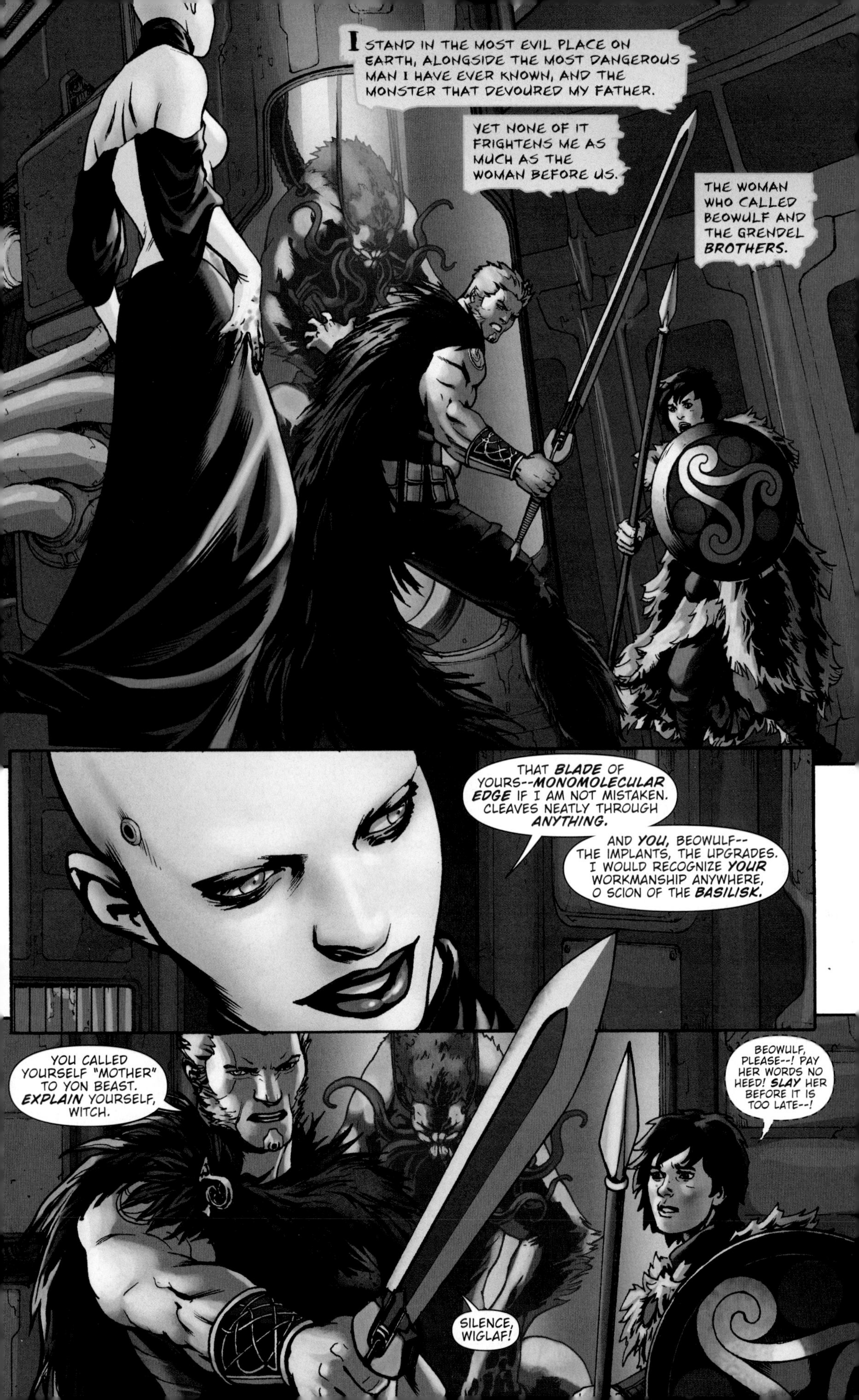
I STAND IN THE MOST EVIL PLACE ON EARTH, ALONGSIDE THE MOST DANGEROUS MAN I HAVE EVER KNOWN, AND THE MONSTER THAT DEVOURED MY FATHER.
YET NONE OF IT FRIGHTENS ME AS MUCH AS THE WOMAN BEFORE US.
THE WOMAN WHO CALLED BEOWULF AND THE GRENDEL BROTHERS.
THAT BLADE OF YOURS--MONOMOLECULAR EDGE IF I AM NOT MISTAKEN. CLEAVES NEATLY THROUGH ANYTHING.
AND YOU, BEOWULF-- THE IMPLANTS, THE UPGRADES. I WOULD RECOGNIZE YOUR WORKMANSHIP ANYWHERE, O SCION OF THE BASILISK.
YOU CALLED YOURSELF "MOTHER" TO YON BEAST. EXPLAIN YOURSELF, WITCH.
BEOWULF, PLEASE--! PAY HER WORDS NO HEED! SLAY HER BEFORE IT IS TOO LATE--!
SILENCE, WIGLAF!

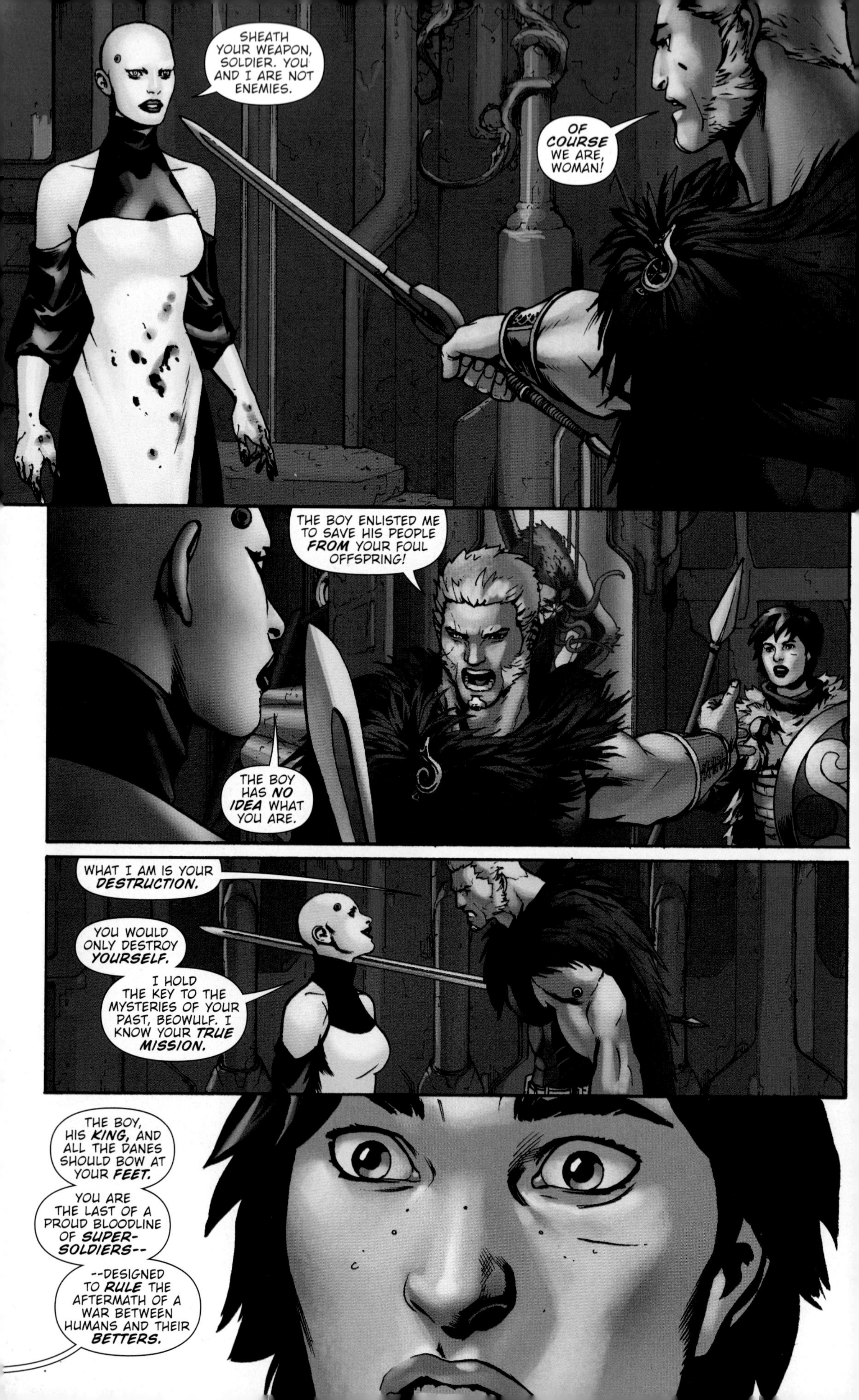

SHEATH YOUR WEAPON, SOLDIER. YOU AND I ARE NOT ENEMIES.
OF COURSE WE ARE, WOMAN!
THE BOY ENLISTED ME TO SAVE HIS PEOPLE FROM YOUR FOUL OFFSPRING!
THE BOY HAS NO IDEA WHAT YOU ARE.
WHAT I AM IS YOUR DESTRUCTION.
YOU WOULD ONLY DESTROY YOURSELF.
I HOLD THE KEY TO THE MYSTERIES OF YOUR PAST, BEOWULF. I KNOW YOUR TRUE MISSION.
THE BOY, HIS KING, AND ALL THE DANES SHOULD BOW AT YOUR FEET.
YOU ARE THE LAST OF A PROUD BLOODLINE OF SUPER-SOLDIERS--
--DESIGNED TO RULE THE AFTERMATH OF A WAR BETWEEN HUMANS AND THEIR BETTERS.

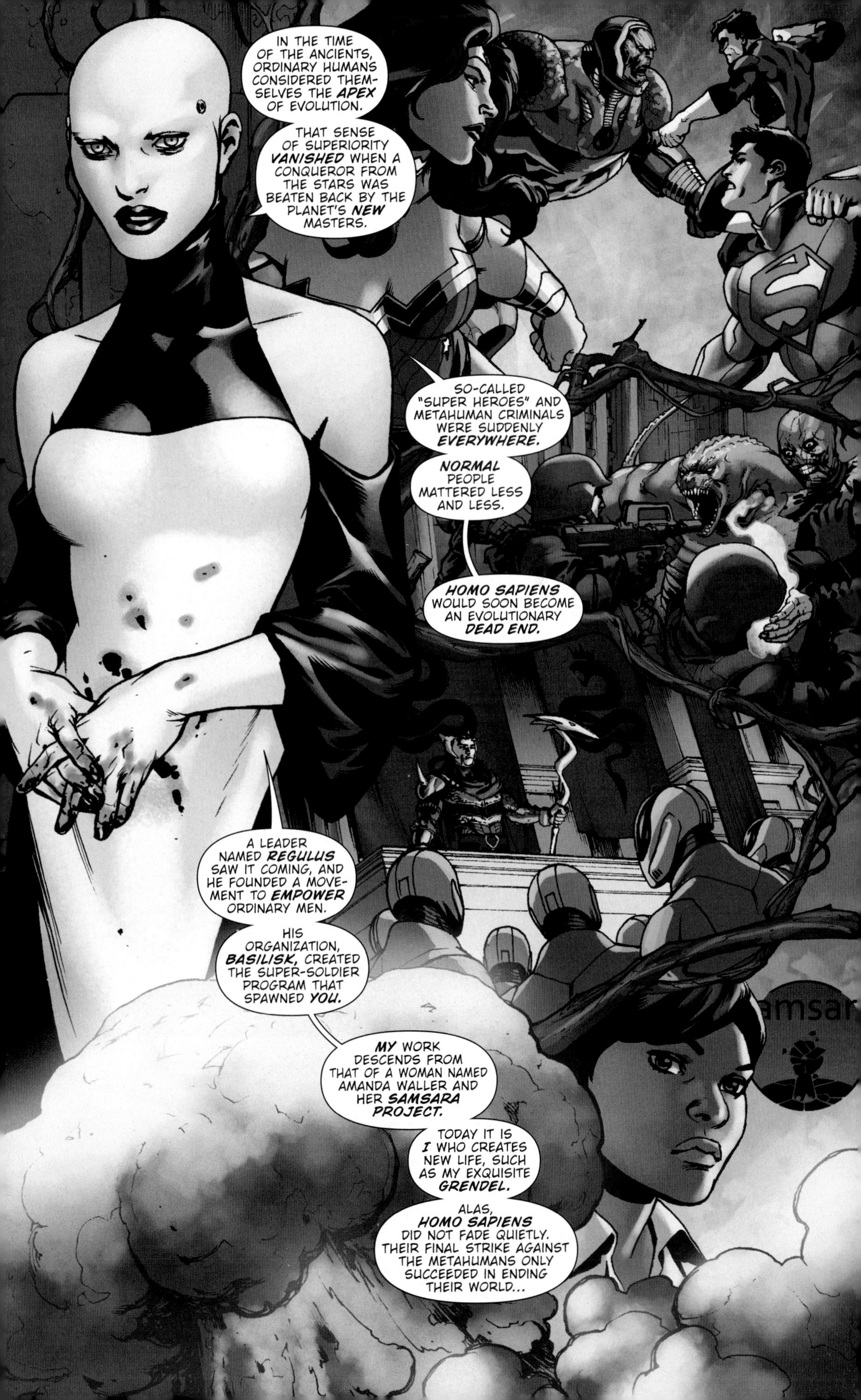
IN THE TIME OF THE ANCIENTS, ORDINARY HUMANS CONSIDERED THEMSELVES THE APEX OF EVOLUTION.
THAT SENSE OF SUPERIORITY VANISHED WHEN A CONQUEROR FROM THE STARS WAS BEATEN BACK BY THE PLANET'S NEW MASTERS.
SO-CALLED "SUPER HEROES" AND METAHUMAN CRIMINALS WERE SUDDENLY EVERYWHERE.
NORMAL PEOPLE MATTERED LESS AND LESS.
HOMO SAPIENS WOULD SOON BECOME AN EVOLUTIONARY DEAD END.
A LEADER NAMED REGULUS SAW IT COMING, AND HE FOUNDED A MOVEMENT TO EMPOWER ORDINARY MEN.
HIS ORGANIZATION, BASILISK, CREATED THE SUPER-SOLDIER PROGRAM THAT SPAWNED YOU.
MY WORK DESCENDS FROM THAT OF A WOMAN NAMED AMANDA WALLER AND HER SAMSARA PROJECT.
TODAY IT IS I WHO CREATES NEW LIFE, SUCH AS MY EXQUISITE GRENDEL.
ALAS, HOMO SAPIENS DID NOT FADE QUIETLY. THEIR FINAL STRIKE AGAINST THE METAHUMANS ONLY SUCCEEDED IN ENDING THEIR WORLD...
amsar

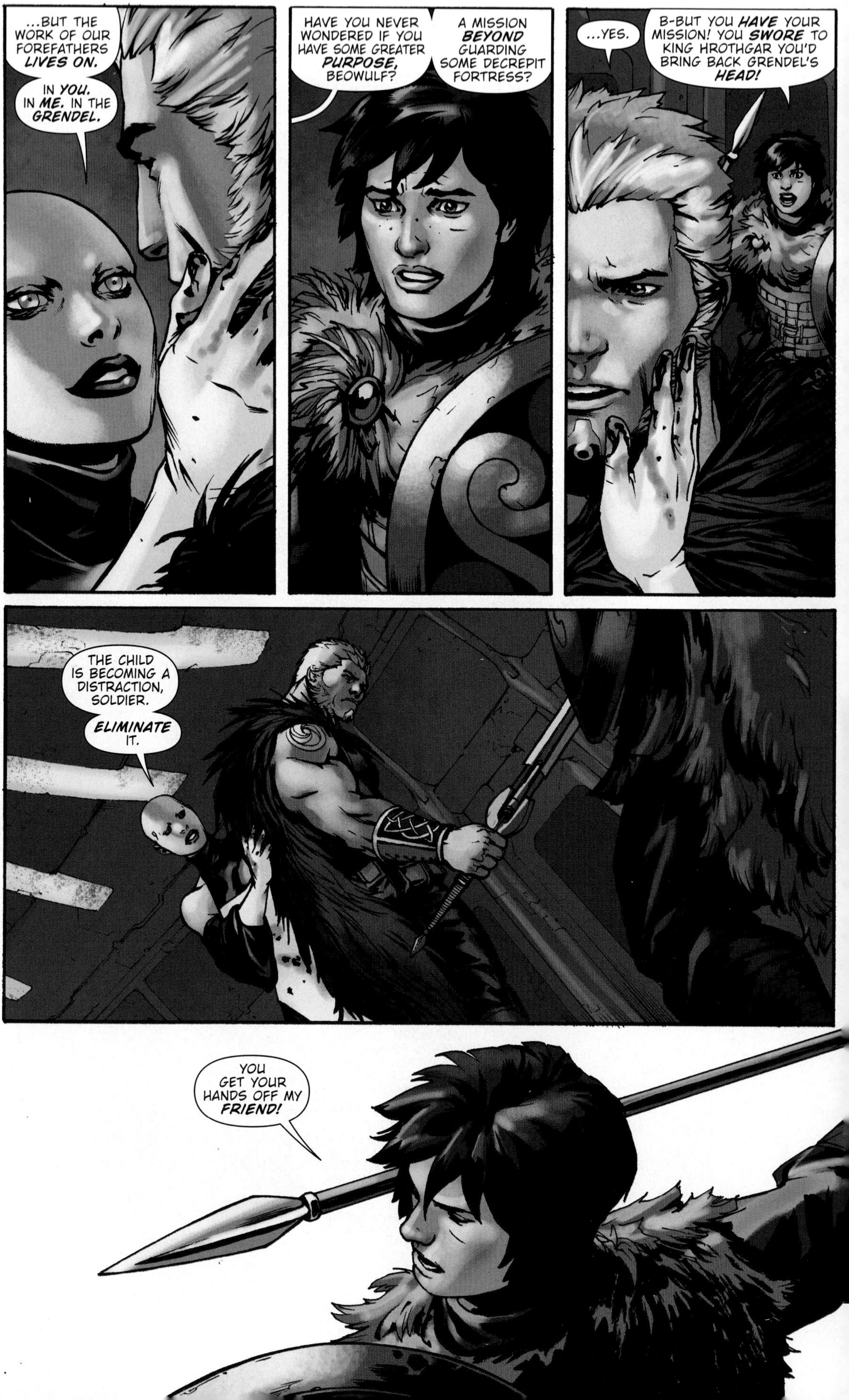
...BUT THE WORK OF OUR FOREFATHERS LIVES ON.
IN YOU. IN ME. IN THE GRENDEL.
HAVE YOU NEVER WONDERED IF YOU HAVE SOME GREATER PURPOSE, BEOWULF?
A MISSION BEYOND GUARDING SOME DECREPIT FORTRESS?
...YES.
B-BUT YOU HAVE YOUR MISSION! YOU SWORE TO KING HROTHGAR YOU'D BRING BACK GRENDEL'S HEAD!
THE CHILD IS BECOMING A DISTRACTION, SOLDIER.
ELIMINATE IT.
YOU GET YOUR HANDS OFF MY FRIEND!

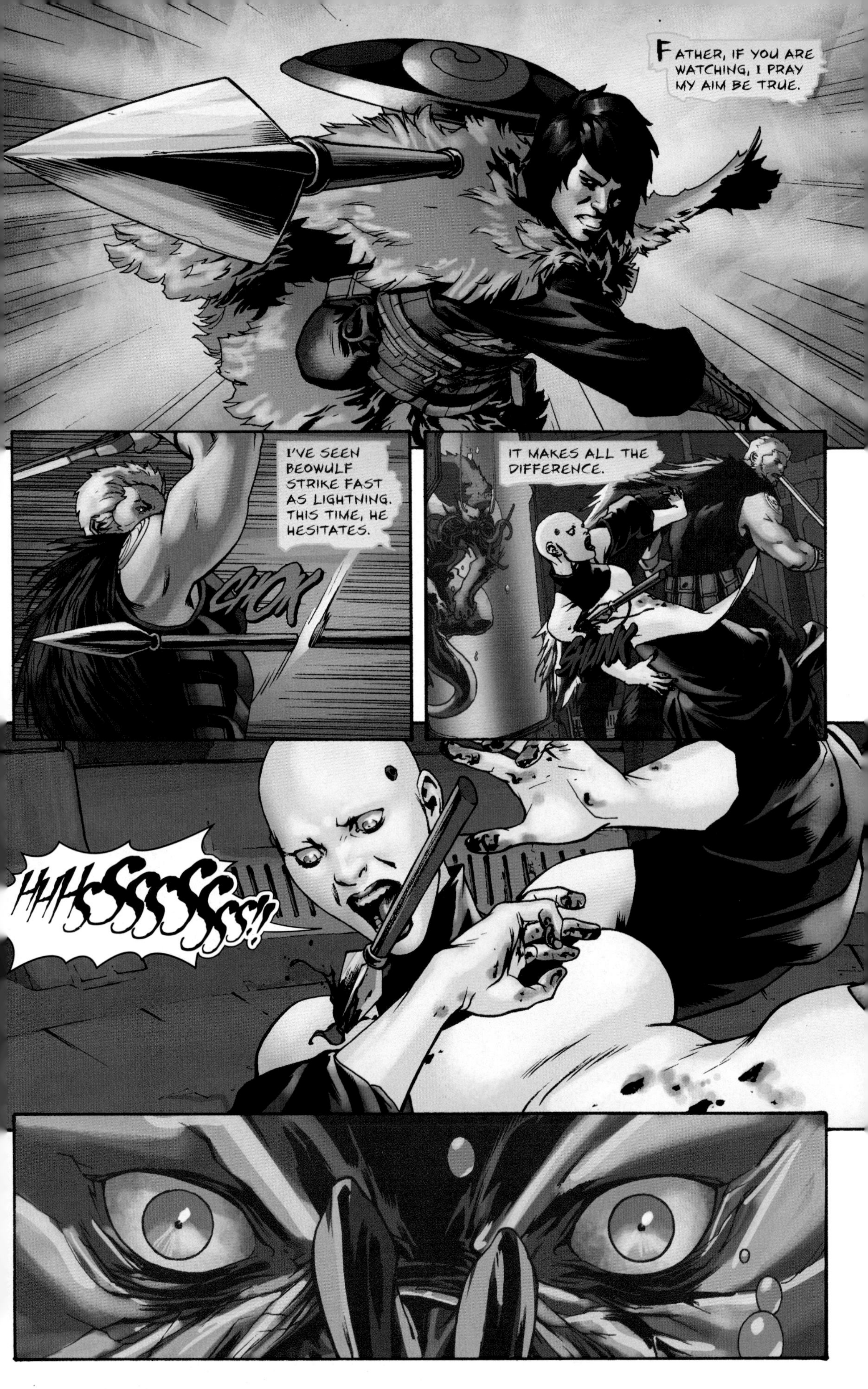
FATHER, IF YOU ARE WATCHING, I PRAY MY AIM BE TRUE.
I'VE SEEN BEOWULF STRIKE FAST AS LIGHTNING. THIS TIME, HE HESITATES.
CHOK
IT MAKES ALL THE DIFFERENCE.
SHUNK
HHHSSSSSSS!!

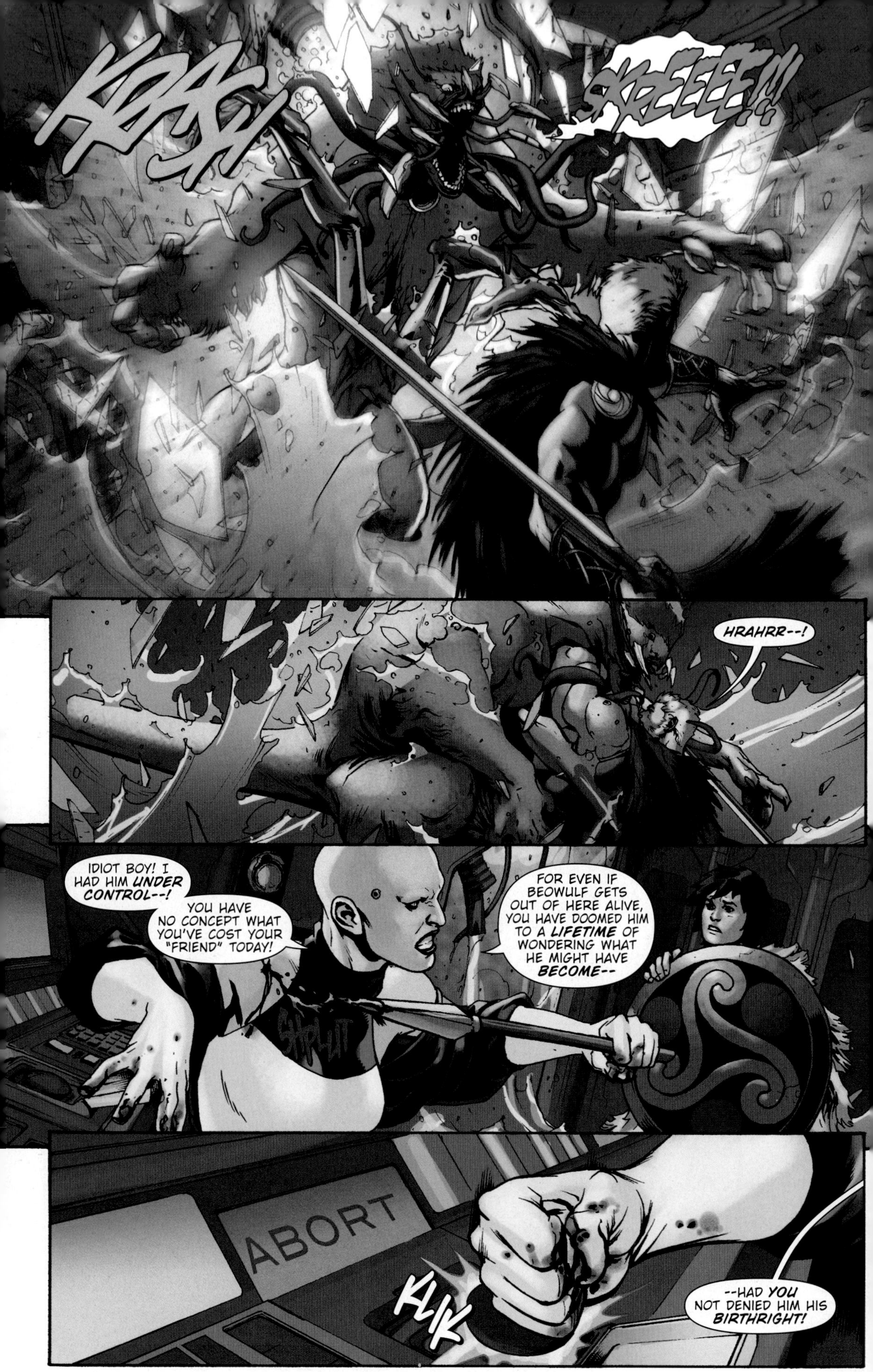
KRAK
SKREEEE!!
HRAHRR--!
IDIOT BOY! I HAD HIM UNDER CONTROL--!
YOU HAVE NO CONCEPT WHAT YOU'VE COST YOUR "FRIEND" TODAY!
FOR EVEN IF BEOWULF GETS OUT OF HERE ALIVE, YOU HAVE DOOMED HIM TO A LIFETIME OF WONDERING WHAT HE MIGHT HAVE BECOME--
SHLUT
ABORT
KLIK
--HAD YOU NOT DENIED HIM HIS BIRTHRIGHT!

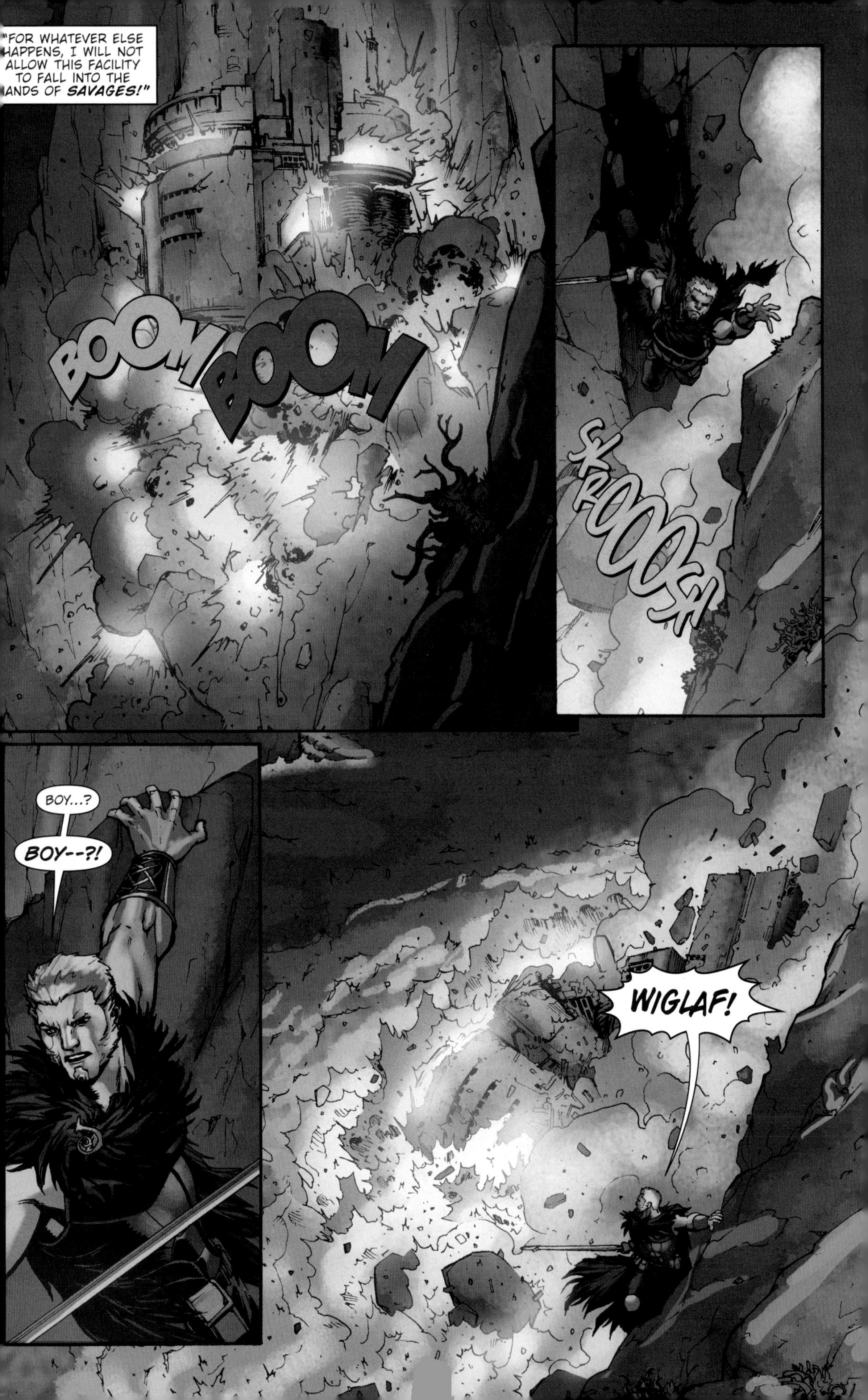
"FOR WHATEVER ELSE HAPPENS, I WILL NOT ALLOW THIS FACILITY TO FALL INTO THE HANDS OF SAVAGES!"
BOOM BOOM
SKROOOSH
BOY...?
BOY--?!
WIGLAF!

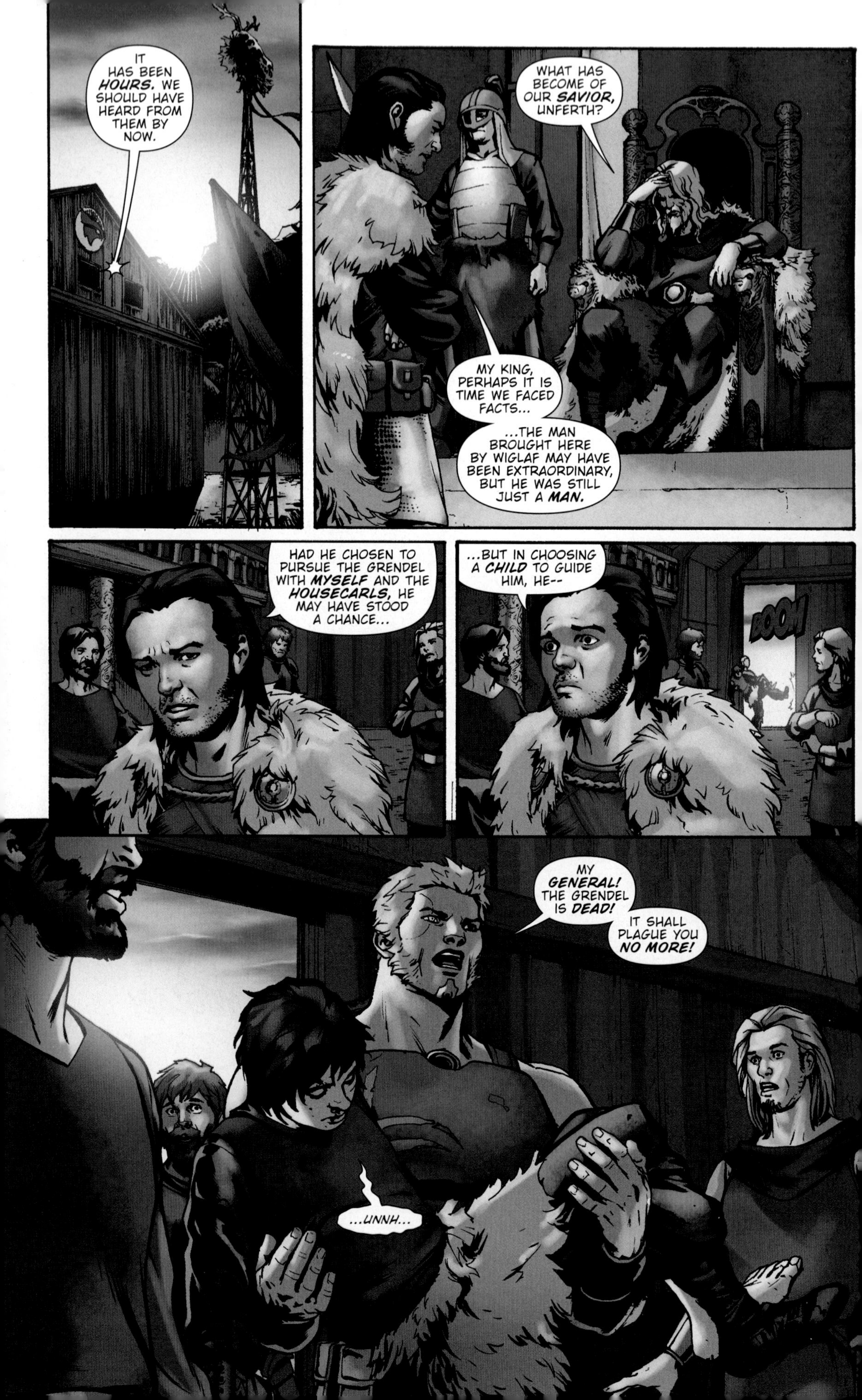
IT HAS BEEN HOURS. WE SHOULD HAVE HEARD FROM THEM BY NOW.
WHAT HAS BECOME OF OUR SAVIOR, UNFERTH?
MY KING, PERHAPS IT IS TIME WE FACED FACTS...
...THE MAN BROUGHT HERE BY WIGLAF MAY HAVE BEEN EXTRAORDINARY, BUT HE WAS STILL JUST A MAN.
HAD HE CHOSEN TO PURSUE THE GRENDEL WITH MYSELF AND THE HOUSECARLS, HE MAY HAVE STOOD A CHANCE...
...BUT IN CHOOSING A CHILD TO GUIDE HIM, HE--
BOOM
MY GENERAL! THE GRENDEL IS DEAD!
IT SHALL PLAGUE YOU NO MORE!
...UNNH...

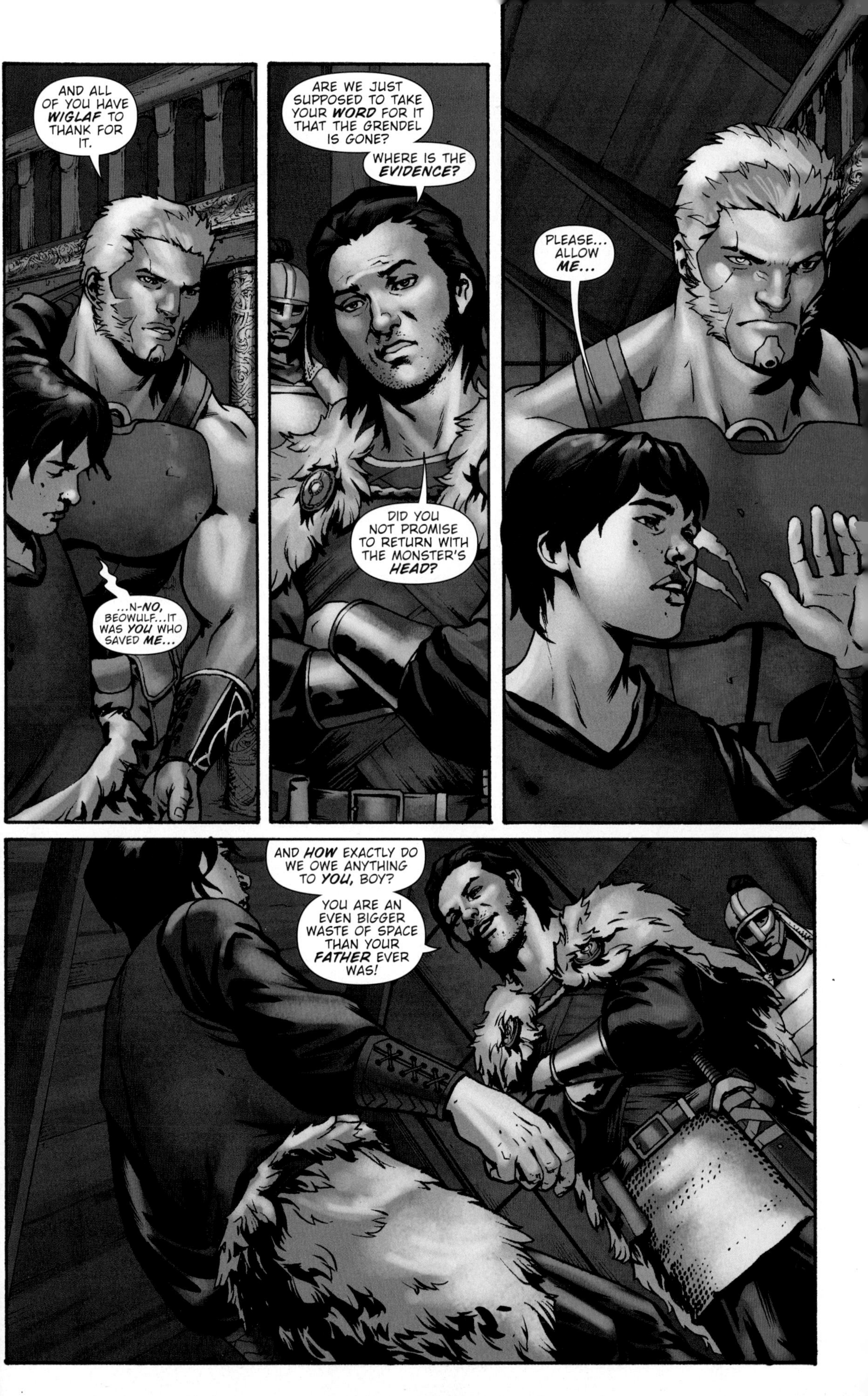
AND ALL OF YOU HAVE WIGLAF TO THANK FOR IT.
...N-NO, BEOWULF...IT WAS YOU WHO SAVED ME...
ARE WE JUST SUPPOSED TO TAKE YOUR WORD FOR IT THAT THE GRENDEL IS GONE?
WHERE IS THE EVIDENCE?
DID YOU NOT PROMISE TO RETURN WITH THE MONSTER'S HEAD?
PLEASE... ALLOW ME...
AND HOW EXACTLY DO WE OWE ANYTHING TO YOU, BOY?
YOU ARE AN EVEN BIGGER WASTE OF SPACE THAN YOUR FATHER EVER WAS!

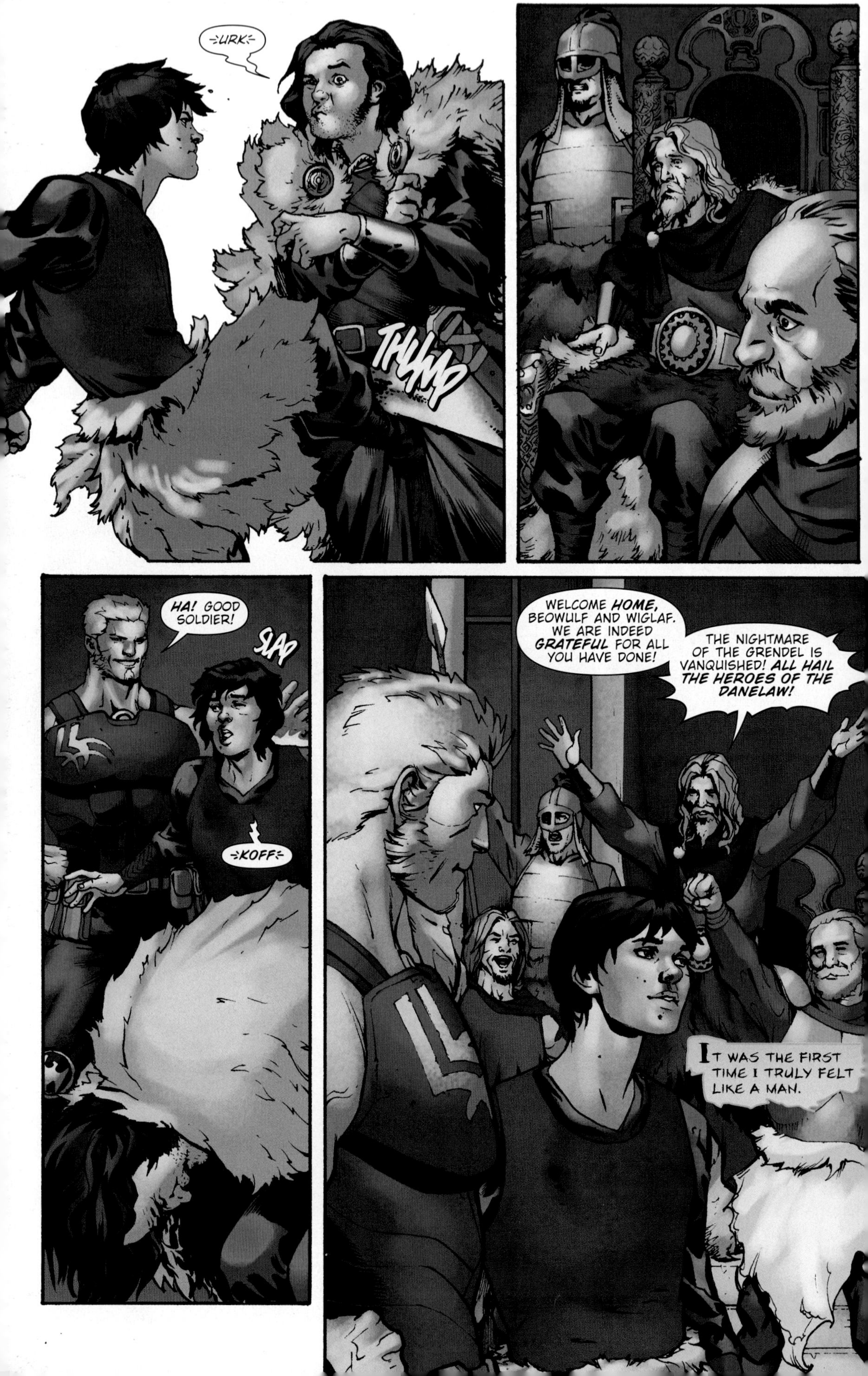
URK
THUMP
HA! GOOD SOLDIER!
SLAP
KOFF
WELCOME HOME, BEOWULF AND WIGLAF. WE ARE INDEED GRATEFUL FOR ALL YOU HAVE DONE!
THE NIGHTMARE OF THE GRENDEL IS VANQUISHED! ALL HAIL THE HEROES OF THE DANELAW!
IT WAS THE FIRST TIME I TRULY FELT LIKE A MAN.

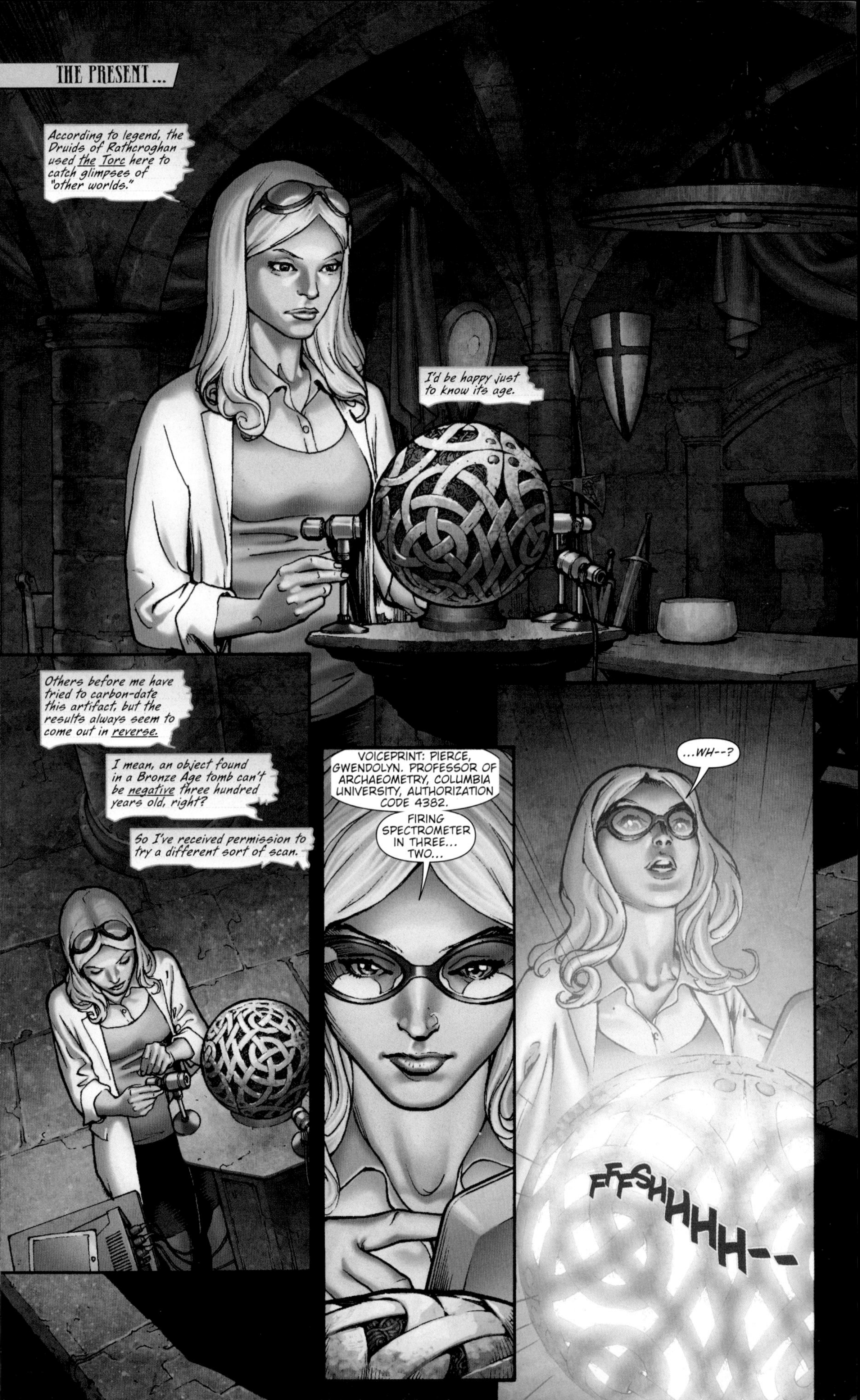
THE PRESENT...
According to legend, the Druids of Rathcroghan used the Torc here to catch glimpses of "other worlds."
I'd be happy just to know its age.
Others before me have tried to carbon-date this artifact, but the results always seem to come out in reverse.
I mean, an object found in a Bronze Age tomb can't be negative three hundred years old, right?
So I've received permission to try a different sort of scan.
VOICEPRINT: PIERCE, GWENDOLYN. PROFESSOR OF ARCHAEOMETRY, COLUMBIA UNIVERSITY, AUTHORIZATION CODE 4382.
FIRING SPECTROMETER IN THREE... TWO...
...WH--?
FFFSHHHHH--

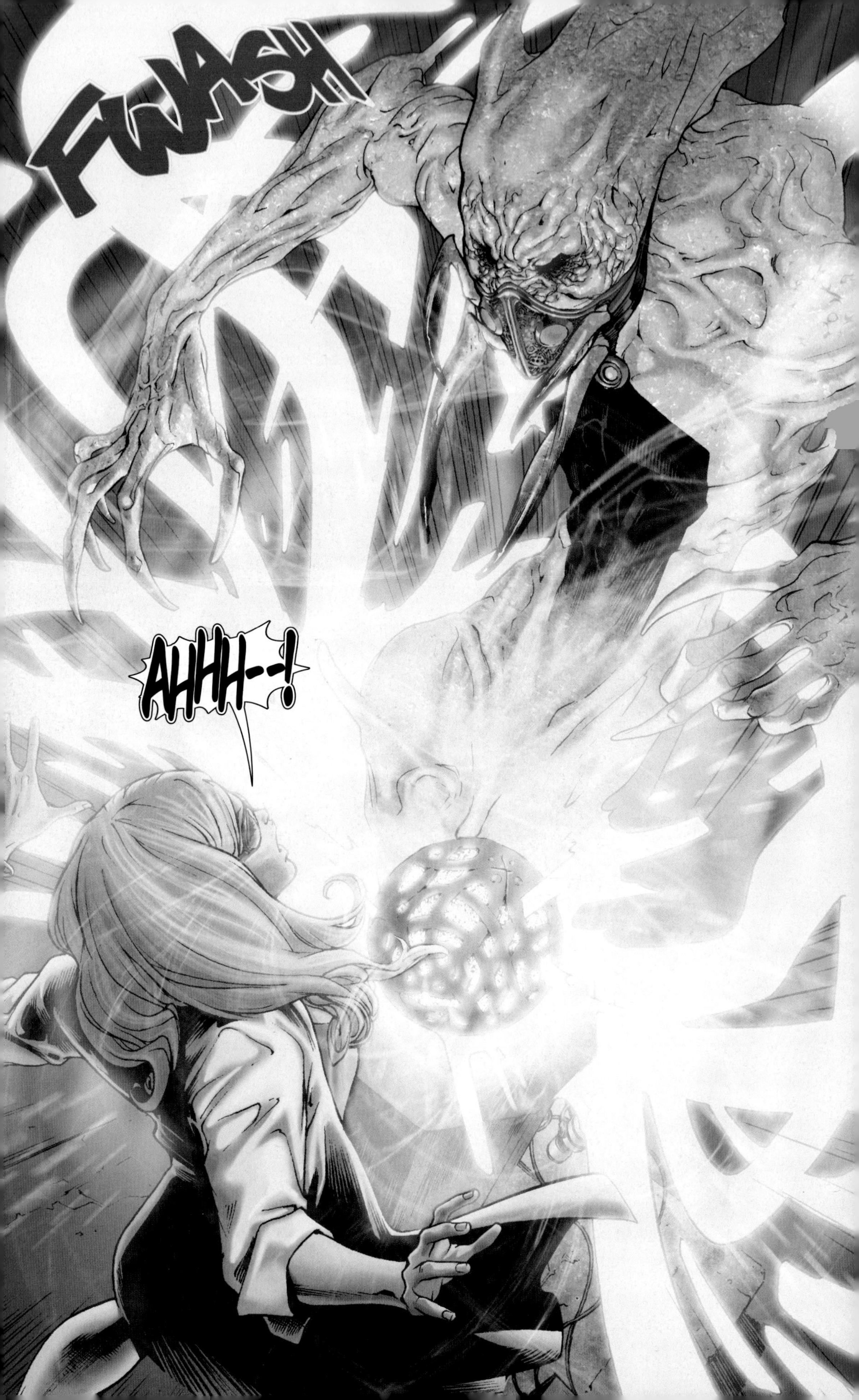
FWASH
AHHH--!

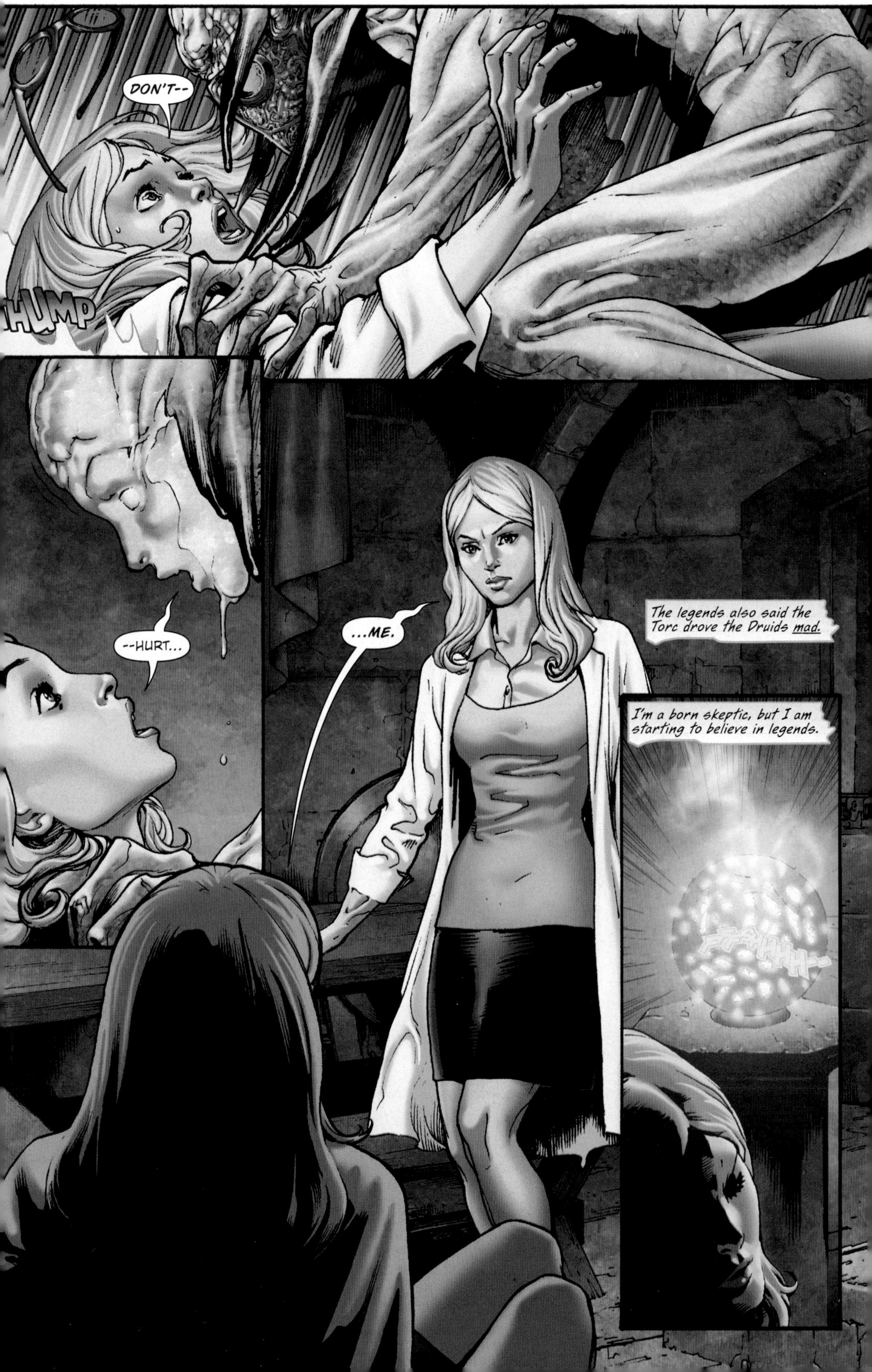
DON'T--
THUMP
--HURT...
...ME.
The legends also said the Torc drove the Druids mad.
I'm a born skeptic, but I am starting to believe in legends.

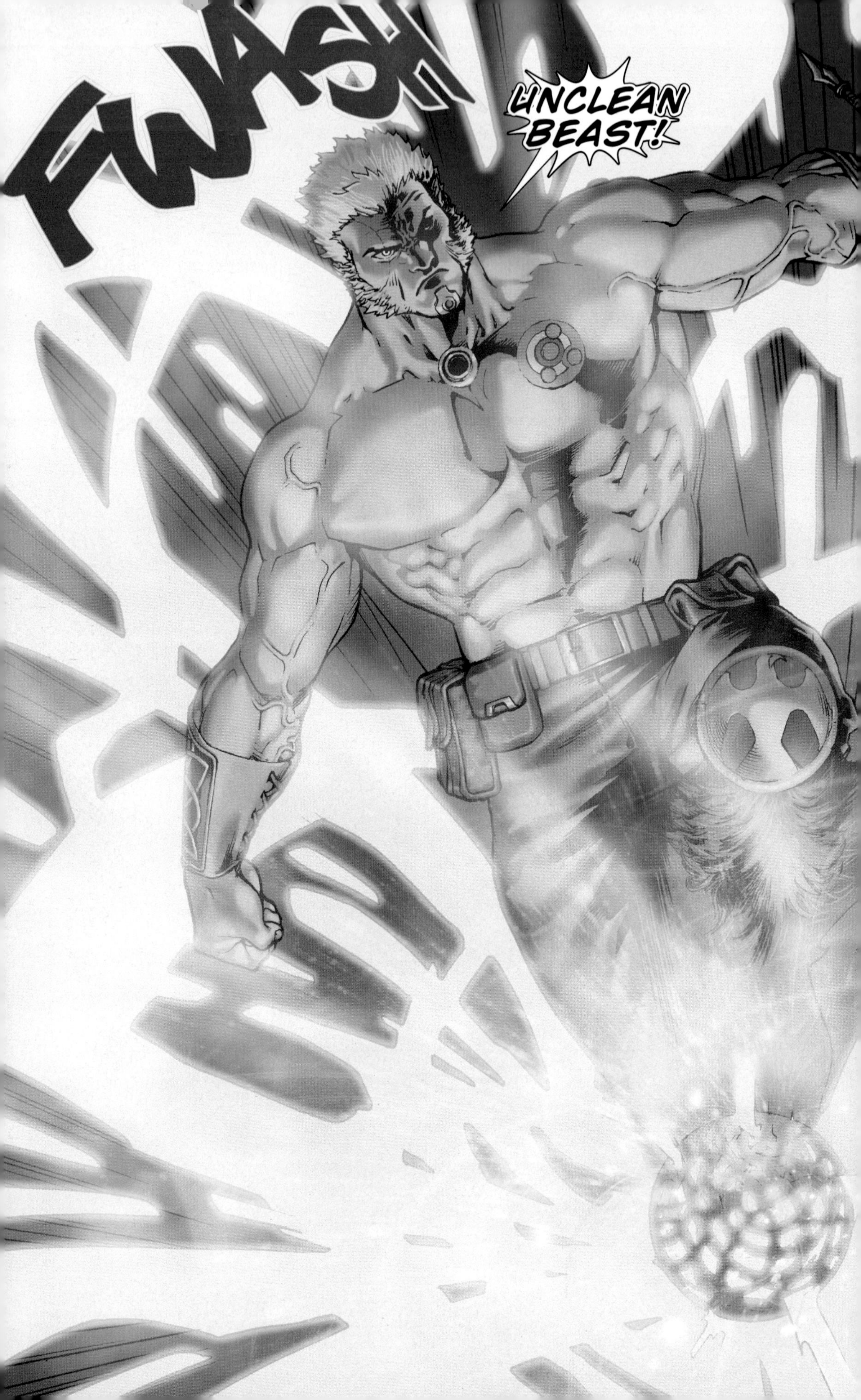
FWASH
UNCLEAN BEAST!

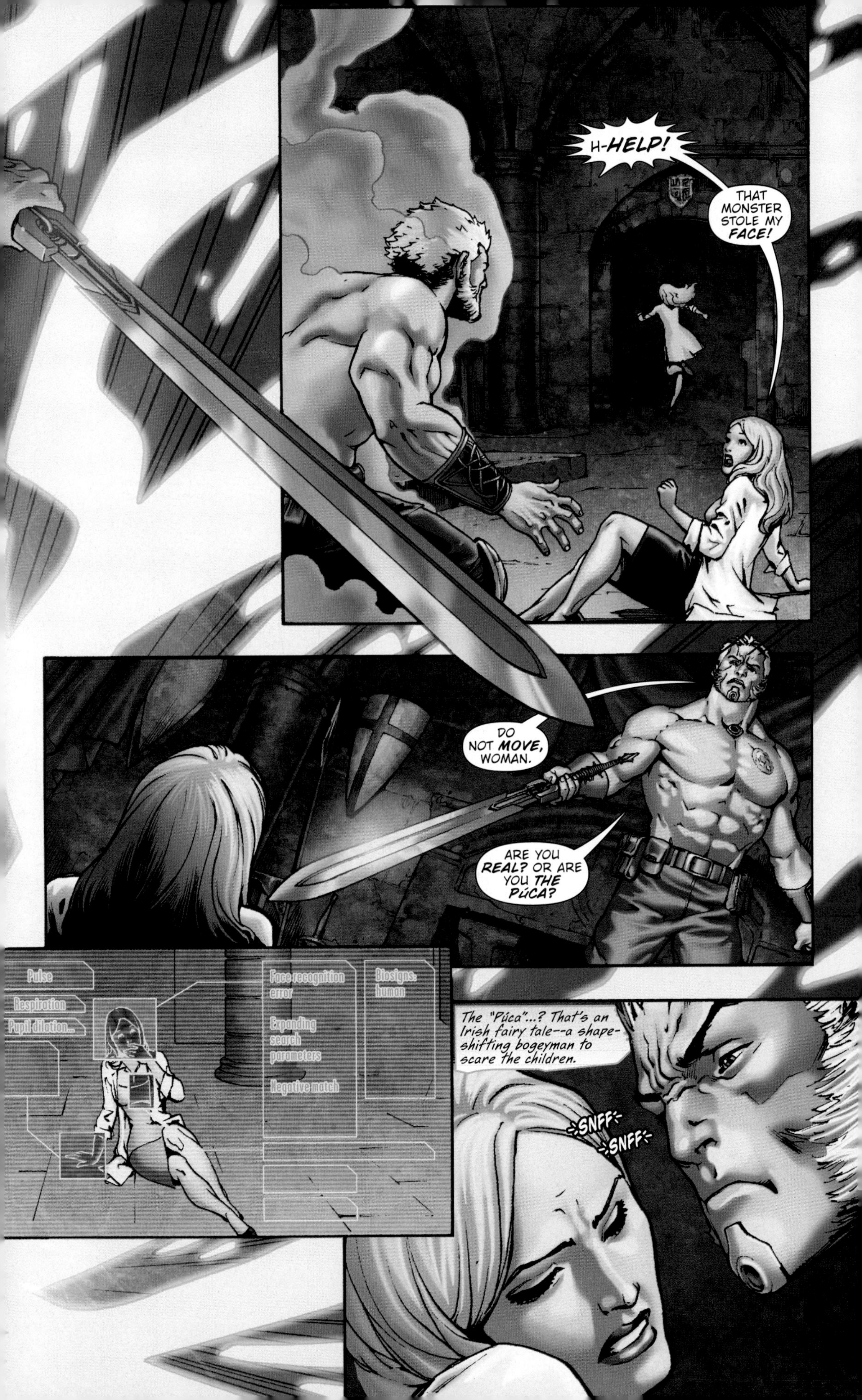
H-HELP!
THAT MONSTER STOLE MY FACE!
DO NOT MOVE, WOMAN.
ARE YOU REAL? OR ARE YOU THE PÚCA?
Pulse
Respiration
Pupil dilation...
Face recognition error
Expanding search parameters
Negative match
Biosigns: human
The "Púca"...? That's an Irish fairy tale--a shape-shifting bogeyman to scare the children.
SNFF
SNFF

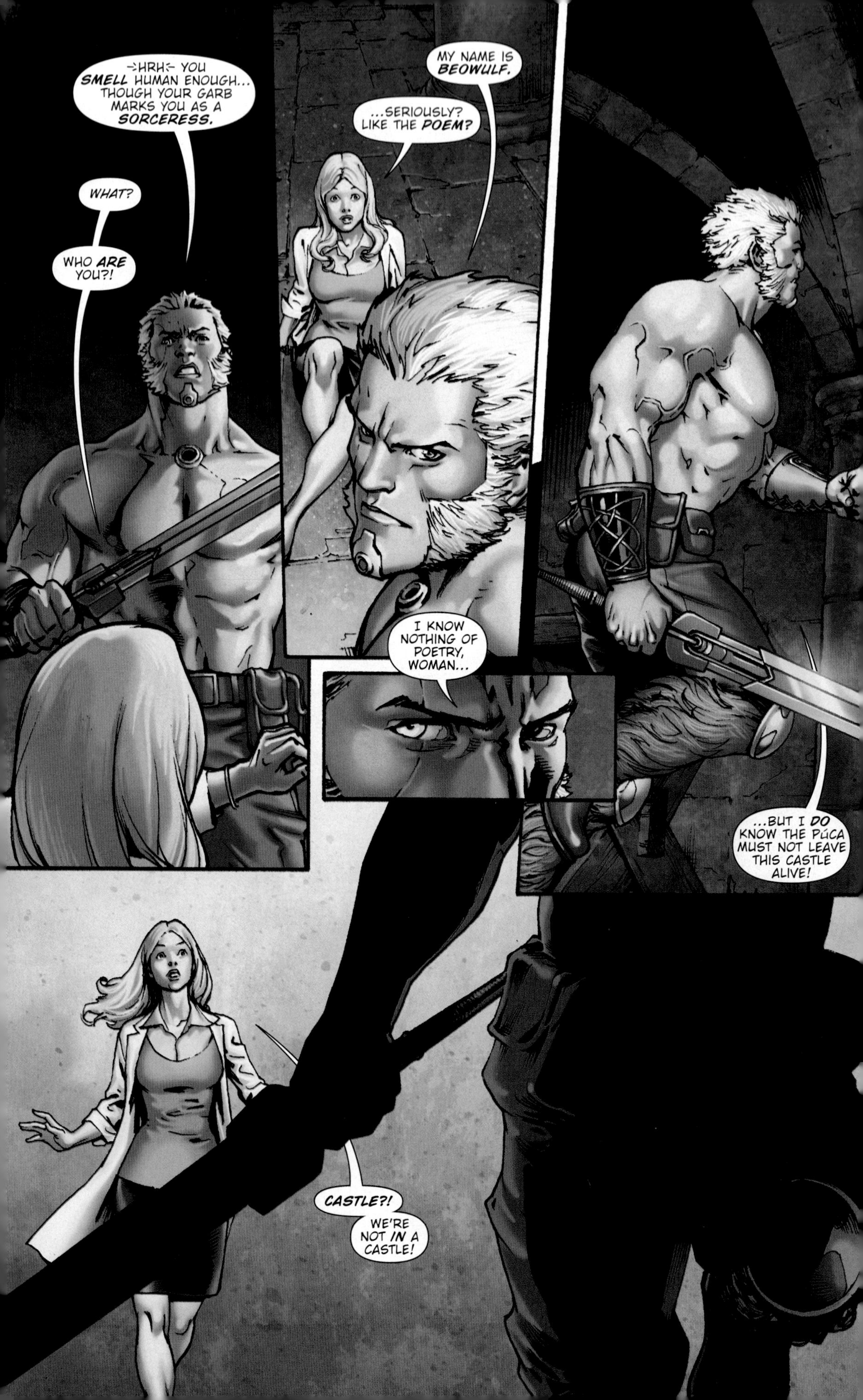

-HRH- YOU SMELL HUMAN ENOUGH... THOUGH YOUR GARB MARKS YOU AS A SORCERESS.
WHAT?
WHO ARE YOU?!
MY NAME IS BEOWULF.
...SERIOUSLY? LIKE THE POEM?
I KNOW NOTHING OF POETRY, WOMAN...
...BUT I DO KNOW THE PÚCA MUST NOT LEAVE THIS CASTLE ALIVE!
CASTLE?!
WE'RE NOT IN A CASTLE!

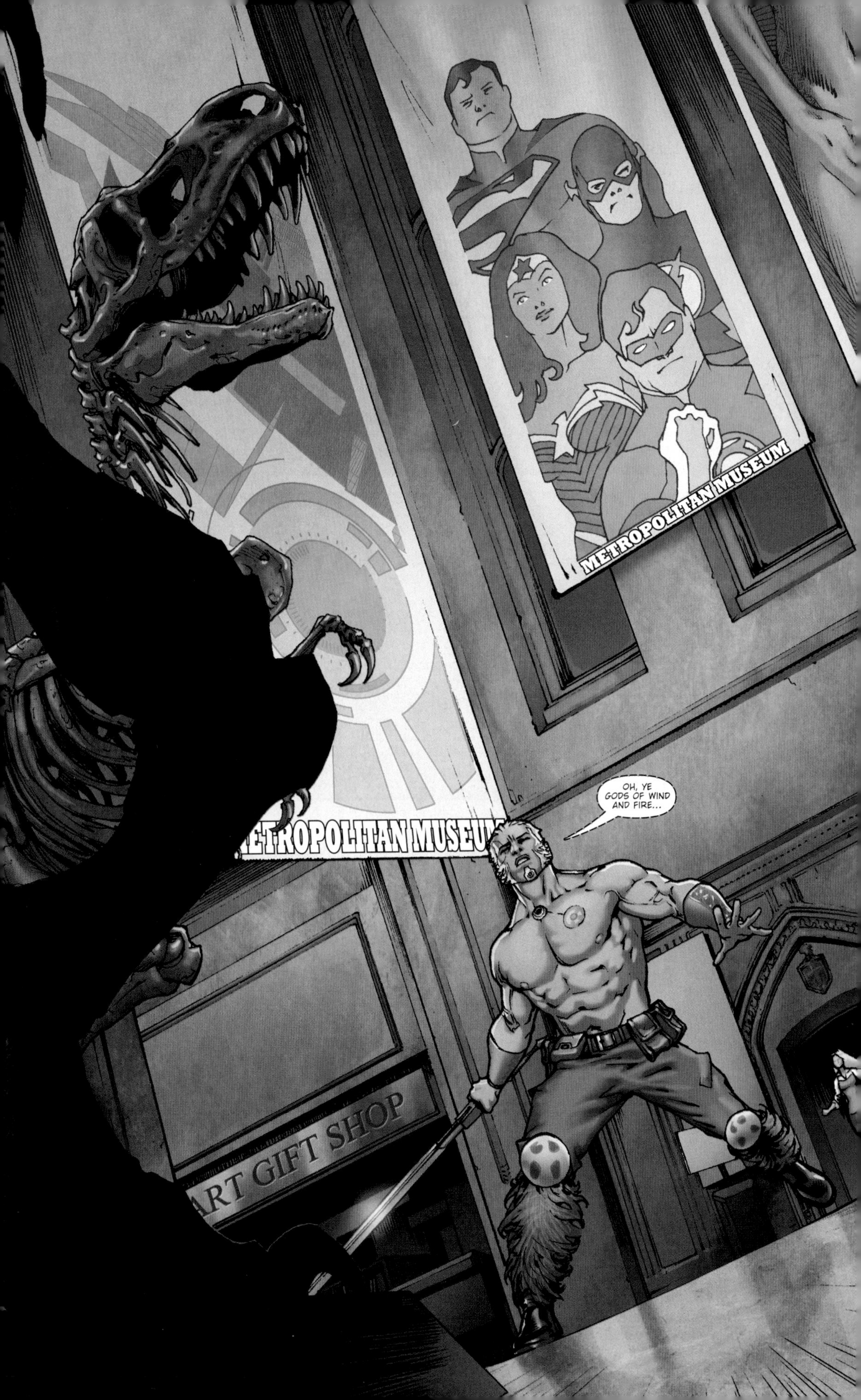
METROPOLITAN MUSEUM
METROPOLITAN MUSEUM
OH, YE GODS OF WIND AND FIRE...
ART GIFT SHOP

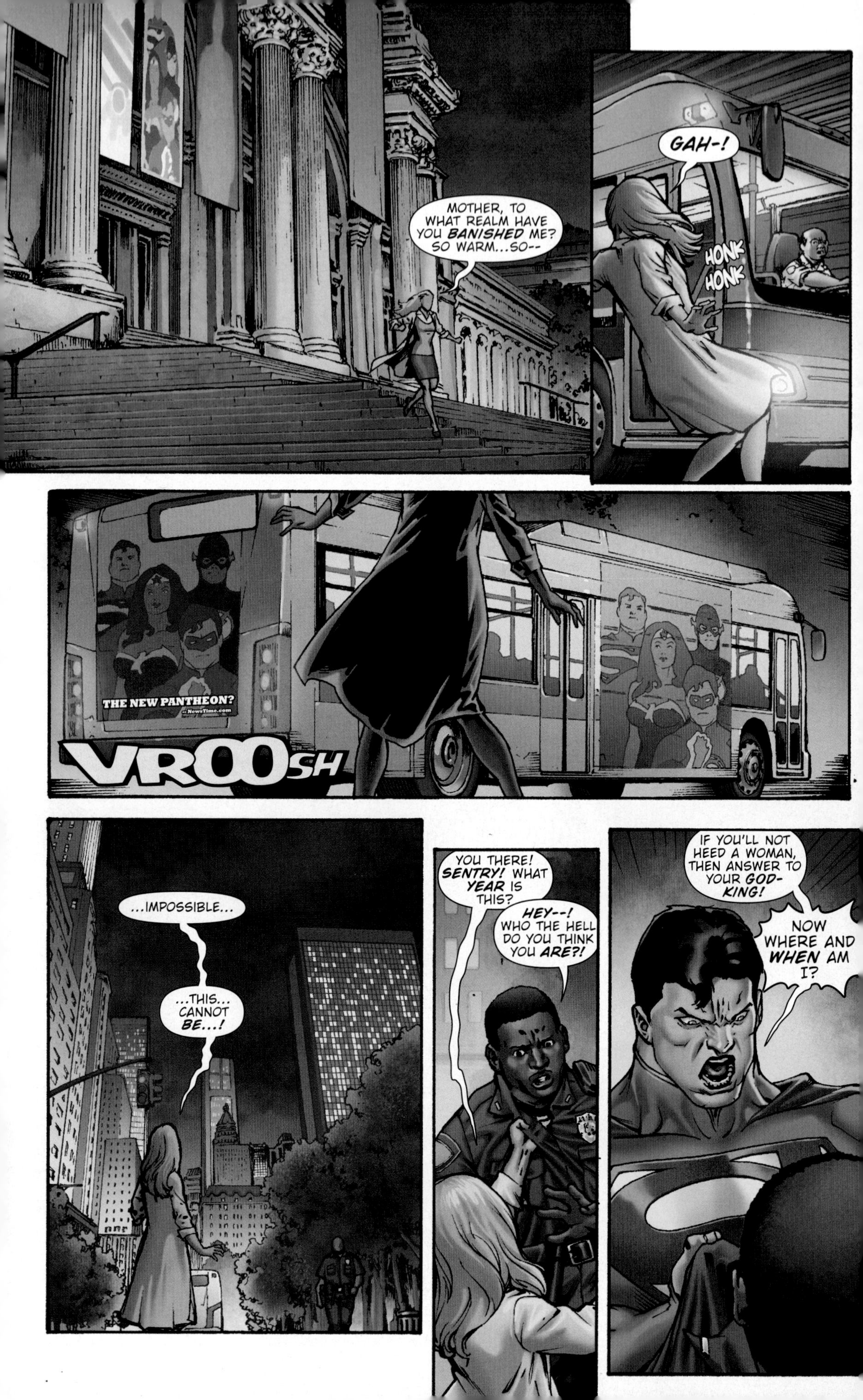
MOTHER, TO WHAT REALM HAVE YOU BANISHED ME? SO WARM...SO--
GAH-!
HONK HONK
THE NEW PANTHEON?
—NewsTime.com
VROOSH
...IMPOSSIBLE...
...THIS... CANNOT BE...!
YOU THERE! SENTRY! WHAT YEAR IS THIS?
HEY--! WHO THE HELL DO YOU THINK YOU ARE?!
IF YOU'LL NOT HEED A WOMAN, THEN ANSWER TO YOUR GOD-KING!
NOW WHERE AND WHEN AM I?

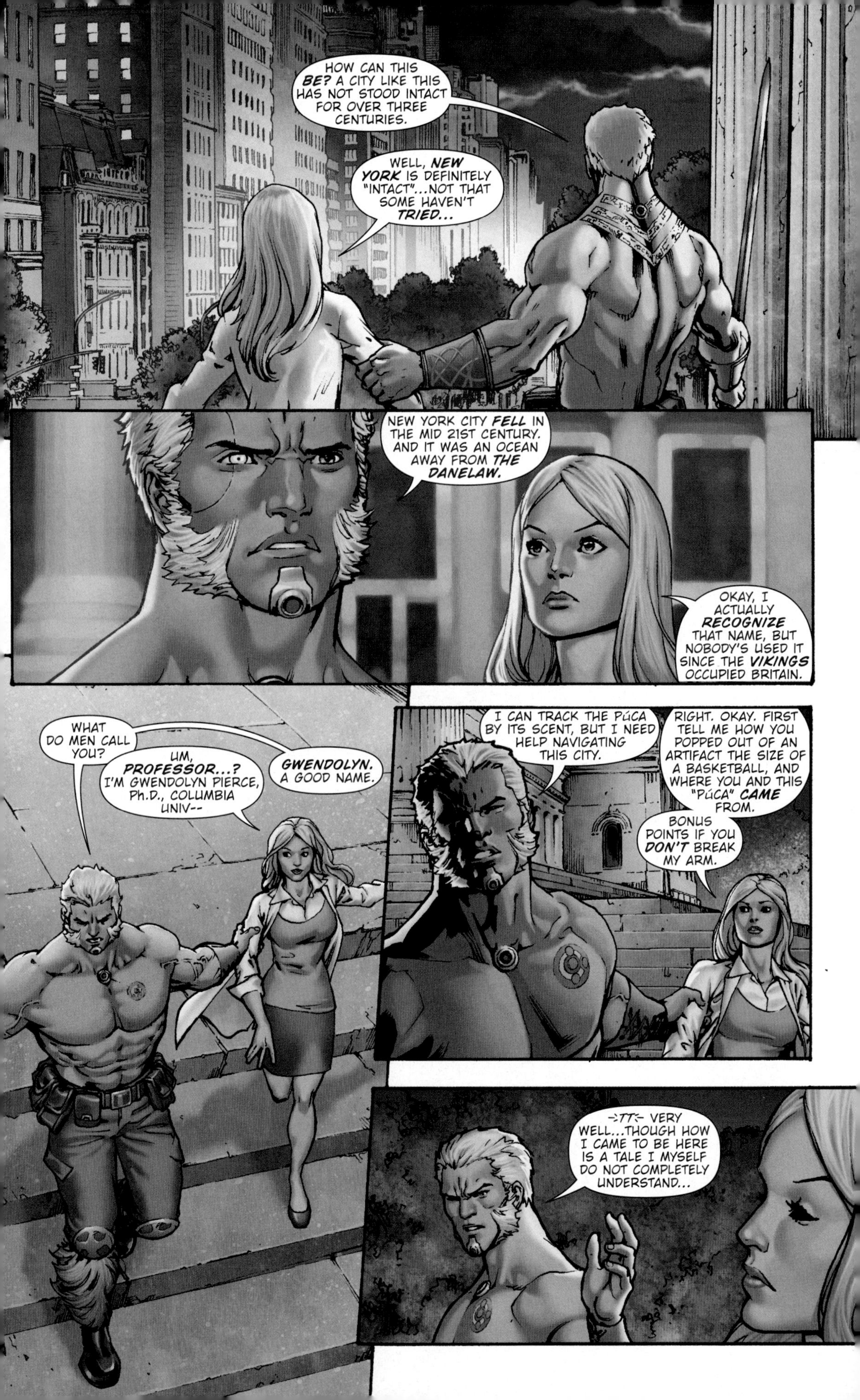
HOW CAN THIS BE? A CITY LIKE THIS HAS NOT STOOD INTACT FOR OVER THREE CENTURIES.
WELL, NEW YORK IS DEFINITELY "INTACT"...NOT THAT SOME HAVEN'T TRIED...
NEW YORK CITY FELL IN THE MID 21ST CENTURY. AND IT WAS AN OCEAN AWAY FROM THE DANELAW.
OKAY, I ACTUALLY RECOGNIZE THAT NAME, BUT NOBODY'S USED IT SINCE THE VIKINGS OCCUPIED BRITAIN.
WHAT DO MEN CALL YOU?
UM, PROFESSOR...? I'M GWENDOLYN PIERCE, Ph.D., COLUMBIA UNIV--
GWENDOLYN. A GOOD NAME.
I CAN TRACK THE PÚCA BY ITS SCENT, BUT I NEED HELP NAVIGATING THIS CITY.
RIGHT. OKAY. FIRST TELL ME HOW YOU POPPED OUT OF AN ARTIFACT THE SIZE OF A BASKETBALL, AND WHERE YOU AND THIS "PÚCA" CAME FROM.
BONUS POINTS IF YOU DON'T BREAK MY ARM.
-TT- VERY WELL...THOUGH HOW I CAME TO BE HERE IS A TALE I MYSELF DO NOT COMPLETELY UNDERSTAND...

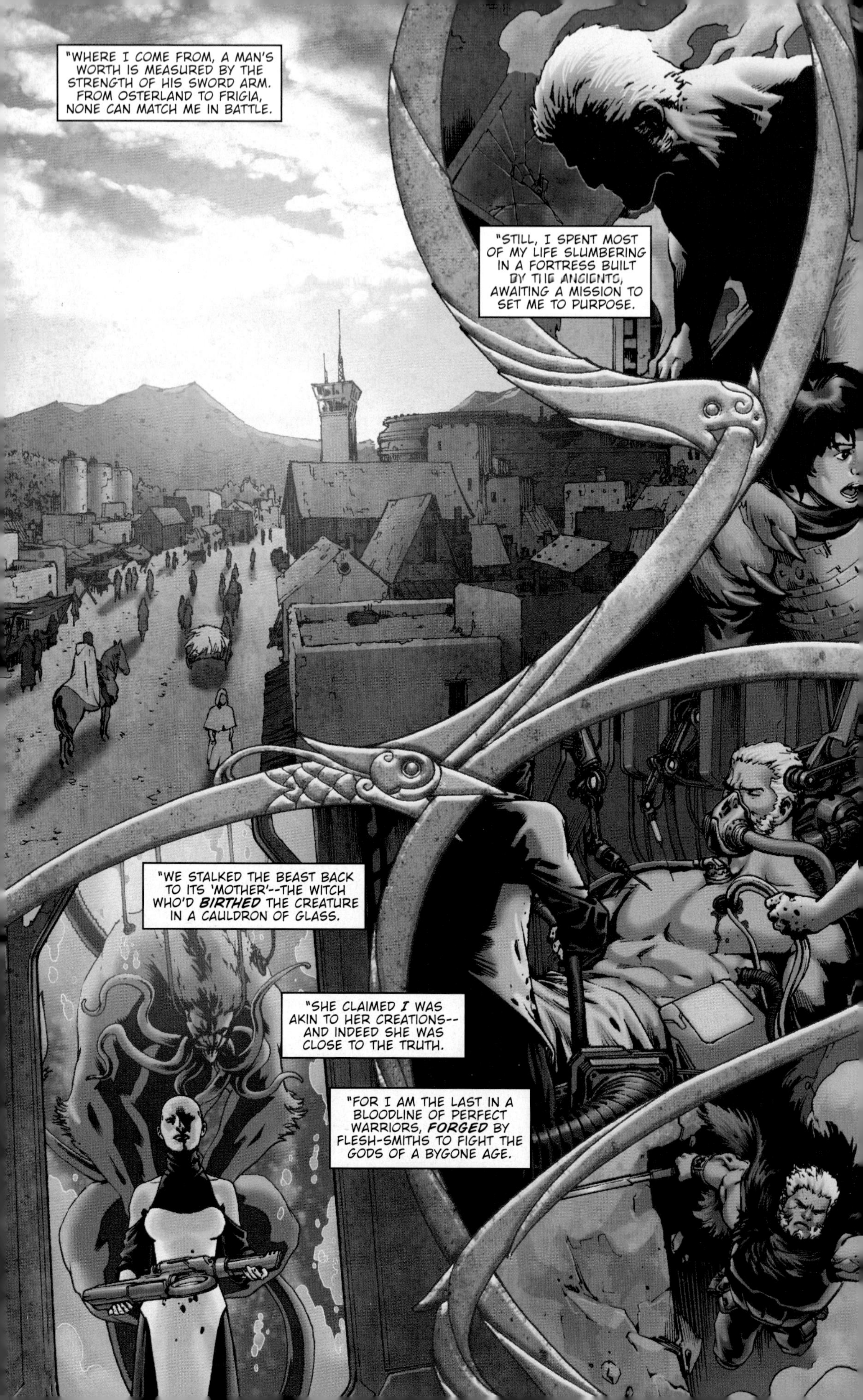
"WHERE I COME FROM, A MAN'S WORTH IS MEASURED BY THE STRENGTH OF HIS SWORD ARM. FROM OSTERLAND TO FRIGIA, NONE CAN MATCH ME IN BATTLE.
"STILL, I SPENT MOST OF MY LIFE SLUMBERING IN A FORTRESS BUILT BY THE ANCIENTS, AWAITING A MISSION TO SET ME TO PURPOSE.
"WE STALKED THE BEAST BACK TO ITS 'MOTHER'--THE WITCH WHO'D BIRTHED THE CREATURE IN A CAULDRON OF GLASS.
"SHE CLAIMED I WAS AKIN TO HER CREATIONS--AND INDEED SHE WAS CLOSE TO THE TRUTH.
"FOR I AM THE LAST IN A BLOODLINE OF PERFECT WARRIORS, FORGED BY FLESH-SMITHS TO FIGHT THE GODS OF A BYGONE AGE.

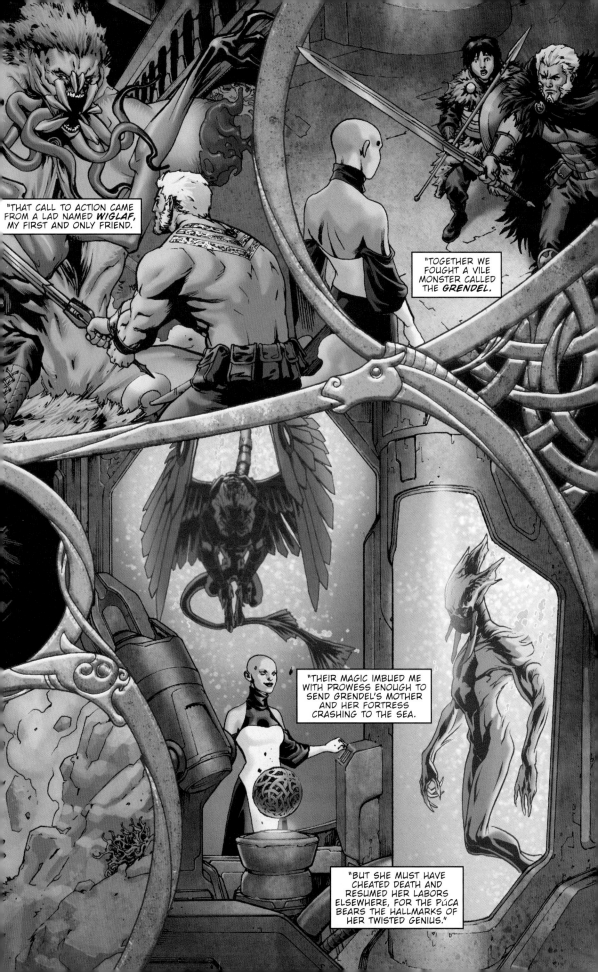

"THAT CALL TO ACTION CAME FROM A LAD NAMED *WIGLAF*, MY FIRST AND ONLY FRIEND."

"TOGETHER WE FOUGHT A VILE MONSTER CALLED THE *GRENDEL.*"

"THEIR MAGIC IMBUED ME WITH PROWESS ENOUGH TO SEND GRENDEL'S MOTHER AND HER FORTRESS CRASHING TO THE SEA."

"BUT SHE MUST HAVE CHEATED DEATH AND RESUMED HER LABORS ELSEWHERE, FOR THE *PÚCA* BEARS THE HALLMARKS OF HER TWISTED GENIUS."

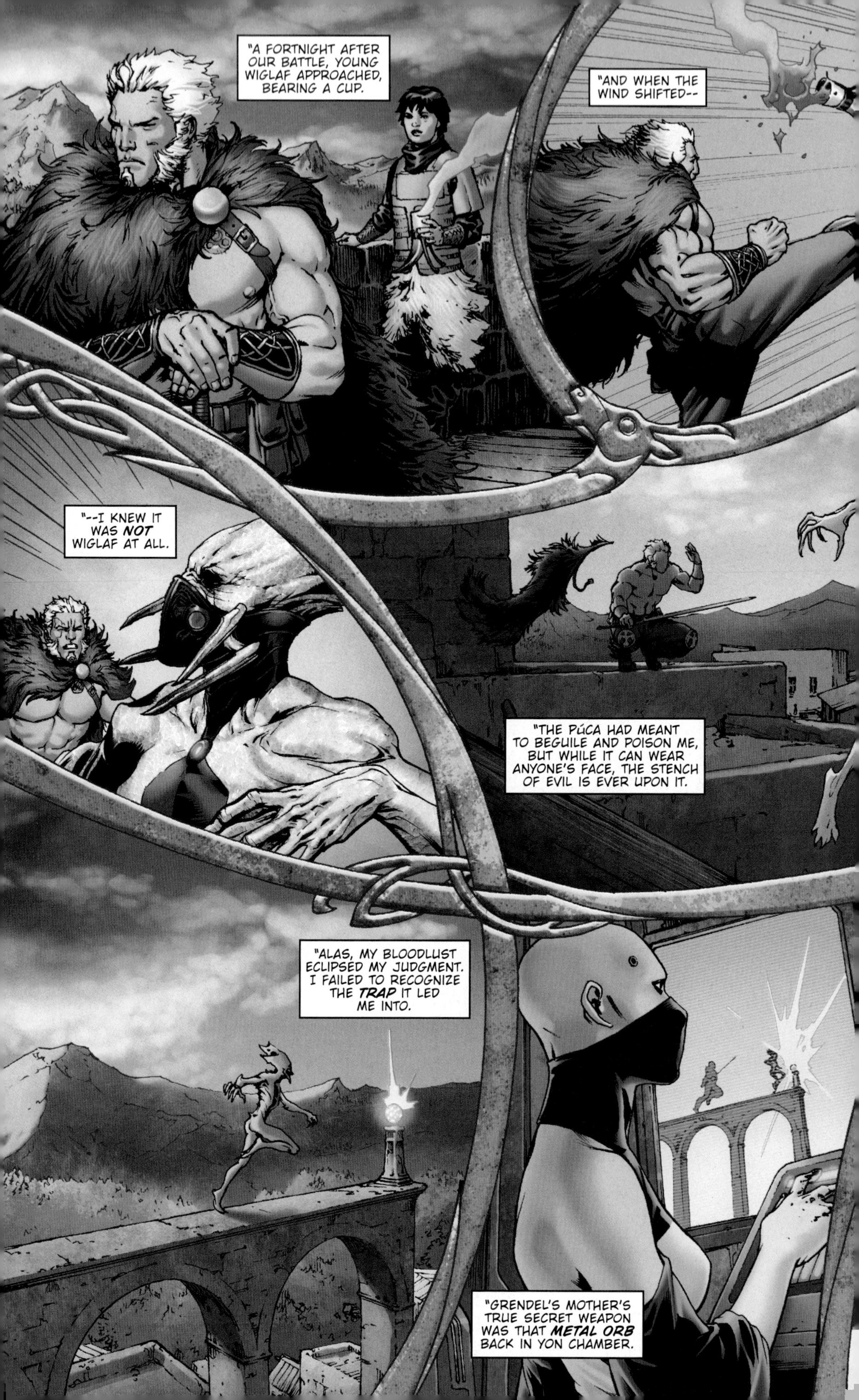
"A FORTNIGHT AFTER OUR BATTLE, YOUNG WIGLAF APPROACHED, BEARING A CUP.
"AND WHEN THE WIND SHIFTED--
"--I KNEW IT WAS **NOT** WIGLAF AT ALL.
"THE PÚCA HAD MEANT TO BEGUILE AND POISON ME, BUT WHILE IT CAN WEAR ANYONE'S FACE, THE STENCH OF EVIL IS EVER UPON IT.
"ALAS, MY BLOODLUST ECLIPSED MY JUDGMENT. I FAILED TO RECOGNIZE THE **TRAP** IT LED ME INTO.
"GRENDEL'S MOTHER'S TRUE SECRET WEAPON WAS THAT **METAL ORB** BACK IN YON CHAMBER.

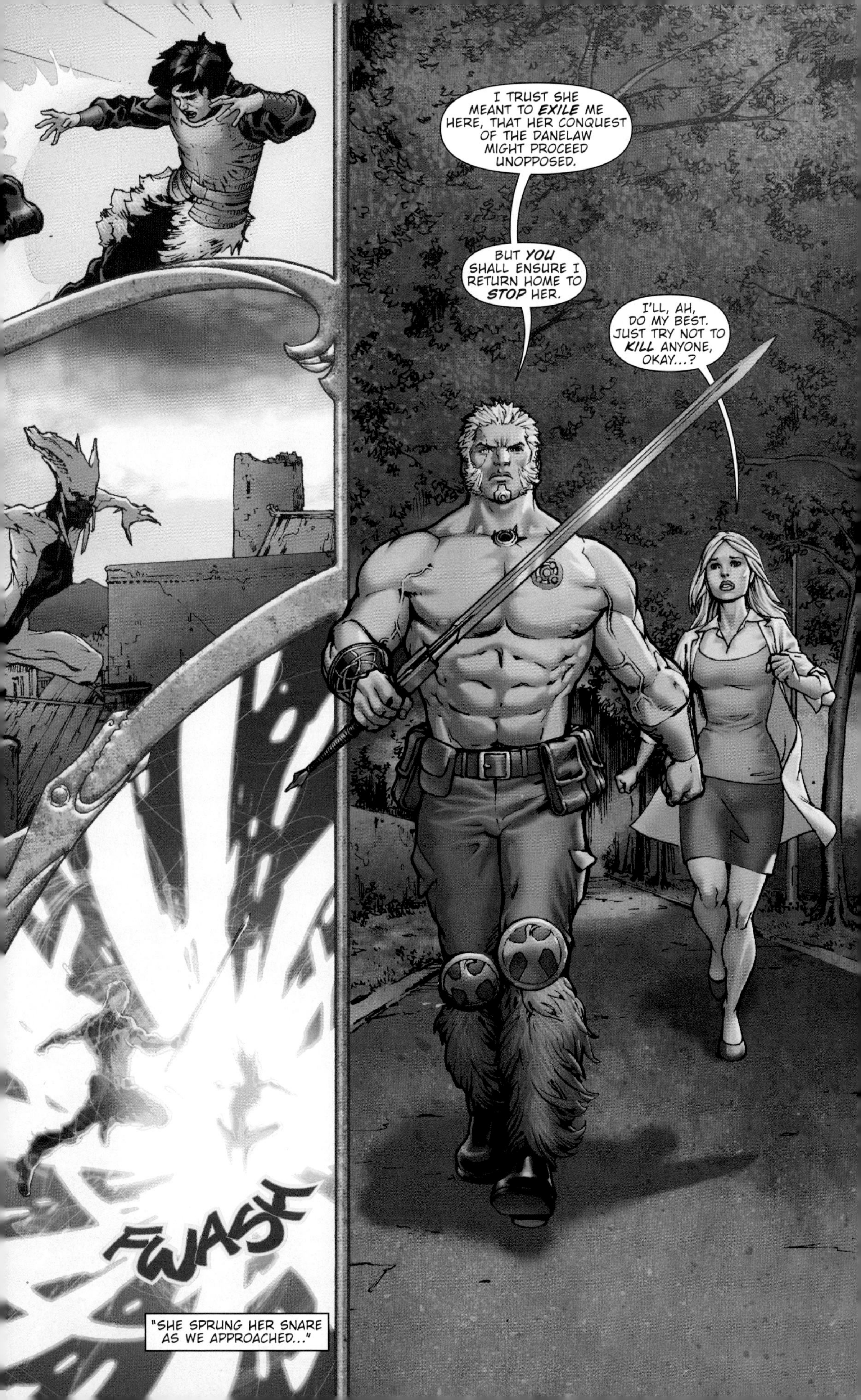
FWASH
"SHE SPRUNG HER SNARE AS WE APPROACHED..."
I TRUST SHE MEANT TO EXILE ME HERE, THAT HER CONQUEST OF THE DANELAW MIGHT PROCEED UNOPPOSED.
BUT YOU SHALL ENSURE I RETURN HOME TO STOP HER.
I'LL, AH, DO MY BEST. JUST TRY NOT TO KILL ANYONE, OKAY...?

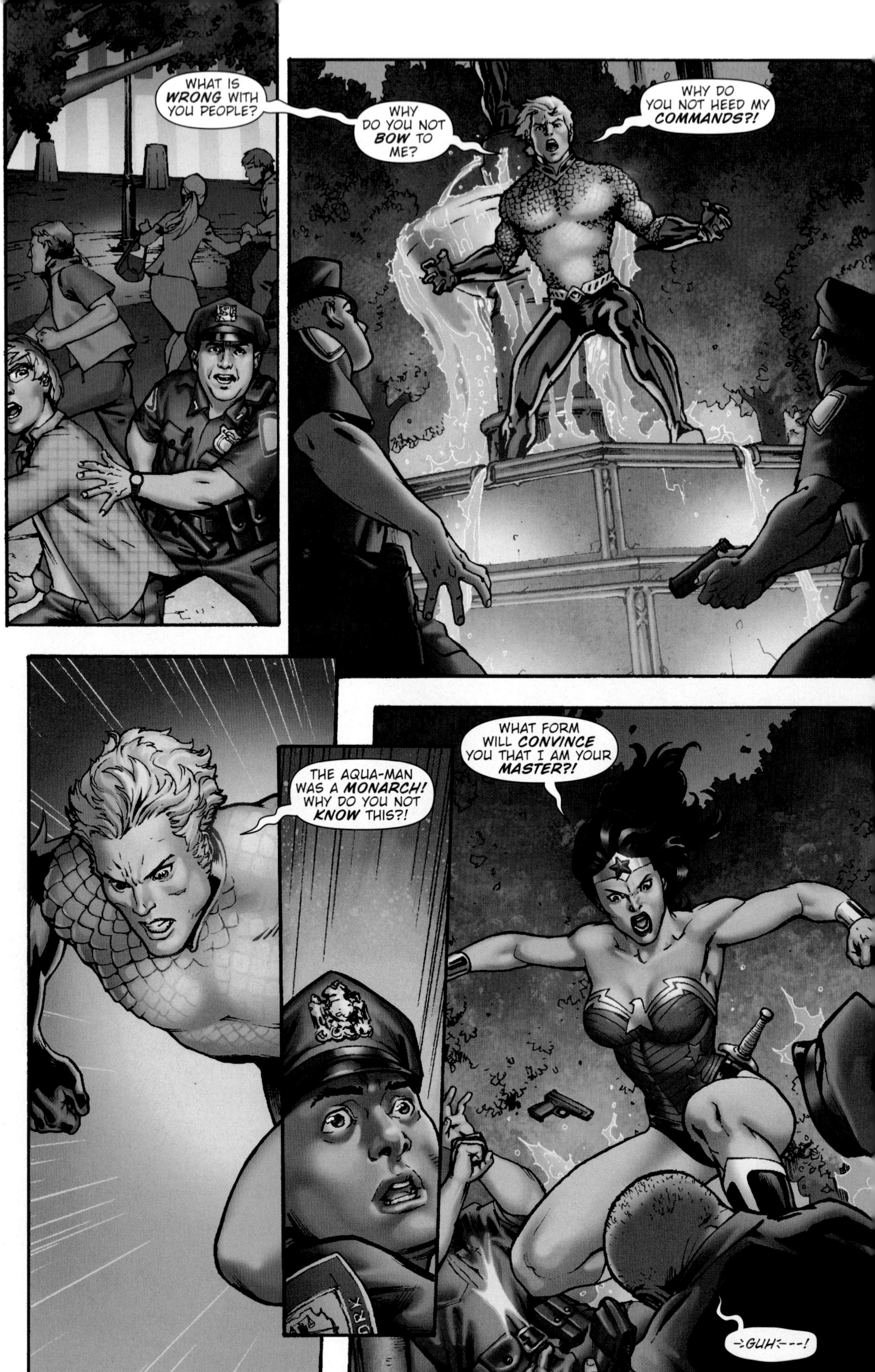
WHAT IS WRONG WITH YOU PEOPLE?
WHY DO YOU NOT BOW TO ME?
WHY DO YOU NOT HEED MY COMMANDS?!
THE AQUA-MAN WAS A MONARCH! WHY DO YOU NOT KNOW THIS?!
WHAT FORM WILL CONVINCE YOU THAT I AM YOUR MASTER?!
GUH---!

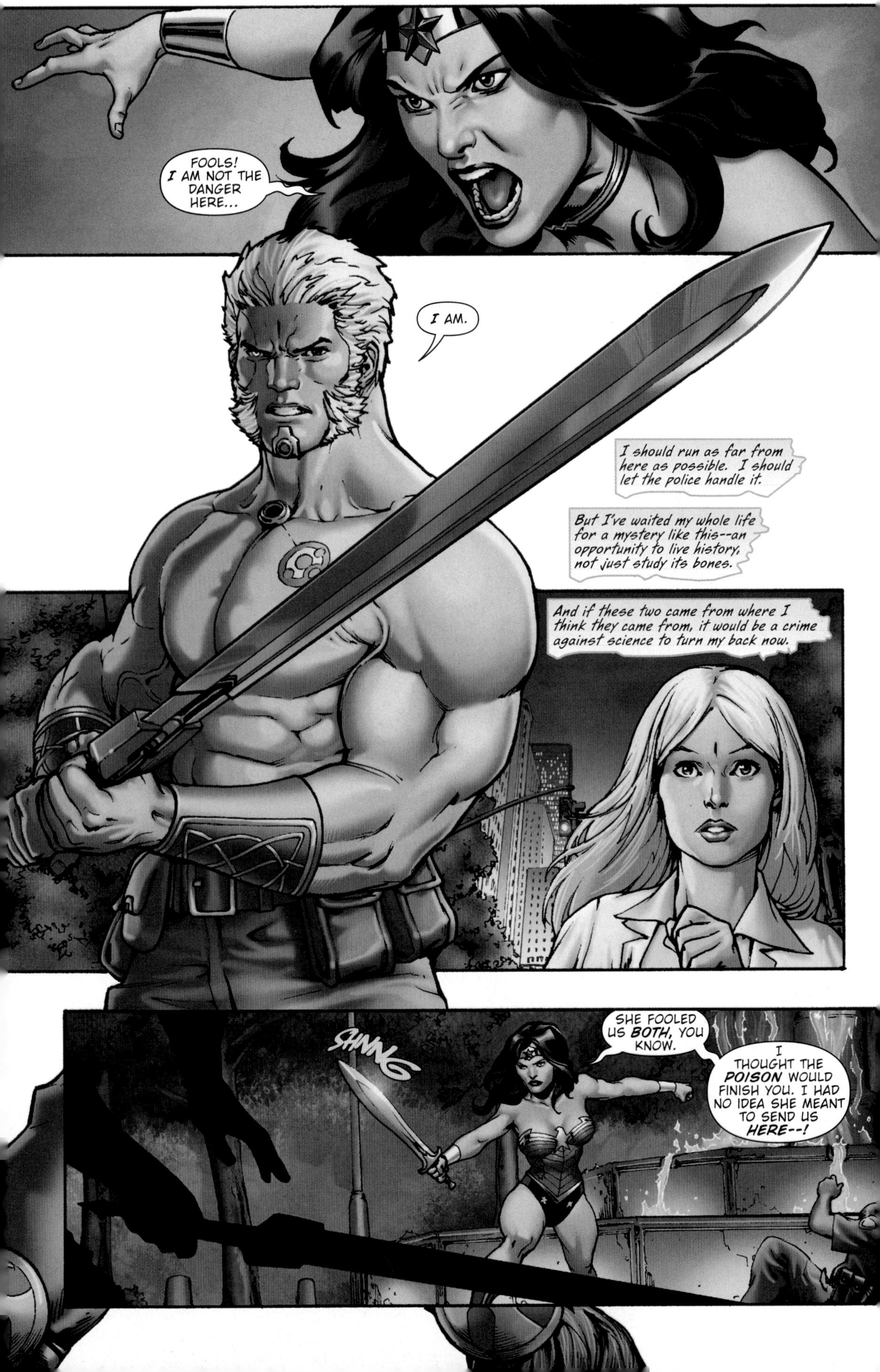
FOOLS! I AM NOT THE DANGER HERE...
I AM.
I should run as far from here as possible. I should let the police handle it.
But I've waited my whole life for a mystery like this--an opportunity to live history, not just study its bones.
And if these two came from where I think they came from, it would be a crime against science to turn my back now.
SHING
SHE FOOLED US BOTH, YOU KNOW.
I THOUGHT THE POISON WOULD FINISH YOU. I HAD NO IDEA SHE MEANT TO SEND US HERE--!

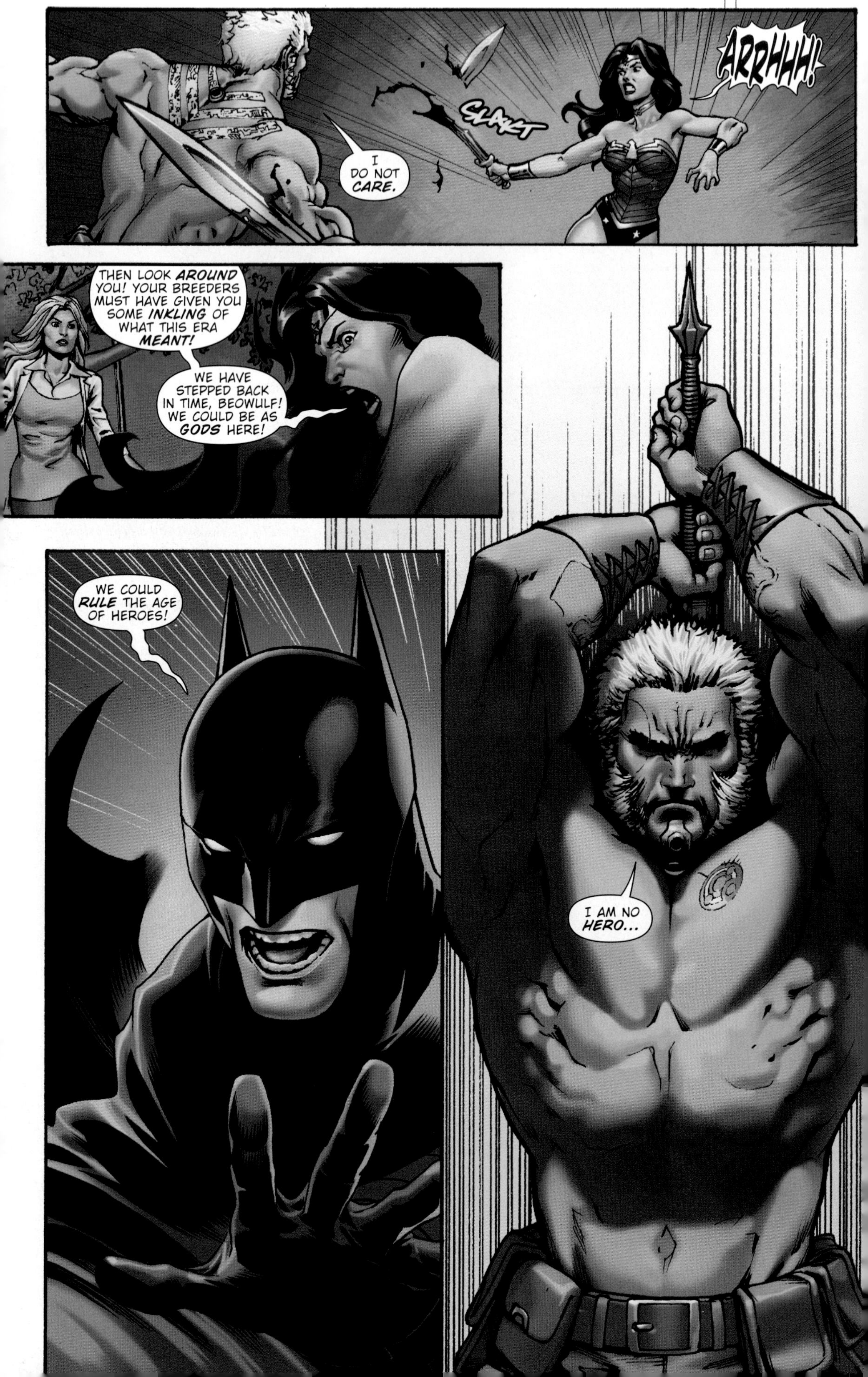
ARRHHH!
SLAKT
I DO NOT CARE.
THEN LOOK AROUND YOU! YOUR BREEDERS MUST HAVE GIVEN YOU SOME INKLING OF WHAT THIS ERA MEANT!
WE HAVE STEPPED BACK IN TIME, BEOWULF! WE COULD BE AS GODS HERE!
WE COULD RULE THE AGE OF HEROES!
I AM NO HERO...

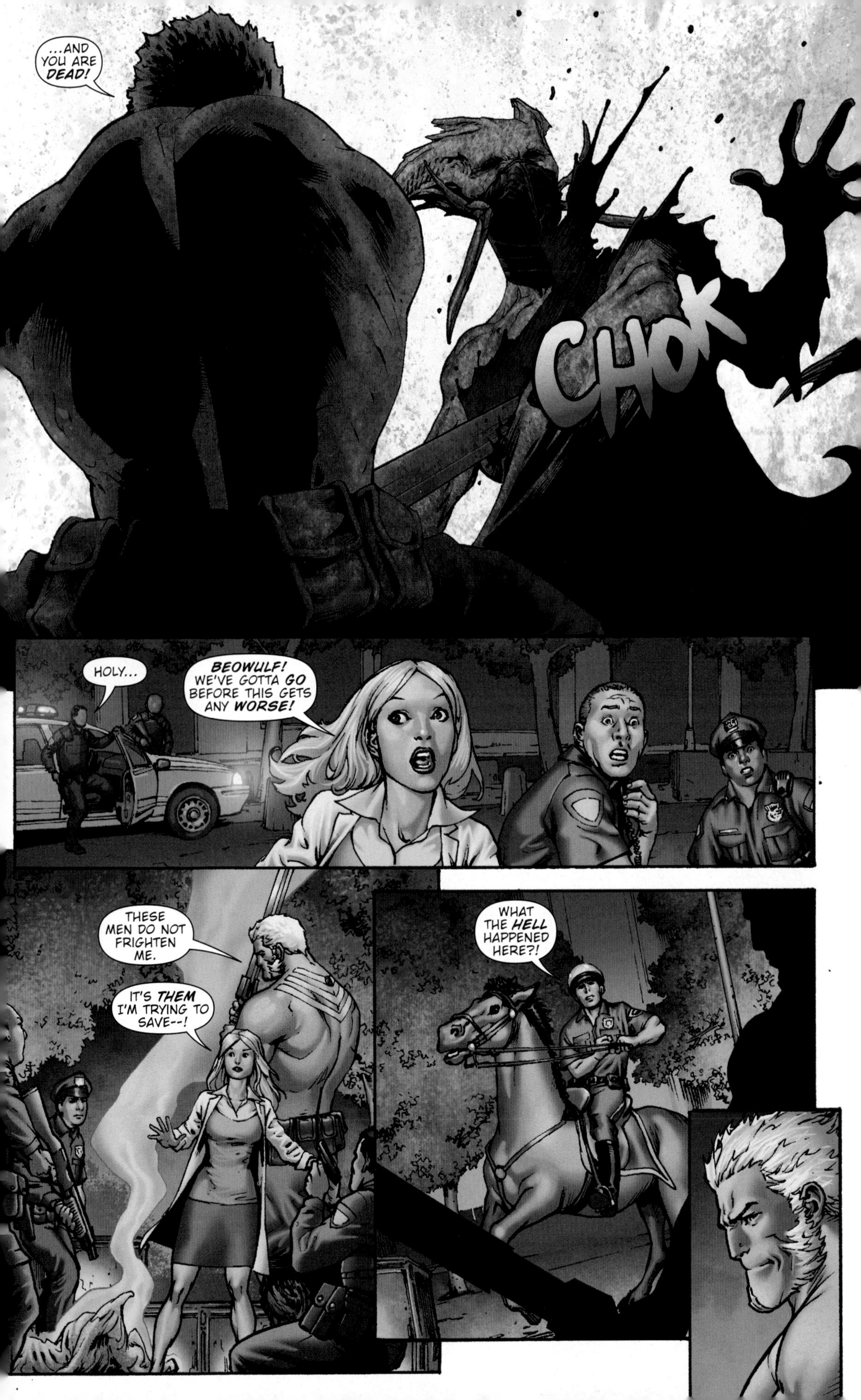
...AND YOU ARE DEAD!
CHOK
HOLY...
BEOWULF! WE'VE GOTTA GO BEFORE THIS GETS ANY WORSE!
THESE MEN DO NOT FRIGHTEN ME.
IT'S THEM I'M TRYING TO SAVE--!
WHAT THE HELL HAPPENED HERE?!

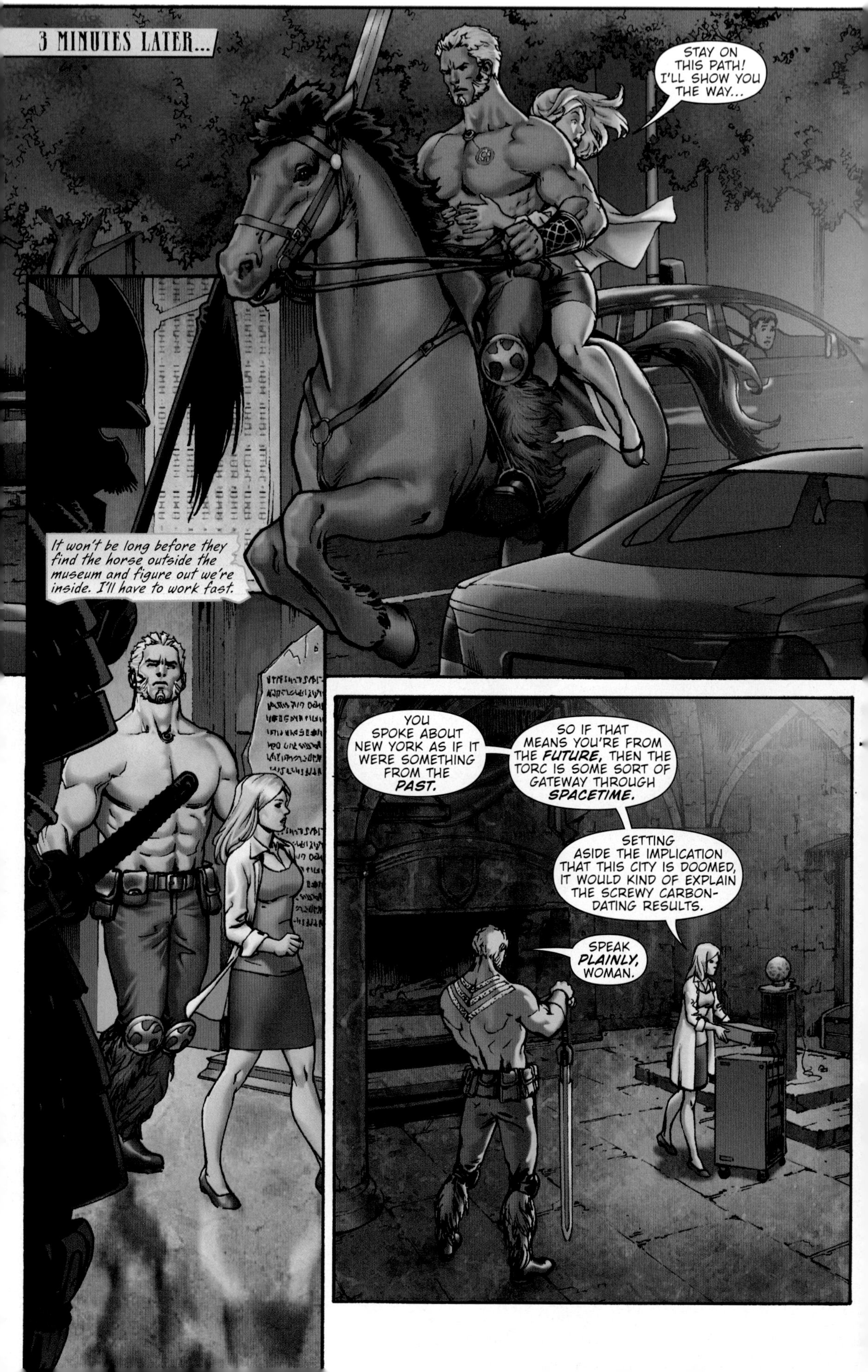
3 MINUTES LATER...
STAY ON THIS PATH! I'LL SHOW YOU THE WAY...
It won't be long before they find the horse outside the museum and figure out we're inside. I'll have to work fast.
YOU SPOKE ABOUT NEW YORK AS IF IT WERE SOMETHING FROM THE PAST.
SO IF THAT MEANS YOU'RE FROM THE FUTURE, THEN THE TORC IS SOME SORT OF GATEWAY THROUGH SPACETIME.
SETTING ASIDE THE IMPLICATION THAT THIS CITY IS DOOMED, IT WOULD KIND OF EXPLAIN THE SCREWY CARBON-DATING RESULTS.
SPEAK PLAINLY, WOMAN.

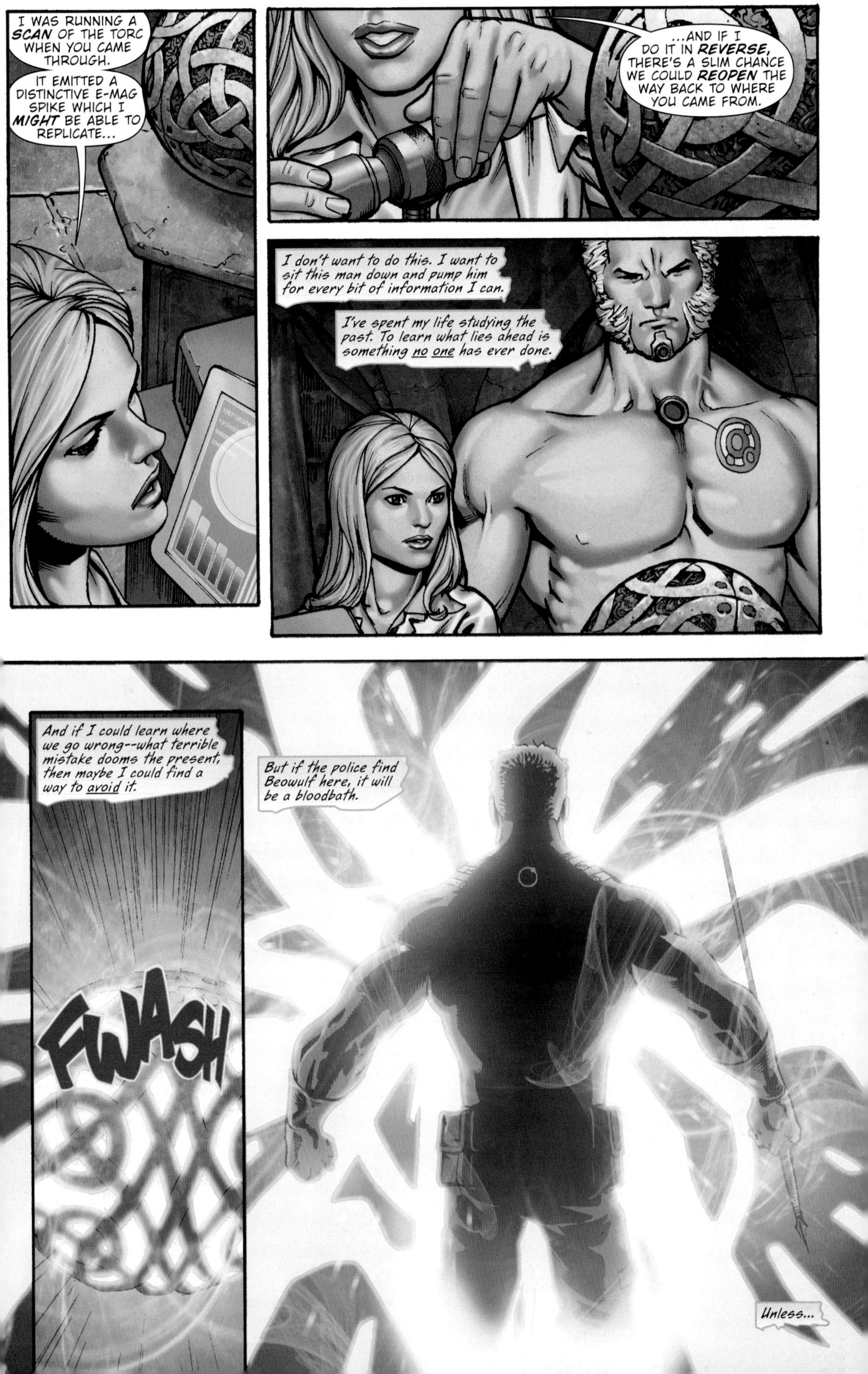

I WAS RUNNING A SCAN OF THE TORC WHEN YOU CAME THROUGH.
IT EMITTED A DISTINCTIVE E-MAG SPIKE WHICH I MIGHT BE ABLE TO REPLICATE...
...AND IF I DO IT IN REVERSE, THERE'S A SLIM CHANCE WE COULD REOPEN THE WAY BACK TO WHERE YOU CAME FROM.
I don't want to do this. I want to sit this man down and pump him for every bit of information I can.
I've spent my life studying the past. To learn what lies ahead is something no one has ever done.
And if I could learn where we go wrong--what terrible mistake dooms the present, then maybe I could find a way to avoid it.
FWASH
But if the police find Beowulf here, it will be a bloodbath.
Unless...

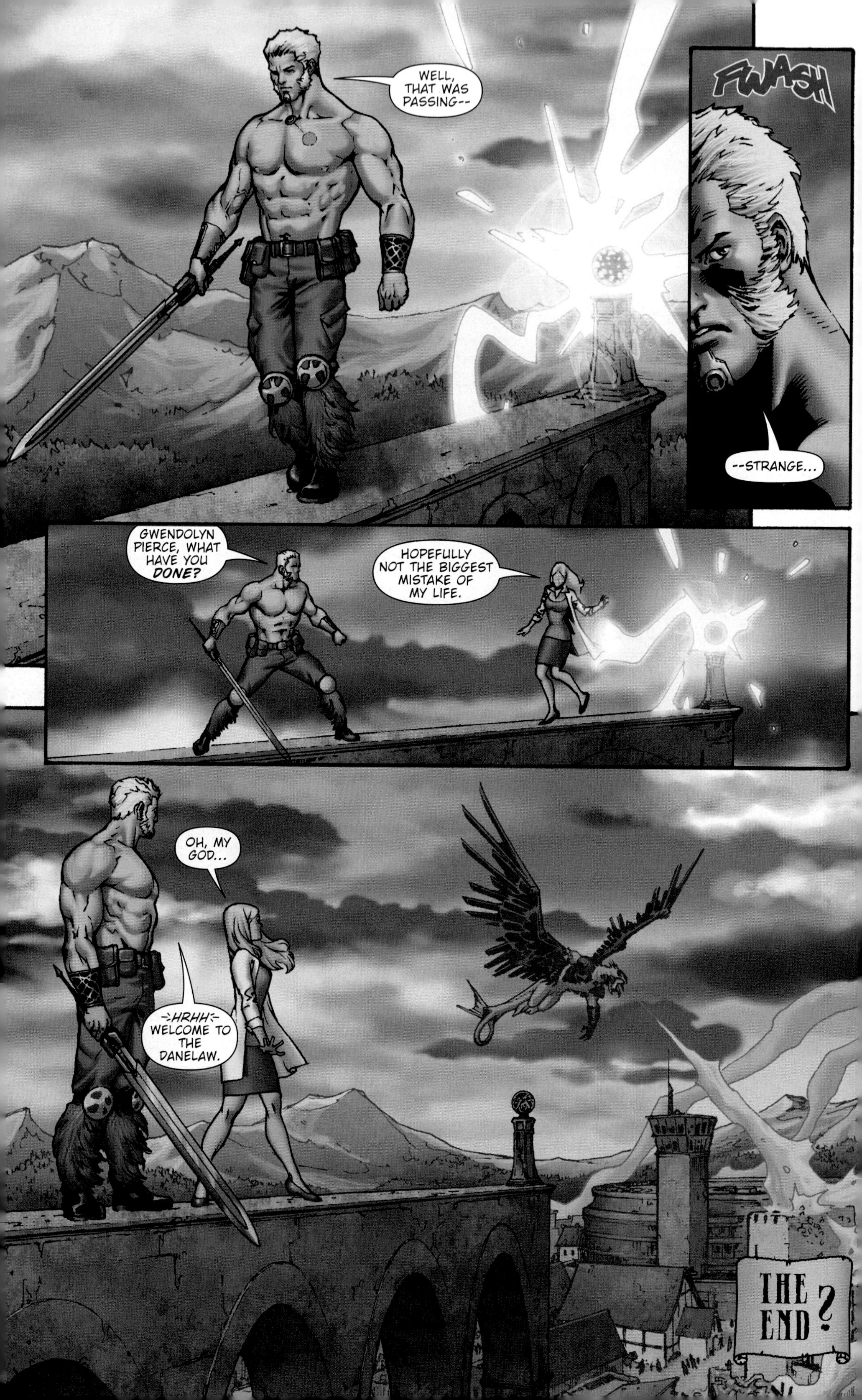
WELL, THAT WAS PASSING--
FWASH
--STRANGE...
GWENDOLYN PIERCE, WHAT HAVE YOU DONE?
HOPEFULLY NOT THE BIGGEST MISTAKE OF MY LIFE.
OH, MY GOD...
HRHH WELCOME TO THE DANELAW.
THE END?

STALKER

MARC ANDREYKO
writer

ANDREI BRESSAN
artist

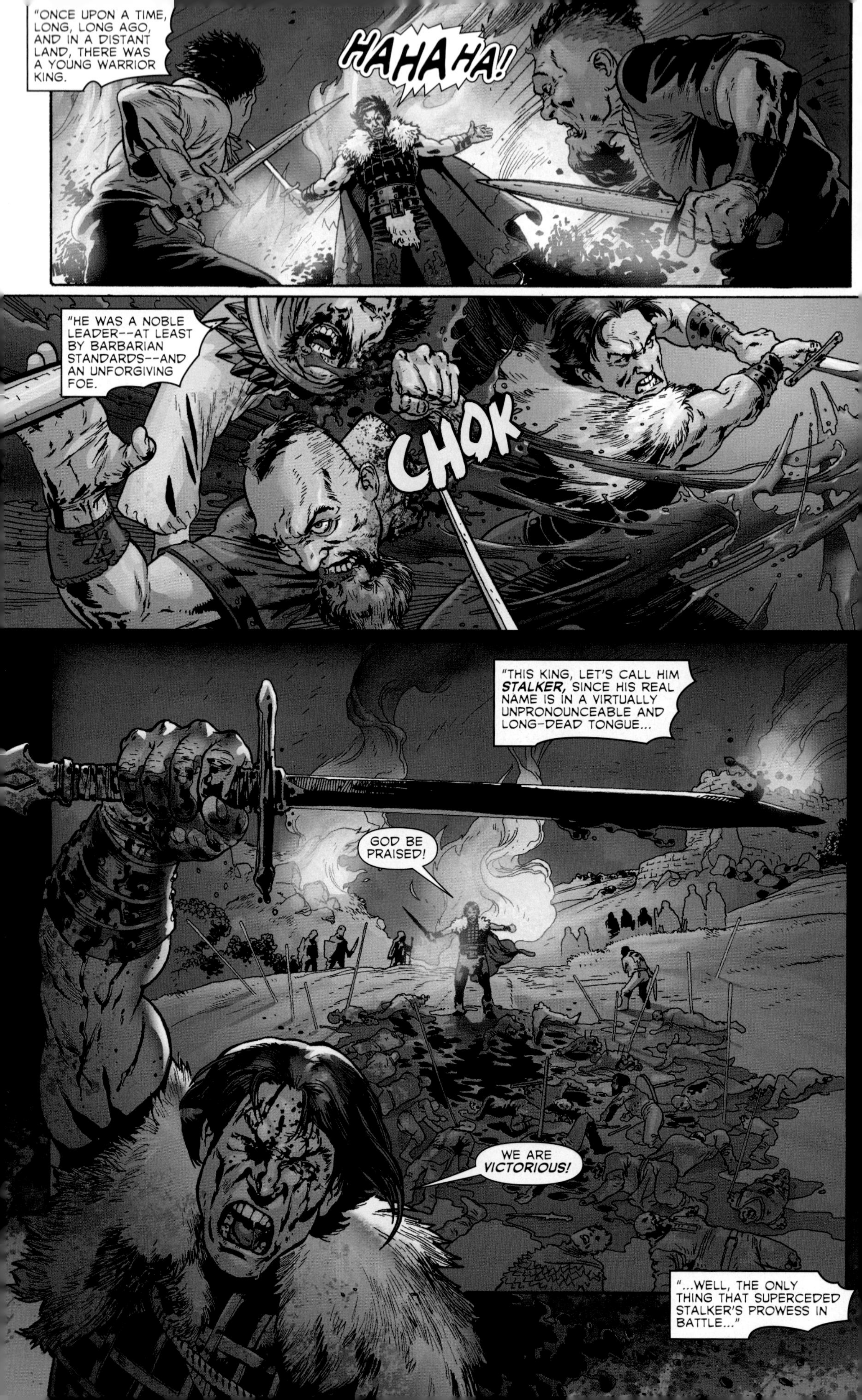
"ONCE UPON A TIME, LONG, LONG AGO, AND IN A DISTANT LAND, THERE WAS A YOUNG WARRIOR KING.
HAHAHA!
"HE WAS A NOBLE LEADER--AT LEAST BY BARBARIAN STANDARDS--AND AN UNFORGIVING FOE.
CHOK
"THIS KING, LET'S CALL HIM *STALKER,* SINCE HIS REAL NAME IS IN A VIRTUALLY UNPRONOUNCEABLE AND LONG-DEAD TONGUE...
GOD BE PRAISED!
WE ARE *VICTORIOUS!*
"...WELL, THE ONLY THING THAT SUPERCEDED STALKER'S PROWESS IN BATTLE..."

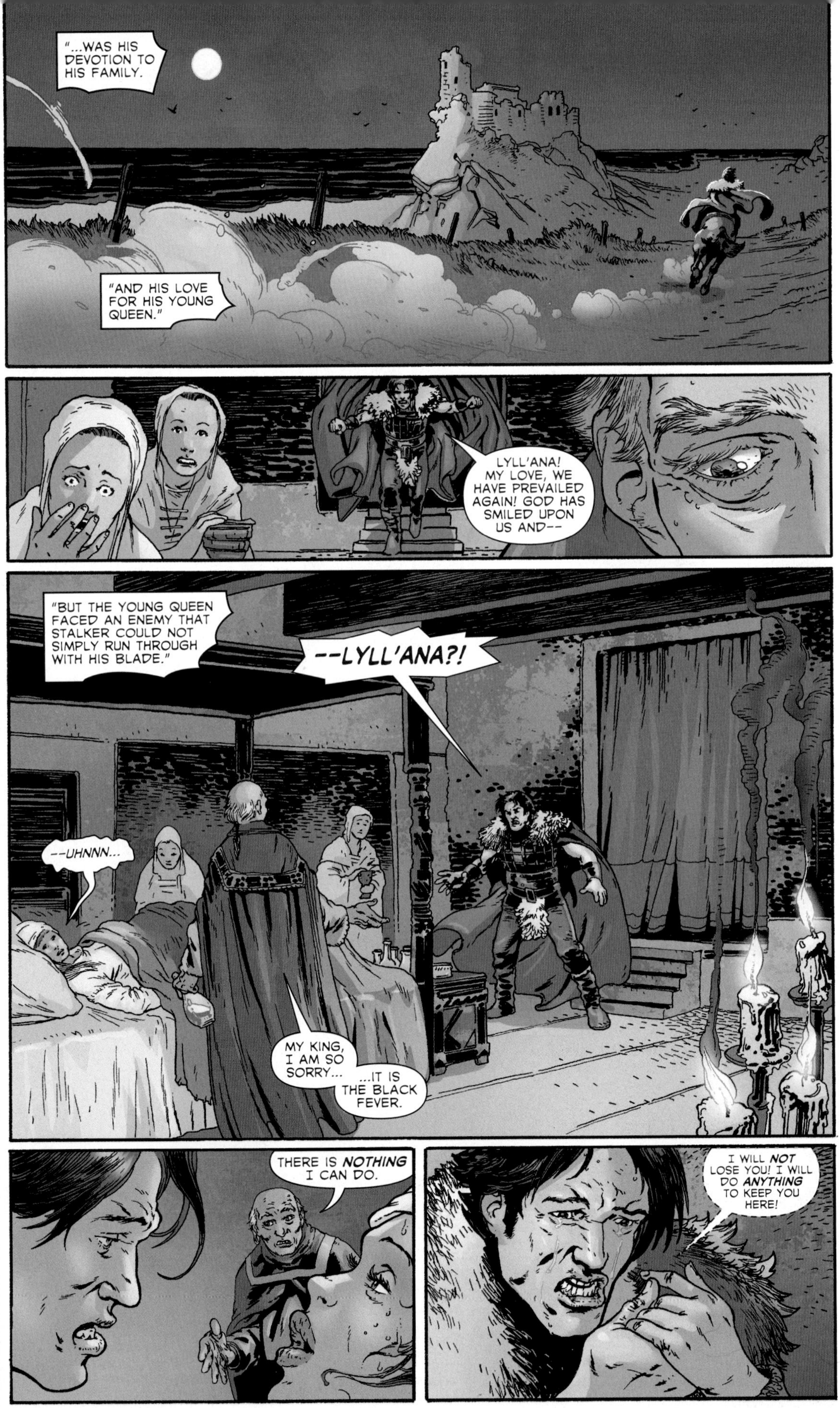
"...WAS HIS DEVOTION TO HIS FAMILY.
"AND HIS LOVE FOR HIS YOUNG QUEEN."
LYLL'ANA! MY LOVE, WE HAVE PREVAILED AGAIN! GOD HAS SMILED UPON US AND--
"BUT THE YOUNG QUEEN FACED AN ENEMY THAT STALKER COULD NOT SIMPLY RUN THROUGH WITH HIS BLADE."
--LYLL'ANA?!
--UHNNN...
MY KING, I AM SO SORRY...
...IT IS THE BLACK FEVER.
THERE IS NOTHING I CAN DO.
I WILL NOT LOSE YOU! I WILL DO ANYTHING TO KEEP YOU HERE!

MY LORD, I HAVE BEEN YOUR FAITHFUL AND RIGHTEOUS SERVANT. I HAVE SERVED YOU UNFAILINGLY.

MY LIFE IS YOURS FOR THE TAKING. ALL I ASK OF YOU IS THIS ONE THING--*SAVE* MY BELOVED AND OUR *UNBORN* CHILD.

"THE POOR, DESPERATE KING WAS RUNNING OUT OF OPTIONS."

"AND HIS GOD? HIS GOD WAS NOTICEABLY *QUIET*."

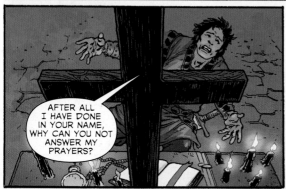

AFTER ALL I HAVE DONE IN YOUR NAME, WHY CAN YOU NOT ANSWER MY PRAYERS?

PERHAPS YOUR GOD IS NO LONGER THERE?

WHO *DARES* SPEAK SUCH BLASPHEMY TO THEIR KING?

"HIS PRAYERS WERE ANSWERED, BUT NOT BY WHO HE HAD HOPED."

I DO, O KING.

HALT OR I SHALL *RUN* YOU *THROUGH*!

GREAT KING, I MEAN YOU NO HARM.

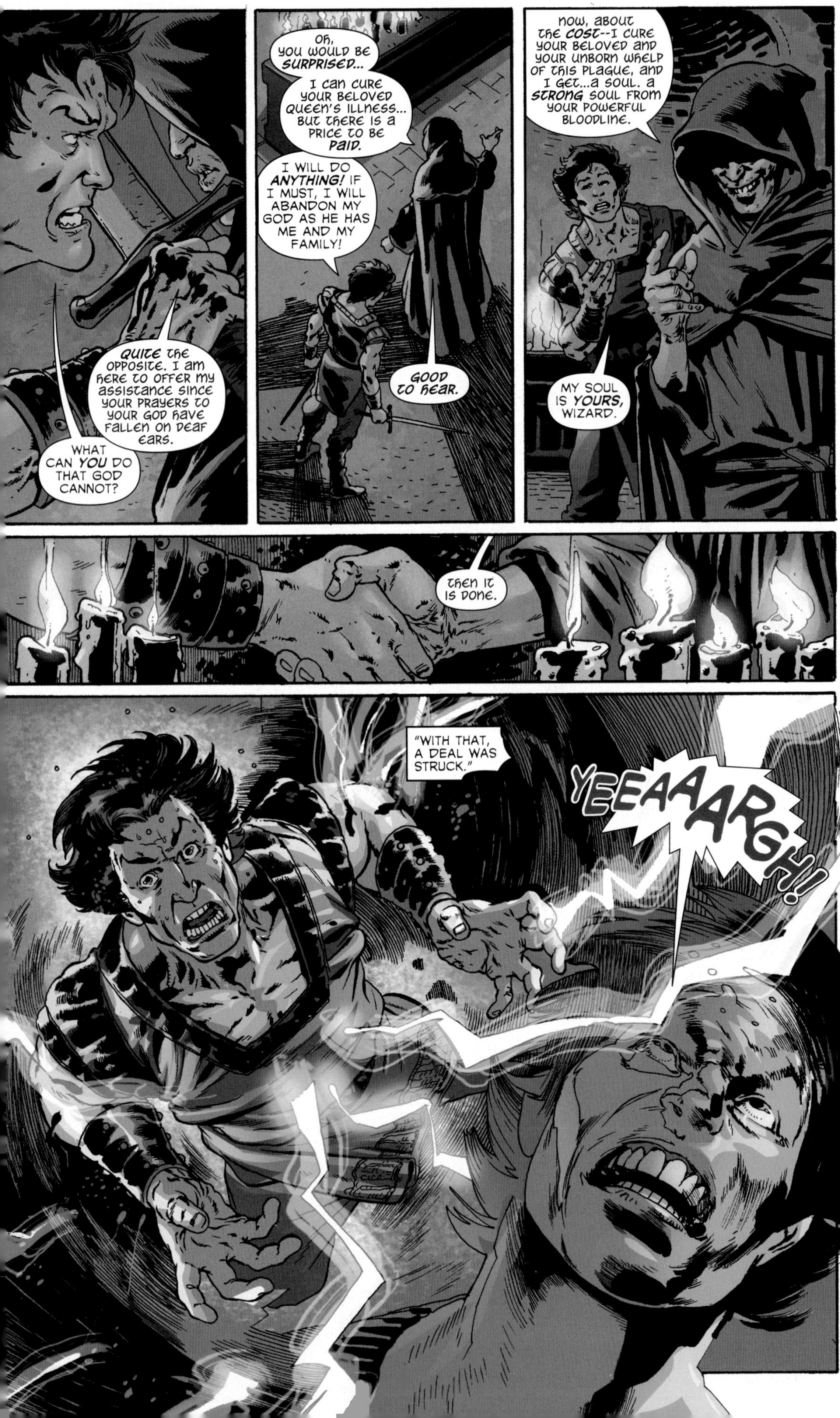
QUITE THE OPPOSITE. I AM HERE TO OFFER MY ASSISTANCE SINCE YOUR PRAYERS TO YOUR GOD HAVE FALLEN ON DEAF EARS.
WHAT CAN YOU DO THAT GOD CANNOT?
OH, YOU WOULD BE SURPRISED...
I CAN CURE YOUR BELOVED QUEEN'S ILLNESS... BUT THERE IS A PRICE TO BE PAID.
I WILL DO ANYTHING! IF I MUST, I WILL ABANDON MY GOD AS HE HAS ME AND MY FAMILY!
GOOD TO HEAR.
NOW, ABOUT THE COST--I CURE YOUR BELOVED AND YOUR UNBORN WHELP OF THIS PLAGUE, AND I GET...A SOUL. A STRONG SOUL FROM YOUR POWERFUL BLOODLINE.
MY SOUL IS YOURS, WIZARD.
THEN IT IS DONE.
"WITH THAT, A DEAL WAS STRUCK."
YEEAAARGH!!

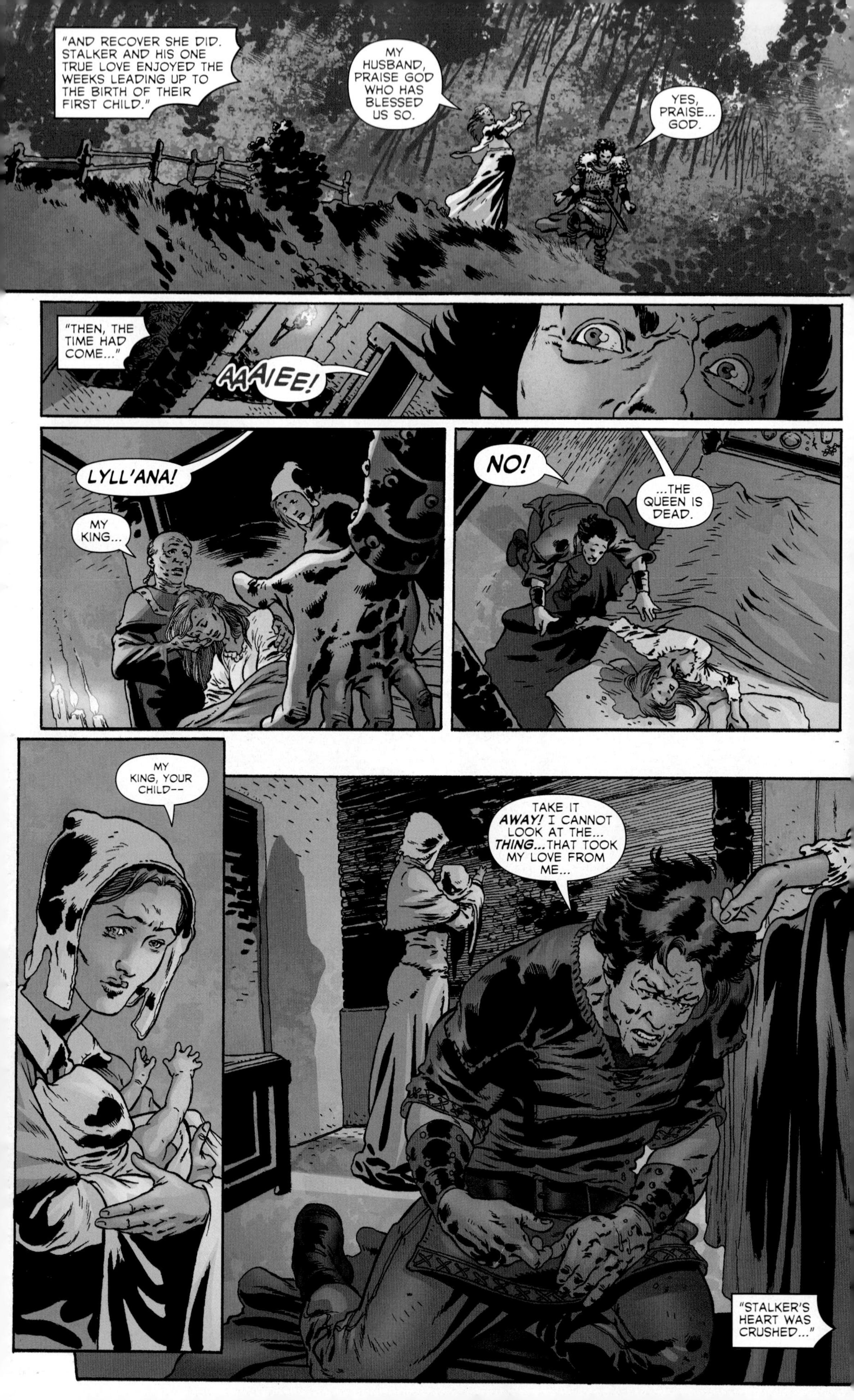
"AND RECOVER SHE DID. STALKER AND HIS ONE TRUE LOVE ENJOYED THE WEEKS LEADING UP TO THE BIRTH OF THEIR FIRST CHILD."
MY HUSBAND, PRAISE GOD WHO HAS BLESSED US SO.
YES, PRAISE... GOD.
"THEN, THE TIME HAD COME..."
AAAIEE!
LYLL'ANA!
MY KING...
NO!
...THE QUEEN IS DEAD.
MY KING, YOUR CHILD--
TAKE IT AWAY! I CANNOT LOOK AT THE... THING...THAT TOOK MY LOVE FROM ME...
"STALKER'S HEART WAS CRUSHED..."

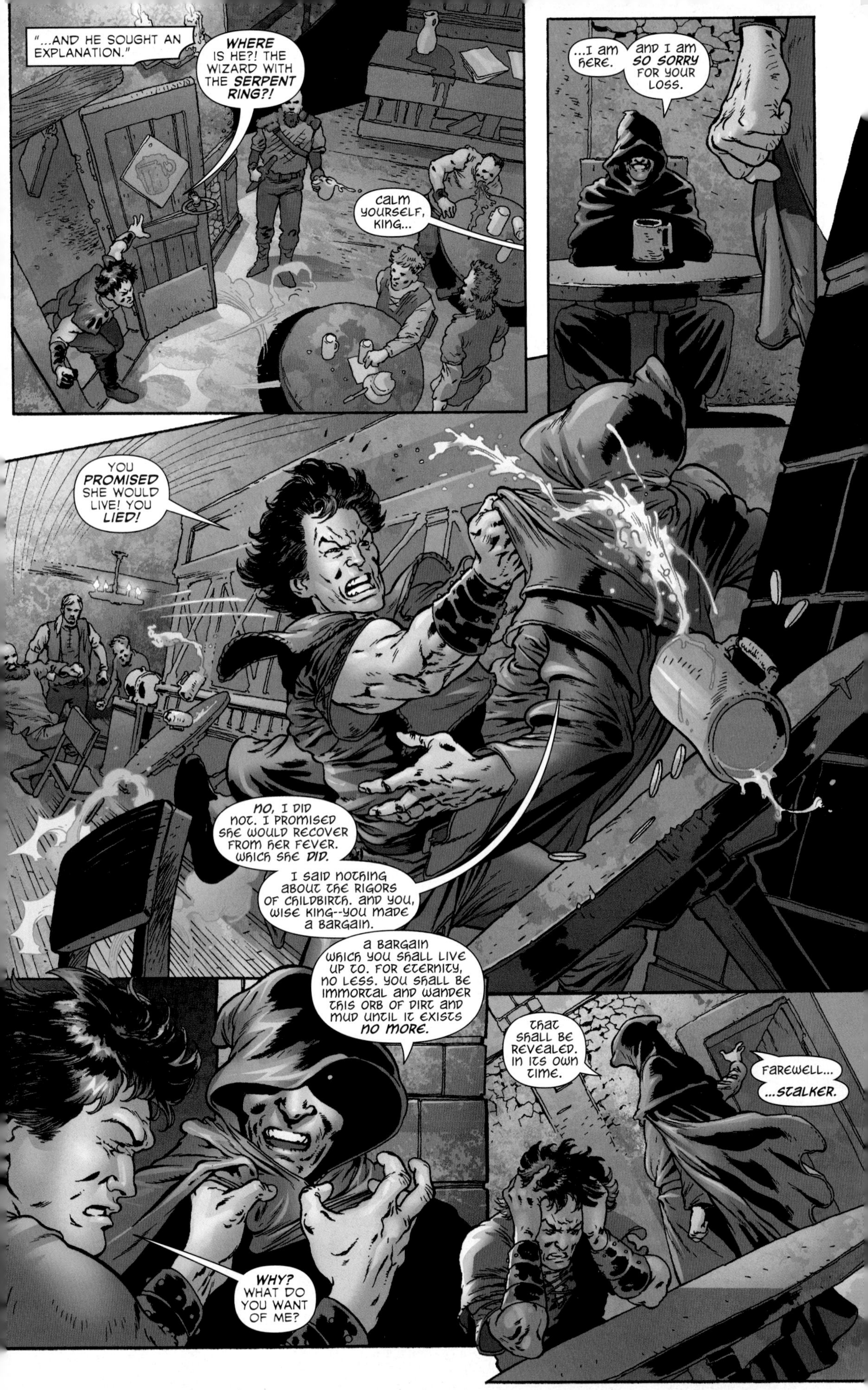
"...AND HE SOUGHT AN EXPLANATION."
WHERE IS HE?! THE WIZARD WITH THE SERPENT RING?!
CALM YOURSELF, KING...
...I AM HERE.
AND I AM SO SORRY FOR YOUR LOSS.
YOU PROMISED SHE WOULD LIVE! YOU LIED!
NO, I DID NOT. I PROMISED SHE WOULD RECOVER FROM HER FEVER. WHICH SHE DID.
I SAID NOTHING ABOUT THE RIGORS OF CHILDBIRTH. AND YOU, WISE KING--YOU MADE A BARGAIN.
A BARGAIN WHICH YOU SHALL LIVE UP TO. FOR ETERNITY, NO LESS. YOU SHALL BE IMMORTAL AND WANDER THIS ORB OF DIRT AND MUD UNTIL IT EXISTS NO MORE.
WHY? WHAT DO YOU WANT OF ME?
THAT SHALL BE REVEALED. IN ITS OWN TIME.
FAREWELL...
...STALKER.

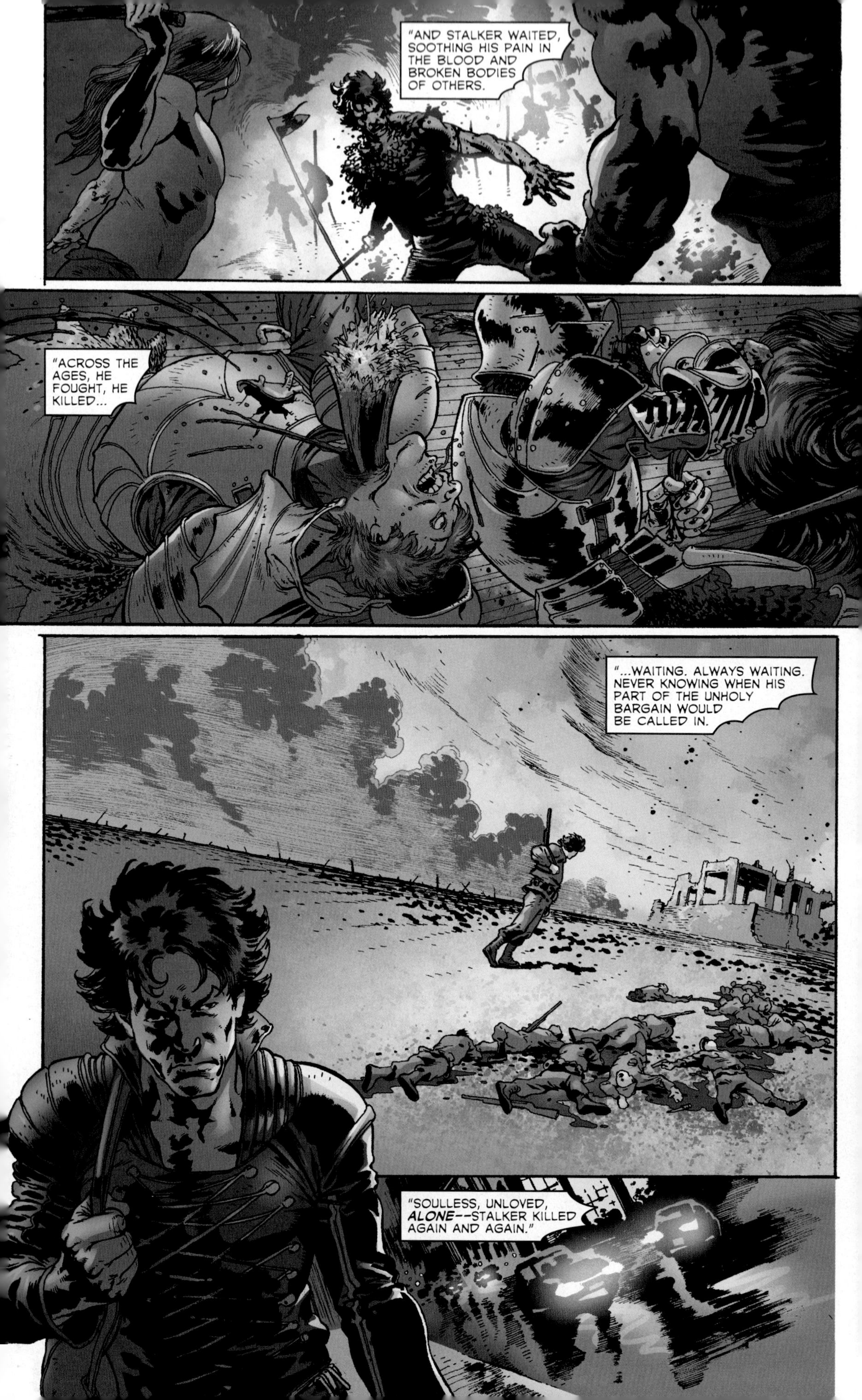
"AND STALKER WAITED, SOOTHING HIS PAIN IN THE BLOOD AND BROKEN BODIES OF OTHERS.
"ACROSS THE AGES, HE FOUGHT, HE KILLED...
"...WAITING. ALWAYS WAITING. NEVER KNOWING WHEN HIS PART OF THE UNHOLY BARGAIN WOULD BE CALLED IN.
"SOULLESS, UNLOVED, ALONE--STALKER KILLED AGAIN AND AGAIN."

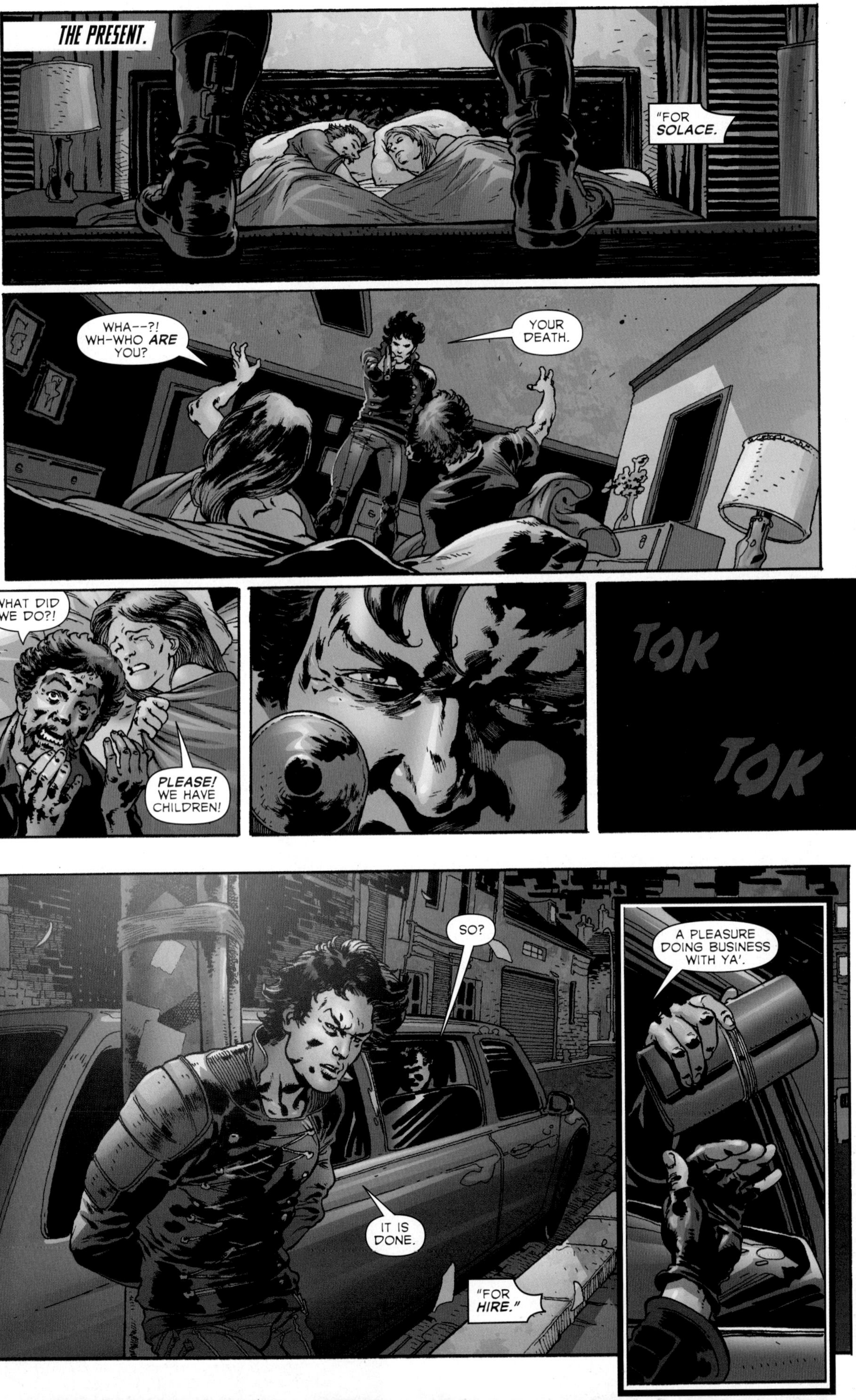
THE PRESENT.
"FOR SOLACE.
WHA--?! WH-WHO ARE YOU?
YOUR DEATH.
WHAT DID WE DO?!
PLEASE! WE HAVE CHILDREN!
TOK
TOK
SO?
IT IS DONE.
"FOR HIRE."
A PLEASURE DOING BUSINESS WITH YA'.

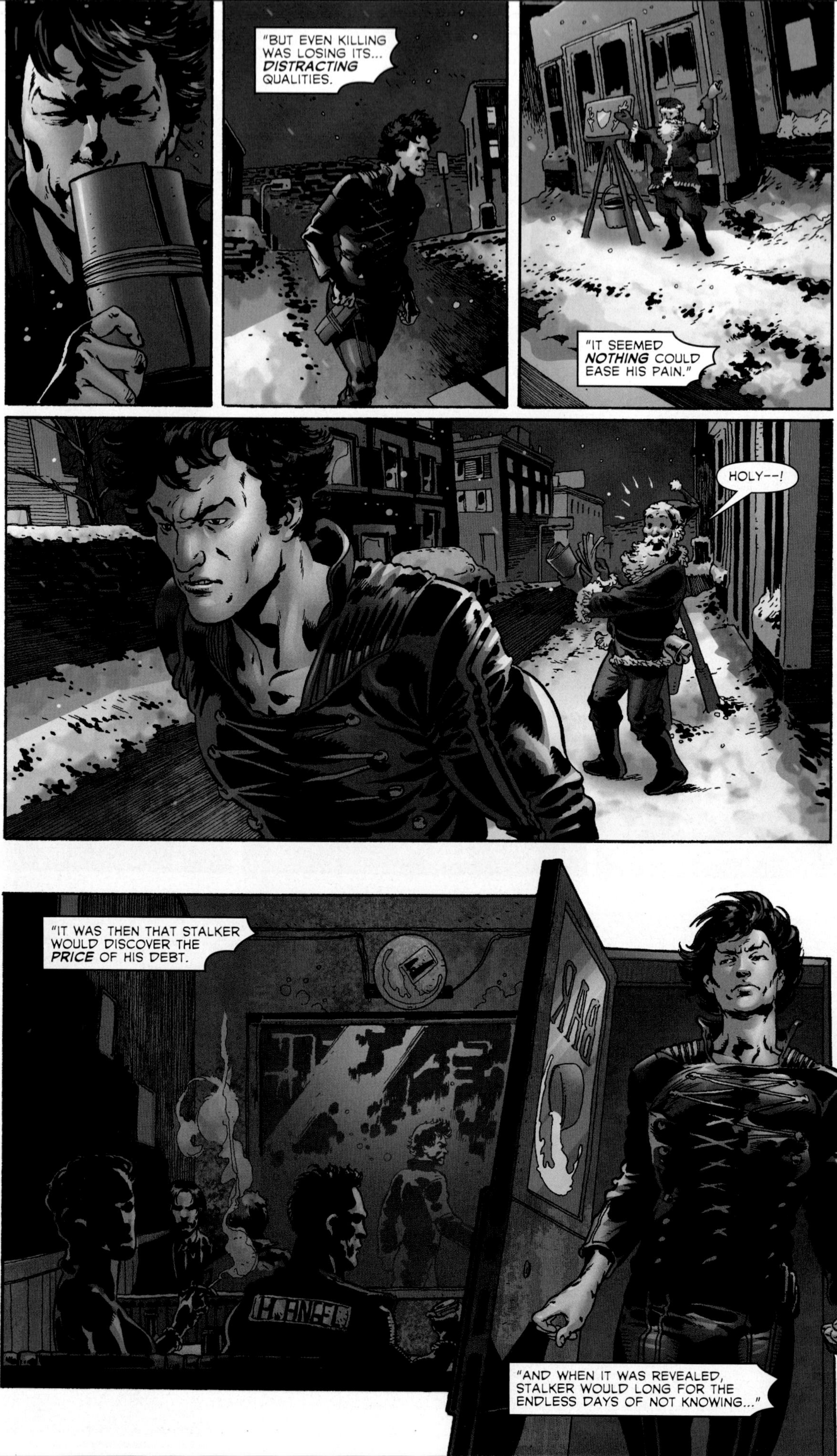
"BUT EVEN KILLING WAS LOSING ITS... DISTRACTING QUALITIES.
"IT SEEMED NOTHING COULD EASE HIS PAIN."
HOLY--!
"IT WAS THEN THAT STALKER WOULD DISCOVER THE PRICE OF HIS DEBT.
"AND WHEN IT WAS REVEALED, STALKER WOULD LONG FOR THE ENDLESS DAYS OF NOT KNOWING..."

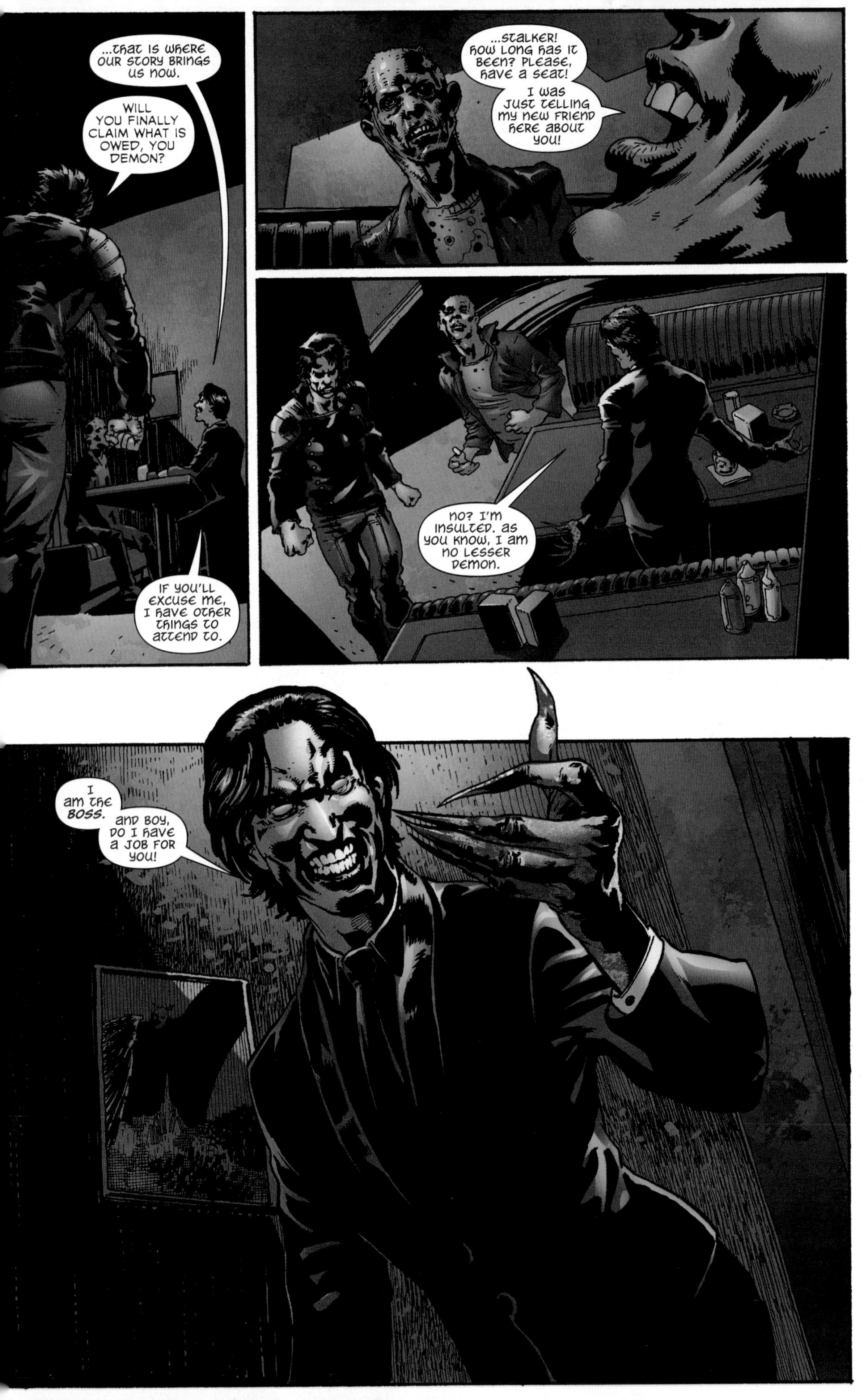
...THAT IS WHERE OUR STORY BRINGS US NOW.
WILL YOU FINALLY CLAIM WHAT IS OWED, YOU DEMON?
IF YOU'LL EXCUSE ME, I HAVE OTHER THINGS TO ATTEND TO.
...STALKER! HOW LONG HAS IT BEEN? PLEASE, HAVE A SEAT!
I WAS JUST TELLING MY NEW FRIEND HERE ABOUT YOU!
NO? I'M INSULTED. AS YOU KNOW, I AM NO LESSER DEMON.
I AM THE BOSS.
AND BOY, DO I HAVE A JOB FOR YOU!

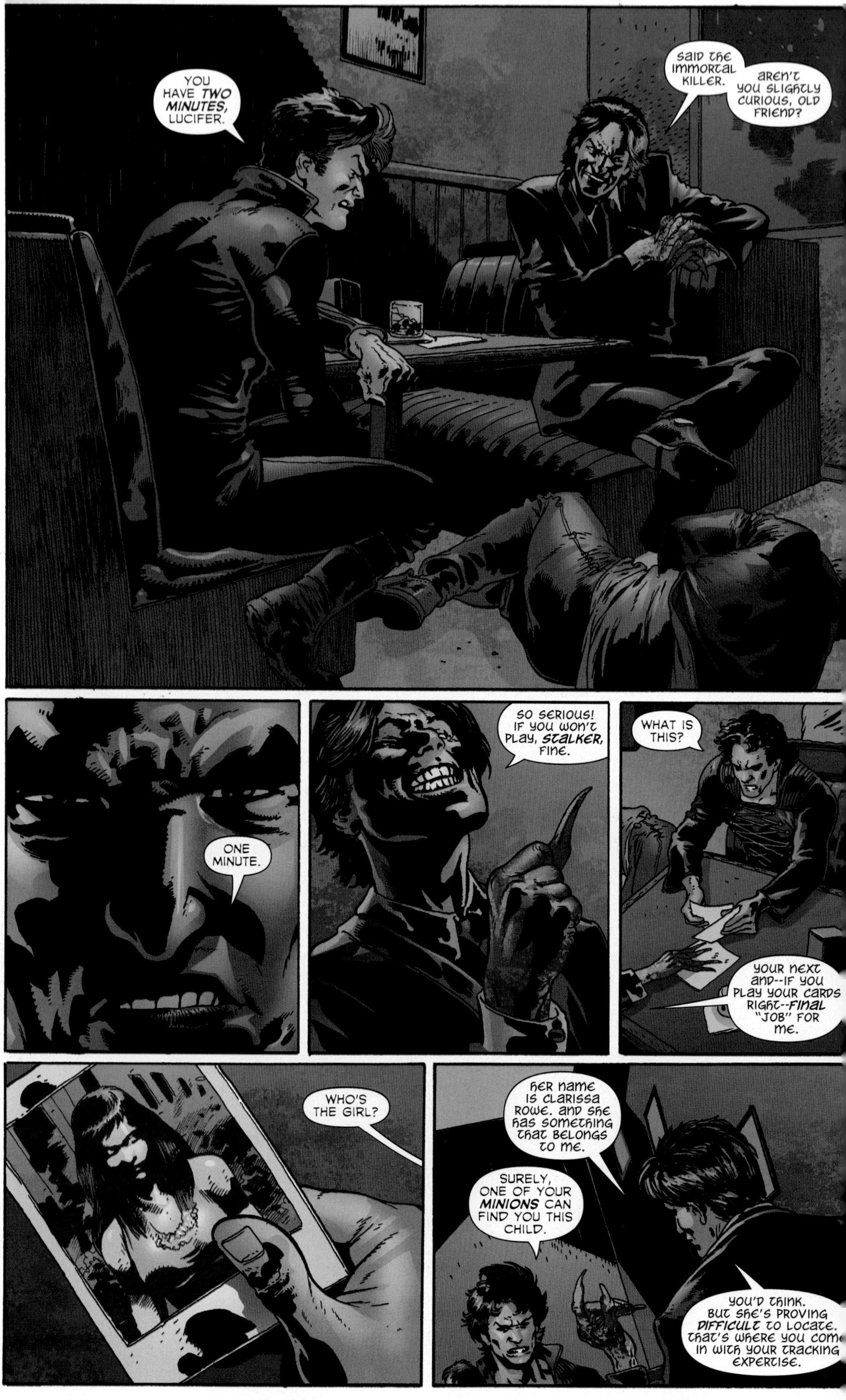

YOU HAVE TWO MINUTES, LUCIFER.
SAID THE IMMORTAL KILLER.
AREN'T YOU SLIGHTLY CURIOUS, OLD FRIEND?
ONE MINUTE.
SO SERIOUS! IF YOU WON'T PLAY, STALKER, FINE.
WHAT IS THIS?
YOUR NEXT AND--IF YOU PLAY YOUR CARDS RIGHT--FINAL "JOB" FOR ME.
WHO'S THE GIRL?
HER NAME IS CLARISSA ROWE. AND SHE HAS SOMETHING THAT BELONGS TO ME.
SURELY, ONE OF YOUR MINIONS CAN FIND YOU THIS CHILD.
YOU'D THINK. BUT SHE'S PROVING DIFFICULT TO LOCATE. THAT'S WHERE YOU COM IN WITH YOUR TRACKING EXPERTISE.

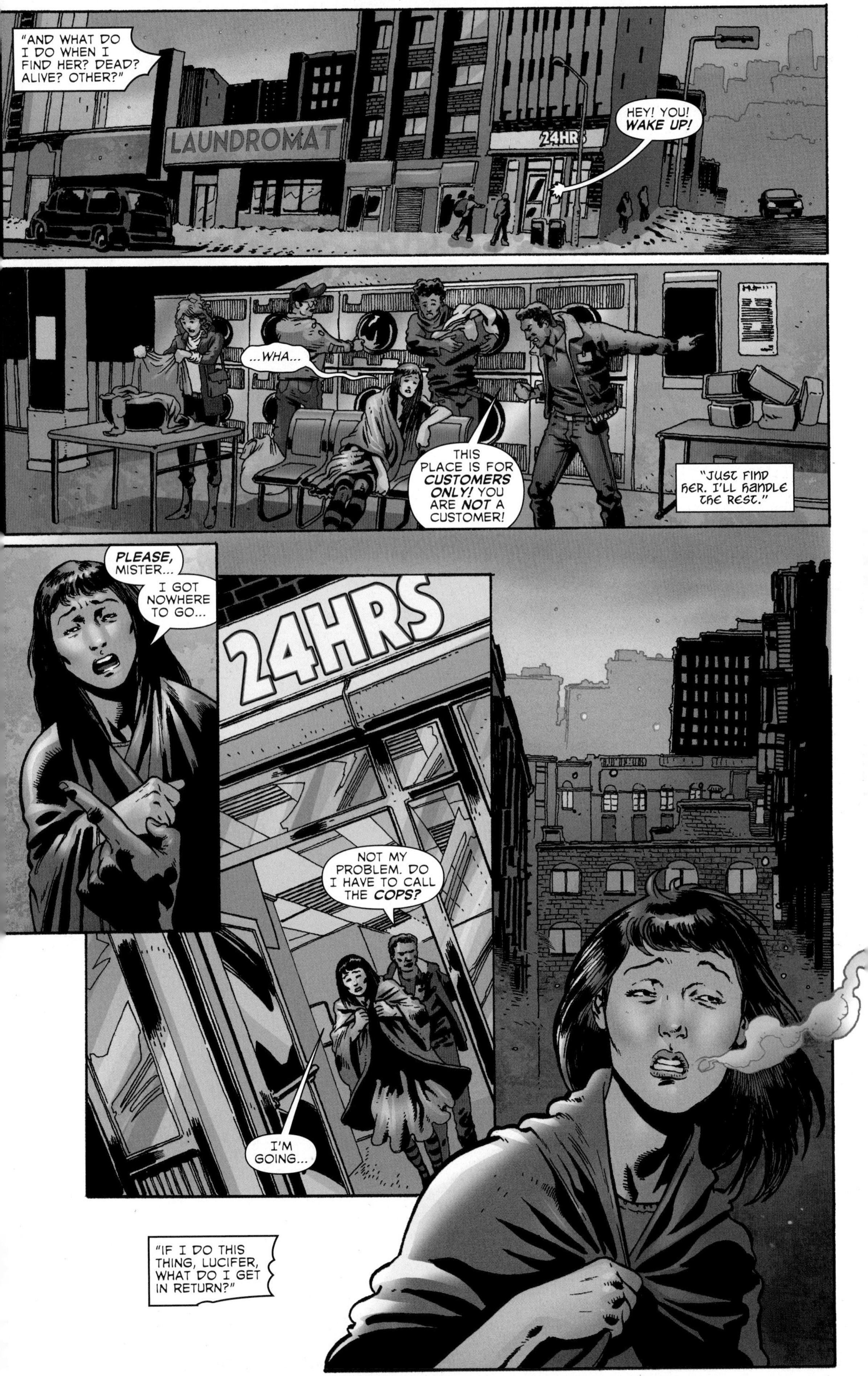
"AND WHAT DO I DO WHEN I FIND HER? DEAD? ALIVE? OTHER?"
LAUNDROMAT
24HRS
HEY! YOU! WAKE UP!
...WHA...
THIS PLACE IS FOR CUSTOMERS ONLY! YOU ARE NOT A CUSTOMER!
"JUST FIND HER. I'LL HANDLE THE REST."
PLEASE, MISTER...
I GOT NOWHERE TO GO...
24HRS
NOT MY PROBLEM. DO I HAVE TO CALL THE COPS?
I'M GOING...
"IF I DO THIS THING, LUCIFER, WHAT DO I GET IN RETURN?"

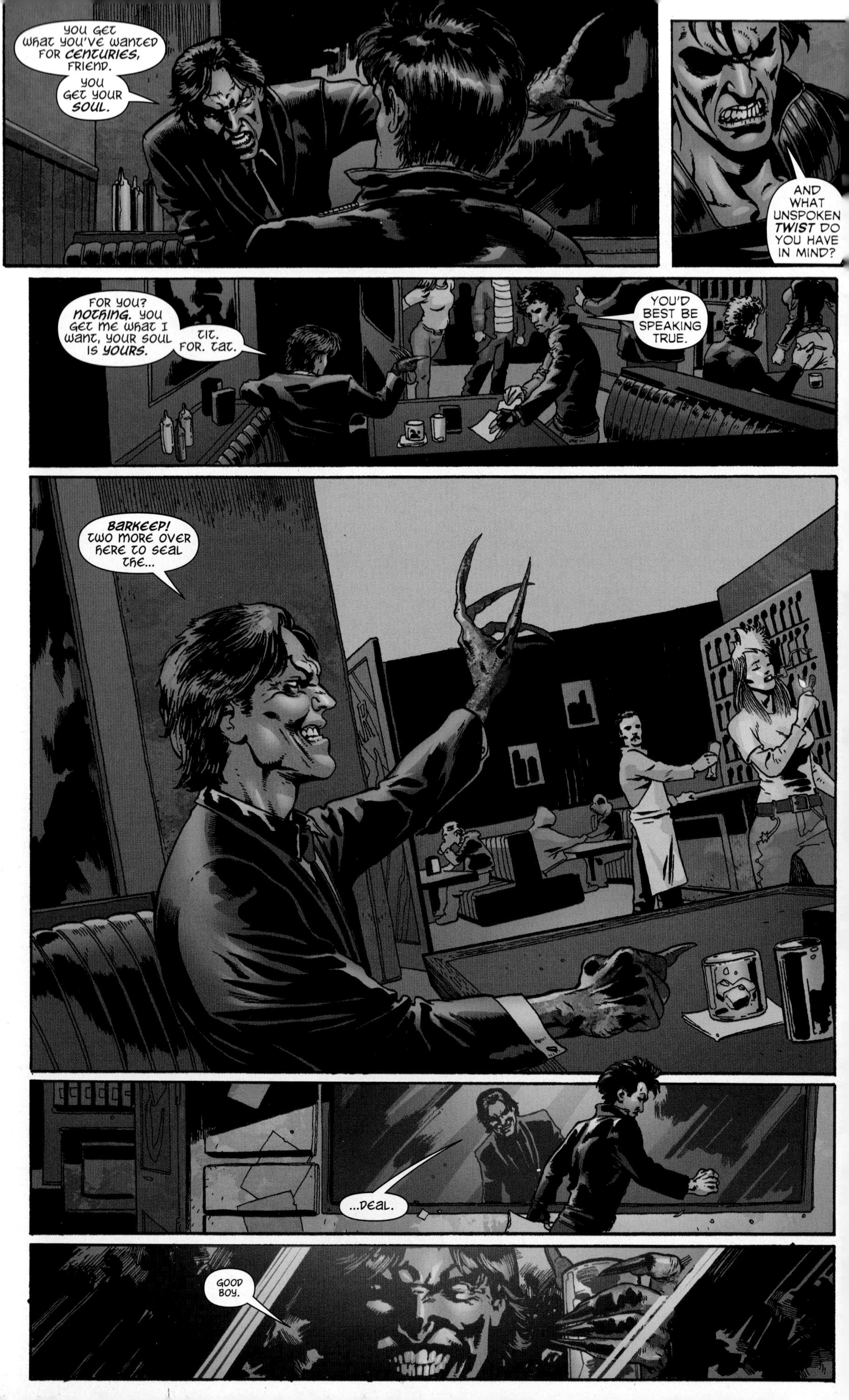
YOU GET WHAT YOU'VE WANTED FOR CENTURIES, FRIEND.
YOU GET YOUR SOUL.
AND WHAT UNSPOKEN TWIST DO YOU HAVE IN MIND?
FOR YOU? NOTHING. YOU GET ME WHAT I WANT, YOUR SOUL IS YOURS.
TIT. FOR. TAT.
YOU'D BEST BE SPEAKING TRUE.
BARKEEP! TWO MORE OVER HERE TO SEAL THE...
...DEAL.
GOOD BOY.

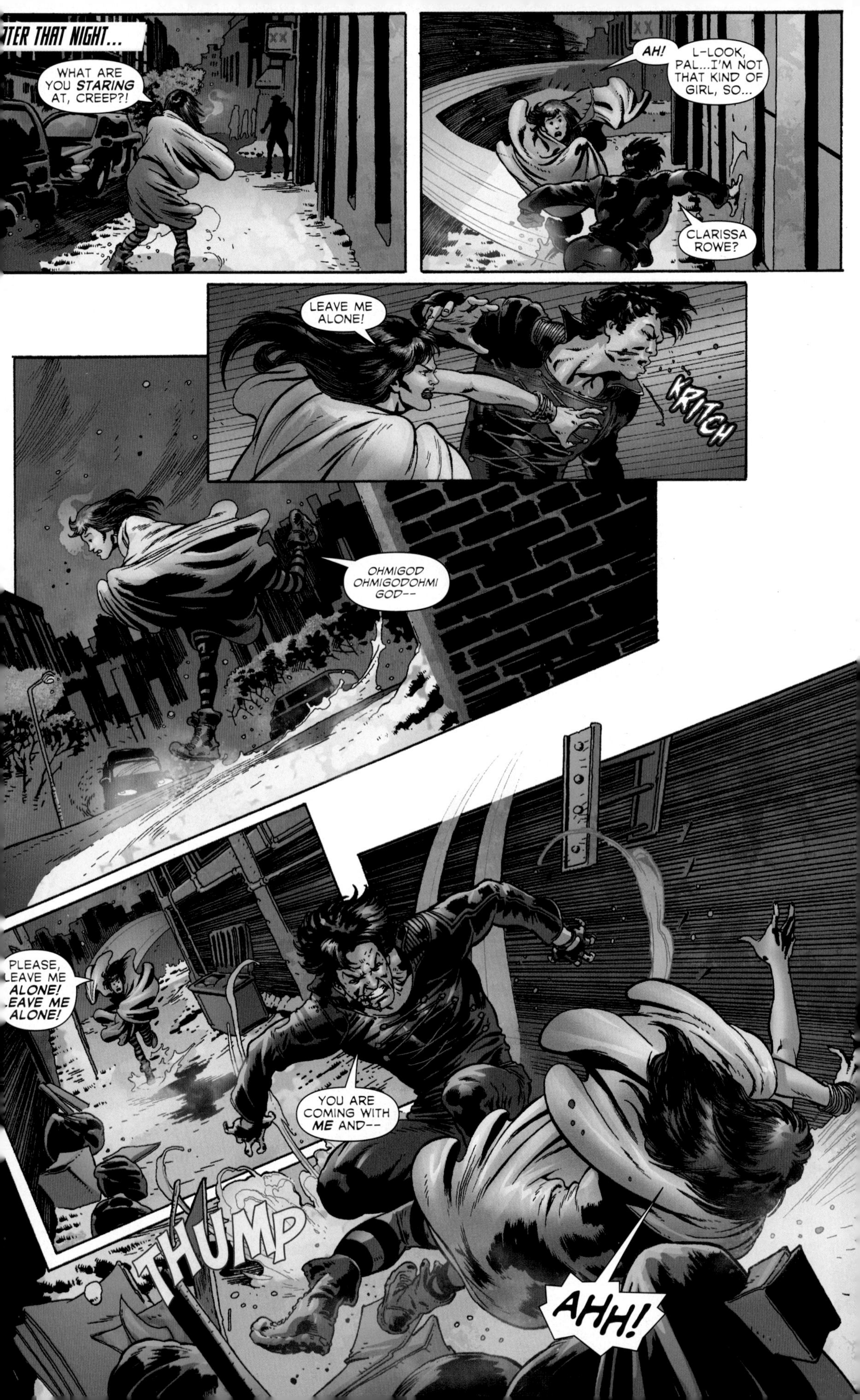

TER THAT NIGHT...
WHAT ARE YOU STARING AT, CREEP?!
AH!
L-LOOK, PAL...I'M NOT THAT KIND OF GIRL, SO...
CLARISSA ROWE?
LEAVE ME ALONE!
KRITCH
OHMIGOD OHMIGODOHMI GOD--
PLEASE, LEAVE ME ALONE! LEAVE ME ALONE!
YOU ARE COMING WITH ME AND--
THUMP
AHH!

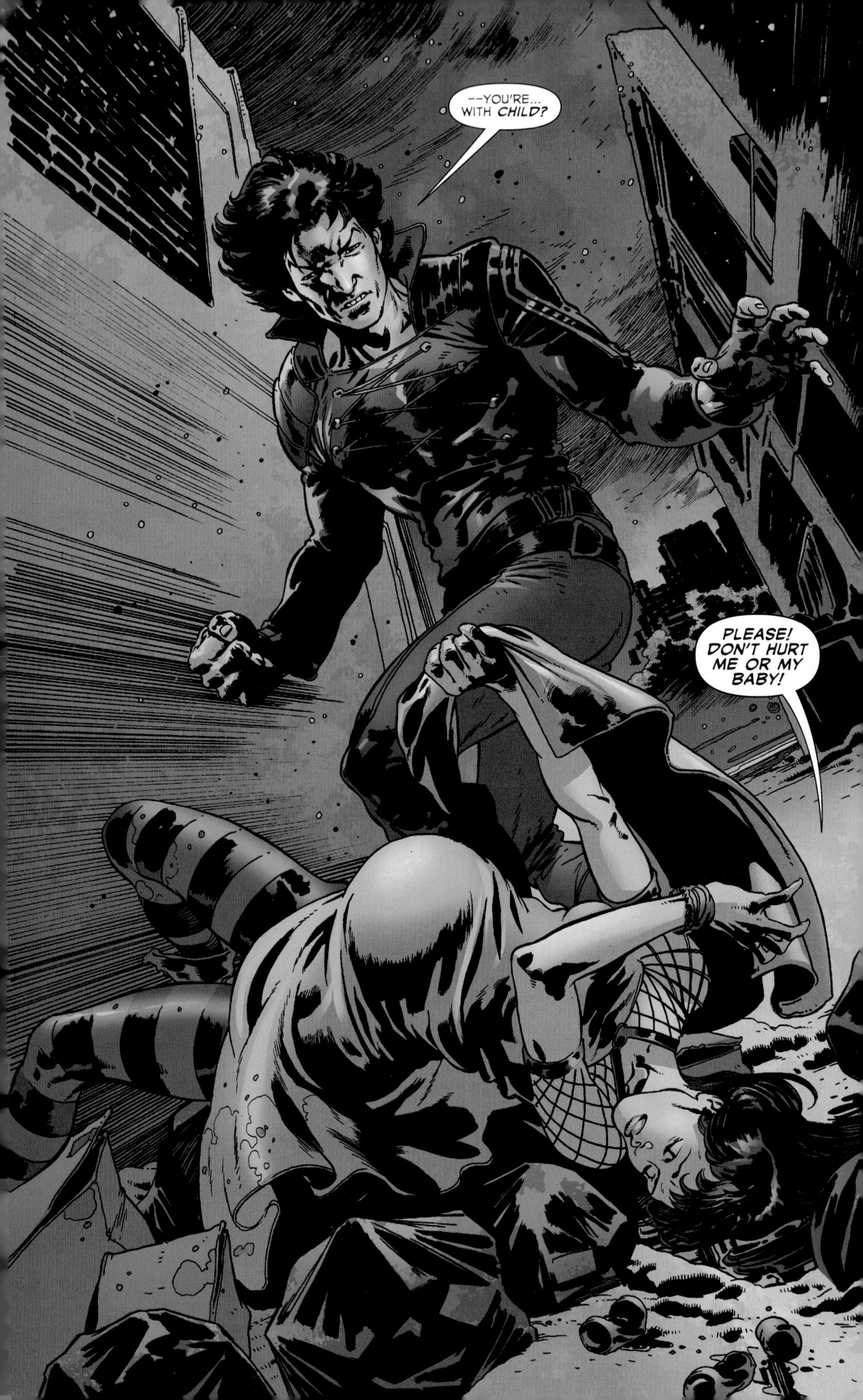
--YOU'RE... WITH CHILD?
PLEASE! DON'T HURT ME OR MY BABY!

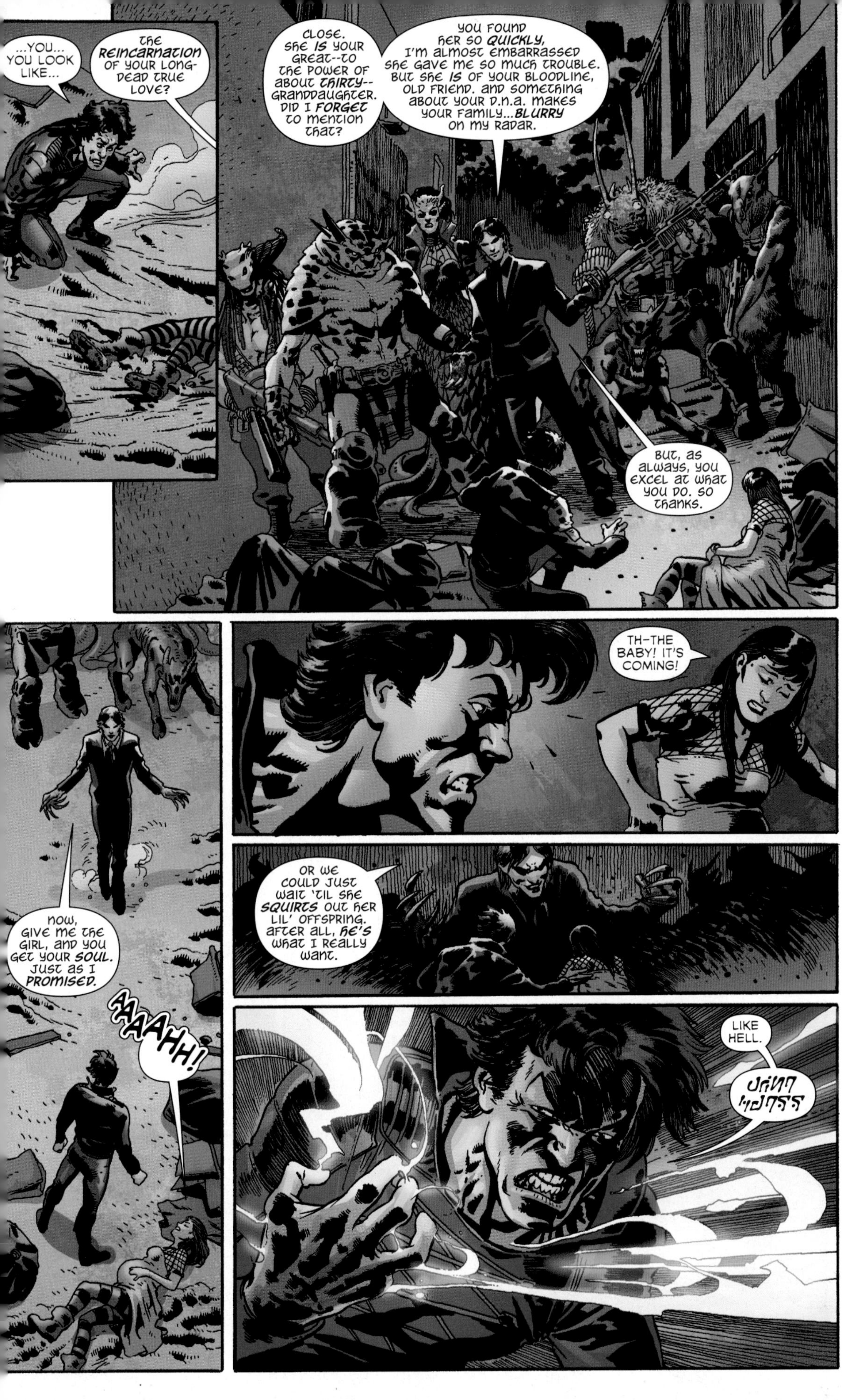
...YOU... YOU LOOK LIKE...
THE REINCARNATION OF YOUR LONG-DEAD TRUE LOVE?
CLOSE. SHE IS YOUR GREAT--TO THE POWER OF ABOUT THIRTY--GRANDDAUGHTER. DID I FORGET TO MENTION THAT?
YOU FOUND HER SO QUICKLY, I'M ALMOST EMBARRASSED SHE GAVE ME SO MUCH TROUBLE. BUT SHE IS OF YOUR BLOODLINE, OLD FRIEND. AND SOMETHING ABOUT YOUR D.N.A. MAKES YOUR FAMILY...BLURRY ON MY RADAR.
BUT, AS ALWAYS, YOU EXCEL AT WHAT YOU DO. SO THANKS.
NOW, GIVE ME THE GIRL, AND YOU GET YOUR SOUL. JUST AS I PROMISED.
TH-THE BABY! IT'S COMING!
AAAAHH!
OR WE COULD JUST WAIT 'TIL SHE SQUIRTS OUT HER LIL' OFFSPRING. AFTER ALL, HE'S WHAT I REALLY WANT.
LIKE HELL.

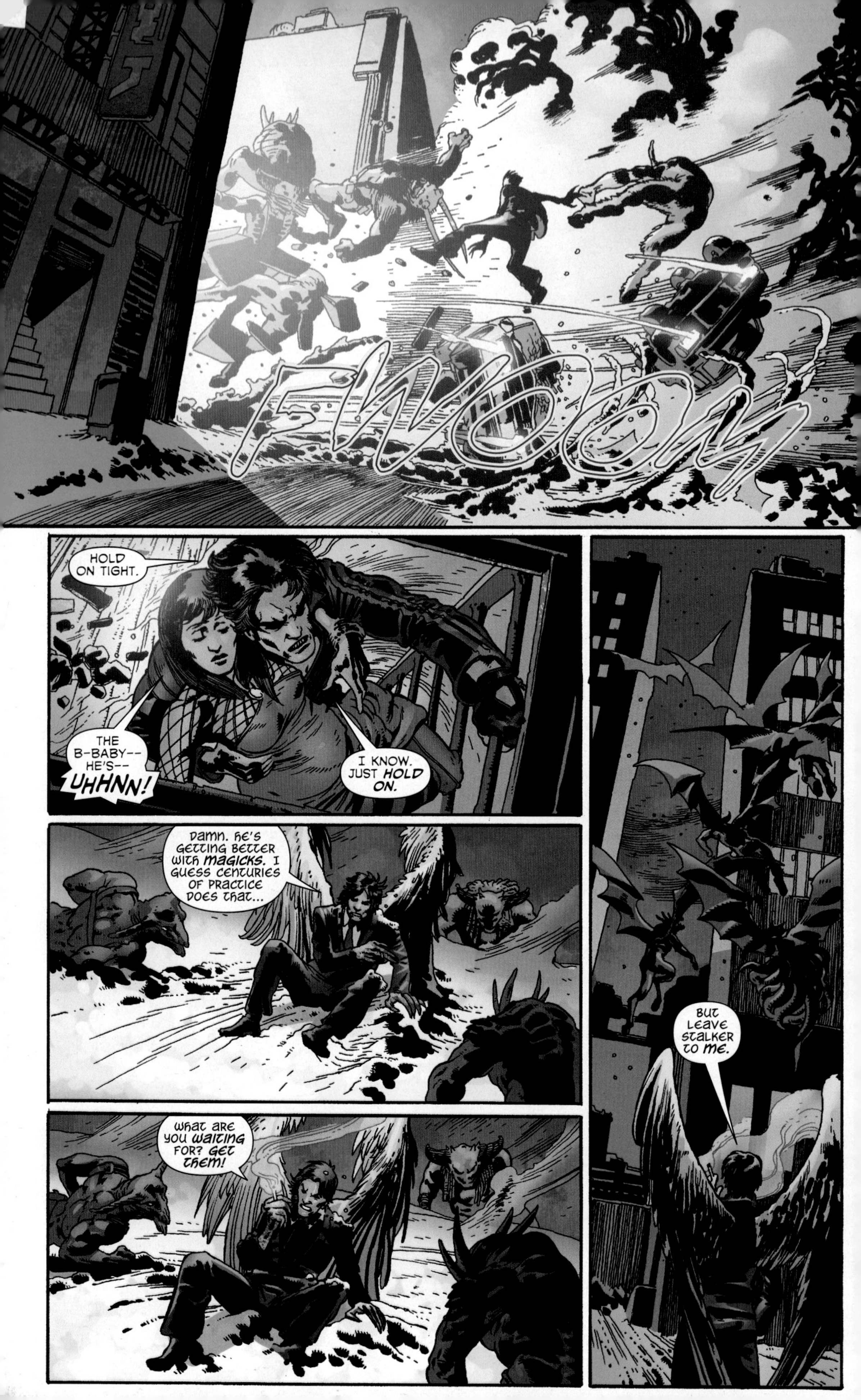
FWOOM
HOLD ON TIGHT.
THE B-BABY-- HE'S-- UHHNN!
I KNOW. JUST HOLD ON.
Damn. He's getting better with MAGICKS. I guess centuries of practice does that...
What are you waiting for? Get them!
But leave Stalker to me.

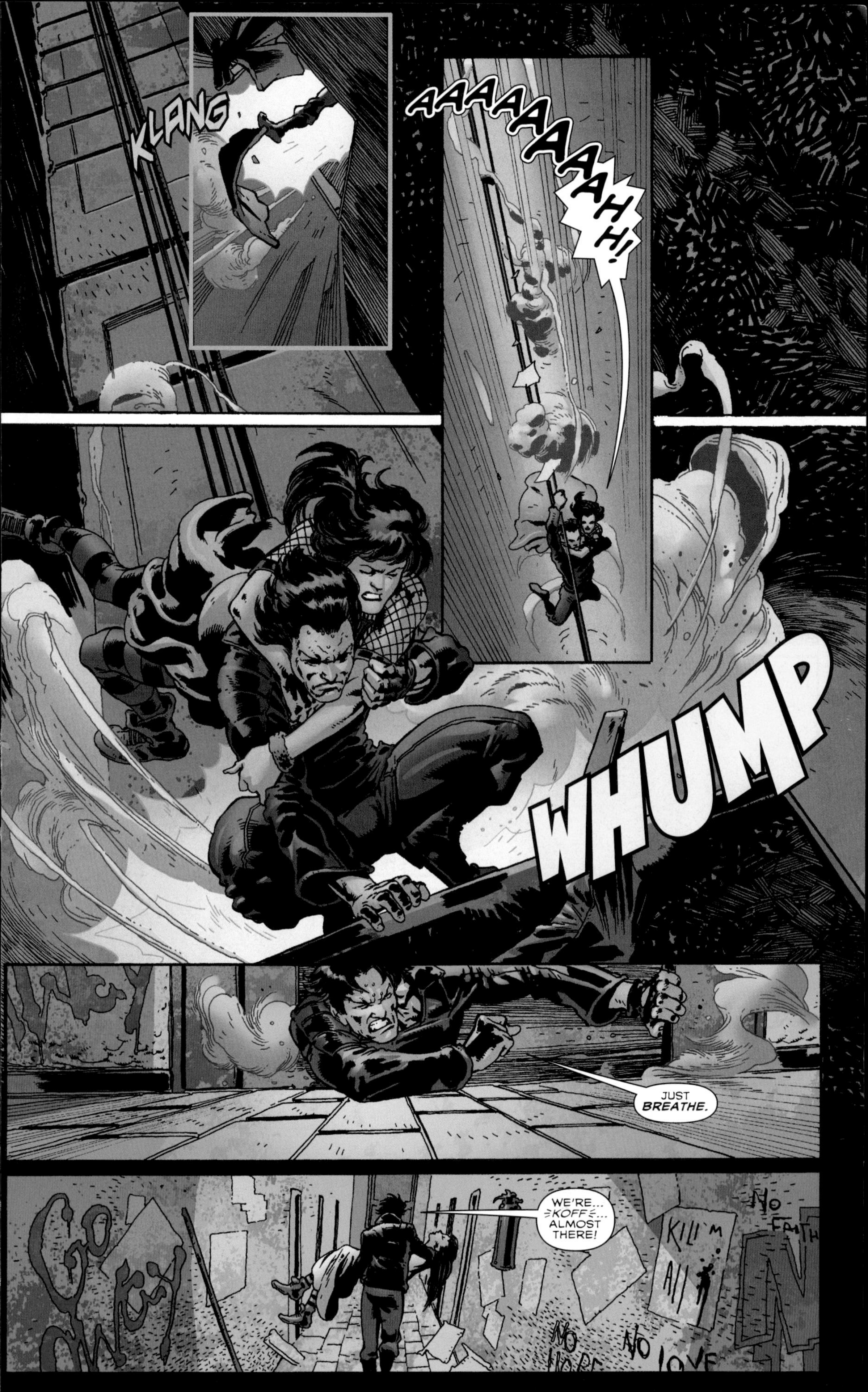
KLANG
AAAAAAAAAH!
WHUMP
JUST BREATHE.
WE'RE... KOFF... ALMOST THERE!
NO FAITH
KILL 'M ALL
NO HOPE
NO LOVE

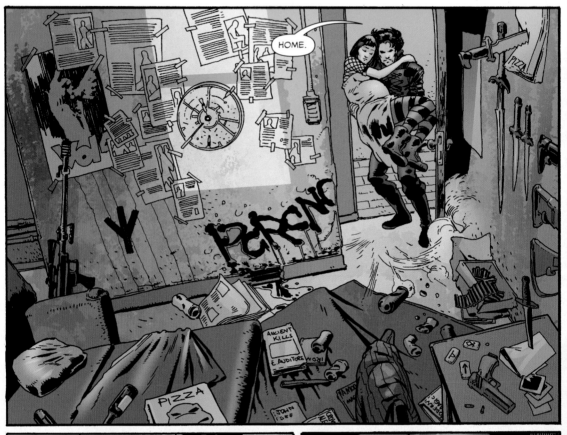

HOME.
ANCIENT KILLS
E. AUDITORE
PIZZA
A-ARE YOU O-OKAY? Y-YOU LOOK WORSE THAN I F-FEEL!
MAGICKS TAKE MUCH OUT OF ME. I WILL BE FINE, BUT YOU--
MAGICKS? WHAT THE HELL IS H-HAPPENING?
WHO *ARE* YOU?
WHY DOES THAT MAN WANT MY BA--
AAAHH!
EXPLANATIONS ARE FOR ANOTHER TIME.
NOW WE MUST DEAL WITH YOUR ONCOMING CHILD AND--
YEAAARGH!
NOT AGAIN...
THIS REMINDS ME OF THAT NIGHT IN BETHLEHEM!

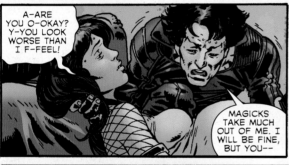

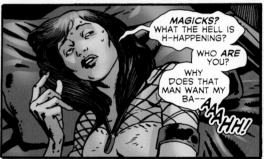

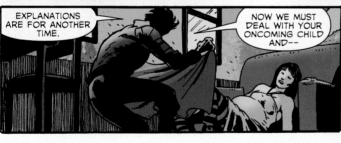

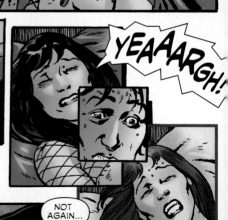

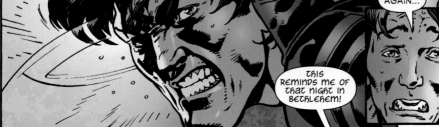

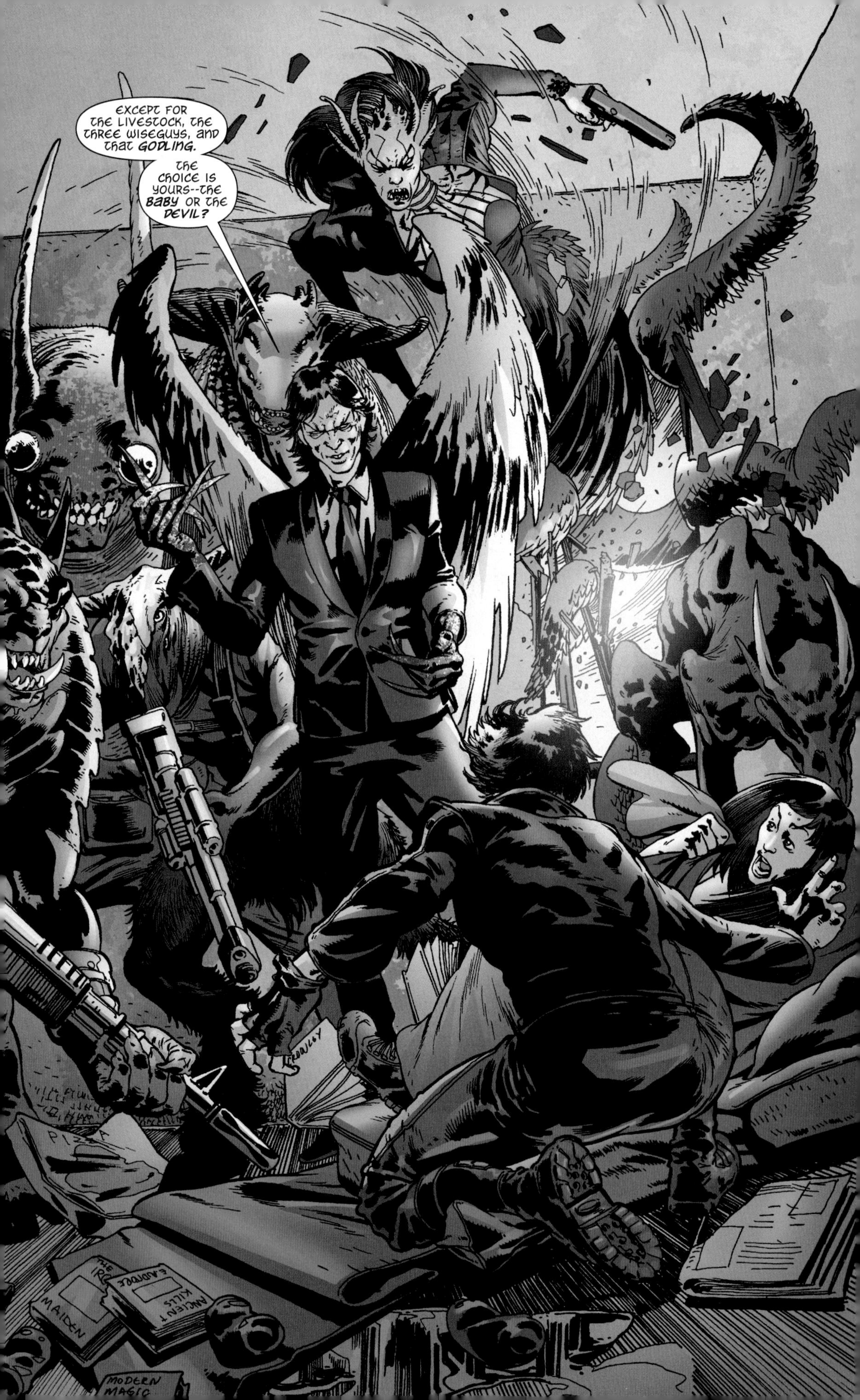
EXCEPT FOR THE LIVESTOCK, THE THREE WISEGUYS, AND THAT GODLING.
THE CHOICE IS YOURS--THE BABY OR THE DEVIL?
MODERN MAGIC

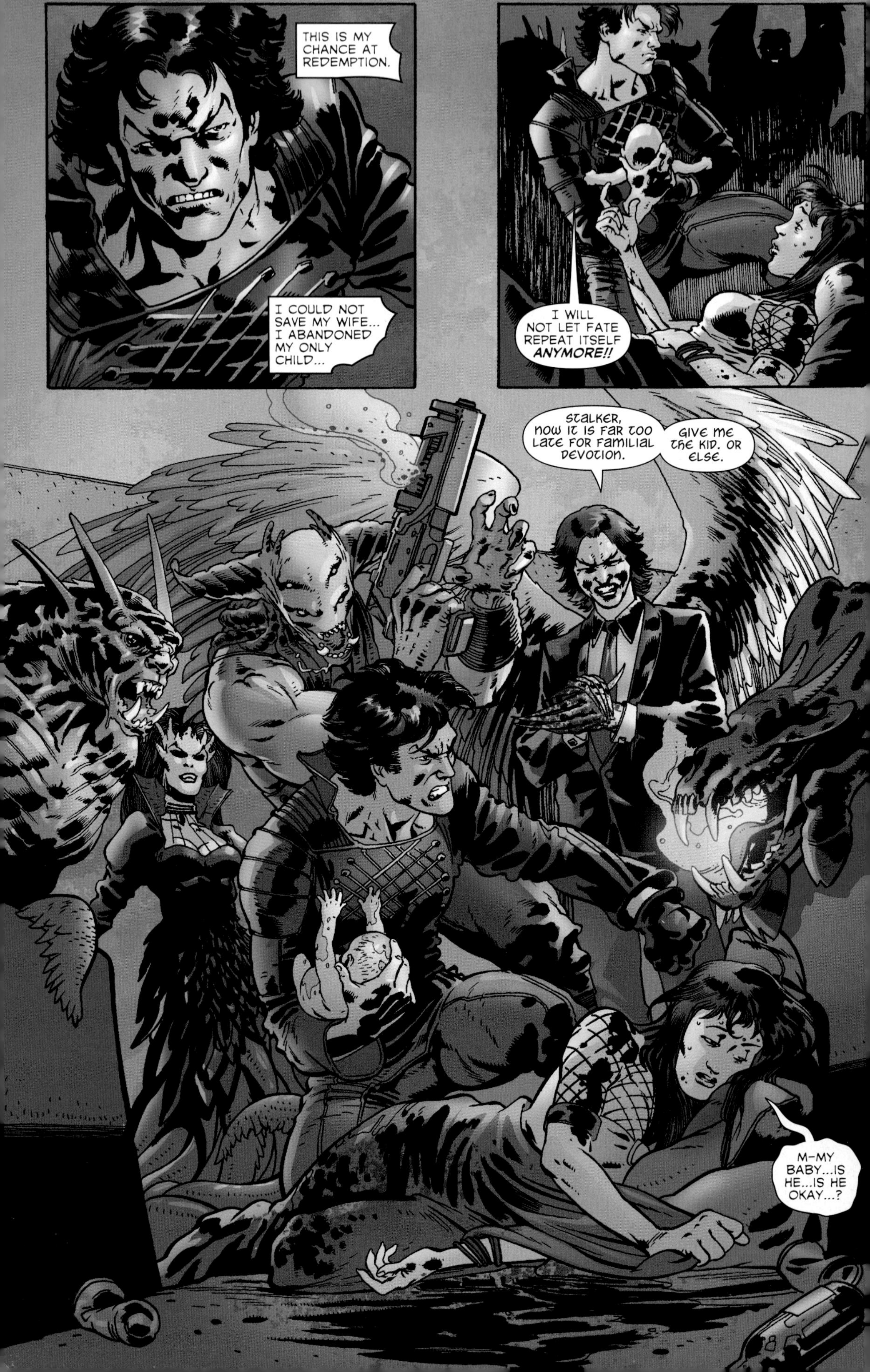
THIS IS MY CHANCE AT REDEMPTION.
I COULD NOT SAVE MY WIFE... I ABANDONED MY ONLY CHILD...
I WILL NOT LET FATE REPEAT ITSELF ANYMORE!!
STALKER, NOW IT IS FAR TOO LATE FOR FAMILIAL DEVOTION.
GIVE ME THE KID. OR ELSE.
M-MY BABY...IS HE...IS HE OKAY...?

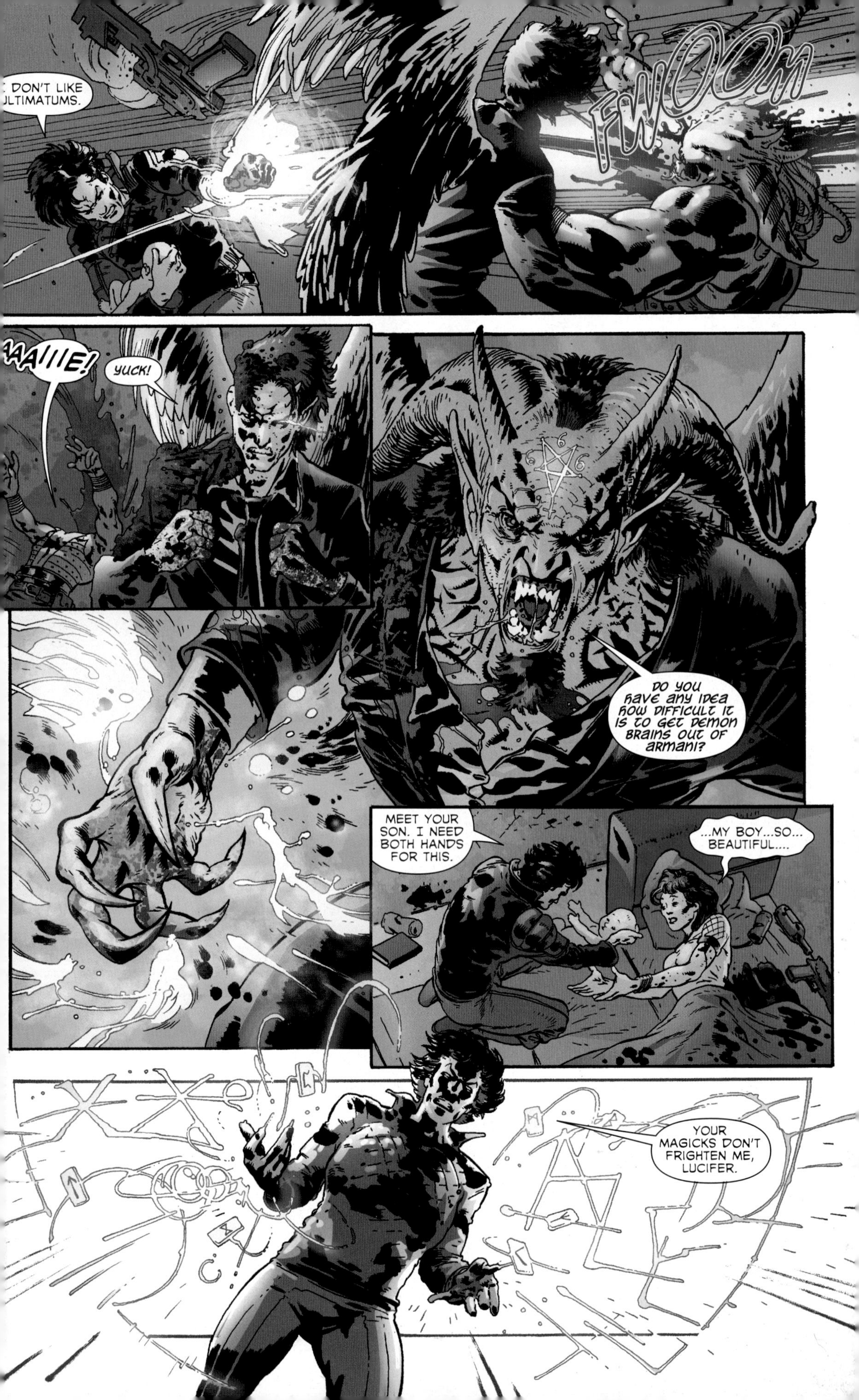

DON'T LIKE
ULTIMATUMS.
FWOOM
AAAIIIE!
YUCK!
DO YOU HAVE ANY IDEA HOW DIFFICULT IT IS TO GET DEMON BRAINS OUT OF ARMANI?
MEET YOUR SON. I NEED BOTH HANDS FOR THIS.
...MY BOY...SO... BEAUTIFUL....
YOUR MAGICKS DON'T FRIGHTEN ME, LUCIFER.

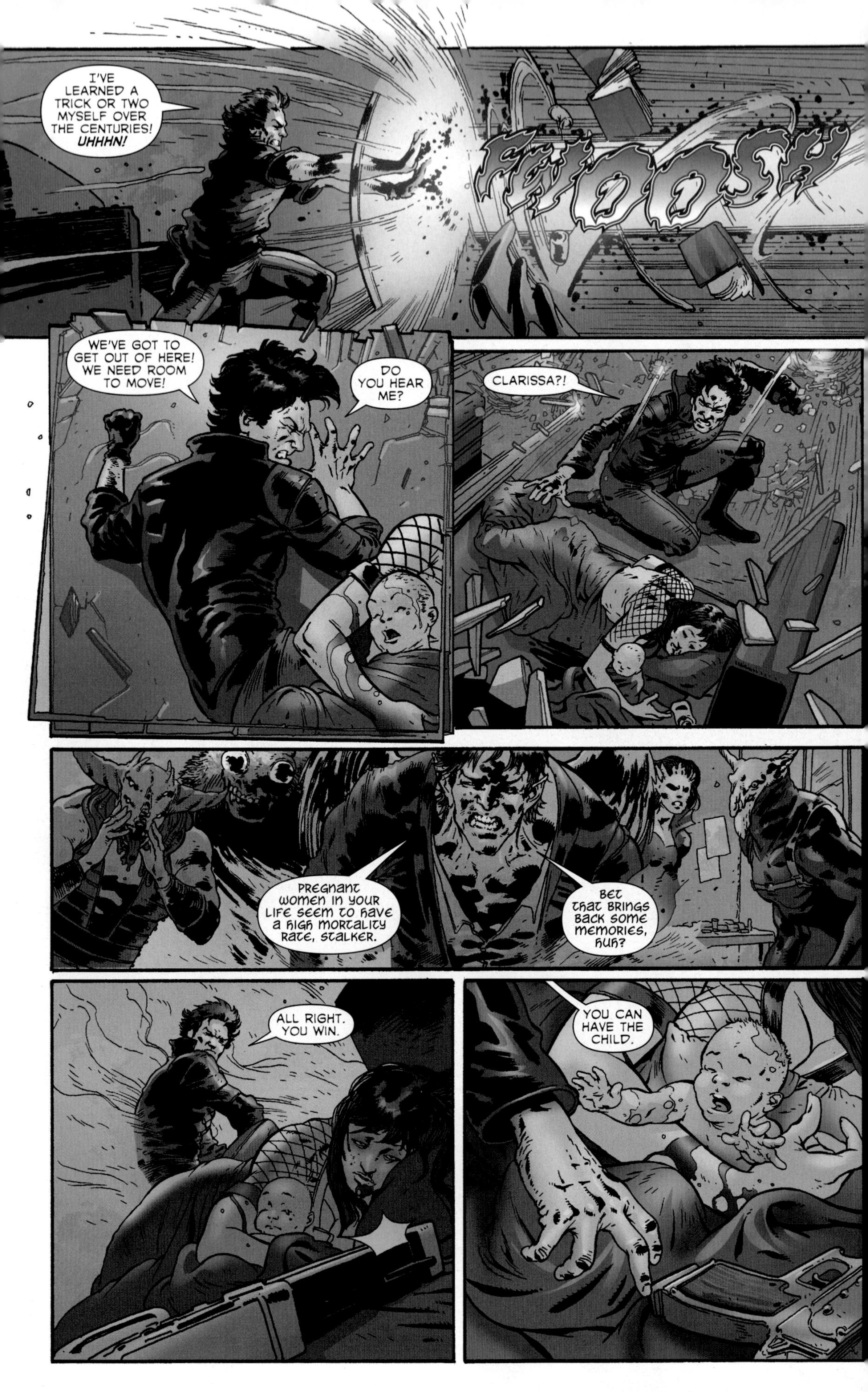

I'VE LEARNED A TRICK OR TWO MYSELF OVER THE CENTURIES! *UHHHN!*
FWOOSH
WE'VE GOT TO GET OUT OF HERE! WE NEED ROOM TO MOVE!
DO YOU HEAR ME?
CLARISSA?!
PREGNANT WOMEN IN YOUR LIFE SEEM TO HAVE A HIGH MORTALITY RATE, STALKER.
BET THAT BRINGS BACK SOME MEMORIES, HUH?
ALL RIGHT. YOU WIN.
YOU CAN HAVE THE CHILD.

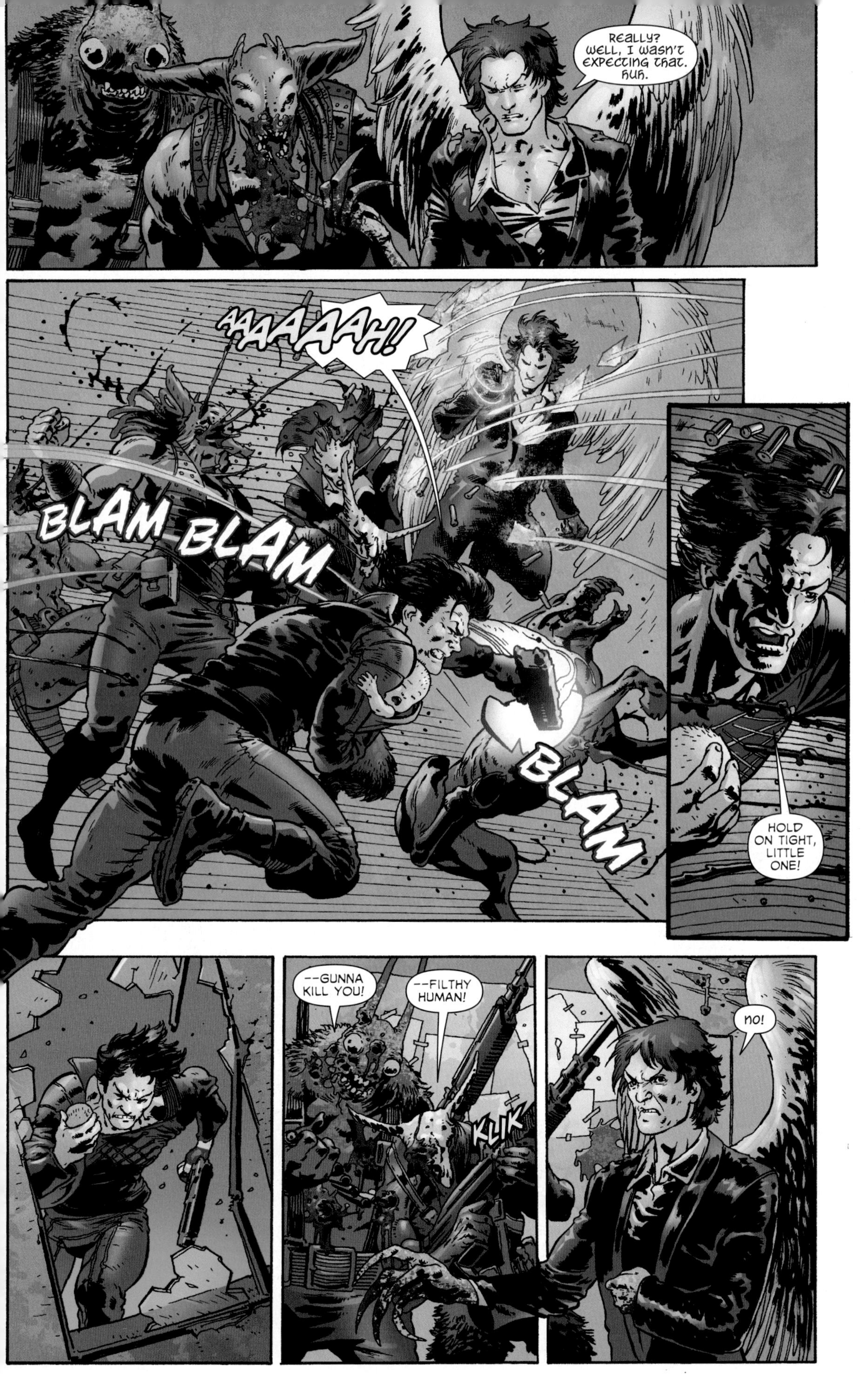
REALLY? WELL, I WASN'T EXPECTING THAT. HUH.
AAAAAAH!
BLAM BLAM
BLAM
HOLD ON TIGHT, LITTLE ONE!
--GUNNA KILL YOU!
--FILTHY HUMAN!
KLIK
NO!

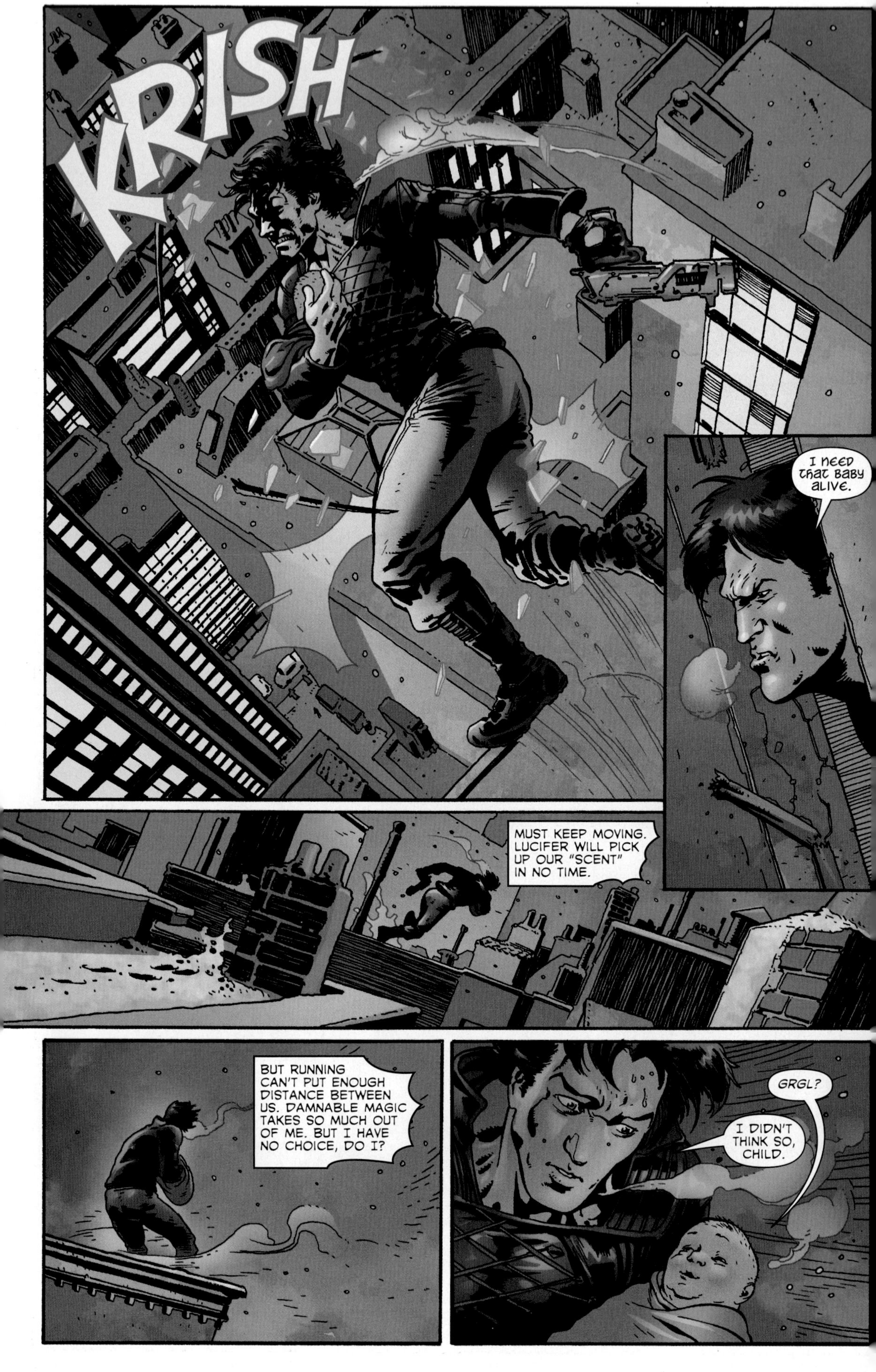
KRISH
I NEED THAT BABY ALIVE.
MUST KEEP MOVING. LUCIFER WILL PICK UP OUR "SCENT" IN NO TIME.
BUT RUNNING CAN'T PUT ENOUGH DISTANCE BETWEEN US. DAMNABLE MAGIC TAKES SO MUCH OUT OF ME. BUT I HAVE NO CHOICE, DO I?
GRGL?
I DIDN'T THINK SO, CHILD.

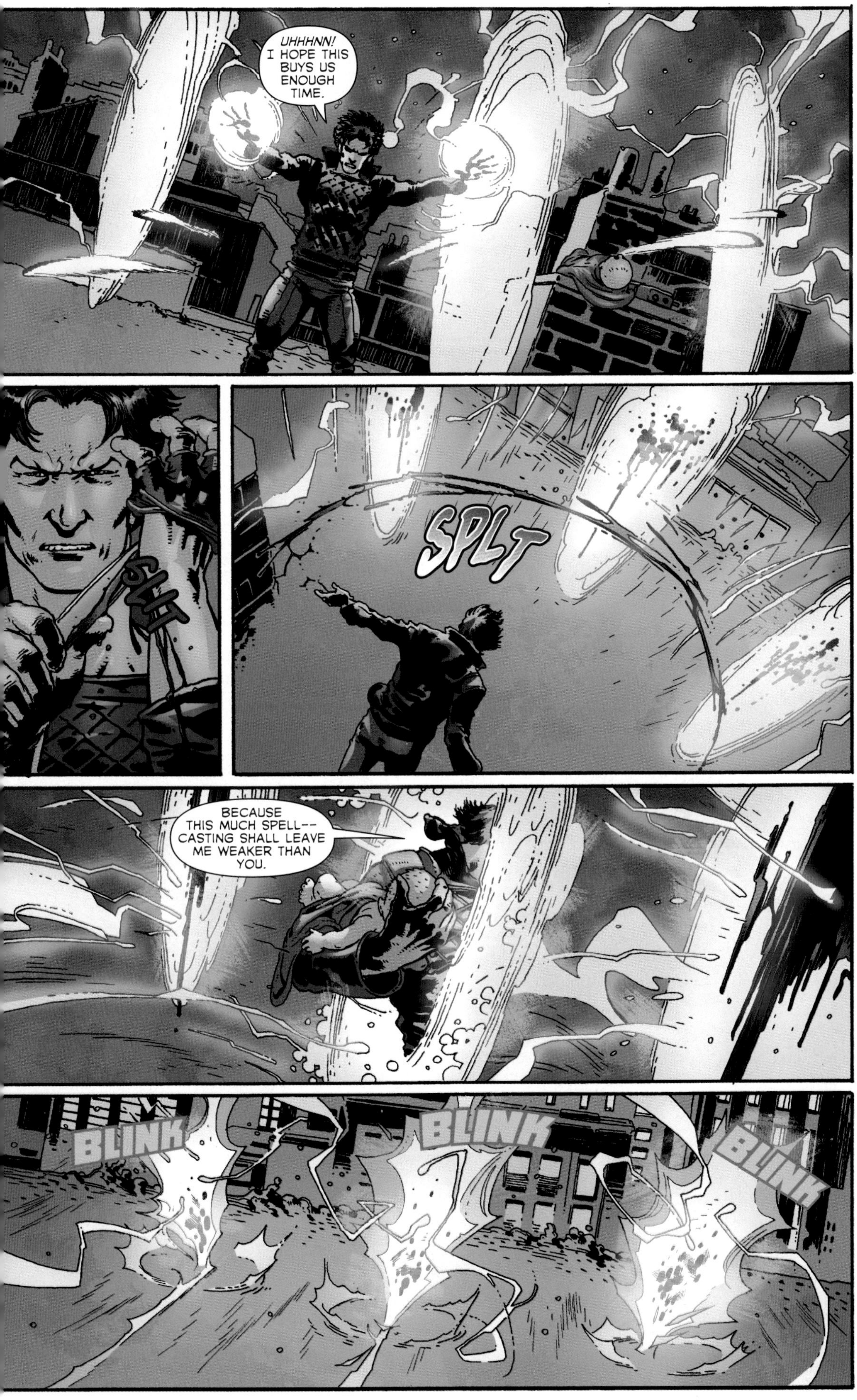
UHHHNN! I HOPE THIS BUYS US ENOUGH TIME.
SPLT
BECAUSE THIS MUCH SPELL-- CASTING SHALL LEAVE ME WEAKER THAN YOU.
BLINK
BLINK
BLINK

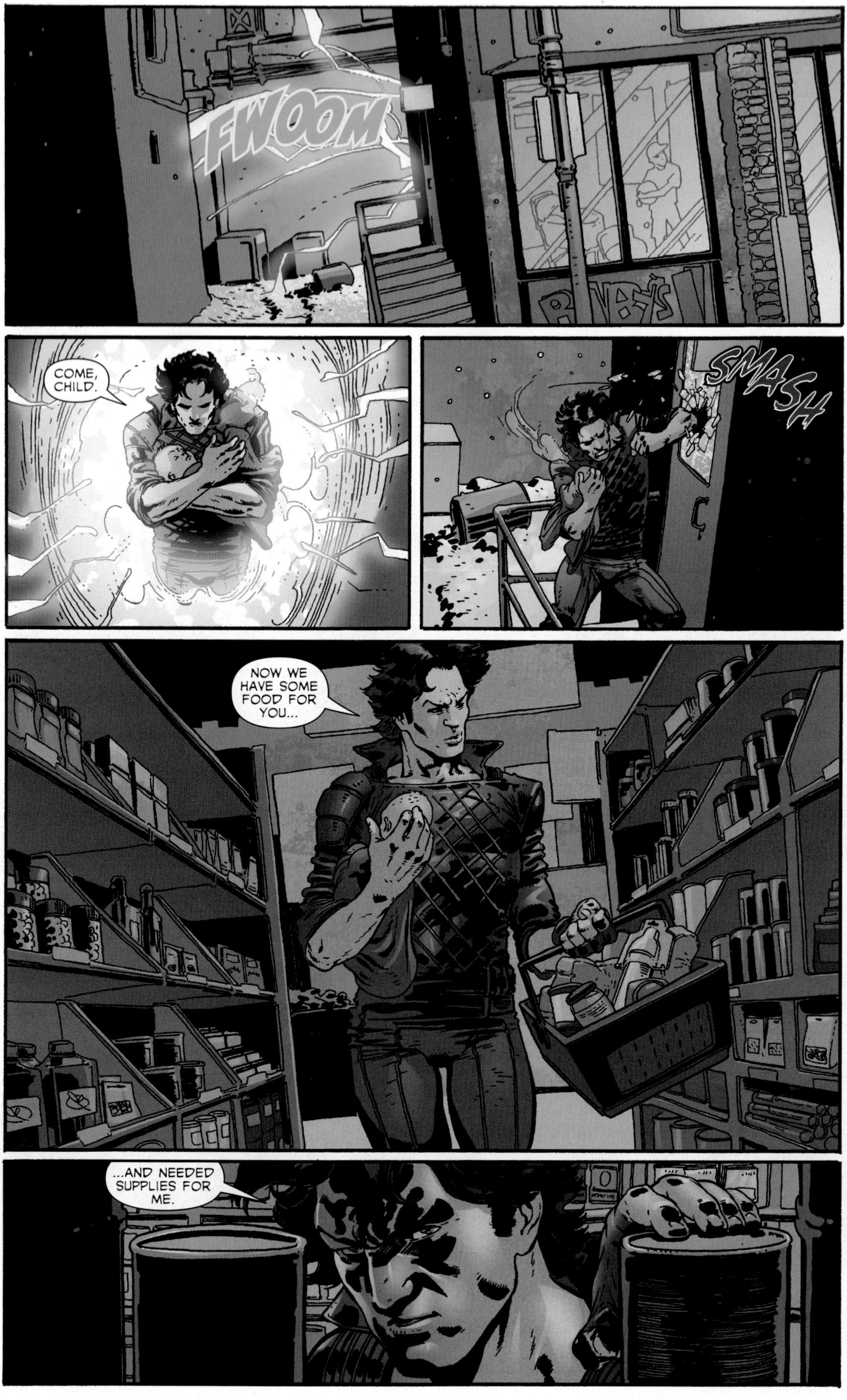
FWOOM
COME, CHILD.
SMASH
NOW WE HAVE SOME FOOD FOR YOU...
...AND NEEDED SUPPLIES FOR ME.

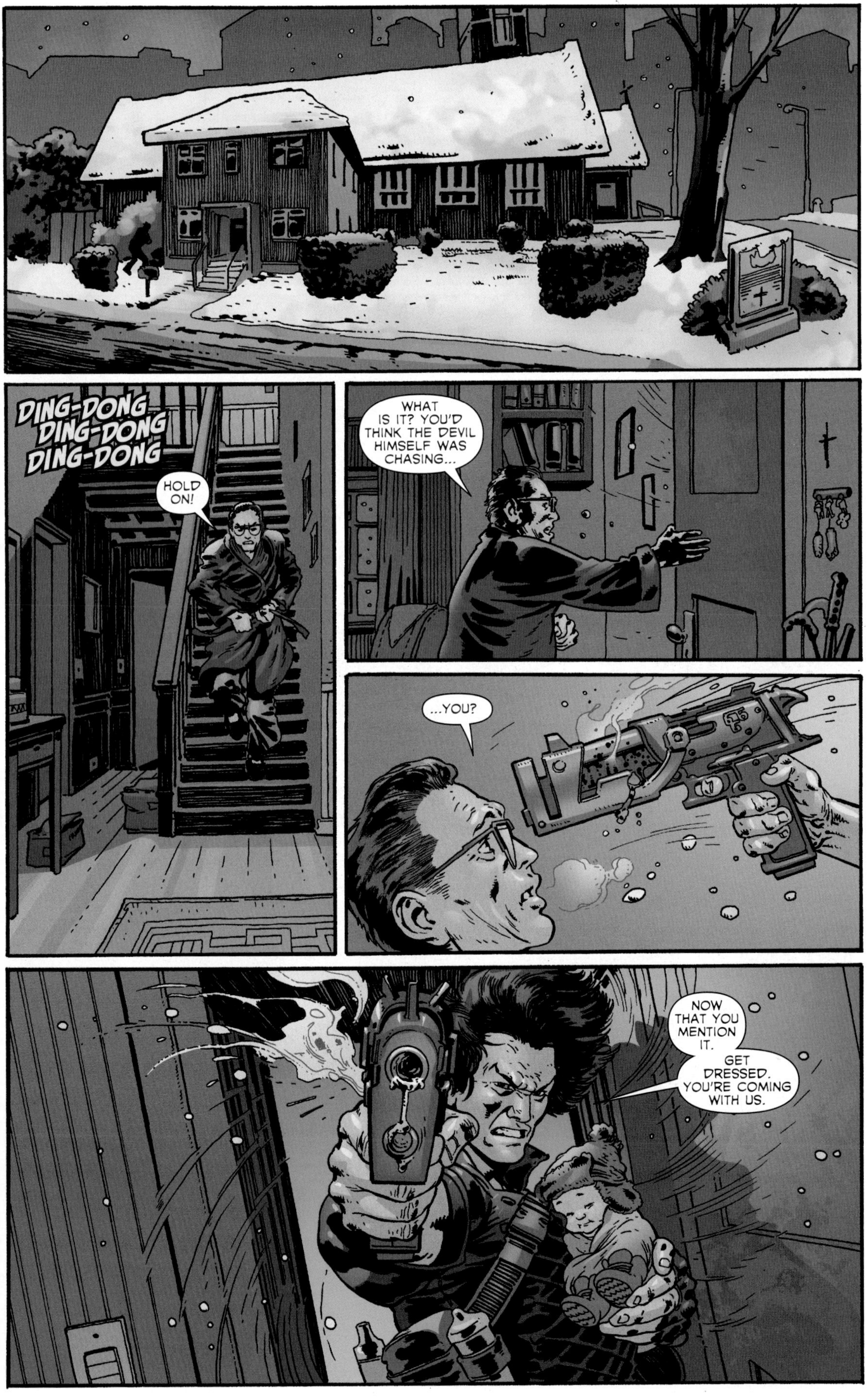
DING-DONG
DING-DONG
DING-DONG
HOLD ON!
WHAT IS IT? YOU'D THINK THE DEVIL HIMSELF WAS CHASING...
...YOU?
NOW THAT YOU MENTION IT.
GET DRESSED. YOU'RE COMING WITH US.

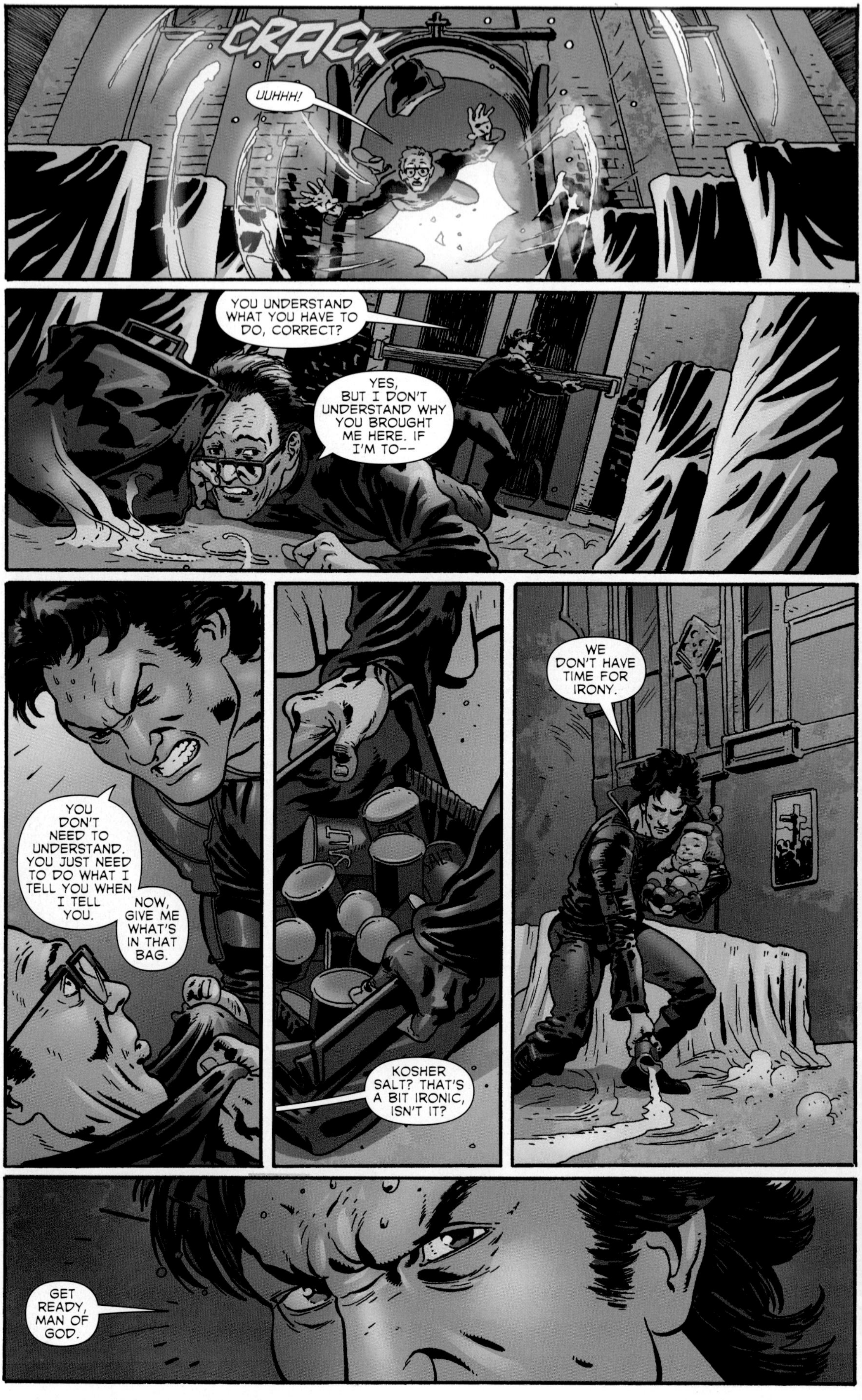
CRACK
UUHHH!
YOU UNDERSTAND WHAT YOU HAVE TO DO, CORRECT?
YES, BUT I DON'T UNDERSTAND WHY YOU BROUGHT ME HERE. IF I'M TO--
YOU DON'T NEED TO UNDERSTAND. YOU JUST NEED TO DO WHAT I TELL YOU WHEN I TELL YOU.
NOW, GIVE ME WHAT'S IN THAT BAG.
KOSHER SALT? THAT'S A BIT IRONIC, ISN'T IT?
WE DON'T HAVE TIME FOR IRONY.
GET READY, MAN OF GOD.

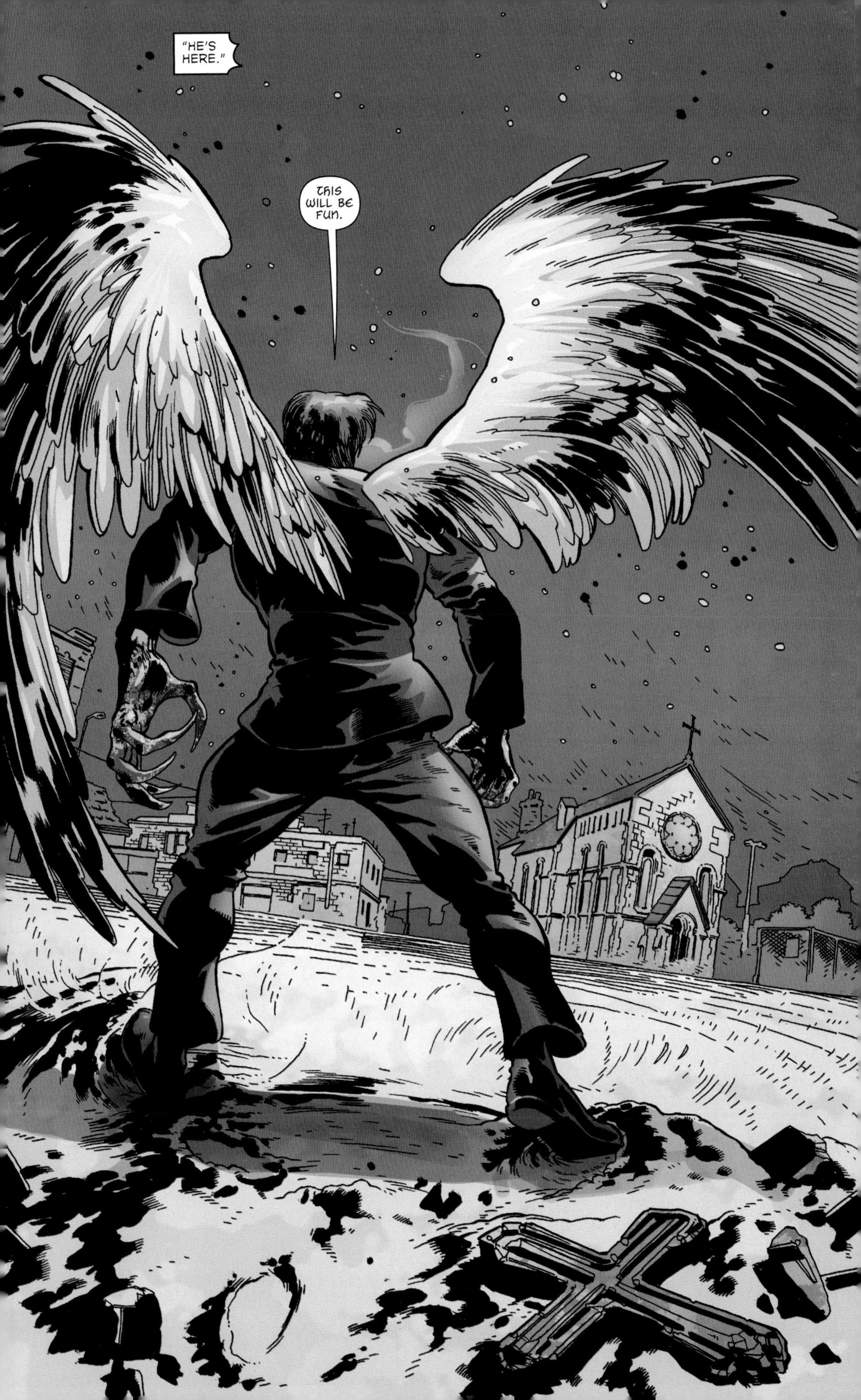
"HE'S HERE."
THIS WILL BE FUN.

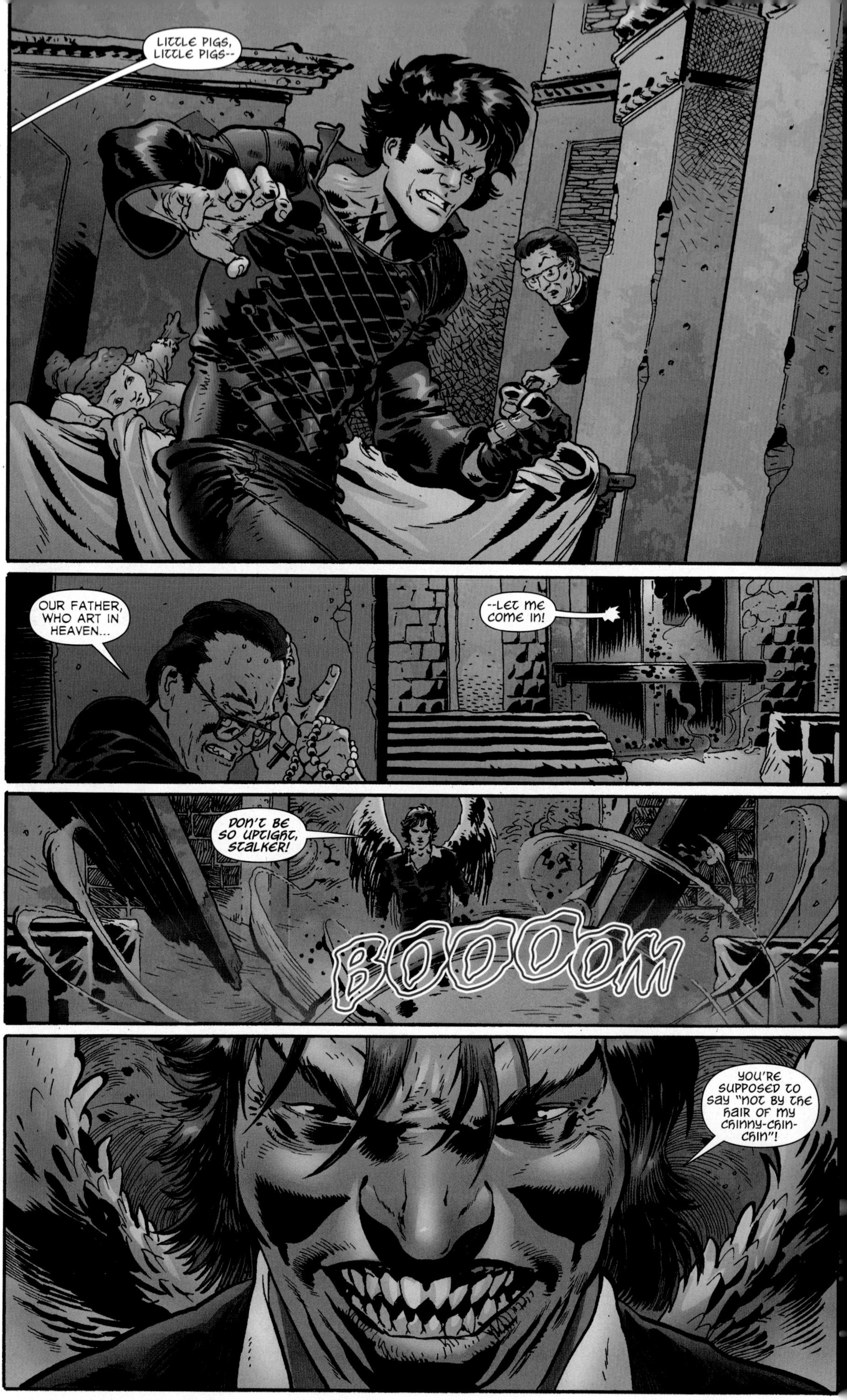
LITTLE PIGS, LITTLE PIGS--
OUR FATHER, WHO ART IN HEAVEN...
--LET ME COME IN!
DON'T BE SO UPTIGHT, STALKER!
BOOOOOM
YOU'RE SUPPOSED TO SAY "NOT BY THE HAIR OF MY CHINNY-CHIN-CHIN"!

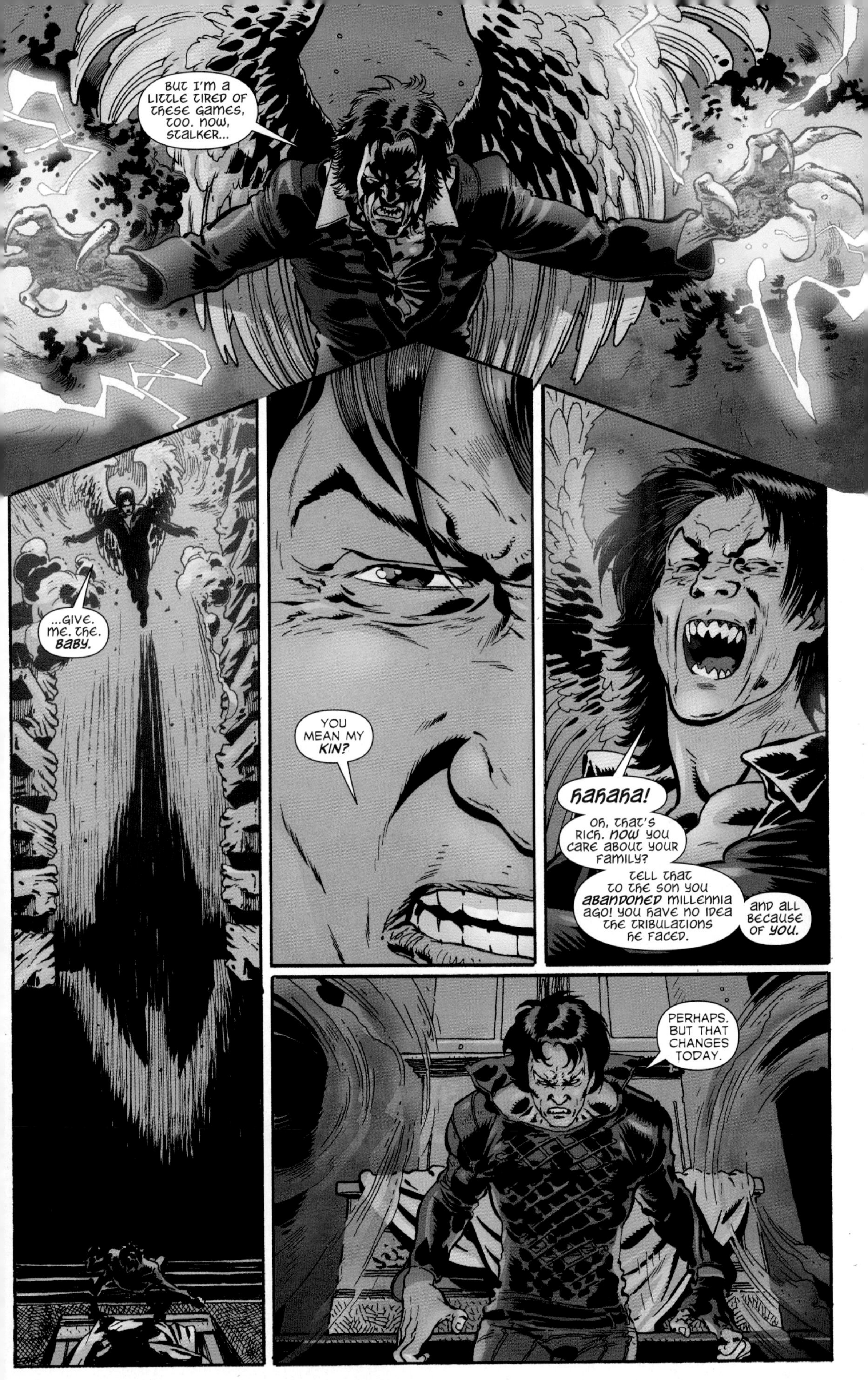
BUT I'M A LITTLE TIRED OF THESE GAMES, TOO. NOW, STALKER...
...GIVE. ME. THE. BABY.
YOU MEAN MY KIN?
HAHAHA!
OH, THAT'S RICH. NOW YOU CARE ABOUT YOUR FAMILY?
TELL THAT TO THE SON YOU ABANDONED MILLENNIA AGO! YOU HAVE NO IDEA THE TRIBULATIONS HE FACED.
AND ALL BECAUSE OF YOU.
PERHAPS. BUT THAT CHANGES TODAY.

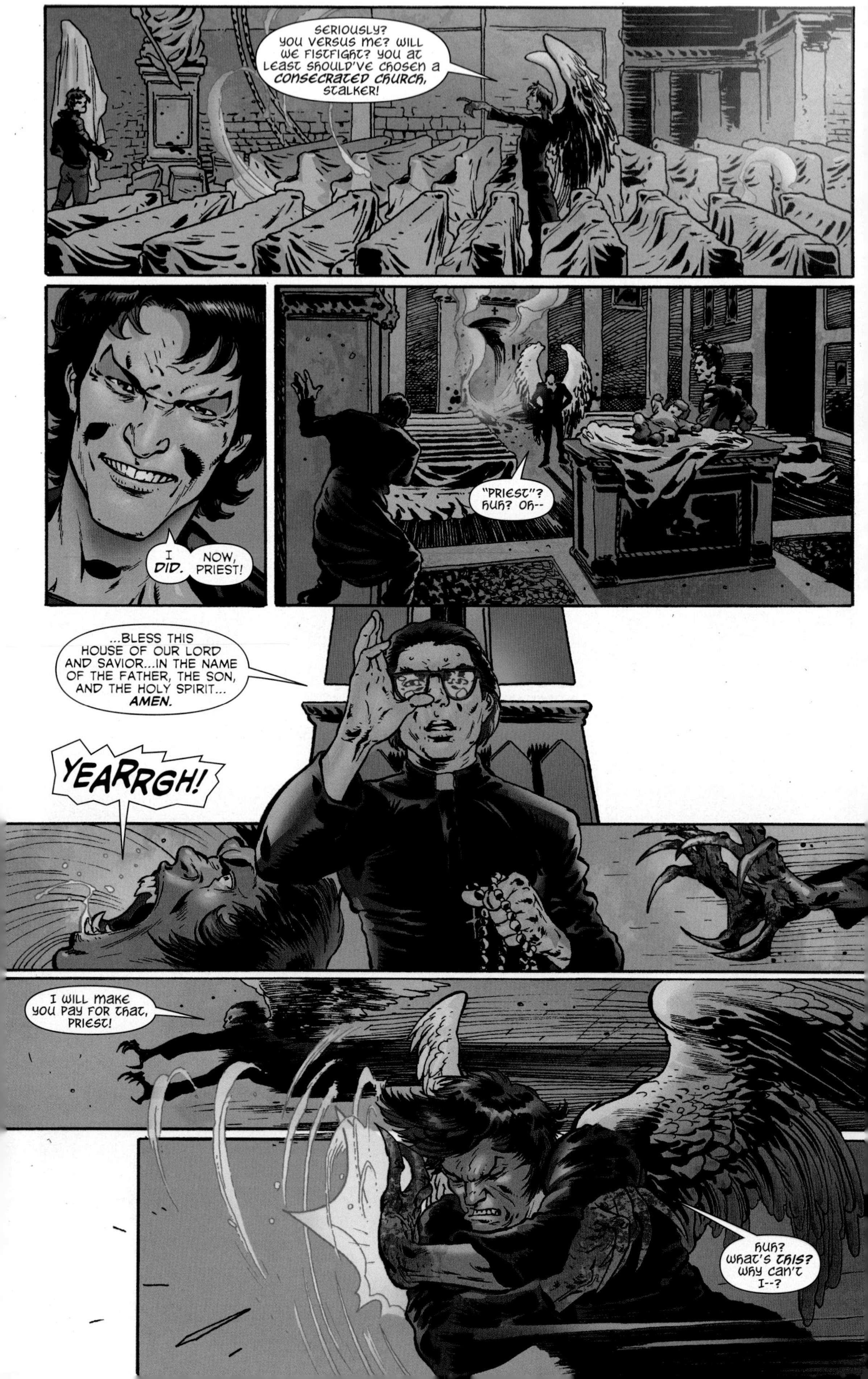
SERIOUSLY? YOU VERSUS ME? WILL WE FISTFIGHT? YOU AT LEAST SHOULD'VE CHOSEN A CONSECRATED CHURCH, STALKER!
I DID.
NOW, PRIEST!
"PRIEST"? HUH? OH--
...BLESS THIS HOUSE OF OUR LORD AND SAVIOR...IN THE NAME OF THE FATHER, THE SON, AND THE HOLY SPIRIT... AMEN.
YEARRGH!
I WILL MAKE YOU PAY FOR THAT, PRIEST!
HUH? WHAT'S THIS? WHY CAN'T I--?

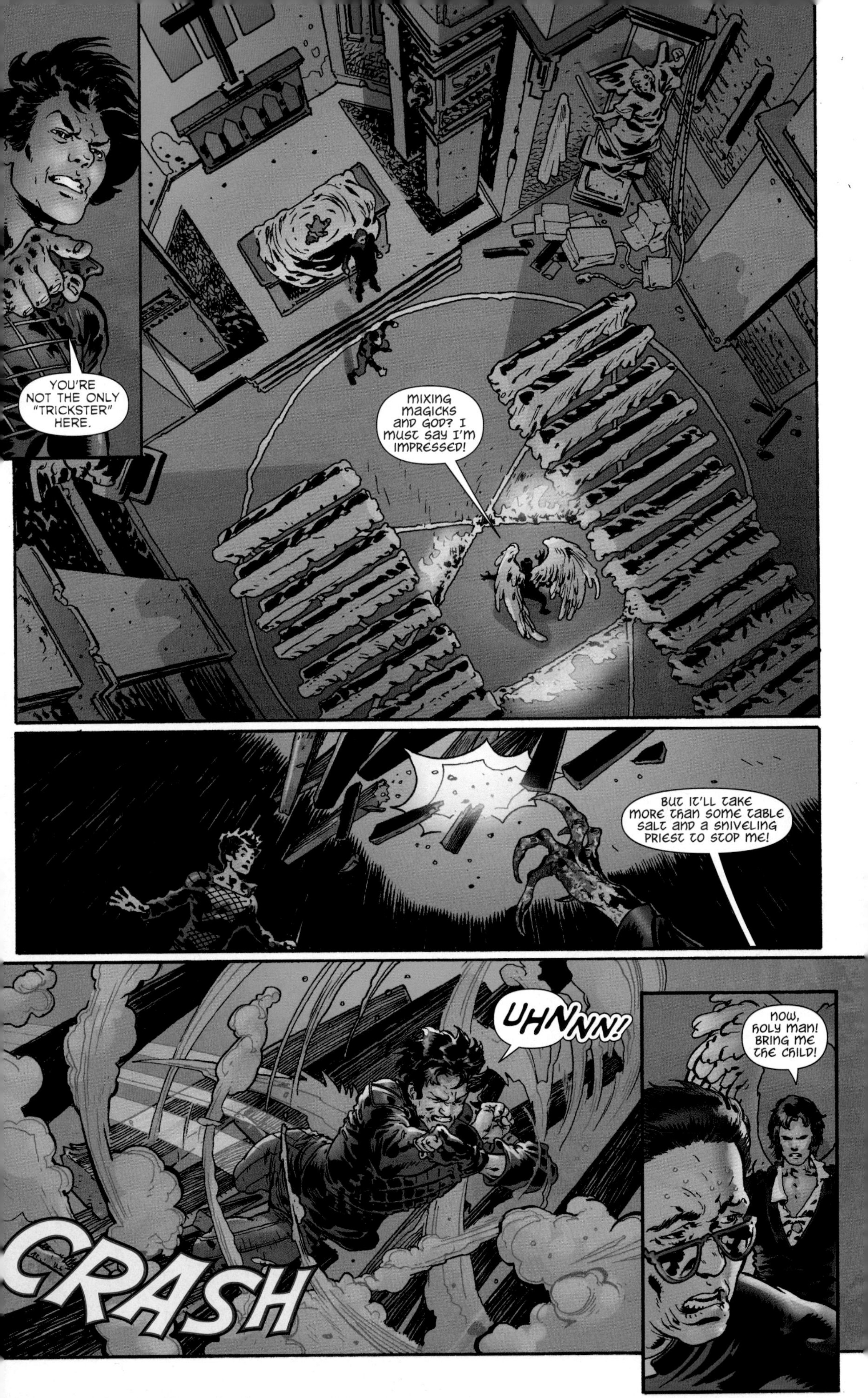
YOU'RE NOT THE ONLY "TRICKSTER" HERE.
MIXING MAGICKS AND GOD? I MUST SAY I'M IMPRESSED!
BUT IT'LL TAKE MORE THAN SOME TABLE SALT AND A SNIVELING PRIEST TO STOP ME!
UHNNNN!
CRASH
NOW, HOLY MAN! BRING ME THE CHILD!

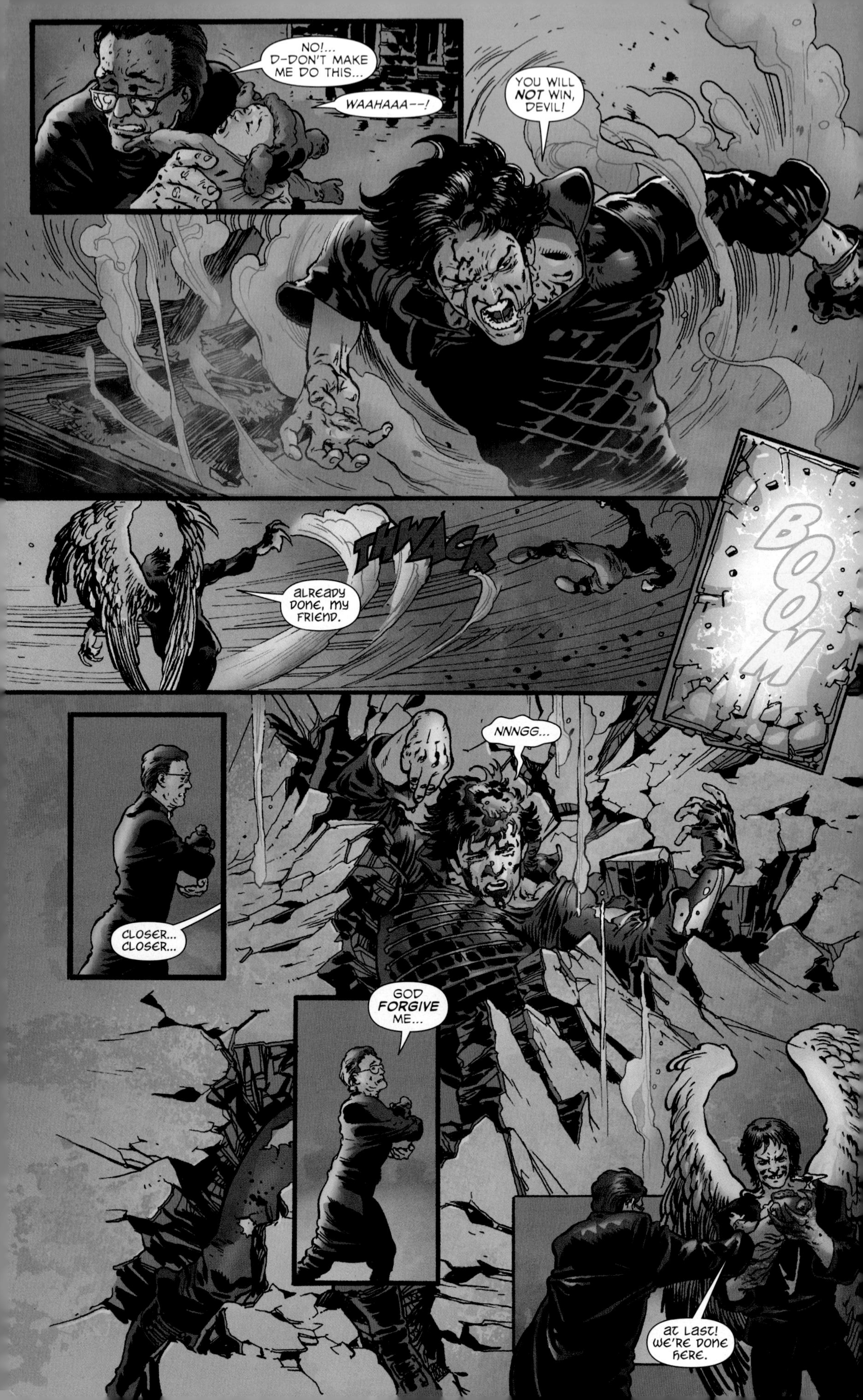
NO!... D-DON'T MAKE ME DO THIS...
WAAHAAA--!
YOU WILL NOT WIN, DEVIL!
THWACK
already done, my friend.
BOOM
NNNGG...
CLOSER... CLOSER...
GOD FORGIVE ME...
at last! we're done here.

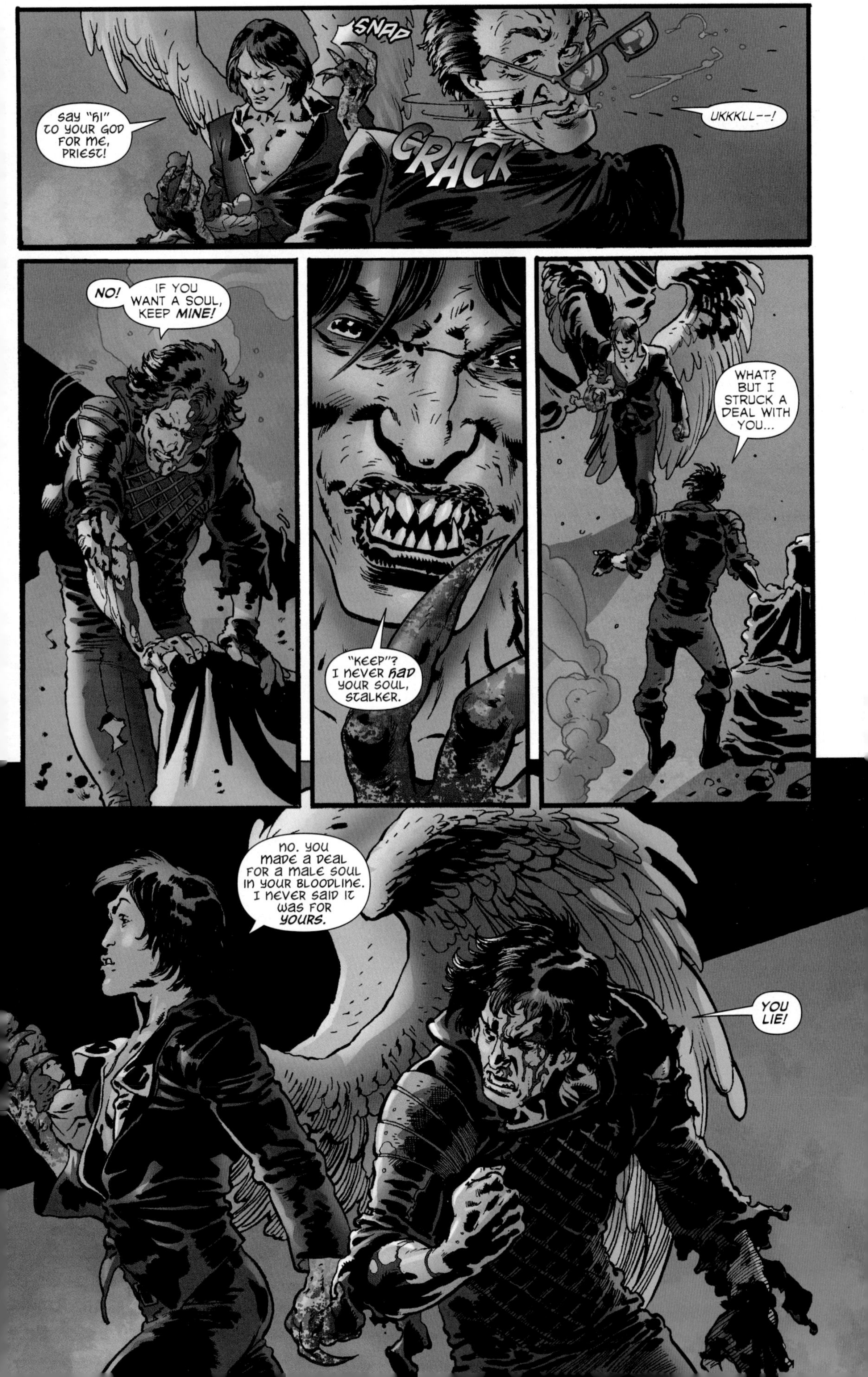
SNAP
SAY "HI" TO YOUR GOD FOR ME, PRIEST!
CRACK
UKKKLL--!
NO!
IF YOU WANT A SOUL, KEEP MINE!
"KEEP"? I NEVER HAD YOUR SOUL, STALKER.
WHAT? BUT I STRUCK A DEAL WITH YOU...
NO. YOU MADE A DEAL FOR A MALE SOUL IN YOUR BLOODLINE. I NEVER SAID IT WAS FOR YOURS.
YOU LIE!

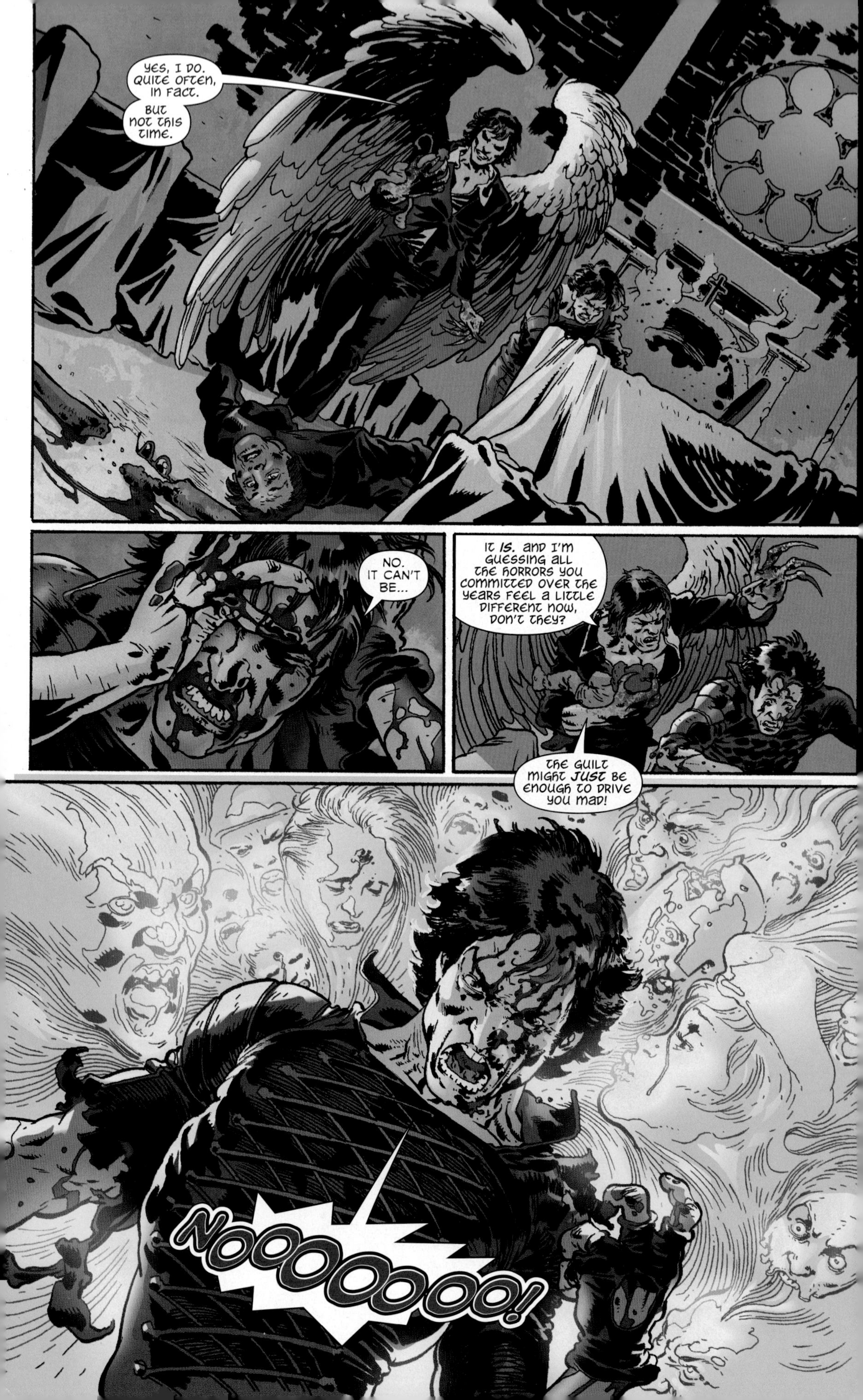
YES, I DO. QUITE OFTEN, IN FACT.
BUT NOT THIS TIME.
NO. IT CAN'T BE...
IT *IS.* AND I'M GUESSING ALL THE HORRORS YOU COMMITTED OVER THE YEARS FEEL A LITTLE DIFFERENT NOW, DON'T THEY?
THE GUILT MIGHT **JUST** BE ENOUGH TO DRIVE YOU MAD!
NOOOOOOOO!

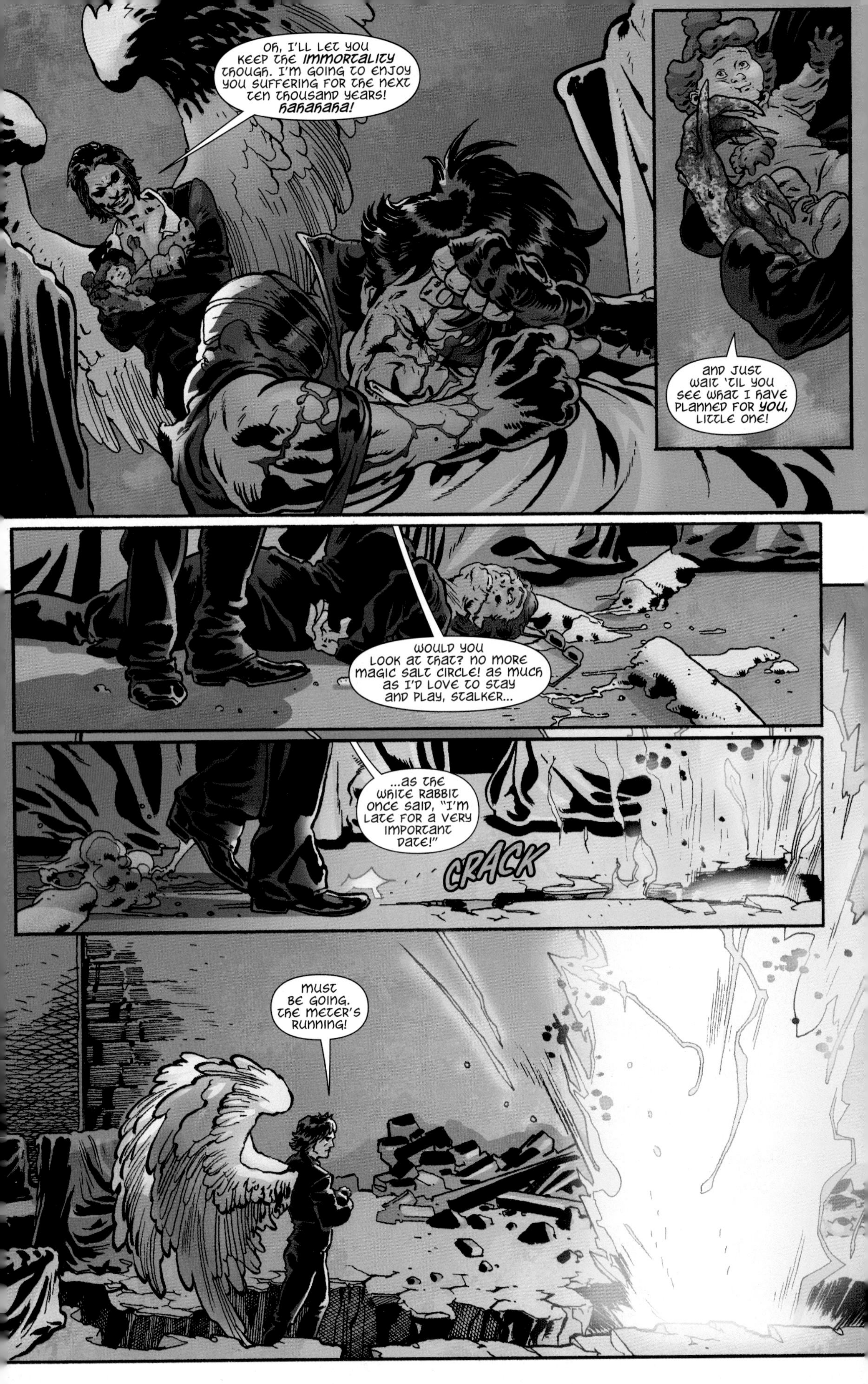
OH, I'LL LET YOU KEEP THE IMMORTALITY THOUGH. I'M GOING TO ENJOY YOU SUFFERING FOR THE NEXT TEN THOUSAND YEARS! HAHAHAHA!
AND JUST WAIT 'TIL YOU SEE WHAT I HAVE PLANNED FOR YOU, LITTLE ONE!
WOULD YOU LOOK AT THAT? NO MORE MAGIC SALT CIRCLE! AS MUCH AS I'D LOVE TO STAY AND PLAY, STALKER...
...AS THE WHITE RABBIT ONCE SAID, "I'M LATE FOR A VERY IMPORTANT DATE!"
CRACK
MUST BE GOING. THE METER'S RUNNING!

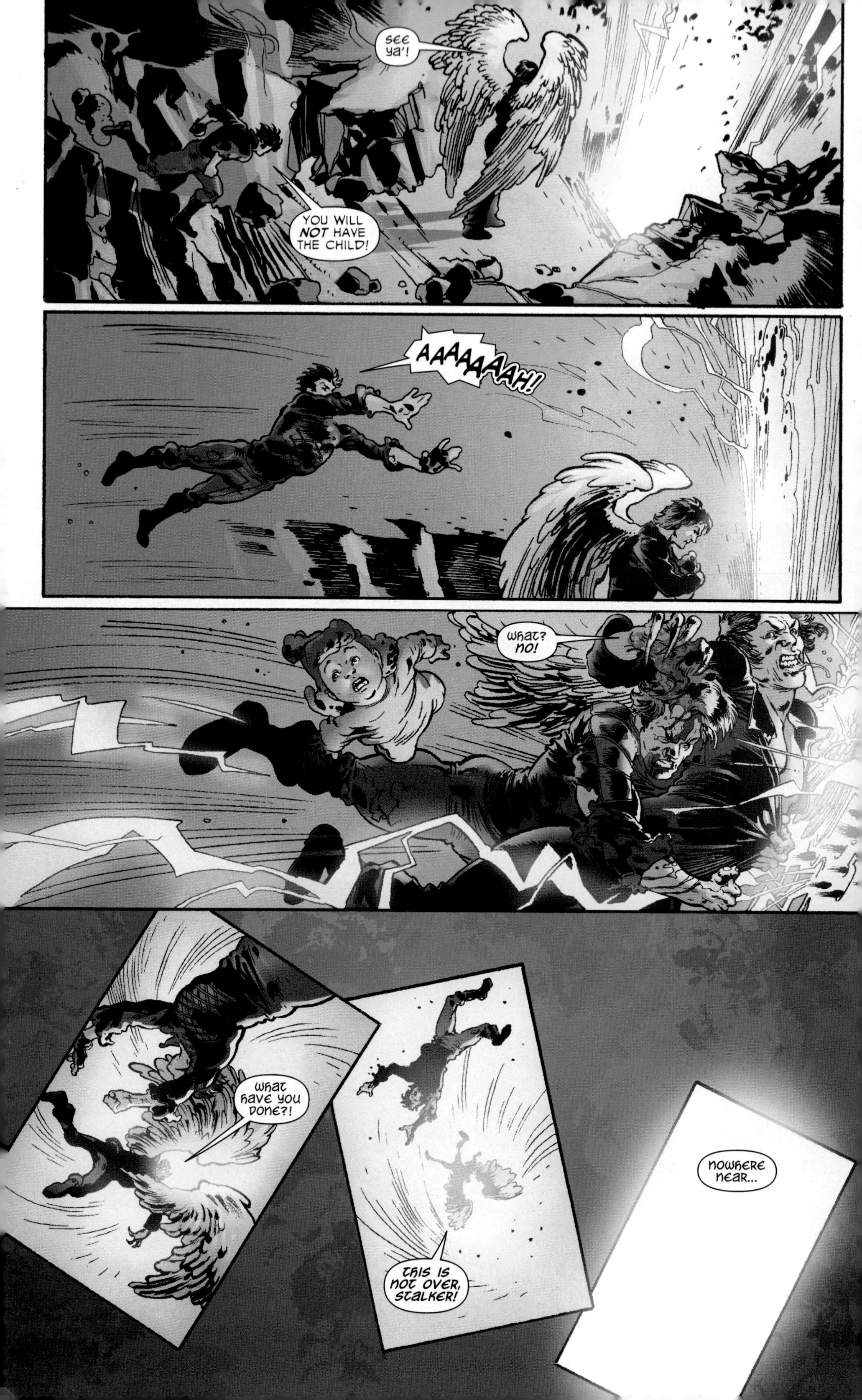
SEE YA'!
YOU WILL NOT HAVE THE CHILD!
AAAAAAAH!
WHAT? NO!
WHAT HAVE YOU DONE?!
THIS IS NOT OVER, STALKER!
NOWHERE NEAR...

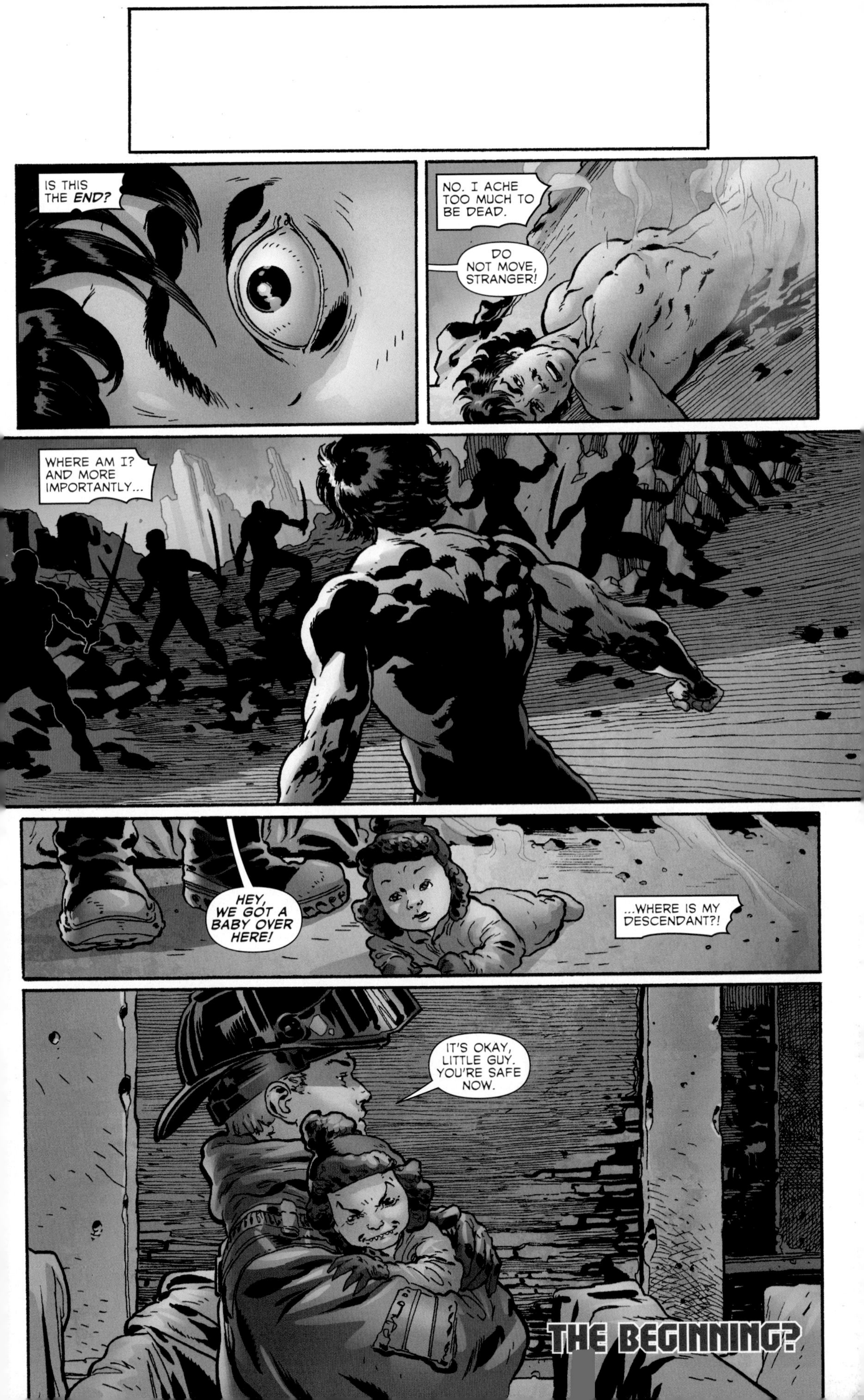
IS THIS THE END?
NO. I ACHE TOO MUCH TO BE DEAD.
DO NOT MOVE, STRANGER!
WHERE AM I? AND MORE IMPORTANTLY...
HEY, WE GOT A BABY OVER HERE!
...WHERE IS MY DESCENDANT?!
IT'S OKAY, LITTLE GUY. YOU'RE SAFE NOW.
THE BEGINNING?

DC UNIVERSE PRESENTS #19 Cover by JESÚS MERINO & BLOND

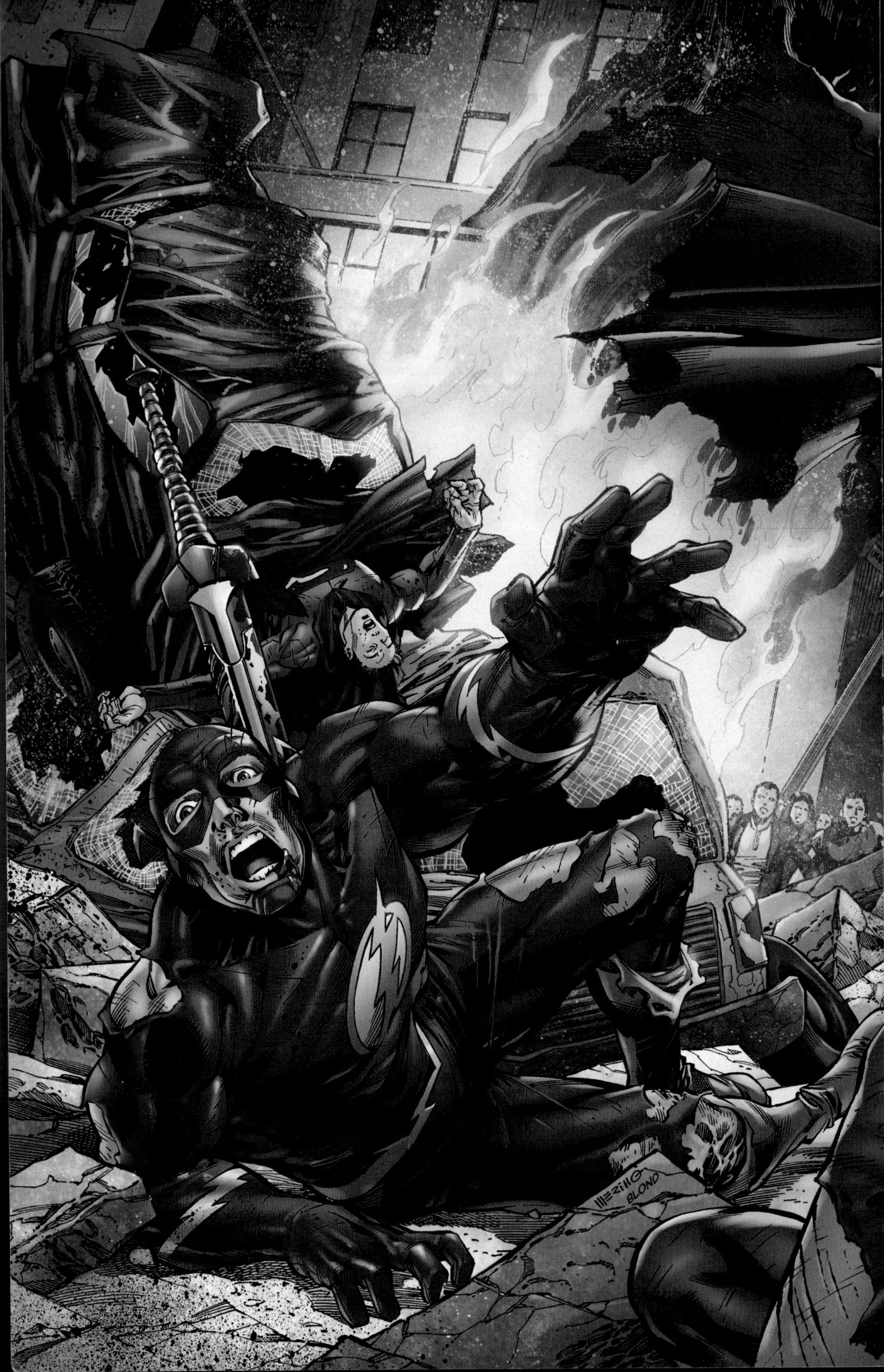

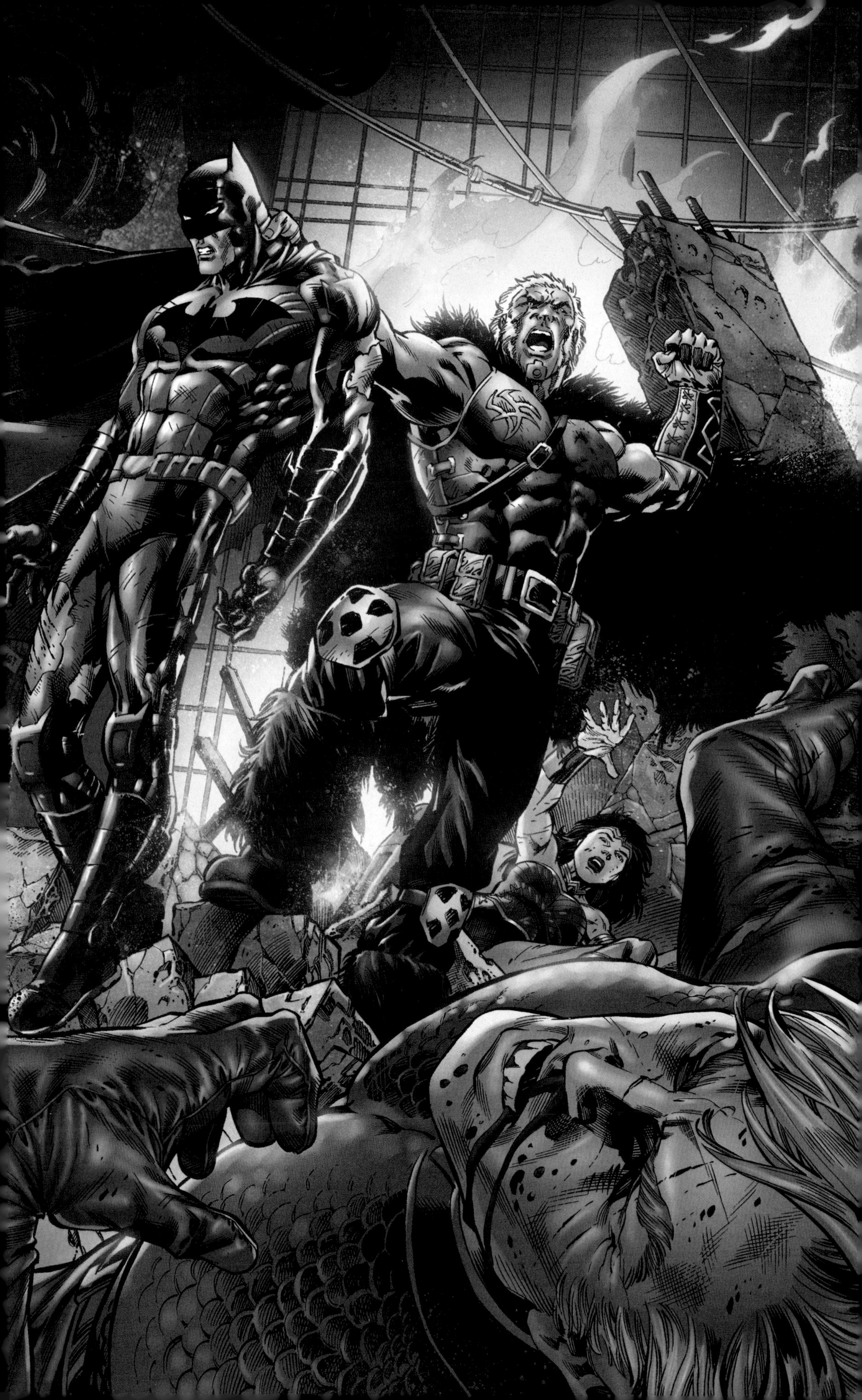

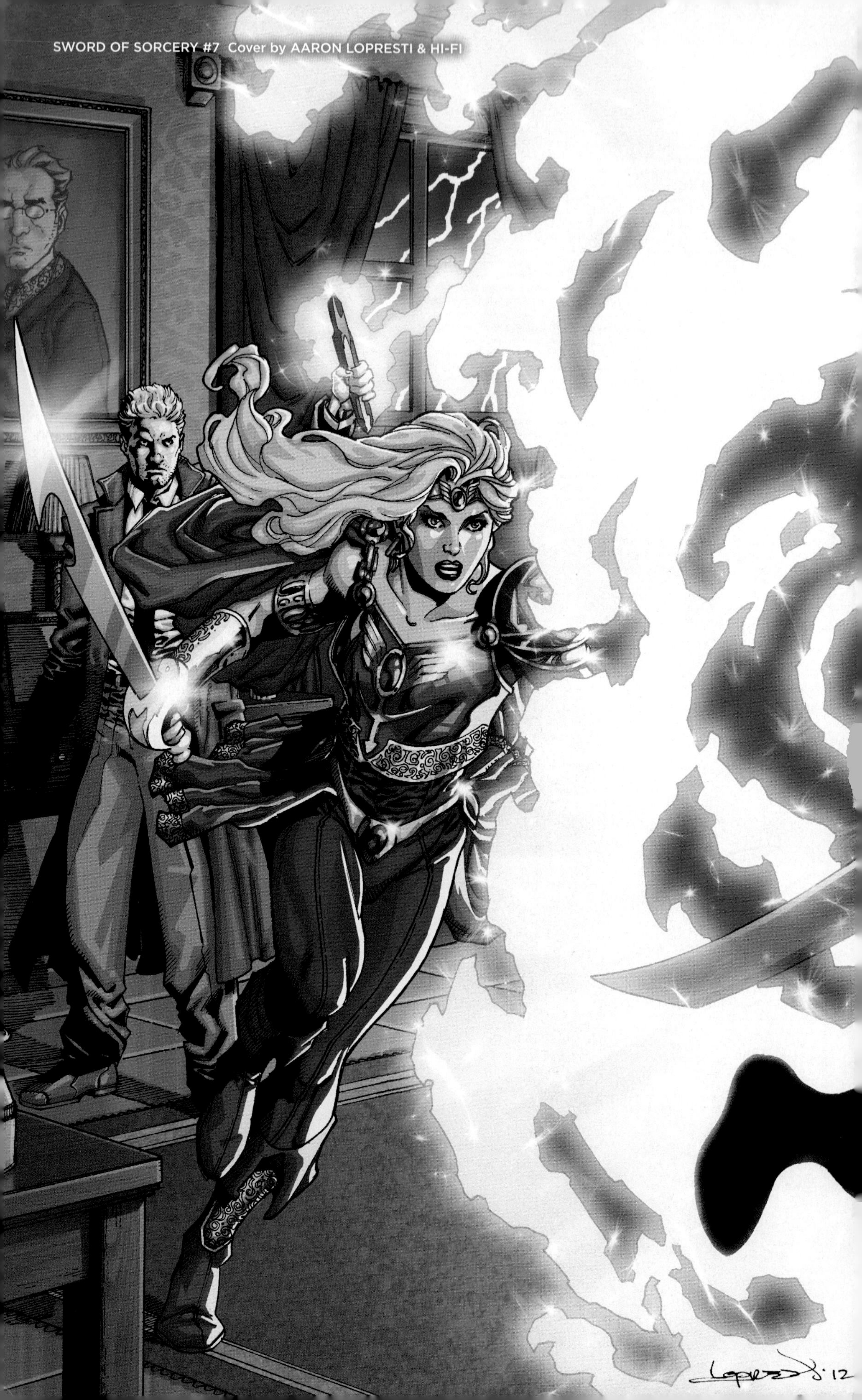

SWORD OF SORCERY #7 Cover by AARON LOPRESTI & HI-FI

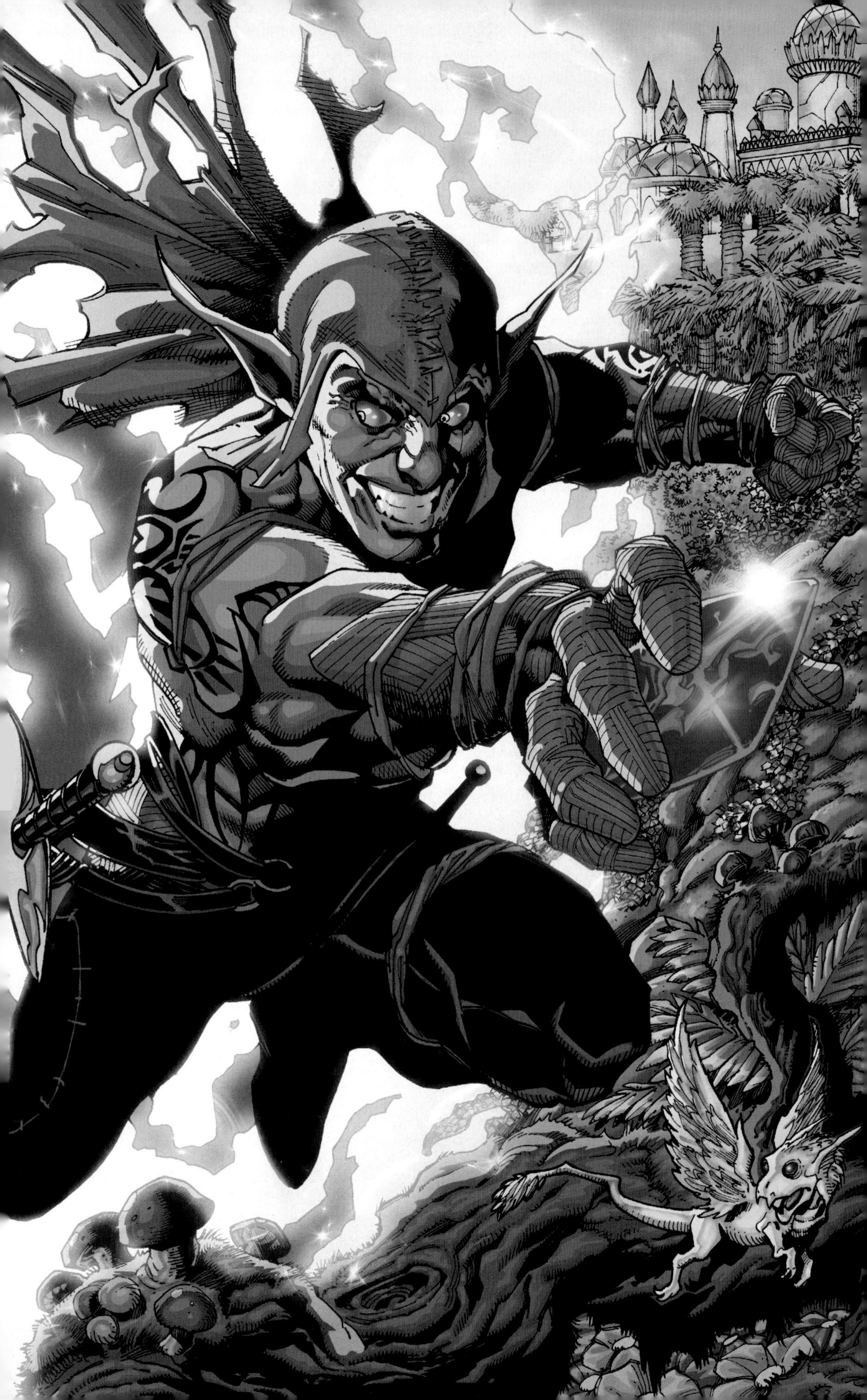

SWORD OF SORCERY #1 Variant cover by RYAN SOOK

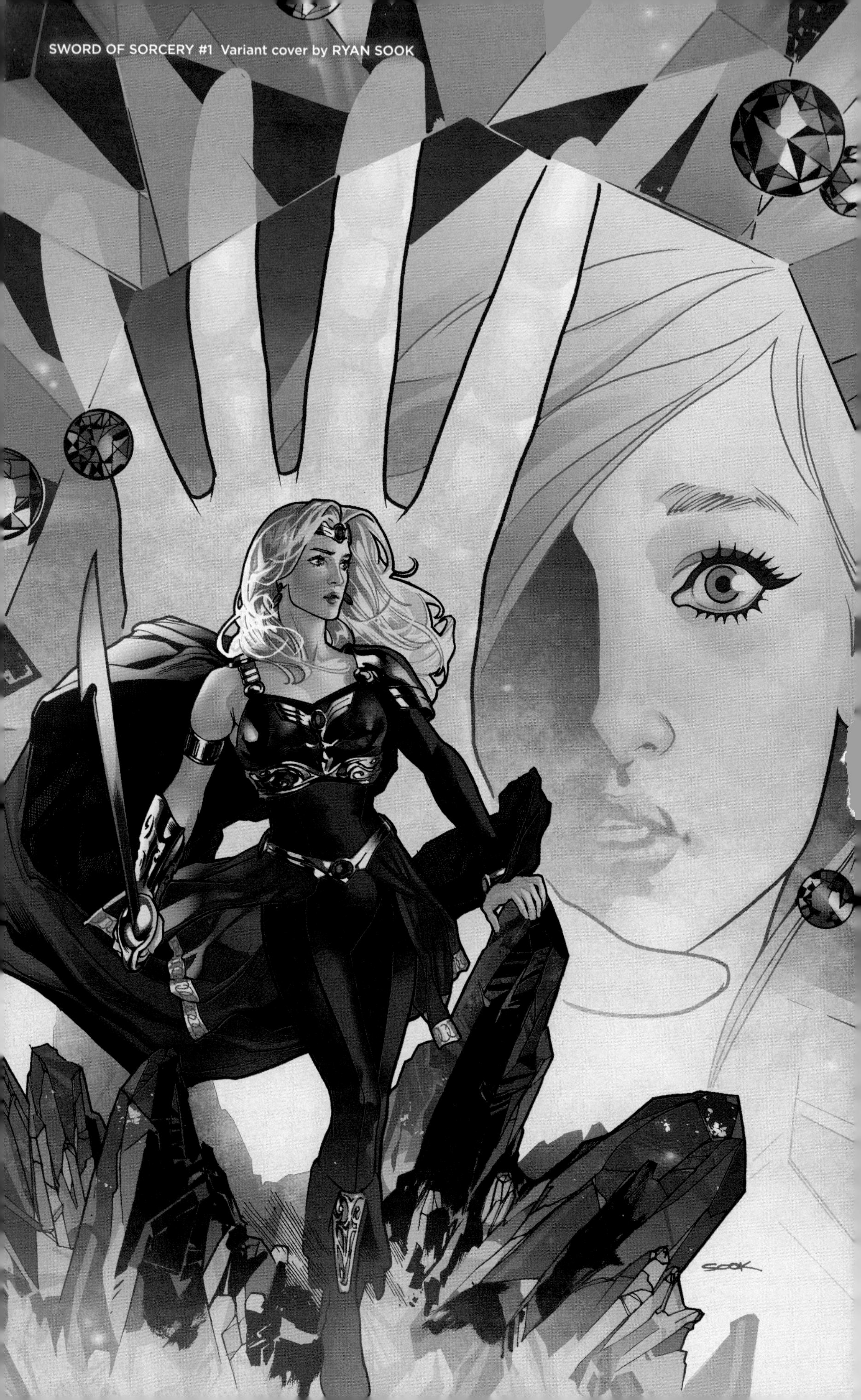
SOOK

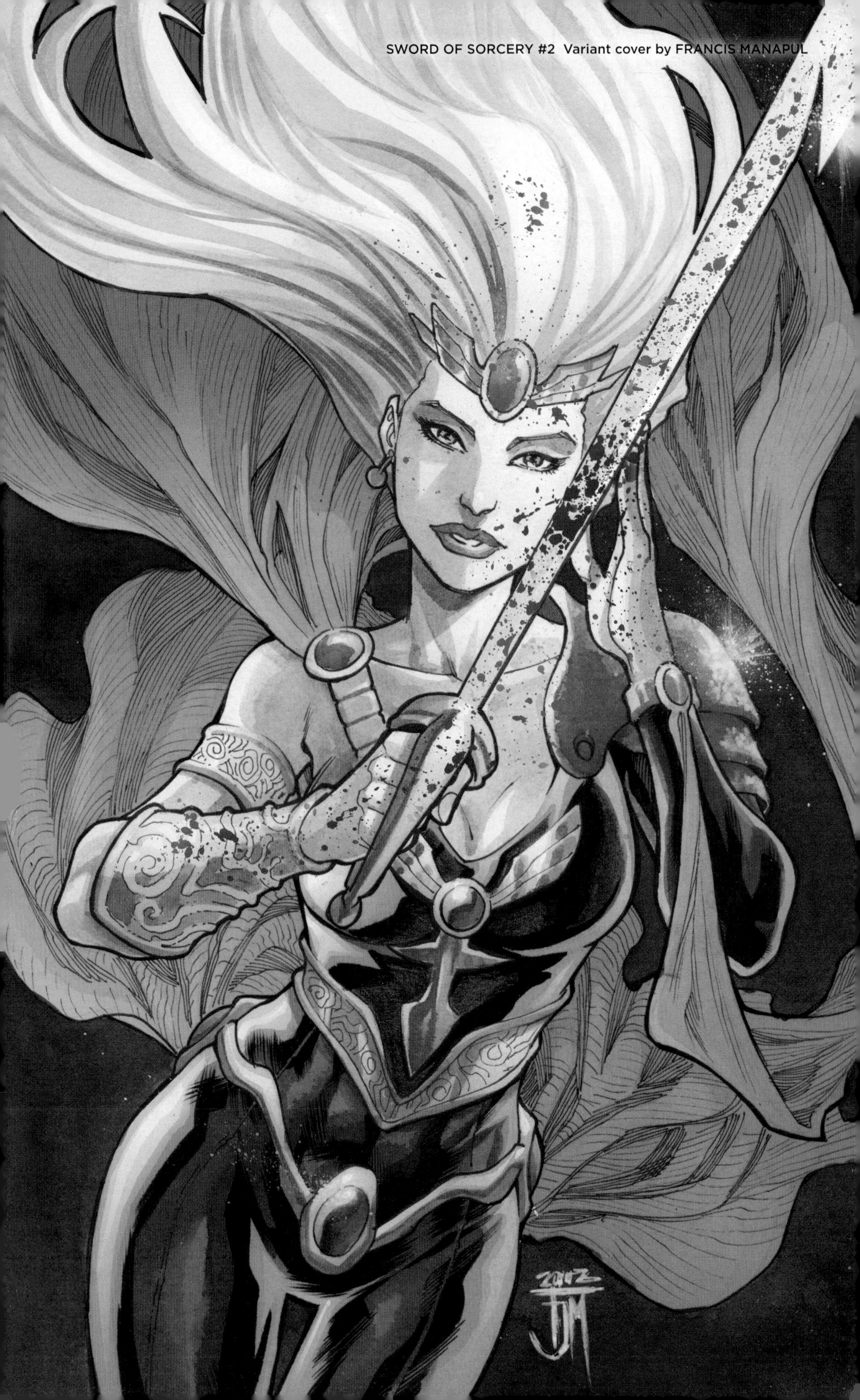

SWORD OF SORCERY #2 Variant cover by FRANCIS MANAPUL

SWORD OF SORCERY #3 Variant cover by CHRIS BURNHAM & NATHAN FAIRBAIRN

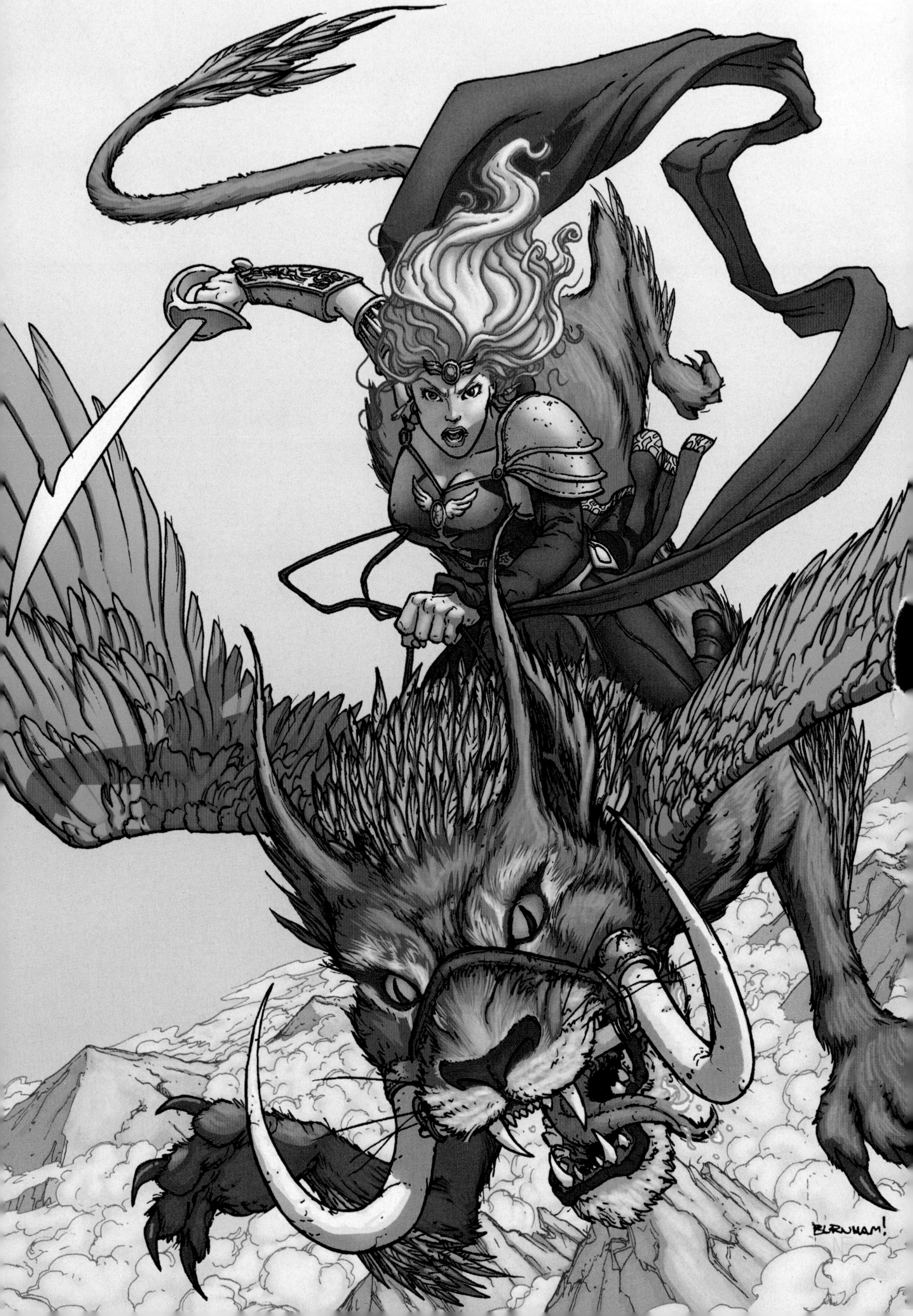
BURNHAM!

"MORDIEL"

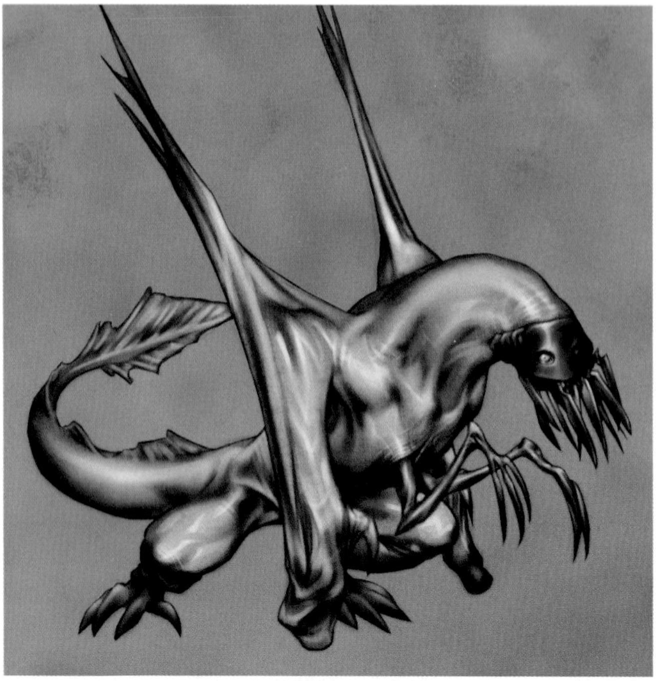

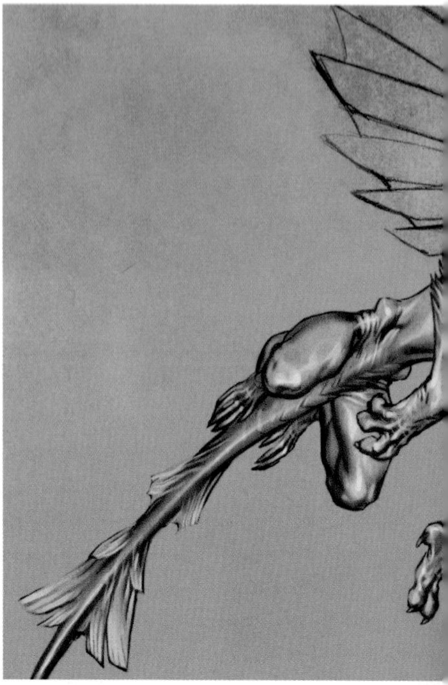

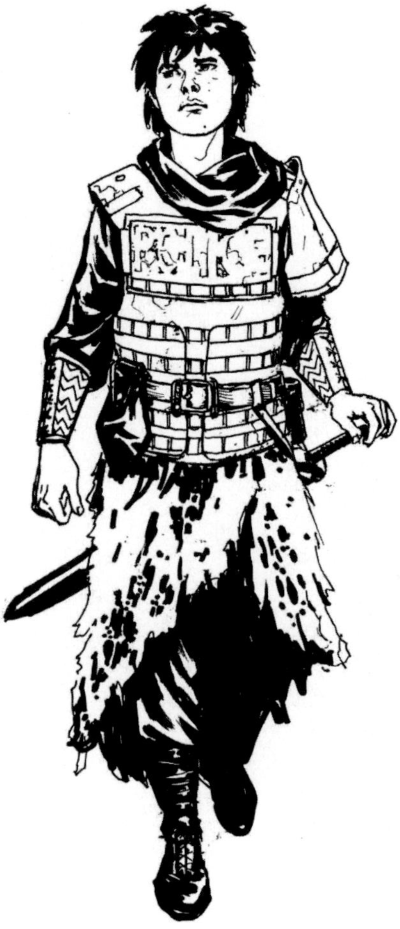

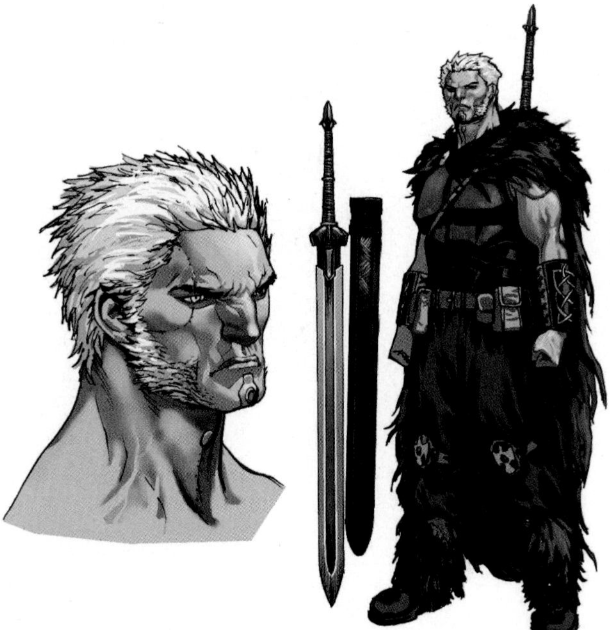

Beowulf designs by Jesús Saíz